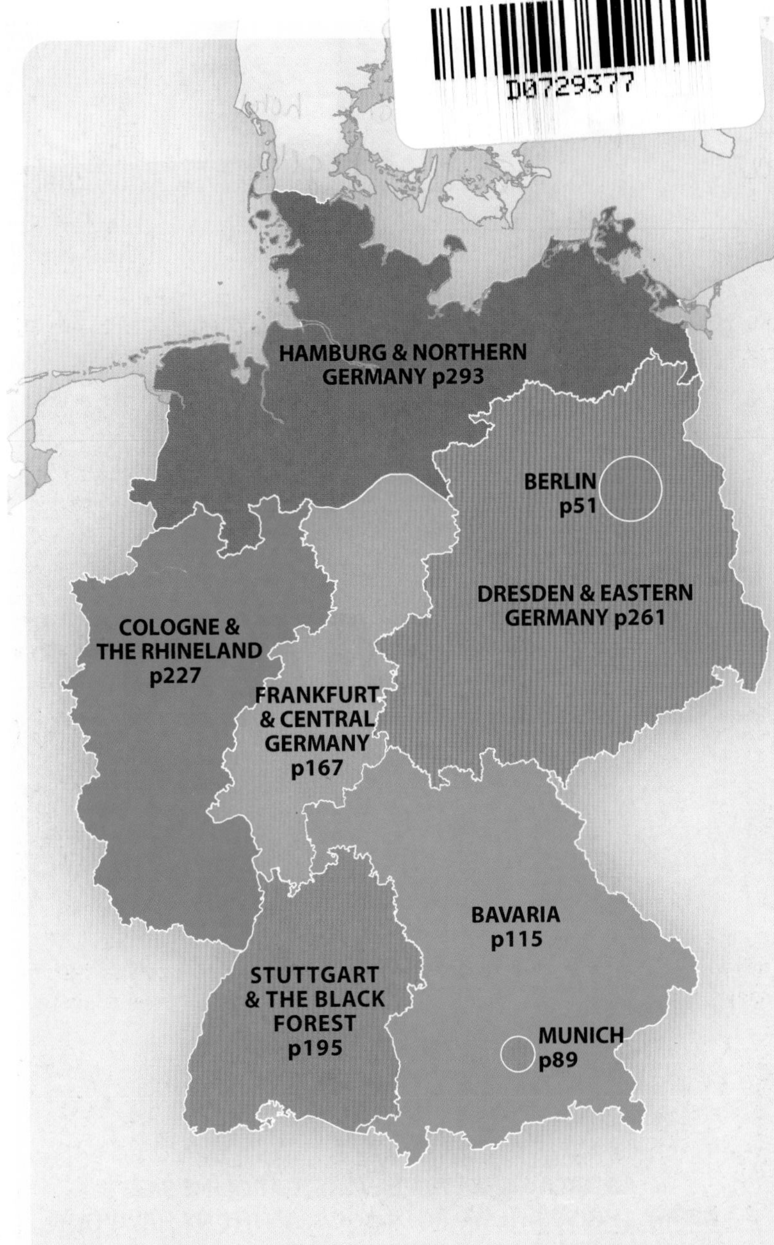
HAMBURG & NORTHERN GERMANY p293
BERLIN p51
DRESDEN & EASTERN GERMANY p261
COLOGNE & THE RHINELAND p227
FRANKFURT & CENTRAL GERMANY p167
BAVARIA p115
STUTTGART & THE BLACK FOREST p195
MUNICH p89

discover GERMANY

ANDREA SCHULTE-PEEVERS, CAROLINE SIEG
KERRY CHRISTIANI, MARC DI DUCA, ANTHONY HAYWOOD,
CATHERINE LE NEVEZ, DANIEL ROBINSON

GERMANY'S TOP 25 EXPERIENCES

1

↘ BEWITCHED BY BERLIN

Berlin (p51) is utterly amazing. I love being able to walk everywhere, enjoying an amazing building or piece of architecture or being part of history wherever you stop. The amalgamation of the old and new works so well in Berlin – your heart wants to cry for the history and smile for the present and future.

Natalie Ler-Davies, Traveller, United Arab Emirates

ROMANTIC RAMBLINGS

2

Be sure to have your camera at the ready as you travel along the **Romantic Road** (p126), an enchanting ribbon of villages, cities and medieval castles winding from Würzburg's vineyard-ribboned hills to Füssen at the foot of the Alps. Take your sweet time: the route reveals its greatest magic if savoured in sips, not gulped in haste.

3

MAD FOR NEUSCHWANSTEIN

Ever since I first saw a picture of **Schloss Neuschwanstein** (p140) I was determined to make it there. We were stoked to get our rental car upgraded to a Mercedes. What could be more perfect for the autobahn! When we finally arrived, the sheer magnificence (and gaudiness) of the castle was amazing.

Michaela Caughlan, Lonely Planet Staff

1 FGU/IMAGEBROKER; 2 DWB/IMAGEBROKER; 3 DAVID TOMLINSON

1 Brandenburger Tor (Brandenburg Gate; p63), Berlin; 2 Cycling south of Wieskirche (p124); 3 Schloss Neuschwanstein (p140), near Füssen

INSPIRED BY HEIDELBERG

4

A sight I'll never forget was my first glimpse of the bridge over the Neckar River in **Heidelberg** (p210), the university city that inspired William Turner's paintbrush with its whimsical castle, and Mark Twain's pen with its raucous nightlife.

Kerry Christiani, Lonely Planet Author, Germany

5

BIKE CRUISING IN HAMBURG

Getting around **Hamburg** (p304), Germany's sprawling 'harbour-polis', is a breeze thanks to simple, cheap and often wonderfully scenic transport options, including boat, rail and bus networks. But perhaps the most enjoyable way to explore the country's second-largest city is under your own steam.

Catherine Le Nevez, Lonely Planet Author, France

ROMANCE THE RHINE RIVER

Though it rained incessantly during our trip to the **Rhine River** (p252), one of the highlights was a lunch cruise past fairy-tale scenes of castles and vineyards. Traditional German food and music made it a magical trip.

Emma Kinton, Traveller, UK

6

4 MANFRED GOTTSCHALK; 5 MARK DAFFEY; 6 KAK/IMAGEBROKER

4 Neckar River and Altstadt, Heidelberg (p210); 5 Cycling by the Alster Lakes, Hamburg (p304); 6 Burg Stahleck, located in the Rhine village of Bacharach (p255)

SEDUCED BY SANSSOUCI

Potsdam's glorious **Sanssouci** (p274) park and palace shows what happens if a king has good taste, plenty of cash and access to the finest architects and artists. I never tire of seeing Frederick the Great's petite retreat atop the vine-draped terrace or of discovering romantic corners in the rambling park.

Andrea Schulte-Peevers, Lonely Planet Author, Germany

7

8

PARTY LIKE IT'S 1999

Are you a beer lover? Well, then the **Munich Oktoberfest** (p108) is for you! I spent my first day sitting with some here for their 27th straight year; after 10 minutes they treated me like a life-long friend. Then with three hours sleep, I got up and did it again, only to find another amazing bunch of friends!

Damian Hughes, Traveller, Australia

FLOORED BY A WALL

9

It's been more than 20 years since the **Berlin Wall** (p78) collapsed, but you can still sense the ghosts of the Cold War when standing in the shadow of a surviving section of this grim and grey divider of humanity.

Andrea Schulte-Peevers, Lonely Planet Author, Germany

7 JEAN-PIERRE LESCOURRET; 8 KRZYSZTOF DYDYNSKI; 9 JERRY GALEA

7 Terraced gardens at Schloss Sanssouci (p274), Potsdam; 8 Oktoberfest (p92) in the Theresienwiese fairgrounds, Munich; 9 A remaining section of the Berlin Wall (p78)

10

DRESDEN'S ARTISTIC ALCHEMY

If you like art, architecture and history and want to be blown away, then the Dresden **Zwinger** (p279) is a must! If it wasn't a beautiful fountain, then it was a cute cherub to look at. The Zwinger has so much going on – make sure you have lots of time in this gorgeous city.

Clara Monitto, Traveller, Germany

DARK MOMENTS IN DACHAU

11

I was with my family in a secluded garden area at **Dachau Concentration Camp Memorial** (p113) – parts of it are unexpectedly peaceful. This was where people were taken to be shot; we were all standing there quietly comparing the incongruousness of the spot's carefully mown lawn and pretty flower beds with its not-so-distant history.

Anna Demant, Lonely Planet Staff

GLIDE ALONG THE MOSELLE

12

Rowing the **Moselle River** (p256) to the Rhine is a fantastic opportunity to see the country from a position few get to experience. The grape vines clinging to the hills, the castles on high peaks, being passed by enormous barges, witnessing the densely populated summer caravan parks, passing through locks and sipping the fabulous riesling!

Gail Irvine, Traveller, Canada

13

QUAFFING IN FRANKFURT

I came to the rustic tavern in Frankfurt's Sachsenhausen quarter with a mission: to try **Ebbelwei** (apple wine; p184). I poured, tasted and thought, 'Aha, this is why they say it's an acquired taste!' Two pitchers later I was on a first-name basis with the waiter and had declared *Ebbelwei* my favourite tipple.

Caroline Sieg, Lonely Planet Author, Germany

10 ANDREA SCHULTE-PEEVERS; 11 ANDREA SCHULTE-PEEVERS; 12 ZKI/IMAGEBROKER; 13 HOLGER LEUE

10 The Zwinger (p279), Dresden; 11 Entrance gates to Dachau Concentration Camp Memorial (p113); 12 Cochem's Reichsburg (p259), set above the Moselle River; 13 Pouring *Ebbelwei* (apple wine; p184) in Frankfurt

14

FEEL FRISKY IN FREIBURG

I returned to **Freiburg** (p218) 30 years after studying there, fulfilling a promise to myself to go back some day. Upon my return I proposed to my (now) wife, who also studied there 30 years before. We now travel there for several weeks each year, visiting friends all over Germany and in Freiburg. A promise fulfilled!

Robert Purrenhage, Traveller, USA

CYCLING LAKE CONSTANCE (THE BODENSEE)

Freewheeling around glittering **Lake Constance** (p223) with your chain singing, a blue sky overhead and the Alps drifting into view is a true joy. Nothing encourages serious pedalling like the surprises around these corners, including medieval castles and farms selling fresh-pressed cider.

Kerry Christiani, Lonely Planet Author, Germany

15

14 View past Martinstor (p218), Freiburg; 15 The town of Sipplingen, Lake Constance (p223)

ONCE UPON A TIME...

My childhood memories of *Grimms Märchen* (Grimms Fairy Tales) came to life when I tooled along the **Fairy-Tale Road** (p188). It almost felt as though I was going to see Rapunzel waving down from her tower any minute.

Caroline Sieg, Lonely Planet Author, Germany

16

17

LAPPING UP HISTORY IN LEIPZIG

The first time I walked into the **Nikolaikirche** (p283) church in Leipzig, I was mesmerised. When I found out about the peace prayers it has hosted since 1982 and the infamous demonstrations in 1989, it all came together: this church is an exquisite element of history, and a constant source of tranquillity.

BIRTHPLACE OF MODERNISM

Chances are you have a little Bauhaus in your house, too: perhaps the chair you sit on or the table at which you dine. 'Form follows function' was the main credo of this influential 20th-century architectural and design movement. Come to **Dessau-Rosslau** (p289) to see where practitioners like Gropius, Klee and Kandinsky did their best work.

18

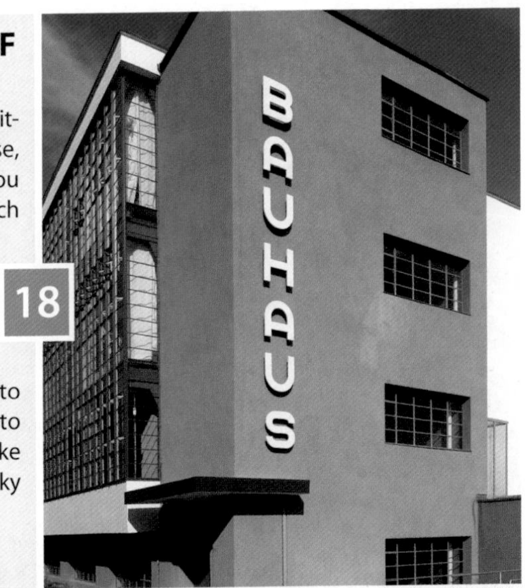

16 DAVID PEEVERS; 17 SBE/IMAGEBROKER; 18 SOM/IMAGEBROKER

16 Gerhard Marcks' *Bremer Stadtmusikanten* (Town Musicians of Bremen) sculpture (p319), Bremen; 17 Interior of Nikolaikirche (p283), Leipzig; 18 Bauhausgebäude (Bauhaus Building; p290), Dessau-Rosslau

AWESTRUCK IN AACHEN

No matter how many times I set foot inside majestic **Aachener Dom** (p249), Charlemagne's palace chapel and burial site, I'll always be awed by the harmony of its design, the iridescent stained-glass windows, the precious works of art and the momentous sense of history that hangs above it all.

19

20

POTTY OVER PORCELAIN

One of the most fascinating days I spent on the road in Saxony was at the **Meissen porcelain factory** (p281). Having seen the incredible care and dexterity of the throwers, sculptors and glazers, the price of the pieces in the factory gift shop suddenly didn't seem all that inflated!

Marc Di Duca, Lonely Planet Author, UK

19 BOE/IMAGEBROKER; 20 DAVID PEEVERS

19 Aachener Dom (p249); 20 Meissen porcelain (p281)

21

VERSED IN WURST

Every time my husband and I travel back to Germany, visiting a sausage stand is one of our top priorities. There are a lot of varieties of **wurst** (p333), but my all-time favourite is the *Currywurst*, a pork sausage cut into slices and seasoned with a sauce generally consisting of ketchup and curry powder.

Birgit Jordan, Traveller, Australia

22

BREMEN'S HANSEATIC COOL

Much about **Bremen** (p318) comes as a surprise – from the stunning red-brick architecture of the town hall in the city itself to the interesting foreshore of Bremerhaven, with its emigration centre. Most surprising of all, however, is its relaxed folk – best typified by the playful *Bremer Stadtmusikanten* (The Town Musicians of Bremen).

Anthony Haywood, Lonely Planet Author, Germany

PROST!

23

On our first night we bumped into an outdoor **beer garden** (p354). It took some time and experimentation to translate the beer and sausage menus from the stalls around the garden, but it was all very tasty. The crowd was mostly locals having furious or relaxed discussions, and a scattering of families all enjoying the evening twilight.

Ryan Incoll, Traveller, Australia

24

RAMBLING THROUGH REGENSBURG

At once ancient and vibrant, **Regensburg** (p160) is one of Bavaria's most beautiful cities and among the best-preserved medieval towns in Europe. Its magic reveals itself in countless, often surprising, places. You'll find it in a leafy beer garden on the banks of the Danube, in the Altstadt's honeycomb of laneways and beneath the soaring spires of the Dom (cathedral).

21 Wurst stand, Nuremberg (p149); 22 *Knight Roland* statue (p318), Bremen; 23 A Munich beer garden (p109); 24 Steinerne Brücke (p161), Regensburg

HAPPY AT THE HOFBRÄUHAUS

A night out at Munich's celebrated **Hofbräuhaus** (p109), the world's most famous beer hall, is unmissable. Order a large wet one, have a sway to the oompah band and watch the crowd get tipsier and more boisterous as the evening progresses.

Marc Di Duca, Lonely Planet Author, UK

25

25 MSI/IMAGEBROKER

25 Hofbräuhaus (p109), Munich

GERMANY'S TOP ITINERARIES

TRIUMPHANT TRIO

FIVE DAYS BERLIN TO MUNICH

Five days may not be long, but it's enough to whet your appetite for this fascinating country by visiting its three finest cities. Hop on this urban rollercoaster in scene-stealing Berlin, train it to maritime Hamburg and fly on to marvellous Munich.

❶ BERLIN

Spend Day One in the German capital ticking off the blockbuster sights: first scaling the **Reichstag dome** (p69) for dazzling views, followed by a stroll along **Unter den Linden** (p66) and stops at the **Brandenburger Tor** (Brandenburg Gate; p63), the **Holocaust Memorial** (p65) and **Checkpoint Charlie** (p73). Before dinner, forage for local fashions, art and accessories in the charismatic **Scheunenviertel** (p68) quarter. On Day Two, marvel at monumental antiquities in the **Pergamonmuseum** (p67) and flirt with Egyptian queen Nefertiti in the **Neues Museum** (p68), then spend the afternoon touring the city's finest royal pad, **Schloss Charlottenburg** (p77), and the famous **KaDeWe** (p87) department store.

❷ HAMBURG

It's a mere 100-minute train ride from Berlin to this breezy port city. Get your fill of Klee and Koons at the **Hamburger Kunsthalle** (p305), tour the baroque **Rathaus** (town hall; p304) and break for lunch in the pretty canal-front **Alsterarkaden** (p304). In the afternoon, explore the atmospheric **Speicherstadt** (p305) warehouse quarter by boat, also getting a preview of the emerging **HafenCity** (p308) quarter. No

RUSSELL MOUNTFORD

Holocaust Memorial (p65), Berlin

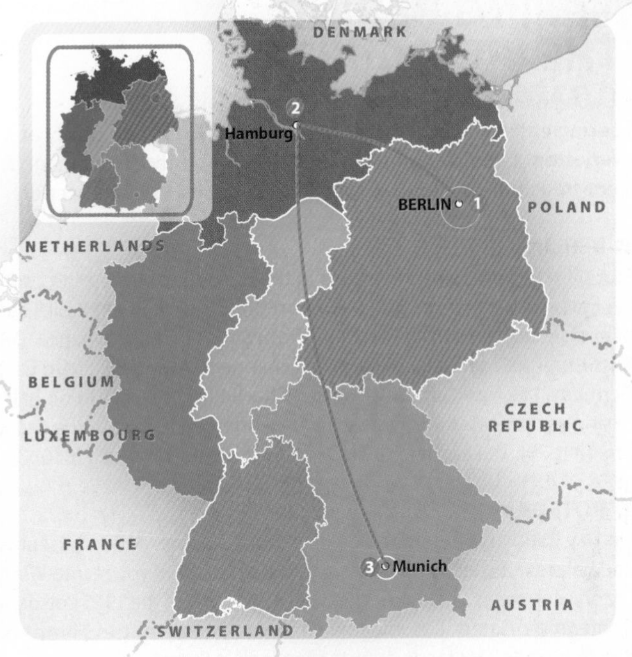

visit to Hamburg would be complete without at least a peak at the notorious **Reeperbahn** (p309), where you can also pay your respects to the Fab Four at the **Beatles-Platz** (p309) and **Beatlemania Museum** (p309). Finish your day with a civilised dinner in a trendy **Elbmeile** (p308) restaurant.

❸ MUNICH

Kick off in the historic Altstadt (old town) by getting your bearings from the **St Peterskirche tower** (p98), then peruse the colourful bounty at the **Viktualienmarkt** (p99). Keep a tab on the city's evolution at the **Stadtmuseum** (p99) and the nearby **Jüdisches Museum** (p99), and compare the lavishly baroque **Asamkirche** (p103) with the Gothic starkness of the landmark **Frauenkirche** (p103). In the afternoon, pick your favourite **Pinakothek museum** (p103), then ring in the evening with a pilgrimage to the **Hofbräuhaus** (p107). Have dinner here or, better yet, at the locals' favourite **Augustiner-Grossgaststätte** (p109). On Day Two, tour the royal splendour of the **Residenz** (p102), then relax in the **Englischer Garten** (English Garden; p105) before reporting to the stunning **BMW Museum** (p105) or confronting the ghosts at **Dachau Concentration Camp** (p113).

DIPPING BEHIND 'THE IRON CURTAIN'

10 DAYS BERLIN TO WEIMAR

Touring eastern Germany by car or train delivers eye candy at every stop. Classic and quirky discoveries abound, from magnificent treasures to cities steeped in history and sublime scenery.

❶ BERLIN

Kick off your tour with three days in the once-divided German capital. For an introduction, join **Berlin on Bike's** (p75) Berlin Wall Tour or explore the city's 'Wild East' on a **Trabi Safari** (p70). While the **DDR Museum** (p68) provides a rather saccharine look at daily life in East Germany, the **Haus am Checkpoint Charlie** (p73) zeroes in on hair-raising escape attempts, whose failures often ended up at the **Stasi Prison** (p70). The former Stasi HQ is now the **Stasi Museum** (p70).

❷ POTSDAM

On Day Four, take a train to Potsdam, famous for its parks, museums and palaces – especially **Schloss Sanssouci** (p274). If you're into WWII history, don't miss **Schloss Cecilienhof** (p275), site of the 1945 Potsdam Conference. Cinephiles, meanwhile, should head out to **Filmpark Babelsberg** (p276) for an entertaining look at German film history.

❸ DESSAU-ROSSLAU

The following day point the compass to Dessau-Rosslau, where the Bauhaus came of age. You can still see the original school building, the **Bauhausgebäude** (p290); as well as the **Meisterhäuser** (p291), the private homes of Gropius, Kandinsky and other pioneering practitioners.

LEFT: DAVID PEEVERS; RIGHT: MARTIN MOOS

Left: The Berlin Wall's East Side Gallery (p78); Right: Dresden's Zwinger (p279)

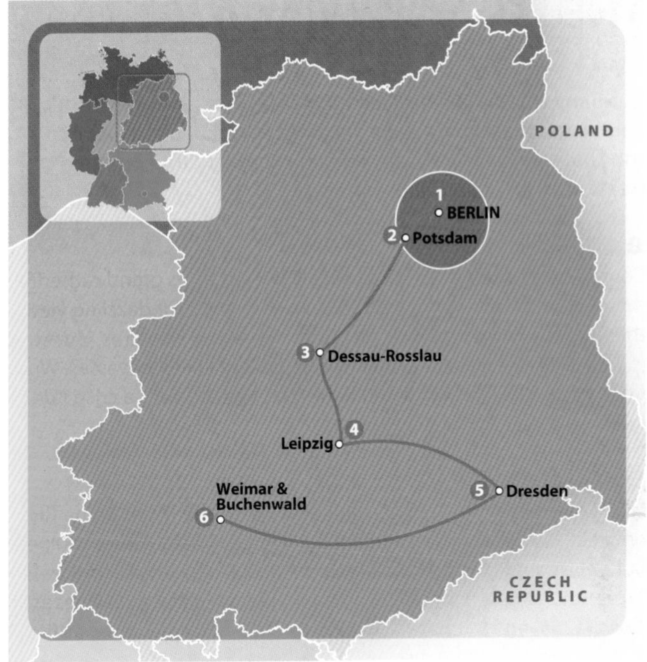

❹ LEIPZIG

Find out why Leipzig is known as the 'City of Heroes' on Day Six by visiting the **Nikolaikirche** (p283), the **Stasi Museum** (p283) and the **Zeitgeschichtliches Forum** (p283). Also pay homage to Johann Sebastian Bach at the **Bach-Museum** (p283) and the **Thomaskirche** (p283), and to Goethe at **Auerbachs Keller** (p284).

❺ DRESDEN

Dresden warrants a couple of days. Since completion of the **Frauenkirche** (p277), its historic silhouette is intact again. Visit the treasures of the **Grünes Gewölbe** (p279) and the **Zwinger** (p279) and, at sunset, stroll along the waterfront or catch a cruise down the **Elbe** (see p281).

❻ WEIMAR & BUCHENWALD

Wrap up your trip in this small Thuringian town where a pantheon of German intellectual giants resided in the 18th century. Check out Goethe's old digs in the **Goethe Haus** (p287); compare them with the relatively modest **Schiller Haus** (p287) where his friend and colleague, Friedrich Schiller, lived with his family. Sadly, Weimar's glorious legacy was tainted during the Nazi years with the construction of **Buchenwald Concentration Camp** (p289) nearby.

THE BIG ENCHILADA

TWO WEEKS COLOGNE TO FRANKFURT

Germany is a rich quilt of exciting cities, soul-stirring scenery and historic landmarks – as you'll discover on this epic road trip that peels away the layers, exposing you to a banquet of treats, treasures and temptations.

❶ COLOGNE

Contagiously energetic, Cologne is embodied by its grand cathedral, the mighty **Kölner Dom** (p230). Climb to the top for dazzling views, then dig for Roman roots at the **Römisch-Germanisches Museum** (p240) or flock to **Museum Ludwig** (p240) for killer canvasses. Wrap up in a **beer hall** (p242) with Rhenish fare paired with a crisp *Kölsch* beer.

❷ ROMANTIC RHINE

Like a fine wine, the show-stopping scenery along the Rhine River between Koblenz and Rüdesheim demands to be sipped, not gulped. Budget a couple of days to pay your respects to the mythical **Loreley** (p255) and sample fine vintages in such higgledy-piggledy villages as **St Goar** (p255) and **Bacharach** (p255), serenaded by medieval castles.

❸ HEIDELBERG

Mark Twain and William Turner were smitten by it, and so will you be. Take in the classic Heidelberg view – the proudly crumbling **Schloss** (p211), the sprightly Neckar River and the **Alte Brücke** (p212) – while wandering along the **Philosophenweg** (p212).

MARTIN LLADO

Heidelberg's Alte Brücke (p212)

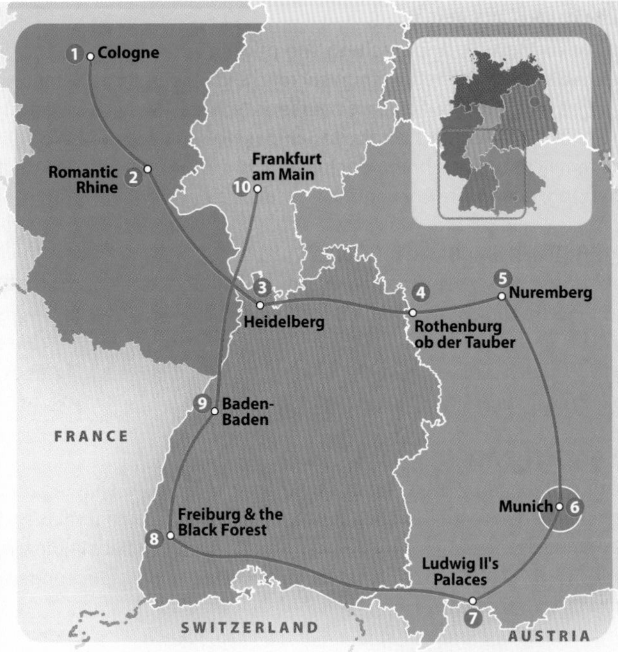

❹ ROTHENBURG OB DER TAUBER

Admire **Rothenburg's** (p129) turrets and massively thick walls from afar, then join the inner-wall crowd for a spin around this delightful pastiche of Hansel-and-Gretel houses, spidery cobbled lanes and hidden quiet corners. Don't forget to indulge in a **Schneeballen** (p132), the local sweet speciality.

❺ NUREMBERG

Home of **kaisers** (emperors; p152), birthplace of **Albrecht Dürer** (p152) and a **Nazi mass rally site** (p152) – Nuremberg has certainly had its moments in German history. Take the city's pulse around the **Hauptmarkt** (p151), site of the famous **Christkindlesmarkt** (p329), and sink your teeth into a famous grilled **wurst** (sausage; p154).

❻ MUNICH

It's impossible not to be charmed by the Bavarian capital. Spend a couple of days checking out such landmark sights as the **Residenz** (p102), legendary beer halls such as the **Hofbräuhaus** (p109) and top-ranked art in the **Pinakothek museums** (p103). After a metro-intense day, seek refuge in the vast **Englischer Garten** (p105).

❼ LUDWIG II'S PALACES

South of Munich, approaching the mighty Alps, Bavaria's most-beloved king sought refuge from encroaching modernity in his fantasy palaces. The most famous, of course, is **Schloss Neuschwanstein** (p140), a sugary confection above **Schloss Hohenschwangau** (p139), the family's ancestral home. Secluded **Schloss Linderhof** (p145) is, if anything, even more enchanting.

❽ FREIBURG & BLACK FOREST

Take gorgeous scenery, mix in a medieval Altstadt, sprinkle with 20,000 students and add a liberal dash of cool – eh voilà! – you have **Freiburg** (p218). Spend one day here, then plunge on into the **Black Forest** (p198), which weaves a patchwork of wrinkled valleys and fir trees, rolling highlands and glacial lakes.

❾ BADEN-BADEN

Baden-Baden (p216) is the grande dame of German spas, ageing but still elegant with its *belle époque* townscape of palatial villas and tree-lined avenues. Get invigorated with a Roman-Irish bath in the historic **Friedrichsbad** (p216) or splash around the pools of the modern **Caracalla-Therme** (p217).

❿ FRANKFURT

The business of Frankfurt is business, but that's not all – as you'll discover taking in the impressive skyline mirrored in the Main River; poking around great art in the **Städel museum** (p181); quaffing *Ebbelwei* in a **Sachsenhausen tavern** (p184) and snooping around Goethe's family home, the **Goethe-Haus** (p180).

BRUCE ESBIN

The Black Forest (p198)

↘ PLANNING YOUR TRIP

GERMANY'S BEST…

CASTLES & PALACES

- **Schloss Neuschwanstein** (p140) King Ludwig II was not quite of this world; neither is his most sugary palace.
- **Wartburg** (p290) History pours from every nook and cranny of Eisenach's medieval beauty.
- **Sanssouci Schloss** (p274) Fall under the spell of this frilly pleasure palace in Potsdam.
- **Burg Eltz** (p260) Fancy yourself knight or damsel at this turreted beauty near the Moselle River.

VIEWS

- **Eagle's Nest** (p147) Be bedazzled by the Berchtesgadener Alps from this mountaintop roost with a sinister past.
- **Fernsehturm** (TV Tower; p68) Put Berlin at your feet from atop the country's tallest building.
- **Kölner Dom** (p238) Clamber up Cologne's cathedral for gob-smacking panoramas of the city and the Rhine River.
- **Zugspitze** (p142) Rack and pinion your way to the top of Germany's mightiest peak.

FOOTSTEPS OF GENIUS

- **Weimar** (p287) Goethe to Gropius, Schiller to Nietzsche – a veritable pantheon of German greats once resided in this provincial town.
- **Wittenberg** (p291) Where Martin Luther kick-started the Reformation in 1517.
- **Bonn** (p246) This former German capital was Beethoven's birthplace.
- **Hamburg** (p304) To quote John Lennon, 'I was born in Liverpool, but I grew up in Hamburg.'

LEFT: DAVID BORLAND; RIGHT: DENNIS JOHNSON

Left: Wartburg castle (p290), Eisenach; Right: Lion statue in Tiergarten (p71), Berlin

MUSEUMS

- **Pergamonmuseum** (p67) This Berlin treasure trove opens a window onto antiquity.
- **Deutsches Museum** (p105) Munich's science museum takes you from the future back to the stone age.
- **Kunsthalle Hamburg** (p305) Hit the artistic mother lode in this great northern city.
- **Grünes Gewölbe** (p279) Dresden's real-life equivalent of Aladdin's Cave.

GARDENS

- **Englischer Garten** (p105) Quaff a beer, watch the surfers or get naked at Munich's splendid oasis.
- **Herrenhäuser Gärten** (p185) Spend a relaxing afternoon in Hanover's mini-Versailles.
- **Park Sanssouci** (p274) This popular Potsdam gem is big enough to enable you to escape the crowds.
- **Tiergarten** (p71) Berlin's perfect urban-velocity antidote.

ROMANTIC TOWNS

- **Rothenburg ob der Tauber** (p129) Drain your camera batteries snapping this story-book medieval town.
- **Heidelberg** (p210) It's love at first sight for most, including Mark Twain.
- **Bacharach** (p255) Hold hands while sauntering along the cobbled lanes of this storied Romantic Rhine wine town.
- **Schiltach** (p217) Fall head over heels for this half-timbered Black Forest jewel.

ICONIC SIGHTS

- **Brandenburger Tor** (Brandenburg Gate; p63) This Berlin city gate's the ultimate symbol of German reunification.
- **Frauenkirche** (p277) Reduced to rubble in WWII, this rebuilt landmark church restored Dresden's classic skyline.
- **Holstentor** (p313) This mighty twin-towered red-brick gate was once part of Lübeck's fortifications.
- **St Michaeliskirche** (p309) Feel your spirits soar when faced with Hamburg's hilltop church, better known as 'Michel'.

ODES TO THE AUTO

- **BMW Museum** (p105) Munich's grand collection of beemers is almost upstaged by the stunning building housing them.
- **Mercedes-Benz Museum** (p209) In a giant double-helix building in Stuttgart, this is a virtual place of worship in a town where the car is god.
- **Autostadt** (p192) Volkswagen offers up interactive fun even for those who can't tell a piston from a carburettor.
- **Porsche Museum** (p209) This gleaming white jewel, in Stuttgart, is a temple of torque for the posh set.

THINGS YOU NEED TO KNOW

AT A GLANCE

- **ATMs** Omnipresent in cities, towns and most villages
- **Credit Cards** Visa and MasterCard increasingly accepted, but don't count on it
- **Currency** The euro (€)
- **Language** German, but English is widely spoken
- **Smoking** Generally banned in public spaces, but with confusing exceptions – ask!
- **Tipping** Service charge is included, but it's customary to add 5% or 10%
- **Visas** Not required for most nationalities (see p372)

ACCOMMODATION

- **Ferienwohnung** Holiday flat, ideal for groups and families; often requires minimum stay
- **Gasthof or Gasthaus** Small countryside inn with simple rooms and attached restaurant
- **Hostels** Both HI-affiliated and independents are ubiquitous; many offer private and family rooms
- **Hotels** Available in all price ranges and comfort levels, from small family-run inns to international chains
- **Pension** The German version of a B&B
- **Privatzimmer** A guest room in a private home; popular in rural areas; booked through tourist offices

ADVANCE PLANNING

- **Three months before** Shop around for flight deals, book accommodation if travelling during major festivals (see p46) or holidays (see p365), and reserve tickets for major performances

MARTIN MOOS

Trains at the Hauptbahnhof (main train station), Leipzig (p282)

- **One month before** Make car-hire reservations, get rail passes, book tickets for Europabus (see p126).
- **One week** Order tickets for major sights (eg Schloss Neuschwanstein, p140); book table at Michelin-starred restaurants
- **One day** Make seat reservations for long-distance train travel; make weekend reservations at fine-dining restaurants

BE FOREWARNED

- **Crowds** Expect heavy traffic and crowds at tourist sights around public holidays and in July and August
- **Restaurants** It varies, but generally open for lunch between noon and 2.30pm and dinner between 6pm and 10pm; in cities often open all day
- **Shops** Closed on Sunday and public holidays (except in tourist towns) and daily at lunchtime in suburbs and rural areas

COSTS

- **€40-60 per day** Survival budget will have you hostelling, eating cheap meals, travelling by public transport and limiting your entertainment
- **€120-180** Enough for midrange hotels, three meals a day, seeing the sights and hiring an economy car
- **€250 and up** Germany is your oyster: stay at five-star hotels, eat fancy meals, get front-row seats at the opera and put the pedal to the metal in a hired Mercedes

EMERGENCY NUMBERS

- **Ambulance** ☎ 112
- **Fire** ☎ 112
- **Police** ☎ 110

GETTING AROUND

- **Bicycle** Germany is superb cycling territory, with 200 signposted long-distance routes, and bike lanes in cities
- **Car** Ditch in cities, but handy for getting around the countryside
- **Train** Deutsche Bahn (www.bahn.de) operates a comprehensive and comfortable rail network

GETTING THERE & AWAY

- **Air** Frankfurt and Munich are the biggest airports; budget airlines often serve smaller, remote ones
- **Bus** The Eurolines (www.eurolines.com) network of coach operators connects German cities with 500 destinations across Europe
- **Train** Overnight trains link Germany with major European cities; Eurostar from London requires a change in Paris or Brussels

TECH STUFF

- **Internet cafes** Tend to have the lifespan of a fruit fly, so check with tourist office for current locations
- **Hotels** In this guide, the computer icon (💻) indicates places sporting guest PCs with online access, and the wi-fi icon (📶) indicates…you guessed it…wi-fi
- **Wi-fi** Increasingly common in hotels, cafes, public areas and airports. Track down hot spots at www.hotspot-locations.de

WHAT TO BRING

- **Foul weather gear** For those days when the sun's a no-show
- **Good maps or GPS** For finding your way around the countryside
- **Loose pants** To accommodate a growing beer belly
- **Nerves of steel** For driving on the autobahn
- **Smart clothes & shoes** For hitting fancy restaurants, the opera or big-city clubs
- **Valid travel and health insurance** (see p366)

WHEN TO GO

- **Beat the crowds** October, November, January to March, except in ski areas
- **Best beer garden weather** May to September
- **Fun on the slopes** December to late March

MSI/IMAGEBROCKER

A beer garden in Regensburg (p160)

GET INSPIRED

BOOKS

- **Grimms Märchen** (Grimms Fairy Tales; 1812) Jacob and Wilhelm Grimm's fairy tales, passed down orally through generations.
- **A Tramp Abroad** (1880) Mark Twain's timelessly witty observations about Germany.
- **Mr Norris Changes Trains** (1935) and **Goodbye to Berlin** (1939) Christopher Isherwood's chronicle of early-1930s' Berlin formed the basis of the movie *Cabaret*.
- **The Rise & Fall of the Third Reich** (1960) William Shirer's definitive tome about Nazi Germany remains a powerful reportage.
- **New Lives** (2007) Ingo Schulze's gripping account of the aftermath of German reunification.

FILMS

- **Das Boot** (1981) Dives into the claustrophobic world of WWII U-boat warfare.
- **Good Bye, Lenin!** (2003) Comedy about a young East Berliner replicating the GDR for his mother after the fall of the Wall.
- **Der Untergang** (Downfall; 2004) Chilling account of Hitler's last 12 days in his Berlin bunker.
- **Das Leben der Anderen** (The Lives of Others; 2006) Academy Award winner; reveals the absurdity and destructiveness of the Stasi.
- **Valkyrie** (2008) Relates the ill-fated true-story assassination plot against Hitler in July 1944 led by Colonel Claus von Stauffenberg.

MUSIC

- **Nine Symphonies** (1800–24) Beethoven pulled out all the stops.
- **Ring of the Nibelungen** (1848–74) Richard Wagner's epic opera cycle.
- **The Threepenny Opera** (1928) Runaway hit musical by Brecht and Weill.
- **Cabaret** (1972) Soundtrack of Bob Fosse's acclaimed film musical.
- **Atem** (1973) Groundbreaking album by electronic-music pioneers Tangerine Dream.
- **Sehnsucht** (1994) Industrial metal band Rammstein's international break-through album.

WEBSITES

- **Deutsche Welle** (www.dw-world.de) Keep abreast of German affairs.
- **Deutschland Portal** (www.deutschland.de) Ultimate gateway to online information about Germany.
- **Facts about Germany** (www.tatsachen-ueber-deutschland.de) Comprehensive reference about all aspects of German society.
- **German Films** (www.german-films.de) Anything you ever wanted to know about movies from Germany.
- **German National Tourist Office** (www.germany-tourism.de) Official tourism office site.
- **Online German Course** (www.deutsch-lernen.com) Free language lessons.

CALENDAR

JAN FEB MAR APR

TOM/IMAGEBROCKER

Partygoers are entertained by German DJ Felix Kröcher

FEBRUARY

KARNEVAL/FASCHING

The pre-Lenten season is celebrated with costumed street partying, parades, satirical shows and general revelry, primarily in Düsseldorf, Cologne and Mainz, but also in the Black Forest and Munich. Ends Ash Wednesday – 40 days before Easter.

BERLIN INTERNATIONAL FILM FESTIVAL

Berlinale (www.berlinale.de) draws stars, directors, critics and the world's A-to-Z-list celebrities to Berlin in February for two weeks of screenings and parties.

MARCH

KURT WEILL FESTIVAL

Every March Dessau-Rosslau honours its famous son, composer Kurt Weill, with a prestigious festival (www.kurt-weill.de) reprising and updating his collaborations with Bertolt Brecht, such as *The Threepenny Opera*.

LEIPZIGER BUCHMESSE

In mid- to late March literature fans flock to the prestigious Leipzig Book Fair (www.leipziger-buchmesse.de), first held in the 17th century and now Germany's second-biggest after Frankfurt.

APRIL

WALPURGISNACHT 30 APR

The pagan Witches' Sabbath festival has Harz villages roaring to life with young and old dressing up as witches and warlocks and parading through the streets singing and dancing.

MAIFEST 30 APR

Villagers celebrate the end of winter by chopping down a tree (*Maibaum*);

painting, carving and decorating it; and staging a merry revelry with traditional costumes, singing and dancing.

ART COLOGNE

Top-ranked international contemporary art fair (www.artcologne.de) that brings together leading galleries, collectors and the merely curious.

MAY–JUNE

HAMBURGER HAFENGEBURTSTAG

Hamburg's biggest annual event is the three-day Harbour Birthday (www.hafengeburtstag.de) in early May. It commemorates Emperor Barbarossa granting Hamburg customs exemption and is energetically celebrated with harbourside concerts, funfairs and gallons of beer.

JHX/IMAGEBROCKER

Berlin International Film Festival

BEC/IMAGEBROCKER

Karneval der Kulturen, Berlin

KARNEVAL DER KULTUREN

Berlin's answer to London's Notting Hill Carnival, the Carnival of Cultures (www.karneval-berlin.de) celebrates the city's multicultural spirit with parties, exotic nosh and a parade of flamboyantly costumed dancers, singers, DJs, artists and musicians.

BACH FESTIVAL

Famous musicians and orchestras come to Leipzig in late May or early June for the 10-day Bach Festival (www.bach-leipzig.de), celebrating the genius of the composer who was cantor at the local Thomas Church for nearly three decades.

WAVE-GOTIK-TREFFEN

The world's largest Goth gathering takes over Leipzig during the long Whitsuntide (Pentecost) weekend.

CALENDAR

CHRISTOPHER STREET DAY

No matter your sexual persuasion, everybody's welcome to paint the town pink at huge pride parades (www.csd-deutschland.de) bursting with naked torsos and strutting trannies and queens. The biggest is in Cologne but Berlin isn't far behind; Frankfurt and Hamburg also put on a good show.

RHEIN IN FLAMMEN

See the Rhine in a whole new light: boats lit up like Christmas trees and castles swathed in eerie 'flames' are part of the Rhine in Flames Festival (www.rhein-in-flammen.com) held in Rhine villages between May and September.

JULY–AUGUST

WINE FESTIVALS

As soon as the grapes have been harvested, the wine festival season starts, with wine tastings, folkloric parades, fireworks and the election of wine queens.

SCHLESWIG-HOLSTEIN MUSIC FESTIVAL

Leading international musicians and promising young artists perform mid-July–August throughout Germany's northernmost state. (www.shmf.de).

SAMBA FESTIVAL

This orgy of song and dance (www.samba-festival.de) draws around 90 bands and up to 200,000 visitors to Coburg in mid-July.

SEPTEMBER–OCTOBER

CANNSTATTER VOLKSFEST

Stuttgart's answer to Oktoberfest, this beer bash (www.cannstatter-volksfest.de), held over three consecutive weekends from late September to

NEX/IMAGEBROCKER

Oktoberfest (p92), Munich

mid-October, lifts spirits with oompah music, fairground rides and fireworks.

OKTOBERFEST

Despite the name, the world's biggest drink-a-thon (see p92) actually gets under way in late September on Munich's Theresienwiese grounds.

TAG DER DEUTSCHEN EINHEIT 3 OCT

Raise a toast to German reunification on the country's national holiday. The best celebrations are in Berlin.

FRANKFURTER BUCHMESSE

The world's largest book fair (www.frankfurt-book-fair.com) draws 7300 exhibitors from over 100 countries.

ERNTEDANKFEST

In late September or early October, rural towns celebrate harvest festivals with decorated church altars, processions *(Erntedankzug)* and folkloric costumes.

NOVEMBER–DECEMBER

ST MARTINSTAG 10 NOV

St Martin, known for his humility and generosity, is honoured with a lantern procession and re-enactment of his famous cutting in half of his coat to share with a beggar; followed by a feast of stuffed, roasted goose.

NIKOLAUSTAG 5 DEC

Children put boots outside the door hoping St Nick will fill them with sweets and toys overnight. Ill-behaved children, though, may find only a prickly rod left by St Nick's helper, Knecht Ruprecht.

DAVID PEEVERS

Christopher Street Day Parade, Tiergarten, Berlin

CHRISTMAS MARKETS

Mulled wine, gingerbread and shiny ornaments are typical features of German Christmas markets, taking over town centres for a month from late November. Nuremberg's Christkindlesmarkt is especially famous. Also see p329.

SILVESTER 31 DEC

New Year's Eve is called Silvester here, in honour of the 4th-century pope under whom the Romans adopted Christianity as their official religion. The new year is greeted with fireworks launched by thousands of amateur pyromaniacs.

Also see the boxed text on p135 for popular festivals held in Bavaria.

BERLIN

BERLIN

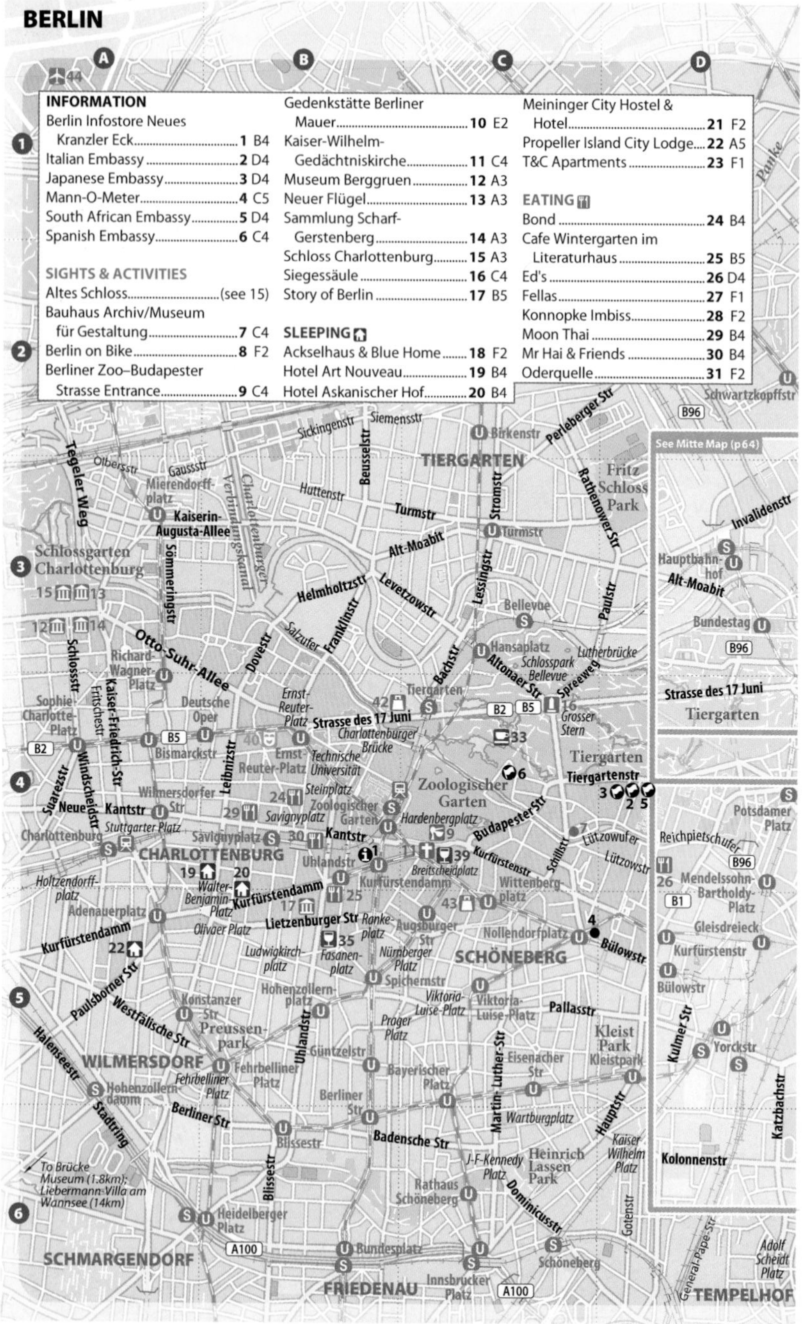

A
B
C
D
1
2
3
4
5
6
INFORMATION
Berlin Infostore Neues Kranzler Eck 1 B4
Italian Embassy 2 D4
Japanese Embassy 3 D4
Mann-O-Meter 4 C5
South African Embassy 5 D4
Spanish Embassy 6 C4
SIGHTS & ACTIVITIES
Altes Schloss (see 15)
Bauhaus Archiv/Museum für Gestaltung 7 C4
Berlin on Bike 8 F2
Berliner Zoo–Budapester Strasse Entrance 9 C4
Gedenkstätte Berliner Mauer 10 E2
Kaiser-Wilhelm-Gedächtniskirche 11 C4
Museum Berggruen 12 A3
Neuer Flügel 13 A3
Sammlung Scharf-Gerstenberg 14 A3
Schloss Charlottenburg 15 A3
Siegessäule 16 C4
Story of Berlin 17 B5
SLEEPING
Ackselhaus & Blue Home 18 F2
Hotel Art Nouveau 19 B4
Hotel Askanischer Hof 20 B4
Meininger City Hostel & Hotel 21 F2
Propeller Island City Lodge 22 A5
T&C Apartments 23 F1
EATING
Bond 24 B4
Cafe Wintergarten im Literaturhaus 25 B5
Ed's 26 D4
Fellas 27 F1
Konnopke Imbiss 28 F2
Moon Thai 29 B4
Mr Hai & Friends 30 B4
Oderquelle 31 F2
See Mitte Map (p64)
TIERGARTEN
CHARLOTTENBURG
SCHÖNEBERG
WILMERSDORF
SCHMARGENDORF
FRIEDENAU
TEMPELHOF
Schlossgarten Charlottenburg
Zoologischer Garten
Tiergarten
Fritz Schloss Park
Kleist Park
Heinrich Lassen Park
Preussen-park
Strasse des 17 Juni
Kurfürstendamm
Kantstr
Otto-Suhr-Allee
Alt-Moabit
Turmstr
Budapester Str
Hauptbahnhof
Bundestag
Potsdamer Platz
To Brücke Museum (1.8km); Liebermann-Villa am Wannsee (14km)

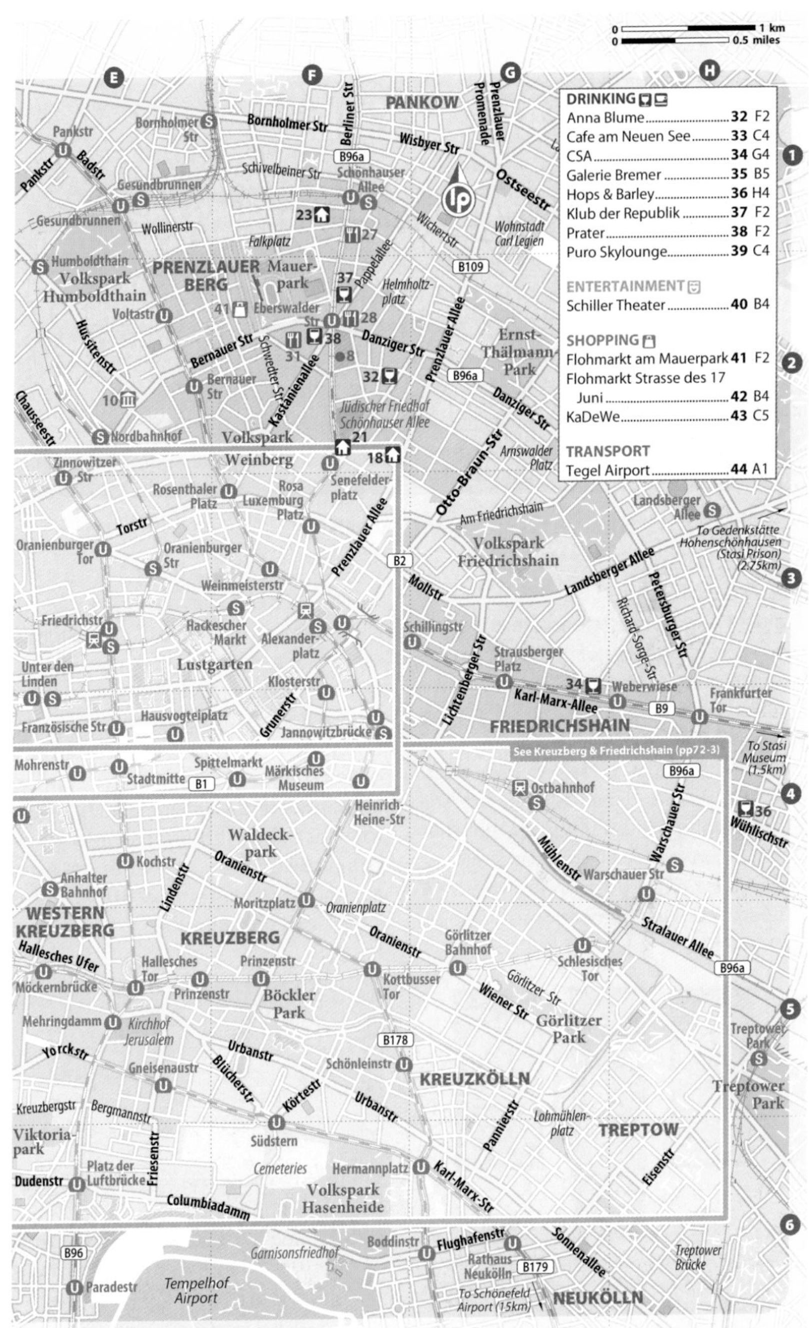
0 1 km
0 0.5 miles
E
F
G
H
1
2
3
4
5
6
DRINKING
Anna Blume 32 F2
Cafe am Neuen See 33 C4
CSA 34 G4
Galerie Bremer 35 B5
Hops & Barley 36 H4
Klub der Republik 37 F2
Prater 38 F2
Puro Skylounge 39 C4
ENTERTAINMENT
Schiller Theater 40 B4
SHOPPING
Flohmarkt am Mauerpark 41 F2
Flohmarkt Strasse des 17 Juni 42 B4
KaDeWe 43 C5
TRANSPORT
Tegel Airport 44 A1
PANKOW
Pankstr
Bornholmer Str
Bornholmer Str
Berliner Str
B96a
Wisbyer Str
Prenzlauer Promenade
Ostseestr
Schivelbeiner Str
Schönhauser Allee
Gesundbrunnen
Wollinerstr
Falkplatz
Wichertstr
Wohnstadt Carl Legien
Humboldthain
Volkspark Humboldthain
PRENZLAUER BERG
Mauerpark
Pappelallee
Helmholtzplatz
B109
Voltastr
Eberswalder Str
Hussitenstr
Bernauer Str
Schwedter Str
Kastanienallee
Danziger Str
Prenzlauer Allee
Ernst-Thälmann-Park
B96a
Jüdischer Friedhof Schönhauser Allee
Chausseestr
Nordbahnhof
Volkspark Weinberg
Arnswalder Platz
Otto-Braun-Str
Zinnowitzer Str
Rosenthaler Platz
Rosa Luxemburg Platz
Senefelderplatz
Landsberger Allee
Torstr
Am Friedrichshain
Volkspark Friedrichshain
To Gedenkstätte Hohenschönhausen (Stasi Prison) (2.75km)
Oranienburger Tor
Oranienburger Str
B2
Landsberger Allee
Weinmeisterstr
Mollstr
Petersburger Str
Richard-Sorge-Str
Friedrichstr
Hackescher Markt
Alexanderplatz
Schillingstr
Strausberger Platz
Unter den Linden
Lustgarten
Klosterstr
Lichtenberger Str
Weberwiese
Frankfurter Tor
Karl-Marx-Allee
B9
Französische Str
Hausvogteiplatz
Grunerstr
Jannowitzbrücke
FRIEDRICHSHAIN
See Kreuzberg & Friedrichshain (pp72-3)
Mohrenstr
Stadtmitte
Spittelmarkt
B1
Märkisches Museum
B96a
To Stasi Museum (1.5km)
Ostbahnhof
Heinrich-Heine-Str
Wühlischstr
Waldeckpark
Mühlenstr
Warschauer Str
Warschauer Str
Kochstr
Oranienstr
Anhalter Bahnhof
Lindenstr
Moritzplatz
Oranienplatz
WESTERN KREUZBERG
KREUZBERG
Oranienstr
Görlitzer Bahnhof
Stralauer Allee
Hallesches Ufer
Hallesches Tor
Prinzenstr
Kottbusser Tor
Schlesisches Tor
B96a
Möckernbrücke
Prinzenstr
Böckler Park
Görlitzer Str
Wiener Str
Mehringdamm
Kirchhof Jerusalem
Görlitzer Park
Treptower Park
Yorckstr
Urbanstr
B178
Gneisenaustr
Blücherstr
Schönleinstr
KREUZKÖLLN
Treptower Park
Körtestr
Urbanstr
Kreuzbergstr
Bergmannstr
Pannierstr
Lohmühlenplatz
TREPTOW
Viktoriapark
Südstern
Friesenstr
Platz der Luftbrücke
Cemeteries
Hermannplatz
Karl-Marx-Str
Eisenstr
Dudenstr
Columbiadamm
Volkspark Hasenheide
Boddinstr
Flughafenstr
Sonnenallee
B96
Garnisonsfriedhof
Rathaus Neukölln
B179
Treptower Brücke
Paradestr
Tempelhof Airport
To Schönefeld Airport (15km)
NEUKÖLLN

HIGHLIGHTS

1 BERLIN ART SCENE

BY MIRIAM BERS, ART HISTORIAN AND CO-OWNER GO-ART! TOURS AND CONSULTING

Berlin is *the* place for contemporary art. Some 10,000 artists live here and there are over 600 galleries – more than in New York City. Many collectors have moved here and the entire art world gets together for events like the Berlin Biennale. It's an inspiring, constantly evolving city; and it's still cheap: artists can afford to have an apartment *and* a studio.

MIRIAM BERS' DON'T MISS LIST

❶ GALLERY QUARTER SCHEUNENVIERTEL

Mitte's Auguststrasse and Linienstrasse were the birthplaces of Berlin's post-Wall contemporary art scene. Some have since moved on to bigger digs, but key players **Eigen+Art** (www.eigenart.de; Auguststrasse 26) and **Neugerriemschneider** (www.neugerriemschneider.com; Linienstrasse 155) are still there, alongside exciting new galleries like **Kunstagenten** (www.kunstagenten.de; Linienstrasse 155) and the innovative **DNA Galerie** (www.dna-galerie.de; Auguststrasse 20).

❷ GALLERY QUARTER SCHÖNEBERG

Over the past three years, the slightly seedy area around Potsdamer Strasse and Kurfürstenstrasse has emerged as one of Berlin's most exciting art quarters. It's a great mix of established galleries like **Giti Nourbahksch** (www.nourbakhsch.de; Kurfürstenstrasse 12), which focuses on installations, and newcomers like **Sommer + Kohl** (www.sommerkohl.com; Kurfürstenstrasse 13/14), which specialises in sculpture.

Clockwise from top: Murals and street art in Berlin; Piece by XOOOOX at Sammlung Boros; Sammlung Boros is housed in a WWII bunker; Eigen+Art, Scheunenviertel

CLOCKWISE FROM TOP: DAVID PEEVERS; DAVID PEEVERS; DAVID PEEVERS; UWE WALTER;

❸ GALLERY QUARTER CHECKPOINT CHARLIE

There's long been a cluster of important galleries on Zimmerstrasse and Rudi-Dutschke-Strasse in Kreuzberg, but of late a new corner has opened up on Markgrafenstrasse and Charlottenstrasse. Keep an eye out for **Carlier Gebauer** (www.carliergebauer.com; Markgrafenstrasse 67), **Barbara Weiss Gallerie** (www.galeriebarbaraweiss.de; Zimmerstrasse 88) and **Antje Wachs Gallerie** (www.antjewachs.de; Charlottenstrasse 3).

❹ STREET ART

Berlin has some of the best street art anywhere. There's fantastic work in Kreuzberg, especially the large-scale works by Italian artist Blu at Falckenstrasse 48 and at the corner of Cuvrystrasse and Schlesische Strasse. **Boxhagener Platz** in Friedrichshain is another hot spot, as is **Brauerei Friedrichshöhe** at Landsberger Allee 54, also in Friedrichshain. **ATM Gallerie** (www.atmberlin.de; Brunnenstrasse 24, Mitte) also focuses on street art.

❺ SAMMLUNG BOROS

This is a great **collection** (www.sammlung-boros.de; Reinhardstrasse 20, Mitte) in a spectacular location – an old WWII bunker! What makes it special is how the space has been adapted for art and also how the artists have reacted to the space. There's one artist who's created a series of works that correspond with one another across several floors, opening up constantly changing perspectives.

➘ THINGS YOU NEED TO KNOW

GoArt! (www.goart-berlin.de) specialises in art and fashion tours, consulting and studio visits. **Gallery hopping** Gallery Weekend (www.gallery-weekend-berlin.de; May) is a great time to visit Berlin. **Festival** Urban Affairs (www.urbanaffairs.de; July/August) is an international street-art festival.

HIGHLIGHTS

2 BERLIN WALL

BY MARTIN 'WOLLO' WOLLENBERG, OWNER OF BERLIN ON BIKE AND WALL EXPERT

What's so unusual about Berlin is that one of its main attractions has almost disappeared from the cityscape. Mostly, you can only see indirectly where the Berlin Wall once stood: an empty lot, some fallow land, maybe some mounts to which Wall segments or a fence were fastened, and a double row of cobbled stones along its former course.

↘ MARTIN 'WOLLO' WOLLENBERG'S DON'T MISS LIST

❶ BORDER CROSSING BORNHOLMER STRASSE

The Bornholmer Brücke steel bridge was the first border crossing to open on 9 November, 1989. Masses of East Berliners headed here on that night, completely overwhelming the border guards who had no choice but to open the gates.

❷ MAUERPARK

This park was built right on top of the Berlin Wall and is hugely popular, especially on Sundays when there's a great flea market (p87) and outdoor karaoke.

❸ GEDENKSTÄTTE BERLINER MAUER

This is the only site where you can still see all the elements of the Wall and the death strip: a section of original wall with its rounded top to make it harder to climb over; the sand strip patrolled by motorised guards; the lamps that bathed the strip in fierce light at night; and even an original guard tower. The

Clockwise from top: Art on the Mauerpark section of the Wall; A memorial at Gedenkstätte Berliner Mauer (p78); Checkpoint Charlie (p73); An outdoor cafe at Mauerpark; Mauerpark

CLOCKWISE FROM TOP: DAVID PEEVERS; MARTIN MOOS; KRZYSZTOF DYDYNSKI; DAVID PEEVERS; CHR/IMAGEBROCKER

Documentation Centre (p78) has lots of interesting background information.

❹ GEDENKSTÄTTE GÜNTER LITFIN

Günter Litfin was the first person shot dead by GDR border guards as he tried to flee to West Berlin a few days after the Wall was built. His brother Jürgen keeps alive his legacy with a small **exhibit** (☎ **0163-379 7290; Kieler Strasse 2; admission free;** 🕒 **noon-5pm Mar-Oct**) in an authentic GDR watchtower. It's the only such tower accessible and open on a regular basis. Jürgen is often around to answer questions.

❺ CHECKPOINT CHARLIE

Internationally, Checkpoint Charlie (p73) is the best-known border crossing. Berliners were not allowed to use it; it was only for foreigners and diplomats. This was the only place during the entire Cold War where there was a direct confrontation between the US and the Soviets when tanks faced off shortly after the Wall went up.

➘ THINGS YOU NEED TO KNOW

Tour Berlin on Bike (p75) runs Wall tours in English (11am Tuesday, Thursday, Saturday April–October). **Museums** For more on the Wall's history, visit Haus am Checkpoint Charlie (p73). **Original** The Wall's longest surviving stretch is the East Side Gallery (p78). **See the boxed text, p78, for more info**

HIGHLIGHTS

3

↘ MUSEUMINSEL (MUSEUM ISLAND)

Berlin's 'Louvre on the Spree' is a cluster of five museums, and a Unesco World Heritage Site. Feast your eyes on majestic antiquities at the **Pergamonmuseum** (p67) and **Altes Museum** (p67), make a date with Nefertiti at the **Neues Museum** (p68), take in Friedrich's brooding landscapes at the **Alte Nationalgalerie** (p66) and marvel at medieval sculptures at the **Bodemuseum** (p67).

4

↘ UNTER DEN LINDEN

Berlin's most splendid boulevard, **Unter den Linden** (p66), is a 1.5km-long ribbon of baroque beauties and haughty neoclassical edifices stretching from the Brandenburger Tor to Museuminsel. Originally a riding path to the hunting grounds in Tiergarten park, it was developed into a showpiece road in the 18th century. A stroll along here offers a handy introduction to the city's Prussian past.

5

↘ REICHSTAG

This famous Berlin **landmark** (p69) has been set on fire, bombed, left to crumble and wrapped in fabric before emerging as the proud home of the German parliament, the Bundestag, in 1999. The plenary hall can only be seen on guided tours, but you're free to catch the lift to the sparkling rooftop glass dome any time.

6

↘ CURRYWURST

For better or wurst (pardon the pun), Berlin's most beloved homegrown snack is the *Currywurst:* a slivered, subtly spiced pork sausage swimming in tomato sauce and sprinkled with curry powder. The iconic treat is as much part of the city's cultural tapestry as the Brandenburger Tor. Sample it at such cult purveyors as **Konnopke Imbiss** (p79) or **Curry 36** (p80).

7

↘ SCHEUNENVIERTEL

Scheunenviertel (p68) is among Berlin's most charismatic quarters, as best revealed in the villagelike labyrinth of lanes off Oranienburger Strasse, its main drag. You'll find surprises lurking around every corner: an intriguing public sculpture, a bleeding-edge gallery, cosy watering hole, 19th-century ballroom or flower-festooned hidden courtyard.

3 Pergamonmuseum (p67); 4 Staatsoper (State Opera), Unter den Linden (p66); 5 Reichstag (p69); 6 Currywurst being seasoned with curry powder; 7 Hackesche Höfe, Scheunenviertel (p68)

THE BEST...

CAPITAL VIEWS

- **Panoramapunkt** (p71) Potsdamer Platz from above.
- **Reichstag dome** (p69) Historic Mitte at your feet.
- **Solar** (p82) Cocktails with a view.
- **Fernsehturm** (TV Tower; p68) Germany's tallest building.
- **Weekend** (p83) Dancing in the sky.

FREEBIES

- **East Side Gallery** (p78) The longest surviving stretch of the Berlin Wall.
- **Holocaust Memorial** (p65) Massive memorial gets under your skin.
- **Reichstag** (p69) Close-ups of Foster's fantastic glass dome.
- **Tiergarten park** (p71) Central oasis of greenery.
- **Unter den Linden** (p66) Boulevard of historic beauties.

RIVERSIDE PLEASURES

- **Badeschiff** (p81) Swim and party in an old cargo barge moored in the Spree.
- **Boat cruises** (p75) Drift past the sights of the historic centre.
- **Kiki Blofeld** (p81) Quirky beach bar gives you that summer feeling.
- **Riverside Promenade** (p69) Jog, stroll, blade or bike through the government district.

QUIRKY SLEEPS

- **Arte Luise Kunsthotel** (p76) Unique lodging created by artists.
- **Eastern Comfort Hostel Boat** (p77) Let the 'waves' rock you to sleep.
- **Hotel Askanischer Hof** (p78) Flashback to the Golden Twenties.
- **Ostel** (p70) A must for *Good Bye, Lenin!* fans.
- **Propeller Island City Lodge** (p78) Sleep in the *Twilight Zone*.

LEFT: DAVID PEEVERS; RIGHT: BEC/IMAGEBROKER

Left: Fernsehturm (TV Tower; p68); Right: Cycling in Tiergarten park (p71)

THINGS YOU NEED TO KNOW

VITAL STATISTICS

- **Population** 3.43 million
- **Phone code** ☎ 030
- **Best time to visit** May–October

KEY DISTRICTS IN A NUTSHELL

- **Charlottenburg** Shopping, royals and chichi joints.
- **Friedrichshain** Socialist-era flavoured student quarter.
- **Kreuzberg** Gritty nightlife and Turkish flair.
- **Mitte** Blockbuster sights.
- **Potsdamer Platz** Showcase of edgy architecture.
- **Prenzlauer Berg** Boho-chic shopping and cafes.

ADVANCE PLANNING

- **As early as possible** Suss out flights and rooms if visiting around major events or trade shows (see www.visitberlin.de for dates).
- **One month before** Book tickets (see p82) for upcoming shows and events.
- **One week before** Make weekend reservations at trendy restaurants like Grill Royal (p79) and Cookies Cream (p79) and get online tickets for the Neues Museum (p68).

RESOURCES

- **Berlin Tourism** (www.visitberlin.de, www.visitBerlin.tv) Official tourist-office websites.
- **Berlin Unlike** (http://berlin-unlike.net) Hip guide with reviews, happenings and a free newsletter.
- **ExBerliner** (www.exberliner.de) English-language city mag.
- **Museumsportal Berlin** (www.museumsportal-berlin.de)

EMERGENCY NUMBERS

- **Call-a-Doc** (☎ 01804-2255 2362) Nonemergency medical assistance and treatment referral.
- **Charité Hospital** (☎ 450 50; Charité-Platz 1) 24/7 ER.
- **Fire & ambulance** (☎ 112)
- **Police** (☎ 110)

GETTING AROUND

- **Bicycle** Rent bicycles from **Fahrradstation** (☎ central reservations 0180-510 8000; www.fahrradstation.de), with six central locations.
- **Boats** (p75) Cruise along the Spree and the city canals.
- **Public transport** (p88) Runs around the clock.
- **Taxi** (p88) Ride 2km for €4 with the *Kurzstreckentarif*.

BE FOREWARNED

- **Museum savings** The SchauLust Museum pass (adult/child €19/5.50) buys three days of admission to 70 museums; available at Berlin Infostores (p63) and participating museums.
- **Party** Berlin nightlife starts notoriously late with some clubs only kicking into high gear around 4am at weekends.
- **Shopping** Most smaller stores don't accept credit cards.

DISCOVER BERLIN

Twenty years after German reunification, Berlin is a city throbbing with vitality, still struggling for an identify, yet poised for a great future. Head-spinning museums to eclectic galleries, grand opera to guerrilla clubs, gourmet outposts to ethnic snack shacks – no matter whether your tastes run to posh or punk, you can sate them in this city.

When it comes to fashion, art, design and music, Berlin is the city to watch. All this trendiness is a triumph for a town that's long been in the crosshairs of history: Berlin staged a revolution, headquartered fascists, was bombed to bits, ripped in half and finally reunited – and that was just in the 20th century! Perhaps it's because of its historical burden that Berlin is throwing itself into tomorrow. Cafes are jammed at all hours, drinking is a religious rite and clubs host their scenes of hedonism until the wee hours. Sleep? *Way* overrated.

BERLIN IN…

One Day

Get up early to beat the crowds to the **Reichstag** (p69), then snap a picture of the **Brandenburger Tor** (opposite) before exploring the maze of the **Holocaust Memorial** (p65). From there saunter along **Unter den Linden** (p66) with a detour to **Gendarmenmarkt** (p66). After lunch, peek inside the **Berliner Dom** (p68) before being awed by Nefertiti at the **Neues Museum** (p68) and the Pergamon Altar at the **Pergamonmuseum** (p67). Finish up at the **Scheunenviertel** (p68) where you should have no trouble sourcing good spots for dinner, drinks and dancing.

Two Days

Follow the one-day itinerary, then revisit Cold War history at **Checkpoint Charlie** (p73) and **Haus am Checkpoint Charlie** (p73). Spend the rest of the morning at the **Jüdisches Museum** (p73) before heading to Berlin's showcase of urban renewal, **Potsdamer Platz** (p71). Stop at the **Museum für Film und Fernsehen** (p71) or walk a few steps west to the **Kulturforum** (p71) and **Gemäldegalerie** (p71). Later, sample the cuisine and bars of **Prenzlauer Berg** (p79 and p81).

Three Days

After following the two-day itinerary, spend a morning at **Schloss Charlottenburg** (p77); don't miss the Neuer Flügel (New Wing) and Schlossgarten (palace park). Go shopping in the **KaDeWe** (p87), and have an early dinner before catching a show at the **Chamäleon Variete** (p86), followed by a nightcap at **Tausend** (p81).

ORIENTATION

Berlin is made up of 12 administrative districts, of which Mitte, Kreuzberg, Prenzlauer Berg, Charlottenburg and Friedrichshain are of most interest to visitors.

INFORMATION

Berlin Tourismus Marketing (BMT; ☎ call centre 250 025; www.visitberlin.de; call centre 8am-7pm Mon-Fri, 9am-6pm Sat & Sun) operates four walk-in offices (extended hours April to October, except Hauptbahnhof branch):

Berlin Infostore Alexa Shopping Center (Map p64; ground fl, Grunerstrasse 20, near Alexanderplatz; 10am-8pm Mon-Sat)

Berlin Infostore Brandenburger Tor (Map p64; south wing; 10am-6pm)

Berlin Infostore Hauptbahnhof (Map p64; ground fl, enter from Europaplatz; 8am-10pm)

Berlin Infostore Neues Kranzler Eck (Map pp52-3; Kurfürstendamm 21; 10am-8pm Mon-Sat, to 6pm Sun)

SIGHTS

MITTE

Mitte is the glamorous heart of Berlin, a cocktail of culture, architecture and history. Packed with blockbuster sights, this is likely where you'll concentrate your sightseeing time, where you'll come to play and learn, to admire and marvel, to be astounded and charmed.

BRANDENBURGER TOR & PARISER PLATZ

A symbol of division during the Cold War, the landmark **Brandenburger Tor** (Brandenburg Gate; Map p64) now

CLOCKWISE FROM TOP: RUSSELL MOUNTFORD; CRE/IMAGEBROKER; JWD/IMAGEBROKER; TOM/IMAGEBROKER

Clockwise from top: Brandenburger Tor (Brandenburg Gate); Street cafe in Prenzlauer Berg (p79); Holocaust Memorial (p65); Gendarmenmarkt (p66)

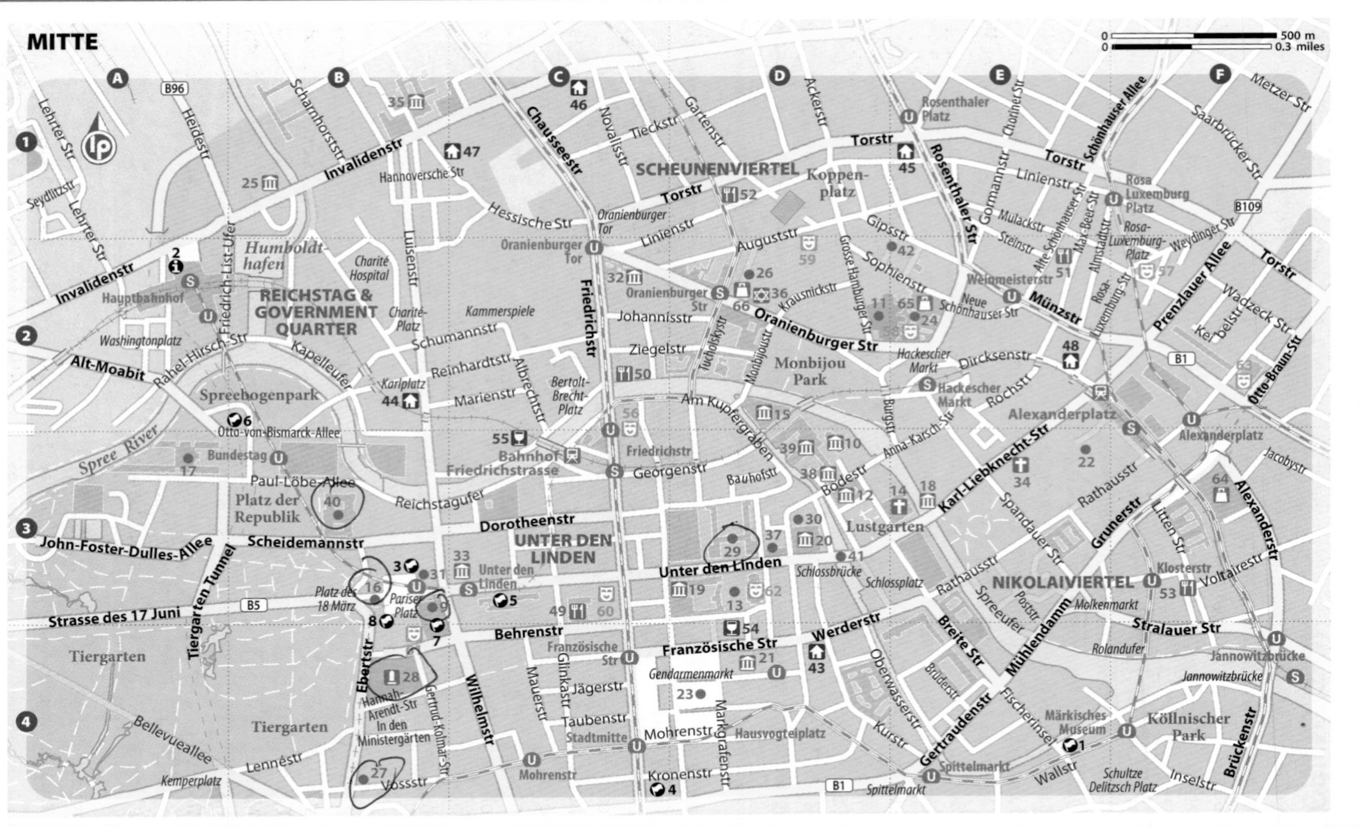
MITTE
500 m
0.3 miles
SCHEUNENVIERTEL
NIKOLAIVIERTEL
UNTER DEN LINDEN
REICHSTAG & GOVERNMENT QUARTER
Alexanderplatz
Monbijou Park
Tiergarten
Platz der Republik
Spreebogenpark
Humboldt-hafen
Köllnischer Park
Koppen-platz
Lustgarten
Spree River
Hauptbahnhof
Bahnhof Friedrichstrasse
Charité Hospital
Kammerspiele
Friedrichstr
Torstr
Chausseestr
Invalidenstr
Oranienburger Str
Karl-Liebknecht-Str
Alexanderstr
Grunerstr
Stralauer Str
Mühlendamm
Gertraudenstr
Breite Str
Französische Str
Behrenstr
Wilhelmstr
Unter den Linden
Dorotheenstr
Scheidemannstr
John-Foster-Dulles-Allee
Strasse des 17 Juni
Tiergarten Tunnel
Ebertstr
Rosenthaler Str
Münzstr
Prenzlauer Allee
Schönhauser Allee
Alt-Moabit
Heidestr
Lehrter Str
Werderstr
Brückenstr
Markgrafenstr
Gendarmenmarkt
Pariser Platz
Platz des 18 März
Märkisches Museum
Hackescher Markt

INFORMATION
Australian Embassy 1 E4
Berlin Infostore Alexa Shopping Centre (see 64)
Berlin Infostore Brandenburger Tor (see 16)
Berlin Infostore Hauptbahnhof 2 A2
French Embassy 3 B3
New Zealand Embassy 4 C4
Russian Embassy 5 C3
Swiss Embassy 6 B2
UK Embassy 7 B4
US Embassy 8 B3

SIGHTS & ACTIVITIES
Hotel Adlon 9 B3
Alte Nationalgalerie 10 D3
Alter Jüdischer Friedhof 11 D2
Altes Museum 12 D3
Bebelplatz 13 D3
Berliner Dom 14 E3
Bodemuseum 15 D2
Brandenburger Tor 16 B3
Bundeskanzleramt 17 A3
DDR Museum 18 E3
Deutsche Guggenheim 19 D3
Deutsches Historisches Museum 20 D3
Emil Nolde Museum 21 D4
Fernsehturm 22 E3
Gendarmenmarkt 23 D4
Hackesche Höfe 24 E2
Hamburger Bahnhof 25 B1
Heckmannhöfe 26 D2
Hitler's Bunker 27 B4
Holocaust Memorial (Memorial to the Murdered European Jews) 28 B4
Humboldt Universität 29 D3
IM Pei Bau 30 D3
Kennedy Museum 31 B3
Kunsthaus Tacheles 32 C2
Madame Tussauds 33 C3
Marienkirche 34 E3
Museum für Naturkunde 35 B1
Neue Synagogue 36 D2
Neue Wache 37 D3
Neues Museum 38 D3
Ort der Information (see 28)
Pergamonmuseum 39 D3
Reichstag 40 B3
Schlossbrücke 41 D3
Sophie-Gips-Höfe 42 E2

SLEEPING
Arcotel John F 43 D4
Arte Luise Kunsthotel 44 B2
Circus Hotel 45 E1
Honigmond Garden Hotel 46 C1
Miniloft Berlin 47 C1
Motel One Berlin-Alexanderplatz 48 E2

EATING
Cookies Cream 49 C3
Grill Royal 50 C2
Monsieur Vuong 51 E2
Schwarzwaldstuben 52 D1
Zur Letzen Instanz 53 F3

DRINKING
Barcomi's Deli (see 42)
Bebel Bar 54 D4
Tausend 55 C3

ENTERTAINMENT
Admiralspalast 56 C2
Babylon Mitte 57 F2
Chamäleon Varieté 58 E2
Clärchens Ballhaus 59 D2
Cookies 60 C3
Felix clubrestaurant 61 B4
Staatsoper Unter den Linden 62 D3
Weekend 63 F2

SHOPPING
Alexa 64 F3
Berlinerklamotten 65 E2
Bonbonmacherei 66 D2

epitomises German reunification. The 1791 structure by Carl Gotthard Langhans is the only surviving one of 18 city gates and is crowned by the *Quadriga* sculpture, a horse-drawn chariot piloted by the winged goddess of victory. The gate stands sentinel over **Pariser Platz**, an elegant square once again framed by embassies and bank buildings as it was during its 19th-century heyday as the 'emperor's reception hall'.

The first one was the faithfully rebuilt **Hotel Adlon** (now called the Adlon Hotel Kempinski; Map p64). A celeb magnet since its 1907 opening, it has sheltered Charlie Chaplin, Albert Einstein and even Michael Jackson. Remember him dangling his baby out the window? It happened at the Adlon.

US president John F Kennedy of *'Ich bin ein Berliner'* fame is the focus of the small **Kennedy Museum** (**Map p64; ☎ 2065 3570; www.thekennedys.de; Pariser Platz 4a; adult/concession €7/3.50; 10am-6pm**), an intimate, nonpolitical exhibit set up like a walk-through family photo album.

HOLOCAUST MEMORIAL

The football-field-sized **Memorial to the Murdered European Jews** (Map p64; colloquially known as the Holocaust Memorial) by American architect Peter Eisenman consists of 2711 sarcophagi-like concrete columns rising in sombre silence from undulating ground. For context visit the subterranean **Ort der Information** (**information centre; Map p64; ☎ 7407 2929; www.holocaust-mahnmal.de; Cora-Berliner-Strasse 1; admission free, audioguide adult/concession €3/1.50; 10am-8pm Tue-Sun Apr-Sep, to 7pm Oct-Mar, last admission 45min before closing**), whose exhibits will leave no one untouched.

HITLER'S BUNKER

Berlin was burning and Soviet tanks advancing relentlessly when Adolf Hitler, holed up in his bunker (Map p64), put a gun to his head in the final days of WWII.

Today, there's just a parking lot on the site along with an information panel (in German and English) with a diagram of the vast bunker network, technical data on how it was constructed and what happened to it after WWII.

UNTER DEN LINDEN

Berlin's most splendid boulevard (Map p64) extends for about 1.5km east of the Brandenburger Tor with grand old buildings lining up like soldiers for inspection. First up, though, is the historical ribbon's newest tourist attraction, **Madame Tussauds** (**Map p64; ☎ 4000 4600; www.madametussauds.com/berlin; Unter den Linden 74; adult/child 3-14yr €18.50/13.50; ⏲ 10am-7pm, last admission 6pm**). High-brow types will likely prefer to steer straight towards the **Deutsche Guggenheim** (**Map p64; ☎ 202 0930; www.deutsche-guggenheim.de; Unter den Linden 13-15; adult/concession/family €4/3/8, Mon free; ⏲ 10am-8pm Fri-Wed, 10am-10pm Thu**), a small, minimalist gallery spotlighting top-notch contemporary artists, such as Eduardo Chillida and Gerhard Richter.

Next up is the **Humboldt Universität** (Map p64), Berlin's oldest university where Marx and Engels studied and the Brothers Grimm and Albert Einstein taught. It occupies the palace of Prince Heinrich, brother of King Frederick the Great, whose pompous **equestrian statue** stands on Unter den Linden outside the university.

It was Frederick who created the ensemble of stately structures framing **Bebelplatz** (Map p64), the site of the first big official Nazi book-burning in May 1933. Beneath a glass pane at the square's centre Micha Ullmann's *Empty Library* commemorates the barbaric event.

Opposite, the neoclassical **Neue Wache** (**Map p64; admission free; ⏲ 10am-6pm**) was originally a Prussian guardhouse and is now an antiwar memorial with an austere interior dominated by Käthe Kollwitz's emotional sculpture *Mother and her Dead Son*.

If you're wondering what the Germans have been up to for the past 2000 years, pop next door into the excellent **Deutsches Historisches Museum** (**German Historical Museum; Map p64; ☎ 203 040; www.dhm.de; Unter den Linden 2; adult/under 18yr €5/free; ⏲ 10am-6pm**). High-calibre temporary exhibits take up a strikingly geometrical annexe, called **IM Pei Bau** (Map p64), named for the architect that designed it.

GENDARMENMARKT

Berlin's most graceful square (Map p64) was once a thriving market place and derives its name from the Gens d'Armes, a Prussian regiment recruited from French Huguenot immigrants. Plenty of luxury hotels and fancy restaurants are nearby.

MUSEUMSINSEL

East of the Deutsches Historisches Museum, the sculpture-studded **Schlossbrücke** (Palace Bridge; Map p64) leads to the little Spree island where Berlin's settlement began in the 13th century. Its northern half, Museumsinsel (Museum Island), is a fabulous treasure trove of art, sculptures and objects spread across five museums.

ALTE NATIONALGALERIE

A Greek-temple building by August Stüler is an elegant backdrop for the exquisite collection of 19th-century European art at the **Alte Nationalgalerie** (**Old National Gallery; Map p64; ☎ 2090 5577; Bodestrasse 1-3; adult/concession €8/4; ⏲ 10am-6pm Tue, Wed & Fri-Sun, to 10pm Thu**). Drawcards include Caspar David Friedrich's mystical landscapes, sensitive portraits by Max Liebermann and the light-hearted canvasses of Monet and Renoir.

EPI/IMAGEBROKER

Ishtar Gate, Pergamonmuseum

PERGAMONMUSEUM

An Aladdin's cave of treasures from ancient worlds, the Pergamonmuseum is the one museum in Berlin that should not be missed. Note that some sections may be closed while the museum is undergoing renovation over the next five years.

The undisputed highlight of the Collection of Classical Antiquities is, of course, the museum's namesake, the **Pergamon Altar** (165 BC) from today's Turkey. It's a gargantuan raised marble shrine surrounded by a vivid frieze of the gods doing battle with the giants. The next room is dominated by the immense **Market Gate of Miletus** (2nd century AD), a masterpiece of Roman architecture. Pass through it and enter another culture and century: Babylon during the reign of King Nebuchadnezzar II (604–562 BC). You're now in the Museum of Near Eastern Antiquities where top billing goes to the radiantly blue and ochre **Ishtar Gate**. Upstairs, in the Museum of Islamic Art, standouts include the fortresslike 8th-century **caliph's palace** from Mshatta in today's Jordan, and the **Aleppo Room** from 17th-century Syria with its richly painted, wood-panelled walls.

Things you need to know: **Map p64; ☎ 2090 5555; Am Kupfergraben; adult/concession incl audioguide €12/6; 🕑 10am-6pm Fri-Wed, to 10pm Thu**

ALTES MUSEUM

Karl Friedrich Schinkel pulled out all the stops for the 1830 **Altes Museum** (**Map p64; ☎ 2090 5577; Am Lustgarten; adult/concession €8/4; 🕑 10am-6pm Fri-Wed, to 10pm Thu**). An architectural highlight is the Pantheon-inspired rotunda, which displays a prized collection of Greek and Roman art and sculpture.

BODEMUSEUM

This mighty **museum** (**Map p64; ☎ 2090 5577; Monbijou-brücke; adult/concession €8/4; 🕑 10am-6pm Fri-Wed, to 10pm Thu**), in a neobaroque edifice by Ernst von Ihne, houses Byzantine art, a coin collection, old paintings and, most importantly, European sculpture from the Middle Ages to the 18th century.

NEUES MUSEUM

After 10 years and €200 million, the reconstructed **Neues Museum** (**New Museum; Map p64; ☎ 2090 5555; www.smb.spk-berlin.de; adult/concession €10/5; 🕙 10am-6pm Sun-Wed, to 8pm Thu-Sat**) finally opened in October 2009. David Chipperfield harmoniously incorporated remnants of the war-damaged structure into the new building, which presents the Egyptian Museum (including the famous bust of Queen Nefertiti) and the Papyrus Collection.

BERLINER DOM

Pompous yet majestic, the 1905 neo-Renaissance **Berliner Dom** (**Berlin Cathedral; Map p64; ☎ 2026 9136; Am Lustgarten; adult/under 14yr/concession without audioguide €5/free/3, with audioguide €8/free/6; 🕙 9am-8pm Mon-Sat, noon-8pm Sun Apr-Sep, to 7pm Oct-Mar**) was once the royal court church and now does triple duty as house of worship, museum and concert hall.

ALEXANDERPLATZ & AROUND

Eastern Berlin's main commercial hub, Alexanderplatz ('Alex' for short; Map p64) was named in honour of Tsar Alexander I on his 1805 visit to Berlin. Despite postreunification attempts to temper the socialist look created during the 1960s, Alexanderplatz remains an oddly cluttered, soulless square that's all concrete with no trees.

The main sight around here is the **Fernsehturm** (**TV Tower; Map p64; ☎ 242 3333; adult/child under 16yr €10/5.50, VIP ticket €19.50; 🕙 9am-midnight Mar-Oct, 10am-midnight Nov-Feb**), at 368m the tallest structure in Germany. Come early (or buy a VIP ticket and skip the line) to beat the queue for the lift to the panorama level at 203m, where views are unbeatable on clear days. Pinpoint city landmarks from here or the upstairs cafe, which makes one revolution in 30 minutes.

To find some open space, wander west of the TV Tower and linger among the flower beds and fountains next to the 13th-century **Marienkirche** (**Church of St Mary; Map p64; ☎ 242 4467; Karl-Liebknecht-Strasse 8; admission free; 🕙 10am-9pm Apr-Oct, 10am-6pm Nov-Mar**), Berlin's second-oldest church. Nearby, the **DDR Museum** (**GDR Museum; Map p64; ☎ 847 123 731; Karl-Liebknecht-Strasse 1; adult/concession €5.50/3.50; 🕙 10am-8pm Sun-Fri, to 10pm Sat**) teaches the rest of us about daily life behind the Iron Curtain.

SCHEUNENVIERTEL

It's hard to imagine that, until reunification, the dapper Scheunenviertel (literally 'Barn Quarter') was a neglected, down-at-heel barrio with tumbledown buildings and dirty streets. Fanning out northwest of Alexanderplatz, it's since catapulted from drab to fab and teems with restaurants, bars, clubs, cabarets, concept stores, owner-run boutiques and even a fair amount of resident celebrities.

The Scheunenviertel has also reprised its legacy as a centre of Jewish life with the gleaming gold dome of the **Neue Synagoge** (**New Synagogue; Map p64; ☎ 8802 8300; www.cjudaicum.de; Oranienburger Strasse 28-30; adult/concession €3/2; 🕙 10am-8pm Sun & Mon, to 6pm Tue-Thu, to 5pm Fri Apr-Sep, reduced hours Oct-Mar**) being its most striking landmark. The dome can be climbed. From the top you can easily spot a crumbling building that, upon closer inspection, looks like the 'Sistine Chapel of Graffiti'. It's the **Kunsthaus Tacheles** (**Map p64; ☎ 282 6185; Oranienburger Strasse 54-56; admission free**), a one-time department store turned artists squat after reunification and now a beloved alternative art and culture space.

A particularly enchanting feature of the Scheunenviertel is the quarter's *Höfe*, interlinked hidden courtyards filled with cafes, boutiques and party venues. The best known is the **Hackesche Höfe** (Map p64) but also check out the quiet and dignified **Sophie-Gips-Höfe** (Map p64) and the breezy **Heckmannhöfe** (Map p64).

The quarter's Jewish heritage is never far away either. Everywhere you look you'll see small brass **paving stones** commemorating Nazi victims. The great Enlightenment philosopher Moses Mendelssohn was among the 12,000 people buried at **Alter Jüdischer Friedhof** (Map p64), the city's oldest Jewish cemetery, on Grosse Hamburger Strasse.

North of here, you can meet dinosaurs and travel back to the beginning of time at the beautiful **Museum für Naturkunde** (Natural History Museum; Map p64; ☎ 2093 8591; Invalidenstrasse 43; adult/concession/family €3.50/2/7; ⏲ 9.30am-5pm Tue-Fri, 10am-6pm Sat & Sun). Star of the show is the world's largest mounted lizard, a 23m-long and 12m-high brachiosaurus, who's joined by a dozen other Jurassic buddies and an ultrarare archaeopteryx.

THOMAS WINZ

Bodemuseum (p67) and Fernsehturm (TV Tower; p68)

REICHSTAG & GOVERNMENT QUARTER

Germany's federal government quarter snuggles into the Spreebogen, a horseshoe-shaped bend of the Spree River. A leisurely stroll along the **river promenade** takes you past beer gardens and beach bars and allows for interesting perspectives.

The quarter's historical anchor is the 1894 **Reichstag** (Map p64; Platz der Republik 1), where the German parliament, the Bundestag, has been hammering out its policies since 1999. It's well worth queuing for the **lift ride** (admission free; ⏲ 8am-midnight, last entry 10pm) to the top to take in the knock-out panorama and close-ups of the dome and the mirror-clad funnel at its centre. Queues are shortest early morning and at night.

In the 1990s several other government buildings sprouted around the Reichstag, most notably the **Bundeskanzleramt** (Federal Chancellery; Map p64; Willy-Brandt-Strasse 1), an unusual H-shaped compound where Germany's chancellor keeps their office.

North of the Spree looms the spaceship-like **Hauptbahnhof** (main train station; Map p64), which looks most impressive at night. East of here, a defunct 19th-century train station has been reborn as Berlin's hotbed of contemporary art. Called the **Hamburger Bahnhof** (Map p64; ☎ 3978 3439; Invalidenstrasse 50-51; adult/under 16yr/concession €8/free/4, last 4hr Thu free; ⏲ 10am-6pm Tue-Fri, 11am-8pm Sat, 11am-6pm Sun), it displays career-spanning bodies of work by Andy Warhol, Roy Lichtenstein, Anselm Kiefer, Joseph Beuys and other 20th-century heavyweights.

DAVID PEEVERS

Stasi Museum, housed in the former Stasi Headquarters

IF YOU LIKE...

If you've enjoyed wallowing in 'Ostalgie' (nostalgia for East Germany) at the **DDR Museum** (p68), you may want to supplement your impressions at these places:

- **Stasi Museum** (off Map pp52-3; ☎ 553 6854; Ruschestrasse 103, House 1; adult/concession €3.50/3; 11am-6pm Mon-Fri, 2-6pm Sat & Sun) Cunningly low-tech surveillance devices, a prisoner transport van and the obsessively neat offices of Stasi chief Erich Mielke are among the starring exhibits in the ex-Stasi HQ. Take the U-Bahn to Magdalenenstrasse, walk north on Ruschestrasse, turn right after about 100m and walk towards the building in front of you.
- **Stasi Prison** (off Map pp52-3; ☎ 9860 8230; Genslerstrasse 66; tour adult/concession €4/2, Mon free; tours 11am & 1pm Mon-Fri, also 3pm Mar-Dec, hourly 10am-4pm Sat & Sun) Victims of Stasi persecution often ended up in this grim prison. Tours (some in English, call ahead) reveal the full extent of the terror perpetrated upon suspected regime opponents. Take tram M5 from Alexanderplatz to Freienwalder Strasse, then walk 10 minutes along Freienwalder Strasse.
- **Trabi Safari** (www.trabi-safari.de; cnr Wilhelmstrasse & Zimmerstrasse; 1/2/3/4 passengers per person €60/40/35/30) Spend an hour exploring Berlin's Wild East behind the wheel – or as a passenger – of a GDR-era Trabant (Trabi for short).
- **Ostel** (Map pp72-3; ☎ 2576 8660; www.ostel.eu; Wriezener Karree 5; dm €9, d from €33) This unique hostel resuscitates GDR charm with original furnishings sourced from flea markets, grannies' attics and eBay. Stay in a Pioneer Room dorm, a '70s holiday apartment, a prefab flat or the bugged Stasi Suite.
- **CSA** (Map pp52-3; ☎ 2904 4741; Karl-Marx-Allee 96; from 8pm May-Oct, from 7pm Nov-Apr) Carved out of the former Czechoslovakian national airline office, this chic bar exudes an ironic Soviet vintage vibe. Dim lights, clear design lines and strong cocktails make this a favourite of the grown-up set.

POTSDAMER PLATZ & TIERGARTEN

Potsdamer Platz is Berlin's newest quarter, built on terrain once bifurcated by the Berlin Wall. It became a showcase of urban renewal in the late 1990s, drawing some of the world's finest architects, including Renzo Piano, Richard Rodgers and Helmut Jahn. For the best bird's-eye views in the city, take what is billed as Europe's fastest lift to the observation deck of the **Panoramapunkt** (Map pp72-3; ☎ 2529 4372; www.panoramapunkt.de; Potsdamer Platz 1; adult/concession €5/4; 🕑 11am-8pm). Germany's film history, meanwhile, gets the star treatment year-round in the engaging **Museum für Film und Fernsehen** (Museum of Film & TV; Map pp72-3; ☎ 300 9030; Potsdamer Strasse 2; adult/concession/family €6/4.50/12; 🕑 10am-6pm Tue, Wed & Fri-Sun, to 8pm Thu) in the Sony Center. Make use of the excellent audioguide as you skip around galleries dedicated to pioneers such as Fritz Lang, ground-breaking movies such as *Olympia* by Leni Riefenstahl and legendary divas such as Marlene Dietrich.

KULTURFORUM

It's easy to spend a day or more mingling with masters old and modern in the five top-notch museums that make up this stellar cultural complex just west of Potsdamer Platz. The first of the Kulturforum museums to be completed was the **Neue Nationalgalerie** (New National Gallery; Map pp72-3; ☎ 266 2651; Potsdamer Strasse 50; adult/concession €8/4; 🕑 10am-6pm Tue, Wed & Sun, to 10pm Thu, to 8pm Fri & Sat), an edgy glass temple by Ludwig Mies van der Rohe that shelters early-20th-century European paintings and sculpture. Expect all the usual suspects from Picasso to Dalí, plus an outstanding collection of German expressionists such as Georg Grosz and Ernst Ludwig Kirchner.

Older masters grace the walls of the **Gemäldegalerie** (Picture Gallery; Map pp72-3; ☎ 266 2951; Matthäikirchplatz 8; adult/concession incl audioguide €8/4; 🕑 10am-6pm Tue, Wed & Fri-Sun, to 10pm Thu), a gallery of European art from the 13th to the 18th centuries that is famous for its exceptional quality and breadth. Take advantage of the audioguide to get the low-down on selected works by Rembrandt, Dürer, Hals, Vermeer and Gainsborough.

Nearby, the cavernous **Kunstgewerbemuseum** (Museum of Decorative Arts; Map pp72-3; ☎ 266 2951; Tiergartenstrasse 6; adult/concession €8/4; 🕑 10am-6pm Tue-Fri, 11am-6pm Sat & Sun) brims with precious objects created through the ages from gold, silver, ivory, wood, porcelain and other fine materials.

The honey-coloured building east of here is Scharoun's famous **Berliner Philharmonie** (Map pp72-3). Its auditorium feels like the inside of a finely crafted instrument and boasts supreme acoustics and excellent sightlines thanks to a clever terraced vineyard design.

TIERGARTEN PARK

Tiergarten is bisected east–west by Strasse des 17 Juni, home to a Soviet WWII memorial and the Flohmarkt Strasse des 17 Juni (p87). Big festivals and the annual Christopher Street Day parade (p48) are staged along here, usually culminating at the landmark **Siegessäule** (Victory Column; Map pp52-3; ☎ 391 2961; adult/concession €2.20/1.50; 🕑 9.30am-6.30pm Mon-Fri, 9.30am-7pm Sat & Sun Apr-Oct, 10am-5pm Mon-Fri, 10am-5.30pm Sat & Sun Nov-Mar), a triumphal column envisioned as a monument to Prussian military exploits.

South of Tiergarten park, the Diplomatic Quarter is home to several striking embassy buildings. Architecture buffs, meanwhile, gravitate west along the canal where the **Bauhaus Archiv/ Museum für Gestaltung** (**Bauhaus Archive/Museum of Design; Map pp52-3; ☎ 254 0020; Klingelhöferstrasse 14; adult/concession €6/3; 🕑 10am-5pm Wed-Mon**) occupies an avant-garde building by Bauhaus school founder Walter Gropius. The study notes, workshop pieces, models, blueprints and other items by Klee, Kandinsky, Schlemmer and other Bauhaus practitioners underline the movement's enormous influence on all aspects of 20th-century architecture and design.

KREUZBERG

Kreuzberg gets its street cred from being delightfully edgy, wacky and, most of all, unpredictable. The western half around Bergmannstrasse and Mehringdamm is solidly in the hands of upmarket bohemians and also harbours the essential-viewing Jewish Museum. Eastern Kreuzberg (still called SO36, after its pre-reunification postal code), by contrast, is a multicultural, multigenerational mosaic with the most dynamic nightlife in town.

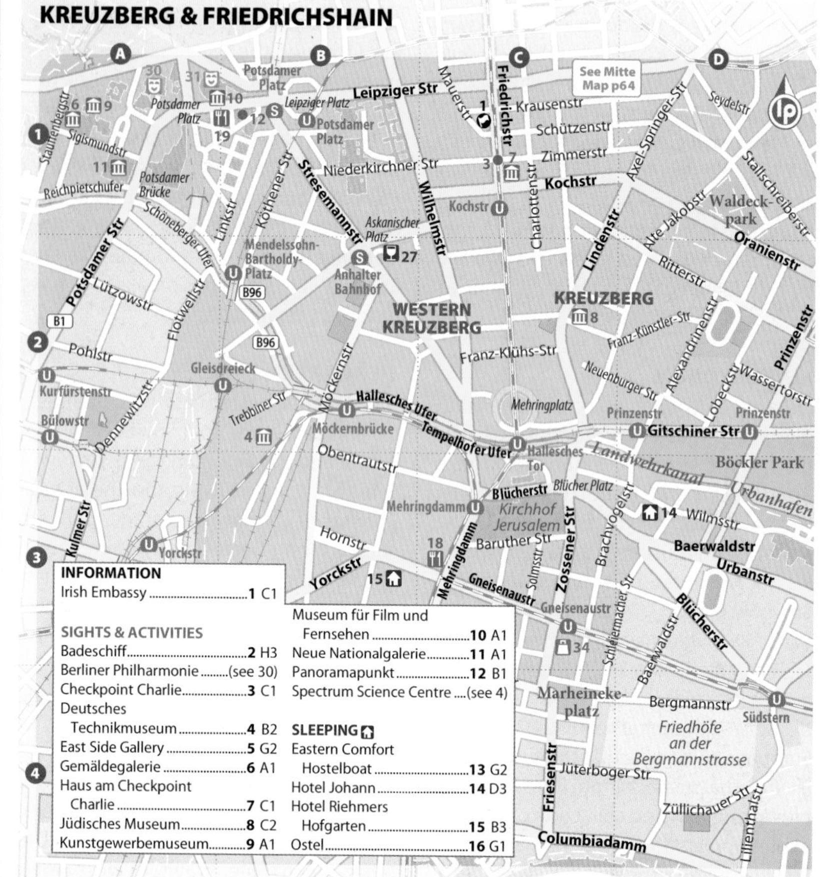

INFORMATION
Irish Embassy 1 C1

SIGHTS & ACTIVITIES
Badeschiff 2 H3
Berliner Philharmonie .... (see 30)
Checkpoint Charlie 3 C1
Deutsches Technikmuseum 4 B2
East Side Gallery 5 G2
Gemäldegalerie 6 A1
Haus am Checkpoint Charlie 7 C1
Jüdisches Museum 8 C2
Kunstgewerbemuseum 9 A1
Museum für Film und Fernsehen 10 A1
Neue Nationalgalerie 11 A1
Panoramapunkt 12 B1
Spectrum Science Centre .... (see 4)

SLEEPING
Eastern Comfort Hostelboat 13 G2
Hotel Johann 14 D3
Hotel Riehmers Hofgarten 15 B3
Ostel 16 G1

JÜDISCHES MUSEUM

For an eye-opening, emotional and interactive exploration of 2000 years of Jewish history in Germany visit the impressive **Jüdisches Museum** (**Jewish Museum; Map pp72-3; ☎ 2599 3300; www.jmberlin.de; Lindenstrasse 9-14; adult/concession/family €5/2.50/10; 🕑 10am-10pm Mon, to 8pm Tue-Sun**). You'll learn about Jewish cultural contributions, holiday traditions, the difficult road to Emancipation, and outstanding individuals, such as jeans inventor Levi Strauss and philosopher Moses Mendelssohn.

CHECKPOINT CHARLIE

Checkpoint Charlie (Map pp72-3) was the principal gateway for Allies, other non-Germans and diplomats between the two Berlins from 1961 to 1990. Unfortunately, this potent symbol of the Cold War has become a tacky tourist trap where uniformed actors pose with tourists (for tips) next to a replica guardhouse. The Cold War years, especially the history and horror of the Berlin Wall, are haphazardly, but well-meaningly, chronicled in the private **Haus am Checkpoint Charlie** (**Map pp72-3; ☎ 253 7250; www.mauermuseum.de; Friedrichstrasse 43-45;**

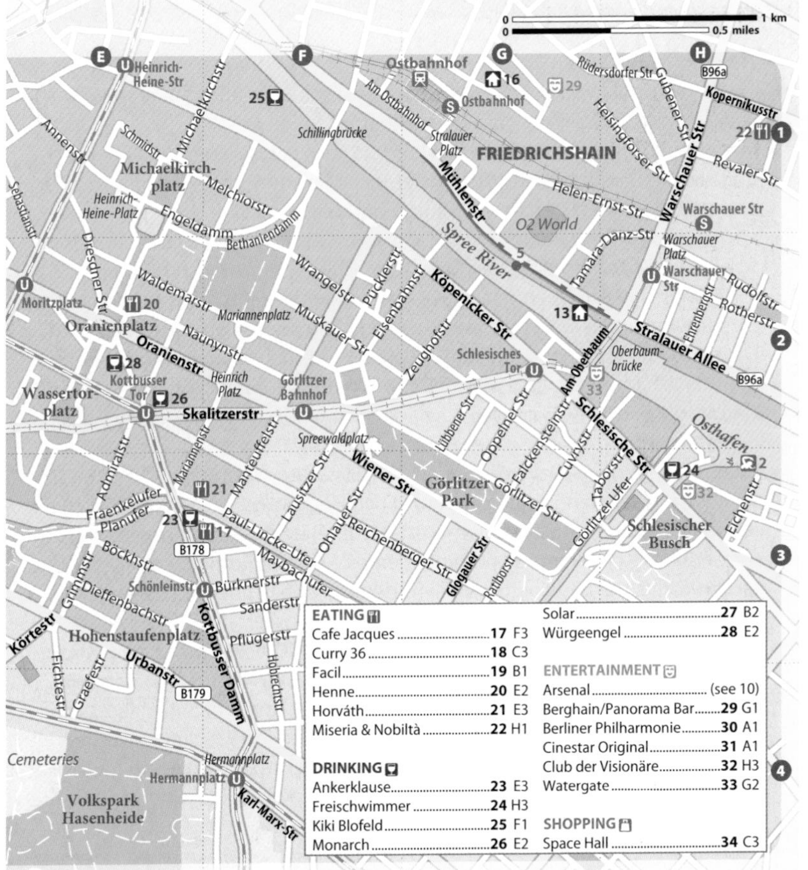

JAE/IMAGEBROKER

Liebermann-Villa am Wannsee

IF YOU LIKE...

If you didn't get your fill of fabulous paintings at the **Gemäldegalerie** (p71), make a beeline to these great galleries for another art fix:

- **Museum Berggruen** (Map pp52-3; ☎ 3269 5815; www.smb.museum/mb; Schlossstrasse 1, Charlottenburg; admission €8; 10am-6pm Tue-Sun) Small but exquisite museum with a special focus on Picasso, Klee, Matisse and Giacometti.
- **Sammlung Scharf-Gerstenberg** (Map pp52-3; ☎ 3435 7315; www.smb.museum/ssg; Schlossstrasse 70, Charlottenburg; adult/under 16 yr/concession €8/free/4, last 4hr Thu free; 10am-6pm Tue-Sun) Open since 2008, this stellar museum trains the spotlight on surrealist artists with an impressive body of works by Magritte, Max Ernst, Dalí, Dubuffet and their 18th-century precursors such as Goya and Piranesi.
- **Emil Nolde Museum** (Map p64; ☎ 4000 4690; www.nolde-stiftung.de; Jägerstrasse 55, Mitte; admission €10; 10am-7pm) A selection of works by Nolde, a key German expressionist.
- **Brücke Museum** (off Map pp52-3; ☎ 831 2029; Bussardsteig 9; admission €4; 11am-5pm Wed-Mon) In 1905 Karl Schmidt-Rottluff, Erich Heckel and Ernst Ludwig Kirchner founded Germany's first modern-artist group, Die Brücke, and paved the way for German expressionism and other genres. Schmidt-Rottluff's personal collection forms the basis of this small museum in the Grunewald Forest (U-Bahn to Oskar-Helene-Heim, then bus 115 to Pücklerstrasse).
- **Liebermann-Villa am Wannsee** (off Map pp52-3; ☎ 8058 5900; www.max-liebermann.de; Colomierstrasse 3; admission €6; 11am-6pm Wed-Mon, to 8pm Thu Apr-Sep, 11am-5pm Wed-Mon Oct-Mar) This lakeside villa was the summer home of Berlin Secession founder Max Liebermann from 1909 until his death in 1935. Influenced by French Impressionism, Liebermann loved the lyricism of nature and gardens in particular and often painted the scenery right outside his window. Take the U-Bahn to Wannsee, then bus 114 to Colomierstrasse.

adult/concession €12.50/9.50; 9am-10pm). The best bits are about ingenious escapes to the West through tunnels, in hot-air balloons, concealed compartments in cars and even a one-man submarine.

DEUTSCHES TECHNIKMUSEUM

Fantastic for kids, the **Deutsches Technikmuseum** (German Museum of Technology; Map pp72-3; ☎ 902 540; Trebbiner Strasse 9; adult/concession €4.50/2.50, under 18yr after 3pm free; 9am-5.30pm Tue-Fri, 10am-6pm Sat & Sun) is a giant shrine to technology that counts the world's first computer, an entire hall of vintage locomotives and extensive exhibits on aviation and navigation among its top attractions. At the adjacent **Spectrum Science Centre** (Map pp72-3; enter from Möckernstrasse 26; admission incl; as above) you can participate in some 250 experiments.

FRIEDRICHSHAIN

Friedrichshain, in the former East Berlin, is a shape-shifter, a slippery creature, still unsettled in its world view and offering a rambunctious stage for good times and DIY surprises. Conventional tourist sites are limited to the **East Side Gallery**, the longest remaining stretch of the Berlin Wall (see p78), and the **Karl-Marx-Allee** (Map pp52-3), a grand boulevard built between 1952 and 1960 that is the epitome of Stalinist pomposity. The exhibit at Cafe Sybille at No 72 has more background.

CHARLOTTENBURG

KURFÜRSTENDAMM & AROUND

The 3.5km-long Kurfürstendamm (Ku'damm for short) is a ribbon of commerce that began as a bridle path to the royal hunting lodge in the Grunewald forest. On Breitscheidplatz, the boulevard's eastern terminus, the bombed-out tower of the landmark **Kaiser-Wilhelm-Gedächtniskirche** (Emperor-William-Memorial-Church; Map pp52-3; admission free; 9am-7pm) serves as an antiwar memorial, standing quiet and dignified amid the roar. Near the church, an exotic Elephant Gate leads inside the **Berlin Zoo** (Map pp52-3; ☎ 254 010; enter on Hardenbergplatz or on Budapester Strasse; adult/child/student zoo or aquarium €12/6/9, zoo & aquarium €18/9/14; 9am-7pm mid-Mar–mid-Oct, to 6pm mid-Sep–mid-Oct, to 5pm mid-Oct–mid-Mar), Germany's oldest animal park. Some 14,000 furry, feathered and flippered creatures from all continents, 1500 species in total, make their home here.

Further west on Ku'damm, the **Story of Berlin** (Map pp52-3; ☎ 8872 0100; Kurfürstendamm 207-208; adult/concession/family €9.80/8/21; 10am-8pm, last admission & bunker tour 6pm) is a multimedia museum that breaks down 800 years of Berlin history into bite-sized chunks that are easy to swallow but substantial enough to be satisfying. The Cold War comes creepily to life during a tour of a still fully functional atomic bunker beneath the building.

TOURS

Bus 100 & 200 One of Berlin's best bargains is a self-guided city tour aboard public buses 100 or 200. Routes check off nearly every major sight in the city centre for the price of a standard bus ticket (€2.10, day pass €6.10).

Berlin on Bike (Map pp52-3; ☎ 4373 9999; www.berlinonbike.de; Knaackstrasse 97; tours incl bike €17, with own bike €12, discounts available for children, students and Berlin Welcome Card holders; Apr-Oct)

Berlin Walks (☎ 301 9194; www.berlinwalks.de) The first English-language walking-tour company founded after the fall of the Wall, and still tops.

New Berlin Tours (☎ 0179-973 0397; www.newberlintours.com) Pioneered the concept of 'free tour' and notorious pub crawl.

A lovely way to experience Berlin on a warm day is from the deck of a boat cruising along the city's rivers, canals and lakes. Tours range from one-hour spins around the historic centre (from €7) to longer trips to Schloss Charlottenburg and beyond (from €16). **Stern & Kreisschiffahrt** (www.stern undkreis.de) is one of the main operators.

SLEEPING

Also see p82 for holiday apartments.

MITTE

Motel One Berlin-Alexanderplatz (Map p64; ☎ 2005 4080; www.motel-one.de; Dircksenstrasse 36; d €74-124, breakfast €6.50; P ⊠ ✣ ≋) This stylish crash pad for the cash-strapped has smallish rooms but up-to-the-minute touches (flat-screen TVs, rainforest showers) that are normally the staple of posher players.

Circus Hotel (Map p64; ☎ 2839 1433; www.circus-berlin.de; Rosenthaler Strasse 1; s €68, d €78-98; ⊠ 💻 ≋) The Circus crew has upped the ante once again with this awesome outpost perfect for grown-up backies. It gets rave reviews for its friendly, professional staff, colour-drenched rooms, excellent breakfast, eco-conscious approach and progressive touches, such as iPod and baby-phone rentals.

Arte Luise Kunsthotel (Map p64; ☎ 284 480; www.luise-berlin.com; Luisenstrasse 19; s €80-115, d €100-210, breakfast €11; P ⊠ ≋) At this 'gallery with rooms' you might sleep in a bed built for giants, in the company of astronauts or inside a boudoir-red 'Cabaret'. Smaller, bathless rooms are also available. Courtyard rooms are quieter.

Honigmond Garden Hotel (Map p64; ☎ 2844 5577; www.honigmond-berlin.de; Invalidenstrasse 122; s €105-175, d €125-235; P ⊠ 💻 ≋) Never mind the busy thoroughfare: this 20-room guesthouse is a sweet retreat where antique-filled rooms overlook a flowery garden with koi pond.

Arcotel John F (Map p64; ☎ 405 0460; www.arcotel.at; Werderscher Markt 11; r €108-280, breakfast €18; P ⊠ ✣ 💻 ≋) This urbane lifestyle hotel pays homage to John F Kennedy with plenty of whimsical detail, including hand-carved rocking chairs (because the President used one to combat a bad back) and curvaceous lamps inspired by Jackie's ball gown.

PRENZLAUER BERG

Meininger City Hostel & Hotel (Map pp52-3; ☎ 6663 6100; www.meininger-hostels.de; Schönhauser Allee 19; dm/s/d/tr €19/52/70/102, breakfast €3.50; P ⊠ 💻 ≋) Run with panache and professionalism, this top-flight hotel-hostel combo is ideal for savvy nomads seeking plenty of comfort without dropping buckets of cash. Check the website for the other four Berlin locations, including a new one at the Hauptbahnhof.

Ackselhaus & Blue Home (Map pp52-3; ☎ 4433 7633; www.ackselhaus.de; Belforter Strasse 21; 1-/2-room apt from €110-180; ≋) This charismatic contender brings 'sexy' back in 10 apartments spread across two 19th-century buildings. Themed from naughty to nautical, elegant to Eastern, each sports a small living room and kitchenette.

KREUZBERG & FRIEDRICHSHAIN

Hotel Johann (Map pp72-3; ☎ 225 0740; www.hotel-johann-berlin.de; Johanniterstrasse 8; s €70-90, d €95-105; ⊠ ≋) This 33-room hotel consistently tops the popularity charts thanks to its eager-to-please service and gorgeous rooms, some with scalloped ceilings, exposed brick walls and other historic touches.

Hotel Riehmers Hofgarten (Map pp72-3; ☎ 7809 8800; www.riehmers-hofgarten.de;

RICHARD NEBESKY

The main gate of Schloss Charlottenburg

↘ SCHLOSS CHARLOTTENBURG

The grandest of Berlin's surviving nine former royal pads is **Schloss Charlottenburg**. It consists of the main palace and two outbuildings in the lovely **Schlossgarten** (palace park). Each building charges separate admission, but it's best to invest in the *Tageskarte* that gives you an entire day to see everything except the Neuer Flügel (New Wing).

The Schloss began as the summer residence of Sophie Charlotte, wife of King Friedrich I. Their baroque living quarters in the palace's oldest section, the **Altes Schloss** (Old Palace), are an extravaganza in stucco, brocade and overall opulence. The most beautiful rooms, though, are the flamboyant private chambers of Frederick the Great in the **Neuer Flügel**, designed by star architect du jour Georg Wenzeslaus von Knobelsdorff in 1746.

Things you need to know: Schloss Charlottenburg (**Charlottenburg Palace; Map pp52-3; ☎ 320 911; www.spsg.de; Spandauer Damm; day pass adult/concession €12/9; Richard-Wagner-Platz, then 145**); Altes Schloss (**☎ 320 911; adult/concession incl guided tour or audioguide €10/7; 10am-6pm Tue-Sun Apr-Oct, to 5pm Nov-Mar**); Neuer Flügel (**☎ 320 911; adult/concession incl audioguide €6/5; 10am-6pm Wed-Mon Apr-Oct, to 5pm Nov-Mar**)

Yorckstrasse 83; s €100, d €138-145;) Near Viktoriapark, this charismatic boutique hotel is part of a protected 1891 building complex with a lush inner courtyard certain to delight romantics. Large double French doors lead to mostly spacious, high-ceilinged rooms that are modern but not stark. Gourmet restaurant.

Eastern Comfort Hostelboat (**Map pp72-3; ☎ 6676 3806; www.eastern-comfort.com; Mühlenstrasse 73-77; dm €16-19, 2nd-class s/d/tr/q €50/58/69/76, 1st-class s/d €64/78, linen €5;**) Moored right by the East Side Gallery, this floating hostel puts you within staggering distance of top party venues. Cabins are carpeted and trimmed

THE BERLIN WALL

For 28 years the Berlin Wall, the most potent symbol of the Cold War, divided not only the city but the world. Construction began shortly after midnight of 13 August 1961, when East German soldiers rolled out miles of barbed wire that would soon be replaced with prefab concrete slabs. The demise of the Wall came as unexpectedly as its creation. On 9 November 1989 SED spokesperson Günter Schabowski made a surprise announcement on GDR TV: all travel restrictions to the West had been lifted – effective immediately. Amid scenes of wild partying and mile-long parades of GDR-made Trabant cars, the two Berlins came together again.

Only little more than 1.5km of the Berlin Wall still stands as a symbol of the triumph of freedom over oppression. The longest, best-preserved and most interesting stretch is the **East Side Gallery** (Map pp72-3), a 1.3km-long section paralleling the Spree, which was turned into an open-air gallery by international artists in 1990.

For more background, swing by the **Gedenkstätte Berliner Mauer** (Map pp52-3; ☎ 464 1030; www.berliner-mauer-gedenkstaette.de; Bernauer Strasse 111; admission free; 🕑 10am-6pm Apr-Oct, to 5pm Nov-Mar), a soon-to-be-expanded memorial that combines a documentation centre, an art installation, a short section of original Wall, a chapel and an outdoor gallery. A high-tech way to walk the Wall is with the **Mauerguide** (www.mauerguide.de; adult/concession per 4hr €8/5, per day €10/7), a nifty handheld minicomputer that maps its course via GPS and provides intelligent commentary and historic audio and video.

in wood, but pretty snug (except for '1st-class'); all but the dorms have their own shower and loo.

CHARLOTTENBURG

OUR PICK **Propeller Island City Lodge** (Map pp52-3; ☎ 8am-noon 891 9016, noon-8pm 0163-256-5909; www.propeller-island.de; Albrecht-Achilles-Strasse 58; r €65-180, breakfast €7; ⊠) To be stranded on Propeller Island means waking up on the ceiling, in a prison cell or inside a kaleidoscope. This is no conventional hotel, so don't expect pillow treats or other trappings.

Hotel Askanischer Hof (Map pp52-3; ☎ 881 8033; www.askanischer-hof.de; Kurfürstendamm 53; s €105-130, d €117-155; P ⊠ wi-fi) In a city that likes to teeter on the cutting edge, this 17-room jewel warps you back in time to the roaring '20s, albeit with updated amenities.

Hotel Art Nouveau (Map pp52-3; ☎ 327 7440; www.hotelartnouveau.de; Leibnizstrasse 59; s €96-146, d €126-176, tr €151-191; P ⊠ 💻 wi-fi) A rickety belle-époque lift drops you off at one of Berlin's finest boutique *Pensionen*. Its rooms neither skimp on space nor on charisma and offer a unique blend of youthful flair and tradition.

EATING

MITTE

Schwarzwaldstuben (Map p64; ☎ 2809 8084; Tucholskystrasse 48; mains €7-14; 🕑 9am-midnight; wi-fi) The tongue-in-cheek olde-worlde decor is as delicious as the authentic southern German food served in gut-busting portions at this cosy corner joint.

Monsieur Vuong (Map p64; ☎ 3087 2643; Alte Schönhauser Strasse 46; mains €7.50; ⏰ noon-midnight) This upbeat Indochina nosh stop hasn't lost a step despite becoming a fixture on the tourist circuit. From the flavour-packed soups to the fragrant rice and noodle dishes, it's all delicious even if the steady queue does not make for leisurely meals.

Zur Letzten Instanz (Map p64; ☎ 242 5528; Waisenstrasse 14-16; mains €9-18; ⏰ noon-1am Mon-Sat) Oozing folksy Old Berlin charm, this rustic eatery has been an enduring hit since 1621 and has fed everyone from Napoleon to Angela Merkel. It's one of the best places in town for classic Berlin fare.

Cookies Cream (Map p64; ☎ 2749 2940; Friedrichstrasse 158; 3-course meal €30; ⏰ dinner Tue-Sat) Combining coolness with substance, this great hidden eatery is reached via the service alley of the Westin Grand Hotel. Upstairs awaits an elegantly industrial space where flesh-free but flavour-packed dishes are brought to linen-draped tables.

Grill Royal (Map p64; ☎ 2887 9288; Friedrichstrasse 105b; mains €16-48; ⏰ dinner) A platinum card is a handy accessory at this 'look-at-me' temple, where politicians, Russian oligarchs, pouting models and 'trustafarians' can be seen slurping oysters and tucking into *wagyū* steak.

PRENZLAUER BERG

Konnopke Imbiss (Map pp52-3; ☎ 442 7765; Schönhauser Allee 44a; dishes €1.30-3.90; ⏰ 6am-8pm Mon-Fri, noon-7pm Sat) Legendary *Currywurst* kitchen.

Fellas (Map pp52-3; ☎ 4679 6314; Stargarder Strasse 3; mains €7-18; ⏰ 10am-1am; 📶) This unhurried bistro employs cooks surely destined for fancier places. The regular menu has great salads and schnitzel, but the most creativity goes into the big-flavoured weekly specials.

Oderquelle (Map pp52-3; ☎ 4400 8080; Oderberger Strasse 27; mains €8-16; ⏰ dinner) If this restaurant weren't so darn popular, you'd just pop in for a beer and a casual but well-crafted German meal. But, alas, without a reservation, chances of scoring a table after 8pm are practically nil, although the bar stools might do in a pinch.

POTSDAMER PLATZ & TIERGARTEN

Edd's (Map pp52-3; ☎ 215 5294; Lützowstrasse 81; mains €14-25; ⏰ lunch Tue-Fri, dinner Tue-Sun) Edd's grandma used to cook for Thai royals and the man himself has regaled Berlin foodies for over three decades with such palate-pleasers as twice-roasted duck, chicken steamed in banana leaves and curries that are poetry on a plate.

JEAN-PIERRE LESCOURRET

Sony Center (p71), near Potsdamer Platz

DAVID PEEVERS

Greta Csatlòs, Berlin Wall's East Side Gallery (p78)

JEAN-PIERRE LESCOURRET

An outdoor restaurant by the Spree

Facil (Map pp72-3; ☎ 590 051 234; 5th fl, Mandala Hotel, Potsdamer Strasse 3; 1-/2-course lunch €18/28, 4-/7-course dinner €80/120; ⏰ lunch & dinner Mon-Fri) With its sleek Donghia chairs, alabaster lamps and honey-hued natural stone, this glass garden at the Mandala Hotel is as breathtaking as Michael Kempf's Michelin-starred fare.

KREUZBERG & FRIEDRICHSHAIN

Henne (Map pp72-3; ☎ 614 7730; Leuschnerdamm 25; half chicken €7.50; ⏰ dinner Tue-Sun) At this Berlin institution the name is the menu: roast chicken it is, take it or leave it. It's a concept that's been a cult for over a century, so who are we to argue?

Cafe Jacques (Map pp72-3; ☎ 694 1048; Maybachufer 8; mains €7.50-15; ⏰ dinner) Fresh flowers, flattering candlelight, delicious wine – this intimate cafe might just be the perfect date spot. But, frankly, you only have to be in love with good food to enjoy supper choices rooted in French or North African cuisine.

Horváth (Map pp72-3; ☎ 6128 9992; Paul-Lincke-Ufer 44a; mains €20-28, 3-/4-course menu €37/45; ⏰ dinner Tue-Sun) At this jewel on 'bistro row' along Landwehr canal, Wolfgang Müller translates influences from Asia, Germany and the Mediterranean into something uniquely his own.

Curry 36 (Map pp72-3; ☎ 251 7368; Mehringdamm 36; snacks €2-6; ⏰ 9am-4am Mon-Sat, 11am-3am Sun) One of the town's top *Currywurst* purveyors.

Miseria & Nobiltà (Map pp72-3; ☎ 2904 9249; Kopernikusstrasse 16; mains €12-22; ⏰ dinner Tue-Sun) When Eduardo Scarpetti penned the comedy *Poverty and Nobility* in 1888, he didn't know that it would inspire the name of this popular family-run trattoria. You'll definitely feel more king than pauper here when digging into the deftly prepared southern Italian compositions.

CHARLOTTENBURG

Cafe Wintergarten im Literaturhaus (Map pp52-3; ☎ 882 5414; Fasanenstrasse 23; mains €8-16; ⏰ 9.30am-midnight) You don't have to be the literary type in order to enjoy a coffee or light lunch at this genteel art-nouveau villa. Get a dose of Old Berlin flair in the gracefully stucco-ornamented rooms or repair to the idyllic garden.

Mr Hai & Friends (Map pp52-3; ☎ 3759 1200; Savignyplatz 1; mains €8-16; ⏰ 11am-1am) Stylish Vietnamese restaurant packed with locals lusting after fresh and aromatic fare.

Bond (Map pp52-3; ☎ 5096 8844; Knesebeckstrasse 16; mains €8-30; ⏰ lunch Sun-Sat, dinner nightly) If you're in Berlin *On Her Majesty's Secret Service*, you'll impress *The Living Daylights* out of your date at this chill designer den decked out in royal purple, ebony and gold. The standard menu is heavy on, well, standards, like grilled meats, club sandwiches and burgers, but the specials are more inventive.

Moon Thai (Map pp52-3; ☎ 3180 9743; Kantstrasse 32; mains €10-17; noon-midnight) Sunset-coloured walls accented with exotic art create an upbeat ambience that's a perfect foil for dishes so perky they might get you out of the doldrums.

DRINKING

MITTE

Barcomi's Deli (Map p64; ☎ 2859 8363; 2nd courtyard, Sophie-Gips-Höfe, Sophienstrasse 21; 9am-9pm Mon-Sat, 10am-9pm Sun) Train your java radar onto this buzzing New York–meets-Berlin deli where latte-rati, families and expats meet for coffee, bagels with lox and some of the best brownies and cheesecake this side of the Hudson River.

Bebel Bar (Map p64; ☎ 460 6090; Behrenstrasse 37; from 9am) Channel your inner Cary Grant and belly up to the bar at this mood-lit thirst parlour at the Hotel de Rome.

Kiki Blofeld (Map pp72-3; Köpenicker Strasse 48/49; from 2pm Mon-Fri, from noon Sat & Sun) Spree-side Kiki will have you swinging in a hammock, lounging on natural grassy benches, chilling on the riverside beach or wooden deck, catching an offbeat flick or shaking it in an East German army boat patrol bunker.

Tausend (Map p64; ☎ 460 6090; Schiffbauerdamm 11; from 9pm Tue-Sat) The living room of the see-and-be-seen scene. Inside the black, metal tunnel, find expert cocktails and eye-candy fellow sippers.

PRENZLAUER BERG

Klub der Republik (Map pp52-3; Pappelallee 81, from 10pm) There's no sign for this ballroom-turned-bar; just look up until you see steamy windows. Teeter up the wobbly staircase to join happy hipsters amid GDR-trash-Ostalgie and wall projections for electronic sounds and cheap drinks.

Prater (Map pp52-3; ☎ 448 5688; Kastanienallee 7-9; from noon Apr-Sep) Berlin's oldest beer garden (since 1837) oozes traditional charm and is a fun spot for guzzling a cold one beneath the chestnut trees.

Anna Blume (Map pp52-3; ☎ 4404 8749; Kollwitzstrasse 83; 10am-midnight) Named for a Kurt Schwitters poem, this corner cafe lures patrons into its art-nouveau interior perfumed by potent java, homemade cakes and flowers from the attached shop. Fantastic people-watching terrace, too.

POTSDAMER PLATZ & TIERGARTEN

Cafe am Neuen See (Map pp52-3; ☎ 254 4930; Lichtenstein-allee 2; mains €4-12; from 10am daily Mar-Oct, Sat & Sun Nov-Feb) This lakeside Bavarian-style beer garden in Tiergarten

PLAY IT COOL BY THE POOL

Viva Berlin! Take an old river barge, fill it with water, moor it in the Spree and – voilà – an urban lifestyle pool is born. In summer a hedonistic Ibiza-vibe reigns at the artist-designed **Badeschiff** (Map pp72-3; ☎ 533 2030; www.arena-berlin.de; Eichenstrasse 4; admission €3; from 8am), with bods bronzing in the sand or cooling off in the water and a bar to fuel the fun. On scorching days come before noon or risk a long wait. After-dark action includes parties, bands, movies and simply chilling. In winter an ethereally glowing plastic membrane covers up the pool and a deliciously toasty chill zone with saunas and bar.

park feels like a micro-vacation from the city bustle.

Solar (Map pp72-3; ☎ 0163-765 2700; www.solar-berlin.de; Stresemannstrasse 76) The door's tight, service slow and the cocktails only so-so but the views – oh, the views – really are worth the vertigo-inducing trip aboard an exterior glass lift to this 17th-floor Manhattan wannabe. The entrance is off-street in an ugly high-rise behind the Pit Stop auto shop.

KREUZBERG & FRIEDRICHSHAIN

Ankerklause (Map pp72-3; ☎ 693 5649; Kottbusser Damm 104; from 4pm Mon, from 10am Tue-Sun) This nautical kitsch tavern in an old harbour-master's shack is a great place for quaffing and waving to the boats puttering along the Landwehrkanal.

Freischwimmer (Map pp72-3; ☎ 6107 4309; Vor dem Schlesischen Tor 2; from 2pm Mon-Fri, from 11am Sat & Sun, winter hr vary) Few places are more idyllic than this rustic ex-boathouse with sunny terrace above a canal.

Würgeengel (Map pp72-3; ☎ 615 5560; Dresdner Strasse 122; from 7pm) For a swanky night out, point the compass to this dimly lit cocktail cave. The interior is pure '50s with a striking glass ceiling, chandeliers and shiny-black tables.

Monarch (Map pp72-3; Skalitzerstrasse 134; from 9pm Tue-Sat) Bonus points if you can find this upstairs bar right away. Tip: the unmarked entrance is next to the *Döner* shop near the Kaiser's supermarket. Behind the steamed-up windows awaits an ingenious blend of trashy sophistication infused with bouncy electro, strong drinks and a relaxed vibe.

Hops & Barley (Map pp52-3; ☎ 2936 7534; Wühlischstrasse 38) Conversation flows as freely as the beer (and cider) produced right at this congenial microbrewery. Share a table with low-key locals swilling post-work pints and munching rustic *Treberbrot*, a hearty bread made with a natural by-product from the brewing process.

HOLIDAY FLATS

For self-caterers, independent types, wallet-watchers, families and anyone in need of plenty of privacy, a short-term furnished-flat rental may well be the cat's pyjamas. Plenty of options have been popping up lately, but these are our favourites:

Brilliant Apartments (☎ 8061 4796; www.brilliant-apartments.de; apt €80-120; ⊠ 🛜)

Miniloft Berlin (Map p64; ☎ 847 1090; www.miniloft.de; Hessische Strasse 5; apt from €105)

T&C Apartments (Map pp52-3; ☎ 405 046 612; www.tc-apartments-berlin.de; Kopenhagener Strasse 72; apt from €50)

CHARLOTTENBURG & SCHÖNEBERG

Galerie Bremer (Map pp52-3; ☎ 881 4908; Fasanenstrasse 37; from 8pm Mon-Sat) Entering this tiny bar tucked behind an art gallery feels like slipping into a swanky '20s speakeasy. The air, though, is rather genteel, grown-up and completely devoid of debauchery.

Puro Skylounge (Map pp52-3; ☎ 2636 7875; Tauentzienstrasse 11; from 8pm Tue-Sat) Puro has quite literally raised the bar in Charlottenburg, by moving it to the top of the Europa Center, that is. Mind erasers of choice are Moët, martinis and cosmos.

ENTERTAINMENT

Zitty (www.zitty.de) and **Tip** (www.tip-berlin.de) are the most widely read of the biweekly German-language listings magazines available at newsstands.

BMT (p63) sells tickets to events in person (at their Infostores), by phone and on-

OHA/IMAGEBROKER

Fountain in front of the Brandenburger Tor (Brandenburg Gate; p63)

line. Discounts of up to 50% are available for select same-day performances.

NIGHTCLUBS

Berghain/Panorama Bar (Map pp72-3; www.berghain.de; Am Wriezener Bahnhof, Friedrichshain; Fri & Sat) Only the best techno and house vinyl masters heat up this hedonistic bass junkie haven inside a labyrinthine ex-power plant. Strict door and no cameras.

Clärchens Ballhaus (Map p64; ☎ 282 9295; Auguststrasse 24, Mitte; from 10pm Mon, from 9pm Tue-Thu, from 8pm Fri & Sat, from 3pm Sun) Yesteryear is now at this late, great 19th-century dance hall where groovers and grannies swing their legs to tango, swing, waltz, disco and pop.

Club der Visionäre (Map pp72-3; ☎ 6951 8942; Am Flutgraben 1, Kreuzberg) This summertime chill and party playground in an old canalside boat shed is great for a drink or two at any time of day or night.

Cookies (Map p64; www.cookies-berlin.de; Friedrichstrasse 158-164, Mitte; Tue, Thu & Sat) This legendary party palace used to be midweek only but now also runs a Saturday party called 'Crush'. There's no sign, a tough door, great cocktails and a grown-up ambience. Enter next to the KPM store.

Felix clubrestaurant (Map p64; ☎ 206 2860; Behrenstrasse 72, Mitte; Thu-Sat) Once past the velvet rope of this exclusive supper club at the Adlon, you too can shake your booty to 'international club sounds', sip champagne cocktails and – who knows? – maybe even meet your very own Carrie or 'Mr Big'. Great after-work party on Thursday (from 9pm).

Watergate (Map pp72-3; ☎ 6128 0394; www.water-gate.de; Falckensteinstrasse 49a, Kreuzberg; Fri & Sat) Watergate has a fantastic location with a lounge overlooking the Spree and a floating terrace actually on it. Top DJs keep the two floors hot and sweaty with a head-spinning mix of techno, breakbeat, house and drum 'n' bass.

Weekend (Map p64; www.week-end-berlin.de; Am Alexanderplatz 5, Mitte; Thu-Sat) This hot 'n' heavy club in a GDR-era office building delivers awesome views, sleek

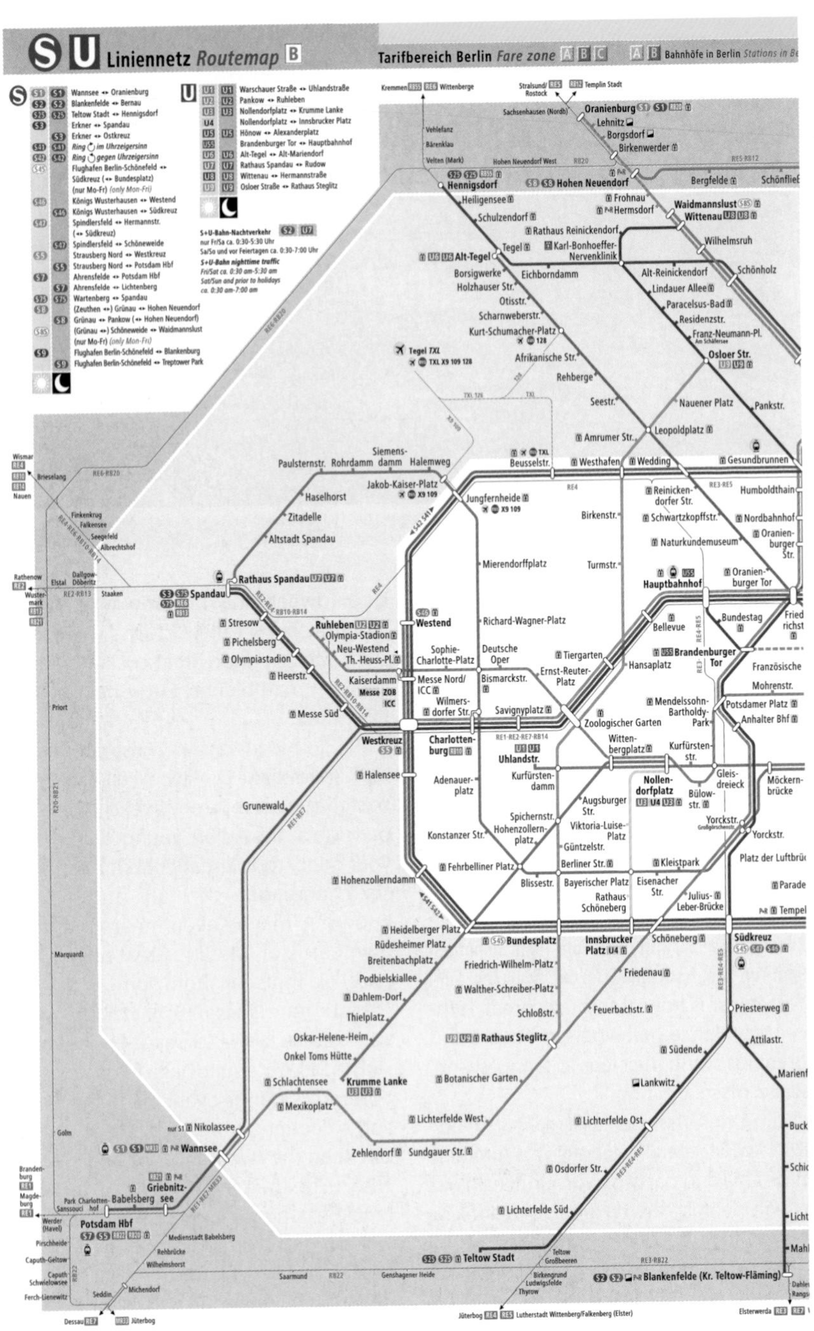
S U Liniennetz Routemap B
Tarifbereich Berlin Fare zone A B C
A B Bahnhöfe in Berlin Stations in Be
S1 Wannsee ↔ Oranienburg
S2 Blankenfelde ↔ Bernau
S25 Teltow Stadt ↔ Hennigsdorf
S3 Erkner ↔ Spandau
S3 Erkner ↔ Ostkreuz
S41 Ring im Uhrzeigersinn
S42 Ring gegen Uhrzeigersinn
S45 Flughafen Berlin-Schönefeld ↔ Südkreuz (↔ Bundesplatz) (nur Mo-Fr) (only Mon-Fri)
S46 Königs Wusterhausen ↔ Westend
S46 Königs Wusterhausen ↔ Südkreuz
S47 Spindlersfeld ↔ Hermannstr. (↔ Südkreuz)
S47 Spindlersfeld ↔ Schöneweide
S5 Strausberg Nord ↔ Westkreuz
S5 Strausberg Nord ↔ Potsdam Hbf
S7 Ahrensfelde ↔ Potsdam Hbf
S7 Ahrensfelde ↔ Lichtenberg
S75 Wartenberg ↔ Spandau
S8 (Zeuthen ↔) Grünau ↔ Hohen Neuendorf
S8 Grünau ↔ Pankow (↔ Hohen Neuendorf)
S85 (Grünau ↔) Schöneweide ↔ Waidmannslust (nur Mo-Fr) (only Mon-Fri)
S9 Flughafen Berlin-Schönefeld ↔ Blankenburg
S9 Flughafen Berlin-Schönefeld ↔ Treptower Park
U1 Warschauer Straße ↔ Uhlandstraße
U2 Pankow ↔ Ruhleben
U3 Nollendorfplatz ↔ Krumme Lanke
U4 Nollendorfplatz ↔ Innsbrucker Platz
U5 Hönow ↔ Alexanderplatz
U55 Brandenburger Tor ↔ Hauptbahnhof
U6 Alt-Tegel ↔ Alt-Mariendorf
U7 Rathaus Spandau ↔ Rudow
U8 Wittenau ↔ Hermannstraße
U9 Osloer Straße ↔ Rathaus Steglitz
S+U-Bahn-Nachtverkehr S2 U7
nur Fr/Sa ca. 0:30-5:30 Uhr
Sa/So und vor Feiertagen ca. 0:30-7:00 Uhr
S+U-Bahn nighttime traffic
Fri/Sat ca. 0:30 am-5:30 am
Sat/Sun and prior to holidays ca. 0:30 am-7:00 am
Kremmen Wittenberge
Stralsund/Rostock Templin Stadt
Oranienburg
Sachsenhausen (Nordb)
Lehnitz
Borgsdorf
Birkenwerder
Vehlefanz
Bärenklau
Velten (Mark)
Hohen Neuendorf West
Hennigsdorf
Hohen Neuendorf
Bergfelde
Schönfließ
Heiligensee
Schulzendorf
Frohnau
Hermsdorf
Waidmannslust
Wittenau
Rathaus Reinickendorf
Tegel
Karl-Bonhoeffer-Nervenklinik
Wilhelmsruh
Alt-Tegel
Borsigwerke
Holzhauser Str.
Otisstr.
Scharnweberstr.
Kurt-Schumacher-Platz
Eichborndamm
Alt-Reinickendorf
Lindauer Allee
Paracelsus-Bad
Residenzstr.
Franz-Neumann-Pl.
Am Schäfersee
Schönholz
Osloer Str.
Tegel TXL
TXL X9 109 128
Afrikanische Str.
Rehberge
Seestr.
Nauener Platz
Pankstr.
Leopoldplatz
Amrumer Str.
Gesundbrunnen
Beusselstr.
Westhafen
Wedding
Paulsternstr.
Rohrdamm
Siemensdamm
Halemweg
Jakob-Kaiser-Platz
Jungfernheide
Haselhorst
Zitadelle
Altstadt Spandau
Reinickendorfer Str.
Schwartzkopffstr.
Humboldthain
Nordbahnhof
Oranienburger Str.
Birkenstr.
Naturkundemuseum
Mierendorffplatz
Turmstr.
Hauptbahnhof
Oranienburger Tor
Wismar
Brieselang
Nauen
Finkenkrug
Falkensee
Seegefeld
Albrechtshof
Rathenow
Elstal
Dallgow-Döberitz
Staaken
Wustermark
Rathaus Spandau
Spandau
Stresow
Pichelsberg
Olympiastadion
Heerstr.
Messe Süd
Ruhleben
Olympia-Stadion
Neu-Westend
Th.-Heuss-Pl.
Kaiserdamm
Messe ZOB ICC
Westend
Richard-Wagner-Platz
Sophie-Charlotte-Platz
Deutsche Oper
Messe Nord/ICC
Bismarckstr.
Wilmersdorfer Str.
Savignyplatz
Tiergarten
Ernst-Reuter-Platz
Bellevue
Bundestag
Friedrichstr.
Brandenburger Tor
Hansaplatz
Französische
Mohrenstr.
Zoologischer Garten
Mendelssohn-Bartholdy-Park
Potsdamer Platz
Anhalter Bhf
Westkreuz
Charlottenburg
Uhlandstr.
Wittenbergplatz
Kurfürstenstr.
Halensee
Adenauerplatz
Kurfürstendamm
Augsburger Str.
Nollendorfplatz
Bülowstr.
Gleisdreieck
Möckernbrücke
Grunewald
Priort
Konstanzer Str.
Spichernstr.
Hohenzollernplatz
Viktoria-Luise-Platz
Güntzelstr.
Yorckstr.
Großgörschenstr.
Platz der Luftbrücke
Fehrbelliner Platz
Berliner Str.
Kleistpark
Blissestr.
Bayerischer Platz
Eisenacher Str.
Rathaus Schöneberg
Julius-Leber-Brücke
Parade
Tempelhof
Hohenzollerndamm
Heidelberger Platz
Rüdesheimer Platz
Bundesplatz
Innsbrucker Platz
Schöneberg
Südkreuz
Breitenbachplatz
Friedrich-Wilhelm-Platz
Friedenau
Podbielskiallee
Walther-Schreiber-Platz
Marquardt
Dahlem-Dorf
Feuerbachstr.
Priesterweg
Thielplatz
Schloßstr.
Oskar-Helene-Heim
Rathaus Steglitz
Attilastr.
Onkel Toms Hütte
Südende
Schlachtensee
Krumme Lanke
Botanischer Garten
Lankwitz
Mariendorf
Mexikoplatz
Lichterfelde West
Lichterfelde Ost
Buckower
Golm
Nikolassee
nur S1
Wannsee
Zehlendorf
Sundgauer Str.
Osdorfer Str.
Schichauweg
Brandenburg
Magdeburg
Griebnitzsee
Park Sanssouci
Charlottenhof
Babelsberg
Lichterfelde Süd
Lichtenrade
Werder (Havel)
Potsdam Hbf
Medienstadt Babelsberg
Pirschheide
Rehbrücke
Caputh-Geltow
Wilhelmshorst
Teltow Stadt
Teltow Großbeeren
Mahlow
Caputh Schwielowsee
Saarmund
Genshagener Heide
Birkengrund
Ludwigsfelde
Thyrow
Blankenfelde (Kr. Teltow-Fläming)
Dahlewitz
Rangsdorf
Ferch-Lienewitz
Seddin
Michendorf
Dessau
Jüterbog
Lutherstadt Wittenberg/Falkenberg (Elster)
Elsterwerda

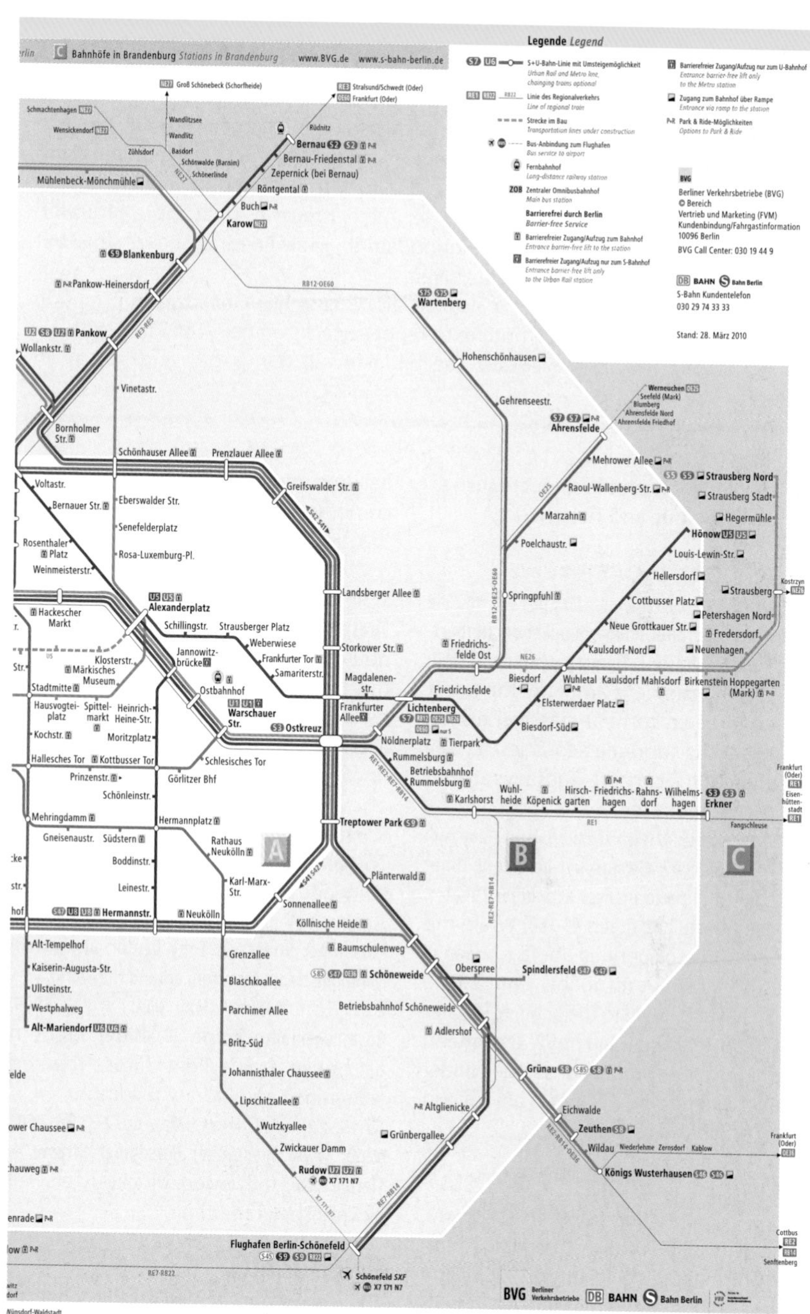

GAY & LESBIAN BERLIN

Berlin's legendary liberalism has spawned one of the world's biggest, most fabulous and diverse LGBT playgrounds. The rainbow flag has proudly flown in Motzstrasse and Fuggerstrasse in Schöneberg since the 1920s. Prenzlauer Berg has the hippest gay scene in eastern Berlin, with hubs along Greifenhagener Strasse, Gleimstrasse and Schönhauser Allee. Kreuzberg has more of an alt-flavoured feel (Oranien-strasse, Mehringdamm), while Friedrichshain's small but up-and-coming scene is student-driven.

Mann-O-Meter (Map pp52-3; ☎ 216 8008; Bülowstrasse 106) One-stop information centre that also operates a hotline to report attacks on gays (☎ 216 3336)

Siegessäule (www.siegessaeule.de) The bible for all things gay and lesbian in Berlin.

design and high-profile spinners such as Dixon, Phonique and Tiefschwarz.

CLASSICAL & OPERA

Berliner Philharmonie (Map pp72-3; ☎ 2548 8999; www.berliner-philharmoniker.de; Herbert-von-Karajan-Strasse 1, Tiergarten; tickets €7-150) The Philharmonie is arguably the finest place in town to hear classical music, thanks to its supreme acoustics. Bonus: free lunchtime concerts Tuesdays at 1pm (September to June).

Staatsoper Unter den Linden (Map p64; ☎ 2035 4555; www.staatsoper-berlin.org; Unter den Linden 7, performances at Schiller Theater, Bismarckstrasse 110; tickets €5-160) While the grand dame of Berlin's opera houses is getting a facelift (probably until 2013), you'll have to travel to the Schiller Theater in Charlottenburg (Map pp52-3) to attend the high-calibre productions staged under Daniel Barenboim. All operas are sung in their original language.

CABARET & VARIETÉ

Admiralspalast (Map p64; ☎ 4799 7499; www.admiralspalast.de, in German; Friedrichstrasse 101-102) This beautifully restored 1920s party palace stages crowd-pleasing plays, concerts and musicals in its elegant historic hall, and more intimate shows – including comedy, readings, dance, concerts and theatre – on two smaller stages.

Chamäleon Varieté (Map p64; ☎ 4000 5930; www.chamaeleon-variete.de; Rosenthaler Strasse 40/41, Mitte) An alchemy of art-nouveau charms and high-tech theatre, this intimate former ballroom presents classy variety shows – comedy, juggling acts and singing – often in sassy, sexy and unconventional fashion.

CINEMAS

The venues listed here all screen English-language films.

Arsenal (Map pp72-3; ☎ 2695 5100; Filmhaus, Potsdamer Strasse 2, Sony Center, Tiergarten) Nonmainstream fare from around the world.

Babylon Mitte (Map p64; ☎ 242 5969; Rosa-Luxemburg-Strasse 30, Mitte) Modern art-house fare, silent films, themed screenings and literary readings.

Cinestar Original (Map pp72-3; ☎ 2606 6260; www.cinestar.de; Potsdamer Strasse 4, Tiergarten) Hollywood blockbusters, all in English, all the time.

SHOPPING

The closest the German capital comes to having a retail spine is Kurfürstendamm and its extension, Tauentzienstrasse. Getting the most out of shopping here means venturing into the various districts, each of which has its own identity and mix of stores calibrated to the needs, tastes and pockets of locals.

KaDeWe (Kaufhaus des Westens; Map pp52-3; ☎ 212 10; Tauentzienstrasse 21) This century-old department store has an assortment so vast that a pirate-style campaign is the best way to plunder its bounty, especially in the legendary 6th-floor gourmet food hall.

Alexa (Map p64; ☎ 269 3400; Grunerstrasse 20) Power shoppers love this XXL-sized mega-mall that cuts a rose-hued presence near Alexanderplatz.

Flohmarkt am Mauerpark (Map pp52-3; Bernauer Strasse 63; 10am-5pm Sun) This flea market has all sorts of vendors, with everything from T-shirt designers and families who've cleaned out their closets to down-at-heelers hawking trash.

Flohmarkt Strasse des 17 Juni (Map pp52-3; 10am-5pm Sat & Sun) Come here for Berlin memorabilia, stuff from granny's closet and jewellery.

Bonbonmacherei (Map p64; ☎ 4405 5243; Oranienburger Strasse 32, Heckmannhöfe, Mitte) The old-fashioned art of handmade sweets has been lovingly revived in this basement-store-cum-show-kitchen.

Berlinerklamotten (Map p64; www.berlinerklamotten.de; Court III, Hackesche Höfe, Mitte) Flip through the racks of this arbiter of fashion-cool to dig up urban, cheeky outfits and accessories made right here in the German capital.

Space Hall (Map pp72-3; ☎ 694 7664; Zossener Strasse 33, Kreuzberg) This galaxy for electronic-music gurus has four floors filled with everything from acid to techno by way of drum 'n' bass, neotrance, dubstep and so on.

GETTING THERE & AWAY

AIR

Berlin has two international airports, Tegel (TXL; Map pp52-3), about 8km northwest from the city centre, and Schönefeld (SFX, off Map p52-3), about 22km southeast. For information about either, go to www.berlin-airport.de or call ☎ 0180-500 0186.

TRAIN

Berlin is well connected by train to other German cities, as well as to popular European destinations, including Prague, Warsaw and Amsterdam. While all long-distance trains converge at the Hauptbahnhof, some also stop at other stations such as Spandau, Ostbahnhof, Gesundbrunnen and Südkreuz.

DAVID PEEVERS

Telephos frieze at Pergamonmuseum (p67)

DAVID PEEVERS

A beach bar in Potsdamer Platz (p81)

GETTING AROUND

TO/FROM THE AIRPORTS

SCHÖNEFELD

Schönefeld airport is served twice hourly by the AirportExpress train from Bahnhof Zoo (30 minutes), Friedrichstrasse (23 minutes), Alexanderplatz (20 minutes) and Ostbahnhof (15 minutes). There are more frequent S9 trains, but the service is slower (40 minutes from Alexanderplatz, 50 minutes from Bahnhof Zoo). The S45 line goes straight to the trade-fair grounds. Trains stop about 400m from the terminals, which are served by a free shuttle bus every 10 minutes. Walking takes about five to 10 minutes. The fare for any of these trips is €2.80.

Budget about €35 for a cab ride to central Berlin.

TEGEL

Tegel is connected to Mitte by the JetExpressBus TXL (30 minutes) and to Bahnhof Zoo in Charlottenburg by express bus X9 (20 minutes). Tegel is not directly served by U-Bahn, but both bus 109 and X9 stop at Jakob-Kaiser-Platz (U7), the station closest to the airport. Any of these trips cost €2.10.

Taxi rides cost about €20 to Bahnhof Zoo and €23 to Alexanderplatz.

PUBLIC TRANSPORT

Berlin's public transport system is run by **BVG** (**☎ 194 49; www.bvg.de**) and consists of the U-Bahn, S-Bahn, regional trains, buses and trams.

Bus drivers sell single tickets and day passes, but all other tickets must be purchased before boarding, either from orange vending machines (with instructions in English) located in U- or S-Bahn stations or from any kiosk or shop bearing the BVG logo. Tickets must be stamped (validated) at station platform entrances. The on-the-spot fine for getting caught without a valid ticket is €40.

The network is divided into fare zones A, B and C, with tickets available for zones AB, BC and ABC. The short-trip ticket (*Kurzstreckenticket*, €1.30) is good for three stops on any U-Bahn or S-Bahn or six on any bus or tram. The group day pass is valid for up to five people travelling together. Children aged six to 14 qualify for reduced *(ermässigt)* rates, while kids under six travel for free.

Buses run frequently between 4.30am and 12.30am. From Sunday to Thursday, night buses take over in the interim, running roughly every 30 minutes. Trams only operate in the eastern districts. The M10, N54, N55, N92 and N93 offer continuous service nightly.

S-Bahn trains make fewer stops than U-Bahns and are therefore handy for longer distances, but they don't run as frequently. They operate from around 4am to 12.30am and all night on Friday, Saturday and public holidays.

The most efficient way to travel around Berlin is by U-Bahn. Trains operate from 4am until about 12.30am and throughout the night on Friday, Saturday and public holidays (all lines except the U4).

TAXI

Flag fall is €3.20, then it's €1.58 per kilometre up to 7km and €1.20 for each kilometre after that. Taxis can also be ordered on ☎ 443 322, 210 202 or 263 000. For short hops you can use the €4 *Kurzstreckentarif* (short-trip rate), which entitles you to ride for up to 2km. You must flag down a moving taxi and request this special rate before the driver has activated the meter. If you want to continue past 2km, regular rates apply to the entire trip.

MUNICH

GREATER MUNICH

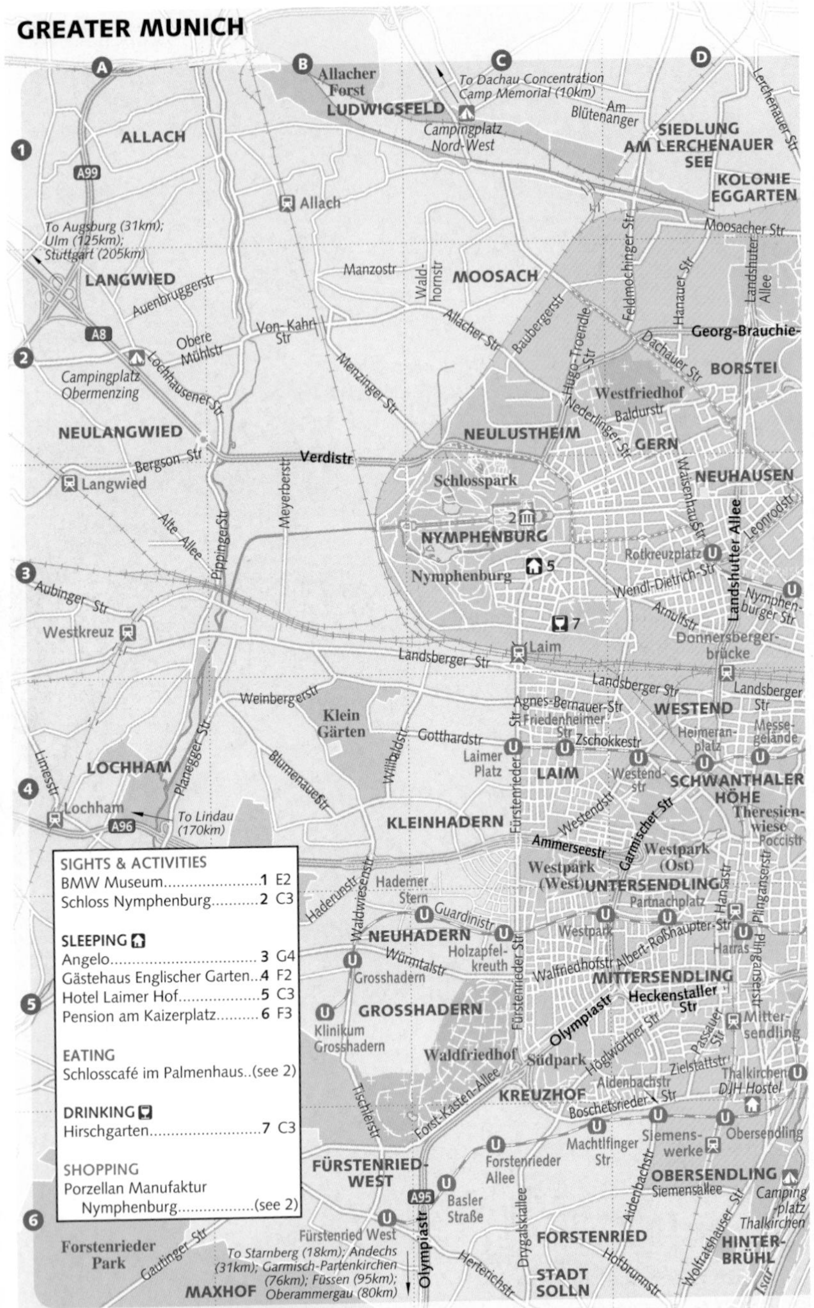

SIGHTS & ACTIVITIES
BMW Museum........................1 E2
Schloss Nymphenburg............2 C3

SLEEPING
Angelo...................................3 G4
Gästehaus Englischer Garten..4 F2
Hotel Laimer Hof...................5 C3
Pension am Kaizerplatz..........6 F3

EATING
Schlosscafé im Palmenhaus..(see 2)

DRINKING
Hirschgarten..........................7 C3

SHOPPING
Porzellan Manufaktur
Nymphenburg...................(see 2)

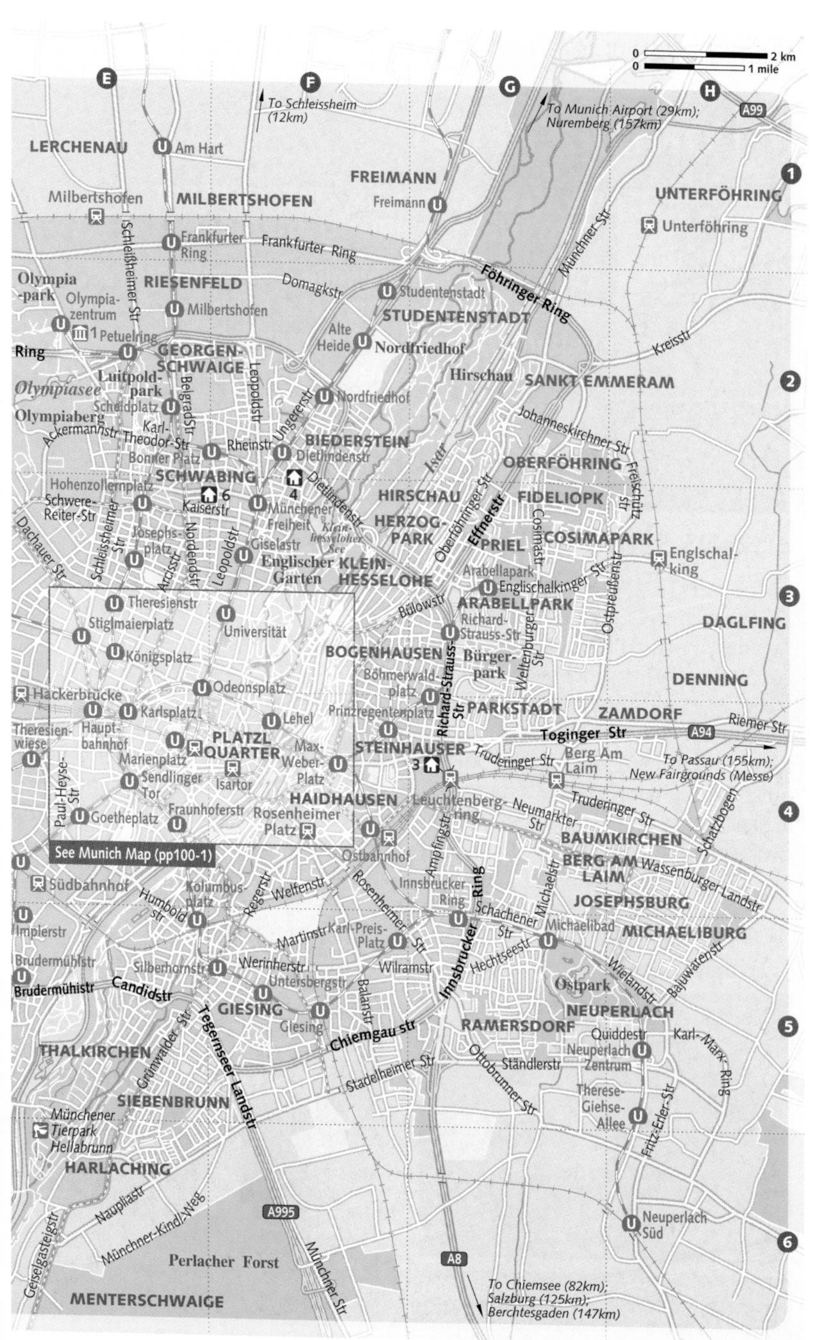
0 2 km
0 1 mile
E
F
G
H
To Schleissheim (12km)
To Munich Airport (29km); Nuremberg (157km)
A99
LERCHENAU
Am Hart
FREIMANN
Freimann
MILBERTSHOFEN
Milbertshofen
UNTERFÖHRING
Unterföhring
Frankfurter Ring
Olympia -park
Olympia-zentrum
RIESENFELD
Domagkstr
Studentenstadt
STUDENTENSTADT
Föhringer Ring
Münchner Str
Milbertshofen
1 Petuelring
Ring
GEORGEN-SCHWAIGE
Alte Heide
Nordfriedhof
Kreisstr
Hirschau
SANKT EMMERAM
Luitpold-park
Olympiasee
Scheidplatz
Olympiaberg
Belgradstr
Leopoldstr
Ungererstr
Nordfriedhof
Johanneskirchner Str
Ackermannstr
Karl-Theodor-Str
Rheinstr
BIEDERSTEIN
Dietlindenstr
Bonner Platz
SCHWABING
6
4
Isar
OBERFÖHRING
Freischütz str
Hohenzollernplatz
Schwere-Reiter-Str
Kaiserstr
Münchener Freiheit
Dietlindenstr
HIRSCHAU
Oberföhringer Str
Effnerstr
FIDELIOPK
Dachauer Str
Schleissheimer Str
Josephs-platz
Nordendstr
Leopoldstr
Giselastr
Kleinhesseloher See
HERZOG-PARK
Cosimastr
COSIMAPARK
PRIEL
Englschal-king
Arcisstr
Englischer Garten
KLEIN-HESSELOHE
Arabellapark
Englischalkinger Str
Ostpreußenstr
Theresienstr
Universität
Bülowstr
ARABELLPARK
Stiglmaierplatz
Richard-Strauss-Str
DAGLFING
Königsplatz
BOGENHAUSEN
Bürger-park
Weltenburger Str
Böhmerwald-platz
DENNING
Hackerbrücke
Odeonsplatz
Karlsplatz
Richard-Strauss-Str
Prinzregentenplatz
PARKSTADT
ZAMDORF
Riemer Str
Theresien-wiese
Haupt-bahnhof
Lehel
PLATZL QUARTER
STEINHAUSER
Toginger Str
A94
Marienplatz
Max-Weber-Platz
3
Truderinger Str
Berg Am Laim
To Passau (155km); New Fairgrounds (Messe)
Paul-Heyse-Str
Sendlinger Tor
Isartor
HAIDHAUSEN
Leuchtenberg-ring
Neumarkter Str
Truderinger Str
Goetheplatz
Fraunhoferstr
Rosenheimer Platz
Ostbahnhof
BAUMKIRCHEN
Schatzbogen
See Munich Map (pp100-1)
Amplingstr
BERG AM LAIM
Wassenburger Landstr
Südbahnhof
Kolumbus-platz
Welfenstr
Regerstr
Rosenheimer Str
Innsbrucker Ring
Ring
Michaelistr
JOSEPHSBURG
Humboldstr
Implerstr
Martinstr
Karl-Preis-Platz
Schachener Str
Michaelibad
MICHAELIBURG
Brudermühlstr
Silberhornstr
Werinherstr
Wilramstr
Innsbrucker Ring
Hechtseestr
Wielandstr
Bajuwarenstr
Brudermühlstr
Candidstr
Untersbergstr
Ostpark
GIESING
Balanstr
NEUPERLACH
Giesing
Chiemgau str
RAMERSDORF
Quiddestr
Karl-Marx-Ring
THALKIRCHEN
Grünwalder Str
Tegernseer Landstr
Neuperlach Zentrum
Ständlerstr
Stadelheimer Str
Ottobrunner Str
SIEBENBRUNN
Therese-Giehse-Allee
Münchener Tierpark Hellabrunn
Fritz-Erler-Str
HARLACHING
Naupliastr
A995
Neuperlach Süd
Münchner-Kindl-Weg
Geiselgasteigstr
Perlacher Forst
A8
Münchner Str
To Chiemsee (82km); Salzburg (125km); Berchtesgaden (147km)
MENTERSCHWAIGE
1
2
3
4
5
6

MUNICH HIGHLIGHTS

1 OKTOBERFEST

BY HANS SPINDLER, OKTOBERFEST ORGANISER & PROUD BAVARIAN

Oktoberfest is the highlight of the year for residents, and visitors get a full dose of Bavarian culture. You rejoice with millions of fellow beer drinkers, sample dozens of different types of beer in a variety of beer tents and watch costume-clad parades celebrating German traditions.

↘ HANS SPINDLER'S DON'T MISS LIST

❶ TRACHTEN- & SCHÜTZENZUG

Try to catch the Costume & Rifleman's Parade on the first Sunday of the Oktoberfest. This procession starts at 10am at Max-Joseph-Platz (p102) and marches for 7km through the city centre to the fairgrounds. The parade – an impressive insight into the customs rooted in Bavaria and other German states – includes regional costume groups leading oxen, 'troops' in historical uniforms, marching bands, riflemen, trumpeters on horseback, flag-throwers and decorated drays from Munich breweries.

❷ BIERZELTE (BEER TENTS)

The atmosphere inside the beer tents is unforgettable – around 5000 guests all packed in, sitting at long tables, watching costume-clad waiters marching through the crowds with four, five or more litre-sized mugs in each fist! Each tent is hosted by a different brewery and serves quality mugs of foamy goodness. But if you want to hang out with lots of Müncheners (Munich residents) head to the Augustiner tent – it's the local favourite.

Clockwise from top: View over Oktoberfest at dawn; Beer tent interior, Theresienwiese fairgrounds; Kegs on a beer wagon; Traditional costume parade; Steins of beer

❸ REVELLING AT LONG TABLES

One of most enjoyable parts of the festival is sitting at the long tables with strangers and friends and spontaneously breaking into song and rocking side to side as a group. Suddenly you've got a table of smiling new friends eager to exclaim *Prost!* (Cheers!) with you.

❹ LOOPING AROUND FIVE TIMES

Aside from the beer drinking, the Oktoberfest is one big amusement park. One of my favourites is the modern Olympialooping, a gigantic roller coaster which makes no less than five dizzying loops. For a more traditional way to lurch your stomach to your knees, hop on the *Teufelsrad* (Devil's Wheel); it's been spinning folk around since 1910 (the aim is to stay standing as long as possible). This ride is as much fun to watch as it is to ride!

↘ THINGS YOU NEED TO KNOW

Top tip To avoid crowds, visit during the week. **Mugs cost** A litre-sized *Mass* (mug, pronounced 'maas') costs around €8 to €9. **Opening hours** Beer tents are open 10am to 11.30pm weekdays (from 9am weekends) but stop serving beer about an hour before closing. **See our author's review on p108.**

MUNICH HIGHLIGHTS

2

THE ALTERNATIVE OKTOBERFEST

OK, there's no replacing the real thing. Sorry. But if you can't visit during the festival, you can do the next best thing – start with a visit to the **Bier & Oktoberfestmuseum** (p102) to learn about the history of German beer and its most famous beer event. After, kick back a litre-sized mug in one of Munich's best beer halls, like the **Hofbräuhaus** (p107) or the (less touristy) **Augustiner-Grossgaststätte** (p109).

3

DACHAU CONCENTRATION CAMP MEMORIAL

This inscription greets you at the **Nazis' first concentration camp** (p113): 'The Way to freedom is to follow one's orders, exhibit honesty, orderliness, cleanliness, sobriety, truthfulness, the ability to sacrifice and love of the fatherland'. A tour takes you through photos and models of officers and inmates, descriptions of scientific experiments and exhibits including a bunker where inmates were tortured.

4

LOLLING IN THE ENGLISCHER GARTEN

Munich's massive city park, the **Englischer Garten** (English Garden; p105), is a mix of contradictions: the Chinese Tower is a beer garden, there are no English flower beds and in summer you'll see hundreds of naked sunbathers with their jackets, ties and dresses stacked neatly beside them.

5

MUNICH JEWISH MUSEUM

The **Jüdisches Museum München** (Munich Jewish Museum; p99) has gone to great lengths to come up with sensitive exhibits that attempt to come to grips with the history of Judaism in Germany. A selection of objects gives you insight into the Jewish history of Munich as well as the variety of Jewish identities in the cultural history of the country.

6

GALLERY OF BEAUTIES

All the rooms are sumptuous at **Schloss Nymphenburg** (p105), but most majestic is the **Schönheitengalerie** (Gallery of Beauties), home to 38 portraits of women chosen by an admiring King Ludwig I. The most famous is of Helene Sedlmayr, a shoemaker's daughter wearing a lavish frock the king gave her for the sitting.

2 Hofbräuhaus (p107); 3 Nandor Glid sculpture, Dachau Concentration Camp Memorial (p113); 4 Chinese Tower in the Englischer Garten (p105); 5 Jüdisches Museum München (p99); 6 Gardens in front of Schloss Nymphenburg (p105)

THE BEST...

THINGS FOR FREE

- **Glockenspiel** (p98) Marienplatz's carillon performs two to three times daily.
- **Viktualienmarkt** (p99) Enjoy the sights and smells of Munich's lively market.
- **Michaelskirche** (p103) Gape at the barrel-vaulted ceiling in the city's finest church.

MOST ENTERTAINING BEER HALLS

- **Hofbräuhaus** (p107) It's touristy and crowded, but it's a must-do for at least a litre of the golden potion.
- **Augustiner-Grossgaststätte** (p109) An old-school, traditional spot to kick one back (or two, or three...)
- **Löwenbräukeller** (p109) Oompah bands, beer and stone-lifting contests.

PLACES TO CHILL

- **Schloss Nymphenburg** (p105) Relax in the elaborate surrounding gardens.
- **Englischer Garten** (p105) Munich's colossal city park is the best antidote after an evening sampling Munich's outstanding beer.
- **Japanisches Teehaus** (Japanese Teahouse; p105) Traditional tea ceremonies are held in summer.

CHEAP EATS

- **Weisses Bräuhaus** (p107) Try Munich's best *Weisswurst* (veal sausage) and other southern German specialities in this convivial space.
- **Königsquelle** (p107) A crowd-pleasing mix of German and pan-European fare.
- **Café Rischart** (p108) OK, we're cheating. This cafe is where you come to eat cake. But after a slice at this Munich stalwart, you won't need dinner.

INT/IMAGEBROKER

Cheese stall at the Viktualienmarkt (p99)

THINGS YOU NEED TO KNOW

VITAL STATISTICS

- **Population** 12.5 million
- **Best times to visit** April–October

ADVANCE PLANNING

- **One year before** So you want to go to the Oktoberfest, just like six million other beer lovers. Unless you can beg your German cousin to let you sleep on their sofa bed, you've gotta book your hotel *way* ahead.

RESOURCES

- **www.munichfound.de** The city's informative expat magazine.
- **www.gomuenchen.com** Popular listing and events magazine.
- **www.in-muenchen.de** Munich's best source of entertainment information; available free at bars, restaurants and ticket outlets.

EMERGENCY NUMBERS

- **Ambulance** (☎ 192 22)
- **Fire** (☎ 112)
- **Police** (☎ 110)
- **Ludwigs-Apotheke** (☎ 260 3021) An English-speaking pharmacy. (Might come in handy after a night of overindulgence at the beer hall?)

GETTING AROUND

- **U-Bahn** (Map p112) Get around underground between 4am and 12.30am weekdays (to 1.30am weekends).

BE FOREWARNED

- **Drunk people** During Oktoberfest (p108), crime and staggering drunks are major problems, especially at the southern end of the Hauptbahnhof late in the evening – there are dozens of assaults every year. Leave early or stay *very* cautious.
- **One litre beers** *All* beers at the Hofbräuhaus (p107) are litre-sized, with one exception: the Münchner Weisse (comes in a 0.5L portion).
- **Static crazy** The *Föhn* (pronounced foon) is a weather-related annoyance peculiar to southern Germany. Static-charged wind brings dense pressure that sits on the city, causing headaches and general crankiness – similar to Marseille's *mistral* effects. (Visiting filmmaker Ingmar Bergman once said the *Föhn* makes 'nice dogs bite, and cats spew lightning'.)
- **Museums** Most are closed Monday or Tuesday.

DISCOVER MUNICH

Pulsing with prosperity and *Gemütlichkeit* (cosiness), Munich (München) revels in its own contradictions. Age-old traditions exist side by side with sleek BMWs, designer boutiques and high-powered industry. Its museums include world-class collections of artistic masterpieces, and its music and cultural scenes give Berlin a run for its money.

Wistful Germans say Munich is the most popular place to live – and in a blink you'll see why. Balmy summer evenings at one of its streetside cafes make the city feel like a Florence or a Milan. Alpine landscapes and crystal-clear lakes lie at its doorstep. And during Oktoberfest visitors descend on the Bavarian capital in their thousands to raise a glass to this fascinating city.

Despite all its sophistication, Munich retains a touch of provincialism that visitors find charming. The people's attitude is one of live-and-let-live – and Müncheners will be the first to admit that their 'metropolis' is little more than a *Weltdorf*, a world village.

INFORMATION

Tourist office Hauptbahnhof (☎ 2339 6500; Bahnhofsplatz 2; 9am-8pm Mon-Sat, 10am-6pm Sun); Marienplatz (☎ 2339 6500; Neues Rathaus; 10am-8pm Mon-Fri, to 4pm Sat, to 2pm Sun)

SIGHTS

MARIENPLATZ & AROUND

The heart and soul of the Altstadt (old town) is **Marienplatz,** the old town square. At the northwest corner stands the **Mariensäule** (Marian Column), erected in 1638 to celebrate the removal of Swedish forces at the end of the Thirty Years War. Topped with a golden figure of the Virgin Mary dating from 1590, it was one of the first Marian columns erected north of the Alps.

NEUES RATHAUS

The soot-blackened facade of the neo-Gothic **Neues Rathaus** (New Town Hall) is festooned with gargoyles and statues, including a dragon scaling the turrets. Inside, six grand courtyards host festivals and concerts throughout the year.

Huge crowds regularly gather on Marienplatz to watch the **Glockenspiel** (carillon). Note the three levels: two portraying the *Schäfflertanz* (a dance) and another the Ritterturnier, a knights' tournament held in 1568 to celebrate a royal marriage. The characters spring into action for a neck-stiffening 12 minutes at 11am and noon (also 5pm November to April). The night scene featuring the Münchener Kindl (a girl in a monk's robe) and a *Nachtwächter* (nightwatchman) runs at 9pm.

ST PETERSKIRCHE

Opposite the Neues Rathaus stands the **St Peterskirche** (Church of St Peter). Severely Gothic in inspiration, the baroque interior is a subdued affair compared to some, but does have a magnificent high altar and eye-catching statues of the four church fathers (1732) by Egid Quirin Asam.

ALTES RATHAUS

The Gothic **Altes Rathaus** (Old Town Hall; 1474) was destroyed by lightning and bombs, and then rebuilt in a plainer style after WWII. In its south tower is the city's **Spielzeugmuseum** (Toy Museum; ☎ 294 001; Alter Rathausturm; adult/child/family €3/1.50/7; 🕓 10am-5.30pm) with a huge collection of toys, Barbie dolls and teddy bears.

VIKTUALIENMARKT & AROUND

The bustling **Viktualienmarkt** is one of Europe's great food markets. In summer the entire place is transformed into one of the finest and most expensive beer gardens around, while in winter people huddle for warmth and schnapps in the small pubs around the square. The merchandise and food are of the finest quality, and prices tend to be high. The enormous **maypole** bears artisans' symbols and the traditional blue-and-white Bavarian stripes. On the south side of the square you'll see a statue of Karl Valentin, Germany's most celebrated comedian.

STADTMUSEUM

To mark the city's 850th birthday in 2008, the **Stadtmuseum** (City Museum; ☎ 2332 2370; St-Jakobs-Platz; adult/concession €4/2; 🕓 10am-6pm, closed Mon) restructured its collections to create the 'Typisch München' (Typically Munich) exhibition. This condenses Munich's tangled past into five easily digestible periods, with a chronological walking route leading through the rambling building. Exhibits in each section represent what is most typical for the time, and explain why.

JÜDISCHES MUSEUM MÜNCHEN

Many decades in the planning, the **Jüdisches Museum München** (Munich Jewish Museum; ☎ 2339 6096; www.juedisches-museum-muenchen.de; St Jakobs-Platz 16; adult/concession €6/3; 🕓 10am-6pm, closed Mon) is a major undertaking that attempts to come to terms with one of the most sinister chapters in the city's history. Contained within a modernist glass cube, the exhibits aim to show in a balanced, sensitive fashion the Jewish place in Munich's

Fountain on Marienplatz, in front of the Neues Rathaus

MZJ/IMAGEBROKER

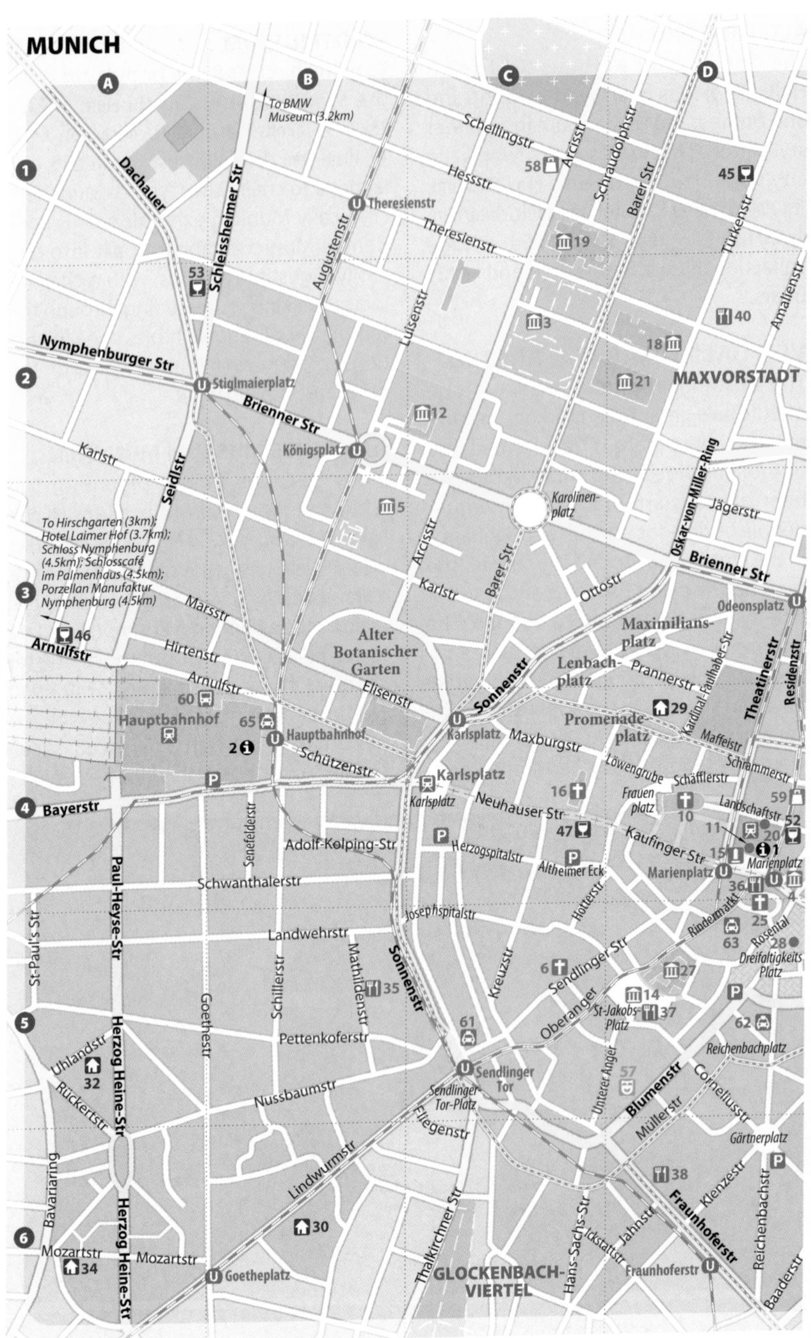
MUNICH
To BMW Museum (3.2km)
Schellingstr
Hessstr
Theresienstr
Dachauer
Schleissheimer Str
Augustenstr
Luisenstr
Arcisstr
Schraudolphstr
Barer Str
Türkenstr
Amalienstr
MAXVORSTADT
Nymphenburger Str
Stiglmaierplatz
Brienner Str
Königsplatz
Karlstr
Seidlstr
Karolinen-platz
Jägerstr
Oskar-von-Miller-Ring
Brienner Str
Odeonsplatz
To Hirschgarten (3km); Hotel Laimer Hof (3.7km); Schloss Nymphenburg (4.5km); Schlosscafé im Palmenhaus (4.5km); Porzellan Manufaktur Nymphenburg (4.5km)
Marsstr
Ottostr
Arnulfstr
Hirtenstr
Alter Botanischer Garten
Maximilians-platz
Lenbach-platz
Prannerstr
Kardinal-Faulhaber-Str
Theatinerstr
Residenzstr
Elisenstr
Sonnenstr
Hauptbahnhof
Promenade-platz
Maffeistr
Karlsplatz
Maxburgstr
Schützenstr
Löwengrube
Schäfflerstr
Schrammerstr
Bayerstr
Neuhauser Str
Frauen platz
Landschaftstr
Senefelderstr
Adolf-Kolping-Str
Herzogspitalstr
Kaufinger Str
Altheimer Eck
Marienplatz
Schwanthalerstr
Josephspitalstr
Hotterstr
Rindermarkt
Rosental
Dreifaltigkeits Platz
St-Paul's-Str
Paul-Heyse-Str
Landwehrstr
Mathildenstr
Sendlinger Str
Kreuzstr
Goethestr
Schillerstr
Oberanger
St-Jakobs-Platz
Pettenkoferstr
Reichenbachplatz
Uhlandstr
Herzog Heine-Str
Sendlinger Tor
Sendlinger-Tor-Platz
Unterer Anger
Corneliusstr
Rückertstr
Nussbaumstr
Blumenstr
Müllerstr
Fliegenstr
Gärtnerplatz
Bavariaring
Lindwurmstr
Klenzestr
Reichenbachstr
Thalkirchner Str
Hans-Sachs-Str
Jahnstr
Fraunhoferstr
Ickstattstr
Mozartstr
Goetheplatz
GLOCKENBACH-VIERTEL
Fraunhoferstr
Baaderstr

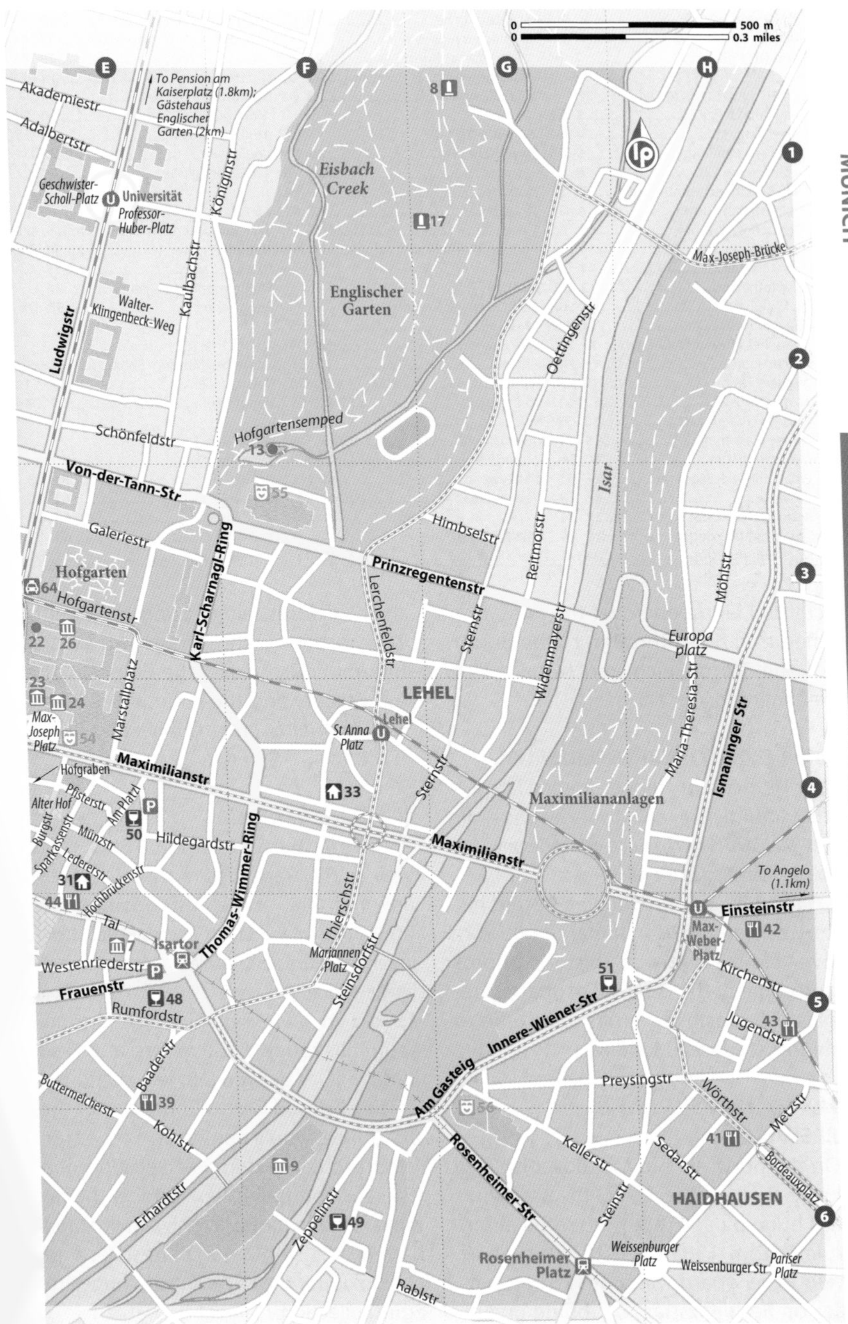

500 m
0.3 miles
To Pension am Kaiserplatz (1.8km); Gästehaus Englischer Garten (2km)
Akademiestr
Adalbertstr
Geschwister-Scholl-Platz
Universität
Professor-Huber-Platz
Königinstr
Eisbach Creek
Englischer Garten
Walter-Klingenbeck-Weg
Kaulbachstr
Ludwigstr
Max-Joseph-Brücke
Oettingenstr
Schönfeldstr
Hofgartensemped
Von-der-Tann-Str
Galeriestr
Hofgarten
Hofgartenstr
Karl-Scharnagl-Ring
Himbselstr
Prinzregentenstr
Reitmorstr
Isar
Möhlstr
Europaplatz
Lerchenfeldstr
Sternstr
Widenmayerstr
LEHEL
Maria-Theresia-Str
Ismaninger Str
Marstallplatz
Max-Joseph-Platz
St Anna Platz
Lehel
Maximilianstr
Hofgraben
Alter Hof
Pfisterstr
Am Platzl
Burgstr
Sparkassenstr
Münzstr
Ledererstr
Hochbrückenstr
Hildegardstr
Thomas-Wimmer-Ring
Maximiliananlagen
To Angelo (1.1km)
Einsteinstr
Max-Weber-Platz
Tal
Isartor
Westenriederstr
Frauenstr
Rumfordstr
Thierschstr
Mariannen Platz
Steinsdorfstr
Kirchenstr
Jugendstr
Innere-Wiener-Str
Am Gasteig
Preysingstr
Wörthstr
Metzstr
Baaderstr
Buttermelcherstr
Kohlstr
Erhardtstr
Zeppelinstr
Rosenheimer Str
Kellerstr
Sedanstr
Steinstr
Bordeauxplatz
HAIDHAUSEN
Rosenheimer Platz
Weissenburger Platz
Weissenburger Str
Pariser Platz
Rablstr
MUNICH

INFORMATION
Tourist Office 1 D4
Tourist Office 2 B4

SIGHTS & ACTIVITIES
Alte Pinakothek 3 C2
Altes Rathaus 4 D4
Antikensammlungen 5 B3
Asamkirche 6 C5
Bier & Oktoberfestmuseum 7 E5
Chinesischer Turm 8 G1
Deutsches Museum 9 F6
Frauenkirche 10 D4
Glockenspiel 11 D4
Glyptothek 12 C2
Hofbräuhaus ...... (see 50)
Japanisches Teehaus 13 F2
Jüdisches Museum München 14 D5
Mariensäule 15 D4
Michaelskirche 16 C4
Monopteros 17 G1
Museum Brandhorst 18 D2
Neue Pinakothek 19 C1
Neues Rathaus 20 D4
Pinakothek der Moderne 21 D2
Residenz 22 E3
Residenzmuseum 23 E4
Schatzkammer der Residenz 24 E4
Spielzeugmuseum ...... (see 4)
St Peterskirche 25 D5
Staatliches Museum Ägyptischer Kunst 26 E3
Stadtmuseum 27 D5
Viktualienmarkt 28 D5

SLEEPING
Bayerischer Hof 29 D4
Cocoon 30 B6
Cortiina 31 E4
Hotel Uhland 32 A5
Opera-Garni 33 F4
Pension Westfalia 34 A6

EATING
Café Osteria La Vecchia Masseria 35 B5
Café Rischart 36 D4
Einstein 37 D5
Fraunhofer 38 D6
Königsquelle 39 E5
Nido 40 D2
Taverna Diyar 41 H6
Unionsbräu Haidhausen 42 H5
Wasserwerk 43 H5
Weisses Bräuhaus 44 E5

DRINKING
Alter Simpl 45 D1
Augustiner Keller 46 A3
Augustiner-Grossgaststätte 47 C4
Braunauer Hof 48 E5
Chinesischer Turm ...... (see 8)
Dreigroschenkeller 49 F6
Hofbräuhaus 50 E4
Hofbräukeller 51 G5
Jodlerwirt 52 D4
Löwenbräukeller 53 A2

ENTERTAINMENT
Jazzclub Unterfahrt im Einstein ...... (see 42)
Nationaltheater 54 E4
P1 ...... 55 F3
Philharmonie im Gasteig 56 G5
Registratur 57 D5

SHOPPING
Deutsches Museum Shop ...... (see 9)
Holareidulijö 58 C1
Manufactum 59 D4

TRANSPORT
BerlinLinienBus 60 A4
Taxi Rank 61 C5
Taxi Rank 62 D5
Taxi Rank 63 D5
Taxi Rank 64 E3
Taxi Rank 65 B4

cultural landscape over the ages, from medieval times through to the horrors of the Third Reich and today's slow regeneration.

BIER & OKTOBERFESTMUSEUM

In a 14th-century timber-framed house is the cute little **Bier & Oktoberfestmuseum** (☎ 2423 1607; www.bier-und-oktoberfestmuseum.de; Sterneckerstrasse 2; adult/concession €4/2.50; 1-5pm Tue-Sat), providing a potted history of Germany's national tipple. Pore over old brewing vats, historic photos and some of the earliest Oktoberfest regalia. The earthy tavern is open 6pm to midnight (closed Monday).

MAX-JOSEPH-PLATZ

RESIDENZ

On the north side of Max-Joseph-Platz looms the oldest section of the **Residenz,** the huge palace that housed Bavarian rulers from 1385 to 1918. Statues of **two lions** guard the gates to the palace on Residenzstrasse; rubbing one of their shields is said to bring you wealth. The northern wings open into several interior courtyards – the Emperor, the Apothecary and the Fountain – as well as two smaller ones, Chapel and King's Tract.

RESIDENZMUSEUM

The Wittelsbachs' amazing treasures, as well as the trappings of their lifestyles, are on display at the **Residenzmuseum** (☎ 290 671; enter from Max-Josephs-Platz 3; adult/under 18yr with parents/concession €6/free/5, combiticket with Schatzkammer €9/free/8; 9am-6pm Apr–mid-Oct, 10am-5pm mid-Oct–Mar). The museum has roughly 130 rooms, and is so large that it's divided into two sections.

The enclosed Grotto Court, one of the first places you'll see when you enter, features the wonderful Perseusbrunnen (Perseus Fountain). Next door is the famous Antiquarium, a lavishly ornamented barrel vault, smothered in frescoes and built to house the Wittelsbachs' huge antique collection.

SCHATZKAMMER DER RESIDENZ

The Residenzmuseum entrance also leads to the **Schatzkammer der Residenz** (**Residence Treasury; ☎ 290 671; enter from Max-Joseph-Platz 3; adult/under 18yr with parents/concession €6/free/5; 9am-6pm Apr–mid-Oct, 10am-5pm mid-Oct–Mar**). It exhibits an Aladdin's cave of baubles and precious objects. Included among the mind-boggling treasures are portable altars, the pearl-studded golden cross of Queen Gisela of Hungary, the Bavarian crown jewels, and 'exotic handicrafts' from Turkey, Iran, Mexico and India.

ODEONSPLATZ TO KARLSPLATZ

Munich's main shopping drag is Kaufinger Strasse, which becomes Neuhauser Strasse in the west. Along it, the **Michaelskirche** (St Michael's Church) is one of the city centre's most spectacular churches. The ceiling is a 20m-wide barrel-vaulted expanse with no supporting columns, thus creating a large, pew-filled space.

FRAUENKIRCHE

Visible from just about anywhere in the Altstadt, the twin copper onion domes of the **Frauenkirche** (Church of Our Lady) are often used as an emblem for the city. In contrast to its red-brick Gothic exterior, the interior is a soaring passage of light. The tomb of Ludwig the Bavarian, guarded by knights and noblemen, can be found in the choir.

ASAMKIRCHE

Near the **Sendlinger Tor**, a 14th-century gate, you'll come upon the pint-sized St Johann Nepomuk church, better known as the **Asamkirche** (**Sendlinger Strasse 62**). Designed and built in the 18th century as a private chapel by the prolific Asam brothers (who lived next door), the over-the-top baroque interior – with not an inch of unembellished wall or column – must have been an awe-inspiring sight for 18th-century Müncheners, as it is today.

PINAKOTHEKS

The **Alte Pinakothek** (**☎ 2380 5216; Barer Strasse 27, enter from Theresienstrasse; adult/child €5.50/4, Sun €1; 10am-6pm, to 8pm Tue, closed Mon**) is a veritable treasure trove of works by Old European Masters and an unmissable part of any visit to the city. Housed in a neoclassical temple built by King Ludwig I, it is one of the most important collections in the world.

Picking up where the Alte Pinakothek leaves off, the **Neue Pinakothek** (**☎ 2380 5195; Barer Strasse 29; adult/child €7/5, Sun €1; 10am-6pm, to 8pm Wed, closed Tue**) contains an extensive collection of 18th-

BAI/IMAGEBROKER

Hallway inside the Residenz

HLI/IMAGEBROKER

Museum Brandhorst

IF YOU LIKE...

If you like Munich's tremendous **museum scene**, try these exceptional masterpieces:

- **Glyptothek** (☎ 286 100; Königsplatz 3; adult/concession €3.50/2.50, Sun €1, combined with Antikensammlungen €5.50/3.50; 10am-5pm, 10am-8pm Thu, closed Mon) Munich's oldest museum is a piece of Greek fantasy. Classical busts, portraits of Roman kings and sculptures from a Greek temple in Aegina are among its prized exhibits.
- **Antikensammlungen** (☎ 598 359; Königsplatz 1; adult/concession €3.50/2.50, Sun €1; 10am-5pm, 10am-8pm Wed, closed Mon) One of Germany's best antiquities collections, featuring vases, gold and silver jewellery and ornaments, bronze work, and Greek and Roman sculptures and statues.
- **Museum Brandhorst** (☎ 2380 5118; www.museum-brandhorst.de; Theresienstrasse 35a; adult/child €7/5, Sun €1; 10am-6pm, to 8pm Thu, closed Mon) This multicoloured structure was purpose-built to house a 700-piece private collection of modern and contemporary works belonging to Udo and Annette Brandhorst. Wow-factor is provided by Picasso, Warhol, Cy Twombly and even Damien Hirst, plus a number of lesser-known artists.
- **Staatliches Museum Ägyptischer Kunst** (Egyptian Art Museum; ☎ 298 546; enter from Hofgartenstrasse 1; adult/concession €6/4; 9am-5pm Tue-Fri, also 5-9pm Tue, 10am-5pm Sat & Sun) German explorers of the Near East brought back treasures that made their way into this excellent collection of Egyptian art, which dates from the Old, Middle and New Kingdoms (2670–1075 BC).

to early-20th-century paintings and sculpture, from rococo to Jugendstil (art nouveau).

Opened in 2002 after six years of construction, **Pinakothek der Moderne** (☎ 2380 5360; Barer Strasse 40; adult/child €10/7, Sun €1; 10am-6pm, to 8pm Thu, closed Mon) is

Germany's biggest collection of modern art. The spectacular interior is dominated by a huge eyelike dome, spreading natural light throughout the soft white galleries over four floors.

ENGLISCHER GARTEN & AROUND

The **Englischer Garten** (English Garden) is one of Europe's most monumental city parks – bigger even than London's Hyde Park or Central Park in New York. It was laid out in the late 18th century by an American-born physicist, Benjamin Thompson, an adviser to the Bavarian government and at one time its war minister. There are no English flower beds, but it's a great place for strolling, jogging, drinking and even surfing, conveniently located between the Isar River and the Schwabing district.

Several follies add some architectural interest. The **Chinesischer Turm** (Chinese Tower), dating back to 1789, rises from a thicket of green benches belonging to the city's best-known beer garden. Just south of here is the heavily photographed **Monopteros**, a faux Greek temple with pearly white columns. The **Japanisches Teehaus** (Japanese Teahouse) was built during the 1972 Olympics, and holds authentic tea ceremonies every second and fourth weekend in summer at 3pm, 4pm and 5pm.

BMW MUSEUM

Redesigned from scratch and reopened in 2008, the **BMW Museum** (**Map pp90-1; ☎ 0180-211 8822; www.bmw-museum.com; Am Olympiapark 2; adult/child €12/6; 🕒 9am-6pm Tue-Fri, 10am-8pm Sat & Sun**) is like no other car museum on the planet. The seven themed 'houses' examine the development of BMW's product line and include sections on motorcycles and motor racing. However, the interior design of this truly unique building, with its curvy retro feel, futuristic bridges, squares and huge backlit wall screens, almost upstages the exhibits.

SOUTH OF THE ALTSTADT

You could spend days exploring the **Deutsches Museum** (**☎ 217 91; www.deutsches-museum.de; Museumsinsel 1; adult/child under 6yr/concession/family €8.50/free/7/17; 🕒 9am-5pm**), said to be the world's largest science and technology collection.

SCHLOSS NYMPHENBURG

Commanding **Schloss Nymphenburg** (**Map pp90-1; ☎ 179 080; combined ticket to everything adult/concession €10/8**) and its lavish gardens sprawl about 5km northwest of the Altstadt. Begun in 1664 as a villa for Electress Adelaide of Savoy, the palace and gardens were expanded over the next century to create the royal family's summer residence. Franz Duke of Bavaria, the head of the once royal Wittelsbach family, still occupies an apartment within the palace complex.

SLEEPING

AROUND THE HAUPTBAHNHOF

our pick **Cocoon** (**☎ 5999 3907; www.hotel-cocoon.de; Lindwurmstrasse 35; s/d €69/89;** ⊠ ❄ 💻 📶) If retro design is your thing, you just struck gold. Things kick off in the reception with its faux '70s veneer and suspended '60s ball chairs, and continue in the rooms, all identical and decorated in cool retro oranges and greens. Every room has LCD TV, iPod dock, 'laptop cabin' and the hotel name above every bed in 1980s robotic lettering.

our pick **Cortiina** (**☎ 242 2490; www.cortiina.com; Ledererstrasse 8; s €165-270, d €225-390;** P ⊠ ❄ 💻) This stunning hotel offers modern stylish elegance minus the usual antique knick-knacks. The design is chic and minimalist without losing any comfort.

ALTSTADT & AROUND

Bayerischer Hof (☎ 212 00; www.bayerischerhof.de; Promenadeplatz 2-6; s €221-480, d €338-480; P ⊠ ⁙ 🖳 ☰ 🏊) Room doors fold away into the stucco mouldings at the Hof, one of the grande dames of the Munich hotel trade. It boasts a super-central location, a pool and a jazz club. Marble, antiques and oil paintings abound, and you can dine till you drop at any one of the three fabulous restaurants.

SCHWABING

Pension am Kaiserplatz (Map pp90-1; ☎ 349 190; fax 339 316; Kaiserplatz 12; s €31-47, d €49-59) The facade of this Jugendstil villa is a throwback to more romantic times, when Schwabing was awash with art and culture. The superb-value rooms (just 10, all with hall bathrooms) are lovingly decorated with a family touch, and breakfast is delivered to your door by the congenial host herself.

LEE FOSTER

Glockenspiel (p98), Neues Rathaus

Gästehaus Englischer Garten (Map pp90-1; ☎ 383 9410; www.hotelenglischergarten.de; Liebergesellstrasse 8; s €65-169, d €75-169; P) Wake up to the quack of ducks in the adjacent Englischer Garten at this cosy pension occupying a graceful old ivy-covered mill with a private garden for breakfast (€9.50 extra).

NYMPHENBURG, NEUHAUSEN & AROUND

Hotel Laimer Hof (Map pp90-1; ☎ 178 0380; www.laimerhof.de; Laimer Strasse 40; s/d from €69/89; P) Run by Bavaria's friendliest couple, this cute listed villa has a relaxed country feel, despite being just five minutes' walk from Schloss Nymphenburg. Of the 23 rooms, those on the upper floors have the most character and best views.

HAIDHAUSEN

Angelo (Map pp90-1; ☎ 189 0860; www.angelo-munich.com; Leuchtenbergring 20; s/d from €110/130; ⊠ ☰) From the open-plan jazz-themed reception-bar to the superbly composed rooms, the restaurant's clean lines to the crisp bathrooms, Munich's newest design hotel is a slick and minimalist affair, but warm and welcoming at the same time. It's already a firm favourite among Bavaria's power dressers. The downside is the location in the unfashionable, traffic-plagued end of Haidhausen, but it's a mere four stops on the S-Bahn from Marienplatz.

Opera-Garni (Hotel Opéra; ☎ 210 4940; www.hotel-opera.de; St Annastrasse 10; r €190-275, ste €285-365; ⊠ 🖳) Step inside the Opera and you'll step back in time. This hotel is pure old-world elegance and refinement. Breakfast is served in the garden between graceful statues, and the rooms are stunningly decorated with individual combinations of rich colours and fabrics, antiques, chandeliers and Persian carpets.

WESTEND & LUDWIGSVORSTADT

Pension Westfalia (☎ **530 377; www.pension-westfalia.de; Mozartstrasse 23; s/d from €35/50;**) You don't have far to stagger from the Oktoberfest meadow to this stately four-storey villa. Outside the beer festival this cosy, family-run pension is a peaceful base for sightseeing. Rooms are all reached by lift, and most have private bathrooms.

Hotel Uhland (☎ **543 350; www.hotel-uhland.de; Uhlandstrasse 1; s €67-145, d €81-190;**) A stein's throw from the Theresienwiese, this attractively renovated art-nouveau villa has a relaxed atmosphere and English-speaking staff. Some large rooms come with a tiny balcony, and there's a quaint garden.

EBO/IMAGEBROKER

Hofbräuhaus interior

HOFBRÄUHAUS

No visit to Munich would be complete without a visit to the Hofbräuhaus, Bavaria's (and possibly the world's) most celebrated beer hall. The swigging hordes of tourists tend to eclipse the fabulous interior, where dainty twirled flowers adorn the medieval vaults.

Things you need to know:
☎ **221 676; Am Platzl 9**

EATING

Café Rischart (☎ **231 7000; Marienplatz 18; dishes €4-8**) Some of the best views of the Marienplatz combine with Munich's finest cakes and pastries at this city institution.

Königsquelle (☎ **220 071; Baaderplatz 2; mains €5-16; dinner**) Something of a Munich institution for its attentive service and dark, well-stocked hardwood bar, the food here is consistently excellent, straightforward but expertly prepared.

Weisses Bräuhaus (☎ **229 9875; Im Tal 10; mains €6-15**) The *Weisswurst* (veal sausage) served here sets the city's standard; wash a pair down with the excellent Schneider *Weissbier*. Of an evening the dining halls are charged with red-faced, beer-fuelled hilarity and Alpine whoops to the strains of a rabble-rousing oompah band.

Wasserwerk (☎ **4890 0020; Wolfgangstrasse 19; mains €6-15; dinner only**) This quirky bistro – strewn with ducts, pipes and wheels – plays up the waterworks theme to marvellous effect. Expect a consistently delicious range of quality international cuisine.

Schlosscafé im Palmenhaus (**Map pp90-1**; ☎ **175 309; Schloss Nymphenburg; mains €7-12**) The glass-fronted 1820 palm house, where Ludwig II used to keep his exotic house plants warm in winter, is now a high-ceilinged and pleasantly scented cafe. It's just behind the palace.

Café Osteria La Vecchia Masseria (☎ **550 9090; Mathildenstrasse 3; mains €7-15**) This is one of the best Italian places in Munich, loud but unquestionably romantic. Earthy wood tables, antique tin buckets, baskets and clothing irons conjure up the ambience of an Italian farmhouse.

Nido (☎ 2880 6103; Theresienstrasse 40; mains €7.50-13) This popular place is a trendy spot with lots of brushed aluminium and big picture windows. It serves a small menu of simple Italian-influenced dishes and a large dose of unpretentious cool.

Fraunhofer (☎ 266 460; Fraunhoferstrasse 9; mains €7.50-16) This bustling restaurant is a homely place where the old-world atmosphere and decor (featuring mounted animal heads and a portrait of Ludwig II) contrasts with the menu. Its fresh takes on classical fare draw a hip, intergenerational crowd.

Unionsbräu Haidhausen (☎ 477 677; Einsteinstrasse 42; mains €7.50-16.50) This sophisticated brewpub has eight separate spaces where a mixed clientele of business types, locals and tourists slurp the house brew and feast on meat platters.

Taverna Diyar (☎ 4895 0497; Wörthstrasse 10; mains €10-18) At its best when heaving with punters after 9pm on a Friday and Saturday, and just as the belly dancer gets into full wobble, this places cooks up authentic platters of fish, kebabs and grilled lamb with lots of Kurdish and Turkish zing.

Einstein (☎ 202 400 332; St-Jakobs-Platz 18; mains €14-23; 🕒 closed Sat) Reflected in the plate-glass windows of the Jewish Museum, this is the only kosher eatery in the city centre. The ID and bag search entry process is worth it for the restaurant's uncluttered lines, smartly laid tables and soothing ambience.

OKTOBERFEST

It all started as an elaborate wedding toast – and turned into the world's biggest collective booze-up. In October 1810 the future king, Bavarian Crown Prince Ludwig I, married Princess Therese, and the newlyweds threw an enormous party at the city gates, complete with a horse race. The next year Ludwig's fun-loving subjects came back for more. The festival was extended and, to fend off autumn, was moved forward to September. As the years drew on the racehorses were dropped and sometimes the party had to be cancelled, but the institution called Oktoberfest (www.oktoberfest.de) was here to stay.

Nearly two centuries later, this 16-day extravaganza draws over six million visitors a year to celebrate a marriage of good cheer and outright debauchery. A special beer is brewed for the occasion (Wies'nbier), which is dark and strong. Müncheners spend the day at the office in lederhosen and dirndl in order to hit the festival right after work.

On the meadow called Theresienwiese (Wies'n for short), a temporary city is erected, consisting of beer tents, amusements and rides – just what drinkers need after several frothy ones! The action kicks off with the Brewer's Parade at 11am on the first day of the festival. The parade begins at Sonnenstrasse and winds its way to the fairgrounds via Schwanthalerstrasse. At noon, the lord mayor stands before the thirsty crowds at Theresienwiese and, with due pomp, slams a wooden tap into a cask of beer. As the beer gushes out, the mayor exclaims, *O'zapft ist's!* (It's tapped!).

DRINKING

ALTSTADT

Hofbräuhaus (☎ 221 676; Am Platzl 9) This is certainly the best-known and most celebrated beer hall in Bavaria, but apart from a few local yokels you'll be in the company of tourists. A live band is condemned to play Bavarian folk music most of the day.

Augustiner-Grossgaststätte (☎ 2318 3257; Neuhauser Strasse 27) This sprawling place has a less raucous atmosphere and superior food to the usual offerings. Altogether it's a much more authentic example of an old-style Munich beer hall, complete with secluded courtyards and hunting trophies.

Braunauer Hof (☎ 223 613; Frauenstrasse 42) This pleasantly warped beer garden has a hedge maze, a bizarre wall mural and a golden bull that's illuminated at night.

Jodlerwirt (☎ 221 249; Altenhofstrasse 4; from 6pm Tue-Sat) One of Munich's earthiest pubs has an accordion-playing host and stand-up comic who spread good cheer in yodelling sessions at the upstairs bar. By the end of the evening you'll find yourself swaying arm in arm with complete strangers.

ENGLISCHER GARTEN

Chinesischer Turm (☎ 383 8730; Englischer Garten 3) This is an institution known to every Münchener from an early age. The popular watering hole derives extra atmosphere from a classic Chinese pagoda and entertainment by a good-time oompah band (in an upper floor of the tower, fenced in like the Blues Brothers).

NEUHAUSEN

Augustiner Keller (☎ 594 393; Arnulfstrasse 52) Every year this leafy 5000-seat beer garden, about 500m west of the Hauptbahnhof, buzzes with activity from the first hint of springtime. It's a beautiful spot with a laid-back atmosphere ideal for leisurely drinking.

MSI/IMAGEBROKER

Hirschgarten

IF YOU LIKE...

If you like the convivial atmosphere of beer halls like the **Hofbräuhaus** (p107), try these less-touristy alternatives:

- **Löwenbräukeller** (☎ 526 021; Nymphenburger Strasse 2) This enormous beer hall is a local fixture for its regular Bavarian music and heel-slapping dances. During the *Starkbierzeit* (the springtime 'strong beer season'), the famous stone-lifting contests are held here. A beer garden rambles round the entire complex.
- **Hirschgarten** (Map pp90-1; ☎ 172 591; Hirschgartenallee 1) Locals and savvy visitors flock to the Hirschgarten, just south of Schloss Nymphenburg. This quaint country beer garden has deer wandering just the other side of the fence. To get there take the S-Bahn to Laim.

HAIDHAUSEN

Hofbräukeller (☎ 448 7376; Innere Wiener Strasse 19) Not to be confused with its better-known cousin in the city centre, this sprawling, very atmospheric restaurant-cum-beer garden retains an early-20th-century air. Locals in *Tracht* (traditional costume) come here to guzzle big mugs of foaming beer alongside the regular specials of roast pork.

Dreigroschenkeller (☎ 489 0290; Lilienstrasse 2) A cosy and labyrinthine cellar pub with rooms based upon Bertolt Brecht's *Die Dreigroschenoper* (The Threepenny Opera), ranging from a prison cell to a red satiny salon. There are nine types of beer to choose from and an extensive menu of hearty German soak-up material.

SCHWABING

Alter Simpl (☎ 272 3083; Türkenstrasse 57) This watering hole has good jazz, a reasonable menu (mains €6 to €13) and an art-house vibe. Thomas Mann and Hermann Hesse were among the writers and artists that used to meet here in the early 20th century.

ENTERTAINMENT

NIGHTCLUBS

P1 (☎ 211 1140; Prinzregentenstrasse 1) A bit of a Munich institution and still the see-and-be-seen place for the city's wannabes, with extremely choosy and effective bouncers, snooty staff and the occasional celebrity.

Registratur (☎ 2388 7758; Blumenstrasse 4) No mistake, the dusty halls and '60s panelling of this old city building have the charm of an off-licence. The humour isn't lost on the (mostly 20s) crowd, who come for a diet of African beats, shock rock and indie pop.

LIVE MUSIC

Philharmonie im Gasteig (☎ 480 980; www.gasteig.de; Rosenheimer Strasse 5) As home to the city's Philharmonic Orchestra, Munich's premier high-brow cultural venue has a packed schedule. The Symphonieorchester des Bayerischen Rundfunks (Bavarian Radio Symphony Orchestra) is also based here, and performs on Sundays throughout the year.

Nationaltheater (☎ box office 218 501; www.staatstheater.bayern.de; Max-Joseph-Platz 2) The Bayerische Staatsoper (Bavarian State Opera) performs here. Its prestigious opera festival takes place in July. You can buy tickets at regular outlets or at the box office.

KLS/IMAGEBROKER

Neues Rathaus and Marienplatz (p98)

Jazzclub Unterfahrt im Einstein (☎ 448 2794; Einsteinstrasse 42) This is perhaps the best-known place in town, with live music from 9pm and regular international acts. Sunday nights feature an open jam session.

SHOPPING

Deutsches Museum Shop (☎ 2138 3892; Museuminsel 1) Perhaps the most fascinating museum gift shop you'll ever visit, with heaps of man-gadgets, working models, kids' science sets, unusual toys, unique 3-D postcards and museum-related knick-knacks and souvenirs. There's another branch at Rindermarkt 17.

Holareidulijö (☎ 271 7745; Schellingstrasse 81; noon-6.30pm Tue-Fri, 10am-1pm Sat) Munich's only secondhand traditional clothing emporium, and worth a look even if you don't intend to buy. Apparently, wearing hand-me-down lederhosen reduces the risk of chafing.

Manufactum (☎ 2354 5900; Dienerstrasse 12) Anyone with an admiration for top-quality German design classics should make a beeline for this place. Last-a-lifetime household items compete for shelf space with retro toys, Bauhaus lamps and times-gone-by stationary.

Porzellan Manufaktur Nymphenburg (Map pp90-1; ☎ 1791 9710; Schloss Nymphenburg; 10am-5pm Mon-Fri) It has made fine porcelain for Bavarian royals and quite a few commoners since being founded in 1747. There's a more central store at Odeonsplatz 1.

GETTING THERE & AWAY

AIR

Munich's **international airport** (MUC; ☎ 089-975 00; www.munich-airport.de) is second in importance only to Frankfurt for international and domestic flights.

STR/IMAGEBROKER

The Monopteros (p105) in the Englischer Garten

BUS

BerlinLinienBus (☎ 09281-2252; www.berlinlinienbus.de) runs daily buses between Berlin and Munich (one way/return €47/88, 9½ hours), via Ingolstadt, Nuremberg, Bayreuth and Leipzig.

TRAIN

There are direct IC and ICE trains to Berlin (€113, six hours), Hamburg (€127, six hours), Frankfurt (€89, 3¼ hours) and Stuttgart (€52, 2½ hours).

GETTING AROUND

TO/FROM THE AIRPORT

Munich's **Flughafen Franz-Josef Strauss** (www.munich-airport.de) is connected by the S8 to the Ostbahnhof, Hauptbahnhof (central train station) and Marienplatz

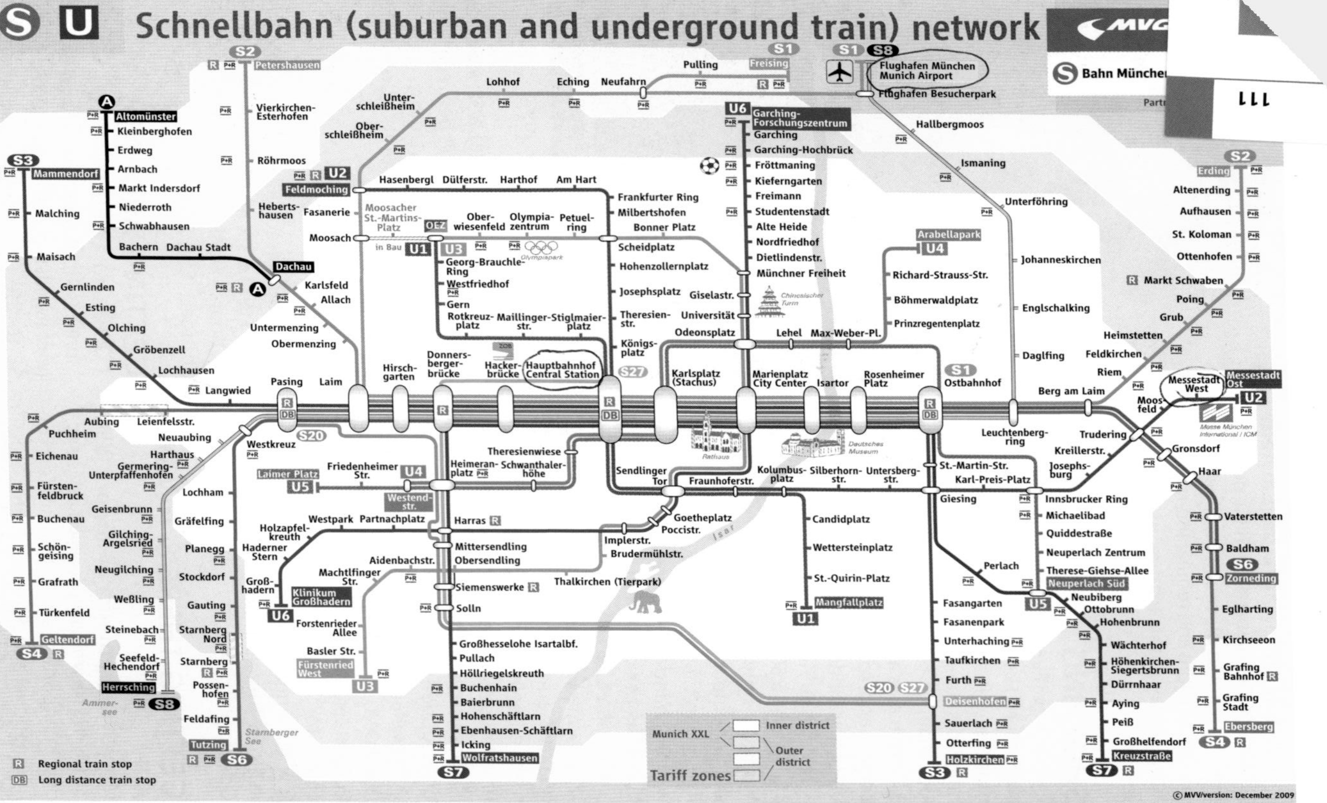
Schnellbahn (suburban and underground train) network
MVG
S Bahn München
Flughafen München
Munich Airport
Flughafen Besucherpark
S1 S8
S1 Freising
Pulling
Neufahrn
Eching
Lohhof
Unter-schleißheim
Ober-schleißheim
S2 Petershausen
Vierkirchen-Esterhofen
Röhrmoos
Hebertshausen
Dachau
Karlsfeld
Allach
Untermenzing
Obermenzing
Altomünster
Kleinberghofen
Erdweg
Arnbach
Markt Indersdorf
Niederroth
Schwabhausen
Bachern
Dachau Stadt
S3 Mammendorf
Malching
Maisach
Gernlinden
Esting
Olching
Gröbenzell
Lochhausen
Langwied
Pasing
Laim
Hirsch-garten
Donners-berger-brücke
Hacker-brücke
Hauptbahnhof
Central Station
Karlsplatz (Stachus)
Marienplatz City Center
Isartor
Rosenheimer Platz
Ostbahnhof
Leuchtenberg-ring
Berg am Laim
Trudering
Gronsdorf
Haar
Vaterstetten
Baldham
S6 Zorneding
Eglharting
Kirchseeon
Grafing Bahnhof
Grafing Stadt
S4 Ebersberg
S2 Erding
Altenerding
Aufhausen
St. Koloman
Ottenhofen
Markt Schwaben
Poing
Grub
Heimstetten
Feldkirchen
Riem
Moosfeld
Messestadt West
Messestadt Ost
U2
Messe München International / ICM
Hallbergmoos
Ismaning
Unterföhring
Johanneskirchen
Englschalking
Daglfing
U6 Garching-Forschungszentrum
Garching
Garching-Hochbrück
Fröttmaning
Kieferngarten
Freimann
Studentenstadt
Alte Heide
Nordfriedhof
Dietlindenstr.
Münchner Freiheit
Giselastr.
Universität
Odeonsplatz
Lehel
Max-Weber-Pl.
Arabellapark U4
Richard-Strauss-Str.
Böhmerwaldplatz
Prinzregentenplatz
Chinesischer Turm
U2 Feldmoching
Hasenbergl
Dülferstr.
Harthof
Am Hart
Frankfurter Ring
Milbertshofen
Bonner Platz
Scheidplatz
Hohenzollernplatz
Josephsplatz
Theresien-str.
Königs-platz
S27
Fasanerie
Moosach
Moosacher St.-Martins-Platz
in Bau
OEZ
U1 U3
Ober-wiesenfeld
Olympia-zentrum
Petuel-ring
Olympiapark
Georg-Brauchle-Ring
Westfriedhof
Gern
Rotkreuz-platz
Maillinger-str.
Stiglmaier-platz
ZOB
Aubing
Leienfelsstr.
Puchheim
Eichenau
Fürsten-feldbruck
Buchenau
Schön-geising
Grafrath
Türkenfeld
S4 Geltendorf
Neuaubing
Westkreuz
S20
Harthaus
Germering-Unterpfaffenhofen
Geisenbrunn
Gilching-Argelsried
Neugilching
Weßling
Steinebach
Seefeld-Hechendorf
Herrsching
S8
Ammersee
Lochham
Gräfelfing
Planegg
Stockdorf
Gauting
Starnberg Nord
Starnberg
Possen-hofen
Feldafing
Tutzing
S6
Starnberger See
Friedenheimer Str.
U4
Laimer Platz
U5
Westend-str.
Theresienwiese
Heimeran-platz
Schwanthaler-höhe
Westpark
Partnachplatz
Holzapfel-kreuth
Haderner Stern
Groß-hadern
Klinikum Großhadern
U6
Forstenrieder Allee
Basler Str.
Fürstenried West
U3
Machtlfinger Str.
Aidenbachstr.
Harras
Mittersendling
Obersendling
Siemenswerke
Solln
Großhesselohe Isartalbf.
Pullach
Höllriegelskreuth
Buchenhain
Baierbrunn
Hohenschäftlarn
Ebenhausen-Schäftlarn
Icking
Wolfratshausen
S7
Sendlinger Tor
Fraunhoferstr.
Goetheplatz
Poccistr.
Implerstr.
Brudermühlstr.
Thalkirchen (Tierpark)
Kolumbus-platz
Silberhorn-str.
Untersberg-str.
Candidplatz
Wettersteinplatz
St.-Quirin-Platz
Mangfallplatz
U1
Rathaus
Deutsches Museum
Isar
St.-Martin-Str.
Karl-Preis-Platz
Giesing
Kreillerstr.
Josephs-burg
Innsbrucker Ring
Michaelibad
Quiddestraße
Neuperlach Zentrum
Therese-Giehse-Allee
Neuperlach Süd
U5
Perlach
Neubiberg
Ottobrunn
Hohenbrunn
Wächterhof
Höhenkirchen-Siegertsbrunn
Dürrnhaar
Aying
Peiß
Großhelfendorf
Kreuzstraße
S7
Fasangarten
Fasanenpark
Unterhaching
Taufkirchen
Furth
Deisenhofen
S20 S27
Sauerlach
Otterfing
Holzkirchen
S3
Munich XXL
Inner district
Outer district
Tariff zones
R Regional train stop
DB Long distance train stop
© MVV/version: December 2009

(€9.20). The trip to the Hauptbahnhof takes about 40 minutes and trains run every 20 minutes from around 4am until 1am. For northern and eastern suburbs take the S8.

PUBLIC TRANSPORT

Short rides (four bus or tram stops; two U-Bahn or S-Bahn stops) cost €1.20, while longer trips cost €2.30. It's marginally cheaper to buy a strip-card of 10 tickets called a *Streifenkarte* for €11, and stamp one strip per adult on rides of two or less tram or U-Bahn stops, two strips for longer journeys.

AROUND MUNICH

DACHAU CONCENTRATION CAMP MEMORIAL

Dachau was the Nazis' first concentration camp, built by Heinrich Himmler in March 1933 to house political prisoners. All in all it 'processed' more than 200,000 inmates, killing at least 43,000, and is now a haunting memorial. A new **visitors centre** (**☎ 669 970; www.kz-gedenkstaette-dachau.de; Alte Römerstrasse 75**) opened in May 2009 housing a bookshop, cafe and tour booking desk.

You pass into the compound itself through the **Jourhaus**, originally the only entrance. Set in wrought iron, the chilling slogan 'Arbeit Macht Frei' (Work Sets You Free) hits you at the gate.

The **museum** (**admission free; 9am-5pm Tue-Sun**) is at the southern end of the camp. Here a 22-minute English-language documentary runs at 11.30am, 2pm and 3.30pm. Either side of the small cinema extends an exhibition relating the camp's harrowing story. This includes photographs of the camp, its officers and prisoners, and of horrifying 'scientific experiments' carried out by Nazi doctors.

GETTING THERE & AWAY

The westbound S2 makes the journey from Munich Hauptbahnhof to Dachau Hauptbahnhof in 21 minutes.

TJO/IMAGEBROKER

Main entrance to the Dachau Concentration Camp Memorial

KKR/IMAGEBROKER

Versailles-inspired Schloss Herrenchiemsee, Herreninsel

CHIEMSEE

☎ 08051

An island just 1.5km across the Chiemsee from Prien, Herreninsel is home to Ludwig II's Versailles-inspired **Schloss Herrenchiemsee** (☎ 688 70; www.herren-chiemsee.de; adult/under 18yr/concession €7/free/6; ⏲ tours continuously 9am-6pm Apr–mid-Oct, 9.40am-4.15pm mid-Oct-Mar). Begun in 1878, it was never intended as a residence but as a homage to absolutist monarchy, as epitomised by Ludwig's hero, the French Sun King, Louis XIV.

The rooms that were completed outdo each other in opulence. The vast **Gesandtentreppe** (Ambassador Staircase), a double staircase leading to a frescoed gallery and topped by a glass roof, is the first visual knockout on the guided tour, but that fades in comparison to the stunning **Grosse Spiegelgalerie** (Great Hall of Mirrors). It sports 52 candelabra and 33 great glass chandeliers with 7000 candles, which took 70 servants half an hour to light. But it's the king's bedroom, the **Kleines Blaues Schlafzimmer** (Little Blue Bedroom), that really takes the cake. The room is bathed in a soft blue light emanating from a glass globe at the foot of the bed.

To reach the palace, take the ferry from Prien-Stock (€6.50 return, 15 to 20 minutes) or from Bernau-Felden (€8, 25 minutes, May to October). From the boat landing on Herreninsel, it's about a 20-minute walk through pretty gardens to the palace. Palace tours, offered in German or English, last 30 minutes.

GETTING THERE & AWAY

Prien and Bernau are served by hourly trains from Munich (€15.20, one hour). Hourly RVO bus 9505 connects the two lake towns.

➘ BAVARIA

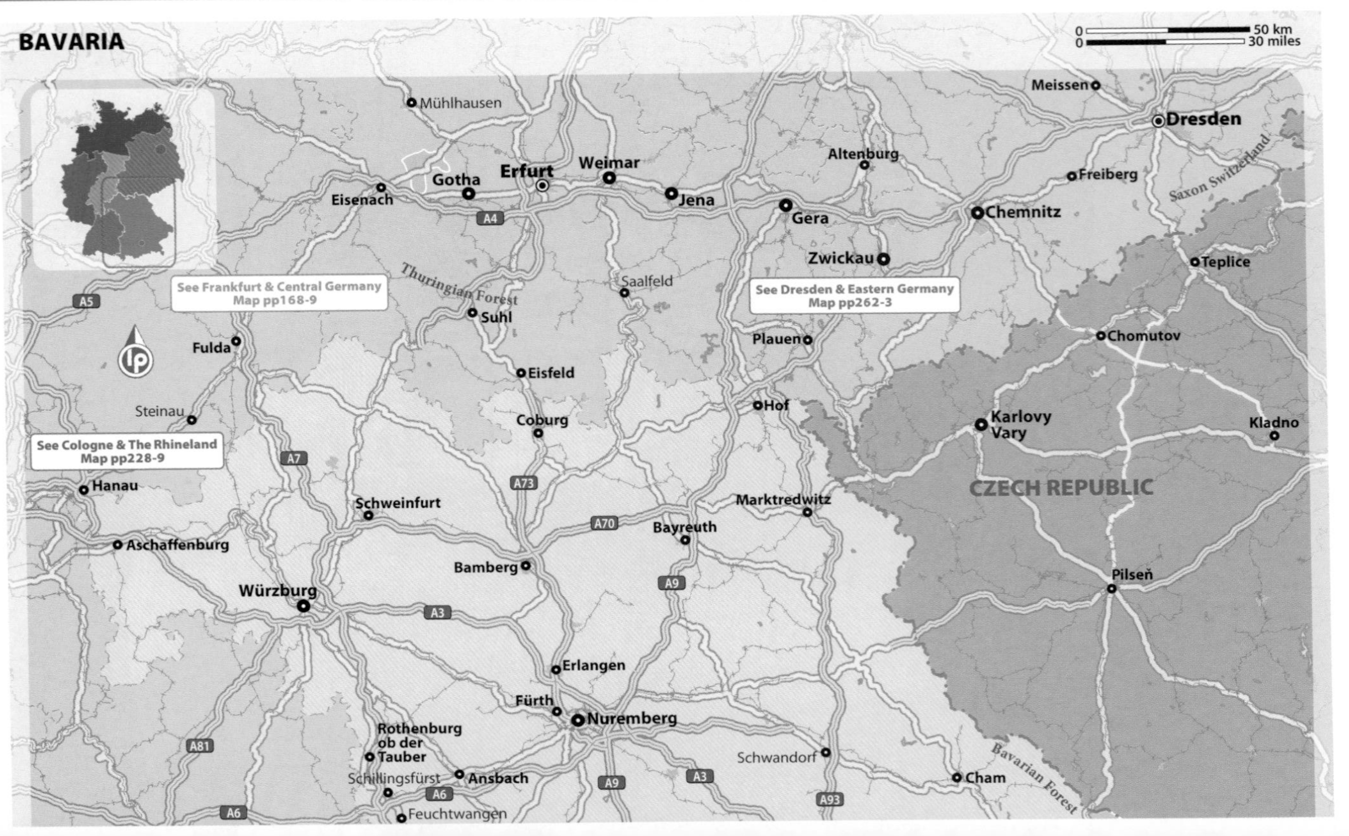

BAVARIA
0 50 km
0 30 miles
See Frankfurt & Central Germany Map pp168-9
See Dresden & Eastern Germany Map pp262-3
See Cologne & The Rhineland Map pp228-9
CZECH REPUBLIC
Thuringian Forest
Saxon Switzerland
Bavarian Forest
Mühlhausen
Meissen
Dresden
Gotha
Erfurt
Weimar
Jena
Eisenach
Altenburg
Gera
Freiberg
Chemnitz
Zwickau
Teplice
Saalfeld
Suhl
Fulda
Plauen
Chomutov
Eisfeld
Steinau
Hof
Coburg
Karlovy Vary
Kladno
Hanau
Schweinfurt
Marktredwitz
Bayreuth
Aschaffenburg
Bamberg
Würzburg
Pilseň
Erlangen
Fürth
Nuremberg
Rothenburg ob der Tauber
Schillingsfürst
Ansbach
Feuchtwangen
Schwandorf
Cham
A3
A4
A5
A6
A7
A9
A70
A73
A81
A93

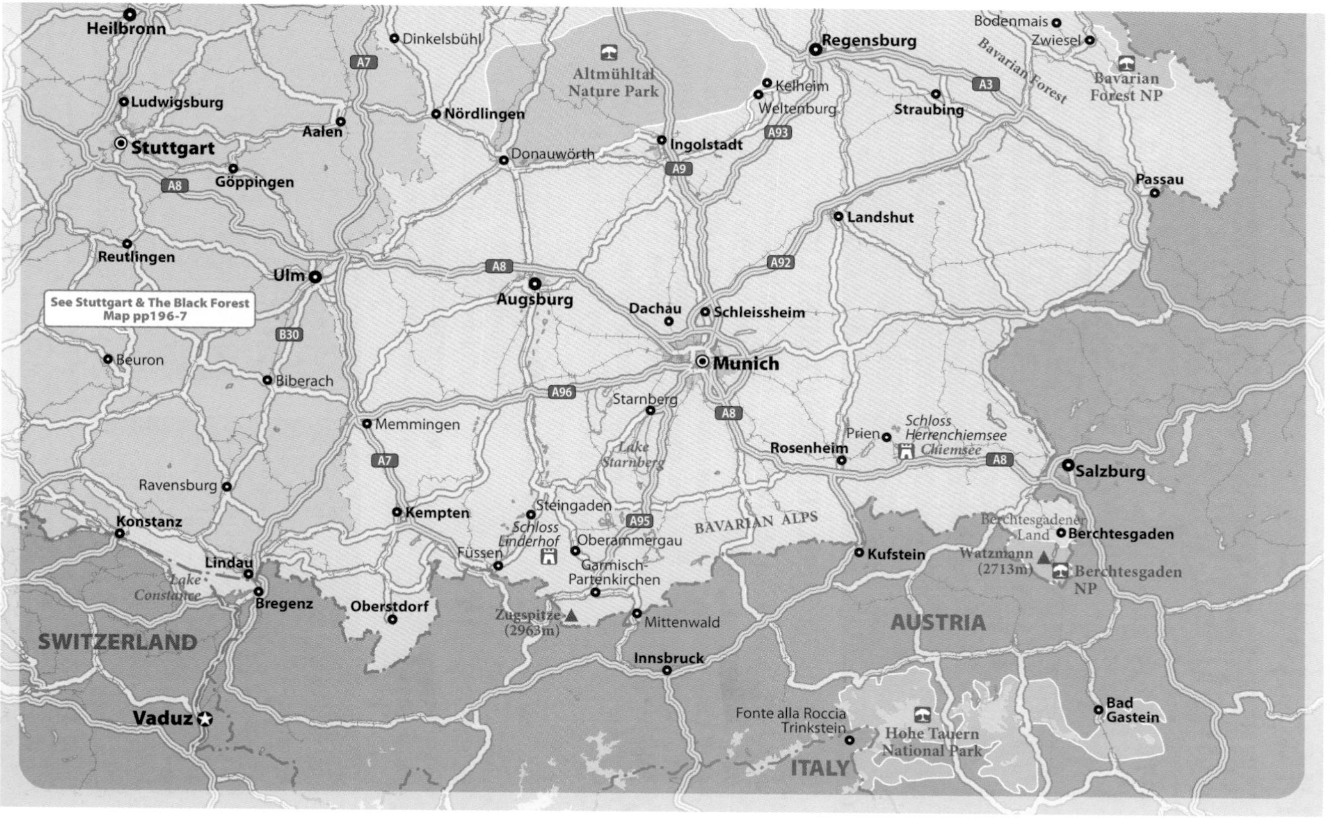
Heilbronn
Ludwigsburg
Stuttgart
A8
Göppingen
Aalen
A7
Dinkelsbühl
Nördlingen
Donauwörth
Altmühltal Nature Park
Ingolstadt
A9
A93
Kelheim
Weltenburg
Regensburg
Straubing
A3
Bavarian Forest
Bodenmais
Zwiesel
Bavarian Forest NP
Passau
Landshut
A92
Reutlingen
Ulm
A8
Augsburg
Dachau
Schleissheim
See Stuttgart & The Black Forest Map pp196-7
B30
Beuron
Biberach
Munich
A96
Starnberg
A8
Memmingen
Schloss Herrenchiemsee
Prien
Chiemsee
Rosenheim
Lake Starnberg
A7
A8
Salzburg
Ravensburg
Kempten
Steingaden
Schloss Linderhof
A95
BAVARIAN ALPS
Berchtesgadener Land
Berchtesgaden
Konstanz
Füssen
Oberammergau
Kufstein
Watzmann (2713m)
Berchtesgaden NP
Lindau
Lake Constance
Bregenz
Garmisch-Partenkirchen
Oberstdorf
Zugspitze (2963m)
Mittenwald
AUSTRIA
SWITZERLAND
Innsbruck
Vaduz
Fonte alla Roccia Trinkstein
Hohe Tauern National Park
ITALY
Bad Gastein

HIGHLIGHTS

1 THE MAGIC OF LUDWIG II

BY CORNELIA ZIEGLER, AUTHOR OF A DEFINITIVE GUIDEBOOK ON LUDWIG II

A few years ago as I gazed upon Schloss Neuschwanstein from Mary's Bridge, I suddenly understood the genius of King Ludwig II. Never before had I seen a structure that blended so perfectly with nature as Neuschwanstein does with the gorgeous scenery around Schwangau.

CORNELIA ZIEGLER'S DON'T MISS LIST

❶ SCHLOSS NEUSCHWANSTEIN

Ludwig dreamed of flying. In fact, it was one of the reasons he was declared mad. But then, a mere five years after his death, Otto Lilienthal started his first flying experiments… I often remember this strange irony when riding the cable car to the top of Tegelberg mountain and looking down at the **castle** (p140).

❷ SCHLOSS LINDERHOF

When visiting Ludwig's enchanting residential **palace** (p145), don't skip the park with its exotic buildings. Travel to the Orient in the Moorish Kiosk, channel ancient Germanic tribes in the Hundinghütte or delve into a Wagner-inspired dream world in the famous Venus Grotto where the king enjoyed floating in a shell-shaped boat.

❸ LAKE STARNBERG

Annually on the Sunday following the anniversary of Ludwig's death, a festive memorial service is held in a chapel on **Lake Starnberg** (Map pp116-17).

Clockwise from top: Schloss Neuschwanstein (p140); Schloss Nymphenburg (p105); Ludwig II memorial, Lake Starnberg (p142); Latona fountain, Schloss Herrenchiemsee (p114); Schloss Linderhof (p145)

Afterwards, a wreath is sunk at the spot where the king drowned in 1886. There's truly no better place to get a sense of the intense fascination this mysterious monarch still exudes to this day.

❹ SCHLOSS HERRENCHIEMSEE

Before or after visiting **Herrenchiemsee palace** (p114), pop by the local history museum (*Heimatmuseum*) in Prien. The original 19th-century farmhouse contains a cosy parlour decorated with a portrait of the king, as was typical back then in rural Bavaria. On Herrenchiemsee itself, take your sweet time to explore this enchanting island on foot.

❺ MUNICH

Ludwig was born in **Schloss Nymphenburg** (p105) in Munich, one of the loveliest park-and-palace ensembles in all of Europe. The room where he was born and the collection of magnificent royal coaches in the **Marstall Museum** are major highlights. In the town centre, don't miss the **Cuvilliés Theatre** (at the Residenz, p102), a rococo jewel, where the king attended many private performances.

↘ THINGS YOU NEED TO KNOW

Hear Classical music at the Herrenchiemsee Festival in July. **Eat** Bleckenau inn (www.berggasthaus-bleckenau.de) above Neuschwanstein serves dishes from Ludwig's times. **Read** Cornelia Ziegler's *Bayern – auf den Spuren von König Ludwig II* (in German). **See p142 for more on Ludwig II**

HIGHLIGHTS

2

ALPINE GRANDEUR

In the Bavarian Alps nature has been as prolific and creative as Picasso in his prime. A gorgeous patchwork of mountains, lakes, forests and meadows, it should convert even the most dedicated lummox to the great outdoors. **Oberstdorf** (p146), **Garmisch-Partenkirchen** (p141) and **Berchtesgaden** (p146) make excellent bases of operation.

3

BAMBERG: BISHOPS & BEER

Bisected by rivers and canals, **Bamberg** (p154) is magnificently sited on seven hills, with an atmospheric jumble of crooked lanes, medieval buildings and a skyline punctured by church steeples. A contagious energy bubbles away in its many brewpubs where you must try the unique local *Rauchbier*, a smoky beer with a century-old tradition.

4

ROTHENBURG OB DER TAUBER

Romantic Road darling **Rothenburg** (p129) is often deluged by visitors, but it's not hard to escape the crowds. Find peaceful nooks by wandering the winding lanes, their cobblestones worn smooth by centuries of use. Or watch the sun set over the Tauber Valley from the gardens outside the city gate.

5

WÜRZBURG RESIDENZ

The Unesco-listed **Residenz** (p128) was made possible by the deep pockets of local bishops and the genius of two of the finest creative minds of the period, Balthasar Neumann and Giovanni Tiepolo. One of Germany's key baroque palaces and such a successful alchemy of art and architecture, it will leave you stunned and inspired.

6

THIRD REICH LEGACY

The dark legacy of the Third Reich is never far in many German cities, especially in places that played key roles in Nazi Germany. Visit two of them – **Berchtesgaden** (p146) and **Nuremberg** (p149) – to see how they are dealing with this horrific history in an honest, responsible and comprehensive fashion.

2 GRANT DIXON; 3 DMP/IMAGEBROKER; 4 BRUCE ESBIN; 5 MSI/IMAGEBROKER; 6 NPR/IMAGEBROKER

2 Hikers near Garmisch-Partenkirchen (p141); 3 Bamberg's Altes Rathaus (p154); 4 View over Rothenburg ob der Tauber (p129); 5 Hofgarten, Würzburg's Residenz (p128); 6 Reichsparteitagsgelände (p152), Nuremberg

THE BEST...

CHRISTMAS MARKETS

- **Augsburg** (p137) Angel musicians and a magical town hall.
- **Nuremberg** (p149) Germany's most famous market.
- **Regensburg** (p160) Three markets, including a torch-lit one at the palace.
- **Rothenburg ob der Tauber** (p129) Stalls sparkling in an idyllic maze of medieval lanes.

BEER HALLS & GARDENS

- **Klosterschenke Weltenburg** (p163) Monastic brew in idyllic setting.
- **Kneitinger, Regensburg** (p162) Quintessential Bavarian brewpub.
- **Weib's Brauhaus, Dinkelsbühl** (p134) Delicious suds from a woman brew master.
- **Wirtshaus zum Schlenkerla, Bamberg** (p156) Try its famous *Rauchbier*.

INSPIRING HIKES

- **Bavarian Forest National Park** (p166) Germany's first national park; home to deer and others.
- **Eiskapelle** (p147) A 200m-high ice cavern near Königssee.
- **Jagdschloss Schachen** (p143) King Ludwig II's exotic mountain retreat.
- **Partnachklamm** (p143) Narrow 750m-long gorge, in winter with icicles and frozen waterfalls.
- **Zugspitze** (p143) For experienced hikers only.

CURIOSITIES

- **Echo Wall, Berchtesgaden** (p147) Echoes bounce off the rocky walls.
- **Felsengänge, Nuremberg** (p152) Underground medieval passages.
- **Käthe Wohlfahrt Weihnachtsdorf, Rothenburg ob der Tauber** (p133) It's Christmas – year-round.
- **Walhalla** (p163) Marble temple to giants of thought and deed.

MARTIN MOOS

Stall selling *Lebkuchen* (gingerbread) hearts at Christkindlesmarkt (p153), Nuremberg

THINGS YOU NEED TO KNOW

VITAL STATISTICS

- **Population** 12.5 million
- **Area** 70,549 sq km
- **Best time to visit** April–October for hiking and outdoor activities, December–March for winter sports
- **Points of entry** Frankfurt, Munich, Lake Constance

ADVANCE PLANNING

- **As early as possible** Book accommodation, especially in summer, around Oktoberfest and December during the Christmas-market season (especially in Nuremberg).
- **One week before** Buy online tickets for Schloss Neuschwanstein (p140) and Hohenschwangau (p139).
- **One day before** Make wine-tasting reservations, eg in Würzburg (p128).

RESOURCES

- **Bayern Tourismus** (www.bayern.by) Regional tourist office.
- **Kinderland Bavaria** (www.kinderland.by) Information on family travel.
- **Romantic Road Tourist Office** (☎ 09851-551 387; www.romantische-strasse.de) In Dinkelsbühl (p133).

EMERGENCY NUMBERS

- **Fire & ambulance** ☎ 112
- **Police** ☎ 110

GETTING AROUND

- **Air** Frankfurt and Munich are the main gateways to Bavaria.
- **Bicycle** The Romantic Road (p126) and the Altmühltal Nature Park (p159) are especially suited for bike touring.
- **Bus** Check out the Europabus (see p126) for travelling along the Romantic Road.
- **Car** Having a car is perfect for tooling around the countryside, and pretty much essential in the remote Bavarian Forest (p165).
- **Trains** For small groups, the Bayern-Ticket (€28; www.bahn.de) is a steal – giving up to five adults unlimited 2nd-class regional train travel for one weekday, or from midnight to 3am on weekends.

BE FOREWARNED

- **Minimum stay** Some lodging providers require you to stay for two or three days in peak season, or pay a surcharge.
- **Private rooms** Tourist offices can help you find inexpensive homestays (*Privatzimmer*).
- **Regional buses** Public bus service often stops early in the evening and is suspended on weekends.
- **Resort tax** Many resort and spa towns charge their overnight guests a *Kurtaxe*. Fees range from €2 to €3 per night and are added to your hotel bill.

BAVARIAN ITINERARIES

ALPINE ADVENTURE Three Days

This driving tour twists and turns through the foothills of the muscular Bavarian Alps. Kick off in **(1) Garmisch-Partenkirchen** (p141), Germany's posh winter resort where an ingenious train-and-cable-car combo whisks you to the peak of the Zugspitze, the country's highest mountain. Ski hounds will be on cloud nine exploring over 100km of downhill runs spread over three ski fields. First up the next day is **(2) Oberammergau** (p144), an impossibly cute – if over touristed – village famous for its Passion Play (performed every 10 years), 500-year-old wood-carving tradition and fresco-festooned facades. Afterwards, drop by **(3) Schloss Linderhof** (p145), King Ludwig II's most romantic castle, or head straight to Chiemsee lake to wander around the ultra-lavish **(4) Schloss Herrenchiemsee** (p112), the king's 'Bavarian Versailles'.

Spend Day 3 immersing yourself in the scenery of **(5) Berchtesgaden** (p146), where must-do's include a boat trip on the emerald-green Königssee, the jaw-dropping ride up to (and views from) the Eagle's Nest and a stop at the Dokumentation Obersalzberg.

ROMANTIC ROAD Five Days

Tailor-made for road trippers, Germany's most famous holiday route is a trail of walled towns, ancient watchtowers and mighty castles. There are endless possibilities for interim stops, but here are a few highlights: start with **(1) Würzburg** (p126), a lively city shaped by wine, bishops and great architecture. Head south to **(2) Rothenburg ob der Tauber** (p129), the fairy-tale looks and charming lanes of which make for an irresistible sightseeing cocktail. Plunge on to **(3) Dinkelsbühl** (p133) and **(4) Nördlingen** (p136), both medieval gems encircled by ancient town walls. Continue to energetic **(5) Augsburg** (p137), shaped by the Romans as well as medieval artisans and traders. In summer its grand squares and canal-woven backstreets spill over with *joie de vivre*. Of the many churches along this route, the one packing the biggest punch is the luminous **(6) Wieskirche** (p131), near the village of Steingaden, a rococo composition of heavenly proportions. The tour's coda is what many consider the road's crowning glory: Füssen's fairy-tale **(7) Schloss Neuschwanstein** (p140), the embodiment of both the genius and tragedy of its creator, King Ludwig II.

BIGGEST HITS One Week

This grand sweep of Bavaria's blockbusters travels through centuries of German history, ticking off bustling cities, Unesco-listed Heritage Sites and romantic towns along the way. The first stop on your epic road trip is **(1) Bamberg** (p154), which will wow you with atmosphere-steeped

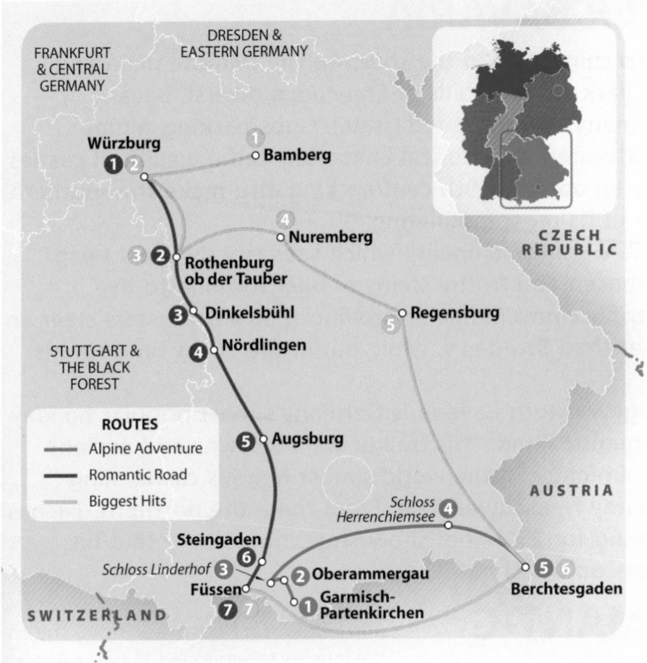

backstreets and a stunning collage of stately medieval buildings. Hook west to **(2) Würzburg** (p126), the *pièce de résistance* of which – the former bishop's residence – showcases the splendour of baroque art and architecture. A short drive south, pretty **(3) Rothenburg ob der Tauber** (p129) should enchant even hopelessly unromantic types, especially if you stay into the evening after the tour buses. Cut across to **(4) Nuremberg** (p149), a modern city that gave birth both to Renaissance master Albrecht Dürer and Nazi mass rallies. Don't overlook **(5) Regensburg** (p160), sitting pretty on the Danube, with a vibrant blend of medieval architecture and 21st-century verve. Leave the cities behind in **(6) Berchtesgaden** (p146), a dreamy pastiche of mountains, meadows and mirror-still lakes. Your final stop is Füssen's **(7) Schloss Neuschwanstein** (p140), King Ludwig II's fairy-tale fantasy, prettily embedded in the forested Alpine foothills.

DISCOVER BAVARIA

From the sky-scraping Alps in the south to the Danube plain and beyond to the dark wooded hills of Franconia, diverse Bavaria (Bayern) is Germany's largest *Land* (state). Gobsmacking Alpine vistas, towns saturated in historical character, and a wealth of castles bequeathed by an oddball 19th-century king also make the southern 'free state' one of its most fascinating.

Bavaria enjoys a split personality which sees city dwellers swap weekend lederhosen and frothy steins of beer for nine-to-five laptops and cappuccinos. Munich's provincial power dressers steer an economy bigger than Sweden's, while out in the sticks time stands still.

Slicing through western Bavaria is Germany's most popular holiday route – the Romantic Road. This trail of walled towns and ancient watchtowers culminates in the world's most famous castle, King Ludwig II's dreamy Neuschwanstein. From there the northern reaches of the Alps extend for 250km of show-stopping scenery that has hikers and skiers on cloud nine.

THE ROMANTIC ROAD

Two million people ply the Romantic Road (Romantische Strasse) every year, making it by far the most popular of Germany's holiday routes. Despite the hordes of visitors, it's worth falling for the sales pitch – you won't be alone, but you certainly won't be disappointed. The Romantic Road runs north–south through western Bavaria, covering 420km between Würzburg and Füssen near the Austrian border. Though Frankfurt is the most popular gateway for the Romantic Road, Munich is a good choice as well.

GETTING AROUND

The ideal way to travel is by car, though many foreign travellers prefer to take Deutsche Touring's Europabus, which can get incredibly crowded in summer. From April to October the special coach runs daily in each direction between Frankfurt and Füssen (for Neuschwanstein); the entire journey takes around 11 hours. There's no charge for breaking the journey and continuing the next day.

Tickets are available for short segments of the trip, and reservations are only necessary during peak-season weekends. Reservations can be made through travel agents, **Deutsche Touring** (☎ **069-790 3501; www.touring.de**), **EurAide** (☎ **089-593 889; www.euraide.de**) in Munich, and Deutsche Bahn's Reisezentrum offices in the train stations.

WÜRZBURG

☎ 0931 / pop 134,500

This scenic town straddles the Main River and is renowned for its art, architecture and delicate wines. A large student population guarantees a laid-back vibe, and plenty of hip nightlife pulsates though its cobbled streets. For centuries the resident prince-bishops wielded enormous power and wealth, and the city grew in opulence under their rule. Their crowning glory is the Residenz, one of the finest baroque structures in Germany and a Unesco World Heritage Site.

INFORMATION

Tourist office Am Congress Centrum (☎ 372 335; Am Congress Centrum; 8am-5pm Mon-Thu, 8am-1pm Fri); Marktplatz (☎ 372 398; www.wuerzburg.de; Falkenhaus; 10am-6pm Mon-Fri, 10am-2pm Sat Apr-Dec & Sun May-Oct, 10am-4pm Mon-Fri, 10am-2pm Sat Jan-Mar)

SIGHTS

FESTUNG MARIENBERG

Perched high on the Main's left bank, the **Festung Marienberg** (Marienberg Fortress) has presided over Würzburg since the city's prince-bishops commissioned a 'new' castle in 1201. It was only ever taken once, by Swedish troops in the Thirty Years War. The lovely walk up from the river via the vine-covered hill takes 20 minutes, or bus 9 will get you there from Juliuspromenade.

The fortress is home to two museums. The **Fürstenbaumuseum** (☎ 355 1750; adult/concession €4/3; 9am-6pm Tue-Sun mid-Mar–Oct) serves as the city's history museum, while the **Mainfränkisches Museum** (☎ 205 940; adult/concession €4/3, combined ticket for both museums €5/4; 10am-7pm Tue-Sun Apr-Oct, to 4pm Tue-Sun Nov-Mar) in the baroque Zeughaus (armoury) contains a famous collection of works by local 15th-century master sculptor Tilman Riemenschneider. An exhibit on winemaking can be found in the Kelterhalle, where grapes once fermented.

MUSEUM AM DOM & DOMSCHATZ

Housed in a beautiful building by the cathedral, the **Museum am Dom** (☎ 386 261; Domerschulstrasse 2; adult/concession €3.50/2.50, combined ticket with Domschatz €4.50; 10am-6pm Apr-Oct, to 5pm Nov-Mar, closed Mon) displays collections of modern art on Christian themes. Works of international renown by Joseph Beuys, Otto Dix and Käthe Kollwitz are on display, as well as

MSI/IMAGEBROKER

Würzburg's vine-covered Schlossberg

masterpieces of the Romantic, Gothic and baroque periods.

At the Würzburger **Domschatz** (Cathedral Treasury; ☎ 3856 5600; Plattnerstrasse; adult/student €2/1.50; 2-5pm Tue-Sun) you can wander through a rich display of church artefacts from the 11th century to the present.

TOURS

At the centre of the Franconian wine industry, you can sample some of the region's finest vintages on tours of these historic wine cellars (reservations are advised):

Bürgerspital Weingut (☎ 350 3403; Theaterstrasse 19; tours €6; tours 2pm Sat

JAMIE OTTERSTETTER

A walkway at Würzburg's Residenz

RESIDENZ

A symbol of wealth and prestige for the Würzburg bishops, the Unesco-listed Residenz is one of southern Germany's most important and eye-catching palaces.

Almost immediately upon entering you'll see the brilliant **grand staircase** come into view on the left. Miraculously, the vaulted ceiling survived the war intact and Tiepolo's magnificent fresco *The Four Continents* (1750–53) – said to be the world's largest above a staircase – dazzles in all its glory. Look closely to see Balthasar Neumann, architect of the Residenz, perched smugly on a cannon.

For opulence, the bishops' imperial apartments rivalled those of kings. The **Kaisersaal** (Imperial Hall) is a combination of marble, gold stucco and more incredible frescoes. The **Spiegelsaal** (Hall of Mirrors) is the most memorable, with gilded stucco dripping from the ceiling, and walls lined with glasslike panels. In the building's southern wing is the magnificent **Hofkirche** (Court Church; admission free), an early example of Neumann's penchant for spatial illusions.

Things you need to know: ☎ 355 170; www.residenz-wuerzburg.de; Balthasar-Neumann-Promenade; adult/concession €5/4; 9am-6pm Apr-Oct, 10am-4.30pm Nov-Mar, English-language tours 11am & 3pm

Mar-Oct) At the Bürgerspital Weinstuben; includes a small bottle of wine.

Weingut Juliusspital (☎ 393 1400; Juliuspromenade 19; tours €6-10; tours in German 5pm Fri & Sat Apr-Dec) In the splendid complex with the Juliusspital wine bar.

SLEEPING

Sleep in Würzburg comes slightly cheaper than in other Bavarian cities.

our pick **Babelfish** (☎ 304 0430; www.babelfish-hostel.de; Haugerring 2; dm €16-20, s/d €40/58;) Recently moved to flashy premises opposite the train station, the spanking new Babelfish has 74 beds spread over two floors, a sunny rooftop terrace, 24-hour reception, wheelchair-friendly facilities and little extras like card keys and a laundry room.

Hotel zum Winzermännle (☎ 541 56; www.winzermaennle.de; Domstrasse 32; s €62-75, d €92-105) This former winery was rebuilt in its original style after the war by the same charming family. Rooms range from broom cupboards to palatial but all are tastefully furnished. It's right in the pedestrian zone with parking nearby.

Hotel Rebstock (☎ 309 30; www.rebstock.com; Neubaustrasse 7; s €83-119, d €133-169; P) Class, hospitality and a touch of nostalgia are the characteristics of this elegant hotel, one of Würzburg's best snooze temples. Meticulously restored, this rococo mansion has superbly furnished rooms and amenities galore.

EATING

our pick **Bürgerspital Weinstuben** (☎ 352 880; Theaterstrasse 19; mains €5-10) The cosy nooks of this labyrinthine medieval place are among Würzburg's most popular eating and drinking spots. Choose from a broad selection of Franconian wines and wonderful regional dishes, including *Mostsuppe*, a tasty wine soup.

Alte Mainmühle (☎ 167 77; Mainkai 1; mains €6-25) Accessed straight from the old bridge, tourists and locals alike cram onto the double-decker terrace suspended above the Main River to savour modern twists on old Franconian favourites. Summer alfresco dining is accompanied by pretty views of the Festung Marienberg.

Backöfele (☎ 590 59; Ursulinergasse 2; mains €7-20) For romantic atmosphere, it's hard to beat this rustic restaurant set around a pretty courtyard. The menu features innovative twists on traditional game, steak and fish dishes.

GETTING THERE & AWAY

There are frequent train connections to Frankfurt (€27, one hour), Bamberg (€17.60, one hour) and Nuremberg (from €17.80, one hour). Travelling to Rothenburg ob der Tauber (€11.30, 1¼ hours) requires a change in Steinach.

ROTHENBURG OB DER TAUBER

☎ 09861 / pop 11,200

A well-polished gem from the Middle Ages, Rothenburg ob der Tauber (meaning 'above the Tauber River') is the main tourist stop along the Romantic Road. With its web of cobbled lanes, higgledy-piggledy houses and towered walls, the town is impossibly charming. Preservation orders here are the strictest in Germany – and at times it feels like a medieval theme park – but all's forgiven in the evenings, when the yellow lamplight casts its spell long after the last tour buses have left.

INFORMATION

Tourist office (☎ 404 800; www.rothenburg.de; Marktplatz 2; 9am-7pm Mon-Fri, 10am-5pm Sat & Sun May-Oct, 9am-5pm Mon-Fri,

10am-1pm Sat Nov-Apr) Out-of-hours electronic room-booking board in the foyer, plus free internet.

SIGHTS

The **Rathaus** (town hall) on the Markt (square), begun in Gothic style in the 14th century, was completed during the Renaissance. Climb 220 steps to the **Rathausturm** (**adult/concession €2/0.50; 9.30am-12.30pm & 1-5pm Apr-Oct & Dec, noon-3pm Nov & Jan-Mar**) viewing platform for widescreen views of the Tauber.

North of the Marktplatz, the recently sandblasted **Jakobskirche** (**Klingengasse 1; adult/concession €2/0.50, during services free; 9am-5.15pm Apr-Oct, 10am-noon & 2-4pm Nov & Jan-Mar, 10am-4.45pm Dec**) is Rothenburg's major place of pilgrimage. The main draw is the carved **Heilig Blut Altar** (Holy Blood Altar), set on a raised platform at the western end of the nave. It depicts the Last Supper with Judas, unusually, at the centre, receiving bread from Christ. The rock crystal inside is said to contain a drop of Christ's blood.

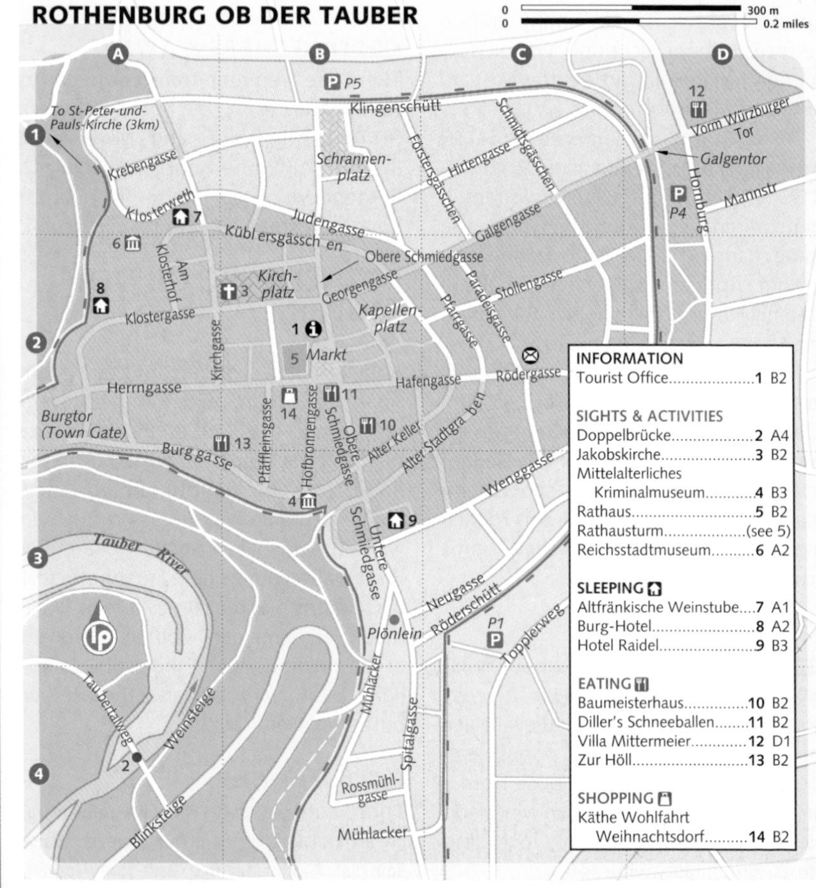

GLENN VAN DER KNIJFF

The interior of Wieskirche, near Steingaden

IF YOU LIKE...

If the **Würzburg Residenz** (p128) gave you a taste for baroque architecture, the following masterpieces will likely make you swoon as well:

- **Wieskirche** (www.wieskirche.de) Near the village of Steingaden, this Unesco site is the magnum opus of artist-brothers Dominikus and Johann Baptist Zimmermann. About a million art and spiritual pilgrims flock here annually.
- **Asamkirche Maria de Victoria** (☎ 175 18; Neubaustrasse 11/2; adult/concession €2/1.50; 9am-noon & 1-5pm Tue-Sun Mar-Oct, 1-4pm Nov-Feb) The brothers Cosmas Damian and Egid Quirin Asam collaborated on this glorious church lidded by the world's largest ceiling fresco (full of stunning optical illusions) painted on a flat surface. Stand on the little circle in the diamond tile near the door and everything snaps into 3-D. It's in Ingolstadt, about 80km north of Munich.
- **Basilika Vierzehnheiligen** (☎ 09571-950 80; www.vierzehnheiligen.de; admission free; 6.30am-7pm Apr-Oct, 7.30am-dusk Nov-Mar) Residenz architect Balthasar Neumann also designed this 18th-century pilgrimage church, 25km south of Coburg. The intersecting oval rotundas, play of light and trompe l'oeil ceiling create an optical illusion, making the interior appear larger than it is and creating a sense of constant motion. There's also an attached monastery brewery.
- **Neues Schloss Schleissheim** (☎ 315 8720; www.schloesser-schleissheim.de; Max-Emanuel-Platz 1; adult/under 18yr/concession €4/free/3; 9am-6pm Apr-Sep, 10am-4pm Oct-Mar, closed Mon) This is the crown jewel among the three palaces in the northern Munich suburb of Schleissheim. Modelled after Versailles, it's filled with stylish period furniture, oil paintings and a vaulted ceiling with 3-D frescoes by Cosmas Damian Asam.
- **Basilika St Emmeram** (www.bistum-regensburg.de) Another masterpiece by the Asams, this Regensburg church near the town palace features two giant ceiling frescoes and, in its crypt, the remains of Sts Emmeram, Wolfgang and Ramwold, all early bishops.

Brutal implements of torture and punishment from medieval times are on display at the curiously fascinating **Mittelalterliches Kriminalmuseum** (Medieval Crime Museum; ☎ 5359; Burggasse 3; adult/concession €3.80/2.20; 11am-5pm Apr, 10am-6pm May-Oct, 2-4pm Nov, Jan & Feb, 1-4pm Dec). Displays include chastity belts, masks of disgrace for gossips, a cage for errant bakers, a neck brace for quarrelsome women and a beer-barrel pen for drunks.

For the most impressive views, go to the west side of town, where a sweeping view of the Tauber Valley includes the **Doppelbrücke**, a double-decker bridge. Also visible is the head of a trail that leads down the valley and over to the lovely Romanesque **St-Peter-und-Pauls-Kirche** (☎ 5524; Detwang; adult/child €1/0.50; 8.30am-noon & 1.30-5pm Apr-Oct, 10am-noon & 2-4pm Nov-Mar, closed Mon), which contains a stunning Riemenschneider altar. There's a beer garden (Unter den Linden) about halfway along the trail.

The city's showcase of local art, culture and history is the **Reichsstadtmuseum** (Imperial City Museum; ☎ 939 043; Klosterhof 5; adult/child €3.50/2; 9.30am-5.30pm Apr-Oct, 1-4pm Nov-Mar), which is housed in a former convent. Highlights include the superb *Rothenburger Passion* (1494) by Martinus Schwarz, and the convent rooms themselves, including a 14th-century kitchen.

SLEEPING

our pick **Hotel Raidel** (☎ 3115; www.romanticroad.com/raidel; Wenggasse 3; s with/without bathroom €39/24, d € 59/49; P) With 500-year-old exposed beams studded with wooden nails, antiques throughout and a welcoming owner, as well as musical instruments for the guests to play, this is the place to check in if you're craving some genuine romance on the Romantic Road.

Altfränkische Weinstube (☎ 6404; www.romanticroad.com/altfraenkische-weinstube; Am Klosterhof 7; s €58, d €64-75) Hiding in a quiet side street near the Reichsstadtmuseum, this enchantingly characterful inn has atmosphere-laden rooms, all with bathtubs and most with four-poster or canopied beds. The restaurant (open for dinner only) serves up sound regional fare with a dollop of medieval cheer.

Burg-Hotel (☎ 948 90; www.burghotel.rothenburg.de; Klostergasse 1-3; r €100-170; P) The best views in town are from this charming 15-room hotel, built right into the town fortifications. All rooms have private sitting areas, and there's an elegant guest lounge with an antique baby grand piano.

EATING

Rothenburg's most obvious speciality is a sweet called *Schneeballen*. Some 23 different types are produced at **Diller's Schneeballen** (☎ 938 010; Hofbronnengasse 16), though a more limited range is available all over town.

Zur Höll (☎ 4229; Burggasse 8; dishes €6-18) This medieval wine tavern, with an appreciation for slow food, is in the town's oldest original building, dating back to the year 900. The menu of regional specialities is limited but refined, though it's the wine that people really come for.

Baumeisterhaus (☎ 947 00; Obere Schmiedgasse 3; mains €9-16) This traditional German inn is one of the town's most atmospheric, and that's saying something. The woody dining area is set around a beautiful vine-clad courtyard and bristles with old hunting relics. The daily menu has a wealth of fine traditional fare.

Villa Mittermeier (☎ 945 40; Vorm Würzburger Tor; mains €18-28) The kitchen dynamos at this classy establishment serve

UKR/IMAGEBROKER
Cobbled street, Rothenburg ob der Tauber

top-notch Michelin-starred cuisine in five settings, including a black-and-white tiled 'Temple', an alfresco terrace and a barrel-shaped wine cellar. The artistic chefs rely on locally harvested produce, and the wine list (400-plus varieties) is probably Franconia's best.

SHOPPING

Käthe Wohlfahrt Weihnachtsdorf (☎ 4090; Herrngasse 1) With its mind-boggling assortment of Yuletide decorations and ornaments, this shop lets you celebrate Christmas every day of the year (to go with the snowballs). Many of the items are handcrafted with amazing skill and imagination, and prices are accordingly high.

GETTING THERE & AWAY

You can go anywhere by train from Rothenburg, as long as it's Steinach. Change here for services to Würzburg (€11.30, one hour). Travel to and from Munich (from €35, three hours) can involve up to three different trains.

GETTING AROUND

The city has five car parks right outside the walls. The town centre is closed to nonresident vehicles from 11am to 4pm and 7pm to 5am weekdays, and all day at weekends; hotel guests are exempt.

DINKELSBÜHL

☎ 09851 / pop 12,000

Some 40km south of Rothenburg, immaculately preserved Dinkelsbühl proudly traces its roots to a royal residence founded by Carolingian kings in the 8th century. Saved from destruction in the Thirty Years War and ignored by WWII bombers, this is arguably the Romantic Road's quaintest and most authentically medieval halt. For a good overall impression of the town, walk along the fortified walls with their 18 towers and four gates.

INFORMATION

The **tourist office** (☎ 902 440; www.dinkelsbuehl.de; Altrathausplatz 14; 9am-6pm Mon-Fri, 10am-5pm Sat & Sun Apr-Oct, 10am-5pm

daily Nov-Mar) recently moved to the new Haus der Geschichte.

SIGHTS

Near the Wörnitzer Tor, Dinkelsbühl's history comes under the microscope at the new **Haus der Geschichte** (**History House; ☎ 902 440; Altrathausplatz 14; adult/child €4/2; 9am-6pm Mon-Fri, 10am-5pm Sat & Sun May-Oct, 10am-5pm daily Nov-Apr**), which occupies the old town hall. There's an interesting section on the Thirty Years War and a gallery with paintings depicting Dinkelsbühl at the turn of the century.

Continue into the historical centre to find the **Weinmarkt**, the main square lined with a row of splendid Renaissance mansions. The corner building is the step-gabled **Ratsherrntrinkstube**, the erstwhile weigh house which later hosted important guests such as Emperor Karl V and King Gustav Adolf of Sweden.

Standing sentry over Weinmarkt is **Münster St Georg**, one of southern Germany's purest late-Gothic hall churches. Rather austere from the outside, the interior stuns with an incredible fan-vaulted ceiling. A curiosity is the **Pretzl Window** donated by the bakers' guild, in the upper section of the last window in the right aisle.

Just outside the western town gate, the **Museum of the 3rd Dimension** (**☎ 6336; Nördlinger Tor; adult/concession €9/7; 10am-6pm Apr-Oct, 11am-4pm Sat & Sun Nov-Mar**) has three floors of holographic images, stereoscopes and 3-D imagery.

BAH/IMAGEBROKER

Dinkelsbühl's Münster St Georg and Weinmarkt

SLEEPING & EATING

our pick **Dinkelsbühler Kunststuben** (**☎ 6750; www.kunst-stuben.de; Segringer Strasse 52; s €50, d €55-80;**) Personal attention and charm by the bucketload make this one of the best guesthouses on the entire Romantic Road. Furniture (including the four-posters) is all handmade by Voglauer, there's a pretty breakfast room and the cosy library is perfect for curling up in with a good read.

Haus Appelberg (**☎ 582 838; Nördlinger Strasse 40; dishes €5-10; 6pm-midnight Tue-Sat**) At Dinkelsbühl's best-kept dining secret, owners double up as cooks to keep tables supplied with traditional dishes such as local carp, Franconian sausages and *Maultaschen* (pork and spinach ravioli). On warm days swap the rustic interior for the secluded terrace, a fine spot for some evening idling over a local Hauf beer or a Franconian white.

Weib's Brauhaus (**☎ 579 490; Untere Schmiedgasse 13; dishes €5-12; closed Tue**) A female brew master presides over the copper vats at this lively restaurant-pub.

The traditional menu includes the popular *Weib's Töpfle* (woman's pot) of pork and deep-fried mashed potatoes and, of course, the house brew.

GETTING THERE & AWAY

Despite a railway line cutting through the town, Dinkelsbühl is not served by passenger trains. Regional buses to and

MSI/IMAGEBROKER

Children celebrating Kinderzeche in Dinkelsbühl

↘ IF YOU LIKE...

If you like the raucous merriment of **Munich's Oktoberfest** (p108), we think you'll also enjoy letting your hair down at these other Bavarian festivals:

- **Historisches Festival 'Der Meistertrunk'** The Historical Festival 'The Master Draught' celebrates a legendary incident that saved Rothenburg ob der Tauber (p129) from destruction during the Thirty Years War. The victorious General Tilly offered to spare the town only if one of its residents could down a huge tankard of wine in one gulp. The mayor took up the challenge...and saved the day. The festival takes place on Whitsuntide weekend, with parades, dances, a medieval market and a reenactment of the Master Draught.
- **Kinderzeche** In Dinkelsbühl (p133), just down the road from Rothenburg, it was the children who persuaded the invading Swedish troops to spare the town from devastation during the Thirty Years War. Every year in July the Children's Festival commemorates the event with a pageant, reenactments, music and other merriment.
- **Gäubodenfest** This 11-day beery roar takes over Straubing, between Regensburg and Passau, in August. The epic drink-a-thon began in 1812 as a social gathering for grain farmers, and more than a million merrymakers now pour into town each year. Despite the crowds, Gäubodenfest remains a traditional celebration that's infinitely less touristy than Munich's famous party.
- **Nördlinger Pfingstmesse** This 10-day festival, held over Whitsuntide/Pentecost in Nördlingen (p136), is a huge party that takes over the old town with beer tents, food stalls and entertainment.

from Nördlingen (€6.30, 45 minutes) stop at the *Busbahnhof* (bus station). Reaching Rothenburg (€8.90, two hours) is a real test of patience without your own car. Change from bus 805 to a train in Ansbach, then change trains in Steinach.

Some hotels have bicycle hire, or try **Fahrrad Krauss** (☎ 3495; Wenggasse 42; per half-day/day €5/10).

NÖRDLINGEN

☎ 09081 / pop 20,100

Charmingly medieval, Nördlingen sees fewer tourists than its better known neighbours and manages to retain an air of authenticity, which is a relief after some of the Romantic Road's worst excesses. The town lies within the Ries Basin, a massive impact crater gouged out by a meteorite more than 15 million years ago. The crater – some 25km in diameter – is one of the best preserved on earth, and has been declared a special 'geopark'. Nördlingen's 14th-century walls, all original, mimic the crater's rim and are almost perfectly circular.

INFORMATION

Tourist office (☎ 841 16; www.noerdlingen.de; Marktplatz 2; ⏰ 10am-6pm Mon-Thu, 10am-4.30pm Fri, 10am-2pm Sat Easter-early Nov, 10am-2pm Sun May-Sep, Mon-Fri only mid-Nov–Easter) Has an out-of-hours foyer with web access and brochures.

SIGHTS

The massive late-Gothic **St Georgskirche** is one of the largest churches in southern Germany. Its elaborate baroque organ and the intricate pulpit (1499) are worth a look, but the real draw is the 90m **Daniel Tower** (adult/concession €2/1.40; ⏰ 9am-6pm Apr-Jun, Sep & Oct, to 7pm Jul & Aug, to 5pm Nov-Mar). Only from the top can you appreciate Nördlingen's shape and the gentle landscape of the Ries crater.

Situated in an ancient barn, the **Rieskrater Museum** (☎ 273 8220; Eugene-Shoemaker-Platz 1; adult/child €4/1.50; ⏰ 10am-4.30pm Tue-Sun) explores the formation of meteorite craters and the consequences of such violent collisions with Earth. Rocks, including a genuine moon rock

MMI/IMAGEBROKER

Christmas decorations in front of Augsburg's Rathaus

(on permanent loan from NASA), fossils and other geological displays shed light on the mystery of meteors.

One of Germany's largest collections of classic steam trains can be found at the **Bayerisches Eisenbahnmuseum** (Bavarian Railway Museum; ☎ 09083-340; www.bayerisches-eisenbahnmuseum.de; Am Hohen Weg 6a; adult/child €5/2.50; noon-4pm Tue-Sat, 10am-5pm Sun May-Sep, Sat & Sun only Mar, Apr & Oct). Its 100 nostalgic vehicles range from sleek high-speed engines for transporting passengers to cute little railyard shunters.

SLEEPING & EATING

Kaiserhof Hotel Sonne (☎ 5067; Marktplatz 3; s €55-65, d €75-120; P) Nördlingen's top sleep has hosted a procession of emperors and their entourages since 1405. Rooms tastefully blend traditional charm with 21st-century comforts, and there's an atmospheric regional restaurant and cellar wine bar.

Sixenbräu Stüble (☎ 3101; Bergerstrasse 17; mains €10-17; closed Mon) An attractive gabled town house near the Berger Tor houses this local institution, which has been plonking wet ones on the bar since 1545. The pan-Bavarian menu has heavy carnivorous leanings, and there's a beer garden for alfresco elbow bending.

GETTING THERE & AWAY

Train journeys to and from Munich (€25, two hours) and Augsburg (€13.30, one hour) require a change in Donauwörth.

AUGSBURG

☎ 0821 / pop 269,000

Bavaria's third-largest city is also one of Germany's oldest, founded by the stepchildren of Roman emperor Augustus over 2000 years ago. As an independent city state from the 13th century, Augsburg was free to raise its own taxes. Public coffers bulged on the proceeds of the textile trade, and banking families such as the Fuggers and the Welsers even lent money to kings and countries. Today this attractive city of spires and cobbles is an easy day trip from Munich or an engaging stop on the Romantic Road.

INFORMATION

Tourist office (☎ 502 070; www.augsburg-tourismus.de; Rathausplatz; 9am-6pm Mon-Fri, 10am-5pm Sat, 10am-2pm Sun Apr-Oct, 9am-5pm Mon-Fri, 10am-2pm Nov-Mar)

SIGHTS

RATHAUSPLATZ

This square at the city's heart is dominated by the twin onion-dome spires of the Renaissance **Rathaus** (1615–20). Its roof is crowned by a 4m pine cone, Augsburg's emblem and an ancient fertility symbol. Inside, the star attraction is the meticulously restored **Goldener Saal** (Golden Hall; ☎ 349 6398; Rathausplatz; admission €2; 10am-6pm), the main meeting hall. It's a dazzling space canopied by a gilded and coffered ceiling, interspersed with frescoes.

For widescreen city views, climb the **Perlachturm** (Perlach Tower; Rathausplatz; adult/concession €1/0.50; 10am-6pm Apr-Nov, 2-6pm Fri-Sun Dec) next door to the Rathaus.

DOM MARIÄ HEIMSUCHUNG

North of Rathausplatz you'll find the cathedral, **Dom Mariä Heimsuchung** (Hoher Weg), which dates back to the 10th century. Architecturally it's a hotchpotch of addition on addition, including the instalment of bronze doors in the 14th century depicting Old Testament scenes. The oldest section is the crypt underneath the west choir, which features a Romanesque Madonna. Other treasures include medieval frescoes, the *Weingartner Altar* by Hans Holbein the Elder, and – dating from the

12th century – the *Prophets' Windows* (depicting Daniel, Jonah, Hosea and Moses), some of the oldest stained-glass windows in Germany.

ST ANNA KIRCHE

Often regarded as the first Renaissance church in Germany, the rather plain-looking **St Anna Kirche** (**Church of St Anna; Im Annahof 2**) contains a bevy of treasures as well as the sumptuous **Fuggerkapelle**, where Jacob Fugger and his brothers lie buried, and the lavishly frescoed **Goldschmiedekapelle** (Goldsmiths' Chapel; 1420). The church played an important role during the Reformation. In 1518 Martin Luther, in town to defend his beliefs before the papal legate, stayed at what was then a Carmelite monastery. His rooms have been turned into the **Lutherstiege**, a small museum about the Reformation.

FUGGEREI

Built to provide homes for poor Catholics, the **Fuggerei** (**☎ 319 8810; adult/child €4/2; 8am-8pm Apr-Oct, 9am-6pm Nov-Mar**) is one of the oldest welfare settlements in the world. Jacob Fugger financed the project in the 16th century and this town within a town is still home to 150 Catholic Augsburgers. For centuries the rent has remained at one Rhenish Gilder (€1 today) per year, plus utilities and three daily prayers.

To see how Fuggerei residents lived in the past, visit the **Fuggereimuseum** (**Mittlere Gasse 14; with Fuggerei admission free; 9am-8pm Mar-Oct, to 6pm Nov-Apr**).

MAXIMILIANSTRASSE

Only the richest merchant families could afford to live on this grand boulevard, which is so wide you might mistake it in parts for a square. The former residence of Jakob Fugger, the **Fugger Stadtpalast**, is at No 36–38. It embraces the Damenhof (Ladies' Court), a gorgeous Italian Renaissance-style inner courtyard. A nearby rococo palace, the **Schaetzlerpalais** (**☎ 324 4102; Maximilianstrasse 56; adult/concession €7/5.50; 10am-8pm Tue, to 5pm Wed-Sun**) was built for a wealthy banker between 1765 and 1770, and today houses the **Deutsche Barockgalerie** (German Baroque Gallery) and the **Staatsgalerie** (Bavarian State Gallery).

SLEEPING

Jakoberhof (**☎ 510 030; www.jakoberhof.de; Jakoberstrasse 41; s €27-74, d €39-89; P**) The best-value option in town is this simple place near the Fuggerei. Bright and airy rooms have few frills and higher rates are for private facilities.

Hotel am Rathaus (**☎ 346 490; www.hotel-am-rathaus-augsburg.de; Am Hinteren Perlachberg 1; s €65-98, d €98-125; P**) As central as it gets, and moments away from Rathausplatz, this boutique hotel has fresh neutral decor and a sunny little breakfast room. The trendy Italian restaurant is surprisingly good.

Steigenberger Drei Mohren Hotel (**☎ 503 60; www.augsburg.steigenberger.de; Maximilianstrasse 40; s/d from €90/135; P**) This landmark hotel, with luxurious decor, is a stunning place where both Mozart and Goethe once stayed. Marble bathrooms, original art and a beautiful garden terrace are among the elegant touches.

EATING

Bayerisches Haus am Dom (**☎ 349 7990; Johannisgasse 4; mains €6-10**) Enjoy an elbow massage from the locals at chunky timber benches while refuelling on Bavarian and Swabian dishes, cheap lunch options (€6) or a sandwich. Erdinger and Andechser are the frothy double act that stimulates nightly frivolity in the beer garden.

Bauerntanz (☎ 153 644; Bauerntanzgässchen 1; mains €7-14) A local institution serving big portions of creative Swabian and Bavarian food.

ENTERTAINMENT

Augsburger Puppenkiste (☎ 450 3450; www.augsburger-puppenkiste.de; Spitalgasse 15; tickets €9-22) The celebrated puppet theatre holds puppet performances of modern and classic fairy-tales that even non-German speakers will enjoy. Advance bookings are essential.

GETTING THERE & AWAY

Regional trains run hourly between Augsburg and Munich (€11.30, 45 minutes), every other hour to Nuremberg (€23.30, two hours).

FÜSSEN

☎ 08362 / pop 17,700

The final halt on the Romantic Road, Füssen is a bustling little tourist town nestled between towering Alpine peaks. It's in the so-called Königswinkel (Royal Corner), home to Germany's biggest tourist attractions: the fantasy castles of Ludwig II (see the boxed text, p142), Neuschwanstein and Hohenschwangau.

Most whiz in and out of the area, checking off fairy-tale castles on a whirlwind coach tour. Those who stay longer escape the crowds into a landscape of gentle hiking trails, Alpine vistas and pretty lakes.

ORIENTATION & INFORMATION

The castles are around 4km east of Füssen via the B17 (Münchener Strasse).

Füssen tourist office (☎ 938 50; www.fuessen.de; Kaiser-Maximilian-Platz 1; 🕑 9am-6.30pm Mon-Fri, 10am-2pm Sat, 10am-noon Sun May-Oct, 9am-5pm Mon-Fri, 10am-2pm Sat Nov-Apr)

NEH/IMAGEBROKER

Views up to Schloss Hohenschwangau

Hohenschwangau tourist office (☎ 819 765; www.schwangau.de; Alpestrasse; 🕑 11am-7pm May-Oct, to 5pm Nov-Apr) At the bus stop below the castles. Provides an informal left-luggage service.

SIGHTS

SCHLOSS HOHENSCHWANGAU

Ludwig spent his formative years at the sun-yellow **Schloss Hohenschwangau** (☎ 930 830; adult/concession €9/8, with Neuschwanstein €17/15; 🕑 8am-5.30pm Apr-Sep, 9am-3.30pm Oct-Mar). His father, Maximilian II, rebuilt this palace in a neo-Gothic style from 12th-century ruins left by Schwangau knights. Far less showy than Neuschwanstein, Hohenschwangau has a distinctly lived-in feel and every piece of furniture is a used original. Some rooms

GLENN VAN DER KNIJFF

Schloss Neuschwanstein, near Füssen

SCHLOSS NEUSCHWANSTEIN

Appearing through the mountaintops like a misty mirage is the world's most famous castle – the model for Disney's citadel – Schloss Neuschwanstein. Ludwig planned this castle with the help of a stage designer rather than an architect, and it provides a fascinating glimpse into the king's state of mind. Built as a romantic medieval castle, it was started in 1869 and, like so many of Ludwig's grand schemes, was never finished. For all the money spent on it, the king spent just over 170 days in residence.

Ludwig imagined his palace as a giant stage to re-create the world of Germanic mythology in the operatic works of Richard Wagner. Its centrepiece is the lavish **Sängersaal** (Minstrels' Hall), created to feed the king's obsession with Wagner and medieval knights. Wall frescoes in the hall depict scenes from the opera *Tannhäuser*. Concerts are held here every September.

Other completed sections include Ludwig's *Tristan and Isolde*–themed **bedroom**, dominated by a huge Gothic-style bed crowned with intricately carved spires; a gaudy artificial grotto (another nod to *Tannhäuser*); and the Byzantine **Thronsaal** (Throne Room) with a mosaic floor of over two million stones.

For the postcard view of Neuschwanstein and the plains beyond, walk 10 minutes up to **Marienbrücke** (Mary's Bridge), which spans the spectacular Pöllat Gorge over a waterfall just above the castle.

Things you need to know: ☎ 930 830; adult/concession €9/8, with Hohenschwangau €17/15; 🕑 8am-5pm Apr-Sep, 9am-3pm Oct-Mar

have frescoes from German history and legend (including the story of the Swan Knight, Lohengrin). The swan theme runs throughout.

TICKETS & TOURS

Both castles must be seen on guided tours (in German or English), which last about 35 minutes (Hohenschwangau is usually first). Timed tickets are only available from the **Ticket Centre** (☎ 930 830; www.ticket-center-hohenschwangau.de; Alpenseestrasse 12) at the foot of the castles. In summer come as early as 8am to ensure you get in that day.

When visiting both castles, enough time is left between tours for the steep 30- to 40-minute walk between the castles. Alternatively, you can shell out €4 for a horse-drawn carriage ride, which is only marginally quicker.

SLEEPING

Pension Kössler (☎ 4069; www.pension-koessler.de; Zalinger Strasse 1; s €35-38, d €70-76; P) This small *Pension* with a friendly atmosphere offers outstanding value. Rooms are simple but comfortable and have private bathroom, TV, phone and balcony – some overlook the attractive garden.

Hotel zum Hechten (☎ 916 00; www.hotel-hechten.com; Ritterstrasse 6; s €46-59, d €86-98; P ⊠) This is one of Füssen's oldest hotels and a barrel of fun. Public areas are traditional in style but the bedrooms are mostly airy and brightly renovated.

EATING

Michelangelo (☎ 924 924; Lechhalde 1; mains €7-15) This sophisticated Italian job at the rear of the Rathaus is run by a real Italian chef who plates up some deliciously simple fare, including 38 different pizzas. The tables in the old monastery gardens afford beautiful views high above the river.

Franziskaner Stüberl (☎ 371 24; Kemptener Strasse 1; mains €10-15) This quaint restaurant specialises in *Schweinshaxe* (pork knuckle) and schnitzel, prepared in more varieties than you can shake a haunch at. Noncarnivores go for the excellent *Kässpätzle* (rolled cheese noodles) and the huge salads.

GETTING THERE & AWAY

If you want to 'do' the castles on a day trip from Munich you'll need to start early. The first train leaves Munich at 4.57am (€22.20, 2½ hours; change in Kaufbeuren), reaching Füssen at 7.24am.

GETTING AROUND

RVO buses 78 and 73 serve the castles from Füssen Bahnhof (train station; €3.50 return), stopping also at the Tegelbergbahn valley station. Taxis to the castles are about €10.

BAVARIAN ALPS

Stretching west from Germany's remote southeastern corner to the Allgäu region near Lake Constance, the Bavarian Alps (Bayerische Alpen) form a stunningly beautiful natural divide along the Austrian border. The region is dotted with quaint frescoed villages, spas and health retreats, and possibilities for skiing, snowboarding, hiking, canoeing and paragliding – much of it year-round.

GARMISCH-PARTENKIRCHEN

☎ 08821 / pop 26,000

A much-loved hang-out for outdoor types and moneyed socialites, the double-barrelled resort of Garmisch-Partenkirchen is blessed with a fabled setting a snowball's throw from the Alps. To say you 'wintered in Garmisch' still has an aristocratic ring, and the area offers some of the best skiing in the land, including runs on Germany's highest peak, the Zugspitze (2964m).

INFORMATION

Tourist office (☎ 180 700; www.gapa.de; Richard-Strauss-Platz 2, Garmisch; 🕑 8am-6pm Mon-Sat, 10am-noon Sun)

SIGHTS & ACTIVITIES

ZUGSPITZE

Views from the top of Germany are literally breathtaking, especially during *Föhn* weather when they extend into four countries. Skiing and hiking are the main activities here.

The **Zugspitzbahn** (☎ 797 01; www.zugspitze.de; return adult/child €36/20) has its own station right behind the Hauptbahnhof (central train station). From here it chugs seven times a day along the mountain base to the Eibsee, a forest lake, before winding its way through a mountain tunnel up to the Schneeferner Glacier (2600m). From there a cable car makes the final ascent to the summit.

Alternatively, the **Eibsee-Seilbahn** (return adult/child €36/20), a steep cable car, sways and swings its way straight up to the summit from the Eibsee lake in about 10 minutes – it's not for the faint-hearted! Most people go up on the train and take the cable car back down, but it works just as well the other way around.

Expect serious crowds at peak times in winter and through much of the summer.

SKIING

Garmisch has two big ski fields: the Zugspitze plateau (2964m) and the Classic Ski Area (Alpspitze, 2628m; Hausberg, 1340m; Kreuzeck, 1651m; day pass adult/child €31/17.50). A Happy Ski Card (two

LUDWIG II, THE FAIRY-TALE KING

Every year on 13 June, a stirring ceremony takes place in Berg, on the eastern shore of Lake Starnberg. A small boat quietly glides towards a cross just offshore and a plain wreath is fastened to its front. The sound of a single trumpet cuts the silence as the boat returns from this solemn ritual in honour of the most beloved king ever to rule Bavaria – Ludwig II.

The cross marks the spot where Ludwig died under mysterious circumstances in 1886. His early death capped the life of a man at odds with the harsh realities of a modern world no longer in need of a romantic and idealistic monarch.

Ludwig was an enthusiastic leader initially, but Bavaria's days as a sovereign state were numbered, and he became a puppet king after the creation of the German Reich in 1871 (which had its advantages, as Bismarck gave Ludwig a hefty allowance). Ludwig withdrew completely to drink, draw castle plans and view concerts and operas in private. His obsession with French culture and the Sun King, Louis XIV, inspired the fantastical palaces of Neuschwanstein, Linderhof and Herrenchiemsee – lavish projects that spelt his undoing.

In January 1886, several ministers and relatives arranged a hasty psychiatric test that diagnosed Ludwig as mentally unfit to rule. That June he was removed to Schloss Berg on Lake Starnberg. A few days later the dejected bachelor and his doctor took a Sunday evening lakeside walk and were found several hours later, drowned in just a few feet of water.

No one knows with certainty what happened that night. Conspiracy theories abound. That summer the authorities opened Neuschwanstein to the public to help pay off Ludwig's huge debts. King Ludwig II was dead, but the myth was just being born.

Snow fields on Zugspitze

days, adult/child €65/39) covers all the slopes, plus other ski areas around the Zugspitze, including Mittenwald and Ehrwald (an incredible 231km of pistes and 106 ski lifts). Local buses serve all the valley stations.

HIKING

Hiking to the **Zugspitze summit** is only possible in summer and is only recommended for those with experience of mountaineering. Another popular route is to King Ludwig II's hunting lodge, **Jagdschloss Schachen** (☎ 920 30; adult/concession €4/3; Jun-Oct), which can be reached via the Partnachklamm in about a four-hour hike. A plain wooden hut from the outside, the interior is surprisingly magnificent; the **Moorish Room** is something straight out of the *Arabian Nights*.

PARTNACHKLAMM

One of the area's main attractions is the dramatically beautiful **Partnachklamm** (☎ 3167; adult/child €2/1), a narrow 700m-long gorge with walls rising up to 80m. A circular walk hewn from the rock takes you through the gorge, which is spectacular in winter when you can walk beneath curtains of icicles and frozen waterfalls.

SLEEPING

Gasthof zum Rassen (☎ 2089; www.gasthof-rassen.de; Ludwigstrasse 45; s €32-53, d €52-90; P ⊠) In this beautifully frescoed 14th-century building, the bright, contemporary rooms provide a contrast with the trad style of the public areas. The massive event hall, formerly a brewery, houses the oldest folk theatre in Bavaria.

Hotel Garmischer Hof (☎ 9110; www.garmischer-hof.de; Chamonixstrasse 10; s €59-94, d €94-136; P) Generations of athletes, artists and outdoor enthusiasts have stayed at this refined chateau, property of the Seiwald family since 1928. The rooms, many with incredible Alpine views, are tasteful and cosy.

Reindl's Partenkirchner Hof (☎ 943 870; www.reindls.de; Bahnhofstrasse 15; s €75-150, d €140-200, ste €210-600; P ⊠) It doesn't get much better than this: an elegant, three-winged luxury hotel stacked with perks, a wine bar and a top-notch gourmet restaurant.

EATING

Bräustüberl (☎ 2312; Fürstenstrasse 23; mains €6-16) This place, a bit outside the centre, is quintessentially Bavarian, complete with enormous enamel coal-burning stove and dirndl-clad waitresses.

Gasthof Fraundorfer (☎ 9270; Ludwigstrasse 24; mains €8-16; closed Tue) Squeeze yourself in between tourists and the odd yokel for this unmissably kitsch part of the Ga-Pa experience. The multilingual menu has a carnivore bias, the decor ranges from baroque cherubs and hunting trophies to the 'Sports Corner', and there's yodelling, shoe-slapping and Bavarian oompah music every evening.

GLENN VAN DER KNIJFF

Interior of the Wieskirche (p131), near Steingaden

Isi's Goldener Engel (☎ 948 757; Bankgasse 5; mains €9-15) This local favourite has hunting-lodge decor that blends frescoes, stag heads and a gilded stucco ceiling. The huge menu ranges from *Leberkäse* (meatloaf) to pepper steak in cognac cream, though the best deal is the generous lunch special.

GETTING THERE & AROUND

Garmisch-Partenkirchen enjoys hourly connections from Munich (€17.60, 1½ hours), and special packages combine the return trip with a Zugspitze day ski pass. RVO bus 9606 travels to Füssen, with stops at Oberammergau, the Wieskirche (p131) and the castles at Neuschwanstein and Hohenschwangau.

OBERAMMERGAU

☎ 08822 / pop 5400

Quaint Oberammergau occupies a wide valley surrounded by the dark forests and snow-dusted peaks of the Ammergauer Alps. The centre is packed with traditional painted houses, woodcarving shops and awestruck tourists who come here to learn about the town's world-famous Passion Play.

The **tourist office** (☎ 922 740; www.ammergauer-alpen.de; Eugen-Papst-Strasse 9a; 9am-6pm Mon-Fri, 10am-2pm Sat, 10am-1pm Sun mid-Jun–mid-Oct, 9am-6pm Mon-Fri, 10am-1pm Sat mid-Oct–mid-Jun) can help find accommodation.

A blend of opera, ritual and Hollywood epic, the Passion Play has been performed every year ending in a zero since the late 17th century as a collective thank you from the villagers for being spared the plague. The next performances will take place between May and October 2010, but tours of the **Passionstheater** (☎ 923

NEH/IMAGEBROKER

Cyclists near Garmisch-Partenkirchen

10; Passionswiese 1; tours adult/concession €4/1; erratic hours, call ahead) enable you to take a peek at the costumes and sets anytime.

The town's other claim to fame is **Lüftmalerei**, the eye-popping house facades painted in an illusionist style. The pick of the crop is the amazing **Pilatushaus** (**923 10; Ludwig-Thoma-Strasse 10; admission with museum ticket; 1-6pm Tue-Sat May-Oct**), the painted columns of which snap into 3-D as you approach.

Oberammergau is also known for its intricate **woodcarvings**. Workshops abound around town, churning out everything from corkscrews to life-sized saints and nativity scenes. Some amazing examples can be seen in the little parish cemetery on Pfarrplatz and in the **Oberammergau Museum** (**941 36; Dorfstrasse 8; adult/child €4/1; 10am-5pm Tue-Sun, closed Feb & Nov**).

Hourly trains connect Munich with Oberammergau (change at Murnau; €16.70, 1¾ hours). RVO bus 9606 goes to Garmisch-Partenkirchen and Füssen almost hourly.

SCHLOSS LINDERHOF

A pocket-sized trove of weird treasures, **Schloss Linderhof** (**920 30; adult/concession Apr-Sep €7/6, Oct-Mar €6/5; 9am-6pm Apr-Sep, 10am-4pm Oct-Mar**) was Ludwig II's smallest but most sumptuous palace, and the only one he lived to see fully completed. Finished in 1878, the palace hugs a steep hillside in a fantasy landscape of French gardens, fountains and follies.

Linderhof's myth-laden, jewel-encrusted rooms are a monument to the king's excesses that so unsettled the governors in Munich. The **private bedroom** is the largest, heavily ornamented and anchored by an enormous 108-candle crystal chandelier weighing 500kg. An artificial waterfall, built to cool the room in summer, cascades just outside the window.

Created by the famous court gardener Carl von Effner, the gardens and outbuildings, open April to October, are as fascinating as the castle itself. The highlight is the oriental-style **Moorish Kiosk**, where Ludwig, dressed in oriental garb, would preside over nightly entertainment from a peacock throne.

Linderhof is about 13km west of Oberammergau and 26km northwest of Garmisch-Partenkirchen. Bus 9622 travels to Linderhof from Oberammergau nine times a day. If coming from Garmisch-Partenkirchen change in Ettal or Oberammergau.

OBERSTDORF

☎ 08322 / pop 11,000

Spectacularly situated in the western Alps, the Allgäu region feels a long, long way from the rest of Bavaria, in both its cuisine (more *Spätzle* than dumplings) and dialect, which is closer to the Swabian of Baden-Württemberg. The Allgäu's chief draw is the car-free resort of Oberstdorf, a major skiing centre a short hop from Austria.

The **tourist office** (**☎ 7000; www.oberstdorf.de; Prinzregenten-Platz 1; 8.30am-noon & 2-6pm Mon-Fri, 9.30am-noon Sat**) and its **branch office** (**☎ 700 217; Bahnhof; 9am-8pm Mon-Sat, 9am-6pm Sun May-Oct, 9am-noon & 2-6pm Nov-Apr**) runs a room-finding service.

Oberstdorf is almost ringed by towering peaks and offers superb hiking. For an exhilarating day walk, ride the Nebelhorn **cable car** (**adult/child €20/9.50**) to the upper station, then hike down via the **Gaisalpseen**, two lovely alpine lakes (six hours).

In-the-know skiers value the resort for its friendliness, lower prices and less-crowded pistes. The village is surrounded by 70km of well-maintained cross-country trails and three ski fields: the **Nebelhorn** (**day/half-day passes €33/28**), **Fellhorn/Kanzelwand** (**day/half-day passes €36/31**) and **Söllereck** (**day/half-day passes €25/20**).

SLEEPING & EATING

Weinklause (**☎ 969 30; www.weinklause.de; Prinzenstrasse 10; s €55-68, d €42-64; P ⊠**) Willing to take one-nighters at the drop of a felt hat, this superb lodge offers all kinds of rooms and apartments, some with kitchenette, some with jaw-dropping, spectacular alpine views. A generous breakfast is served in the restaurant, which comes to life most nights with local live music.

our pick Weinstube am Frohmarkt (**☎ 3988; Am Frohmarkt 2; mains €7-18; 5pm-1am Thu-Tue**) The musty-sweet aroma of wine, cheese and Tyrolean cured ham scents the air at this intimate wine bar. Rub shoulders with locals over the Törggelen buffet downstairs, or retreat upstairs for a quiet glass of wine.

GETTING THERE & AWAY

There are at least five direct trains daily from Munich (€27.80, 2½ hours), otherwise change in Buchloe. RVO buses 81 and 9718 run three times daily between Oberstdorf and Füssen (one way/return €10.20/18, two hours).

BERCHTESGADEN & BERCHTESGADENER LAND

☎ 08652 / pop 7700

Wedged into Austria and framed by six formidable mountain ranges, Berchtesgadener Land is a drop-dead-gorgeous corner of Bavaria. Much of it is protected within the Berchtesgaden National Park, declared a Unesco 'biosphere reserve' in 1990. The village of Berchtesgaden is the obvious base for hiking into the park; away from the trails, the main draws are Eagle's Nest, a mountaintop lodge built for Hitler; and Dokumentation Obersalzberg, a museum chronicling the region's dark Nazi past.

INFORMATION

Tourist office (**☎ 9670; www.berchtesgadener-land.info; Königsseer Strasse 2; 8.30am-6pm Mon-Fri, 9am-5pm Sat, 9am-3pm Sun May–mid-Oct, 8.30am-5pm Mon-Fri, 9am-noon Sat mid-Oct–Apr**)

MARTIN MOOS

Mountains tower over Berchtesgaden

SIGHTS

KÖNIGSSEE

Without doubt the highlight of any visit to the Berchtesgadener Land is a crossing of the emerald-green **Königssee**. Contained by steep mountain walls just 5km south of Berchtesgaden, it's the country's highest lake (603m) with pure water shimmering into fjordlike depths. Departing from the lakeside village of Schönau (take bus 839 or 841 from Berchtesgaden), **Bayerische Seen-Schifffahrt** (☎ 963 60; www.seenschifffahrt.de; return adult/child €12.50/6.30) runs electric boats year-round to **St Bartholomä**, a quaint onion-domed chapel on the western shore. At one point, the boat stops while the captain plays a *Flügelhorn* towards the amazing **Echo Wall** – the melody bounces back after several seconds. About an hour's hike from the dock at St Bartholomä is the **Eiskapelle** (Ice Chapel), where an ice dome grows every winter to heights of over 200m. In late summer the ice melts and the water tunnels a huge opening in the solid ice.

DOKUMENTATION OBERSALZBERG

A quiet mountain retreat 3km east of Berchtesgaden, Obersalzberg became the southern headquarters of Hitler's government. The fascinating **Dokumentation Obersalzberg** (☎ 947 960; Salzbergstrasse 41; adult/child under 16yr €3/free; 🕐 9am-5pm Apr-Oct, 10am-3pm Tue-Sun Nov-Apr) leaves few stones unturned. The forced takeover of the area, the construction of the compound and the daily life of the Nazi elite are documented, and all facets of the Nazi terror regime – Hitler's near-mythical appeal, his racial politics, the resistance movement and the death camps – are covered in extraordinary depth. A section of the underground bunker network is open for touring.

EAGLE'S NEST

Berchtesgaden's most sinister draw is Mt Kehlstein, a sheer-sided peak at Obersalzberg where Martin Bormann, a key henchman of Hitler's, engaged 3000 workers to build a diplomatic meeting-house for the Führer's 50th birthday.

Perched at 1834m, the innocent-looking lodge (called Kehlsteinhaus in German) occupies one of the world's most breathtaking spots.

From mid-May to October, the **Eagle's Nest** is open to visitors. To get there, drive or take bus 849 from the Hauptbahnhof to the Kehlstein bus departure area. From here the road is closed to private traffic and you must take a special **bus** (www.kehlsteinhaus.de; per person €15; 8.55am-4pm) up the mountain (35 minutes). The final 124m stretch to the summit is in a luxurious, brass-clad elevator. The Eagle's Nest now houses a restaurant that donates profits to charity.

SALZBERGWERK

Once a major producer of so-called 'white gold', Berchtesgaden has thrown open its **salt mines** (600 20; adult/child €14/9; 9am-5pm May-Oct, 11.30am-3pm Nov-Apr) for fun-filled tours (90 minutes). The **SalzZeitReise** exhibition opened here in 2007, and sees visitors donning protective overalls and taking a special train into the depths of the mine. Down below, the highlights include the crossing of a 100m-long illuminated lake containing the same concentration of salt as the Dead Sea. It's usually only around 12°C down there, so bring a sweater.

SLEEPING

Hotel-Pension Greti (975 297; www.pension-greti.de; Waldhauserstrasse 20, Schönau; s €25-39, d €44-72; P) Warm and welcoming, and just a 15-minute walk from the Königssee, Greti's rooms are surprisingly voguish and all have balconies.

Hotel Vier Jahreszeiten (9520; www.hotel-vierjahreszeiten-berchtesgaden.de; Maximilianstrasse 20; s €52-73, d €83-104; P) For a glimpse of Berchtesgaden's storied past, stay at this traditional Alpine lodge where Bavarian royalty once entertained. Rooms have panoramic views of the mountains and the in-house restaurant couldn't be more atmospheric.

Hotel Rosenbichl (944 00; www.hotel-rosenbichl.de; Rosenhofweg 24; d €56-68; P) This wellness hotel in the middle of the protected nature zone offers exceptional value. Room decor is a bit naff '90s, but you get a lot of floor space for your euro.

EATING

Holzkäfer (621 07; Buchenhöhe 40; dishes €4-9; 2pm-late, closed Tue) This funky log-cabin restaurant in the hills around

HITLER'S MOUNTAIN RETREAT

Of all the German towns tainted by the Third Reich, Berchtesgaden has a burden heavier than most. Hitler fell in love with nearby Obersalzberg in the 1920s, and bought a small country home, later enlarged into the imposing Berghof.

After seizing power in 1933, Hitler established a part-time headquarters here and brought much of the party brass with him. They bought, or often confiscated, large tracts of land and tore down farmhouses to erect a 7ft-high barbed-wire fence. Obersalzberg was sealed off as the fortified southern headquarters of the NSDAP (National Socialist German Workers' Party).

Little is left of Hitler's Alpine fortress today. In the final days of WWII, the Royal Air Force levelled much of Obersalzberg, though the Eagle's Nest, Hitler's mountaintop eyrie, was left strangely unscathed.

Obersalzberg is a great spot for a night out with fun-loving locals. Crammed with antlers, carvings and backwoods oddities, it's known for its tender pork roasts, dark beers and list of Franconian wines.

Bräustübl (☎ 976 724; Bräuhausstrasse 13; mains €8-14) Enter through the arch painted in Bavaria's white and blue diamonds and pass the old beer barrels to reach a secluded beer garden. The vaulted hall is the scene of heel-whacking Bavarian stage shows every Saturday night.

Gastätte St Bartholomä (☎ 964 937; St Bartholomä; mains €8-15) On the shore of the Königsee, and reached by boat, this is a tourist haunt that actually serves delicious food made with ingredients picked, plucked and hunted from the surrounding forests and the lake.

GETTING THERE & AWAY

Travelling from Munich by train involves a change at Freilassing (€28.50, three hours).

MICHELLE LEWIS

Hitler's Eagle's Nest, Berchtesgaden

FRANCONIA

Somewhere between Ingolstadt and Nuremberg, Bavaria's accent mellows, the oompah bands play that little bit quieter and wine competes with beer as the local tipple. This is Franconia (Franken), and as every local will tell you, Franconians, who inhabit the wooded hills and the banks of the sluggish Main River in Bavaria's northern reaches, are a breed apart from their brash and extrovert siblings to the south.

In the northwest, the region's winemakers produce some exceptional whites sold in a distinctive teardrop-shaped bottle, the *Bocksbeutel*. For outdoor enthusiasts, the Altmühltal Nature Park offers wonderful hiking, biking and canoeing. But it is Franconia's old royalty and incredible cities – Nuremberg, Bamberg and Würzburg (for the latter, see p126) – that draw the biggest crowds.

NUREMBERG

☎ 0911 / pop 500,000

Nuremberg (Nürnberg), Bavaria's second-largest city and the unofficial capital of Franconia, is an energetic place where the nightlife is intense and the beer is as dark as coffee. As one of Bavaria's biggest draws it is alive with visitors year-round, but especially during the spectacular Christmas market.

The Nazis saw in Nuremberg a perfect stage for their activities. It was here that the fanatical party rallies were held, the boycott of Jewish businesses began and the infamous Nuremberg Laws outlawing

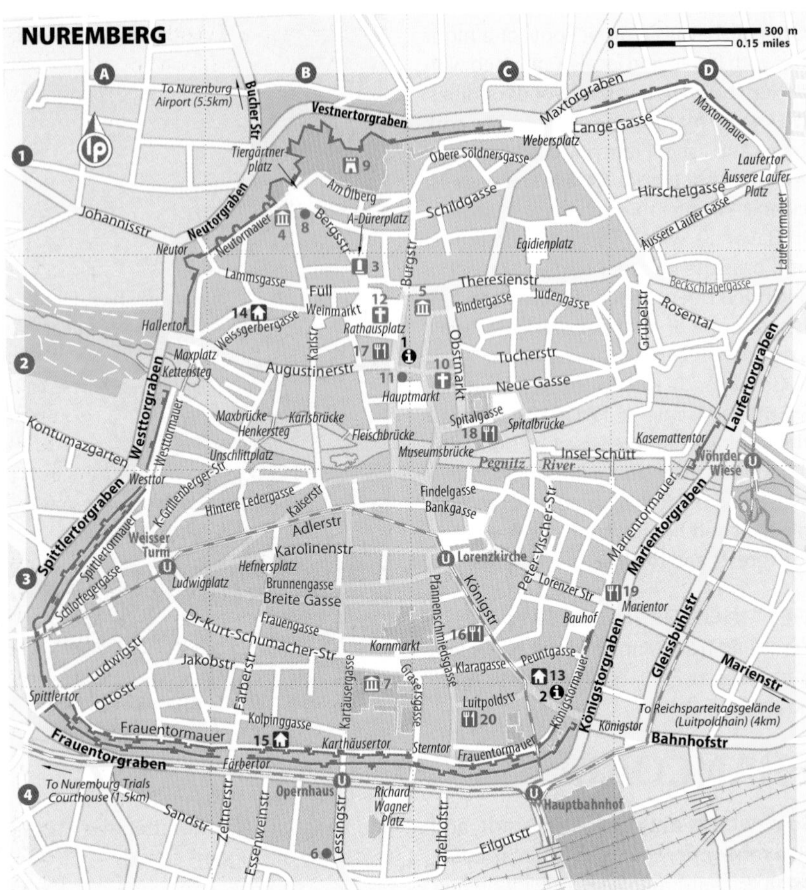

INFORMATION
Tourist Office Hauptmarkt 1 B2
Tourist Office Königstrasse 2 C4

SIGHTS & ACTIVITIES
Albrecht Dürer Monument 3 B2
Albrecht-Dürer-Haus 4 B1
Altes Rathaus 5 C2
Deutsche Bahn Museum 6 B4
Felsengänge .... (see 3)
Germanisches Nationalmuseum 7 B3
Hausbrauerei Altstadthof 8 B1
Kaiserburg 9 B1
Kaiserburg Museum .... (see 9)
Lochgefängnisse .... (see 5)
Old Town Walking Tours .... (see 1)
Pfarrkirche Unsere Liebe Frau 10 C2
Schöner Brunnen 11 B2
St Sebalduskirche 12 B2

SLEEPING
Hotel Drei Raben 13 C3
Hotel Elch 14 B2
Lette 'm Sleep 15 B4

EATING
Barfüsser Kleines Brauhaus 16 C3
Bratwursthäusle 17 B2
Heilig-Geist-Spital 18 C2
Marientorzwinger 19 D3
Vegan Imbiss 20 C4

Jewish citizenship were enacted. After WWII the city was chosen as the site of the War Crimes Tribunal, now known as the Nuremberg Trials. Later, the painstaking reconstruction – using the original stone – of almost all the city's main buildings (flattened in January 1945 by Allied bombers), including the castle and old churches in the Altstadt (old town), returned the city to some of its former glory.

INFORMATION

Tourist office (☎ 233 60; www.tourismus.nuernberg.de) Hauptmarkt (**Hauptmarkt 18; 9am-6pm Mon-Sat, 10am-4pm Sun May-Sep**); Königstrasse (**Königstrasse 93; 9am-7pm Mon-Sat, 10am-4pm Sun**)

SIGHTS

HAUPTMARKT

This bustling square in the heart of the Altstadt is the site of markets including the famous Chriskindlesmarkt (Christmas market). The ornate Gothic **Pfarrkirche Unsere Liebe Frau** (1350–58), better known as the Frauenkirche, was built on the site of a razed synagogue as a repository for the crown jewels of Holy Roman Emperor Charles IV, who, fearing theft, sent them instead to his native Prague for safekeeping.

Protruding from the northwest corner of the square like a half-buried church spire is the 19m **Schöner Brunnen** (Beautiful Fountain). A replica of the late-14th-century original, it is a stunning golden vision of 40 electors, prophets, Jewish and Christian heroes and other allegorical figures. A local superstition has it that if you turn the small **golden rings** on its sides three times your wish will come true.

ALTES RATHAUS & ST SEBALDUSKIRCHE

Beneath the **Altes Rathaus** (1616-22), a hulk of a building with lovely Renaissance-style interiors, you'll find the macabre **Lochgefängnisse** (**Medieval Dungeons; ☎ 231 2690; Rathausplatz 2; tours adult/concession €3/1.50; 10am-4.30pm Tue-Sun Apr-Oct, daily during Christkindlesmarkt**). This 12-cell death row and torture chamber must be seen on a 30-minute guided tour (held every half-hour) and might easily put you off lunch.

Across the cobbles from the Altes Rathaus rises the 13th-century **St Sebalduskirche**, Nuremberg's oldest church. The highlight inside is the bronze shrine of **St Sebald**, a Gothic and Renaissance masterpiece that took its maker, Peter Vischer the Elder, as well as his two sons, more than 11 years to

MZC/IMAGEBROKER

View over Nuremberg's Christkindlesmarkt (p153)

CHERYL FORBES
Mural on Bamberg's Altes Rathaus (p154)

complete. The entire piece is carried by a posse of giant snails.

FELSENGÄNGE

Under the **Albrecht Dürer Monument** on Albrecht-Dürer-Platz are four storeys of dank passageways called the **Felsengänge** (☎ 227 066; adult/concession €4.50/3.50; tours at 11am, 1pm, 3pm & 5pm, 3-person minimum). Burrowed into the sandstone in the 14th century to house a brewery and beer cellar, they also served as an air-raid shelter during WWII. Down in the tunnels, which can only be seen on a tour, things can get pretty chilly even in summer, so take a jacket. Buy tickets from the brewpub **Hausbrauerei Altstadthof** (Bergstrasse 19).

KAISERBURG

Another must-see is the humongous **Kaiserburg** (Imperial Castle; ☎ 244 6590; Burg; adult/concession incl museum €6/5, well & tower only €3/2; 9am-6pm Apr-Sep, 10am-4pm Oct-Mar). Construction began here during the Hohenstaufen reign in the 12th century, and dragged on for almost four centuries. The complex embraces the Kaiser's living quarters, a Romanesque chapel, the Imperial and Knights' Halls and the **Sinwellturm** (Sinwell Tower; 113 steps). There's also the amazing 48m-deep **Tiefer Brunnen** (Deep Well), which still yields drinking water.

The **Kaiserburg Museum** (☎ 200 9540; Burg; adult/concession €5/4) chronicles the history of the castle and sheds light on medieval defence techniques. The grassy knoll in the southeast corner of the castle gardens is **Am Ölberg**, a great spot to sit and gaze out over the city's rooftops.

ALBRECHT-DÜRER-HAUS

Germany's most famous Renaissance draughtsman, Dürer lived and worked at what is now known as the **Albrecht-Dürer-Haus** (☎ 231 2568; Albrecht-Dürer-Strasse 39; adult/concession €5/2.50; 10am-5pm Tue-Sun, to 8pm Thu) from 1509 till his death in 1528. Several originals and copies of his graphic works are on display, and a multimedia version of Agnes, his wife, takes visitors through the master's re-created workshop.

REICHSPARTEITAGSGELÄNDE

If you've ever wondered where the infamous black-and-white images of ecstatic Nazi supporters hailing their Führer were filmed, it was here in Nuremberg. This orchestrated propaganda began as early as 1927, but after 1933 Hitler opted for a purpose-built venue, the **Reichsparteitagsgelände** (Nazi Party Rally

Grounds). Much of the outsized grounds were destroyed during Allied bombing raids, but enough is left to get a sense of the megalomania behind it. A visit to the **Dokumentationszentrum** (Documentation Centre; ☎ 231 5666; Bayernstrasse 110; adult/student €5/2.50; 9am-6pm Mon-Fri, 10am-6pm Sat & Sun) in the north wing of the Kongresshalle helps to put the grounds into some historical context. Don't miss it.

NUREMBERG TRIALS COURTHOUSE

Nazi war criminals were tried for crimes against peace and humanity in the **Schwurgerichtssaal 600** (Courtroom 600; ☎ 231 5666; Fürther Strasse 110). Held in 1945–46, the trials resulted in the conviction and sentencing of 22 Nazi leaders and 150 underlings, and the execution of dozens.

GERMANISCHES NATIONALMUSEUM

One of the most important museums of German culture with over 1.3 million items (not all of which are displayed), the **Germanisches Nationalmuseum** (☎ 133 10; Kartäusergasse 1; adult/concession €6/4; 10am-6pm Tue-Sun, to 9pm Wed) is strangely underrated and undervisited. It features an archaeological collection, arms and armour, musical and scientific instruments and toys – but the jewel in its crown is the **art section**. As you might expect, local lad Dürer gets top billing.

DEUTSCHE BAHN MUSEUM

Nuremberg's impressive **Deutsche Bahn Museum** (German Railways Museum; ☎ 0180-444 2233; www.db-museum.de; Lessingstrasse 6; adult/concession €4/3; 9am-5pm Tue-Fri, 10am-6pm Sat & Sun) explores the history of Germany's legendary rail system. You'll see the country's first engine, the Adler, which ran from Nuremberg to nearby Fürth in 1852. Other fine specimens include Ludwig II's gilded carriage (dubbed the 'rolling Neuschwanstein' for its starry ceiling fresco and lavish decoration) and Bismarck's sober quarters for official visits. A highlight is the hourly demonstration of one of Germany's largest model railways, run by a controller at a huge console of blinking lights and switches.

TOURS

English-language **Old Town walking tours** (adult/child under 14yr €9/free; 1pm May-Oct) are run by the tourist office, and include admission to the Kaiserburg. Tours leave from the Hauptmarkt branch (see p151) and take 2½ hours.

FESTIVALS & EVENTS

From late November to Christmas Eve, the Hauptmarkt is taken over by the most famous **Christkindlesmarkt** (Christmas Market; www.christkindles markt.de) in Germany.

SLEEPING

Accommodation gets tight and rates rocket during the Christmas market and toy fair (trade only) in late January to early February.

Lette 'm sleep (☎ 992 8128; www.backpackers.de; Frauentormauer 42; dm €16-20, d €49, linen €3;) Conveniently located within the old town wall and just five minutes from the Hauptbahnhof, this is a great place to grab some shut-eye and meet fellow travellers. The rooftop apartments boast their own kitchens and are ideal for groups of friends.

OUR PICK **Hotel Elch** (☎ 249 2980; www.hotel-elch.de; Irrerstrasse 9; s/d €69/85;) This dramatically historic hotel, occupying a 14th-century half-timbered house near the Kaiserburg, has petite rooms up a narrow medieval staircase. Breakfast is served in the quaint woody restaurant, the Schnitzelria, which does a good line in Franconian beers and, yes, schnitzel.

Hotel Drei Raben (☎ 274 380; www.hotel-drei-raben.de; Königstrasse 63; s & d €100-185; ⊠ ⓦ) This designer theme hotel builds upon the legend of three ravens perched on the building's chimney stack, who tell each other stories from Nuremberg lore. Each of the 21 rooms uses its style and humour to tell a particular tale – from the life of Dürer to the history of the locomotive.

EATING

Barfüsser Kleines Brauhaus (☎ 204 242; Königstrasse 60; mains €6-15) This Nuremberg institution is housed in an atmospheric old grain warehouse packed with copper vats, enamel advertising plaques and oodles of other knick-knacks. The cavernous vaulted cellar is the place to install yourself in the company of an *Eichenholzfässchen,* a 5L oak-wood keg of beer.

Heilig-Geist-Spital (☎ 221 761; Spitalgasse 12; mains €7-17) Lots of dark carved wood, a herd of hunting trophies and a romantic candlelit half-light make this former hospital one of the most atmospheric dining rooms in town.

our pick Marientorzwinger (☎ 274 2784; Lorenzer- strasse 33; mains €8-17) This is the last remaining *Zwinger* eatery (taverns built between the inner and outer walls when they relinquished their military use) in Nuremberg. Chomp on sturdy Franconian staples or a vegie dish in the simple wood-panelled dining room or the leafy beer garden, and swab the decks with a yard of Fürth-brewed Tucher.

Vegan Imbiss (Luitpoldstrasse 13; dishes €3-6; Ⓥ) Wedged between the facades of Luitpoldstrasse, this tiny snack bar offers meat- and dairy-free noodle-rice-veg combinations with a touch of Asian zing.

Bratwursthäusle (☎ 227 695; Rathausplatz 1; dishes €5-11; ⏲ closed Sun) Seared over a flaming beech-wood grill, the little links sold at this rustic inn arguably set the standards for *Rostbratwürste* across the land.

GETTING THERE & AWAY

Nuremberg airport (☎ 937 00), 5km north of the centre, is served by regional and international carriers, including Lufthansa, Air Berlin and Air France. U-Bahn 2 runs every few minutes from the Hauptbahnhof to the airport (€1.80, 12 minutes). A taxi to/from the airport will cost you about €16.

Trains run at least hourly to/from Frankfurt (€48, two hours) and Munich (€49, one hour).

BAMBERG

☎ 0951 / pop 70,000

With a history-steeped centre, a magnificent cathedral and heaps of romantic charm, it's difficult not to be impressed by Bamberg. Clearly one of Germany's most beautiful cities, this Unesco-listed history lesson was built by archbishops on seven hills, earning it the sobriquet of 'Franconian Rome'. Bamberg is also justly famous for its beer, with 10 breweries in town and another 80 or so in the vicinity.

INFORMATION

Tourist office (☎ 297 6200; www.bamberg.info; Geyerswörthstrasse 3; ⏲ 9.30am-6pm Mon-Fri, to 2.30pm Sat & Sun)

SIGHTS

ALTSTADT

Bamberg's main appeal lies in its sheer number of fine historic buildings, their jumble of styles and the paucity of modern eyesores. Most attractions are sprinkled along the Regnitz River, but the town's incredibly statuesque **Altes**

Rathaus is actually on it, perched on twin bridges like a ship in dry dock (note the cherub's leg sticking out from the fresco on the east side). To the northwest are the charming half-timbered homes of **Klein Venedig** (Little Venice), complete with punts, canals and river docks.

DOM

Bamberg's princely and ecclesiastical roots are felt strongest around Domplatz on the southern bank of the Regnitz. The dominant structure is the soaring **Dom** (8am-5pm Nov-Mar,to 6pm Apr-Oct), the result of a Romanesque-Gothic duel fought by church architects after the original edifice burnt down (twice) in the 12th century. Look out for the **Lächelnde Engel** (Smiling Angel) in the north aisle, who smirkingly hands the martyr's crown to the headless St Denis. In the west choir is the marble tomb of **Pope Clemens II**, the only papal burial spot north of the Alps.

The star turn, however, and Bamberg's enduring mystery, is the statue of the **Bamberger Reiter**, a chivalric king-knight on a steed. Nobody knows for sure who he is, but one leading theory points towards Konrad III, the Hohenstaufen king buried in the cathedral.

On the south side of the Dom, in a separate building off the cloisters, is the **Diözesan Museum** (☎ 502 316; Domplatz 5; adult/concession €3/2.50; 10am-5pm Tue-Sun). Top ranking among its ecclesiastical treasures goes to Heinrich II's Blue Coat of Stars, kept not far from the pontifical knee-socks of Clemens II.

AROUND DOMPLATZ

Northwest of the Dom is the **Alte Hofhaltung** (old court hall), a former prince-bishops' palace that contains the **Historisches Museum** (☎ 519 0746; Domplatz 7; adult/concession €3/2; 9am-5pm Tue-Sun May-Oct). Across the square, you'll spot the stately **Neue Residenz** (☎ 519 390; Domplatz 8; adult/concession €4/3; 9am-6pm Apr-Sep, 10am-4pm Oct-Mar), a huge episcopal palace now housing a significant collection of baroque paintings. The baroque

MARK AVELLINO

Historic buildings in Unesco-listed Bamberg

Rosengarten (Rose Garden) behind the palace has fabulous views over Bamberg's red-tiled roofs.

SLEEPING

Brauereigasthof Fässla (☎ 265 16; www.faessla.de; Obere Königstrasse 19-21; s/d €40/60; P) Those with more than a passing interest in the local brews should try this atmospheric guesthouse, where snug but modern rooms are just up the stairs from the pub and covered courtyard.

Barockhotel am Dom (☎ 540 31; www.barockhotel.de; Vorderer Bach 4; s/d €72/98; P ☒ ▣) The sugary facade, a sceptre's swipe from the Dom, gives a hint of the baroque heritage and original details within. Rooms have sweeping views of the Dom or over the roofs of the Altstadt, and breakfast is served in a 14th-century vault.

our pick **Hotel Sankt Nepomuk** (☎ 984 20; www.hotel-nepomuk.de; Obere Mühlbrücke 9; s/d €95/145; P) Named aptly after the patron saint of bridges, this classy place is located in an A-framed former mill in the middle of the Regnitz. It has rustic rooms, a superb gourmet restaurant on the premises and bicycles for hire.

EATING

Wirtshaus zum Schlenkerla (☎ 560 60; Dominikaner- strasse 6; dishes €5-10) A local legend that's known nationwide, this dark, rustic 16th-century restaurant with long wooden tables serves tasty Franconian specialities and its own superb *Rauchbier,* poured straight from the oak barrel.

Ambräusianum (☎ 509 0262; Dominikanerstrasse 10; dishes €7-15) This outstanding brewpub does a killer *Weisswurst* breakfast – parsley-speckled veal sausage served with a big freshly baked pretzel and a *Weissbier* (€5.50). Sit next to the copper vat and listen to the beer ferment.

Messerschmidt (☎ 297 800; Lange Strasse 41; mains €15-24) In the house where plane engineer Willy Messerschmidt was born, this stylish gourmet eatery oozes old-world tradition, with dark woods, white linens and formal service.

GETTING THERE & AWAY

There are at least hourly RE and RB trains from Nuremberg (€11.30, 45 to 60 minutes) or from Würzburg (€17.60, one hour), as well as ICE trains every hour to/from Munich (€56, two hours) and Berlin (€80, four to five hours).

BAYREUTH

☎ 0921 / pop 75,000

Even without its Wagner connections, Bayreuth would still be an interesting detour from Nuremberg or Bamberg for its baroque architecture and curious palaces. But it's for the annual Wagner Festival that 60,000 opera devotees make a pilgrimage to this neck of the *Wald* (forest), many having waited years in the ticket lottery to do so.

INFORMATION

Tourist office (☎ 885 88; www.bayreuth-tourismus.de; Luitpoldplatz 9; ⏲ 9am-6pm Mon-Fri, to 2pm Sat)

SIGHTS

TOWN CENTRE

Designed by Giuseppe Galli Bibiena, a famous 18th-century architect from Bologna, the **Markgräfliches Opernhaus** (Margravial Opera House; ☎ 759 6922; Opernstrasse; tours adult/under 18yr/concession €5/free/4; ⏲ tours 9am-6pm Apr-Sep, 10am-4pm Oct-Mar) is a stunning baroque masterpiece. Germany's largest opera house until 1871, it has a lavish interior smothered in carved, gilded and marbled wood.

Just south of here is Wilhelmine's **Neues Schloss** (New Palace; ☎ 759 6921; Ludwigstrasse 21; adult/concession €5/4; 9am-6pm Apr-Sep, 10am-4pm Tue-Sun Oct-Mar), which opens into the vast **Hofgarten** (admission free; 24hr). A riot of rococo style, the Margravial residence after 1753 features a collection of 18th-century porcelain made in Bayreuth. Also worth a look is the **Spiegelscherbenkabinett** (Broken Mirror Cabinet), which is lined with irregular shards of broken mirror – supposedly Wilhelmine's response to the vanity of her era.

To learn more about the man behind the myth, visit Haus Wahnfried, Wagner's former home on the northern edge of the Hofgarten. It now houses the **Richard Wagner Museum** (☎ 757 2816; www.wagnermuseum.de; Richard-Wagner-Strasse 48; adult/concession €4/2; 9am-5pm, to 8pm Tue & Thu Apr-Oct). Inside is a thorough, if unexciting, exhibit on Wagner's life, with glass cases crammed with documents, photographs, clothing and private effects. The composer and his wife Cosima are buried in an unmarked, ivy- covered tomb in the garden, with the sandstone grave of his loving canine companion Russ standing nearby.

OUTSIDE THE TOWN CENTRE

North of the Hauptbahnhof, the main venue for Bayreuth's annual Wagner Festival is the **Festspielhaus** (☎ 787 80; Festspielhügel 1-2; adult/concession €5/4; tours 10am & 2pm Dec-Mar, Apr-Aug when rehearsals permit, 10am, 11am, 2pm & 3pm Sep & Oct, closed Mon & Nov), constructed in 1872 with Ludwig II's backing. The structure was specially designed to accommodate Wagner's massive theatrical sets, with three storeys of mechanical works hidden below stage.

About 6km east of the centre lies the **Eremitage**, a lush park girding the

DWH/IMAGEBROKER

Bamberg's Altes Rathaus (p154)

Altes Schloss (☎ 759 6937), Friedrich and Wilhelmine's summer residence. Also in the park is horseshoe-shaped **Neues Schloss** (not to be confused with the one in town), which centres on the amazing mosaic Sun Temple with gilded Apollo sculpture. Around both palaces you'll find numerous grottoes, follies and gushing fountains.

For a fascinating look at the brewing process, head to the enormous **Maisel's Brauerei-und-Büttnerei-Museum** (Maisel's Brewery & Coopers Museum; ☎ 401 234; Kulmbacher Strasse 40; tours adult/concession €4/2) next door to the brewery of one of Germany's finest wheat-beer makers. The 90-minute guided tour (2pm daily, in German) takes you into the bowels of the 19th-century plant, with atmospheric rooms filled with 4500 beer mugs and amusing artefacts.

FESTIVALS & EVENTS

The **Wagner Festival** (**www.bayreuther-festspiele.de**) has been a summer fixture for over 130 years. Demand is insane, with an estimated 500,000 fans vying for less than 60,000 tickets. Tickets are allocated by lottery but preference is given to patrons and Wagner enthusiasts.

SLEEPING

During the Wagner Festival, beds are as hard to come by as the tickets themselves.

Hotel Goldener Hirsch (**☎ 1504 4000; www.bayreuth-goldener-hirsch.de; Bahnhofstrasse 13; s €65-85, d €85-110; P ⊠**) Not far from the train station, this landmark site has had the same name since 1753, and has been a hotel since 1900. Behind its forest-green exterior the '70s and '80s vibe is gradually giving way to clean-cut contemporary decor, but all rooms are spacious and welcoming.

Hotel Goldener Anker (**☎ 650 51; www.anker-bayreuth.de; Opernstrasse 6; s €78-128, d €128-198; P ⊠**) The refined elegance of this hotel, owned by the same family since the 16th century, is hard to beat. It's just a few metres from the opera house, in the pedestrian zone. Many of the rooms are decorated in heavy traditional style with swag curtains, dark woods and antique touches.

EATING

Kraftraum (**☎ 800 2515; Sophienstrasse 16; mains €5.50-8; V**) This vegetarian eatery has plenty to tempt even the most committed meat-eater. Pastas and jacket potatoes hold the fort, alongside some amazing salads and antipasti platters. Sunday brunch has a devoted following.

Oskar (**☎ 516 0553; Maximilianstrasse 33; dishes €6-15**) From the wood-panelled interior to out on the cobbles this updated version of a Bavarian beer hall bustles from morning to night. The menu includes salads and baked potato dishes, but the speciality is anything involving dumplings.

DWH/IMAGEBROKER

Festspielhaus (p157), Bayreuth

Miamiam Glouglou (☎ 656 66; Von-Römer-Strasse 28; mains €7-20) Delightful Parisian-style restaurant with an authentically French menu.

GETTING THERE & AWAY

Bayreuth is well served by rail from Nuremberg (€16.70, one hour). Trains from both Munich (€62, 2½ hours) and Regensburg (€30, 2¼ hours) require a change in Nuremberg.

COBURG

☎ 09561 / pop 42,000

Coburg languished in the shadow of the Iron Curtain during the Cold War, all but closed in by East Germany on three sides, but since reunification the town has undergone a revival. Its proud Veste is one of Germany's finest medieval fortresses.

Coburg's epicentre is the magnificent Markt, a cafe-filled square oozing a colourful, aristocratic charm. The lavish **Schloss Ehrenburg** (☎ 808 832; Schlossplatz; tours in German adult/under 18yr/concession €4/free/3; tours hourly 9am-5pm Tue-Sun Apr-Sep, 10am-3pm Tue-Sun Oct-Mar) was once the town residence of the Coburg dukes. The splendid **Riesensaal** (Hall of Giants) has a baroque ceiling supported by 28 statues of Atlas.

Towering above everything is a storybook medieval fortress, the **Veste Coburg** (courtyard dawn-dusk). It houses the vast collection of the **Kunstsammlungen** (☎ 8790; adult/concession €5/2.50; 9.30am-5pm daily Apr-Oct, 1-4pm Tue-Sun Nov-Mar), with works by star painters such as Rembrandt, Dürer and Cranach the Elder.

At **Café Prinz Albert** (☎ 945 20; Ketschengasse 27; dishes €3-5; 8am-6.30pm) Coburg's links with the British royals are reflected in both the decor and menu. The Prince Albert breakfast – a cross-cultural marriage of sausage, egg and Bamberger croissants – is fit for a queen's consort.

Heavenly (if pricey) food is made with fresh organic ingredients at **Tie** (☎ 334 48; Leopoldstrasse 14; mains €14.50-18; from 5pm Tue-Sun; V), a bright vegetarian restaurant. Dishes range from vegetarian classics to Asian inspirations, with the odd fish or meat dish for the unconverted.

GETTING THERE & AWAY

Direct trains to Bamberg (€10.30, 50 minutes) and Nuremberg (€19.90, 1¾ hours) leave Coburg every other hour. The trip to Bayreuth (€15.20, 1½ hours) requires a change in Lichtenfels.

ALTMÜHLTAL NATURE PARK

The Altmühltal Nature Park is one of Germany's largest nature parks and covers some of Bavaria's most gorgeous terrain. The Altmühl River gently meanders through a region of little valleys and hills before joining the Rhine-Main Canal and eventually emptying into the Danube. For information on the park and for help with planning an itinerary, contact the **Informationszentrum Naturpark Altmühltal** (☎ 08421-987 60; www.naturpark-altmuehltal.de; Notre Dame 1, Eichstätt; 9am-5pm Mon-Sat, 10am-5pm Sun Apr-Oct, 8am-noon & 2-4pm Mon-Thu, 8am-noon Fri Nov-Mar).

The most beautiful section of the river is from Treuchtlingen or Pappenheim to Eichstätt or Kipfenberg, about a 60km stretch that you can do lazily in a kayak or canoe in two to three days. You can hire canoes and kayaks in just about every town along the river. Expect to pay about €15/25 per day for a one-/two-person boat, more for bigger ones. Staff will haul you and the boats to or from your embarkation point for a small fee.

With around 3000km of hiking trails and 800km of cycle trails criss-crossing the landscape, foot and pedal are the best ways to strike out into the park. The most popular cycling route is the Altmühltal Radweg, which runs parallel to the river for 160km. You can hire bikes in almost every town within the park, and prices are more or less uniform.

The Altmühltal-Panoramaweg, stretching 200km west–east between Gunzenhausen and Kelheim, is a picturesque hiking route crossing the entire park.

EASTERN BAVARIA

The sparsely populated eastern reaches of Bavaria may live in the shadow of Bavaria's big-hitting attractions, but they hold many historical treasures to rival their neighbours. Top billing goes to Regensburg, a former capital, and one of Germany's prettiest and liveliest cities. From here the Danube gently winds its way to the Italianate city of Passau. Away from the towns, the Bavarian Forest broods in semi-undiscovered remoteness.

REGENSBURG

☎ 0941 / pop 130,000

A Roman settlement completed under Emperor Marcus Aurelius, Regensburg was the first capital of Bavaria, the residence of dukes, kings and bishops, and for 600 years an imperial free city. Two millennia of history bequeathed the city some of the region's finest architectural heritage, a fact recognised by Unesco in 2006. Though big on the historical wow-factor, today's Regensburg is a laid-back and unpretentious sort of place, and a good springboard into the wider region.

INFORMATION

Tourist office (☎ 507 4410; www.tourismus.regensburg.de; Altes Rathaus; ⌚ 9am-6pm Mon-Fri, 9am-4pm Sat, 9.30am-4pm Sun)

SIGHTS

DOM ST PETER

Regensburg's soaring landmark, the **Dom St Peter** (☎ 597 1660; Domplatz; admission free) ranks among Bavaria's grandest Gothic cathedrals. Inside are kaleidoscopic stained-glass windows above the choir and in the south transept. Another highlight is a pair of charming sculptures (1280), attached to pillars just west of the altar, which features the Angel Gabriel beaming at the Virgin on the opposite pillar as he delivers the news that she's with child.

SCHLOSS THURN UND TAXIS & MUSEUM

In the 15th century, Franz von Taxis (1459–1517) assured his place in history by setting up the first European postal system, which remained a monopoly until the 19th century. In recognition of his services, the family was given a new palace, the former Benedictine monastery St Emmeram, henceforth known as **Schloss Thurn und Taxis** (☎ 504 824; www.thurnundtaxis.de; Emmeramsplatz 5; combined ticket adult/concession €11.50/9; ⌚ tours at 11am, 2pm, 3pm & 4pm Mon-Fri, also 10am & 1pm Sat & Sun Apr-Oct, weekends only Nov-Mar). It was soon one of the most modern palaces in Europe, and featured such luxuries as flushing toilets, central heating and electricity. The palace complex also contains the **Thurn und Taxis-Museum** (☎ 504 8133; adult/concession €4.50/3.50; ⌚ 11am-5pm Mon-Fri, 10am-5pm Sat & Sun). The jewellery, porcelain and precious furnishings on display here belonged, for many years, to the wealthiest dynasty in Germany.

DOCUMENT NEUPFARRPLATZ

Regensburg once had a thriving medieval Jewish community centred around Neupfarrplatz. When the city fell on hard economic times in the early 16th cen-

MANFRED GOTTSCHALK

Cruising through the Danube Gorge (p163) from Kelheim

tury, the townspeople expelled all Jews and burned their quarter to the ground. A multimedia exhibit, the **Document Neupfarrplatz** (☎ 507 3442; tours adult/concession €5/2.50; 2.30pm Thu-Sat, additionally Sun & Mon Jul & Aug) explains events on the square from ancient times right up until the formation of the resistance movement in 1942–43. Tickets are only available from Tabak Götz at Neupfarrplatz 3.

ALTES RATHAUS & REICHSTAGSMUSEUM

The seat of the Reichstag for almost 150 years, the **Altes Rathaus** is now home to Regensburg's three mayors and the **Reichstagsmuseum** (Imperial Diet Museum; ☎ 507 3442; Altes Rathaus; adult/concession €7.50/4; tours in English 3pm Apr-Oct, 2pm Nov-Mar). Tours take in not only the lavishly decorated **Reichssaal** (Imperial Hall) but also the original **torture chambers** in the basement. The interrogation room bristles with tools such as the rack, the Spanish Donkey (a tall wooden wedge on which naked men were made to sit) and spiked chairs.

STEINERNE BRÜCKE

An incredible feat of engineering for its day, Regensburg's **Steinerne Brücke** (Stone Bridge) was at one time the only fortified crossing of the Danube. Ensconced in its southern tower is the **Brückturm-Museum** (☎ 507 5889; Weisse-Lamm-Gasse 1; adult/concession €2/1.50; 10am-5pm Apr-Oct), a small historical exhibit about the bridge.

SLEEPING

Brook Lane Hostel (☎ 690 0966; www.hostel-regensburg.de; Obere Bachgasse 21; dm €15-19, s/d/apt €35/45/140;) Expanded and thoroughly modernised in 2009, Regensburg's only backpacker hostel has spanking-new dorms and bathrooms, and its very own food store.

Petit Hotel D'Orphée (☎ 596 020; www.hotel-orphee.de; Wahlenstrasse 1; s €35-110, d €70-135) Behind a humble door in the heart of the city lies a world of genuine charm, unexpected extras and real attention to detail. Another somewhat grander branch of the hotel is located above the Café Orphée (p162).

Hotel Goldenes Kreuz (☎ 558 12; www.hotel-goldeneskreuz.de; Haidplatz 7; s €75-105, d €95-125; ⊠ Wi-Fi) Surely the best deal in town, the nine fairy-tale rooms at this hotel each bear the name of a crowned head and are fit for a kaiser. Huge mirrors, dark antique and Bauhaus furnishings, four-poster beds, chubby exposed beams and parquet flooring produce a stylish opus in leather, wood, crystal and fabric.

our pick **Hotel Elements** (☎ 941-3819 8600; www.hotel-elements.de; Alter Kornmarkt 3; apt €129-149) Four elements, four rooms – and what rooms they are! This tiny, brand-new theme hotel breaks new ground with its imaginative design, and is the best-kept secret in Bavaria.

EBO/IMAGEBROKER

Interior of Dom St Stephan (p164), Passau

EATING

Spaghetteria (Am Römling 12; dishes €4.90-8.70) Get carbed up at this former 17th-century chapel where you can splatter six types of pasta with 23 types of sauce, and get out the door for the cost of a cocktail in Munich.

Dicker Mann (☎ 573 70; Krebsgasse 6; mains €6-15) One of the oldest restaurants in town, this stylish, very traditional restaurant has dependable Bavarian food, swift service and a lively flair thanks to its young and upbeat staff.

Café Orphée (☎ 529 77; Untere Bachgasse 8; mains €7-18; 🕑 9am-1am) This delightful brasserie, decked out in red velvet, dark wood and plenty of mirrors, is straight off a Parisian street. Pâtés, snacks, coffee or a light lunch all stem from a menu of appetising Gallic cuisine.

Rosenpalais (☎ 599 7579; Minoritenweg 20; bistro mains €11-20, restaurant mains €20-32; 🕑 closed Sun) If it's posh-nosh you're after, try this refined place just off Dachauplatz. Well-heeled clientele head upstairs to the graceful silver-service restaurant, wallet-watching gourmets stay downstairs.

DRINKING

Kneitinger (☎ 524 55; Arnulfsplatz 3; 🕑 9am-11pm) This quintessential Bavarian brewpub is the place to go for some hearty home cooking (mains €5.80 to €15), delicious house suds and outrageous oompah frolics.

Spitalgarten (☎ 847 74; St Katharinenplatz 1) A veritable thicket of folding chairs and slatted tables by the Danube, this is one of the best places in town for some alfresco quaffing. It claims to have brewed beer (today's Spital) here since 1350, so you can assume it probably knows what it's doing by now.

GETTING THERE & AWAY

Regensburg has direct train links to Frankfurt am Main (€63, three hours), Munich (€23.30, 1½ hours) via Landshut (€11.30, 50 minutes), Nuremberg (€17.60, one to two hours) and Passau (from €20.50, one to two hours).

AROUND REGENSBURG

KLOSTERSCHENKE WELTENBURG

When you're this close to the world's oldest monastic brewery, there's just no excuse to miss out. **Klosterschenke Weltenburg** (☎ 09441-675 70; www.klosterschenke-weltenburg.de; Asamstrasse 32; 8am-7pm Apr-Nov, closed Mon-Wed Mar) has been brewing its delicious dark beer since 1050. Now a state-of-the-art brewery, it is a favourite spot for an excursion, and the comely beer garden can get quite crowded on warm weekends and holidays. Not everyone comes for the brew alone, as the complex is also home to a most magnificent church, **Klosterkirche Sts Georg und Martin**, designed by Cosmas Damian and Egid Quirin Asam.

The most dramatic approach to Weltenburg is by boat from the Danube river town of Kelheim (about 30km southwest of Regensburg on the B16) via the **Danube Gorge**, a spectacular stretch of the river as it carves through craggy cliffs and past bizarre rock formations. From mid-March to October, you can take a trip up the gorge for €4.60/8.20 one way/return; bicycles are an extra €2.10/4.

WALHALLA

Modelled on Athens' Parthenon, the **Walhalla** (adult/child €4/3; 9am-5.45pm Apr-Sep, 10-11.45am & 1-3.45pm Oct-Mar) is a breathtaking Ludwig I monument dedicated to the giants of Germanic thought and deed. Marble steps seem to lead up forever from the banks of the Danube to this dazzling marble hall, with a gallery of 127 heroes.

To get there take the Danube Valley country road (unnumbered) 10km east from Regensburg to the village of Donaustauf, then follow the signs. Alternatively, you can take a two-hour boat cruise with **Schifffahrt Klinger** (☎ 0941-521 04; €7.50/10.50 one way/return; 10am & 2pm Apr–mid-Oct), which includes a one-hour stop at Walhalla.

BEFREIUNGSHALLE

Perched on a hill above the Danube, this mustard-coloured tankard of a building is the **Befreiungshalle** (Hall of Liberation; ☎ 09441-682 0710; Befreiungshallestrasse 3; adult/concession €3/2.50; 9am-6pm Apr-Sep, to 4pm Oct-Mar). Erected in 1863, it's an outrageous piece of Bavarian nationalism ordered by King Ludwig I to commemorate the victories over Napoleon (1813–15). Inside you'll find a veritable shrine lorded over by white marble angels modelled on the Roman goddess Victoria.

PASSAU

☎ 0851 / pop 51,000

Gathered around the confluence of three rivers, the Danube, Inn and Ilz, Passau was predestined to become a powerful trading post. The handsome old centre has a distinctly Italian look, with a maze of winding medieval cobbled lanes, underpasses and archways away from the main thoroughfares.

INFORMATION

Tourist office Altstadt (☎ 955 980; www.passau.de; Rathausplatz 3; 8.30am-6pm Mon-Fri, 9am-4pm Sat & Sun, reduced hours mid-Oct–Easter); Hauptbahnhof (☎ 955 980; Bahnhofstrasse 28; 9am-5pm Mon-Fri, 10.30am-3.30 Sat & Sun Easter-Sep, reduced hours Oct-Easter)

SIGHTS

VESTE OBERHAUS

This 13th-century fortress, built by the prince-bishops, towers over the city with patriarchal pomp. Views are superb, either from the castle tower (€1) or from the **Battalion Linde**, a lookout that gives the only bird's-eye view of the three-way confluence down below. Inside the bastion is the **Oberhausmuseum** (☎ 4933 5012; Oberhaus 125; adult/concession €5/4; 9am-5pm Mon-Fri, 10am-6pm Sat & Sun Mar-Nov). Some of the best exhibits here uncover the mysteries of medieval castle-building and a knight's rites of passage.

DOM ST STEPHAN

The characteristic green onion domes of Passau's otherwise whitewashed cathedral, the **Dom** (6.30am-7pm), float serenely above the town silhouette. There has been a church on this spot since the 5th century, but the current baroque look emerged after the Great Fire of 1662. The interior was designed by a crew of Italian artists, notably the architect Carlo Lurago and the stucco master Giovanni Carlone. The frescoes show fascinating scenes of heaven, but the true masterpiece is the industrial-size church organ, one of the world's largest with a staggering 17,974 pipes. Organ recitals are held on weekdays at noon, and on Thursday at 7.30pm from May to October (adult/child €3/1 lunchtime, €5/3 evening).

PASSAUER GLASMUSEUM

If you were wondering why Passau has bilingual signage in Czech and German, visit the **Passauer Glasmuseum** (Passau Museum of Glass; ☎ 350 71; Hotel Wilder Mann, Am Rathausplatz; adult/concession €5/4; 1-5pm), the largest museum of Czech glass and crystal in the world and a magnet for Slavic cross-border raiders. Even if you charge through this amazing collection of over 30,000 pieces displayed in 380 cases, you'll need an hour to view the 36 rooms filled with baroque, classical, art-nouveau and art-deco pieces. Be sure to pick up a floor plan as it's easy to get lost.

SLEEPING

Pension Rössner (☎ 931 350; www.pension-roessner.de; Bräugasse 19; s/d €35/60; P) The price-to-quality ratio is high at this immaculate *Pension* in a restored mansion on the eastern tip of the Altstadt. Each room is uniquely decorated and many also have fortress views. Breakfast is a silly €7 extra.

our pick **Hotel Wilder Mann** (☎ 350 71; www.wilder-mann.com; Am Rathausplatz; s €50-60, d €80-140; P) Royalty and celebrities, from Empress Elizabeth of Austria to Mikhail Gorbachev and Henry Kissinger, have stayed at this historic inn. Rooms seek to recapture a lost grandeur, and some of the carved bedsteads are very grand indeed.

EATING & DRINKING

Diwan (☎ 490 3280; top fl, Stadtturm, Niebelungenplatz 1; mains €3-7) Climb aboard the high-speed lift from street level to this trendy, high-perched cafe-lounge with by far the best views in town.

our pick **Scharfrichter Haus** (☎ 359 00; Milchgasse 2; mains €7.40-16.50; noon-2pm & 6pm-1am) Cafe, cellar restaurant and jazz club rolled into one, this Passau institution draws a sophisticated crowd who enjoy seasonal specials on crisp white linen, before retiring to the intimate cabaret theatre with a glass of Austrian wine.

Heilig-Geist-Stiftsschänke (☎ 2607; Heilig-Geist-Gasse 4; mains €10-19; closed Wed) Traditional food is prepared with

Bavarian Forest National Park (p166)

panache, and served either in the classy walnut-panelled tangle of dining rooms or the leafy beer garden, where hedges create separate dining areas. The candlelit stone cellar is open from 6pm.

GETTING THERE & AWAY

Passau is on the main train line to Nuremberg (€32.90 to €43, two hours) and Regensburg (€20.50 to €26, one hour). There are also direct trains to Munich (€30.20, 2½ hours). The trip to Zwiesel (€19, 1½ hours) and other Bavarian Forest towns requires a change in Plattling.

BAVARIAN FOREST

Together with the Bohemian Forest on the Czech side of the border, the Bavarian Forest (Bayerischer Wald) forms the largest continuous woodland area in Europe. This inspiring landscape of peaceful rolling hills and rounded tree-covered peaks is interspersed with little-disturbed valleys and stretches of virgin woodland, providing a habitat for many species long since vanished from the rest of the region. A large area is protected as the surprisingly wild and remote Bavarian Forest National Park (Nationalpark Bayerischer Wald).

A centuries-old glass-blowing industry is still active in many of the towns along the **Glasstrasse** (Glass Road), a 250km holiday route connecting Waldsassen with Passau. You can visit the studios, workshops, museums and shops and stock up on traditional and contemporary designs.

INFORMATION

Grafenau tourist office (☎ 08552-962 343; www.grafenau.de; Rathausgasse 1; 8am-5pm Mon-Thu, 8am-1pm Fri, 10-11.30am Sat)

Zwiesel tourist office Town centre (☎ 09922-840 523; www.zwiesel-tourismus.de; Stadtplatz 27; 8.30am-5pm Mon-Fri, 10am-1pm Sat); Zwiesel-Süd (10am-noon Mon-Fri) The latter has English-speaking staff and is just outside town on the main road towards Regen.

SIGHTS

Frauenau's dazzlingly modern **Glasmuseum** (☎ 09926-941 020; Am Museumspark 1; adult/child €5/2.50; 9am-5pm Mon-Fri, 10am-4pm Sat & Sun) covers four millennia of glass-making history, starting with the ancient Egyptians and ending with modern glass art from around the world.

On the southern edge of the Bavarian Forest, in Tittling, there's the **Museumsdorf Bayerischer Wald** (☎ 08504-8482; Herrenstrasse 11; adult/child €4/free; 9am-5pm Apr-Oct). This 20-hectare open-air museum features 150 typical Bavarian Forest timber cottages and farmsteads from the 17th to the 19th centuries, with displays ranging from clothing and furniture to pottery and farming implements.

BAVARIAN FOREST NATIONAL PARK

A paradise for outdoor enthusiasts, the Bavarian Forest National Park stretches for about 24,250 hectares along the Czech border, from Bayerisch Eisenstein in the north to Finsterau in the south. Its thick forest, most of it mountain spruce, is criss-crossed by hundreds of kilometres of marked hiking, cycling and cross-country skiing trails. Around 1km northeast of the village of Neuschönau stands the **Hans-Eisenmann-Haus** (☎ 08558-961 50; www.nationalpark-bayerischer-wald.de; Böhmstrasse 35, Neuschönau; 9am-5pm), the national park's main visitor centre.

SLEEPING & EATING

Accommodation in this region is a real bargain; Zwiesel and Grafenau have the best choices.

Hotel-Gasthaus Zum Kellermann (☎ 08552-967 10; www.hotel-zum-kellermann.de; Stadtplatz 8, Grafenau; s/d €37/60; closed Wed; P) Fresh and airy rooms at very reasonable rates make this simple Grafenau guesthouse a good bet. There's a pretty terrace area outside and the restaurant (mains €6 to €12) supplies yummy local fare.

Hotel Hubertus (☎ 08552-964 90; www.hubertus-grafenau.de; Grüb 20, Grafenau; s €47-58, d €78-104; P) This elegant hotel in Grafenau offers incredible value for the weary traveller. The stylish rooms are spacious and most have balconies. Guests are treated to a pool and sauna, and delicious buffet meals.

Hotel Zur Waldbahn (☎ 09922-8570; www.zurwald bahn.de; Bahnhofplatz 2, Zwiesel; s €55-62, d €88-96; P) Tradition and modern comforts blend seamlessly at this friendly inn, conveniently located opposite the Hauptbahnhof. The warm, wood-panelled rooms are tastefully furnished, the restaurant is top-notch, and just check out that pool.

Dampfbräu (☎ 09922-605 30; Stadtplatz 6, Zwiesel; mains €8-15) Rustic hearts cut out of the chunky timber backrests, murals illustrating local industries, simple belly-fillers caught and picked in the surrounding forests, and tankards of locally brewed ale make this the most characterful tavern eatery in town.

GETTING THERE & AWAY

From Munich, Regensburg or Passau, Zwiesel is reached by rail via Plattling. The scenic Waldbahn shuttles directly between Zwiesel and Bodenmais and Zwiesel and Grafenau.

There's also a tight network of regional buses, though service can be infrequent. The Igel-Bus navigates around the national park on four routes.

FRANKFURT &
CENTRAL GERMANY

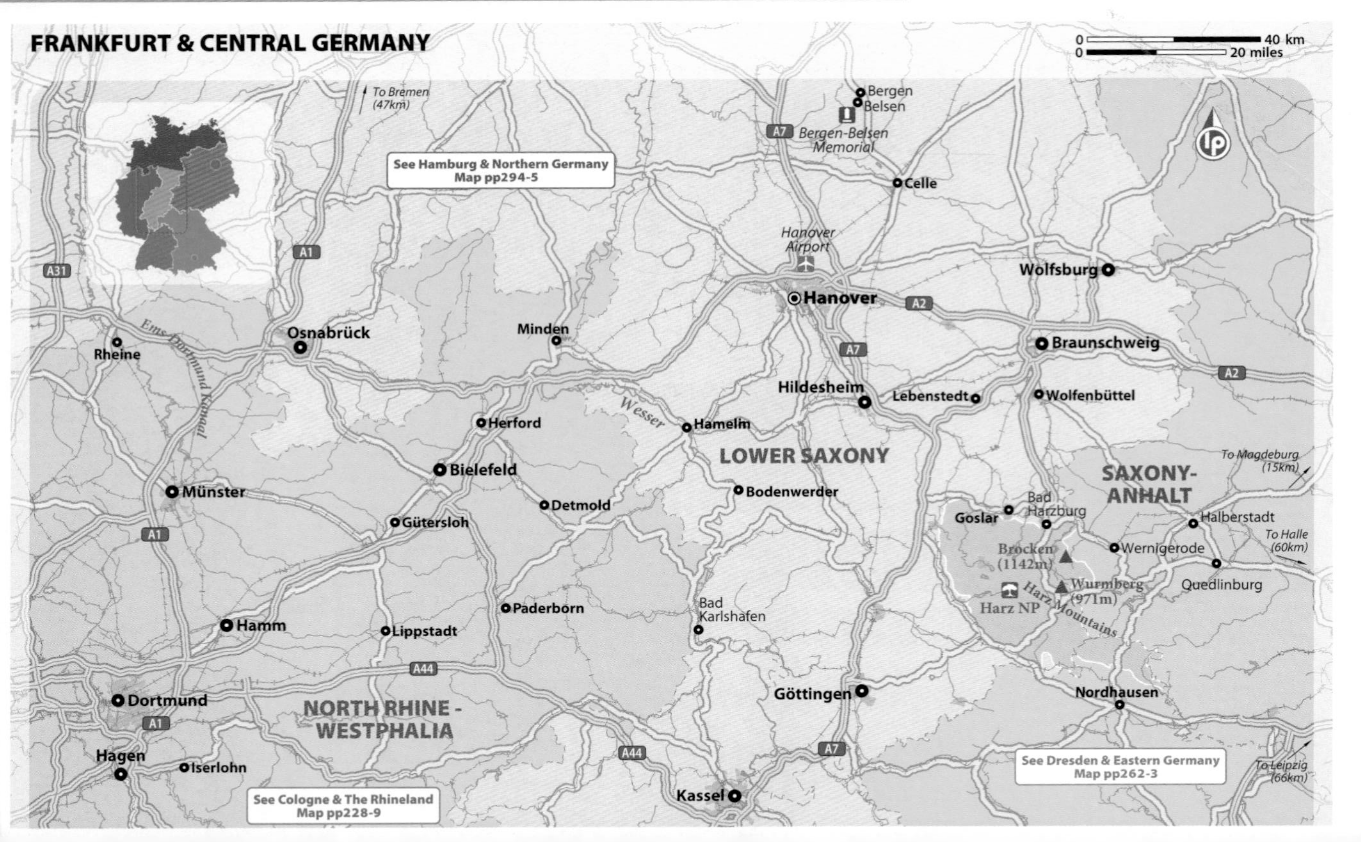
FRANKFURT & CENTRAL GERMANY
0 40 km
0 20 miles
To Bremen (47km)
See Hamburg & Northern Germany Map pp294-5
Bergen
Belsen
Bergen-Belsen Memorial
Celle
Hanover Airport
Hanover
Wolfsburg
Braunschweig
Wolfenbüttel
Lebenstedt
Hildesheim
Rheine
Ems-Dortmund Kanaal
Osnabrück
Minden
Herford
Wesser
Hameln
LOWER SAXONY
Bielefeld
Münster
Detmold
Gütersloh
Bodenwerder
To Magdeburg (15km)
SAXONY-ANHALT
Goslar
Bad Harzburg
Halberstadt
To Halle (60km)
Brocken (1142m)
Wernigerode
Quedlinburg
Wurmberg (971m)
Harz NP
Harz Mountains
Paderborn
Bad Karlshafen
Hamm
Lippstadt
Dortmund
NORTH RHINE - WESTPHALIA
Göttingen
Nordhausen
Hagen
Iserlohn
See Dresden & Eastern Germany Map pp262-3
To Leipzig (66km)
See Cologne & The Rhineland Map pp228-9
Kassel
A1
A2
A7
A31
A44

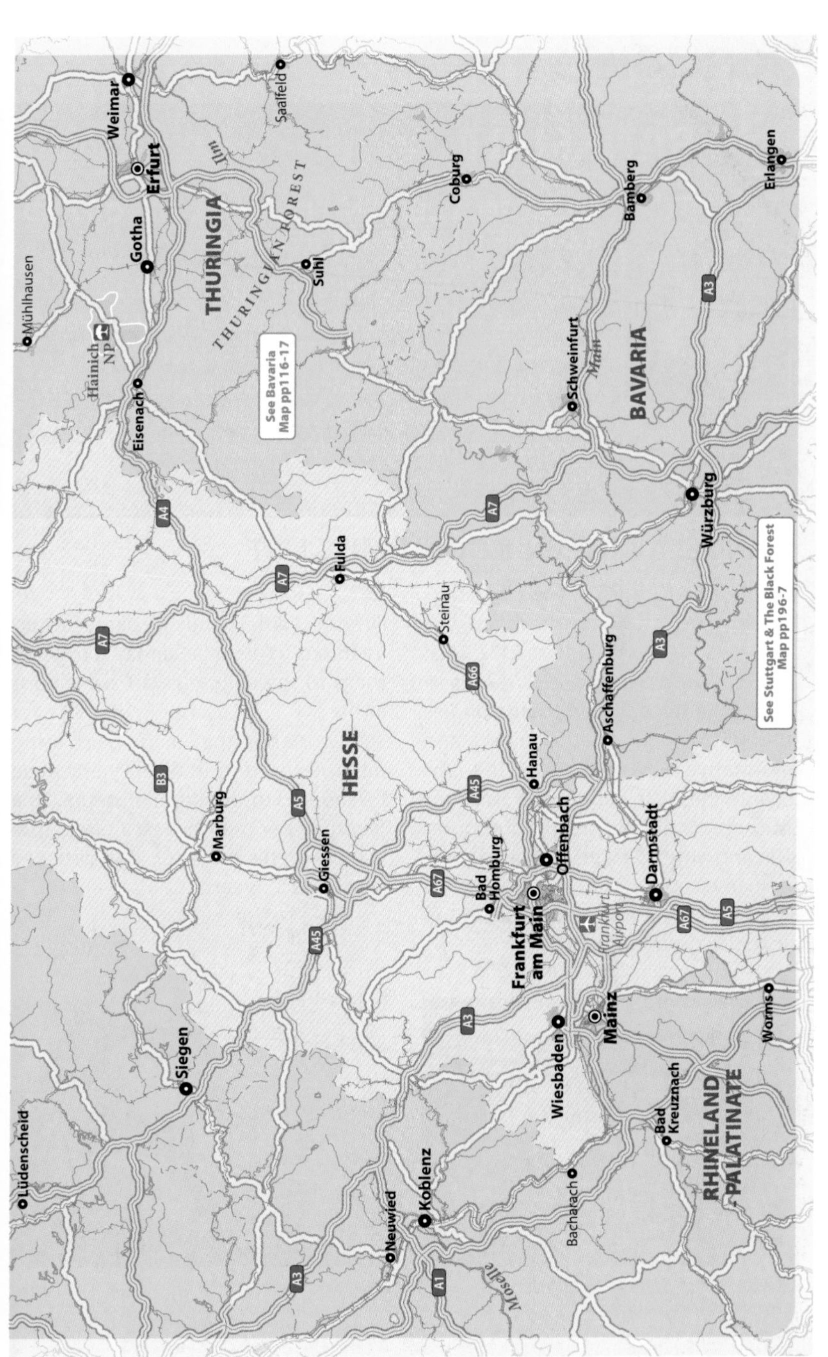
Mühlhausen
Weimar
Erfurt
Gotha
THURINGIA
THURINGIAN FOREST
Ilm
Saalfeld
Coburg
Suhl
Hainich NP
Eisenach
See Bavaria Map pp116-17
Schweinfurt
Main
BAVARIA
Bamberg
Erlangen
A3
A4
A7
Fulda
Würzburg
See Stuttgart & The Black Forest Map pp196-7
Steinau
A66
Aschaffenburg
HESSE
Hanau
A45
Marburg
B3
A5
Giessen
Offenbach
Bad Homburg
A67
Frankfurt am Main
Frankfurt Airport
Darmstadt
Mainz
Wiesbaden
Worms
Siegen
Lüdenscheid
Koblenz
Neuwied
A1
Mosel
Bacharach
Bad Kreuznach
RHINELAND-PALATINATE

HIGHLIGHTS

1 FRANKFURT

BY ANGELA CULLEN, FINANCIAL EDITOR AND 18-YEAR FRANKFURT RESIDENT

You have to hunt a little to find Frankfurt's treasures – it's filled with oodles of hidden facets tucked down alleyways. There's a great quality of life here – green spaces abound and it's really compact and easy to navigate, yet the city is still very international and the museum scene features world-class art.

ANGELA CULLEN'S DON'T MISS LIST

❶ RIDE THE EBBELWEI EXPRESS

It might be a tad touristy, but the **Apple Wine Express** (☎ 2132 2425; www.ebbelwei-express.com; adult/child under 14yr €6/3), a historic tram that trundles through town, is an entertaining and informative way to discover the city. It tours the main sights, but also runs through traditional neighbourhoods, showing you all facets of the city. As the name suggests, you also get to try Frankfurt's local tipple, apple wine, an alcoholic apple cider.

❷ KID-FRIENDLY STÄDEL

I've got children, and one of my favourite things to do on a Sunday is to bring them to the children's art workshops at the **Städel Museum** (p181). At a recent workshop they made paint using methods used in Botticelli's era while I wandered through the museum. One Saturday per month it also offers special children's tours for kids between eight and 13 years.

Clockwise from top: Reflections in the Main River, Frankfurt am Main (p178); Frankfurt skyline; Live jazz at Jazzkeller (p183); Artworks at the Städel Museum (p181); *Ebbelwei Express*

CLOCKWISE FROM TOP: RICHARD I'ANSON; MMX/IMAGEBROKER; HOLGER LEUE; URBANMYTH/ALAMY; HOLGER LEUE

❸ GET UP HIGH

Seeing Frankfurt, with its jagged skyscrapers and abundant green spaces, from a lofty spot is stunning. An alternative to the pricey **Main Tower** (p178) is the 43m-tall wooden tower **Goethe Turm** (**Sachsenhäuser Landwehrweg**) in Sachsenhausen; from the top you get a sweeping view of the city, including the *Bleistift* (pencil; p178) building. The ground-floor **Goetheruh Cafe** (☎ **686 830**) is bliss on a summer's day.

❹ CATCH SOME JAZZ

Frankfurt's got some excellent jazz venues tucked away. My favourite is the **Jazzkeller** (p183), which has been around since 1952. It's a fabulous, atmospheric little stone cellar that showcases an eclectic mix of local and European jazz bands. On Fridays it morphs into a fun dancing den, with Latin beats and funk.

THINGS YOU NEED TO KNOW

Top tip Avoid October – everything's full because of the book fair. **My Main** Over the last few years they've really cleaned up the riverfront along the Main. **Ebbelwei** Apple Wine is an acquired taste – give it a couple of tries and it grows on you. **See our author's review on p178**

HIGHLIGHTS

2

BERGEN-BELSEN CONCENTRATION CAMP

Unlike Auschwitz in Poland, none of the original buildings remain from Bergen-Belsen (p191), the most infamous concentration camp on German soil. Yet the large, peaceful-looking lumps of grassy earth – covered in beautiful purple heather in summer – soon reveal their true identity as mass graves. Signs indicate approximately how many people lie in each – 1000, 5000, an unknown number…

3

THE FAIRY-TALE ROAD

Germany's most famous brothers were inspired by the tranquil forests and towns covering this region, and a long list of fairy tales were set in towns here. The Fairy-Tale Road (p176) is a journey through your childhood memories of straw-spinning Rumpelstiltskin and long-haired Rapunzel, stopping off in such memorable towns as the Pied Piper's Hamelin, with its vast collection of rat statues.

4

HERRENHÄUSER GÄRTEN

A masterpiece of greenery and flowers, Herrenhäuser Gärten (p185), Hanover's expansive royal gardens, is a beautiful example of early-baroque-style gardening. Its 1666 Grosse Garten is the largest in this series of gardens, with a maze of Low German roses and flowers, plus French baroque and rococo touches.

5

GOSLAR

The ancient Hanseatic town of Goslar (p192), at the foot of the Harz Mountains, has a cornucopia of half-timbered houses (over 1000) in its 13th-century streets – but some say their favourite part is the chiming clock in the town centre, where a procession of mechanical miners march out from the clock three times a day.

6

HOME OF THE VOLKSWAGEN

In Wolfsburg (p191), they make sure you know whose turf you're on: a giant VW sign proudly waves from the top of the company HQ. You'll see all the VW marques, like the Bentley and Lamborghini, but it's the icon of Germany's postwar *Wirtschaftswunder* (economic miracle; see p348), the Beetle, that really enchants the masses.

2 Bergen-Belsen concentration camp (p191); 3 Building decoration, Hamelin (p188); 4 Herrenhäuser Gärten (p185), Hanover; 5 Markt, Goslar (p192) ; 6 VW 1200 at the Autostadt (p192), Wolfsburg

THE BEST...

THINGS FOR FREE

- Celle's Synagogue (p191), a beautiful half-timbered house, holds regular services.
- From October to March, Hanover's Herrenhäuser Gärten (p185) doesn't charge admission, but stays gorgeous.
- Goethe Turm (p171) Climb up for a spectacular view of the city.

LOCAL WATERING HOLES

- Markthalle (p187) Hanover's covered market is always great for a snack or bag of gourmet groceries, but on Friday evenings the after-work crowd piles in to imbibe and celebrate the start of the weekend.
- Jazzkeller (p183) Drinks, jazz and sometimes dancing in one of Frankfurt's faves.
- Wein-Dünker (p183) Sick of beer? Sample quality German rieslings in this convivial Frankfurt wine bar.

KID-FRIENDLY SPOTS

- Look for the Pied Piper and rat symbols in the rat catcher's old stomping grounds, Hamelin (p188).
- Watch the city trumpeter climb the tower and blow his horn at Celle's Stadtkirche (p191).
- Ponder Rapunzel's locks at the Brüder Grimm-Museum (Museum of the Brothers Grimm; p185) in Kassel.

MUSEUMS OFF THE RADAR

- Kunstmuseum (p191) Celle's excellent collection of German art.
- Jüdisches Museum (p180) Jewish life in Frankfurt from the Middle Ages onward.
- Goslarer Museum (p194) Covering the history of the Harz mountains.

High-speed train at Frankfurt Airport train station

THINGS YOU NEED TO KNOW

VITAL STATISTICS

- **Population** Frankfurt 659,000; Hesse six million; Lower Saxony eight million
- **Percentage of Frankfurt population that is foreign** 26%
- **Points of entry** Frankfurt and Hanover airports
- **Best time to visit** April–October

ADVANCE PLANNING

- **Six months before** Check to make sure there aren't any major conventions coinciding with your visit (like October's Frankfurt Book Fair) – if something major is going on, book your hotel now.
- **Two weeks before** Pick up a copy of one of the Grimms' fairy tales to read on the trip.

RESOURCES

- **www.frankfurtexpat.de** Local listings website in English, written by resident expats.

EMERGENCY NUMBERS

- **Fire/Ambulance** (☎ 112)
- **Police** (☎ 110)

GETTING AROUND

- **Train** The trains in this region are comfortable, efficient and relaxing – there's absolutely no reason to hire a car, and parking in cities like Frankfurt gets expensive. Plan your journey and book tickets in advance on www.bahn.de.
- **Frankfurt U-Bahn & S-Bahn** (p184) Runs between 4am and 12.30am (until 1am on weekends). So reliable they promise to refund the price of your ticket if you're delayed by more than 10 minutes – it's called the *10-Minuten Garantie* (10-minute guarantee).

BE FOREWARNED

- **Near the train station** The area northeast of the Hauptbahnhof is a base for Frankfurt's trade in sex and illegal drugs. Women in particular might want to avoid Elbestrasse and Taunusstrasse, the main red-light district. Frequent police and private security patrols of the station and the surrounding Bahnhofsviertel keep things under control, but it's always advisable to use big-city common sense.

FRANKFURT & CENTRAL GERMANY ITINERARIES

FRANKFURT OR BUST Three Days

If you're pressed for time, base yourself in Frankfurt and explore it in full, with a day trip to Kassel on the side – there's much more than just a stock market in this financial centre.

Book yourself a room in **(1) Frankfurt** (p181) and take a ride on the **(2) Ebbelwei Express** (p170), which will take you past all the major sights and give you a feel for the city. Round out your day by sampling **(3) Handkäse** (hand cheese; p184) for dinner (no fart jokes, please). The next day, check out what's on at the impressive **(4) Städel Museum** (p181), **(5) Museum für Angewandte Kunst** (p181) and the **(6) Liebieghaus** (p181) – all conveniently located in a row on the *Museumsufer* (Museum Embankment). Pay a visit to **(7) Goethe-Haus** (p180), where the legendary writer was born, and finish off the day with some Turkish fare at **(8) Manolya** (p183) followed by relaxing tunes at the **(9) Jazzkeller** (p183). Next, take a day trip up to **(10) Kassel** (p184), where you can explore the fabulous **(11) Brüder Grimm-Museum** (p185).

FAIRY-TALE ROAD Five Days

Kids and adults alike will love flipping the pages of their favourite fairy tale in these bucolic surroundings. Rent a car and start in the Brothers Grimm university town, **(1) Kassel** (p184), paying a visit to the **(2) Brüder Grimm-Museum** (p185). Continue north to **(3) Hamelin** (p188) and spend a few nights here – you'll need the time to trace the Pied Piper's legacy all over town and to find all those rat symbols. From here, take a day trip to the **(4) Münchhausen Museum** (p190) in Bodenwerder to contemplate one of history's most shameless fibbers, Baron Hieronymous von Münchhausen. Leave Grimm and the liar behind and head north to **(5) Bremen City** (p318), whose **(6) Town Musicians of Bremen** (p319) statue greets you in an oddly quiet fashion.

LITTLE CITY BIG CITY One Week

Spend a week hopping from a small, underrated city to the international financial hub of Germany; this entire itinerary can be done by train. **(1) Hanover** (p185) gets a bad rap, but it is a delightful little city with oodles of day trips on its doorstep. Base yourself here for five nights and start with a visit to its celebrated **(2) Herrenhäuser Gärten** (p185), a series of three impressive gardens that rival Versailles. Next, head to the **(3) Die Nanas** (p186), the voluptuous, fluorescent-coloured 'Sophie', 'Charlotte' and 'Caroline' sculptures – they're

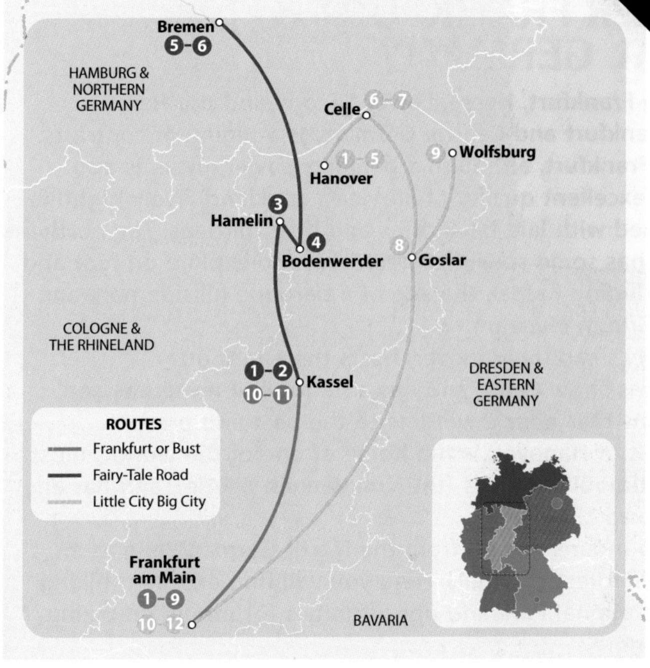

the pride of the city. Stroll through the Altstadt (old town) to see the Gothic (4) Marktkirche (p187) before hopping on a Maschsee-bound bus (number 131) for dinner at (5) Pier 51 (p187), one of Hanover's most revered restaurants. Take a day trip to historic (6) Celle (p190) and explore its multilayered (7) Schloss (p191) and half-timbered houses. Next spend a day in (8) Goslar (p192), the tranquil Unesco World Heritage town flanked by the Harz Mountains, and for a change of pace, hit the (9) Autostadt (p192) in Wolfsburg to see how the Volkswagen Beetle is made. Now it's time to move on to (10) Frankfurt (p178), where you should start with a ride on the (11) Ebbelwei Express (p170) and end with a visit to a traditional (12) Sachsenhausen tavern (p184).

ANKFURT & MANY

Hesse, Lower Saxony and the Harz Central Germany is a region of contrasts. though a banking powerhouse, is also uality of life, leafy parkland, lively nightlife l-back cafes and beer gardens. The northern plendid green areas to explore on foot and by bicycle, including Kassel, the site of a baroque hillside park and the Brothers Grimm Museum.

Lower Saxony's capital, Hanover, hosts the enormous communications show CeBit, and has a handful of museums and historic gardens that offer a window to the past and present. Wolfsburg, east of Hanover, is the home of one of the world's most successful automobile models (the Volkswagen Beetle), and has an unusually relaxed character.

The Harz Mountains rise up from the North German Plain as an 'island' of high, forest-clad hills. Here you will find excellent hiking trails in Harz National Park and opportunities for mountain-biking and road cycling.

HESSE

FRANKFURT AM MAIN

Unashamedly high-rise, Frankfurt-on-the-Main (pronounced 'mine') is unlike any other German city. Bristling with jagged skyscrapers, 'Mainhattan' – the focal point of an urban area with over 5 million inhabitants – is a true capital of finance and business, home base for one of the world's largest stock exchanges as well as the European Central Bank (www.ecb.int). Yet Frankfurt consistently ranks as one of the world's most liveable cities, with a rich collection of museums (second only to Berlin's), lots of parks and greenery, a lively student scene, excellent public transport, fine dining and plenty to do in the evening.

INFORMATION

Tourist office (**☎ 2123 8800, for hotel reservations 2123 0808; www.frankfurt-tourismus.de**) Altstadt (**Römerberg 27, inside Römer; 9.30am-5.30pm Mon-Fri, 9.30am-4pm Sat & Sun; Dom/Römer**); Hauptbahnhof (**8am-9pm Mon-Fri, 9am-6pm Sat & Sun; Frankfurt Hauptbahnhof**) Behind track 13.

SIGHTS & ACTIVITIES

ALTSTADT

A good place to start getting a feel for the city is 200m above it, on the viewing platform atop the **Main Tower** (**☎ 3650 4777; www.maintower-restaurant.de; Neue Mainzer Strasse 52-58; Alte Oper; elevator fee adult/student & senior €5/3.50; 10am-9pm Sun-Thu, 10am-11pm Fri & Sat late Mar-late Oct, 10am-7pm Sun-Thu, 10am-9pm Fri & Sat late Oct-late Mar, weather permitting**). Off to the west is the 256m-high **Messeturm**, which locals call the *Bleistift* (pencil).

The **Frankfurter Dom** (**cathedral; www.dom-frankfurt.de, in German; Dom/Römer; officially 9am-noon & 2.30-6pm, often opens earlier, closes later & stays open at noon**), one of

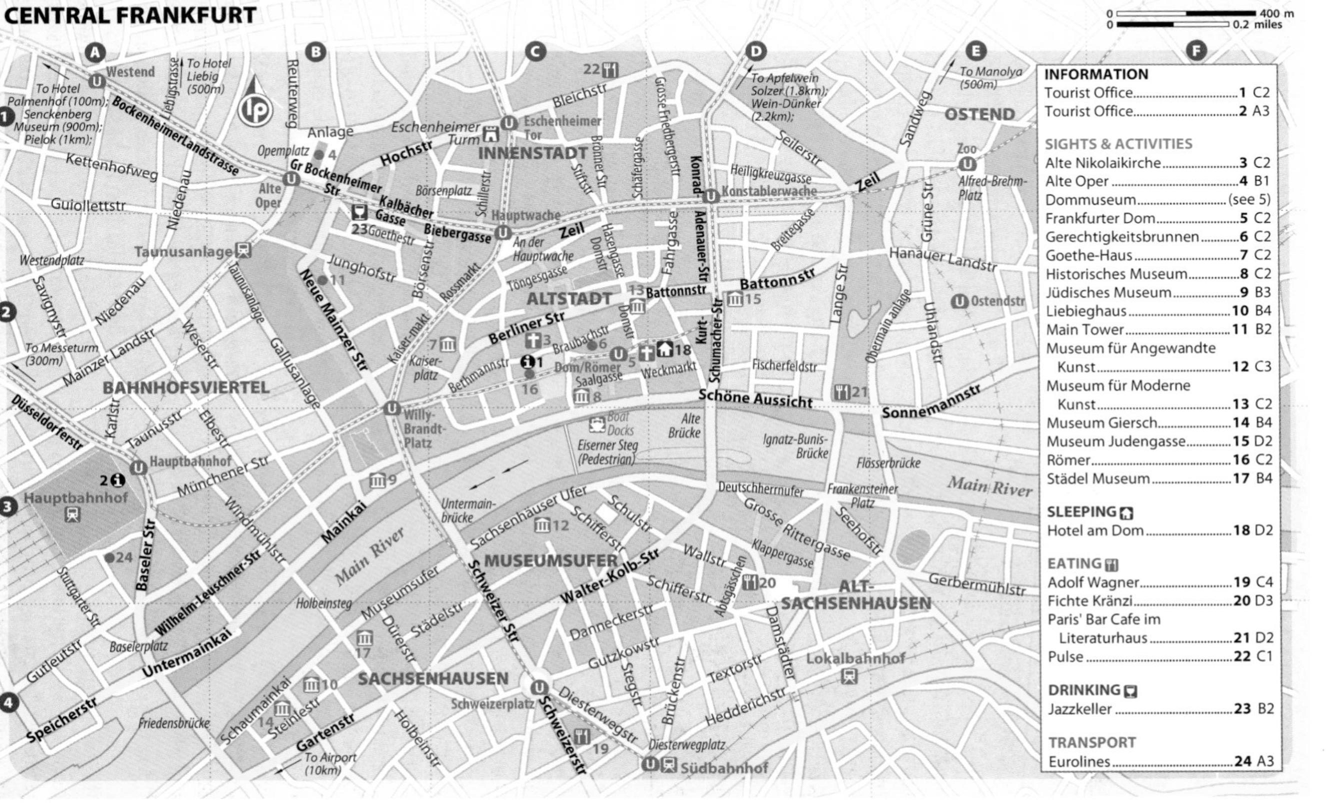
CENTRAL FRANKFURT
0 400 m
0 0.2 miles
INFORMATION
Tourist Office 1 C2
Tourist Office 2 A3
SIGHTS & ACTIVITIES
Alte Nikolaikirche 3 C2
Alte Oper 4 B1
Dommuseum (see 5)
Frankfurter Dom 5 C2
Gerechtigkeitsbrunnen 6 C2
Goethe-Haus 7 C2
Historisches Museum 8 C2
Jüdisches Museum 9 B3
Liebieghaus 10 B4
Main Tower 11 B2
Museum für Angewandte Kunst 12 C3
Museum für Moderne Kunst 13 C2
Museum Giersch 14 B4
Museum Judengasse 15 D2
Römer 16 C2
Städel Museum 17 B4
SLEEPING
Hotel am Dom 18 D2
EATING
Adolf Wagner 19 C4
Fichte Kränzi 20 D3
Paris' Bar Cafe im Literaturhaus 21 D2
Pulse 22 C1
DRINKING
Jazzkeller 23 B2
TRANSPORT
Eurolines 24 A3
To Hotel Palmenhof (100m); Senckenberg Museum (900m); Pielok (1km);
To Hotel Liebig (500m)
To Messeturm (300m)
To Apfelwein Solzer (1.8km); Wein-Dünker (2.2km);
To Manolya (500m)
To Airport (10km)
Westend
INNENSTADT
ALTSTADT
BAHNHOFSVIERTEL
OSTEND
MUSEUMSUFER
SACHSENHAUSEN
ALT-SACHSENHAUSEN
Main River
Hauptbahnhof
Südbahnhof
Lokalbahnhof
Zoo
Hauptwache
Konstablerwache
Willy-Brandt-Platz
Dom/Römer
Alte Oper
Eschenheimer Tor
Eschenheimer Turm
Taunusanlage
Opernplatz
Ostendstr
Alfred-Brehm-Platz
Zeil
Neue Mainzer Str
BockenheimerLandstrasse
Mainzer Landstr
Berliner Str
Konrad-Adenauer-Str
Kurt-Schumacher-Str
Battonnstr
Hanauer Landstr
Sonnemannstr
Schöne Aussicht
Schweizer Str
Walter-Kolb-Str
Schaumainkai
Untermainkai
Mainkai
Sachsenhäuser Ufer
Wilhelm-Leuschner-Str
Baseler Str
Düsseldorferstr
Untermainbrücke
Eiserner Steg (Pedestrian)
Alte Brücke
Ignatz-Bunis-Brücke
Flösserbrücke
Holbeinsteg
Friedensbrücke

HOLGER LEUE

Römerberg facades, Frankfurt

RÖMERBERG

The Römerberg, a long block west of the Dom, is Frankfurt's old central square, where postwar-restored 14th- and 15th-century buildings, including the early Gothic, Protestant Alte Nikolaikirche, provide a glimpse of how beautiful the city once was. In the centre is the Gerechtigkeitsbrunnen (Font of Justice); in 1612, at the coronation of Matthias, the fountain ran with wine!

The old town hall, or Römer, in the northwestern corner of Römerberg, is made up of three re-created step-gabled 15th-century houses. In the time of the Holy Roman Empire, it was the site of celebrations during the election and coronation of emperors; today it's the registry office and houses the office of Frankfurt's mayor. Inside, the Kaisersaal is adorned with portraits of 52 rulers.

Things you need to know: Römerberg (**Dom/Römer**); Kaiseraal (**Imperial Hall; ☎ 2123 4814; adult/student €2/1; 10am-1pm & 2-5pm, closed during events**)

the few structures to survive the 1944 bombing, is dominated by an elegant, Gothic-style tower (95m), begun in the 1400s and completed in the 1860s.

The Dommuseum (**cathedral museum; ☎ 1337 6816; www.dommuseum-frankfurt.de, in German; adult/student €3/2; 10am-5pm Tue-Fri, 11am-5pm Sat, Sun & holidays**) has a collection of precious liturgical objects and sells tickets for Dom tours (**in German; adult/student €3/2; 3pm Tue-Sun**).

The well-regarded Museum für Moderne Kunst (**Museum of Modern Art; ☎ 2123 0447; www.mmk-frankfurt.de; Domstrasse 10; adult/student & senior €8/4; 10am-6pm Tue-Sun, to 8pm Wed; Dom/Römer**), dubbed the 'slice of cake' because of its distinctive triangular footprint, focuses on European and American art from the 1960s to the present, with frequent temporary exhibits.

Fans of the Enlightenment and German literature may want to drop by the Goethe-Haus (**☎ 138 800; www.goethehaus-frankfurt.de; Grosser Hirschgraben 23-25; adult/student €5/2.50; 10am-6pm Mon-Sat, to 5.30pm Sun; Willy-Brandt-Platz**), birthplace of Johann Wolfgang von Goethe (1749–1832). The furnishings are mainly reproductions but original pieces include Goethe's grandmother's writing desk and the great man's childhood puppet theatre.

Inaugurated in 1880, the Renaissance-style Alte Oper (Old Opera House) was burnt out in 1944, narrowly avoided being razed and replaced with 1960s cubes, and was finally reconstructed (1976–81) to resemble the original, its facade graced with statues of Goethe and Mozart.

The Jüdisches Museum (**☎ 2123 5000; www.jewishmuseum.de; Untermainkai 14-15; adult/student €4/2; 10am-5pm Tue-Sun, to 8pm Wed; Willy-Brandt-Platz**), on the north Main bank in the former residence of the Rothschild family, has exhibits on Jewish life in the city from the Middle Ages onward, with details on well-known Frankfurt Jews persecuted, exiled or murdered by the Nazis.

In the northwest corner of Sachsenhausen, museums crowd the south bank of the Main along the Museumsufer (Museum Embankment). From west to east, the Museumsufer museums include the following:

Liebieghaus (☎ **650 0490; www.liebieghaus.de; Schaumainkai 71; adult/under 12yr/student & senior/family €8/free/6/14; 10am-6pm Tue & Fri-Sun, to 9pm Wed & Thu; Schweizerplatz)** The superb collection includes Greek, Roman, medieval, Renaissance and baroque works, plus a recently redone Egyptian section and some items from East Asia.

Museum für Angewandte Kunst (Museum of Applied Arts; ☎ 2123 4037; www.angewandtekunst-frankfurt.de; Schaumainkai 17; adult/concession €5/2.50; 10am-5pm Tue & Thu-Sun, to 9pm Wed; Schweizerplatz) Displays furniture, textiles, metalwork, glass and ceramics from Europe and Asia. Set in lovely gardens, with a smart cafe and outdoor seating.

Städel Museum (☎ 605 0980; www.staedelmuseum.de; Schaumainkai 63; adult/under 12yr/student & senior/family €10/free/8/18, audioguide €4; 10am-6pm Tue & Fri-Sun, to 9pm Wed & Thu; Schweizerplatz) This institution, founded in 1815, has a world-class collection of works by 14th- to 20th-century painters, including Botticelli, Dürer, Van Eyck, Rembrandt, Renoir, Rubens, Vermeer and Cézanne, plus Frankfurt natives such as Hans Holbein.

SLEEPING

Hotel am Dom (☎ 138 1030; www.hotelamdom.de; Kannengiessergasse 3, Altstadt; s/d/apt €90/120/130; Dom/Römer) This unprepossessing, 30-room hotel has immaculate rooms, apartments with kitchenettes and four-person suites just a few paces from the cathedral.

our pick Hotel Liebig (☎ 2418 2990; www.hotelliebig.de; Liebigstrasse 45, Westend; s €112-170, d €138-205, q €360, weekends s/d/q from €95/115/295, d during fairs up to €295; P ; Westend) In the verdant Westend, this Italian-run family hotel has 19 bright rooms with wood floors and stylish bathrooms. Prices include breakfast on weekends only.

RICHARD I'ANSON

Historic buildings on the Römerberg, Frankfurt

FRANKFURT & CENTRAL GERMANY

HESSE

Hotel Palmenhof (☎ 753 0060; www.palmenhof.com; Bockenheimer Landstrasse 89-91, Westend; s €119-149, d €159-175, weekends s €75-90, d €85-100, breakfast €16; P ⊠ 💻; Ⓤ Westend or Bockenheimer Warte) Built in 1890, this veteran establishment has 45 understated but tasteful rooms with classical furnishings.

HOLGER LEUE

Museum Giersch, Frankfurt

IF YOU LIKE...

If you like Frankfurt's exceptional **museum scene**, check out these other exceptional displays of Frankfurt history, Jewish life and natural history:

- **Historisches Museum** (☎ 2123 5599; www.historisches-museum.frankfurt.de, in German; Saalgasse 19; adult/concession €4/2; 10am-6pm Tue-Sun, to 9pm Wed; Ⓤ Dom/Römer) Established to showcase Frankfurt's long and fascinating history, this museum will soon move across the square from its current uninspiring building to several old town houses.
- **Museum Judengasse** (☎ 297 7419; Kurt-Schumacher-Strasse 10; adult/student €2/1, incl same-day entry to Jüdisches Museum €5/2.50; 10am-5pm Tue-Sun, to 8pm Wed; Ⓤ Konstablerwache) Along the northeastern boundaries of the old city fortifications, you can see the excavated remains of houses and ritual baths from the Jewish ghetto, most of which was destroyed by a French bombardment in 1796.
- **Senckenberg Museum** (☎ 754 20; www.senckenberg.de; Senckenberganlage 25; adult/student/senior/family €6/3/5/15, audioguide €3; 9am-5pm Mon, Tue, Thu & Fri, to 8pm Wed, to 6pm Sat, Sun & holidays; Ⓤ Bockenheimer Warte) A solid neobaroque building from the early 1900s houses Frankfurt's fine natural-history museum, which has full-sized dinosaur mock-ups out front – great for the kiddies – and, inside, exhibits on palaeontology, biology and geology.
- **Museum Giersch** (☎ 6330 4128; www.museum-giersch.de, in German; Schaumainkai 83; adult/student €5/2.50; noon-7pm Tue-Thu, noon-5pm Fri, 11am-5pm Sat & Sun; Ⓤ Schweizerplatz) Along the Museumsufer, this local favourite puts on special exhibitions of works by lesser-known Hesse artists from the 19th and early 20th centuries.

our pick Villa Orange (☎ 405 840; www.villa-orange.de; Hebelstrasse 1, Nordend; s/d from €128/158, weekends €90/99, during fairs up to €255/275; P ⊠ ⁙ 🖳 ; Musterschule) Offering tranquillity, modern German design and small-hotel comforts (eg a quiet corner library), this century-old villa has 38 spacious rooms. Breakfast is organic.

EATING & DRINKING

Eckhaus (☎ 491 197; Bornheimer Landstrasse 45; mains €8-17.50; 5pm-midnight Mon-Thu, 5pm-1am Fri, 10am-1am Sat, 10am-midnight Sun; Merianplatz) The smoke-stained walls and ancient floorboards suggest an inelegant, long-toothed past. The hallmark *Kartoffelrösti* (shredded potato pancake; €9) has been served here for over 100 years.

Pielok (☎ 776 468; www.restaurant-pielok.de, in German; Jordanstrasse 3; mains €8.20-15.30; 11.30am-2.30pm & 5.30-10.30pm Mon-Fri & during trade fairs Sun, 5.30-10.30pm Sat; V ; Bockenheimer Warte) Without claiming to be special, this place – run by the same family since 1945 – somehow is: loyal regulars, students and workers tread a path here for *bürgerlich* (good, plain) German fare at reasonable prices.

Manolya (☎ 494 0162; Habsburger Allee 6; mains €9.50-18.50; 5pm-1am Mon-Thu, 11am-2am Fri & Sat, 11am-midnight Sun; Höhenstrasse) This well-regarded Turkish restaurant, opened in 1992, has a convivial atmosphere and outdoor seating.

Pulse (☎ 1388 6802; www.pulse-frankfurt.de/page, in German; Bleichstrasse 38a; mains €11.50-14.50; 10am-1am Sun-Thu, to 4am Fri & Sat; Konstablerwache) A laid-back restaurant, bar and nightclub rolled into one. This place is officially gay but ends up very mixed, especially on weekends.

our pick **Paris' Bar Café im Literaturhaus** (☎ 2108 5985; www.paris-literaturhaus.de, in German; Schöne Aussicht 2; mains €15-23; 11am-midnight Mon-Fri, 6pm-midnight Sat, 11am-6pm Sun; Dom/Römer) Inside an imposing, colonnaded venue for literary events, this semiformal restaurant offers consistently excellent meat and fish, including superlative rump steak (€19).

our pick **Wein-Dünker** (☎ 451 993; Berger Strasse 265; wine per glass from €2.10; noon-2am or 3am Mon-Sat, 6pm-2am or 3am Sun; Bornheim Mitte) This musty little wine cellar, down to the right as you enter the courtyard, is not retro, it's real. Descend, rub your eyes and try some of Germany's finest.

Jazzkeller (☎ 288 537; www.jazzkeller.com; Kleine Bockenheimer Strasse 18a, Innenstadt; admission €5-20; 9pm-2am Tue-Thu, 10pm-3am Fri & Sat, 8pm-2am Sun; Hauptwache) Look hard to find this place – a great jazz venue with mood – hidden in a cellar under an alley that intersects Goethestrasse at an oblique angle.

GETTING THERE & AWAY

AIR

Frankfurt Airport (FRA; ☎ 01805-372 4636; www.frankfurt-airport.com; Flughafen), 12km southwest of downtown, is Germany's busiest airport, with the highest cargo turnover and the third-highest passenger numbers in Europe (after London's Heathrow and Paris' Charles de Gaulle).

BUS

Long-distance buses leave from the south side of the Hauptbahnhof, where you'll find **Eurolines** (☎ 790 3253; www.eurolines.eu; Mannheimer Strasse 15; 7.30am-7.30pm Mon-Fri, 7.30am-2pm Sat, 7.30am-1pm Sun; Frankfurt Hauptbahnhof), with services to most European destinations.

TRAIN

The Hauptbahnhof, west of the centre, handles more departures and arrivals than any other station in Germany, which

EBBELWEI & HANDKÄSE MIT MUSIK

Frankfurt delicacies are best experienced in the city's traditional taverns, which serve *Ebbelwei* (*Ebbelwoi;* Frankfurt dialect for *Apfelwein,* ie apple wine) along with local specialities like *Handkäse mit Musik* (hand-cheese with music).

Handkäse mit Musik is the sort of name you could only find in Germany. It describes a round cheese marinated in oil and vinegar with onions, served with bread and butter and no fork. As you might imagine, this potent mixture tends to give one a healthy dose of wind – the release of which, ladies and gentlemen, is the music part.

Atmospheric joints (most in Sachsenhausen) serving *Ebbelwei* and local dishes:

Adolf Wagner (☎ **612 565; www.apfelwein-wagner.com, in German; Schweizerstrasse 69, Sachsenhausen;** Ⓤ **Schweizerplatz**) Warm and woody.

Apfelwein Solzer (☎ **452 171; www.solzer-frankfurt.de; Berger Strasse 260, Bornheim; Handkäse €2.60;** ⌚ **6pm-midnight Mon-Sat, 1-10pm Sun May-Oct, from 5pm daily in winter;** Ⓤ **Bornheim Mitte**) With wood-panelled walls and a covered courtyard.

Fichte Kränzi (☎ **612 778; www.fichtekraenzi.de; Wallstrasse 5, Sachsenhausen;** ⌚ **5pm-midnight;** Ⓢ **Lokalbahnhof**) Has smoke-stained murals and great atmosphere.

means that there are convenient trains to pretty much anywhere, including Berlin (€111, four hours).

Long-haul services from Frankfurt Airport include ICE trains to Hamburg (€107, four hours), Hanover (€81, 2½ hours) and Stuttgart (€56, 1¼ hours) every two hours; to Cologne (€60, one hour) and Dortmund (€81, 2¼ hours) two or three times an hour; and south towards Basel (€70, three hours, hourly).

GETTING AROUND

TO/FROM THE AIRPORT

S-Bahn lines S8 and S9 shuttle between the airport and the city centre (one way €3.70, 15 minutes), stopping at Hauptbahnhof, Hauptwache and Konstablerwache, as well as Wiesbaden and Mainz.

PUBLIC TRANSPORT

Frankfurt's excellent transport network, run by **traffiQ** (☎ **01805-069 960; www.traffiq.de, in German**), integrates all bus, tram, S-Bahn and U-Bahn lines (in general the U-Bahn is underground only in the city centre).

KASSEL

Postwar reconstruction left Kassel, on the Fulda River two hours north of Frankfurt, with lots of particularly unattractive 1950s buildings. Still, visitors will find a glorious baroque park and some surprisingly interesting museums, including one dedicated to the Brothers Grimm.

INFORMATION

Kassel Tourist Kassel-Wilhelmshöhe train station (☎ **340 54; www.kassel-tourist.de;** ⌚ **9am-6pm Mon-Fri, to 1pm Sat**); Rathaus (☎ **707 707; Obere Königsstrasse 8;** ⌚ **9am-6pm Mon-Fri, to 2pm Sat**)

SIGHTS

Museum Fridericianum (⌚ **707 2720; www.fridericianum-kassel.de; Friedrichsplatz 18**) and, southeast across Friedrichsplatz, the striking documenta Halle (☎ 707 270; www.documentahalle.de, in German; Du-Ry-Strasse 1) host changing exhibitions of contemporary art.

Wilhelm and Jakob Grimm began compiling folk stories while living in Kassel. Their lives and stories, now available in almost 200 languages, are featured at the Brüder Grimm-Museum (Museum of the Brothers Grimm; ☎ 103 235; www.grimms.de; Schöne Aussicht 2; adult/student €1.50/1; 10am-5pm, to 8pm Wed), across the street from the Neue Galerie.

GETTING THERE & AWAY

Rail destinations from Kassel Hauptbahnhof and/or Kassel-Wilhelmshöhe (Fernbahnhof) include Marburg (€17.60, 1¼ hours) and Frankfurt am Main (RE/ICE €30.70/48, 125/80 minutes).

LOWER SAXONY

HANOVER

To most of the world, Hanover is known for its huge CeBit information and communications technology fair, but the city also boasts acres of greenery and its spectacularly baroque Herrenhäuser Gärten (gardens) are a mini-Versailles, featuring a sparkly Niki de Saint Phalle Grotto. The compact centre, only partially reconstructed in a medieval style after WWII bombing, is adjoined to the east by the Eilenreide forest, and you can enjoy some good museums en route to the southern lake Maschsee.

INFORMATION

Hannover Tourismus (☎ information 1234 5111, room reservations 123 4555; www.hannover.de, www.hannover-tourism.de; Ernst-August-Platz 8; 9am-6pm Mon-Fri, to 2pm Sat, also 9am-2pm Sun Apr-Sep)

SIGHTS

An excellent way to get your bearings in Hanover is to visit the Neues Rathaus (built in 1901–13) and travel 98m to the top in the curved lift (elevator; adult/concession €2.50/2; 9.30am-6pm Mon-Fri, 10am-6pm Sat & Sun Apr-Nov) inside its green dome.

Largely modelled on the gardens at Versailles, the Herrenhäuser Gärten (☎ 1684 7576, 1234 5333; www.herrenhaeuser-gaerten.de; 9am-sunset; 4 or 5 to Herrenhäuser Gärten) truly rank among Hanover's most memorable attractions. On the one hand, the Grosser Garten (Large Garden), Berggarten (Mountain Garden) and Georgengarten (Georgian Garden) are prime examples of why Hanover calls itself a city 'in green'. On the other, the statues, fountains and

ANDREA SCHULTE-PEEVERS

A Niki de Saint Phalle *Die Nanas* sculpture (p186)

FRANKFURT & CENTRAL GERMANY

LOWER SAXONY

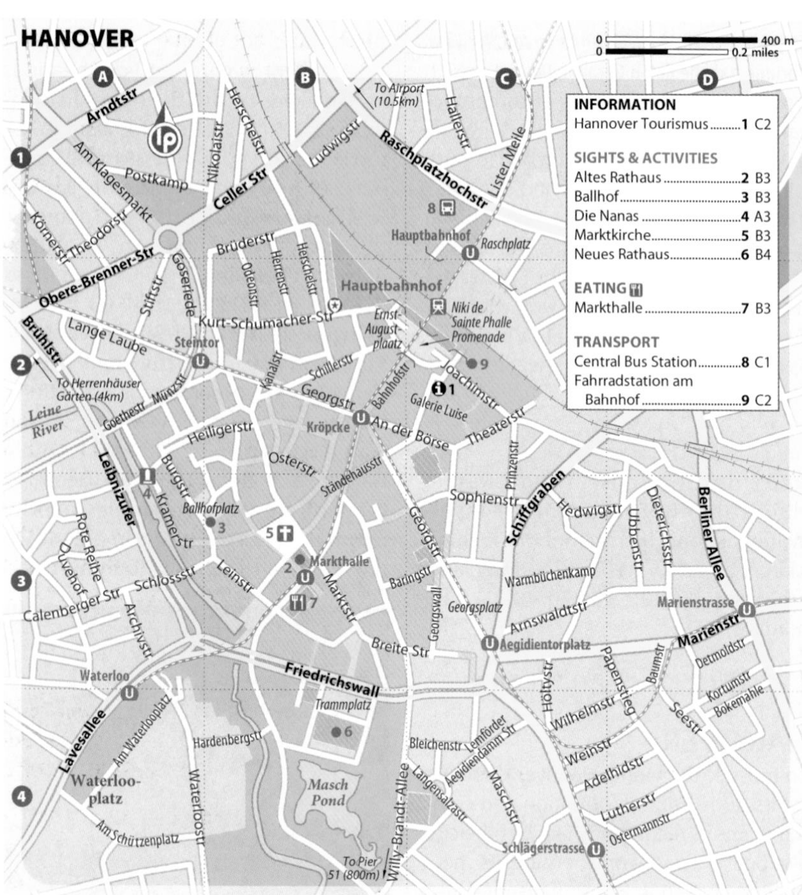

coloured tile walls of the **Niki de Saint Phalle Grotto** (opened after her death in 2002) provide a magical showcase of the artist's work that could one day outshine *Die Nanas*.

With its fountains, neat flowerbeds, trimmed hedges and shaped lawns, the 300-year-old **Grosser Garten** (**admission €3, incl entry to Berggarten €4, child free, Grosser Garten free mid-Oct–Mar**) is the centrepiece of the experience. There's a maze near the northern entrance, while the **Grosse Fontäne** (Big Fountain; the tallest in Europe) at the southern end jets water up to 80m high. In summer, there are **Wasserspiele** (**water games; 11am-noon & 3-5pm Mon-Fri, 11am-noon & 2-5pm Sat & Sun Apr-late Oct**) when all fountains are synchronised.

The city government was inundated with nearly 20,000 letters of complaint when the three earth-mama sculptures, **Die Nanas**, were first installed beside the Leine River in 1974. Now, the voluptuous and fluorescent-coloured 'Sophie', 'Charlotte' and 'Caroline', by French artist Niki de Saint Phalle, are among the city's most recognisable, and most loved, landmarks. Indeed, *Die Nanas* helped make de Saint Phalle famous, and devout fans of her work will find a direct trip to Leibnizufer (U-Bahn stop Markthalle Landtag) rewarding.

Despite WWII bombing, Hanover's restored Altstadt (old town) remains appealingly quaint. The red-brick, Gothic Marktkirche in the market square has original elements, as do both the Altes Rathaus (begun 1455) across the market, and the nearby Ballhof (1649–64), a hall originally built for 17th-century badminton-type games.

SLEEPING & EATING

our pick Loccumer Hof (☎ 126 40; www.loccumerhof.de, in German; Kurt-Schumacher-Strasse 14/16; s/d €99/129; P ⊠ 💻 wifi) Some of the stylish and well-decorated rooms here are themed by nations ('Australia'), elements ('Air') and feng shui. Others are low-allergy, and the artwork (not for sale) is by the owner-manager, who has put together possibly Hanover's most interesting hotel. As well as these walk-in prices, rates are often one-third less for advanced booking.

our pick Markthalle (☎ 341 410; Kamarschstrasse 49; dishes €3.50-8; 🕑 7am-8pm Mon-Wed, to 10pm Thu & Fri, to 4pm Sat; ⊠ V) This huge covered market of food stalls and gourmet delicatessens is fantastic for a quick bite, both carnivorous and vegetarian.

Pier 51 (☎ 807 1800; Rudolf von Bennigsen Ufer 51; starters €9-13, mains €21-23; 🕑 noon-midnight; ⊠) One of Hanover's loveliest restaurants, and very romantic at sundown, Pier 51 is walled with glass and juts out over the Maschsee. The menu is strong on fish, although you can also choose pasta or meat. In summer there's an outside 'Piergarten', decked out with the old-fashioned *Strandkörbe* (straw basket seats) that you see on German beaches.

GETTING THERE & AWAY

AIR

Hanover Airport (HAJ; ☎ 977 1223; www.hannover-airport.de) has many connections, including Lufthansa (☎ 0180-380 3803), and the

DAVID PEEVERS

One of Hanover's many parks

low-cost carriers **Air Berlin** (☎ 01805-737 800; www.airberlin.com) to/from London-Stansted and **TuiFly** (☎ 01805-757 510; www.tuifly.com) to/from Newcastle in Great Britain.

The S-Bahn (S5) takes 18 minutes from the airport to the Hauptbahnhof (€2.80).

TRAIN

Hanover is a major rail hub, with frequent ICE trains to/from Hamburg (€40, 1¼ hours), Munich (€116, 4¼ hours) and Berlin (€61, 1¾ hours), among others.

HAMELIN

If you have a phobia about rats, you might give this picturesque town on the Weser River a wide berth. According to *The Pied Piper of Hamelin* fairy tale, in the 13th century the Pied Piper *(Der Rattenfänger)* was employed by Hamelin's townsfolk to lure its nibbling rodents into the river. When the townsfolk refused to pay him, he picked up his flute again and led their kids away. In the meantime, the rats rule again here – rats that are stuffed, fluffy and cute; wooden rats; and even little rats that adorn the sights around town.

INFORMATION

Hameln Tourist Information (☎ 957 823, 0180-551 5150; www.hameln.de; Diesterallee 1; 🕑 9am-6.30pm Mon-Fri, 9.30am-4pm Sat, 9.30am-1pm Sun May-Sep, 9am-6pm Mon-Fri, 9.30am-1pm Sat & Sun Oct & Apr)

SIGHTS & ACTIVITIES

Look for the rat symbols cropping up throughout the streets along with infor-

FAIRY-TALE ROAD

The 600km **Märchenstrasse** (www.deutsche-maerchenstrasse.de) is one of Germany's most popular tourist routes. It's made up of cities, towns and hamlets in four states (Hesse, Lower Saxony, North Rhine-Westphalia and Bremen), many of them associated with the works of Wilhelm and Jakob Grimm. Click on towns on the website's map for details. Public transport is designed for local commuting, so having a car is a big plus.

The Grimm brothers travelled extensively through central Germany in the early 19th century documenting folklore. Their collection of tales, *Kinder- und Hausmärchen,* was first published in 1812 and quickly gained international recognition. It includes such fairy-tale staples as *Hansel and Gretel, Cinderella, The Pied Piper, Rapunzel* and scores of others.

There are over 60 stops on the Fairy-Tale Road. Major ones include (from south to north): **Hanau**, about 15km east of Frankfurt, the birthplace of Jakob (1785–1863) and Wilhelm (1786–1859); **Steinau**, where the Grimm brothers spent their youth; **Marburg**, in whose university the brothers studied for a short while; **Kassel** (p184), with a museum dedicated to the Grimms; **Göttingen**, at whose university the brothers served as professors before being expelled in 1837 for their liberal views; **Bad Karlshafen**, a meticulously planned white baroque village; **Bodenwerder**, whose rambling Münchhausen Museum is dedicated to the legendary Baron von Münchhausen, (in)famous for telling outrageous tales (see p190); **Hamelin** (Hameln; above), forever associated with the legend of the Pied Piper; and **Bremen** (p319).

mation posts (currently only in German) offering a glimpse into the history of Hamelin and its restored 16th- to 18th-century architecture.

The ornamental Weser Renaissance style prevalent throughout the Altstadt has a strong Italian influence, and the finest example of this is the Rattenfängerhaus (**Rat Catcher's House; Osterstrasse 28**), from 1602, with its typically steep and richly decorated gable. Walking along Osterstrasse towards the Markt, you pass Leisthaus at No 9, built for a patrician grain trader in 1585–89 in the Weser Renaissance style and today housing the Hamelin City Museum (**☎ 202 1215; Osterstrasse 8-9**).

On the corner of Markt and Osterstrasse you find the Hochzeitshaus (1610–17), partly used today as city council offices and as a police station. The Rattenfänger Glockenspiel at the far end of the building chimes daily at 9.35am and 11.35am, while a carousel of Pied Piper figures twirls at 1.05pm, 3.35pm and 5.35pm.

The heart of Hamelin is the Markt (square) and its northern continuation, Pferdemarkt (Equestrian Square), where during the Middle Ages knights fought it out in tournaments.

SLEEPING & EATING

our pick Hotel La Principessa (**☎ 956 920; www.laprincipessa.de; Kupferschmiedestrasse 2; s €72, d €90-99; P ⊠ ⊜**) Cast-iron balustrades, tiled floors throughout and gentle Tuscan pastels and ochre shades make this Italian-themed hotel an unusual and distinguished option in Hamelin. Out the back are some giant rats for the kids to mess with.

Rattenfängerhaus (**☎ 3888; Osterstrasse 28; mains €9-22; ⊙ lunch & dinner Mon-Thu, 10am-10pm Fri-Sun; ⊠**) Hamelin's traditional restaurants are unashamedly aimed at tourists, such as this cute half-timbered tavern with a speciality of 'rats' tails' flambéed at your table (fortunately, like most of the theme dishes here, it's based on pork). Schnitzels, herrings, vegie dishes and 'rat killer' herb liquor are also offered.

DENNIS JOHNSON

Anne Frank's headstone, Bergen-Belsen (p191)

GETTING THERE & AWAY

Frequent S-Bahn trains (S5) head to Hamelin from Hanover's Hauptbahnhof (€10.30, 45 minutes). Regular direct trains connect Hanover's airport with Hamelin (€13.30, one hour).

BODENWERDER

If Bodenwerder's most famous son were to have described his small home town, he'd probably have painted it as a huge, thriving metropolis on the Weser

River. But then Baron Hieronymous von Münchhausen (1720–97) was one of history's most shameless liars. He gave his name to a psychological condition – Münchhausen's syndrome, or compulsive exaggeration of physical illness – and inspired the cult film of British comedian Terry Gilliam, *The Adventures of Baron Munchausen*.

Bodenwerder's principal attraction is the **Münchhausen Museum** (☎ 409 147; Münchhausenplatz 1; adult/child €2/1.50; 🕐 10am-5pm Apr-Oct), which struggles a little with the difficult task of conveying the chaos and fun associated with the 'liar baron' – a man who liked to regale dinner guests with his Crimean adventures, claiming he had, for example, tied his horse to a church steeple during a snow drift and ridden around a dining table without breaking one teacup.

CELLE

With 400 half-timbered houses and its Ducal Palace dating back to the 13th century, Celle is graced with a picture-book town centre that is among the most attractive in the region. The white-and-pink Ducal Palace, Celle's centrepiece set in small gardens, contrasts with the ultramodern Kunstmuseum opposite, which is illuminated at night into a '24-hour' museum and successfully creates an interesting contrast of old and new in this small but fascinating town.

INFORMATION

Tourismus Region Celle (☎ 1212; www.region-celle.com; Markt 14-16; 🕐 9am-6pm Mon-Fri, 10am-4pm Sat, 11am-2pm Sun May-Sep, 9am-5pm Mon-Fri, 10am-1pm Sat Oct-Apr)

SIGHTS

With row upon row of ornate half-timbered houses, all decorated with scrolls and allegorical figures, Celle is a perfect place for a stroll. Even the tourist office is located in a striking building, the **Altes Rathaus** (1561–79), which boasts a wonderful Weser Renaissance stepped gable, topped with the ducal coat of arms and a golden weather vane. One block south of the tour-

ANDREA SCHULTE-PEEVERS

Celle's Schloss

ist office, on the corner of Poststrasse and Runde Strasse, you'll find one of Celle's most magnificent buildings, the ornate Hoppener Haus (1532).

Celle's wedding-cake Schloss (**Ducal Palace; ☎ 123 73; Schlossplatz; adult/concession €5/3, combined Residenzmuseum, Bomann Museum & Kunstmuseum €8/5; 10am-5pm Tue-Sun**), built in 1292 by Otto Der Strenge (Otto the Strict) as a town fortification, was expanded in 1378 and turned into a residence.

Celle's Kunstmuseum (**Art Museum; ☎ 123 55; www.kunst.celle.de; Schlossplatz 7; adult/concession incl Bomann Museum €5/3; 10am-5pm Tue-Sun**), situated across the road from the Schloss, is dedicated to contemporary German artists. In the older building adjacent, you'll find the regional history Bomann Museum (**☎ 125 44; www.bomann-museum.de, in German; Schlossplatz 7; adult/concession incl Kunstmuseum €3/2; 10am-5pm Tue-Sun**). Here, among other things, you can wander through rooms furnished in 19th-century style.

Just west of the Rathaus is the 13th-century Stadtkirche (**☎ 7735; www.stadtkirche-celle.de, in German; tower adult/concession €1/0.50; 10am-6pm Tue-Sat Apr-Dec, to 5pm Jan-Mar, tower 10-11.45am & 2-4.45pm Tue-Sat Apr-Oct**). You can climb up the 235 steps to the top of the church steeple for a view of the city, or just watch as the city trumpeter climbs the 220 steps to the white tower below the steeple for a trumpet fanfare in all four directions. The ascent takes place at 9.30am and 5.30pm daily.

Dating back to 1740, Celle's synagogue (**☎ 124 59; Im Kreise 24; admission free; noon-5pm Tue-Thu, 9am-2pm Fri, 11am-4pm Sun**) is the oldest in northern Germany. Partially destroyed during Kristallnacht (see the boxed text, p348), it looks just like any other half-timbered house from the outside, but a new Jewish congregation formed in 1997 and services are held regularly.

GETTING THERE & AWAY

Several trains each hour to Hanover take from 20 minutes (IC; €10.50) to 45 minutes (S-Bahn; €8.40).

BERGEN-BELSEN

Visiting a former concentration camp memorial in Germany is a moving but also challenging experience, and Bergen-Belsen (**☎ 05051-6011; www.bergenbelsen.de; Lohheide; admission free; 9am-6pm Apr-Sep, to 5pm Oct-Mar**) is no exception – it provides a horrifying punch to the stomach through the sheer force of its atmosphere. In all, 70,000 Jews, Soviet soldiers, political hostages and other prisoners died here. Among them was Anne Frank, whose posthumously published diary became a modern classic.

The revamped Documentation Centre today is one of the best of its kind and deals sensitively but very poignantly with the lives of the people who were imprisoned here – before, during and after incarceration. The exhibition is designed to be viewed chronologically, and these days a better focus is placed on the role of Bergen-Belsen in the early years as a POW camp for mostly Soviet prisoners of war.

GETTING THERE & AWAY

By public transport the journey is best done on a weekday, when you can take bus 1-15 at 10am weekdays from Schlossplatz in Celle direct to Bergen-Belsen Memorial (€5.60, 48 minutes). At 3.04pm, a direct bus returns to Celle. A few other buses run, requiring an easy change to a connecting bus in Bergen.

WOLFSBURG

Arriving in Wolfsburg by train, the first thing you see is an enormous, almost surreal, VW emblem on a building in a scene that could have come from Fritz Lang's classic film *Metropolis*. This is part of the Volkswagen company's nation-sized global headquarters. Wolfsburg is indeed a company town, and because of this it also has an earthy, working-class atmosphere that sets it apart from any other cities in the region.

SIGHTS

Spread across 25 hectares, **Autostadt** (**Car City; ☎ 0800-288 678 238; www.autostadt.de, in German; Stadtbrücke; adult/child/concession/family €15/6/12/38; 9am-6pm**) is a celebration of all things VW.

Things kick off with a broad view of automotive design and engineering in the Konzernforum, while the neighbouring Zeithaus looks back at the history of the Beetle and other VW models. Then, in various outlying pavilions you can learn more about individual marques, including VW itself, Audi, Bentley, Lamborghini, Seat and Skoda. Many exhibits are interactive and most have signage in German and English.

Included in the entrance price is a 45-minute trip into the neighbouring Volkswagen factory, bigger than Monaco and the world's largest car plant.

More low-key, the **AutoMuseum** (**☎ 520 71; Dieselstrasse 35; adult/concession/family €6/3/15; 10am-6pm Fri-Sun, closed 24 Dec-1 Jan**) has a collection that includes a vehicle used in the *Herbie, the Love Bug* movie, a Beetle built from wood, the original 1938 Cabriolet presented to Adolf Hitler on his 50th birthday, and the bizarre 'See-Golf', a Golf Cabriolet from 1983 with hydraulic pontoons that extend outwards to make it amphibious.

The glass-and-concrete building that houses the science centre **Phaeno** (**☎ 0180-106 0600; www.phaeno.de; Willy Brandt-Platz 1; adult/child/concession/family €12/7.50/9/26.50; 9am-5pm Tue-Fri, 10am-6pm Sat & Sun, last entry 1hr before closing**) is truly cutting edge. Sleek, curved and thin, it looks like a stretchy spaceship from Planet Minimalism.

GETTING THERE & AWAY

Frequent ICE train services go to Berlin (€44, one hour). IC trains to Hanover (€17, 30 minutes) are cheaper and barely slower than the ICE.

HARZ MOUNTAINS

GOSLAR

The hub of tourism in the Western Harz, Goslar has a charming medieval Altstadt, which, together with its historic Rammelsberg mine, is a Unesco World Heritage Site.

Founded by Heinrich I in 922, the town's early importance centred on silver and the Kaiserpfalz, the seat of the Saxon kings from 1005 to 1219. It fell into decline after a second period of prosperity in the 14th and 15th centuries, reflecting the fortunes of the Harz as a whole, and relinquished its mine to Braunschweig in 1552 and then its soul to Prussia in 1802.

INFORMATION

Tourist-Information (**☎ 780 60; www.goslar.de; Markt 7; 9.15am-6pm Mon-Fri, 9.30am-4pm Sat, 9.30am-2pm Sun Apr-Oct, 9.15am-5pm Mon-Fri, 9.30am-2pm Sat Nov-Mar**)

SIGHTS

One of the nicest things to do in Goslar is to wander through the historic streets around the Markt. **Hotel Kaiserworth** was erected in 1494 to house the textile guild, and sports almost life-size figures on its orange facade. The impressive late-Gothic **Rathaus** comes into its own at night, when light shining through stained-glass windows illuminates the stone-patterned town square.

The **market fountain**, crowned by an ungainly eagle symbolising Goslar's status as a free imperial city, dates from the 13th century; the eagle itself is a copy – the original is on show in the Goslarer Museum. Opposite the Rathaus is the

OGE/IMAGEBROKER

Teufelsmauer nature reserve, near Quedlinburg

IF YOU LIKE...

If you like **Goslar** (opposite), you'll really fall for **Quedlinburg** (www.quedlinburg.de), another Unesco-designated hamlet tucked away in the Harz mountains, with an intact Altstadt (old town) and over 1400 half-timbered houses dating from six centuries ago:

- **Rathaus** Built in 1320, the town hall has been expanded over the years and was adorned with a Renaissance facade in 1616. Inside, the beautiful Festsaal is decorated with a cycle of frescoes focusing on Quedlinburg's colourful history. The **Roland statue** (1426) in front of it dates from the year Quedlinburg joined the Hanseatic League.
- **Marktkirche St Benedikti** Behind the Rathaus, this striking late-Gothic church has a small house on its tower that was used by town watchmen until 1901.
- There are several fine half-timbered buildings near the Marktkirche, but arguably the most spectacular is the (1612) **Gildehaus zur Rose** at Breite Strasse 39, with a richly carved and panelled interior.
- **Schlossmuseum** (☎ 905 681) The Schlossberg, a pretty hill with a 25m-high plateau above Quedlinburg, was first graced with a church and residence under Henry the Fowler. The present-day Renaissance Schloss is now a revamped museum containing fascinating Ottonian period exhibits dating from 919 to 1056.
- **Stiftskirche St Servatius** (☎ 709 900) This 12th-century church is one of Germany's most significant from the Romanesque period. Its treasury contains valuable reliquaries and early Bibles.

EWR/IMAGEBROKER

Goslar's medieval Aldstadt

Glockenspiel, a chiming clock depicting four scenes of mining in the area.

Goslar's pride and joy is the reconstructed 11th-century Romanesque palace, **Kaiserpfalz** (☎ 311 9693; Kaiserbleek 6; adult/concession €4.50/2.50; 10am-5pm Apr-Oct, to 4pm Nov-Mar). After centuries of decay into a historic pile of rubble, this palace was resurrected in the 19th century and adorned with interior frescoes of idealised historical scenes. On the southern side is **St Ulrich Chapel**, housing a sarcophagus containing the heart of Heinrich III. Below the Kaiserpfalz is the recently restored **Domvorhalle**, displaying the 11th-century Kaiserstuhl, the throne used by Salian and Hohenstaufen emperors.

Situated just east of the Zinnfiguren-Museum, the **Goslarer Museum** (☎ 433 94; Königstrasse 1; adult/concession €4/2; 10am-5pm Tue-Sun Apr-Oct, to 4pm Nov-Mar) offers a good overview of the natural and cultural history of Goslar and the Harz. The **Mönchehaus Museum** (☎ 295 70; Mönchestrasse 3; adult/child €5/1.50; 10am-5pm Tue-Sat), in a 16th-century half-timbered house, has changing exhibits of modern art, including works by the most recent winner of the prestigious Kaiserring art prize – past winners include Henry Moore, Joseph Beuys and Rebecca Horn.

GETTING THERE & AWAY

Bad Harzburg–Hanover trains stop here often, as do trains on the Braunschweig–Göttingen line.

STUTTGART & THE BLACK FOREST

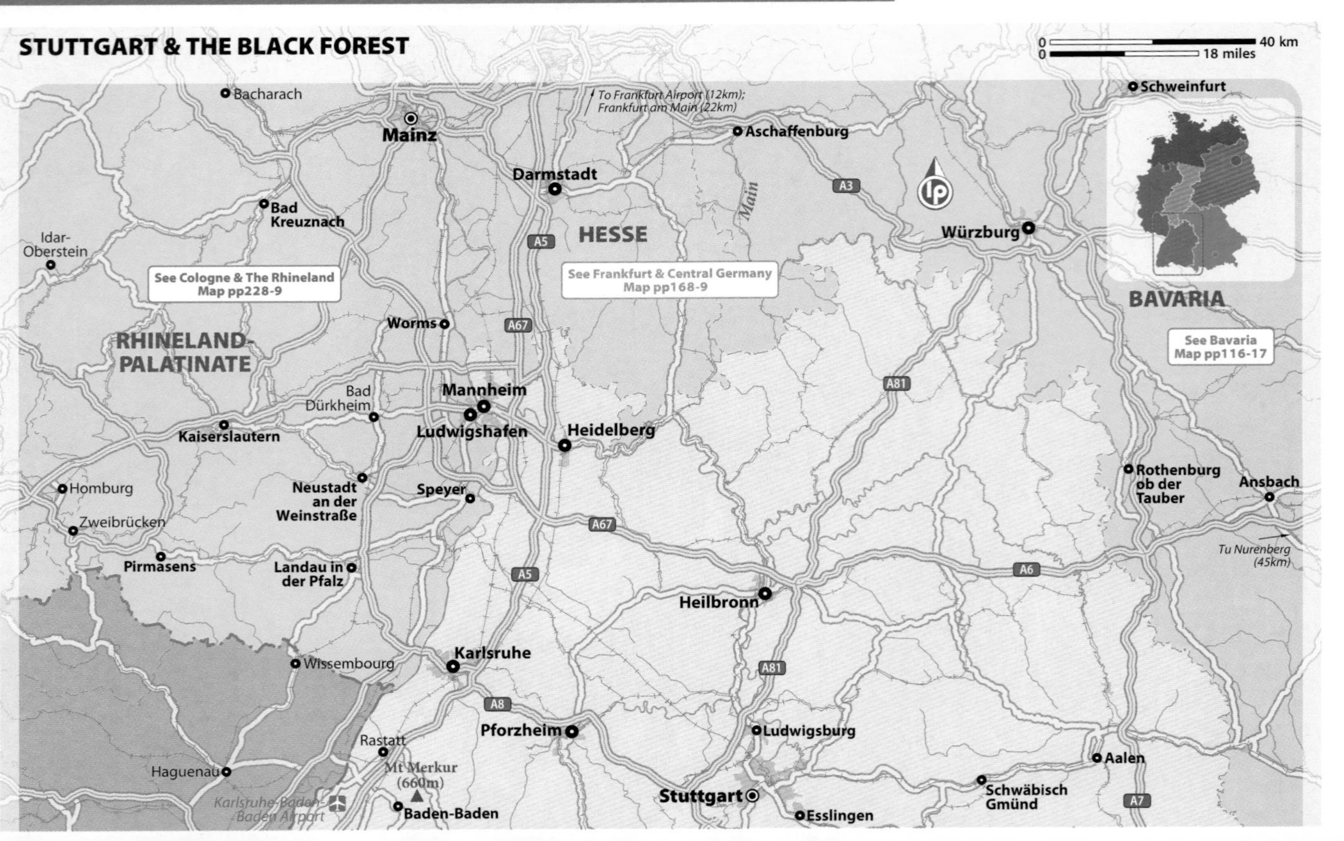

STUTTGART & THE BLACK FOREST
0
0
40 km
18 miles
Bacharach
Mainz
To Frankfurt Airport (12km); Frankfurt am Main (22km)
Aschaffenburg
Schweinfurt
Darmstadt
A3
Main
Bad Kreuznach
Idar-Oberstein
A5
HESSE
Würzburg
See Cologne & The Rhineland Map pp228-9
See Frankfurt & Central Germany Map pp168-9
BAVARIA
Worms
A67
See Bavaria Map pp116-17
RHINELAND-PALATINATE
A81
Bad Dürkheim
Mannheim
Ludwigshafen
Kaiserslautern
Heidelberg
Rothenburg ob der Tauber
Ansbach
Homburg
Neustadt an der Weinstraße
Speyer
Zweibrücken
A67
Tu Nurenberg (45km)
Pirmasens
Landau in der Pfalz
A5
A6
Heilbronn
Karlsruhe
Wissembourg
A81
A8
Pforzheim
Ludwigsburg
Rastatt
Aalen
Haguenau
Mt Merkur (660m)
Schwäbisch Gmünd
Karlsruhe-Baden-Baden Airport
Baden-Baden
Stuttgart
Esslingen
A7

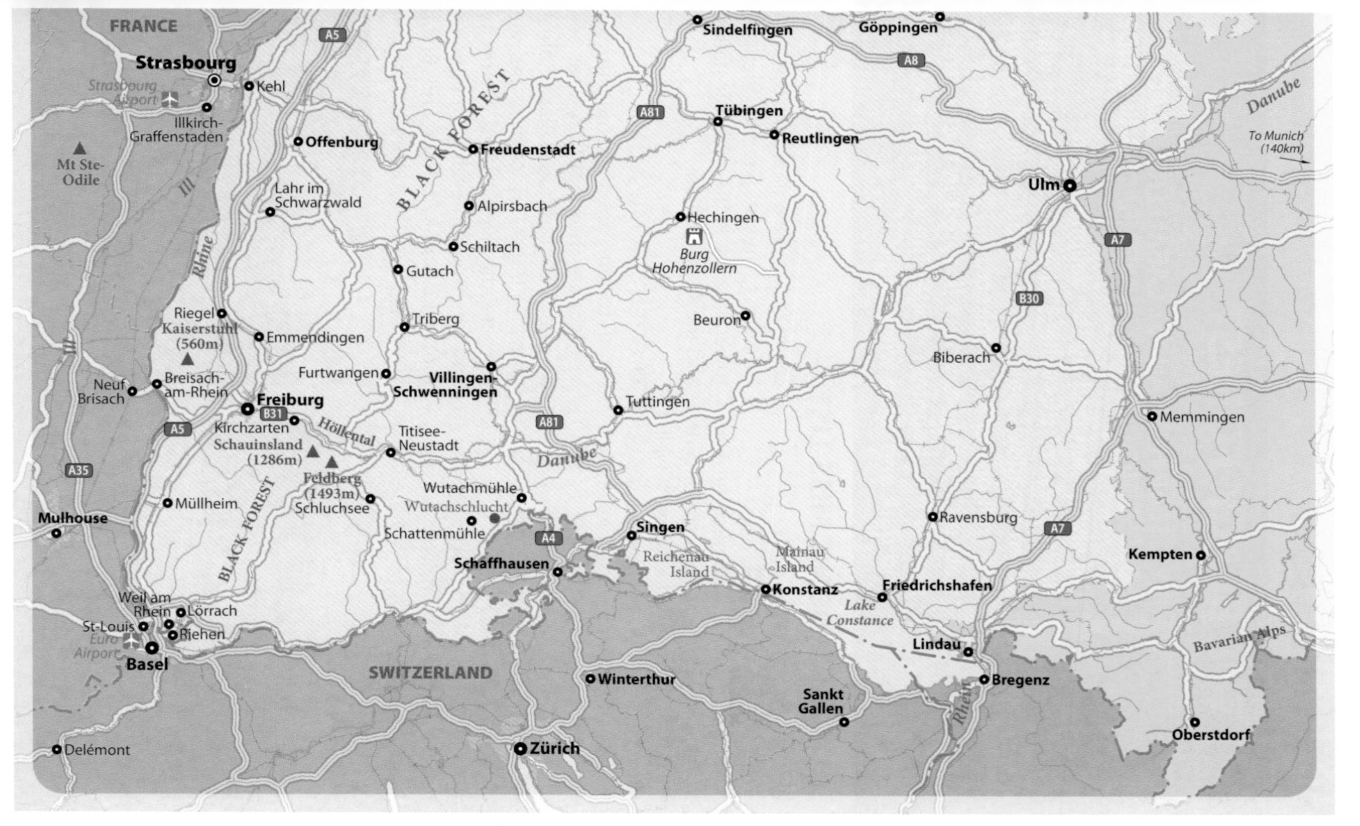
FRANCE
Strasbourg
Strasbourg Airport
Kehl
Illkirch-Graffenstaden
Mt Ste-Odile
Ill
Rhine
Offenburg
Lahr im Schwarzwald
BLACK FOREST
Freudenstadt
Alpirsbach
Schiltach
Gutach
Triberg
Riegel
Kaiserstuhl (560m)
Emmendingen
Furtwangen
Villingen-Schwenningen
Neuf Brisach
Breisach-am-Rhein
Freiburg
B31
A5
Kirchzarten
Höllental
Titisee-Neustadt
Schauinsland (1286m)
Feldberg (1493m)
Schluchsee
A35
Müllheim
BLACK FOREST
Mulhouse
Wutachmühle
Wutachschlucht
Schattenmühle
Danube
A81
Schaffhausen
A4
Singen
Reichenau Island
Mainau Island
Konstanz
Lake Constance
Friedrichshafen
Lindau
Bregenz
Rhein
Weil am Rhein
Lörrach
St-Louis
Riehen
Euro Airport
Basel
SWITZERLAND
Winterthur
Sankt Gallen
Delémont
Zürich
Sindelfingen
Göppingen
A8
A81
Tübingen
Reutlingen
Hechingen
Burg Hohenzollern
Beuron
Tuttingen
Danube
To Munich (140km)
Ulm
A7
B30
Biberach
Memmingen
Ravensburg
A7
Kempten
Bavarian Alps
Oberstdorf

HIGHLIGHTS

1 THE BLACK FOREST

BY ÓSCAR HERNÁNDEZ CABALLERO, BLACK FOREST MIDDLE-NORTH NATURAL PARK GUIDE

I'm always amazed by the deepness and narrowness of the valleys, the soft landscape with green meadows paired with tradition-filled culture and well-preserved architecture. I love taking a walk on a foggy day, in a fir forest in the central part of the mountain range. The woods are old and dark and filled with magic.

ÓSCAR'S DON'T MISS LIST

❶ WALK THE WUTACHSCHLUCHT

Take a day to walk the gorge of the river Wutach, known as the **Wutachschlucht** (p223), in the south. It's the most well-preserved section of the Black Forest and one of the rare places where you can find limestone.

❷ SCOOTING DOWN SCHAUINSLAND

From the top of the **Schauinsland** (p221), near Freiburg, you can try a downhill scooter track. Take the cable car up and have a walk around the top – be sure to investigate the viewing tower. Just ask at the cable car station and they'll set you up.

❸ OPEN-AIR MUSEUM

Head to the open-air museum at **Vogtsbauernhof** (p217). You can see a variety of traditional Black Forest farms from the 16th century and see how people lived before electricity and cars. You can even try traditional food like smoked ham and Black Forest cake in the restaurant (if you

Clockwise from top: A waterfall near Triberg (p221); An old house in the Rötenbachschlucht valley; Cyclists on the Schauinsland (p221); Mummelsee (p222); Black Forest landscape, near Gutach (p217)

CLOCKWISE FROM TOP: ARC/IMAGEBROKER; STA/IMAGEBROKER; JRE/IMAGEBROKER; EMS/IMAGEBROKER; JKI/IMAGEBROKER

ask, they show you how the make the latter!)

❹ TAKE A DRIVE

I highly recommend the Freudenstadt to Baden-Baden portion of the **Schwarzwald-Hochstrasse B500** (see the boxed text, p222) – it's particularly picturesque, and look out for the messy (but interesting) part that still shows signs of the 1999 hurricane Lothar. One of my other favourite drives is the **Deutsche Uhrenstrasse** (see the boxed text, p222), which passes through the central portion of the mountain range and the land of the cuckoo clocks.

↘ THINGS YOU NEED TO KNOW

Top tip Avoid school holidays (August, late October, Easter, Carnival and Pentecost) **Let a guide guide you** They know the most beautiful corners of the range, as well as local history, nature and traditions.

HIGHLIGHTS

2 HEIDELBERG

BY DR ELISABETH SÜDKAMP, ART HISTORIAN AND OFFICIAL HEIDELBERG GUIDE

With its castle ruin, the oldest university in Germany and the surrounding hills of Odenwald Forest, Heidelberg enchants with a fascinating mixture of history, vibrant modern life and nature. It's a magical place with a romantic, bustling and international ambience. But it's impossible to truly explain 'magic': come and experience it yourself!

DR ELISABETH SÜDKAMP'S DON'T MISS LIST

❶ ALTE BRÜCKE

Along with the church steeples and castle ruin, the **Old Bridge** (p212), with its elegant nine arches, is part of the classic view of Heidelberg. Close to the bridge gate is the modern bronze 'bridge monkey': it's said if you touch the mirror you'll get rich; if you touch the paw you'll come back to Heidelberg.

❷ INSPIRING VIEWS

One of my favourite walks is the scenic **Philosophenweg** (Philosopher's Walk, p212), which treats you to beautiful views of the Old Town and the castle. From up here, it's easy to understand why so many artists, philosophers and professors of the romantic movement found their inspiration in Heidelberg.

❸ LOFTY RIDES

For a fun trip, ride the **Bergbahn** (funicular railway, p211) to the top of Königstuhl Mountain, above the castle. The historical wooden wagons are still in use for the last section. At the top are lovely hiking trails and gorgeous valley views.

Clockwise from top: Heidelberg's Marktplatz (p212); Alte Brücke (p212), over the Neckar River; Schloss Heidelberg (p211); Cyclists on the Alte Brücke; View from the Philosophenweg (p212)

❹ SWEET STUFF

Heidelberg's most famous culinary speciality is the **Studentenkuss** (Student's Kiss), a melt-in-your-mouth confection made from nougat, wafers and chocolate. It was created by cafe owner Fridolin Knösel in the late 1800s to help his (male) student customers express their admiration for the beautiful – but constantly chaperoned – young ladies who also frequented the cafe. Presented as a gallant gift, not even the chaperones could object to this 'kiss'.

❺ MARKTPLATZ

A great time to visit the **Marktplatz** (p212) is on Wednesdays and Saturdays when it brims with fresh fruit and vegetables during the farmers market. In springtime, as soon as the first rays of sun show, restaurants, bars and cafes put their tables outside for people to enjoy an alfresco lunch or evening drink. The narrow alleys around here are filled with antique shops, student pubs and small museums.

↘ THINGS YOU NEED TO KNOW

Eat For fabulous German cuisine in an atmospheric setting, head to Haus zum Ritter (www.ritter-heidelberg.de). **Ecofloat** Cruise the Neckar River on a solar-powered boat (www.hdsolarschiff.com). **Relax** Channel Mark Twain at historic student pubs Sepp'l or Roter Ochse. **For more on Heidelberg, see p210**

HIGHLIGHTS

3

↘ ZEPPELIN MUSEUM

Get the full scoop on the airships that first took flight in 1900 under the stewardship of high-flying Count Ferdinand von Zeppelin at this **museum** (p225). See a full-scale mock-up of a 33m section of the *Hindenburg,* the largest airship ever built; an incredible 245m long, outfitted as luxuriously as an ocean liner and hydrogen-filled, it tragically burst into flames (killing 36) while landing in 1937.

4

↘ FAST CARS

Car lovers will go mad in Stuttgart, which is home to two **car museums** (p209): At the Mercedes-Benz museum, look out for legends like the 1888 Daimler Riding Car, the world's first gasoline-powered vehicle. The Porsche Museum take you through the history of Porsche from its 1948 beginnings – break to glimpse the 911 GTI that won Le Mans in 1998.

5

CAKE & CUCKOO CLOCKS

Gorge on the original *Schwarzwälder Kirschtorte* (Black Forest gateau) and hear the world's biggest cuckoo clock call in **Triberg** (p221). Check out its rival (the clock's, that is) up the road. They both claim to be the biggest, but only one made it into the *Guinness Book of World Records.*

6

TAKE TO THE WATERS

After hiking all those high peaks, you deserve to unwind, give your muscles a rest and take a moment to relax in **Baden-Baden** (p216), the swish spa town that heals the mind and the skin. Forget your troubles, close your eyes, and let the curative water soothe your muscles and your worries in Germany's most renowned waters.

7

LIVELY FREIBURG

It's tough to put your finger on why **Freiburg** (p218) has such a fun and relaxing feel – maybe it's the large student population, maybe it's the gorgeous, soothing, ubiquitous red-sandstone buildings, most notably the Gothic Münster on the town square – contemplate it all at one of Freiburg's fine watering holes.

3 WER/IMAGEBROKER; 4 EBO/IMAGEBROKER; 5 KUTTIG/ALAMY; 6 JKL/IMAGEBROKER; 7 DJS/IMAGEBROKER

3 Zeppelin Museum (p225), Friedrichshafen; 4 Mercedes-Benz Museum (p209), Stuttgart; 5 One of the world's biggest cuckoo clocks (p221), Triberg; 6 Kurhaus (p216), Baden-Baden; 7 Konviktstrasse, Freiburg (p218)

THE BEST...

THINGS FOR FREE

- **Schlossgarten** (p208) Stuttgart's palace gardens are a remarkable sanctuary of greenery.
- Tick-tock your way through the **House of 1000 Clocks** (p222) in Triberg.
- **Trinkhalle** (Pump Room; p216) Bring your own bottle and fill it up with medicinal mineral water in Baden-Baden.

HEART-PUMPING HIKES

- **Winzerweg** (Wine Growers' Trail; p221) Fifteen kilometres of forests and vineyards.
- The 13km path from **Schattenmühle to Wutachmühle** (p223) is the best place to view the dramatic Wutachschlucht gorge.
- The 55km **Kaiserstuhltour** (p221) circuit is for hard-core hikers only.

LAZY RIDES

- Hop on the **Kaiserstuhlbahn** (Kaiserstuhl train; p221) for a relaxing loop around volcanic hills.
- Zoom up the 3.6km **Schauinslandbahn** (cable car; p221) for fabulous views of the Black Forest.
- Trundle up to Heidelberg's **Königstuhl** (p211) in an antique rail car.

REGIONAL DISHES

- **Calwer-Eck-Bräu** (p210) serves the gut-filling *Maultaschensuppe* (ravioli soup).
- **Englers Weinkrügle** (p219) offers local fish with local wine, and various other mouth-watering concoctions.
- **Café Schäfer** (p222) for a decadent slice (or two) of *Schwarzwälder Kirschtorte* (Black Forest gateau) made according to the original recipe.

JKI/IMAGEBROKER

Baden-Baden's Trinkhalle (Pump Room; p216)

THINGS YOU NEED TO KNOW

VITAL STATISTICS

- **Population** 10.75 million (Baden-Württemberg)
- **Points of entry** Stuttgart, Freiburg, Friedrichshafen and Basel-Mulhouse (Switzerland/France) airports.
- **Best time to visit** April–October.

ADVANCE PLANNING

- **One month before** Book a guide for an unforgettable hike through the Black Forest – contact the regional tourist offices for names and numbers.
- **One week before** Make sure you pack fleece, hiking boots and water bottles in the suitcase.

RESOURCES

- **www.schwarzwaldverein.de** The Schwarzwaldverein is Germany's first hiking club.
- **www.tourismus-bw.de** State Tourist Board. Stuttgart & the Black Forest is within the state of Baden-Württemberg.

DISCOUNT CARDS

- The three-day **Bodensee Erlebniskarte** (adult/6-15yr €69/37, not including ferries €39/21) allows free travel on almost all boats and mountain cableways on and around Lake Constance and gets you free entry to around 180 tourist attractions and museums. Check with the local tourist offices for details.
- In most parts of the Black Forest your hotel or guesthouse will issue you with the handy **Schwarzwald-Gästekarte** (Guest Card) for discounts or freebies on museums, ski lifts, events and attractions. Versions of the card with the Konus symbol entitle you to free use of public transport.
- Almost all tourist offices in the Black Forest sell the three-day **SchwarzwaldCard** (adult/4-11yr/family €32/21/99) for admission to around 150 attractions in the Black Forest, including museums, ski lifts, boat trips, spas and swimming pools. Details on both cards are available at www.blackforest-tourism.com.

GETTING AROUND

- **www.bodenseeschifffahrt.at** & **www.bsb-online.com** Two ferry companies linking the ports on Lake Constance.
- **www.der-katamaran.de** A sleek catamaran linking Konstanz with Friedrichshafen in 50 minutes.

STUTTGART & THE BLACK FOREST ITINERARIES

TASTE OF THE FOREST Three Days

The Black Forest is vast and dark. If you only have a few days, spend it based in the vibrant university town of Freiburg and make a few day trips to the hills and explore the Forest's noisy export, the cuckoo clock. Base yourself in **(1) Freiburg** (p218); take in its impressive city gate, the **(2) Schwabentor** (p219), then make your way to the nearby trail winding up the leafy **(3) Schlossberg** (p219). From its lovely viewing tower you can catch your first glimpse of the deep colours of the surrounding Black Forest. Next, rent a car and spend a few days taking a cable car up the **(4) Schauinsland** (p221) and exploring the town of **(5) Triberg** (p221), home to two enormous cuckoo clocks, both of which are claimed to be the world's largest. Ponder which is bigger over a slice of Black Forest cake at **(6) Café Schäfer** (p222), which bakes the layers of chocolate, whipped cream and cherries according to the original recipe.

CITY TO THE LAKE Five Days

Work your way from the urban hub of southwestern Germany to the Bavarian Riviera; this entire itinerary can be done by train. Start in **(1) Stuttgart** (p208), a city blessed with an air of relaxed prosperity and a keen sense of style. Stop off at one of the car museums in town – take your pick from the **(2) Mercedes-Benz museum** (p209) and the **(3) Porsche museum** (p209) – and stroll through the **(4) Mittlerer Schlossgarten** (p208), where you can relax with a beverage in its tranquil **(5) Biergarten im Schlossgarten** (p210).

From Stuttgart, take a day trip to **(6) Ulm** (p214), the birthplace of Albert Einstein. Contemplate its impressive **(7) Münster** (p215) and the town's most famous **(8) fountain** (p215), featuring a crazy-haired Einstein. Next head out to **(9) Tübingen** (p214) to admire its gabled architecture and tour the archaeology museum inside its towering castle, **(10) Schloss Hohentübingen** (p214). Then continue on to **(11) Konstanz** (p223) for a relaxing lakeside sojourn; be sure to catch the ferry to the Mediterranean hamlet of **(12) Lindau** (p224) for the day and ponder if you're really still in Germany.

CASTLES & FORESTS One Week

Spend a week in Germany's most famous university towns, stop off and hit the spa and finish in Freiburg, the best bet for exploring the darkest forest you've ever seen. Mark Twain wrote *A Tramp Abroad,* partly set in this region, after spending three months in the university town of **(1) Heidelberg** (p210). Explore its magnificent **(2) Schloss** (p211),

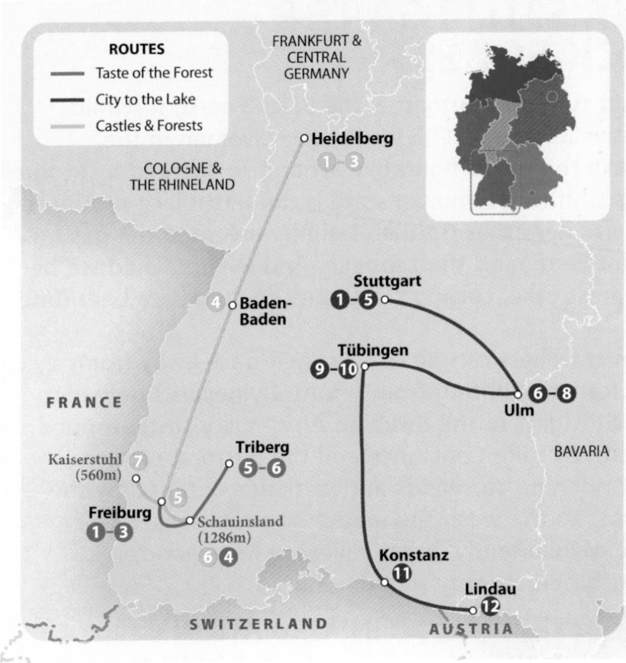

making sure to venture onto the terrace for spectacular views of the Neckar River, then cross over the (3) Alte Brücke (p212) for a glimpse of its infamous brass monkey.

Next move south to the glitzy spa town of (4) Baden-Baden (p216) for a gulp of, or a dip in, its famous waters. After a restorative pause, head to the polar opposite: (5) Freiburg (p218), another lively university town with a laid-back southern German feel. Spend a day admiring its red sandstone architecture, and then start your exploration of the Black Forest beyond its city limits. This is a fantastic base for excursions to (6) Schauinsland (p221), a patchwork of forest and meadows worlds away from the city, or the (7) Kaiserstuhl (p221), a lofty peak wedged between the French Vosges and the German Black Forest.

DISCOVER STUTTGART & THE BLACK FOREST

If one word could sum up Stuttgart & the Black Forest, it would surely be 'inventive'. Some 35,000 years ago, cavemen in the Swabian Alps gave the world figurative art and so sparked a string of firsts. Germany's southwesternmost state is the birthplace of Albert Einstein, and it was here that Gottlieb Daimler invented the gas engine and Count Ferdinand the zeppelin. And where would we be without Black Forest cake, cuckoo clocks and the ultimate beer food, the pretzel?

It's as much as travellers can do to tear their gaze away from the bewitching scenery, shifting from terraced vineyards between Heidelberg and Stuttgart to the Swabian Alps' misty castle-topped crags. Swing south to Lake Constance and the pastoral picture becomes one of ripening cornfields and wetlands outlined by the jagged Swiss Alps. To the west, the fabled Black Forest serves a soothing tonic of luxuriantly green valleys, where woodsy farmhouses crouch below softly rounded hills.

STUTTGART

Ask many Germans their opinion about the Stuttgarters and they will go off on a tangent: they are smooth operators behind a Mercedes wheel, speeding along the autobahn while flashing and gesticulating; they are city slickers in designer suits with a Swabian drawl; they are tight-fisted homebodies who slave away to *schaffe, schaffe, Häusle baue* (work, work, build a house). So much for the stereotypes.

Blessed with a prosperous air, a finger on the pulse of technology and an endearing love of the great outdoors, the real Stuttgart immediately challenges such preconceptions. One minute you're touring space-age car museums, the next you're strapping on boots to hike through vineyards, dining on Michelin-starred cuisine or shimmying beside ubercool 20-somethings in the bars on Theodor-Heuss-Strasse.

INFORMATION

Tourist office (☎ 222 80; www.stuttgart-tourist.de; Königstrasse 1a; 🕑 9am-8pm Mon-Fri, 9am-6pm Sat, 11am-6pm Sun)

SIGHTS

East of the station, the fountain-dotted **Mittlerer Schlossgarten** (Middle Palace Garden) draws thirsty crowds to its terrific beer garden (p210) in summer. The **Unterer Schlossgarten** (Lower Palace Garden) is a ribbon of greenery rambling northeast to the Neckar River and the **Rosensteinpark**, home to the zoo. Sitting south, the **Oberer Schlossgarten** (Upper Palace Garden) is framed by eye-catching landmarks like the columned **Staatstheater** (State Theatre) and the ultramodern glass-clad **Landtag** (State Parliament).

Stepping east, the neoclassical-meets-contemporary **Staatsgalerie** (State Gallery; ☎ 470 400; www.staatsgalerie-stuttgart.de; Konrad-Adenauer-Strasse 30-32; adult/concession €5.50/4,

special exhibitions €10/7; ⏲ 10am-6pm Tue-Sun, to 8pm Tue & Thu) bears British architect James Stirling's curvy, colourful imprint. Alongside big-name exhibitions, the gallery harbours a top-drawer collection of 20th-century art, showcasing works by Rembrandt, Monet, Dalí and pop idols Warhol and Lichtenstein.

Duke Karl Eugen von Württemberg's answer to Versailles was the exuberant three-winged **Neues Schloss** (New Palace), a baroque-neoclassical royal residence that now houses state government ministries. A bronze statue of Emperor Wilhelm I looking dashing on his steed graces nearby **Karlsplatz**.

CAR MUSEUMS

A futuristic swirl on the cityscape, the brand-new **Mercedes-Benz Museum** (**☎ 173 0000; www.museum-mercedes-benz.com; Mercedesstrasse 100; adult/concession €8/4; ⏲ 9am-6pm Tue-Sun; 🚊 Gottlieb-Daimler-Stadion)** takes a chronological spin through the Mercedes empire.

Like a pearly white spaceship preparing for lift-off, the barrier-free **Porsche Museum** (**☎ 9112 0911; www.porsche.com;**

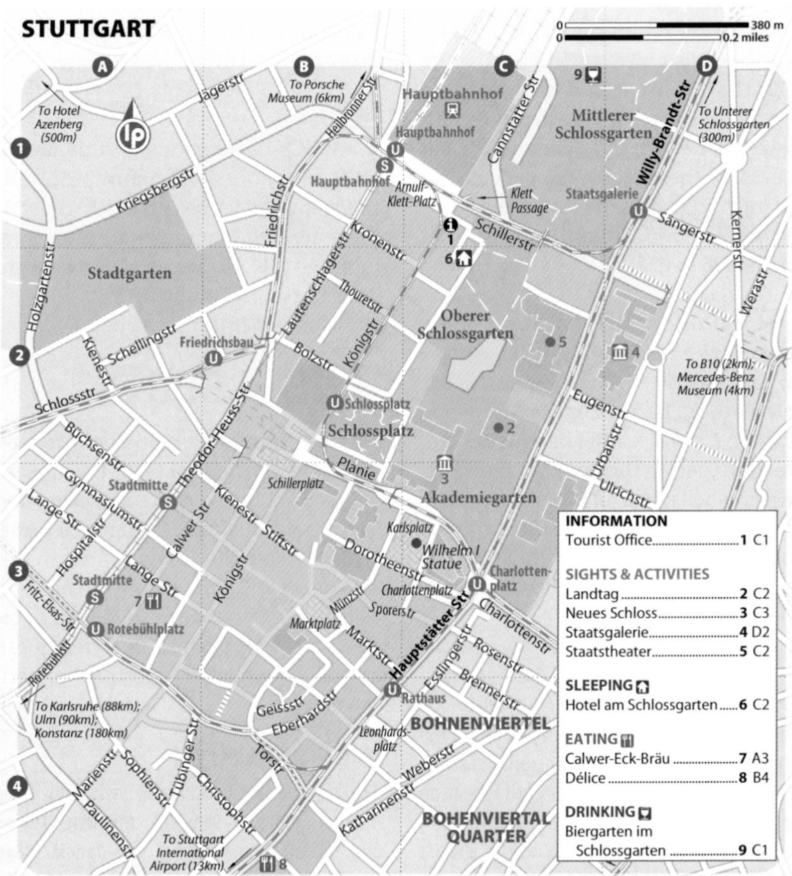

Porscheplatz 1; adult/concession €8/4; 9am-6pm Tue-Sun; Neuwirtshaus) is every little boy's dream.

SLEEPING

our pick **Hotel Azenberg** (**225 5040; www.hotelazenberg.de, in German; Seestrasse 114-116; s €85-145, d €105-165;**) This family-run retreat has plush, individually designed quarters with themes swinging from English country manor to Picasso. Work off breakfast doing laps in the pool. The hotel is a brisk uphill stroll or a short ride on bus 43 from Stadtmitte to Hölderlinstrasse.

Hotel am Schlossgarten (**202 60; www.hotelschlossgarten.com; Schillerstrasse 23; s €120-141, d €164-184;**) Sidling up to the Schloss, this hotel has swish rooms with above-par perks like free newspapers and chocolate; those facing the park are the quietest. Foodies jostle for a table in the Michelin-starred Zirbelstube restaurant (mains €28 to €52).

EATING & DRINKING

Calwer-Eck-Bräu (**2224 9440; Calwer Strasse 31; mains €9-18.50; 11am-midnight Mon-Thu, to 1am Fri & Sat, 10am-midnight Sun**) Dark polished wood and leather banquettes create a cosy feel in this 1st-floor brewpub. Loosen a belt notch for Swabian-Bavarian dishes like *Maultaschensuppe* (ravioli soup) and *Weisswurst* (white veal-pork sausage), which pair nicely with cloudy pilsners.

our pick **Délice** (**640 3222; www.restaurant-delice.de; Hauptstätter Strasse 61; 6.30pm-midnight Mon-Fri**) Save your appetite for dinner (presuming you've booked well ahead) at this vaulted Michelin-starred restaurant. Viennese master chef Friedrich Gutscher uses organic ingredients in taste sensations such as tender pigeon breast on boletus potatoes and curd ice cream with rose water. The sommelier will talk you through the award-winning riesling selection.

Biergarten im Schlossgarten (**226 1274; Mittlerer Schlossgarten; 10am-1.30am May-Oct**) Celebrate summer with beer and pretzels at Stuttgart's best-loved, 2000-seat beer garden in the green heart of the Schlossgarten. Regular live music gets steins a-swinging.

GETTING THERE & AWAY

AIR

Stuttgart International Airport (**STR; 01805-948 444; www.stuttgart-airport.com**), a major hub for **Germanwings** (**www.germanwings.com**), is 13km south of the city.

TRAIN

IC and ICE destinations include Berlin (€126, 5½ hours), Frankfurt (€56, 1¼ hours) and Munich (€46 to €52, 2¼ hours). There are frequent regional services to Tübingen (€11.30, one hour), Schwäbisch Hall's Hessental station (€13.30, 70 minutes) and Ulm (€16.70, one hour).

HEIDELBERG

Whether you go to Heidelberg to tiptoe in the footsteps of Mark Twain, who quipped about its drunken, duelling fraternities and eulogised its ruptured castle in his 1880 novel A *Tramp Abroad;* to see the light of William Turner in the Altstadt (Old Town) and the Neckar River; or to crawl the pubs Goethe-style in a quest for enlightenment, this postcard-perfect city obliges.

INFORMATION

Tourist office (**194 33; www.heidelberg-marketing.de; 9am-7pm Mon-Sat, 10am-6pm Sun & holidays Apr-Oct, 9am-6pm Mon-Sat Nov-Mar**)

BKR/IMAGEBROKER

Schloss Heidelberg

↘ HEIDELBERG'S SCHLOSS

Sticking up above the Altstadt like a picture-book pop-up against a theatrical backdrop of wooded hills, the partly ruined, red sandstone Schloss is Heidelberg's heart-stealer. Palatinate princes, stampeding Swedes, Protestant reformers, raging fires and lightning bolts – this Gothic-Renaissance fortress has seen the lot. Its tumultuous history, story-book looks and changing moods have inspired the pens of Mark Twain and Victor Hugo.

With a capacity of more than 220,000L, the 18th-century **Grosses Fass** (Great Vat) is the world's largest wine cask, shaped from 130 oak trees. Describing it as being 'as big as a cottage', Mark Twain bemoaned its emptiness and mused on its possible functions as a dance floor and gigantic cream churn.

To reach the castle you can either hoof it up the steep, cobbled **Burgweg** in about 10 minutes, or take the **Bergbahn** from the Kornmarkt station.

Things you need to know: Schloss (☎ 538 431; www.schloss-heidelberg.de; adult/concession €3/1.50, gardens free; 🕒 8am-5.30pm); Bergbahn (funicular railway; www.bergbahn-heidelberg.de; adult/6-14yr one way €3/2, return €5/4; 🕒 every 10min)

SIGHTS

KÖNIGSTUHL

For views over hill and dale, hop in one of the century-old rail cars trundling between the castle and the 550m-high **Königstuhl**. The return fare, with a stop at the Schloss, is adult €8 and child six to 14 years €6.

UNIVERSITY

Despite witty accounts of student duels and drunkenness, Mark Twain points out that 'idle students are not the rule' in Heidelberg in his 1880 novel *A Tramp Abroad*. Indeed Germany's oldest university, **Ruprecht-Karls-Universität** (www.uni-heidelberg.de), established in 1386 by Count Palatinate Ruprecht I, has plenty of gravitas – with

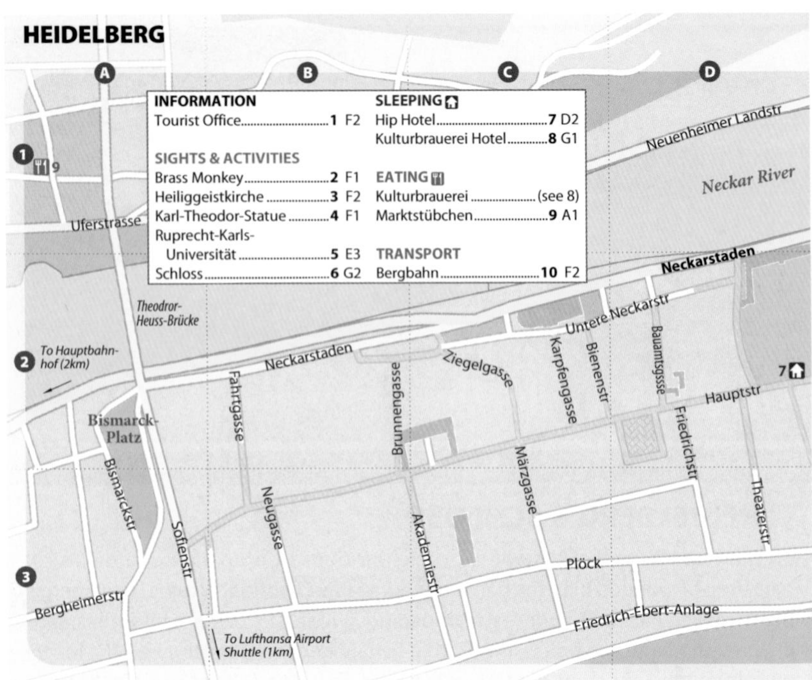

famous alumni such as composer Robert Schumann and chancellor Helmut Kohl.

MARKTPLATZ

Second only to the Schloss on the must-see list is the ochre-red **Heiliggeistkirche** (built 1398–1441) on the Marktplatz, an imposing Gothic church and a Protestant place of worship. See if you can spot the late-medieval markings on the facade, used to ensure that pretzels were of the requisite shape and size. For bird's-eye snapshots of Heidelberg, climb to the top of the **church spire** (**adult/student €1/0.50; 11am-5pm Mon-Sat, 1-5pm Sun mid-Mar–Oct, 11am-3pm Fri & Sat, 12.30-3pm Sun Nov–mid-Mar**).

ALTE BRÜCKE

On the Altstadt side of the bridge, listen for the giggles and clacking cameras to pinpoint a statue of a **brass monkey** holding a mirror and surrounded by mice: touch the mirror for wealth, the outstretched fingers to ensure you return to Heidelberg and the mice for many children. Speaking of fertility, the **Karl-Theodor-Statue** on the bridge refers to the legend that the prince fathered almost 200 illegitimate children.

PHILOSOPHENWEG

If you need solitude from the crowds, take a contemplative amble along the **Philosophenweg** (Philosophers' Way), on the hillside north of the Neckar River. Snaking through steep vineyards and orchards, the trail commands Kodak views of the Altstadt and the Schloss, which inspired German philosopher Georg Wilhelm Friedrich Hegel. The view is captivating at sundown when Heidelberg is bathed in a reddish glow. The walkway is

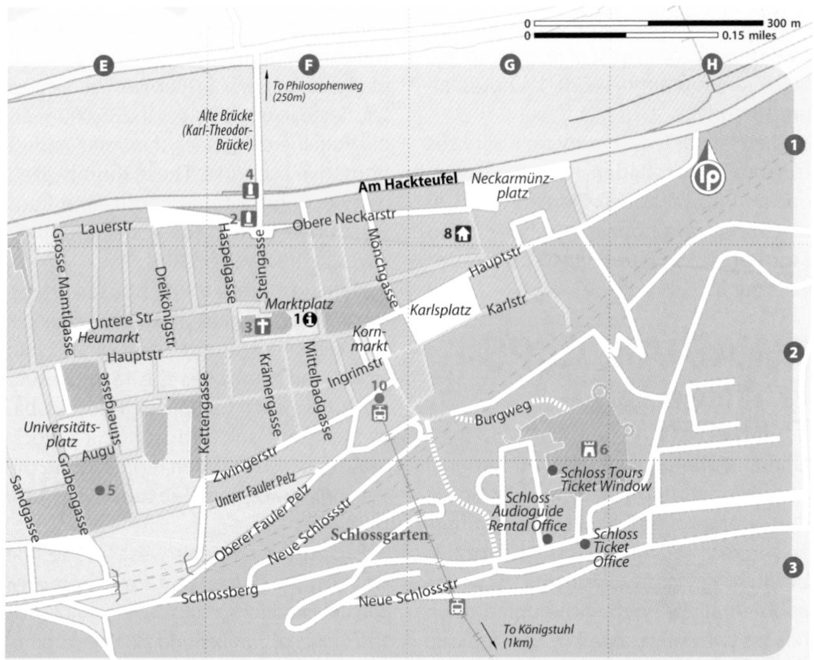

a well-known lovers' haunt, where many a young local is said to have lost their heart (and virginity!).

SLEEPING

Kulturbrauerei Hotel (☎ 502 980; www.heidelberger-kulturbrauerei.de, in German; Leyergasse 6; s €111-140, d €121-160; P) Great beer and grub are a boon at this microbrewery hotel. The stylish rooms are decked out in soft creams with shiny parquet floors and large windows.

our pick Hip Hotel (☎ 208 79; www.hip-hotel.de; Hauptstrasse 115; s €135-180, d €150-210; 💻) Snooze in a Fijian beach shack, a woodsy Canadian hunter's cottage, or a topsy-turvy Down Under room where everything (paintings, doors, bed) is upside down. In an age where cities spawn a theme hotel a minute, this place is truly hip. The globe-trotting Kischka family's eye for detail shines through, whether you plump for a Swiss ski hut or four-poster Prague romance.

EATING & DRINKING

Marktstübchen (☎ 653 0893; Marktplatz, Neuenheim; light meals €6-9) Tots whiz past on tricycles as their parents toast summer with cold beers and perfectly crisp *Flammkuchen* (Alsatian pizzas) on the square at this Alsatian-style bistro in Neuenheim.

KulturBrauerei (☎ 502 980; Leyergasse 6; mains €9.90-19.80) With its chandeliers and time-faded frescoes, this high-ceilinged microbrewery is an atmospheric spot for tucking heartily into *Schäufele* (pork shoulder) with sauerkraut, or quaffing home brews in the beer garden.

GETTING THERE & AWAY

Lufthansa's Airport Shuttle (☎ 0621-651 620; www.lufthansa-airportbus.de) links the

Crowne Plaza Hotel (Kurfürstenanlage 1-3), three blocks southwest of Bismarckplatz, with Frankfurt airport (€20, 1¼ hours, almost hourly).

There are at least hourly train services to/from Baden-Baden (€15.20 to €26, one hour to 1½ hours), Frankfurt (€15.20 to €25.50, one hour to 1½ hours) and Stuttgart (€19.60 to €35, 40 minutes to 1½ hours).

SWABIAN ALPS & AROUND

TÜBINGEN

Liberal students and deeply traditional *Burschenschaften* (fraternities) singing ditties for beloved Germania, ecowarriors and punks – all have a soft spot for this bewitchingly pretty Swabian city, where cobbled alleys lined with gabled town houses twist up to a perkily turreted castle. As did some of the country's biggest brains. It was here that Joseph Ratzinger, now Pope Benedict XVI, lectured on theology in the late 1960s, before fleeing to Bavaria, scandalised by Marxist-inspired student radicalism; and it was here, also, that Friedrich Hölderlin studied stanzas, Johannes Kepler planetary motions and Johann Wolfgang von Goethe the bottom of a beer glass.

INFORMATION

Tourist office (☎ 913 60; www.tuebingen-info.de; An der Neckarbrücke 1; 9am-7pm Mon-Fri, 10am-4pm Sat, plus 11am-4pm Sun May-Sep)

SIGHTS

On its fairy-tale perch above Tübingen, the turreted 16th-century **Schloss Hohentübingen** (Burgsteige 11) overlooks the Altstadt's red rooftops. An ornate Renaissance gate leads to the courtyard and the laboratory where Friedrich Miescher discovered DNA in 1869. Inside, the archaeology **museum** (☎ 297 7384; adult/concession €4/3; 10am-6pm Wed-Sun May-Sep, 10am-5pm Oct-Apr) hides the 35,000-year-old Vogelherd figurines, the world's oldest figurative artworks. These thumb-sized ivory carvings of mammoths and lions were unearthed in the Vogelherdhöhle caves in the Swabian Alps.

Half-timbered town houses frame the Altstadt's main plaza **Am Markt**, a much-loved student hang-out. Rising above the hubbub is the 15th-century **Rathaus** (town hall), with a riotous baroque facade and an astronomical clock. Statues of four women representing the seasons grace the **Neptune Fountain** opposite.

Facing the church's west facade, the **Cottahaus** is the one-time home of Johann Friedrich Cotta, who first published the works of Schiller and Goethe. A bit of a lad, Goethe conducted detailed research on Tübingen's pubs during his week-long stay in 1797. The party-loving genius is commemorated by the plaque *'Hier wohnte Goethe'* (Goethe lived here). On the wall of the grungy student digs next door is the perhaps more insightful sign *'Hier kotzte Goethe'* (Goethe puked here).

GETTING THERE & AWAY

Tübingen is an easy train ride from Stuttgart (€11.30, 45 to 60 minutes, at least two an hour) and Villingen (€17.80 to €22.50, 1½ to two hours, hourly) in the Black Forest.

ULM

Starting with the statistics, Ulm has the crookedest house (as listed in *Guinness*) and one of the narrowest (4.5m wide), the world's oldest zoomorphic sculpture (aged 30,000 years) and tallest cathedral steeple (161.5m high), and is the birthplace of the

RICHARD I'ANSON

Wintertime view over Heidelberg (p210)

all-time brainiest physicist, Albert Einstein. Relatively speaking, of course.

INFORMATION

Tourist office (☎ 161 2830; www.tourismus.ulm.de; Stadthaus, Münsterplatz 50; ⌚ 9am-6pm Mon-Sat, 11am-3pm Sun Apr-Oct, 9am-6pm Mon-Fri, 9am-4pm Sat Nov-Mar)

SIGHTS

Ooh, it's so big…first-time visitors gush as they strain their neck muscles gazing up to the **Münster** (Cathedral; Münsterplatz; admission free; ⌚ 9am-4.45pm Jan & Feb, to 5.45pm Mar & Oct, to 6.45pm Apr-Jun & Sep, to 7.45pm Jul & Aug). It is. And rather beautiful. Celebrated for its 161.5m-high steeple, the world's tallest, this Goliath of cathedrals took a staggering 500 years to build from the first stone laid in 1377. Note the hallmarks on each stone, inscribed by cutters who were paid by the block. Those intent on cramming the Münster into one photo, filigree spire and all, should lie down on the cobbles.

Lording it over the Marktplatz, the 14th-century, step-gabled **Rathaus** sports an ornately painted Renaissance facade and a gilded **astrological clock**. Inside there is a replica of **Berblinger's flying machine**. In front is the **Fischkastenbrunnen**, a fountain where fishmongers kept their catch alive on market days.

A nod to Ulm's most famous son, Jürgen Goertz's bronze **fountain** shows a wild-haired Albert Einstein (who was born in Ulm but left when he was one year old), with his tongue poking out. Standing in front of the 16th-century *Zeughaus* (arsenal), the rocket-snail creation is a satirical play on humanity's attempts to manipulate evolution for its own self-interest. Nearby, at Zeughaus 14, is a single stone bearing the inscription *Ein Stein* (One Stone).

GETTING THERE & AWAY

Ulm is well-served by ICE trains; major destinations include Stuttgart (€16.70 to €24, one hour, several hourly) and Munich (€24.80 to €34, 1½ hours to two hours, several hourly).

JKI/IMAGEBROKER

Half-timbered houses in Schiltach's town centre

BADEN-BADEN

'So nice that you have to name it twice', gushed Bill Clinton. Indeed there is no denying Baden-Baden's allure to royals, the rich and celebrities – Obama and Bismarck, Queen Victoria and Victoria Beckham included. Yet 'nice' hardly does bon vivant Baden-Baden justice; it is without doubt one of Baden-Württemberg's most refined cities – resplendent with chichi boutiques, smart pavement cafes, and manicured gardens where fountains dance and sparkle, and locals walk coiffed poodles.

Locked in an embrace between the Black Forest and France, this grand dame of German spas stills turn heads with her graceful belle époque villas, fortunes in her sumptuous casino, and the moods in her templelike thermal baths that put the *Baden* (bathe) in Baden.

INFORMATION

Main tourist office (☎ 275 200; www.baden-baden.com; Schwarzwaldstrasse 52; 🕑 9am-6pm Mon-Sat, to 1pm Sun)

SIGHTS & ACTIVITIES

KURHAUS & CASINO

Corinthian columns and a frieze of mythical griffins grace the belle époque facade of the monumental **Kurhaus** (☎ 353 202; www.kurhaus-baden-baden.de, in German; Kaiserallee 1), which towers above well-groomed gardens. An alley of chestnut trees, flanked by two rows of boutiques, links the Kurhaus with Kaiserallee.

In the leafy park just north sits the **Trinkhalle** (Pump Room; Kaiserallee 3), where you can wander a 90m-long portico embellished with 19th-century frescoes of local legends. Baden-Baden's elixir of youth, some say, is the free curative mineral water that gushes from a faucet (10am to 2am, until 3am Friday and Saturday) linked to the springs below. A cafe sells plastic cups for €0.20, or bring your own bottle to fill with super water.

SPAS

If it's the body of Venus and the complexion of Cleopatra you desire, take the waters in the sumptuous 19th-century **Friedrichsbad** (☎ 275 920; www.roemisch-irisches-bad.de; Römerplatz 1; 🕑 9am-10pm, last admission 7pm). As Mark Twain put it: 'after 10 minutes you forget time; after 20 minutes, the world'. Modesty, rheumatic aches and the nudity of fellow bathers are soon forgotten as you slip into the regime of steaming, scrubbing, hot-cold bathing and dunking in the **Roman-Irish Bath** (admission €21, incl soap & brush massage €31). With its cupola, mosaics and column-ringed pool, the bathhouse is the vision of a neo-Renaissance palace.

For the modest, there's the glass-fronted **Caracalla-Therme** (☎ 275 940; www.caracalla.de; Römerplatz 11; 2/3/4hr €13/15/17; 8am-10pm, last admission 8pm), where you can keep your swimsuit on in the pools, grottos and surge channels, but not in the saunas upstairs.

SLEEPING & EATING

Heiligenstein (☎ 961 40; www.hotel-heiligenstein.de, in German; Heiligensteinstrasse 19a, Neuweier; s €75-79, d €110-115; P) Insiders know it's worth going the extra mile (or seven) to this sweet hotel overlooking Neuweier's vineyards. The slick rooms come with balconies and guests can put their feet up in the spa and gardens.

Rizzi (☎ 258 38; Augustaplatz 1; mains €15-24; noon-1am) A summertime favourite, this stout pink villa's tree-shaded patio faces Lichtentaler Allee. Italian numbers such as whole sea bass and saffron-infused risotto pair nicely with local rieslings.

GETTING THERE & AWAY

Karlsruhe-Baden-Baden airport (Baden Airpark; www.badenairpark.de), 15km west of town, is linked to London and Dublin by Ryanair.

Baden-Baden is on a major north–south rail corridor. Twice-hourly destinations include Freiburg (€17.80 to €27, 45 to 90 minutes) and Karlsruhe (€9.50 to €14.50, 15 to 30 minutes).

SCHILTACH

Schiltach looks and feels like something out of a children's fairy story, nestling below thick forest and hugging the banks of the Kinzig and Schiltach Rivers. The lovingly restored half-timbered houses, which once belonged to tanners, merchants and raft builders, are a riot of crimson geraniums in summer. Drop off the map for a spell to unwind in what is, perhaps, the fairest village in the Kinzig Valley.

INFORMATION

The **tourist office** (☎ 5850; www.schiltach.de; Marktplatz 6; 9am-noon & 2-5pm Mon-Thu, 9am-noon Fri) in the Rathaus can help find accommodation and offers free internet access. Hiking options are marked on an enamel sign just opposite.

SIGHTS & ACTIVITIES

Centred on a trickling fountain, the sloping, triangular **Marktplatz** is Schiltach at its picture-book best. The frescoes of the step-gabled, 16th-century **Rathaus** opposite depict scenes from local history. Clamber south up **Schlossbergstrasse**, pausing to notice the plaques that denote the trades of one-time residents, such as the *Strumpfstricker* (stocking weaver) at No 6, and the sloping roofs where tanners once dried their skins. Up top there are views over Schiltach's red rooftops to the surrounding hills.

Museum am Markt (☎ 5875; Marktplatz 13; admission free; 11am-5pm Apr-Oct) romps through local history with exhibits from antique spinning wheels to Biedermeier costumes.

GUTACH

Well worth the 4km detour south of the Kinzig Valley, the **Schwarzwälder Freilichtmuseum** (Black Forest Open-Air Museum; ☎ 935 60; www.vogtsbauernhof.org; adult/6-17yr/concession/family €6/3/5/13; 9am-6pm late Mar-early Nov, to 7pm Aug) spirals around the Vogtsbauernhof, a self-contained, early-17th-century farmstead. Farmhouses shifted from their original locations have been painstakingly reconstructed, using techniques such as thatching and panelling, to create this authentic farming hamlet and preserve age-old Black Forest traditions.

FREIBURG

Freiburg is a story-book tableau of gabled town houses, narrow lanes and cobbled squares, given its happy-ever-after by some 22,000 students who add an injection of cool, a love of alfresco dining and attitude-free nightlife to the medieval mix. Crouching at the foot of wooded hills, Freiburg's scenery is pure Black Forest, but its spirit is deliciously southern.

INFORMATION

Tourist office (☎ 388 1880; www.freiburg.de; Rathausplatz 2-4; 🕑 8am-8pm Mon-Fri, 9.30am-5pm Sat, 10am-noon Sun Jun-Sep, 8am-6pm Mon-Fri, 9.30am-2.30pm Sat, 10am-noon Sun Oct-May)

SIGHTS

Freiburg's Gothic **Münster** is the monster of all minsters, a red-sandstone giant that dwarfs the bustling Münsterplatz, with a riot of punctured spires that flush scarlet at dusk. Crane your neck to notice the leering **gargoyles**, including a mischievous one on the southern flank that once spouted water from its backside.

Facing the Münster's south side and embellished with polychrome tiled turrets is the arcaded brick-red **Historisches Kaufhaus**, a 16th-century merchants' hall. The coats of arms on the oriels and the four figures above the balcony symbolise Freiburg's allegiance to the House of Habsburg.

Across the Gewerbekanal, the **Museum für Neue Kunst** (Museum of Modern Art; ☎ 201 2583; Marienstrasse 10; adult/concession €2/1; 🕑 10am-5pm Tue-Sun) highlights 20th-century expressionist and abstract art, including emotive works by Oskar Kokoschka and Otto Dix.

A canal babbles west through the charming former fishing quarter of **Fischerau** to **Martinstor** (Kaiser-Joseph-Strasse), one of Freiburg's two surviving town gates, and, slightly north, **Bertoldsbrunnen** fountain, which marks where the city's thorough-

SIR/IMAGEBROKER

Münster interior, Freiburg

fares have crossed since its foundation in 1091.

Veering east of the Museum für Neue Kunst, you will come to the 13th-century city gate **Schwabentor**, emblazoned with a mural of St George slaying the dragon. Trails nearby twist up to the forested **Schlossberg**, topped by a lookout tower, the **Aussichtsturm**, which is shaped like an ice-cream cone, and commands panoramic views.

The chestnut-shaded **Rathausplatz** is a popular hang-out. On its western side, the **Neues Rathaus** (New City Hall) comprises two Renaissance town houses with arcades that lead through to a cobblestone courtyard. The tower's tinkling **carillon** plays at noon daily.

Linked to the Neues Rathaus by an over-the-street bridge is the step-gabled, oxblood-red **Altes Rathaus** (Old City Hall; 1559), which shelters the tourist office. Freiburg's oldest edifice, the early-14th-century **Gerichtslaube**, is a short hop west along Turmstrasse.

SLEEPING & EATING

Hotel Schwarzwälder Hof (**☎ 380 30; www.schwarzwaelder-hof.eu; Herrenstrasse 43; s €45-70, d €75-105; 💻**) Down the cobbled lane and up the wrought-iron staircase lie well-kept quarters. Choose between 'basic' (but rather nice) and 'modern' rooms with dark-wood floors, flat-screen TVs and Altstadt views. The rustic tavern (mains €8.80 to €16.50) serves regional fare and wines.

Hotel Oberkirch (**☎ 202 6868; www.hotel-oberkirch.de; Münsterplatz 22; s €95-118, d €139-161; P 💻**) Our readers sing the praises of this green-shuttered, 250-year-old hotel, with the Münster views of a million postcards. The countrified rooms reveal a Laura Ashley love of florals, and bathrooms positively sparkle.

BEHOLD THE SUPER BOG

If giant cuckoo clocks and Black Forest cherry cake no longer thrill, how about a trip to the world's largest loo? Drive a couple of minutes south of Gutach on the B33 to Hornberg and there, in all its lavatorial glory, stands the titanic toilet dreamed up by Philippe Starck. Even if you have no interest in designer urinals or home jacuzzis, it's worth visiting the **Duravit Design Centre** (**☎ 07833-700; www.duravit.de, in German; Werderstrasse 36, Hornberg; 🕒 8am-7pm Mon-Fri, noon-4pm Sat**) alone for the tremendous view across the Black Forest from the 12m-high ceramic loo.

Tacheles (**☎ 319 6669; Grünwälderstrasse 17; schnitzels €7.50; 🕒 11.30am-2am Mon-Thu, to 5am Fri & Sat, to 1am Sun**) Eat schnitzel and be merry is the motto at this laid-back courtyard-bar. On the menu: a mind-boggling 300 varieties of breaded veal.

Englers Weinkrügle (**☎ 383 115; Konviktstrasse 12; mains €8-13.50; 🕒 11am-2pm & 5.30pm-midnight Tue-Sun**) Wisteria drapes this woody Baden-style *Weinstube* (traditional tavern), dishing up flavoursome regional fare like trout in various guises (for instance in riesling or almond-butter sauce).

DRINKING

Alte Wache (**☎ 202 870; Münsterplatz 38; 🕒 10am-7pm**) Taste some local Pinot noir wines while gazing up to the Münster's gargoyles on the cobbled terrace of this 18th-century guardhouse turned buzzy wine bar.

Schlappen (**☎ 334 94; Löwenstrasse 2; 🕒 11am-1am Mon-Thu, 11am-3am Fri & Sat, 3pm-1am Sun**) Posters cover every inch of this

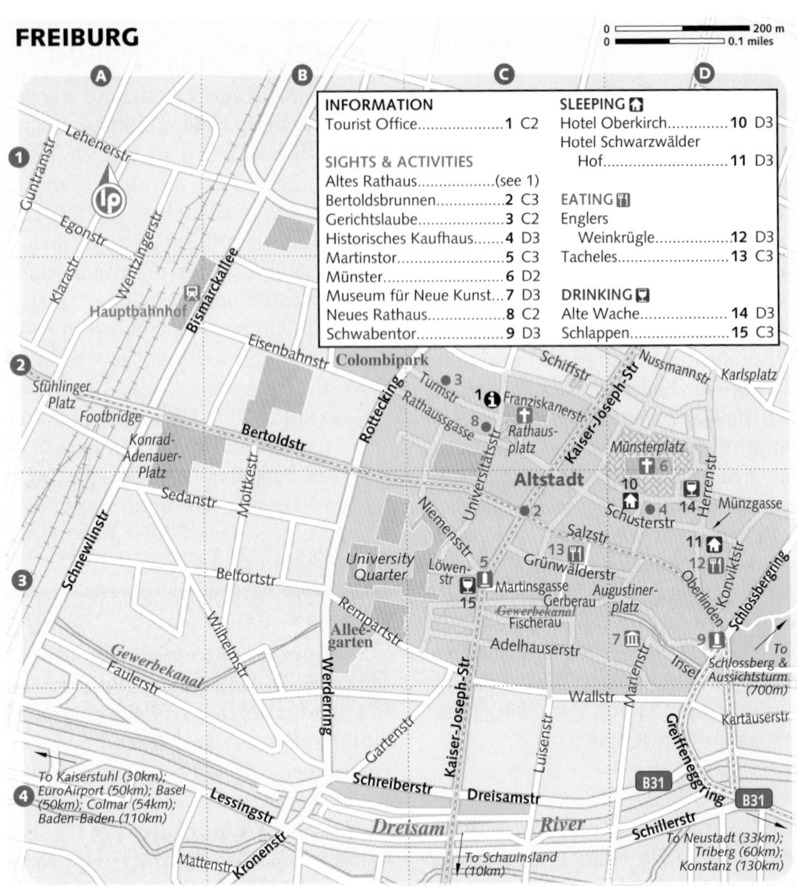

funky watering hole, which attracts a mixed bunch. Some come for the *Flammkuchen* (Alsatian pizza), some to sample different types of absinthe, and some to check out the wacky men's urinal – look in the mirror and watch the water flow…

GETTING THERE & AWAY

AIR

Freiburg shares **EuroAirport** (www.euroairport.com) with Basel (Switzerland) and Mulhouse (France). Low-cost airlines easyJet and Ryanair fly to destinations including London, Berlin, Rome and Alicante from here.

TRAIN

Freiburg is on a major north–south rail corridor with frequent departures for destinations such as Basel (€14.10 to €21.80, 45 to 65 minutes) and Baden-Baden (€17.80 to €27, 45 minutes to 1½ hours). Freiburg is also the western terminus of the Höllentalbahn to Donaueschingen via Titisee-Neustadt (€4.80, 38 minutes, twice an hour).

AROUND FREIBURG

SCHAUINSLAND

Freiburg seems tiny as you drift up above the city and a tapestry of meadows and forest on the 3.6km **Schauinslandbahn** (**cable car; adult/6-14yr/concession return €11.50/7/10.50, one way €8/5/7.50; 9am-5pm, to 6pm Jul-Sep**) to the 1284m **Schauinsland peak** (**www.bergwelt-schauinsland.de, in German**). The lift provides a speedy link between Freiburg and the Black Forest highlands.

Up top there's a lookout tower commanding astounding views to the Rhine Valley and Alps, plus walking, cross-country and cycling trails that allow you to capture the scenery from many angles. For downhill action, try the bone-shaking 8km off-road **scooter track** (**2pm & 5pm Sun May-Jun, Sat & Sun Jul & Sep, Wed-Sun Aug**), which costs €18 including equipment hire. To reach Schauinslandbahn from Freiburg, take tram 4 to Günterstal and then bus 21 to Talstation.

KAISERSTUHL

Squeezed between the Black Forest and French Vosges, these low-lying **volcanic hills** in the Upper Rhine Valley yield some highly quaffable wines including fruity *Spätburgunder* (Pinot noir) and *Grauburgunder* (Pinot gris) varieties.

The grapes owe their quality to a unique microclimate, hailed as Germany's warmest and sunniest, and fertile loess (clay and silt) soil that retains heat during the night. Nature enthusiasts should keep their peepers open for rarities like sand lizards, praying mantis and European bee-eaters.

The Breisach tourist office can advise on cellar tours, wine tastings, bike paths like the 55km **Kaiserstuhltour** circuit, and trails such as the **Winzerweg** (Wine Growers' Trail), an intoxicating 15km hike from Achkarren to Riegel.

The **Kaiserstuhlbahn** does a loop around the Kaiserstuhl. Stops (where you may have to change trains) include Sasbach, Endingen, Riegel and Gottenheim.

TRIBERG

Home to Germany's highest waterfall, heir to the original Black Forest cake recipe and nesting ground of the world's biggest cuckoos – Triberg lays on the superlatives with a trowel. It was here that in bleak winters past folk huddled in snowbound farmhouses to carve the clocks that would drive the planet cuckoo; and here that in a flash of brilliance the waterfall was harnessed to power the country's first electric street lamps in 1884.

INFORMATION

Tourist office (**☎ 866 490; www.triberg.de, in German; Wahlfahrtstrasse 4; 10am-5pm Nov-Apr, to 6pm May-Oct**) Inside the Schwarzwald-Museum, 50m uphill from the river.

SIGHTS

Niagara they ain't, but Germany's highest **waterfalls** (**☎ 2724; adult/8-16yr/family €3/1.50/7; Mar-early Nov, 25-30 Dec**) do exude their own wild romanticism. The Gutach River feeds the seven-tiered falls, which drop a total of 163m. It's annoying to have to pay to experience nature but the fee is at least worth it. The trail up through the wooded gorge is guarded by tribes of red squirrels after the bags of nuts (€1) sold at the entrance.

Triberg is the world's undisputed cuckoo-clock capital. Two timepieces claim the title of *weltgröste Kuckucksuhr* (world's largest cuckoo clock), giving rise to the battle of the birds. Triberg's underdog **World's Biggest Cuckoo Clock** (**☎ 4689; Untertalstrasse 28; adult/6-10yr**

TOP FIVE GREAT DRIVES

More than just pretty drives, many of these routes highlight a theme, such as Franco-German friendship, clock-making and grape-growing. Local tourist offices provide details and brochures.

- **Schwarzwald-Hochstrasse** (Black Forest Hwy) Following the B500, this connects Baden-Baden with Freudenstadt, 60km to the south. It affords expansive views of the Upper Rhine Valley and the Vosges Mountains in Alsace (France). The route skirts a number of lakes, including the pine-fringed Mummelsee.
- **Badische Weinstrasse** (Baden Wine Rd) An oenologist's delight. From Baden-Baden south to Lörrach, this 160km route corkscrews through the red-wine vineyards of Ortenau, the Pinot noir of Kaiserstuhl and Tuniberg, and the white-wine vines of Markgräflerland.
- **Schwarzwald-Tälerstrasse** (Black Forest Valley Rd) Twists 100km from Rastatt to Freudenstadt, affording views across steep valleys (the Murgtal and Kinzig), lush woodlands, granite cliffs and gin-clear streams. High points include Gernsbach's half-timbered houses, Forbach's bridge and freshly tapped beer in Alpirsbach.
- **Deutsche Uhrenstrasse** (German Clock Rd) A 320km loop starting in Villingen-Schwenningen that revolves around the story of clock-making in the Black Forest. Stops include Furtwangen and cuckoo-clock capital Triberg.
- **Grüne Strasse** (Green Rd) Links the Black Forest with the Rhine Valley and the Vosges Mountains in France. Popular with hikers and cyclists, this 160km route takes you through Kirchzarten, Freiburg, Breisach, Colmar and Munster.

€1.20/0.60, 9am-noon & 1-6pm), complete with gear-driven innards, is 1km up the hill in Schonach, inside a snug chalet. Its commercially savvy **rival** (**☎ 962 20; www.uhren-park.de; Schonachbach 27; admission €1.50; 9am-6pm Mon-Sat, 10am-6pm Sun Easter-Oct, 9am-5.30pm Mon-Sat, 11am-5pm Sun Nov-Easter**), listed in the *Guinness World Records,* is at the other end of town on the B33 between Triberg and Hornberg.

A glockenspiel bashes out melodies and a cuckoo greets his fans with a hopelessly croaky squawk on the hour at the **House of 1000 Clocks** (**☎ 963 00; Hauptstrasse 81; 10am-5pm**). Inside, the clocks range from classic to funky; the latest quartz models feature a sensor that sends the cuckoo to sleep after dark. Ah…peace at last!

EATING

Café Schäfer (**☎ 4465; www.cafe-schaefer-triberg.de; Hauptstrasse 33; 9am-6pm Mon-Fri, 8am-6pm Sat, 11am-6pm Sun, closed Wed**) Other Black Forest cakes pale in comparison to Claus Schäfer's masterpiece: layers of moist sponge, fresh cream and sour cherries, with the merest suggestion of *Kirsch* (cherry liqueur). So light you can eat another slice (well it would be rude not to), the *Kirschtorte* at this old-world cafe is baked according to the original recipe.

GETTING THERE & AWAY

The Schwarzwaldbahn railway line loops southeast to Konstanz (€21.50, 1½ hours, hourly), and northwest to Offenburg (€10.30, 40 minutes, hourly).

Bus 7150 travels north to Offenburg; bus 7265 heads south to Villingen via St Georgen. Local buses operate between the Bahnhof and Marktplatz, and to the nearby town of Schonach (hourly).

WUTACHSCHLUCHT

This wild gorge of jagged, near-vertical rock faces was carved out by the swift, serpentine **Wutach** (literally 'angry river'). The river rises almost at the summit of the Feldberg and flows into the Rhine near Waldshut, on the Swiss border. Wildlife spotters will want their binoculars handy in this **nature reserve**, where a microclimate supports orchids and ferns, rare birds from treecreepers to kingfishers, and countless species of butterflies, beetles and lizards.

To truly appreciate the Wutachschlucht, hike the 13km from **Schattenmühle** to **Wutachmühle** (or vice versa). Energy permitting, you can add the lush, 2.5km **Lotenbach-Klamm** (Lotenbach Glen) to your tour. May to September is the best time to tackle the walk. Be sure to carry supplies as there's very little between the trailheads.

The **tourist office** (☎ 07703-7607; www.bonndorf.de, in German; Martinstrasse 5; 9am-noon & 2-6pm Mon-Fri, 10am-noon Sat May-Oct, 9am-noon & 2-5pm Mon-Fri except Wed afternoon Nov-Apr) in Bonndorf, 15km east of Schluchsee, has hiking information, maps and a list of places to stay.

Bus 7258 runs between Bonndorf and Neustadt train station (€4, 40 minutes, hourly Monday to Saturday, every two hours Sunday). Bus 7344 links Bonndorf to Schattenmühle and Wutachmühle (€2.90, 27 minutes, every hour or two Monday to Friday).

LAKE CONSTANCE

KONSTANZ

Hugging the northwestern shore of Lake Constance and clinging to the Swiss border, scored by the Rhine and outlined by the Alps, Konstanz is a natural stunner. Roman emperors, medieval traders and the bishops of the 15th-century Council of Constance all left their mark on this red-roofed town, mercifully spared from the WWII bombings that obliterated other German cities.

When the sun pops its head out, Konstanz is a feel-good university town with a lively buzz and upbeat bar scene, particularly in the cobbled Altstadt and the harbour where the voluptuous *Imperia* turns. In summer locals,

WER/IMAGEBROKER

Lakeside promenade, Lake Constance

MKL/IMAGEBROKER

Meersburg, Lake Constance

KKR/IMAGEBROKER

Lindau's harbour and Mangturm (Old Lighthouse)

IF YOU LIKE...

If you like **Lake Constance**, venture over to **Lindau** (www.lindau.de), Germany's Garden of Eden and the Bavarian Riviera:

- In summer the harbourside **Seepromenade** has Mediterranean flair, with its palms, bobbing boats and well-heeled tourists sunning themselves in pavement cafes.
- Out at the harbour gates, looking across to the Alps, is Lindau's signature 33m-high **Neuer Leuchtturm** (New Lighthouse) and, just in case you forget which state you're in, a statue of the Bavarian lion. The square tile-roofed, 13th-century **Mangturm** (Old Lighthouse) guards the northern edge of the sheltered port.
- Lindau's biggest stunner is the 15th-century, step-gabled **Altes Rathaus** (Bismarckplatz), a frescoed frenzy of cherubs, merry minstrels and galleons. Next door is the candy-pink, baroque **Neues Rathaus** where a glockenspiel plays at 11.45am daily.
- Lions and voluptuous dames dance across the trompe l'oeil facade of the flamboyantly baroque **Haus zum Cavazzen**. Inside, the **Stadtmuseum** (☎ 944 073; Marktplatz 6; adult/concession €3/1.50; 11am-5pm Tue-Fri & Sun, 2-5pm Sat) showcases a fine collection of furniture, weapons and paintings.

nicknamed *Seehasen* (lake hares), head outdoors to inline skate along the leafy promenade and enjoy lazy days in lakefront lidos.

INFORMATION

Tourist office (☎ 133 030; www.konstanz.de/tourismus; Bahnhofplatz 13; 9am-6.30pm Mon-Fri, 9am-4pm Sat, 10am-1pm Sun & holidays Apr-Oct, 9am-12.30pm & 2-6pm Mon-Fri Nov-Mar)

SIGHTS

At the merest hint of a sunray, the tree-fringed, sculpture-dotted **lakefront promenade** lures inline skaters, cyclists, walkers and ice cream–licking crowds.

At the end of the pier, giving ferry passengers a come-hither look from her rotating pedestal, stands **Imperia**. Peter Lenk's 9m-high sculpture of a buxom prostitute, said to have plied her trade in the days of the Council of Constance, is immortalised in a novel by Honoré de Balzac. In her clutches are hilarious sculptures of a naked (and sagging) Pope Martin V and Holy Roman Emperor Sigismund, symbolising religious and imperial power.

The nearby **Zeppelin Monument** shows the airship inventor Count Ferdinand von Zeppelin in an Icarus-like pose. He was born in 1838 on the **Insel**, an islet a short stroll north through the flowery **Stadtgarten** park, where there's a **children's playground**.

North of the Insel, the **Rheinbrücke** links the Altstadt with newer quarters across the Rhine. On the opposite bank, Seestrasse has a row of handsome **art-nouveau villas**.

Towering above Münsterplatz, the sandstone **Münster** (⌚ 9am-6pm Mon-Sat, 10am-6pm Sun), an architectural potpourri of Romanesque, Gothic and baroque styles, was the church of the diocese of Konstanz until 1821. Standouts include the 15th-century **Schnegg**, an ornate spiral staircase in the northern transept, to the left of which a door leads to the 1000-year-old **crypt**. From the crypt's polychrome chapel, you enter the sublime **Gothic cloister**.

Slightly south of the Münster on Kanzleistrasse, the flamboyantly frescoed Renaissance **Rathaus** hides a peaceful arcaded courtyard.

Best explored on foot, Konstanz' historic heart, Niederburg, stretches north from the Münster to the Rhine. The twisting cobbled lanes lined with half-timbered town houses are the place to snoop around galleries, antique shops and 13th-century **Kloster Zoffingen** (Brückengasse 15), Konstanz' only remaining convent, still in the hands of Dominican nuns.

SLEEPING & EATING

Villa Barleben (☎ 942 330; www.hotel-barleben.de, in German; Seestrasse 15; s €95-215, d €165-265) Gregariously elegant, this 19th-century villa's sunny rooms and corridors are sprinkled with antiques and ethnic art. The rambling lakefront gardens are ideal for dozing in a *Strandkörb* (beach lounger), G&T in hand, or enjoying lunch on the terrace.

Brauhaus Johann Albrecht (☎ 250 45; Konradigasse 2; mains €8-16) This step-gabled brewpub pairs light, hoppy beers with roll-me-out-the-door fare like fat pig trotters with sauerkraut. Sit on the terrace in summer.

GETTING THERE & AWAY

Konstanz is Lake Constance's main ferry hub; Konstanz' Hauptbahnhof is the southern terminus of the scenic Schwarzwaldbahn, which trundles hourly through the Black Forest, linking Offenburg with towns such as Triberg and Villingen. To reach Lake Constance's northern shore, you usually have to change in Radolfzell. The Schweizer Bahnhof has connections to destinations throughout Switzerland.

FRIEDRICHSHAFEN

Near the eastern end of Friedrichshafen's lakefront promenade, Seestrasse, is the **Zeppelin Museum** (☎ 380 10; www.zeppelin-museum.de; Seestrasse 22; adult/concession/family €7.50/3/17; ⌚ 9am-5pm Tue-Sun May-Oct, 10am-5pm Tue-Sun Nov-Apr, also Mon Jul & Aug), housed in the Bauhaus-style former Hafenbahnhof, built in 1932.

DWH/IMAGEBROKER

Boats on Lake Constance

IF YOU LIKE...

If you like **Konstanz'** gorgeous setting on Lake Constance, take advantage of the water activities on offer:

- For some ozone-enriched summer fun, grab your bathers and head to **Strandbad Horn** (☎ 635 50; Eichhornstrasse 100; admission free; year-round), 4km northeast of the centre. The lakefront beach has sunbathing lawns, a kiddie pool, playground, volleyball courts and even a naturist area.
- If you would prefer to trundle across the lake, hire a pedalo at **Bootsvermietung Konstanz** (☎ 218 81; per hr €8; 11am-sunset Easter–mid-Oct).
- **La Canoa** (☎ 959 595; www.lacanoa.com, in German; Robert-Bosch-Strasse 4; canoe/kayak per hr €11/16, per day €28/39; 10am-6pm Mon-Fri, to 4pm Sat) rents high-quality canoes and kayaks in Konstanz and from various other Lake Constance locations, including Lindau and Friedrichshafen.

GETTING THERE & AWAY

Ryanair flies from London Stansted to **Friedrichshafen's airport** (www.fly-away.de), frequently linked to the centre by buses 7586 and 7394. **InterSky** (www.intersky.biz) flies mainly to cities in Germany and Italy.

Ferry sailing times are posted on the waterfront just outside the Zeppelin Museum.

From Monday to Friday, seven times a day, express bus 7394 makes the trip to Konstanz (1¼ hours) via Meersburg (30 minutes). Birnau and Meersburg are also served almost hourly by bus 7395.

Friedrichshafen is on the Lake Constance/Bodensee–Gürtelbahn rail line, which runs along the lake's northern shore from Radolfzell to Lindau. There are also regular services on the Bodensee–Oberschwaben–Bahn, which runs to Ravensburg (€3.65, 21 minutes) and Ulm (€17.80, 1¼ hours).

↘ COLOGNE & THE RHINELAND

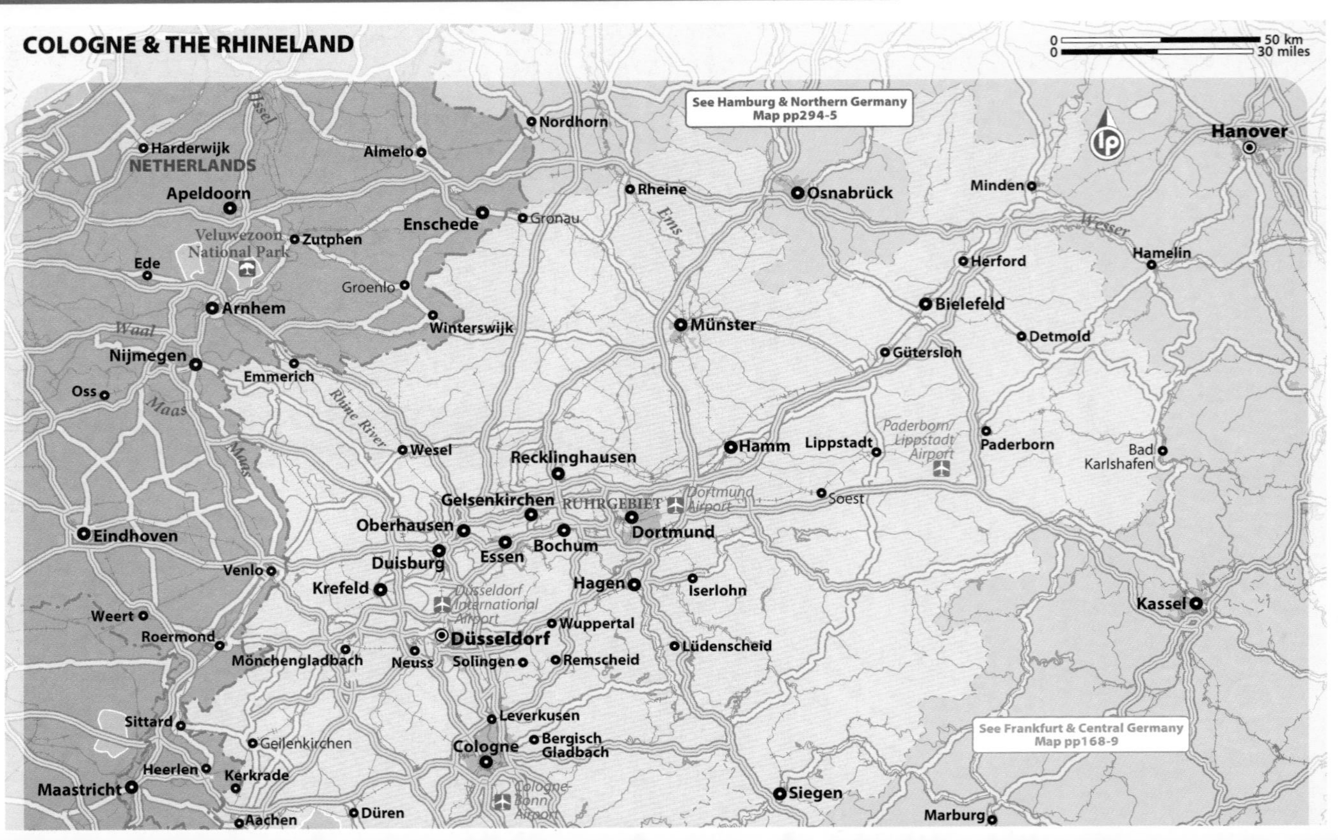

COLOGNE & THE RHINELAND
0 50 km
0 30 miles
See Hamburg & Northern Germany Map pp294-5
See Frankfurt & Central Germany Map pp168-9
Nordhorn
Harderwijk
NETHERLANDS
Almelo
IJssel
Apeldoorn
Enschede
Gronau
Rheine
Ems
Osnabrück
Minden
Wesser
Hanover
Hamelin
Veluwezoon National Park
Zutphen
Ede
Groenlo
Arnhem
Winterswijk
Münster
Herford
Bielefeld
Detmold
Gütersloh
Waal
Nijmegen
Emmerich
Oss
Maas
Rhine River
Wesel
Recklinghausen
Hamm
Lippstadt
Paderborn/ Lippstadt Airport
Paderborn
Bad Karlshafen
Gelsenkirchen
RUHRGEBIET
Dortmund Airport
Soest
Oberhausen
Eindhoven
Essen
Bochum
Dortmund
Duisburg
Venlo
Krefeld
Hagen
Iserlohn
Düsseldorf International Airport
Kassel
Weert
Wuppertal
Roermond
Düsseldorf
Lüdenscheid
Mönchengladbach
Neuss
Solingen
Remscheid
Sittard
Leverkusen
Geilenkirchen
Cologne
Bergisch Gladbach
Heerlen
Kerkrade
Maastricht
Siegen
Cologne Bonn Airport
Düren
Aachen
Marburg

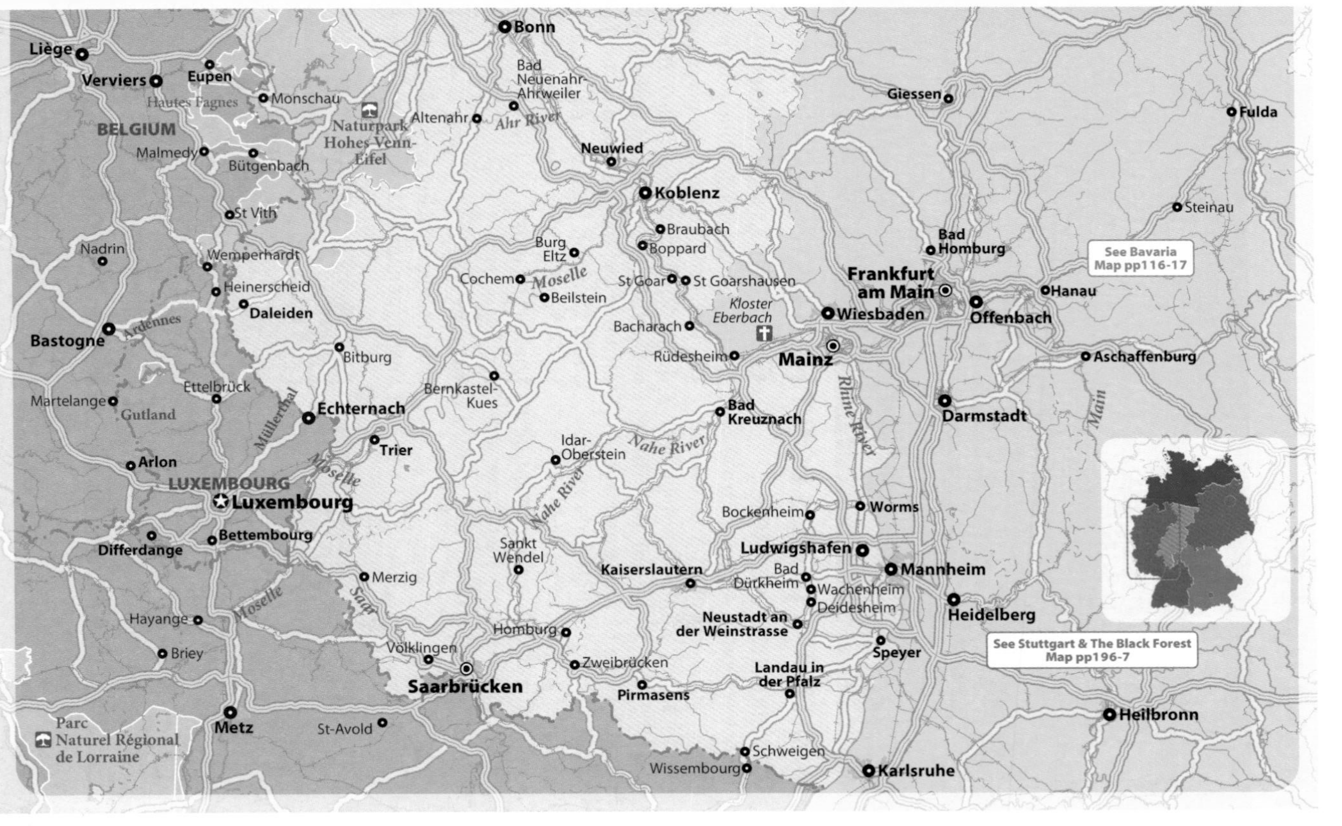
Bonn
Liège
Verviers
Eupen
Monschau
Hautes Fagnes
BELGIUM
Malmedy
Bütgenbach
Naturpark Hohes Venn-Eifel
Altenahr
Bad Neuenahr-Ahrweiler
Ahr River
Neuwied
Koblenz
Braubach
Boppard
Burg Eltz
Cochem
Moselle
Beilstein
St Goar
St Goarshausen
Kloster Eberbach
Bacharach
Rüdesheim
Mainz
Giessen
Fulda
Steinau
Bad Homburg
See Bavaria Map pp116-17
Frankfurt am Main
Hanau
Wiesbaden
Offenbach
Aschaffenburg
Darmstadt
Main
Rhine River
St Vith
Nadrin
Wemperhardt
Heinerscheid
Daleiden
Bastogne
Ardennes
Bitburg
Ettelbrück
Martelange
Gutland
Müllerthal
Echternach
Bernkastel-Kues
Trier
Arlon
LUXEMBOURG
Luxembourg
Idar-Oberstein
Nahe River
Bad Kreuznach
Bockenheim
Worms
Ludwigshafen
Mannheim
Bettembourg
Differdange
Sankt Wendel
Kaiserslautern
Bad Dürkheim
Wachenheim
Deidesheim
Heidelberg
Merzig
Saar
Hayange
Briey
Homburg
Neustadt an der Weinstrasse
Speyer
See Stuttgart & The Black Forest Map pp196-7
Völklingen
Saarbrücken
Zweibrücken
Pirmasens
Landau in der Pfalz
Heilbronn
Metz
St-Avold
Parc Naturel Régional de Lorraine
Schweigen
Wissembourg
Karlsruhe

HIGHLIGHTS

1 KÖLNER DOM

BY MATTHIAS DEML, ART HISTORIAN AT CATHEDRAL WORKSHOP

The Cologne Cathedral is much more than just a city landmark. It was planned as the largest cathedral in central Europe and ended up being a perfect expression of the Gothic architectural style rooted in medieval France. It reflects the long history of the country better than any other structure in Germany.

MATTHIAS DEML'S DON'T MISS LIST

❶ DREIKÖNIGENSCHREIN

The Kölner Dom is a treasure trove of magnificent works of art from over 10 centuries, but an absolute highlight is clearly the **Shrine of the Three Kings**. It's one of the largest and artistically most accomplished medieval reliquaries and the reason why Cologne became the third-most-important pilgrimage site in Europe after Rome and Santiago di Compostela.

❷ STAINED-GLASS WINDOWS

Another remarkable feature is the precious collection of **stained-glass windows**. The oldest one, from 1260, is in the Chapel of the Magi at the back of the choir. The newest one, in the south transept, was created in 2007 by Gerhard Richter, one of Germany's finest living artists.

❸ GEROKREUZ

This **wooden crucifix** is the oldest surviving monumental sculpture in cen-

Clockwise from top: Two different aspects of the Kölner Dom; Cologne's city centre; Stained-glass windows; Shine of the Three Kings

CLOCKWISE FROM TOP: HKE/IMAGEBROKER; WGA/IMAGEBROKER; MSZ/IMAGEBROKER; HSH/IMAGEBROCKER; PSF/IMAGEBROKER

tral Europe in existence since antiquity. It shows Christ hanging on the cross and was carved in the late 10th century and donated to the cathedral by Gero, the archbishop at the time. It is said to have miraculous powers.

❹ VIEWS

One thing's for sure, the Dom is definitely photogenic! The most famous perspective is of the western facade with its elaborate portals and twin towers. For the best view of the choir, which is the oldest part of the cathedral, go to platform 1 of the main train station. To see how the Dom fits within the city panorama, head to the opposite bank of the Rhine River.

❺ SPIRITUAL SIDE

Let's not forget that the Kölner Dom is not a dead monument but an active house of worship. The ambience is at its most spiritual before 9am when there are few visitors and the sunlight filters softly through the stained-glass windows. Of course you can also attend a service or the daily noon prayer.

THINGS YOU NEED TO KNOW

Join a guided tour to make the most of your visit. **Marvel** at the artistry of religious objects displayed in the vaulted treasury. **Catch** your breath while absorbing the stunning city panorama after climbing the 509 steps up the cathedral tower. **See our author's review on p239**

HIGHLIGHTS

2

↘ CASTLES GALORE

The **Romantic Rhine** (p252), the river's prettiest stretch between Koblenz and Rüdesheim, is a magical land where half-timbered villages are serenaded by medieval castles. Nature, history and humankind have collaborated to create a delightful landscape of great beauty and complexity. The region's considerable charms were not lost on Unesco, which declared it a World Heritage Site in 2002.

3

↘ GREAT GRAPES

Some of Germany's finest vintages grow along the **Rhine** (p252) and **Moselle** (p256) river valleys. Terraced vineyards surge skyward in columned symmetry, sheltering the vines from fierce winds, while the slate-rich soil stores up the sun's energy – conditions ideal for the noble riesling grape. Sample it in cosy taverns or at ancient wine estates.

4

↘ DÜSSELDORF'S OLD TOWN

Nicknamed the 'longest bar in the world', the warren of lanes that is Düsseldorf's **Altstadt** (p244) is tailor-made for letting your hair down. Sure, there are plenty of fancy bars, hopping night clubs, riverside cafes and chic lounges, but to soak up the true Rhenish spirit, sample the local brew known as *Altbier* in a traditional brewpub.

5

↘ CHARLEMAGNE'S AACHEN

Sharing a border with Belgium and Holland, **Aachen** (p248) exudes international flair rooted in the 8th century when Charlemagne made it the capital of his vast Frankish empire. Learn all about the 'father of Europe' and his impact along the new Route Charlemagne (www.route-charlemagne.eu).

6

↘ ROMAN ROOTS IN TRIER

It started out as a Roman military camp, founded in the 1st century BC when the Rhine and Moselle formed the Roman empire's northern frontier. Now, **Trier** (p257), Germany's oldest city, boasts some the best-preserved remnants in Europe from this era, including a town gate, an amphitheatre and thermals baths.

2 Rüdesheim (p255), on the Romantic Rhine; 3 Moselle Valley (p256); 4 Rheinuferpromenade (p244), Düsseldorf; 5 Markt, Aachen (p248) ; 6 Porta Nigra (p257), Trier

THE BEST...

HEAVENLY HEIGHTS

- **Festung Ehrenbreitstein** (p253) Mighty castle perched above the Rhine and Moselle.
- **Kölner Dom** (p238) Climb the tower for the ultimate exercise fix.
- **Niederwald Denkmal** (p256) Join Germania in surveying her domain above Rüdesheim.
- **Rheinturm** (p244) Enjoy sunset drinks in Düsseldorf's landmark tower.
- **Vierseenblick** (p254) Unique views from the hills above Boppard.

TRADITIONAL TAVERNS

- **Am Knipp** (p250) Serving hearty tummy fillers in Aachen since 1698.
- **Päffgen** (p242) Pouring Cologne's *Kölsch* beer for over a century.
- **Weinstube Hottum** (p252) Tasty Mainz wines and specialities.
- **Zum Gequetschten** (p248) Carnivore heaven in Bonn.

FAIRY-TALE FANCIES

- **Bacharach** (p255) Half-timbered medieval time warp with great wine taverns.
- **Beilstein** (p260) Higgledy-piggledy village nicknamed 'Sleeping Beauty of the Moselle'.
- **Burg Eltz** (p260) Turreted beauty dreamily cradled by a dense forest.
- **Loreley Rock** (p255) Home of the legendary lady whose beauty lured sailors to their deaths.

HILLTOP CASTLES

- **Burg Rheinfels** (p255) Robber-baron hang-out honeycombed with secret tunnels.
- **Festung Ehrenbreitstein** (p253) One of Europe's largest fortifications.
- **Marksburg** (p254) The only Rhine castle that was never destroyed.
- **Reichsburg** (p259) A neo-Gothic pastiche from the 19th century.

SLU/IMAGEBROKER

Medienhafen (Media Harbour; p244) and Rheinturm (Rhine Tower; p244), Düsseldorf

THINGS YOU NEED TO KNOW

VITAL STATISTICS

- **Population** 22 million
- **Best time to visit** May–October
- **Points of entry** Cologne, Düsseldorf, Frankfurt am Main and Frankfurt/Hahn airports

ADVANCE PLANNING

- **As early as possible** Book lodging for Cologne, Düsseldorf or Mainz during Carnival, or the Moselle and Rhine wine villages in summer.
- **One month before** Order concert tickets for Düsseldorf's Tonhalle (p246) or Cologne's Kölner Philharmonie (p242).

RESOURCES

- **Nordrhein-Westfalen Tourismus** (www.nrw-tourismus.de) Regional tourist board of the state of North-Rhine Westphalia.
- **Rheinland-Pfalz Tourismus** (www.rlp-info.de) Regional tourist office of the state of Rhineland-Palatinate.
- **Upper Middle Rhine World Heritage Site** (www.welterbe-mittelrheintal.de) Comprehensive information about the Unesco-listed Romantic Rhine.
- **German Wines** (www.deutscheweine.de) In-depth information about German grape-growing areas.

GETTING AROUND

- **Bicyling** is lovely on the dedicated trails along the river banks, but stressful in the cities.
- **Boats** link villages along the Rhine and Moselle from April to October. The main operator is Köln-Düsseldorfer (www.k-d.com), but nearly every town has local companies as well. Combine a trip in one direction with a return by bike or train.
- **Cars** are a pain in the cities, but useful, though not essential, when exploring the Rhine and Moselle river valleys, although heavy traffic can be an issue in summer.
- **Public transport** is ubiquitous.
- **Trains** are great for getting around with practically all destinations in this chapter served. Check www.bahn.de for deals such as the Rheinland-Pfalz Ticket and the Nordrhein-Westfalen Ticket.

BE FOREWARNED

- The Rhine and Moselle villages are pretty much deserted from November to February.
- Rooms are scarce and rates skyrocket in the entire region during big trade shows in Cologne and Düsseldorf.

COLOGNE & THE RHINELAND ITINERARIES

ARTY TRIO Three Days

The 'trio' in question is the neighbouring cities of Düsseldorf, Cologne and Bonn, whose world-class museums deliver a fine survey of what's been going on in the Western art world for, oh, the past 700 years or so. All three are linked several times hourly by regional S-Bahn trains. In Düsseldorf, start off at the **(1) K20** (p244) to admire 20th-century art from Picasso to Pollock, then skip over to the **(2) K21** (p244) where Andreas Gursky, Tony Cragg (now director of the city's prestigious art academy) and Nam June Paik are main players. Next day in Cologne don't miss the **(3) Wallraf-Richartz-Museum** (p240), the walls of which are graced by Old Masters like Rembrandt, key impressionists like Monet and Romantic heavyweights like Caspar David Friedrich. Meanwhile at the nearby **(4) Museum Ludwig** (p240), the spotlight is on postmodern art, especially American pop art. Spend Day 3 in Bonn, where the **(5) Kunstmuseum Bonn** (p246) has important 20th-century German art by Macke, Beuys and Kiefer; then check out the latest edgy exhibit next door at the **(6) Kunst- und Ausstellungshalle der Bundesrepublik Deutschland** (p248).

ROMANTIC RAMBLINGS Five Days

Few rivers have captured the imagination of artists and travellers as much as the Rhine. Get a first hint of why by riding the chairlift up to the imposing **(1) Festung Ehrenbreitstein** (p253) in Koblenz and looking down at the narrow, castle-studded and vineyard-draped valley carved by the mighty stream. Most castles were ruined, but one survived nearly intact: the **(2) Marksburg** (p254) in Braubach. If you're motorised, take a detour to dramatically located **(3) Burg Eltz** (p260) before continuing south along the Rhine to St Goar, lorded over by the rambling **(4) Burg Rheinfels** (p255) with its subterranean defensive tunnels. Hop on a boat and cruise past the myth-laden **(5) Loreley Rock** (p255) and several other castles to quaint half-timbered **(6) Bacharach** (p255). Another must is the cable-car float above the vineyards to the **(7) Niederwald Denkmal** (p256) for awesome views and a spin around **(8) Kloster Eberbach** (p256). Conclude your trip in **(9) Mainz** (p256).

FUN FOR FOODIES One Week

Kick off in Düsseldorf's earthy Altstadt tavern **(1) Zum Uerige** (p245) with a glass or two of the indigenous amber *Altbier*, then restore brain balance with a gut-busting *Schweinshaxe* (roast pork leg) at the boisterous gastro-pub **(2) Brauerei im Füchschen** (p245). Next day, head

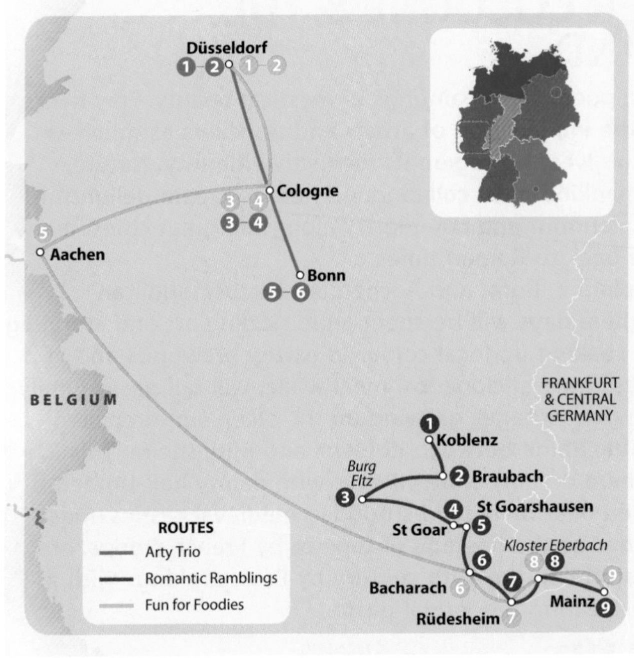

south to Cologne and sample the city's own beer, the pale and hoppy *Kölsch*, in a traditional brewpub such as **(3) Päffgen** (p242). If you have a sweet tooth, swing by the fun **(4) Schokoladen Museum** (Chocolate Museum; p240) before pushing west to Aachen, the birthplace of the famous *Printen,* crunchy spiced cookies drenched in chocolate or frosting. The old-fashioned cafe **(5) Leo van den Daele** (p250) is perfect for trying this speciality. As you work your way south, you trade beer for wine in the romantic villages along the Rhine and Moselle. Take a hike through the vineyards and join a tasting, for instance in pretty **(6) Bacharach** (p255); drink a toast to Bacchus in **(7) Rüdesheim** (p255) or enjoy the famous Rheingau riesling at **(8) Kloster Eberbach** (p256). Wrap up your gastro-tour in Mainz, where you can sample the classic Palatine speciality called *Saumagen* (yes, stuffed sheep's stomach – better than it sounds) in such cosy nosh spots as **(9) Weinstube Hottum** (p252). With the exception of Kloster Eberbach, all towns on this itinerary are frequently served by trains.

DISCOVER COLOGNE & THE RHINELAND

It lives in songs, poems and paintings of mystical beauty. Few rivers have captured the imagination of artists and travellers as much as the Rhine, which gives this region its distinctive identity. Nature, history and humankind have collaborated here to create delightful landscapes of splendour and complexity alongside great cities, many with a pedigree back to Roman times.

Düsseldorf, Cologne, Bonn and Aachen are all cosmopolitan powerhouses where days will be spent amid sizzling art and stunning architecture, or soaking up local colour in earthy brewpubs and riverside terraces. Wine aficionados, meanwhile, will fall passionately in love with the rich vintages growing on the steep sun-drenched banks of Romantic Rhine between Koblenz and Rüdesheim. This is a magical land where dreamy wine villages with dainty half-timbered houses are lorded over by legend-shrouded medieval castles. Most were ruined either by the passage of time or by French troops, but several were restored in the 19th century by Prussian kings with a penchant for re-creating the feudal past.

RHINELAND CITIES

COLOGNE

☎ 0221 / pop 995,500

Cologne (Köln) is like a 3-D history and architecture textbook. You'll find an ancient Roman wall, medieval churches galore, nondescript postwar buildings, avant-garde structures and now also a brand-new postmodern quarter right on the Rhine. For visitors, the city offers the mother lode of attractions, led by its famous cathedral whose filigree twin spires dominate the Altstadt skyline. Cologne's museum landscape is especially strong when it comes to art but also has something in store for fans of chocolate, sports and history.

INFORMATION

Tourist office (Map p239; ☎ 2213 0400; www.koelntourismus.de; Kardinal-Höffner-Platz 1; 9am-8pm Mon-Sat, 10am-5pm Sun)

SIGHTS

KÖLNER DOM

Cologne's geographical and spiritual heart – and its single-biggest tourist draw – is the magnificent **Kölner Dom** (Cologne Cathedral; Map p239; ☎ 1794 0200; 6am-10pm May-Oct, to 7.30pm Nov-Apr). The Dom is Germany's largest cathedral and must be circled to truly appreciate its dimensions. Note how its lacy spires and flying buttresses create a sensation of lightness and fragility despite its mass and height. Soft light filters through the dazzling **stained-glass windows**, including the spectacular new one by Gerhard Richter in the transept – a kaleidoscope of 11,500 squares in 72 colours.

Among the cathedral's numerous treasures, the *pièce de résistance* is the **Shrine of the Three Kings** behind the main altar, a richly bejewelled and gilded sarcophagus said to hold the remains of the kings who followed the star to the stable in Bethlehem where Jesus was born. Other highlights include the **Gero Crucifix** (970), notable for its monumental size and an emotional intensity rarely achieved in those early medieval days; the **choir stalls** from 1310, richly carved from oak; and the **altar painting** by local artist Stephan Lochner from around 1450.

For an exercise fix, climb the 509 steps up the Dom's **south tower** (**adult/concession €2.50/1.50; 9am-6pm May-Sep, to 5pm Mar-Apr & Oct, to 4pm Nov-Feb**) to the base of

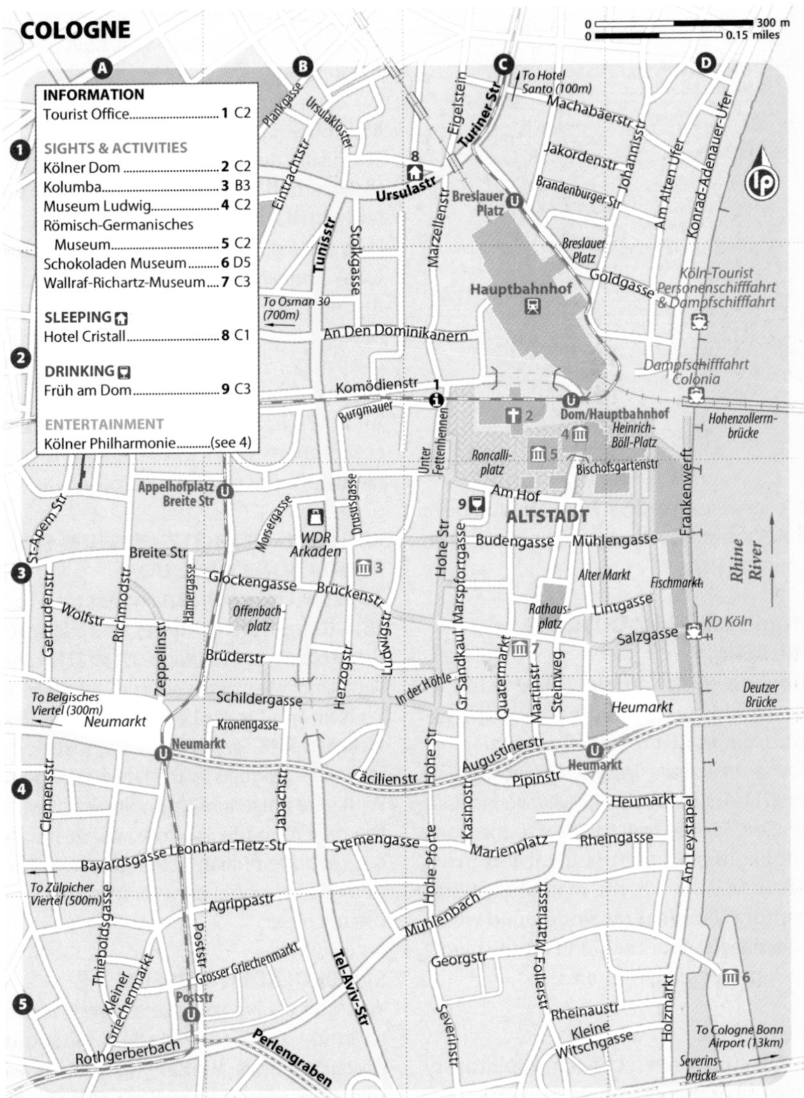

the steeple that dwarfed all buildings in Europe until Gustave Eiffel built a certain tower in Paris.

RÖMISCH-GERMANISCHES MUSEUM

Anyone even remotely interested in Roman history should not skip the extraordinary **Römisch-Germanisches Museum** (**Romano-Germanic Museum; Map p239; ☎ 2212 4438; Roncalliplatz 4; adult/concession €8/4; ⏲ 10am-5pm Tue-Sun**), adjacent to the Dom. Highlights include the giant **Poblicius tomb** (AD 30–40), the magnificent 3rd-century **Dionysus mosaic** around which the museum was built, and astonishingly well-preserved glass items.

KOLUMBA

Art, history, architecture and spirituality form a harmonious tapestry in spectacular new digs for the collection of religious treasures of the Archdiocese of Cologne. Called **Kolumba** (**Map p239; ☎ 933 1930; Kolumbastrasse 4; adult/under 18yr/concession €5/free/3; ⏲ noon-5pm Wed-Mon**), the building encases the ruins of the late-Gothic church St Kolumba, layers of foundations going back to Roman times and the Madonna in the Ruins chapel, built on the site in 1950.

MUSEUM LUDWIG

The distinctive building facade and unorthodox roofline signal that the **Museum Ludwig** (**Map p239; ☎ 2212 6165; Heinrich-Böll-Platz; adult/concession/family €9/6/18, audioguide €3; ⏲ 10am-6pm Tue-Sun**) is no ordinary museum. Considered a mecca of postmodern art, it actually presents a survey of all major 20th-century genres. There's plenty of American pop art, including Andy Warhol's *Brillo Boxes,* alongside a comprehensive Picasso collection and plenty of works by Sigmar Polke.

WALLRAF-RICHARTZ-MUSEUM & FONDATION CORBOUD

A famous collection of paintings from the 13th to the 19th centuries, the **Wallraf-Richartz-Museum** (**Map p239; ☎ 2212 1119; Obenmarspforten; admission varies, usually €6-9; ⏲ 10am-6pm Tue, Wed & Fri, 10am-10pm Thu, 11am-6pm Sat & Sun**) occupies a postmodern cube designed by the late OM Ungers. Works are presented chronologically, with the oldest on the 1st floor where standouts include brilliant examples from the Cologne School, known for its distinctive use of colour.

SCHOKOLADEN MUSEUM

You don't have to have a sweet tooth to enjoy the **Schokoladen Museum** (**Chocolate Museum; Map p239; ☎ 931 8880; Am Schokoladenmuseum 1a; adult/concession/family**

€7.50/7/21; 10am-6pm Tue-Fri, 11am-7pm Sat & Sun), a high-tech temple to the art of chocolate-making. Exhibits on the origin of the 'elixir of the gods', as the Aztecs called it, and the cocoa-growing process are followed by a live-production factory tour and a stop at a chocolate fountain for a sample.

SLEEPING

our pick **Hotel Chelsea** (**Map p240; 207 150; www.hotel-chelsea.de; Jülicher Strasse 1; s €61-122, d €90-235;**) Those fancying an artsy vibe will be well sheltered in this self-proclaimed 'hotel different'. Originals created by international artists in exchange for lodging grace the public areas and 38 rooms and suites.

Hotel Cristall (**Map p239; 163 00; www.hotelcristall.de; Ursulaplatz 9-11; s €72-184, d €90-235;**) This stylish boutique hotel makes excellent use of colour, customised furniture and light accents and manages to appeal both to the suit brigade and city-breakers. Alas, rooms won't fit a tonne of luggage and light sleepers should get one facing away from the busy street.

Hotel Santo (**off Map p239; 913 9770; www.hotelsanto.de; Dagobertstrasse 22-26; s €95-140, d €120-160; Ebertplatz;**) Despite the drab location near the Hauptbahnhof (central train station), this 69-room boutique hotel is an island of sassy sophistication. The design flaunts an edgy, urban feel tempered by playful light effects, soothing colours and natural materials.

Hopper Hotel Et Cetera (**Map p240; 924 400; www.hopper.de; Brüsseler Strasse 26; s €80-270, d €120-295;**) A waxen monk welcomes you to this former monastery whose 49 rooms sport eucalyptus floors, cherry furniture and marble baths along with lots of little pampering touches.

EATING

La Bodega (**Map p240; 257 3610; Friesenstrasse 51; tapas €2.20-5.70; 5pm-1am Sun-Thu, to 3am Fri & Sat**) It's always fiesta time at this buzzy cantina with its cosy vaulted cellar and romantic courtyard. Gobble up

DAVID PEEVERS

Wallraf-Richartz-Museum, Cologne

ALFREDO MAIQUEZ

Kölner Dom (p238), Cologne

the *jamón* (smoked ham), stuffed peppers, nut-encrusted goat cheese and other authentic tapas or go the whole nine yards and order a heaping paella.

Feynsinn (Map p240; ☎ 240 9210; Rathenauplatz 7; lunch €7.50, dinner mains €10-17; ⏰ 10am-1am) What used to be a small cafe famous for its eccentric glass-chard chandelier has morphed into a well-respected restaurant where organic ingredients are woven into sharp-flavoured dishes. Owners have even started to raise their own pigs and cattle!

Bagutta (Map p240; ☎ 212 694; Heinsbergstrasse 20a; mains around €20, 3-/4-/5-course menu €32/37/42; ⏰ 6-11pm Wed-Mon) Leagues of local loyalists keep this knick-knack-filled charmer hopping. Do as they do: ignore the menu and just ask chef Stefan Bierl to put together a 'surprise menu'.

Osman 30 (off Map p239; ☎ 5005 2080; Im Mediapark 8; 3-course menu €44; ⏰ 6pm-1am Mon-Thu, 6pm-3am Fri & Sat, 11am-7pm Sun; Ⓤ Christoph-Strasse/Mediapark) The setting alone of this made-to-impress restaurant on the 30th floor of the KölnTurm is spectacular, but fortunately the Mediterranean food can hold its own with the views.

DRINKING

Beer reigns supreme in Cologne, where over 20 breweries produce the local variety called *Kölsch*, which is served in skinny glasses called *Stangen*. Pick from a selection of stout Rhenish dishes to keep you grounded.

Früh am Dom (Map p239; ☎ 261 30; Am Hof 12-14) This warren of a beer hall near the Dom epitomises Cologne earthiness. It's also known for great breakfasts (€4 to €13, mains €4 to €20).

Päffgen (Map p240; ☎ 135 461; Friesenstrasse 64-66; ⏰ 10am-midnight) Busy, loud and boisterous, Päffgen has been pouring *Kölsch* since 1883 and hasn't lost a step since. Also serves food (mains €6.50 to €17).

ENTERTAINMENT

Kölner Philharmonie (Map p239; ☎ 280 280; www.koelner-philharmonie.de; Bischofsgartenstrasse 1) The famous Kölner Philharmoniker is the 'house band' in this grand, modern concert hall below the Museum Ludwig.

GETTING THERE & AWAY

About 18km southeast of the city centre, **Köln Bonn Airport** (Cologne Bonn Airport; off Map p239; ☎ 02203-404 001; www.airport-cgn.de) has direct flights to 130 cities and is served by 50 airlines, including budget carriers such as Germanwings, Air Berlin and easyJet. The S13 train connects the airport and the Hauptbahnhof every 20 minutes (€2.40, 15 minutes). Taxis charge about €25.

Cologne is linked to Bonn several times hourly by U-Bahn lines U16 and U18 and regional trains (€6.50, 30 minutes).

DÜSSELDORF

☎ 0211 / pop 585,000

Düsseldorf dazzles with boundary-pushing architecture, zinging nightlife and an art scene to rival many larger cities. It's a posh and modern metropolis that seems all buttoned-up business at first glance: Yet all it takes is a few hours of bar-hopping around the Altstadt (old town), the historical quarter along the Rhine, to realise that locals have no problem letting their hair down once they shed those Armani jackets. The Altstadt may still be the 'longest bar in the world' but lately it's been getting competition from the Medienhafen, a redeveloped harbour area and a feast of international avant-garde architecture.

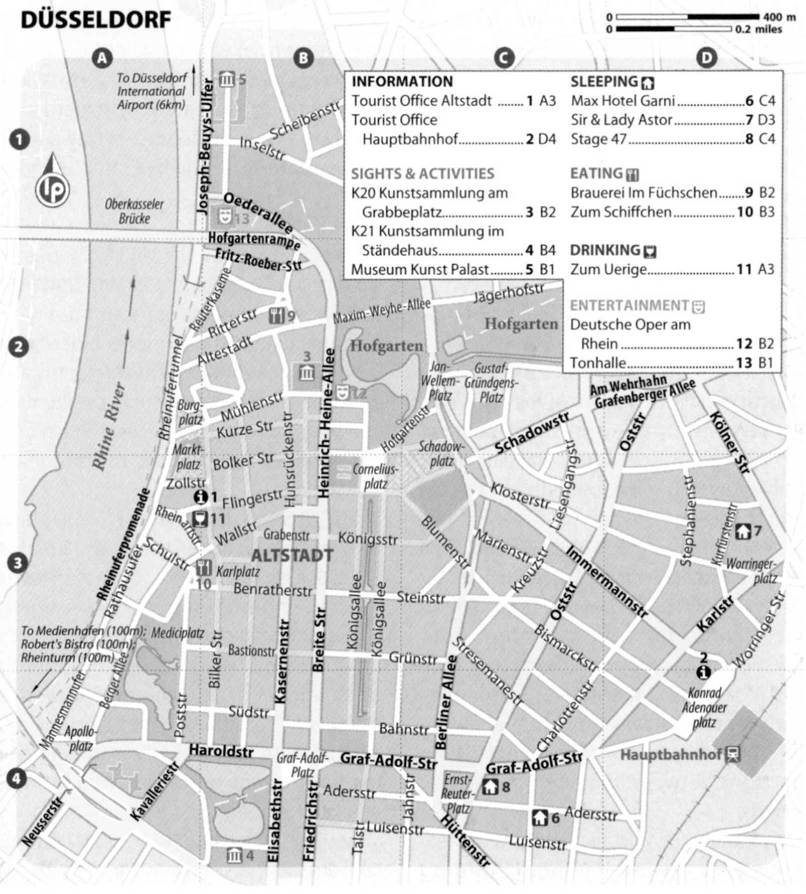

INFORMATION

Tourist office Altstadt (☎ 1720 2840; cnr Marktstrasse & Rheinstrasse; 🕐 10am-6pm)

Tourist office Hauptbahnhof (☎ 1720 2844; Immermannstrasse 65b; 🕐 9.30am-6.30pm Mon-Sat)

SIGHTS

ALTSTADT

Düsseldorf's Altstadt, a mostly pedestrianised web of lanes cuddling up to the Rhine, is rightly (in)famous for its raucous nightlife. Fortunately, it also brims with charming and quiet corners, a smattering of museums and historical sights, plus good shopping to boot. Burgplatz marks the beginning of the **Rheinuferpromenade** (river walk), the cafes and benches of which fill with people in fine weather, creating an almost Mediterranean flair. It follows the Rhine all the way to the Rheinpark and the 240m **Rheinturm** (Rhine Tower; Stromstrasse 20; lift adult/child €3.50/1.90) with a viewing platform and revolving restaurant at 172m.

ART MUSEUMS

A collection that spans the arc of 20th-century artistic vision gives the **K20 Kunstsammlung am Grabbeplatz** (☎ 838 1130; www.kunst sammlung.de; Grabbeplatz 5) an enviable edge in the art world. Nearby, the once stuffy **museum kunst palast** (☎ 899 0200; www.museum-kunst-palast.de; Ehrenhof 5; adult/concession/family €8/6.50/18; 🕐 11am-6pm Tue-Sun) now takes an unconventional approach to presenting its well-respected collection. Old masters find themselves juxtaposed with contemporary young dogs and non-Western works to reveal unexpected connections between the ages and artistic trends.

Speaking of juxtaposition: a stately 19th-century parliament building forms the incongruous setting of the cutting-edge **K21 Kunstsammlung im Ständehaus** (☎ 838 1630; Ständehausstrasse 1; www.kunstsammlung.de; adult/concession/family €6.50/4.50/15; 🕐 10am-6pm Tue-Fri, 11am-6pm Sat & Sun), which brims with canvases, photographs, installations and video art created after 1980 by an international cast of artists.

MEDIENHAFEN

South of the Altstadt, the Medienhafen (Media Harbour) is an office quarter that's been wrought from the remains of the old city harbour. Despite a few trendy restaurants and design shops, there's little life in the streets as of yet, but if you're a fan of bold contemporary architecture, do swing by. The most eye-catching structure is clearly the warped **Neuer Zollhof**, a typically sculptural design by Frank Gehry.

SLEEPING

Max Hotel Garni (☎ 386 800; www.max-hotelgarni.de; Adersstrasse 65; s/d/tr €70/82/99; 💻) Upbeat, contemporary and run with personal flair, this charmer is one of our Düsseldorf favourites. The 11 rooms are good-sized and decked out in bright hues and warm woods. The reception isn't always staffed, so call ahead to arrange an arrival time.

our pick **Sir & Lady Astor** (☎ 173 370; www.sir-astor.de; Kurfürstenstrasse 18 & 23; s €83-170, d €95-240; P ⊠ ❄ 💻 📶) Never mind the ho-hum setting on a residential street near the Hauptbahnhof: this unique twin boutique hotel brims with class, originality and charm. Check-in is at Sir Astor, furnished in 'Scotland-meets-Africa' style, while Lady Astor across the street goes more for French floral sumptuousness.

Stage 47 (☎ 388 030; www.stage47.de; Graf-Adolf-Strasse 47; s/d from €160/180; P ⊠ 💻 📶)

Behind the drab exterior, movie glamour meets design chic at this urban boutique hotel. Rooms are named for famous people, some of whom have actually stayed in these environs dominated by black, white and grey tones.

EATING

our pick **Brauerei im Füchschen** (☎ **137 470; www.fuechschen.de; Ratinger Strasse 28; snacks €3, mains €5-14; 9am-1am**) Boisterous, packed and drenched with local colour – the 'Little Fox', in the Altstadt, is all you expect a Rhenish beer hall to be. The kitchen makes a mean *Schweinshaxe*.

Zum Schiffchen (☎ **132 421; www.brauerei-zum-schiffchen.de; Hafenstrasse 5; mains €7-19; 11.30am-midnight**) History pours out of every nook and cranny in this almost ridiculously cosy Altstadt restaurant, which specialises in gut-busting German and Rhenish meals. We wonder if portions were as huge when Napoleon dropped by here a couple of centuries ago?

Robert's Bistro (☎ **304 821; Wupperstrasse 2; mains €10-22; 11.30am-midnight Tue-Fri, 10am-midnight Sat**) Tables are squished together as tightly as lovers at this *très* French restaurant in the Medienhafen. You should bring both an appetite for hearty Gallic fare (the fish soup is highly recommended) and some patience – it doesn't take reservations, and a queue is guaranteed.

DRINKING

The beverage of choice here is *Altbier*, a dark and semi-sweet beer typical of Düsseldorf.

Zum Uerige (☎ **866 990; Berger Strasse 1; 10am-midnight**) This cavernous beer hall is the best place to soak it all up. The suds flow so quickly from giant copper vats that the waiters – called *Köbes* – simply carry huge trays of brew and plonk down a glass whenever they spy an empty.

ENTERTAINMENT

Mozart to Monteverdi are the bread and butter of Düsseldorf's renowned opera

WER/IMAGEBROKER

Pubs on the Rheinuferpromenade, Düsseldorf

house, the **Deutsche Oper am Rhein** (☎ 892 5211; www.rheinoper.de; Heinrich-Heine-Allee 16a; tickets €15-68), while the imposing domed **Tonhalle** (☎ 899 6123; www.tonhalle-duesseldorf.de; Ehrenhof 1; tickets vary), in a converted 1920s planetarium, is the home base of the Düsseldorfer Symphoniker (Düsseldorf Symphony Orchestra).

GETTING THERE & AWAY

Many domestic and international carriers serve **Düsseldorf International Airport** (☎ 4210; www.duesseldorf-international.de). S-Bahns, regional RE and long-distance trains connect the airport with Düsseldorf Hauptbahnhof, and cities beyond, every few minutes. A taxi into town costs about €16.

BONN

☎ 0228 / pop 311,000

When this friendly, relaxed city on the Rhine became West Germany's 'temporary' capital in 1949 it surprised many, including its own residents. When in 1991 a reunited German government decided to move to Berlin, it shocked many, *especially* its own residents. For visitors, the birthplace of Ludwig van Beethoven has plenty in store, not least the great composer's birth house, a string of top-rated museums, a lovely riverside setting and the nostalgic flair of the old government quarter.

INFORMATION

Tourist office (☎ 775 000; www.bonn.de; Windeckstrasse 1; ⏲ 9am-6.30pm Mon-Fri, 9am-4pm Sat, 10am-2pm Sun) For pretrip planning, go to www.bonn-region.de.

SIGHTS

ALTSTADT

A good place to start exploring Bonn's historic centre is on Münsterplatz, where the landmark **Münster Basilica** (☎ 985 880; www.bonner-muenster.de; admission free; ⏲ 7am-7pm) was built on the graves of the two martyred Roman soldiers who later got promoted to be the city's patron saints. It got its Gothic look in the 13th century but the Romanesque origins survive beautifully in the ageing cloister (open till 5pm). On the square outside the church, a buttercup-yellow baroque Palais (palace; now the post office) forms a photogenic backdrop for the **Beethoven Monument** (1845).

The famous composer first saw the light of day in 1770 in the rather plain **Beethoven Haus** (Beethoven House; ☎ 981 7525; www.beethoven-haus-bonn.de; Bonngasse 20; adult/concession/family €4/3/10; ⏲ 10am-6pm Mon-Sat, 11am-6pm Sun Apr-Oct, to 5pm Nov-Mar). It's now the repository of a pretty static array of letters, musical scores, instruments and paintings. Tickets are also good for the **Digitales Beethoven-Haus** next door, where you can experience the composer's genius during a spacey, interactive 3-D multimedia show or deepen your knowledge in the digital archive.

MUSEUMSMEILE

Bonn's **Museum Mile**, one of the country's finest museum clusters, sits opposite the government quarter, on the western side of the B9. The **Haus der Geschichte der Bundesrepublik Deutschland** (Forum of Contemporary German History; ☎ 916 50; www.hdg.de; Willy-Brandt-Allee 14; admission free; ⏲ 9am-7pm Tue-Sun) presents a highly engaging and intelligent romp through recent German history, starting when the final bullet was fired in WWII.

Beyond its breathtaking foyer, the **Kunstmuseum Bonn** (☎ 776 260; www.kunstmuseum-bonn.de; Friedrich-Ebert-Allee 2;

KNÖLL KNÖLL/PHOTOLIBRARY

Speyer's Kaiserdom

↘ IF YOU LIKE...

If you were in awe of the magnificent **cathedrals** in **Aachen** (p249), **Cologne** (p238) and **Mainz** (p251), we think you should also check out these houses of the worship:

- **Worms** Some 45km south of Mainz, Worms' skyline is dominated by the late-Romanesque Cathedral of St Peter and St Paul. Inside, the lofty dimensions impress as much as the lavish, canopied high altar (1742) by baroque master Balthasar Neumann.
- **Speyer** In 1030 Emperor Konrad II laid the cornerstone of Speyer's Romanesque Kaiserdom (Imperial Cathedral), the square red towers and green copper dome of which float above the town's rooftops. Eight emperors and kings are buried in the darkly festive crypt with candy-striped arches that recall Moorish architecture. It's about 45km south of Worms.
- **Münster** Enter the massive twin-towered Cathedral of St Paul via a porch richly festooned with sculptures of the apostles; pay your respects to St Christopher, the patron saint of travellers; then marvel at the 16th-century astronomical clock. Münster is about 120km north of Düsseldorf.
- **Soest** About 100km northeast of Düsseldorf, Soest is a tranquil town of half-timbered houses and a clutch of treasure-filled medieval churches. Visit the exquisite late-Gothic St Maria zur Wiese with its lacy neo-Gothic twin spires and vibrant stained-glass windows; St Maria zur Höhe, known for its beautiful ceiling frescoes; and the Petrikirche with Romanesque origins, Gothic choir and baroque onion dome.
- **Paderborn** Highlights of the mighty Dom (cathedral) in Paderborn, some 50km east of Soest, include the delicate high altar and the endearing trompe l'oeil *Dreihasenfenster* (Three Hares' Window), which has tracery depicting three bunnies, ingeniously arranged so that each has two ears, even though there are only three ears in all.

adult/concession/family €5/2.50/10; 11am-6pm Tue, Thu-Sun, to 9pm Wed) presents 20th-century works, especially by August Macke and other Rhenish expressionists, as well as such avant-gardists as Beuys, Baselitz and Kiefer.

Next door, the **Kunst- und Ausstellungshalle der Bundesrepublik Deutschland** **(Art and Exhibition Hall of the Federal Republic of Germany; ☎ 917 1200; www.bundeskunsthalle.de; Friedrich-Ebert-Allee 4; adult/concession/family per exhibit €8/5/14, all exhibits €14/9/24.50; 10am-9pm Tue & Wed, to 7pm Thu-Sun)** is another striking space that brings in blockbuster exhibits from around the world.

SLEEPING

Hotel Pastis **(☎ 969 4270; www.hotel-pastis.de, in German; Hatschiergasse 8; s/d €60/95)** This little hotel-restaurant combo is so fantastically French, you'll feel like the Eiffel Tower is just around the corner. After dining on unfussy gourmet cuisine – paired with great wines, *bien sûr* – you'll sleep like a baby in snug, cosy rooms.

Domicil **(☎ 729 090; www.domicil-bonn.bestwestern.de; Thomas-Mann-Strasse 24/26; s/d from €85/120; P ⊠)** This classy hotel sprawls over several buildings grouped around a central courtyard. For something a little special, book the larger deluxe rooms, some of which have romantic stucco ceilings or a courtyard-facing terrace.

EATING & DRINKING

Brauhaus Bönnsch **(☎ 650 610; Sterntorbrücke 4; mains €7-15; 11am-1am)** The unfiltered ale is a must at this congenial brewpub adorned with photographs of famous politicians. Schnitzel, spare ribs and sausage dominate the menu, but the *Flammkuchen* (Alsatian pizza) is still a perennial bestseller.

Zum Gequetschten **(☎ 638 104; Sternstrasse 78; mains €8-17; noon-midnight)** This traditional restaurant-pub is festooned with eye-catching blue tiles and is one of the most storied inns in town. The menu is back-to-basics German, all delicious and served in belt-loosening portions.

GETTING THERE & AWAY

Köln Bonn Airport **(Cologne Bonn Airport; ☎ 02203-404 001; www.airport-cgn.de)** has flights within Germany, Europe and beyond and is served by 50 airlines, including Germanwings, easyJet and Air Berlin. Express bus SB60 makes the trip between the airport and Hauptbahnhof every 20 or 30 minutes between 4.45am and 12.30am (€6.50, 26 minutes). For a taxi to/from the airport budget between €35 and €40.

Bonn is linked to Cologne several times hourly by U-Bahn lines U16 and U18 and regional trains (€6.50, 30 minutes).

AACHEN

☎ 0241 / pop 246,000

The Romans nursed their war wounds and stiff joints in the steaming waters of Aachen's mineral springs, but it was Charlemagne who put the city firmly on the European map. Charlemagne's legacy lives on in the stunning Dom which, in 1978, became Germany's first Unesco World Heritage Site.

INFORMATION

Tourist office **(☎ 180 2960/1; www.aachen-tourist.de; Elisenbrunnen, Friedrich-Wilhelm-Platz; 9am-6pm Mon-Fri, 9am-2pm Sat, also 10am-2pm Sun Easter-Dec)**

SIGHTS

DOMSCHATZKAMMER

The **cathedral treasury** **(☎ 4770 9127; Klostergasse; adult/concession €4/3; 10am-1pm Mon, 10am-5pm Tue-Sun Jan-Mar, 10am-1pm**

KFS/IMAGEBROKER

Aachener Dom interior

↘ AACHENER DOM

It's impossible to overestimate the significance of Aachen's magnificent cathedral. The oldest and most impressive section is Charlemagne's palace chapel, the **Pfalzkapelle**, an outstanding example of Carolingian architecture. Completed in 800, the year of the emperor's coronation, it's an octagonal dome encircled by a 16-sided ambulatory supported by antique Italian pillars. To accommodate the flood of the faithful, a Gothic **choir** was docked to the chapel in 1414 and filled with such priceless treasures as the **pala d'oro**, a gold-plated altar-front depicting Christ's Passion, and the jewel-encrusted gilded copper **pulpit**, both fashioned in the 11th century. At the far end is the gilded **shrine of Charlemagne** that has held the emperor's remains since 1215. In front, the equally fanciful **shrine of St Mary** shelters the cathedral's four premium relics.

Unless you join a guided tour (adult/concession €3/2.50, 45 minutes), you'll only catch a glimpse of Charlemagne's white marble **imperial throne** in the upstairs gallery. Reached via six steps – just like King Solomon's throne – it served as the coronation throne of 30 German kings between 936 and 1531. The 2pm tour is in English.

Things you need to know: ☎ 4770 9144; www.aachendom.de, in German; Münsterplatz; 🕑 7am-6pm Nov-Mar, to 7pm Apr-Oct

Mon, 10am-6pm Tue, Wed, Fri-Sun, 10am-9pm Thu Apr-Dec) is a veritable mother lode of gold, silver and jewels. Focus your attention on the **Lotharkreuz**, a 10th-century processional cross, and the **marble sarcophagus** that held Charlemagne's bones until his canonisation.

RATHAUS

The Dom gazes serenely over Aachen's **Rathaus** (☎ 432 7310; Markt; adult/child/

Beethoven Monument (p246), Münsterplatz, Bonn

concession €2/free/1; 10am-1pm & 2-5pm), a splendid Gothic pile festooned with 50 life-size statues of German rulers, including the 30 kings crowned in town. Inside, the undisputed highlights are the **Kaisersaal** with its epic 19th-century **frescoes** by Alfred Rethel and the replicas of the **imperial insignia**: a crown, orb and sword (the originals are in Vienna).

ART MUSEUMS

Of Aachen's two art museums, the **Suermondt Ludwig Museum** (☎ 479 800; www.suermondt-ludwig-museum.de; Wilhelmstrasse 18; adult/concession €5/2.50; noon-6pm Tue, Thu & Fri, noon-8pm Wed, 10am-6pm Sat & Sun) is especially proud of its medieval sculpture but also has fine works by Cranach, Dürer, Macke, Dix and other masters.

In a former umbrella factory, the **Ludwig Forum für Internationale Kunst** (Ludwig Forum for International Art; ☎ 180 7104; www.ludwigforum.de; Jülicherstrasse 97-109; adult/concession €5/2.50; noon-6pm Tue, Wed & Fri, noon-8pm Thu, 11am-6pm Sat & Sun) trains the spotlight on contemporary art (Warhol, Immendorf, Holzer, Penck, Haring etc) and also stages progressive changing exhibits.

SLEEPING

Hotel Stadtnah (☎ 474 580; http://hotelstadtnah.de; Leydelstrasse 2; s/d from €48/64;) The tab ain't steep but neither do you get the 'Ritz'. Still, if you're fine with basic decor and amenities, this 16-room cheapie near the Hauptbahnhof should do in a snap.

Hotel Drei Könige (☎ 483 93; www.h3k-aachen.de, in German; Büchel 5; s €90-130, d €120-160, apt €130-240;) The radiant Mediterranean decor is an instant mood enhancer at this family-run favourite with its doesn't-get-more-central location. Some rooms are a tad twee but the two-room apartment sleeps up to four.

EATING & DRINKING

Leo van den Daele (☎ 357 24; Büchel 18; dishes €7-11; 9am-6.30pm Mon-Sat, 11am-6.30pm Sun) Leather-covered walls, tiled stoves and antiques forge the yesteryear flair of this rambling cafe institution. Come for all-day breakfast, a light lunch or divine cakes (the strudel and the Belgian Reisfladen, made with rice, are specialities).

Am Knipp (☎ 331 68; Bergdriesch 3; mains €8-17; dinner Wed-Mon) Hungry grazers have stopped by this traditional inn since 1698 and you too will have a fine time spiking your cholesterol level with the hearty German cuisine served amid a flea market's worth of knick-knacks. Lovely beer garden as well.

Gaststätte Postwagen (☎ 350 01; Krämerstrasse 2; mains €10-20; ⏰ noon-midnight) This place, tacked onto the town hall, oozes olde-worlde flair from every nook and cranny and is a good place for classic German meals. The downstairs is made to look like an 18th-century postal coach (hence the name).

GETTING THERE & AWAY

Regional trains to Cologne (€14.40, 70 minutes) run several times hourly. Trips to most cities south of Aachen require a change in Cologne.

MAINZ

☎ 06131 / pop 198,000

The lively city of Mainz, capital of Rhineland-Palatinate, has a sizable university, fine pedestrian precincts and a certain *savoir vivre,* whose origins go back to Napoleon's occupation (1798–1814). Strolling along the Rhine and sampling local wines in a half-timbered Altstadt tavern are as much a part of any Mainz visit as viewing the fabulous Dom, Chagall's ethereal windows in St-Stephan-Kirche or the first printed Bible in the Gutenberg Museum, a bibliophile's paradise.

INFORMATION

Tourist office (☎ 286 210; www.touristik-mainz.de, www.mainz.de; Brückenturm am Rathaus; ⏰ 9am-6pm Mon-Fri, 10am-6pm Sat, 11am-3pm Sun)

SIGHTS

Mainz' famed cathedral, **Dom St Martin** (⏰ 9am-6.30pm Mon-Fri, 9am-4pm Sat, 12.45-3pm & 4-6.30pm Sun & holidays Mar-Oct, to 5pm Sun-Fri Nov-Feb), entered from the Marktplatz, is one of Germany's most magnificent houses of worship. The grandiose, wall-mounted **memorial tombstones** form a veritable portrait gallery of archbishops and other 13th- to 18th-century power mongers, many portrayed alongside their private putti.

St-Stephan-Kirche (Kleine Weissgasse 12; ⏰ 10am-noon & 2-5pm Mon-Thu, 10am-5pm Fri & Sat, noon-5pm Sun Feb-Nov, to 4.30pm Dec & Jan) would be just another Gothic church rebuilt after WWII were it not for the nine brilliant, stained-glass windows created by the Russian-Jewish artist Marc Chagall (1887–1985) in the final years of his life. Bright blue and imbued with a mystical, meditative quality, they serve as a symbol of Jewish-Christian reconciliation.

A heady experience for anyone excited by books, the **Gutenberg Museum** (☎ 122 644; www.gutenberg-museum.de; Liebfrauenplatz 5; adult/student & senior/family €5/3/10; ⏰ 9am-5pm Tue-Sat, 11am-3pm Sun) takes a panoramic look at the technology that made the world as we know it – including this guidebook – possible. Highlights include medieval manuscripts and early printed masterpieces – kept safe in a vault – such as Gutenberg's original 42-line Bible.

SLEEPING

Hotel Hof Ehrenfels (☎ 971 2340; www.hof-ehrenfels.de; Grebenstrasse 5-7; s/d/tr €80/100/120, Fri-Sun discount €10; ⊠) Just steps from the cathedral, this 22-room place, housed in a 15th-century, one-time Carmelite nunnery, has Dom views that are hard to beat.

our pick **Hotel Schwan** (☎ 144 920; www.mainz-hotel-schwan.de; Liebfrauenplatz 7; r €87-117) You can't get any more central than this family-run place, around since 1463. The 22 well-lit rooms have baroque-style furnishings.

EATING & DRINKING

ourpick **Eisgrubbräu** (☎ 221 104; www.eisgrub.de, in German; Weissliliengasse 1a; mains €5.80-17.90; 9am-1am Sun-Thu, to 2am Fri & Sat) Grab a seat in this down-to-earth microbrewery's warren of vaulted chambers, order a mug of *Dunkel* (dark) or *Hell* (light) – or even a 3L/5L *Bierturm* (beer tower; €17.90/28.40) – and settle in for people-watching.

Heiliggeist (☎ 225 757; www.heiliggeist-mainz.de; Mailandsgasse 11; mains €6-20; 4pm-1am Mon-Fri, 9am-1am or 2am Sat, Sun & holidays) Sit beneath the soaring Gothic vaults of a 15th-century hospital and enjoy a drink, snack or full meal from a menu filled with Italian-inspired creations.

Weinstube Hottum (☎ 223 370; Grebenstrasse 3; mains €7.50-13.50; 4pm-midnight) One of the best of the Altstadt wine taverns, Hottum has a cosy, traditional atmosphere, delectable wines and a menu – half of which appears on a tiny slate tablet – with regional dishes such as *Saumagen* (pig's stomach stuffed with meat, potatoes and spices, then boiled, sliced and briefly fried) and *Winzersteak* (vintner-style pork steak).

GETTING THERE & AWAY

From the Hauptbahnhof, S-Bahn line 8 goes to Frankfurt Airport (€3.70, several times hourly), 30km northeast of Mainz.

A major IC rail hub, Mainz has at least hourly regional services to Bingen (€5.70, 15 to 40 minutes) and other Romantic Rhine towns, such as Koblenz (€16.70 by regional train, 50 to 90 minutes).

THE ROMANTIC RHINE

Between Koblenz and Bingen, the **Rhine** (www.romantischer-rhein.de) cuts deeply through the Rhenish slate mountains, meandering between hillside castles and steep fields of grapes to create a magical mixture of wonder and legend. Idyllic villages appear around each bend, their neat half-timbered houses and proud church steeples seemingly plucked from the world of fairy tales.

In 2002 Unesco designated these 65km of riverscape, more prosaically known as the **Oberes Mittelrheintal** (Upper Middle Rhine Valley; www.welterbe-mittelrheintal.de), as a World Heritage Site.

GETTING THERE & AWAY

River travel is a relaxing and very romantic way to see the castles, vineyards and villages of the Romantic Rhine.

From about Easter to October (winter services are very limited), 13 boats run by **Köln-Düsseldorfer** (KD; ☎ 0221-2088 318; www.k-d.com) link villages such as Bingen, St Goar and Boppard on a set timetable. You can travel to the next village or all the way from Mainz to Koblenz (€46.50, downstream/upstream 6/8½ hours).

Villages on the Rhine's left bank (eg Bingen, Boppard and St Goar) are served hourly by local trains on the Koblenz–Mainz run, inaugurated in 1859. Right-bank villages such as Rüdesheim, Assmannshausen and St Goarshausen are linked every hour or two by Koblenz–Wiesbaden services. It takes about 1½ hours to travel by train from Koblenz to either Mainz or Wiesbaden.

Many rail passes (such as Eurail) get you a free ride on normal KD services.

KOBLENZ

☎ 0261 / pop 106,000

Koblenz is a modern town with roots that go all the way back to the Romans, who founded a military stronghold here around 10 BC. An eminently strollable town, it is the northern gateway to the Romantic Rhine.

DAV/IMAGEBROKER

Cruising the Romantic Rhine, near Koblenz

INFORMATION

Tourist office (www.touristik-koblenz.de) Hauptbahnhof (☎ 313 04; Bahnhofsplatz 17; 9am-7pm daily May-Sep, 9am-6pm daily Apr & Oct, 9am-6pm Mon-Fri, 9am-2pm Sat Nov-Mar); Rathaus (☎ 130 920; Jesuitenplatz 2; 9am or 10am-7pm daily May-Sep, 10am-6pm daily Apr & Oct, 9am-6pm Mon-Fri, 10am-4pm Sat Nov-Mar)

SIGHTS

At the point of confluence of the Moselle and the Rhine is the **Deutsches Eck** (literally, 'German corner'), dominated by a **statue of Kaiser Wilhelm I** on horseback, in the bombastic style of the late 19th century.

On the right bank of the Rhine, looming 118m above the Deutsches Eck, the mighty **Festung Ehrenbreitstein** (Ehrenbreitstein Fortress; ☎ 6675 4000; www.festungehrenbreitstein.de) proved indestructible to all but Napoleonic troops, who levelled it in 1801. Behind the stone bulwarks, you'll find a DJH hostel, two restaurants and the **Landesmuseum** (☎ 667 50; www.landesmuseumkoblenz.de, in German; adult/student & senior €4/3; 9.30am-5pm late Mar-Oct), with exhibits on the region's economic history, photography and August Horch, founder of the Audi automotive company.

SLEEPING

our pick **Hotel Jan van Werth** (☎ 365 00; www.hoteljanvanwerth.de, in German; Von-Werth-Strasse 9; s/d €43/64, without bathroom €24/50;) This long-time budget favourite, with a lobby that feels like someone's living room, offers exceptional value – no surprise that the 16 rooms are often booked out, especially when the weather's good.

Diehl's Hotel (☎ 970 70; www.diehls-hotel.de; Rheinsteigufer 1; s €64-98, d €79-134, breakfast €13; P) A family-run hotel on the Rhine's east bank, with a stylish 1980s vibe and 60 comfortable rooms offering watery views of Koblenz. The restaurant has a gorgeous terrace overlooking the Rhine – perfect for a romantic sunset dinner.

EATING & DRINKING

Many of Koblenz' restaurants and pubs are in the Altstadt and along the Rhine.

Kaffeewirtschaft (☎ 914 4702; Münzplatz 14; salads €4.40-8.70, mains €5.20-12.20; ⏰ 9am-midnight Mon-Thu, 9am-2am Fri & Sat, 10am-midnight Sun & holidays) An old-fashioned cafe with minimalist designer decor, old marble tables and weekly specials (including vegetarian options) that take advantage of whatever's in season.

our pick **Cafe Miljöö** (☎ 142 37; www.cafe-miljoeoe.de, in German; Gemüsegasse 12; mains €7.90-11.90; ⏰ 8am-1am or later) 'Milieu' (pronounce it like the French) is a cosy, bistro-like cafe with fresh flowers, changing art exhibits, lots of vegie and vegan options, and a great selection of coffees, teas and homemade cakes.

KIM/IMAGEBROKER

Bacharach

BRAUBACH

☎ 02627 / pop 3200

Framed by forested hillsides, vineyards and Rhine-side rose gardens, the 1300-year-old town of Braubach, about 8km south of Koblenz on the right bank, is centred on the small, half-timbered **Marktplatz**. High above are the dramatic towers, turrets and crenellations of the 700-year-old **Marksburg** (☎ 206; www.marksburg.de; adult/6-18yr/student €5/3.50/4.50; ⏰ 10am-5pm Easter-Oct, 11am-4pm Nov-Easter), one of the area's most interesting castles because, unique among the Rhine fortresses, it was never destroyed. The tour takes in the citadel, the Gothic hall and the large kitchen, plus a grisly torture chamber, with its hair-raising assortment of pain-inflicting nasties.

BOPPARD

☎ 06742 / pop 16,000

Thanks to its historic sites and scenic location on a horseshoe bend in the river, Boppard, about 20km south of Koblenz, makes a particularly atmospheric stop. Be sure to sample the excellent riesling from grapes grown near here in some of the Rhine's steepest vineyards.

Along the riverfront is the eminently strollable **Rheinallee**, a promenade lined with ferry docks, neatly painted hotels and wine taverns. For a spectacular view that gives you the illusion of looking at four lakes instead of a single river, take the 20-minute **Sesselbahn** (☎ 2510; www.sesselbahn-boppard.de; up only/return €4.20/6.50; ⏰ 9.30am-6.30pm Jul & Aug, 10am-5pm or 6pm Apr-Jun, Sep & Oct) from the upriver edge of town up to the **Vierseenblick** viewpoint.

Weinhaus Heilig Grab (☎ 2371; www.heiliggrab.de; Zelkesgasse 12; snacks €3.50-7; ⏰ 3-11pm or later Wed-Mon, closed Christmas–mid-Jan) Across the street from the Hauptbahnhof,

Boppard's oldest wine tavern offers a cosy setting for sipping 'Holy Sepulchre' rieslings (from €2.30). Also has snacks and five rooms for rent (doubles €66 to €76).

ST GOAR

☎ 06741 / pop 3000

St Goar, 10km upriver from Boppard and 28km downriver from Bingen, is lorded over by the sprawling ruins of **Burg Rheinfels** (☎ 383; Schlossberg; adult/6-14yr €4/2; 9am-6pm daily mid-Mar–early Nov, 11am-5pm Sat & Sun in good weather early Nov–mid-Mar), once the mightiest fortress on the Rhine. Built in 1245 by Count Dieter V of Katzenelnbogen as a base for his toll-collecting operations, its size and labyrinthine layout are truly astonishing. Not only kids will love exploring the subterranean tunnels and galleries.

Hotel Zur Loreley (☎ 1614; www.hotel-zur-loreley.de; Heerstrasse 87; s €47, d €60-70, apt per person €38-44, all incl breakfast; P ⊠) A central and welcoming place to hang your hat, this places has eight rooms with tasteful, modern decor and five holiday apartments.

ST GOARSHAUSEN & LORELEY

☎ 06771 / pop 1600

St Goar's twin town on the right bank of the Rhine – the two are connected by car ferry – is **St Goarshausen**, gateway to the most fabled spot along the Romantic Rhine, **Loreley**. This enormous slab of slate owes its fame to a mythical maiden whose siren songs are said to have lured sailors to their death in the treacherous currents, as poetically portrayed by Heinrich Heine in 1823. At the **Loreley Besucherzentrum** (Visitor Centre; ☎ 599 093; www.loreley-besucherzentrum.de; adult/student €2.50/1.50; 10am-6pm Apr–mid-Nov, 10am-5pm Mar, 11am-4pm Sat & Sun Nov-Feb), which has a tourist office branch inside, exhibits (including an 18-minute 3-D film) examine the region's geology, flora and fauna, shipping, winemaking, the Loreley myth and early Rhine tourism in an engaging, interactive fashion.

BACHARACH

☎ 06743 / pop 2100

One of the prettiest of the Rhine villages, tiny Bacharach – 24km downriver from Bingen – conceals its considerable charms behind a time-worn, 14th-century wall. From the B9, go through one of the thick arched gateways under the train tracks and you'll find yourself in a medieval village graced with exquisite half-timbered mansions such as the **Altes Haus**, the **Posthof** and the off-kilter **Alte Münze** – all are along Oberstrasse, the main street, which runs parallel to the Rhine.

Bacharach's **tourist office** (☎ 919 303; www.rhein-nahe-touristik.de; Oberstrasse 45; 9am-5pm Mon-Fri, 10am-3pm Sat, Sun & holidays Apr-Oct, 9am-noon Mon-Fri Nov-Mar) has handy information about the entire area.

Rhein Hotel (☎ 1243; www.rhein-hotel-bacharach.de; Langstrasse 50; s €39-59, d €78-118; closed Jan & Feb; P ⊠) Right on the town's medieval ramparts, this homey, family-run hotel has 14 well-lit rooms with original artwork and compact bathrooms. The restaurant (mains €8.30 to €21; closed Tuesday) specialises in regional dishes such as *Rieslingbraten* (riesling-marinated braised beef).

RÜDESHEIM

☎ 06722 / pop 10,000

Rüdesheim am Rhein, capital of the Rheingau (famous for its rieslings), is on the Rhine's right bank across from Bingen, to which it's connected by passenger and car ferries. Tunnel-like **Drosselgasse** alley is so overloaded with signs that it looks like it might be in Hong Kong, and is the Rhine at its most colourfully touristic – bad German pop wafts out of the pubs, which are filled with rollicking crowds. One island of relative calm, just 50m to the left from the top of Drosselgasse, is **Siegfried's Mechanisches Musikkabinett** (☎ 492 17; www.siegfrieds-musikkabinett.de; Oberstrasse 29; tour adult/student €6/3; 🕒 10am-6pm Mar-Dec), a fun, working collection of 18th- and 19th-century mechanical musical instruments.

For a great panorama head up to the **Niederwald Denkmal** (inaugurated 1883), a bombastic monument on the wine slopes west of town starring **Germania** and celebrating the creation of the German Reich in 1871. You can walk up via the vineyards – trails, including one that begins at the western end of Oberstrasse, are signposted – but it's faster to glide above the vineyards aboard the **Seilbahn** (cable car; ☎ 2402; www.seilbahn-ruedesheim.de; Oberstrasse; adult/5-13yr one way €4.50/2, return €6.50/3; 🕒 late Mar-early Nov & late Nov-23 Dec).

AROUND RÜDESHEIM

KLOSTER EBERBACH

If you saw the 1986 film *The Name of the Rose,* starring Sean Connery, you've already seen parts of this one-time Cistercian **monastery** (☎ 06723-917 80; www.kloster-eberbach.de; adult/student incl English-language brochure €3.50/1.50, 1½hr audioguide for 1/2 people €3.50/5; 🕒 10am-6pm Apr-Oct, 11am-5pm Nov-Mar), in which many of the interior scenes were shot. Today visitors can explore the 13th- and 14th-century **Kreuzgang** (cloister), the monks' baroque **refectory** and their vaulted Gothic **Monchdormitorium** (dormitory), as well as the austere Romanesque **Klosterkirche** (basilica). Kloster Eberbach is about 20km northeast of (ie towards Wiesbaden from) Rüdesheim.

THE MOSELLE VALLEY

While plenty of places in Germany demand that you hustle, the Moselle (in German, Mosel) gently suggests that you should, well…just mosey. The German

KKK/IMAGEBROKER

Drosselgasse (p255), Rüdesheim

section of the river, which rises in France and then traverses Luxembourg, runs 195km from Trier to Koblenz on a slow, serpentine course, revealing new scenery at every bend.

Exploring the vineyards and wineries of the Moselle Valley is an ideal way to get to know German culture, meet German people and, of course, acquire a taste for some wonderful wines.

GETTING THERE & AROUND

Frankfurt-Hahn Airport is only 20km from Traben-Trarbach and 30km from Bernkastel-Kues.

The rail line linking Koblenz with Trier (€19.20, 1½ to two hours, at least hourly) follows the Moselle – and serves its villages – only as far upriver as Bullay (€10.30, 45 to 65 minutes from Koblenz, 40 to 50 minutes from Trier). From there, hourly Moselwein-Strecke shuttle trains head upriver to Traben-Trarbach (€3.10, 25 minutes, hourly).

The villages between Traben-Trarbach and Trier are served by bus 333 (at least six times daily Monday to Friday, twice daily Saturday and Sunday), run by **Moselbahn buses** (☎ 01805-131 619; www.moselbahn.de, in German).

Driving is the easiest way to see the Moselle.

TRIER

☎ 0651 / pop 104,000

A Unesco World Heritage Site since 1986, Trier is home to Germany's finest Roman monuments – including an extraordinary number of elaborate thermal baths – as well as architectural gems from later ages.

INFORMATION

Tourist office (☎ 978 080; www.trier.de; An der Porta Nigra; ⌚ 9am-6pm Mon-Sat Mar-Dec, 10am-5pm Mon-Sat Jan & Feb, 10am-5pm Sun & holidays May-Oct, 10am-3pm Sun Mar, Apr & Nov-late Dec, 10am-1pm Sun late Dec-Feb)

KFS/IMAGEBROKER

A fountain in Trier's Hauptmarkt

SIGHTS & ACTIVITIES

Top billing among Trier's Roman monuments goes to the **Porta Nigra** (☎ 718 1459; Porta-Nigra-Platz; adult/7-18yr/senior & student/family €2.10/1/1.60/5.10; ⌚ 9am-6pm Apr-Sep, to 5pm Mar & Oct, to 4pm Nov-Feb), a brooding 2nd-century city gate that's been blackened by time (the name is Latin for 'black gate'). An engineering marvel, it's held together by nothing but gravity and iron rods.

A block east of the Hauptmarkt looms the fortresslike **Dom** (www.dominformation.de; ⌚ 6.30am-6pm Apr-Oct, to 5.30pm Nov-Mar), built above the palace of Constantine

SLU/IMAGEBROKER

A wine tavern in the Ahrtal

IF YOU LIKE...

If you enjoyed the **wine** taverns, estates and festivals in the **Moselle** (p256) and **Rhine** villages (p252), we bet you'll also like tasting the tipple produced in these nearby growing regions:

- **Ahrtal** The tiny Ahr Valley, along a tributary of the Rhine some 30km south of Bonn, produces racy reds like *Spätburgunder* (Pinot noir) and Portugieser with grapes growing on steeply terraced vineyards.
- **Deutsche Weinstrasse** The German Wine Road is Germany's largest contiguous grape-growing area. Starting in Bockenheim, about 15km west of Worms, it winds 85km south to the French border. Pretty, wisteria-filled villages such as Deidesheim and Wachenheim are famous for their full-bodied rieslings.
- **Nahe** Fragrant Müller-Thurgau, fruity riesling and racy Silvaner are the dominant varietals growing on the steep vineyards hugging the Nahe River, which joins the Rhine just north of Mainz.

the Great's mother, Helena. The present structure is mostly Romanesque with some soaring Gothic and eye-popping baroque embellishments. The brick **Konstantinbasilika** (Konstantinplatz; 10am-6pm Mon-Sat, noon-6pm Sun & holidays Apr-Oct, 11am-noon & 3-4pm Tue-Sat, noon-1pm Sun & holidays Nov-Mar) was constructed in AD 310 as Constantine's throne hall. Its dimensions (67m long and 36m high) are truly mind-blowing considering that it was built by the Romans.

The adjacent **Rheinisches Landesmuseum** (Roman Archaeological Museum; ☎ 977 40; www.landesmuseum-trier.de, in German; Weimarer Allee 1; adult/student/family incl audioguide €5/3/10; 9.30am-5.30pm Tue-Sun) affords an extraordinary look at local Roman life. Highlights include a scale model of 4th-century Trier and rooms filled with tombstones, mosaics, rare gold coins and some fantastic glass.

On the southern edge of the *Palastgarten* (palace garden) stands the **Kaiserthermen** (☎ 436 2550; Weimarer Allee 2; adult/7-18yr/senior

& student/family €2.10/1/1.60/5.10; 9am-6pm Apr-Sep, to 5pm Mar & Oct, to 4pm Nov-Feb), a vast thermal bathing complex created by Constantine. About 700m to the south-east is the Roman **Amphitheater** (730 10; Olewiger Strasse; adult/7-18yr/senior & student/family €2.10/1/1.60/5.10; 9am-6pm Apr-Sep, to 5pm Mar & Oct, to 4pm Nov-Feb), once capable of holding 20,000 spectators during gladiator tournaments and animal fights.

SLEEPING

Hille's Hostel (710 2785, 0171 329 1247; www.hilles-hostel-trier.de; Gartenfeldstrasse 7; dm from €14, d €28-50; reception 8am-noon & 4-6pm;) An independent hostel with a 1970s vibe, this laid-back place has a piano in the kitchen and 10 brightly decorated rooms with private bathrooms.

Hotel Römischer Kaiser (977 0100; www.friedrich-hotels.de, in German; Porta-Nigra-Platz; d €105-150;) Right next to Porta Nigra, this 1894 building offers 43 bright, comfortable rooms with solid wood furnishings, parquet floors and spacious bathrooms.

EATING

Kartoffel Kiste (979 0066; www.kiste-trier.de, in German; Fahrstrasse 13-14; mains €7.20-14.50; 11am- midnight) A local favourite, this place specialises in baked, breaded, soupified and sauce-engulfed potatoes, as well as steaks.

Zum Domstein (744 90; Am Hauptmarkt 5; mains €8.80-16.90, Roman dinner €15-33; 8.30am-midnight) A German-style bistro where you can either dine like an ancient Roman or feast on more conventional German and international fare.

BERNKASTEL-KUES

06531 / pop 6700

This charming twin town, some 50km downriver from Trier, is the hub of the middle Moselle region. Bernkastel, on the right bank, is a symphony in half-timber, stone and slate and teems with wine taverns. On Karlstrasse, the alley to the right as you face the Rathaus, the tiny **Spitzhäuschen** resembles a giant bird's house, its narrow base topped by a much larger, precariously leaning, upper floor.

In Kues, most sights are conveniently grouped next to the bridge in the late-Gothic **St-Nikolaus-Hospital** (2260; Cusanusstrasse 2; admission free; 9am-6pm Sun-Fri, to 3pm Sat), an old-age home founded by Cusanus in 1458 for 33 men (one for every year of Christ's life). The complex also houses the new, multimedia **Mosel-Weinmuseum** (Moselle Wine Museum; 4141; adult/under 12yr/13-18yr €5/free/3; 10am-6pm mid-Apr–Oct, 2-5pm Nov–mid-Apr), with interactive terminals (in German, English and Dutch) and attractions such as an Aromabar (you have to guess what you're smelling). In the cellar **Vinothek**, you can sample Moselle wines by the glass (about €2) or indulge in an 'all you can drink' wine tasting (€15).

our pick **Hotel Moselblümchen** (2335; www.hotel-moselbluemchen.de; Schwanenstrasse 10, Bernkastel; s €39-65, d €66-110;) is a traditional, family-run hotel on a narrow old-town alley behind the tourist office. It has 20 tasteful rooms and a small sauna, and can arrange bike rental.

COCHEM

02671 / pop 5100

Cochem, a picture-postcard village about 55km downriver from Traben-Trarbach, spends much of the year overrun with day trippers. Towering above steep vineyards, the city-owned **Reichsburg** (255; www.reichsburg-cochem.de; adult/6-17yr €4.50/2.50; 9am-5pm mid-Mar–Oct, 10am or 11am-2pm or 3pm Nov-early Jan) – everyone's idealised version of a turreted medieval castle – is

TOM/IMAGEBROKER

Cochem's Reichsburg (p259)

actually a neo-Gothic pastiche built in 1877, making it a full 78 years older than Disneyland.

On the right bank of the Moselle about 12km upriver from Cochem, **Beilstein** (www.beilstein-mosel.de, in German) is a pint-sized village right out of the world of fairy tales. Little more than a cluster of houses surrounded by steep vineyards, its romantic, half-timbered townscape is enhanced by the ruined **Burg Metternich**, a hilltop castle reached via a staircase.

Victor Hugo thought this next fairy-tale castle, hidden away in the forest above the left bank of the Moselle, was 'tall, terrific, strange and dark'. Indeed, 850-year-old **Burg Eltz** (☎ 02672-950 500; www.burg-eltz.de; tour adult/student/family €8/5.50/24; 9.30am-5.30pm Apr-Oct), owned by the same family for more than 30 generations, has a forbidding exterior, softened by turrets crowning it like candles on a birthday cake. The **treasury** features a rich collection of jewellery, porcelain and weapons. By car, you can reach Burg Eltz – which has never been destroyed – via the village of Münstermaifeld.

➘ DRESDEN & EASTERN GERMANY

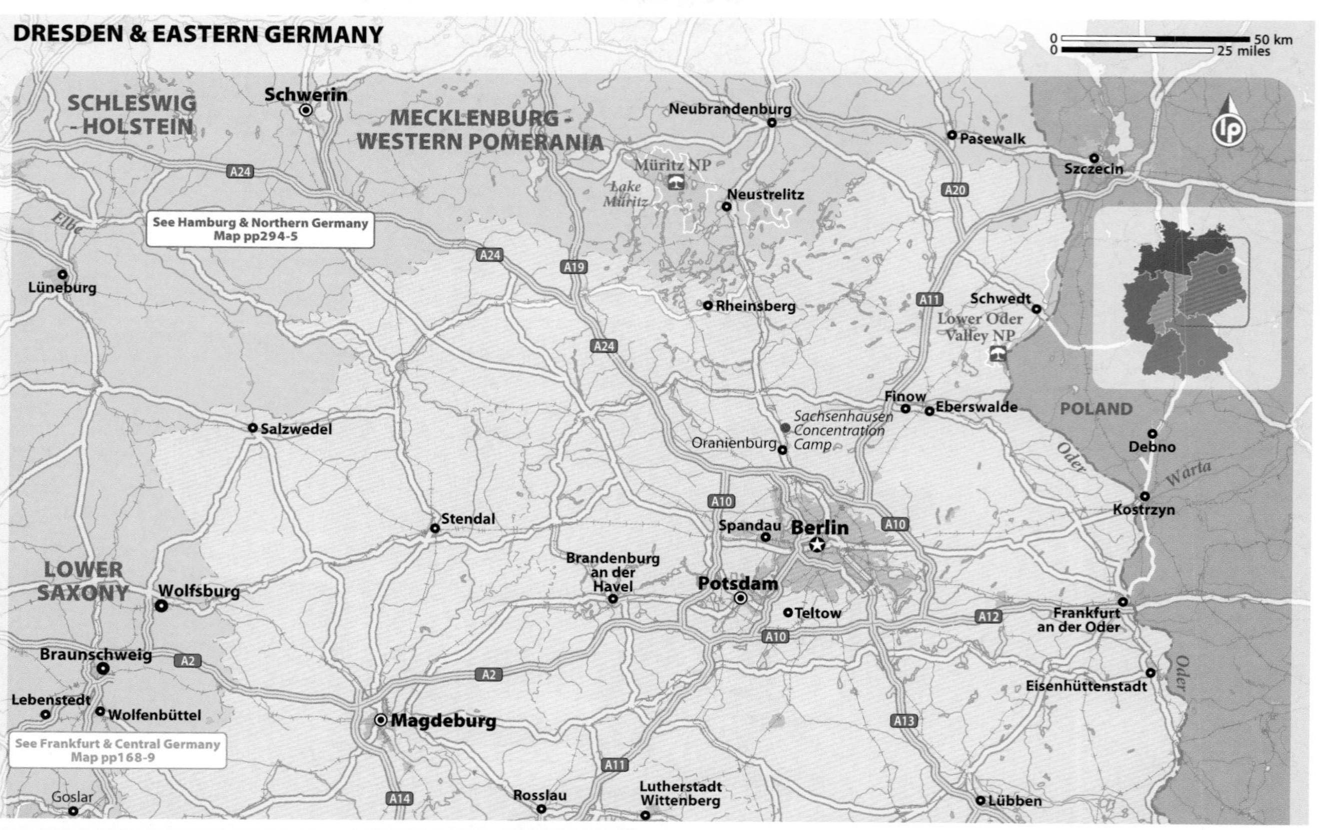
DRESDEN & EASTERN GERMANY
0 50 km
0 25 miles
SCHLESWIG-HOLSTEIN
Schwerin
MECKLENBURG-WESTERN POMERANIA
Neubrandenburg
Pasewalk
Szczecin
A24
Müritz NP
Lake Müritz
Neustrelitz
A20
Elbe
See Hamburg & Northern Germany Map pp294-5
A19
Lüneburg
Rheinsberg
A11
Schwedt
Lower Oder Valley NP
Finow
Eberswalde
POLAND
Salzwedel
Sachsenhausen Concentration Camp
Oranienburg
Oder
Debno
Warta
A10
Kostrzyn
Stendal
Spandau
Berlin
Brandenburg an der Havel
LOWER SAXONY
Wolfsburg
Potsdam
Teltow
A12
Frankfurt an der Oder
Braunschweig
A2
Eisenhüttenstadt
Lebenstedt
Wolfenbüttel
Magdeburg
A13
See Frankfurt & Central Germany Map pp168-9
A14
Goslar
Rosslau
Lutherstadt Wittenberg
Lübben

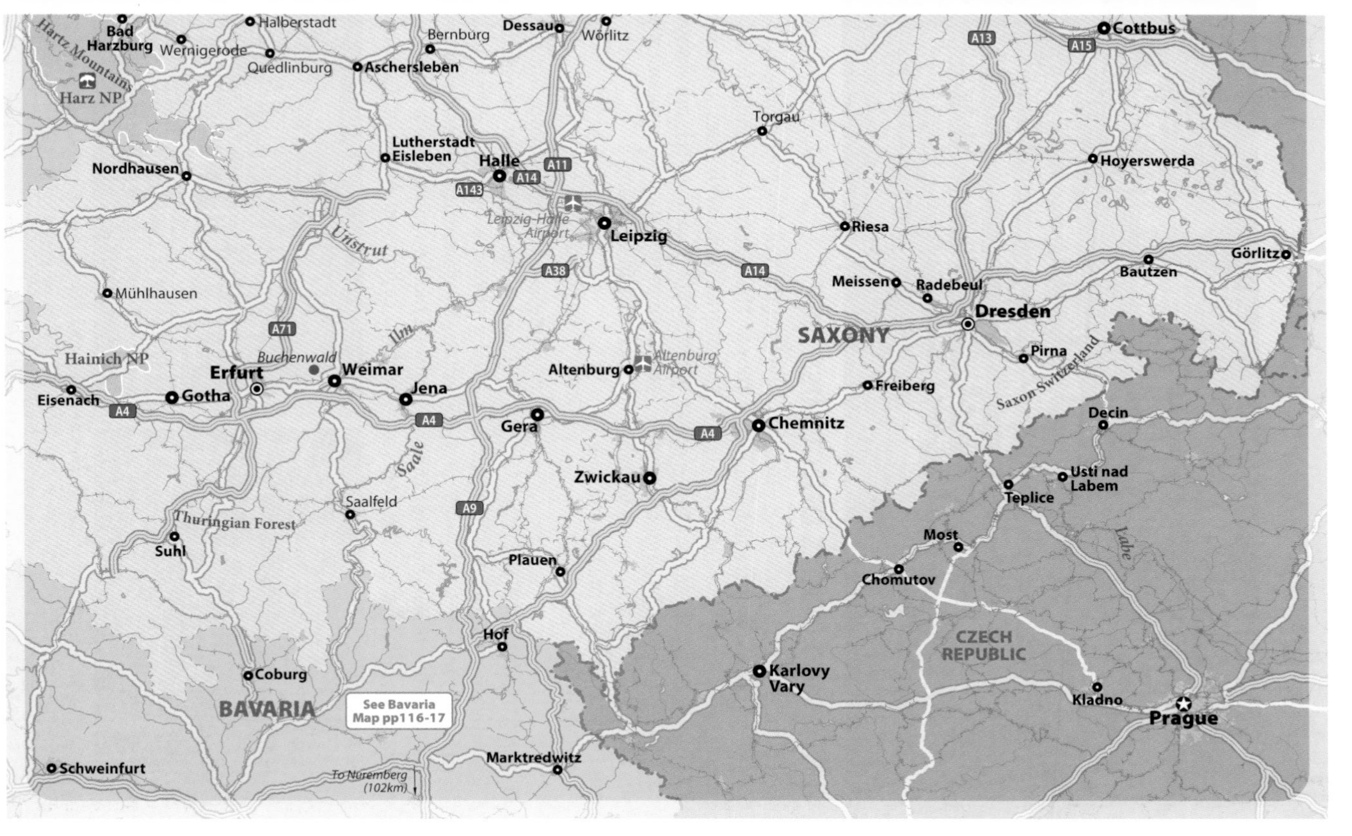
Cottbus
Hoyerswerda
Bautzen
Görlitz
A15
A13
Dresden
Pirna
Saxon Switzerland
Decin
Usti nad Labem
Labe
Prague
Kladno
Teplice
CZECH REPUBLIC
Most
Chomutov
Radebeul
Meissen
Freiberg
Riesa
SAXONY
Chemnitz
Karlovy Vary
Torgau
A14
Altenburg Airport
Altenburg
A4
Zwickau
Leipzig
Wörlitz
Dessau
A11
A14
Leipzig-Halle Airport
A38
Halle
A143
Plauen
Marktredwitz
Gera
Hof
A9
Bernburg
Aschersleben
Lutherstadt Eisleben
Jena
Ilm
Saale
A4
See Bavaria Map pp116-17
To Nuremberg (102km)
Saalfeld
Weimar
Unstrut
Buchenwald
Halberstadt
Quedlinburg
A71
Erfurt
Coburg
BAVARIA
Thuringian Forest
Gotha
Wernigerode
Nordhausen
Mühlhausen
Suhl
Bad Harzburg
Hartz Mountains
Harz NP
Hainich NP
A4
Eisenach
Schweinfurt

HIGHLIGHTS

1 POTSDAM

BY REGINA EBERT, RESIDENT & POTSDAM GUIDE

I've been a guide here for 15 years, and every day I'm inspired by this town's abundant lakes; romantic, palace-filled parks; and remarkable art and extraordinary structures that wow the eyes. Potsdam's allure is endless. No wonder they keep coming in droves!

REGINA EBERT'S DON'T MISS LIST

❶ SANSSOUCI'S MARBLE HALL

Sanssouci has many incredible rooms, but the **Marmorhalle** (Marble Hall; p275) is one of my favourites – it's constructed with 15 types of exquisite marble. This is also where Voltaire used to sit to discuss philosophy when he was in town.

❷ AM I IN HOLLAND?

I love taking visitors to Potsdam's charming **Holländisches Viertel** (Dutch Quarter; p275), built for Dutch workers who came here in the 1730s at the invitation of Friedrich Wilhelm I – though they didn't stay long! The entire district brims with cafes, galleries and restaurants, and visitors are always surprised to find such an authentically Dutch area in Germany.

❸ CHINESISCHES HAUS

Its name is a tad misleading, but the **Chinese House** (p275) in Sanssouci Park is always a hit for children and adults. This fantastical garden pavilion mixes Chinese figures and a Buddha-painted ceiling with Venetian Carnival

Clockwise from top: Orangerieschloss (Orangery Palace; p274); Schloss Sanssouci (p274); Chinesisches Haus (Chinese House; p275), Park Sanssouci; Houses in Holländisches Viertel (Dutch Quarter; p275); Schloss Sanssouci (p274)

CLOCKWISE FROM TOP: RBB/IMAGEBROKER; EWR/IMAGEBROKER; EWR/IMAGEBROKER; OLIVER STREWE; HBA/IMAGEBROKER

details – the entire structure is a feast for the eyes.

❹ WATER TAXI

Potsdam is surrounded by water, and I always encourage people to take advantage of the local **water taxi** (www.potsdamer-wassertaxi.de). You can hop on and off as you please and it stops at all the major sites, except Sanssouci (but that's just a short walk from one of the stops). It's a fun and relaxing way the get around – kids particularly love it!

❺ RAPHAEL ON RED

One of my favourite rooms is the Raphaelsaal (Raphael Hall) in the **Orangerieschloss** (Orangery Palace; p274). This remarkable hall contains 49 reproductions of the Italian's paintings, all hanging on red damask-covered walls – a striking combination of colour and detail.

➘ THINGS YOU NEED TO KNOW

Top tip To avoid Sanssouci's crowds, visit weekday mornings. **Best photo op** Hike up to the Belvedere Pfingstberg, the highest point in town. **Did you know?** Potsdam is filled with *Hinterhöfe* (courtyards); they're tough to find, but the tourist office offers tours of these hidden cafe- and gallery-filled delights.

HIGHLIGHTS

2

WEIMAR

Weimar (p287) experienced its heyday during the 18th-century Age of Enlightenment when it attracted a literal who's who of intellectual and cultural greats, from Goethe to Bach to Kandinsky. You can still explore their old stomping grounds in an array of museums and sights, while the town's quaint streets, parks and gardens lend themselves to quiet contemplation.

3

LUTHERHAUS

Lutherstadt Wittenberg is the very crucible of the Reformation that culminated in the division of the Christian Church into Catholics and Protestants in the 16th century. This is the town where long-term resident Martin Luther wrote his famous 95 theses challenging Catholic practices at that time. The best place to learn about the development of his beliefs is at his former family home, the **Lutherhaus** (p291).

4

ALADDIN'S CAVE IN DRESDEN

Two mind-boggling treasure chambers inhabit Dresden's **Residenzschloss** (p279). The Neues Grünes Gewölbe (New Green Vault) collection includes 132 gem-studded figurines representing a royal court in India; the Historisches Grünes Gewölbe (Historical Green Vault) showcases a further 3000 items.

5

MEISSEN PORCELAIN

Exquisite porcelain gracing tables and display cases around the world is manufactured here in Meissen. At the **Meissen museum** (p281) your tour will include an educational visit to studios where you can watch live demonstrations where artisans painstakingly construct the trademark plates, figurines and teacups. Now the price tag really makes sense!

6

THE TUBULAR CHAIR

The Bauhaus movement – which gave birth to minimalism and the iconic steel-and-black tubular chair gracing design-conscious spaces across the globe – originated in **Dessau-Rosslau** (p289). You can visit the school where Walter Gropius and Mies van der Rohe fathered modern architecture, and a handful of Bauhaus **Meisterhäuser** (Masters' Houses).

2 A monument to Goethe and Schiller, Weimar (p287); 3 Lutherhaus (p291), Lutherstadt Wittenberg; 4 The Grünes Gewölbe (279), Dresden's Residenzschloss; 5 Meissen porcelain (p281); 6 Bauhausgebäude (p290), Dessau-Rosslau

THE BEST...

THINGS FOR FREE

- **Zeitgeschichtliches Forum** (p283) History of the GDR, from division to the fall of the Wall, in Leipzig.
- **Frauenkirche** (p277) Dresden's reconstructed landmark church.
- **Bauhausgebäude** (p290) Modernist masterpieces in Dessau, the epicentre of the Bauhaus movement.
- Contemplate whether Martin Luther really did nail his theses to the doors of Wittenberg's **Schlosskirche** (p292).

PLACES TO CHILL

- Potsdam's **Park Sanssouci** (p274) is a relaxing – and romantic – expanse of greenery.
- The bucolic **Sächsische Dampfschiffahrt** (p281) steam ship is the most tranquil way to travel between Dresden and Meissen.
- Park an der Ilm (Ilm Park) surrounding **Goethes Gartenhaus** (p287) is as serene now as it was in his time.

LITERARY HAUNTS

- Mephistopheles and Faust from Goethe's *Faust – Part I* revelled at **Auerbachs Keller** (p284), a landmark Leipzig restaurant.
- Dramatist Friedrich von Schiller lived and wrote *William Tell* at **Schiller Haus** (p287) in Weimar.
- Visit **Goethe Haus** (p287) in Weimar, where the legend penned *Faust*.

UNESCO HERITAGE SITES

- The Bauhaus element and key structures in **Weimar** (p287).
- **Lutherstadt-Wittenberg's** (p291) many Reformation-related sites.
- The grand dame of Brandenburg, most of **Potsdam** (p272) has had Unesco status since 1990.

Left: An archer in Park Sanssouci (p274), Potsdam; Right: Semperoper (Opera House; p279), Dresden

THINGS YOU NEED TO KNOW

VITAL STATISTICS

- **Population** Brandenburg 2.53 million; Saxony 4.35 million; Thuringia 2.28 million; Saxony–Anhalt 2.41 million
- **Points of entry** Berlin, Dresden and Leipzig airports.
- **Best time to visit** April to October

ADVANCE PLANNING

- **Three months before** Book tickets to see a performance at Dresden's **Semperoper** (p279).
- **One month before** Reserve a table at Leipzig's **Auerbachs Keller** (p284), one of Germany's most memorable restaurants.

RESOURCES

- **www.cybersax.de** Dresden's online city magazine is chock-full of local listings and events. German only, but highlights and headlines are intuitive enough for you to be able to figure out what's going on in town while you visit.
- **www.lutheronline.com** A website dedicated to Martin Luther.

GETTING AROUND

- **Train** The trains in this region are comfortable, efficient and relaxing – there's absolutely no reason to hire a car, and parking in cities like Dresden and Leipzig gets expensive. Plan your journey and book tickets in advance at www.bahn.de.
- **The quickest way to Potsdam** Potsdam (p272) is best done as a day trip from Berlin. From Berlin's city centre, regional trains make the trip in 25 minutes, but S-Bahns take 40 minutes; both journeys cost the same (€2.80).

BE FOREWARNED

- **Buchenwald** (p289) and **Sachsenhausen** (p277) **Concentration Camps** It goes without saying that a visit to either of these former camps is disturbing. Plan for a little down time after your visit – your mind needs time to take it all in.
- **Meissen** (p280) Long waits are common at the Meissen museum. Plan extra time for your visit and take a stroll through the charming Meissen Altstadt (old town) while you wait for your time slot.

DRESDEN & EASTERN GERMANY ITINERARIES

SPLURGE YOURSELF SILLY Three Days

It's easy to travel on a budget in this area, but if you've got some money to spare, you can really go to town – treat yourself to a few memorable days in and around **(1) Dresden** and bring home an exquisite souvenir (just make sure you get your hands on some bubble-wrap). Book yourself into a room at the **(2) Hotel Bülow Residenz** (p280) – a refined small hotel that holds the revered, high-end Relais & Chateau designation of excellence. Be sure to indulge in a meal at its well-respected restaurant, too. Take in a performance at the **(3) Semperoper** (p279), the neo-Renaissance stunner that hosts classical concerts and operas (remember to book tickets far in advance, particularly for those coveted seats in the first few rows). Next hop on a ferry to the **(4) Meissen museum** (p281) for the day. Here you can learn how handmade porcelain is crafted and, of course, buy yourself a distinguished piece (or a full table-setting) to show off back home. You can return to Dresden by train, or opt to glide back on the ferry.

WRITERS, REFORMERS & COMPOSERS Five Days

Dresden and eastern Germany inspired some of the most famous writers and composers of our time. It's also where the Reformation began. Base yourself in **(1) Leipzig** (p282) and book dinner for your first night at the exceptional **(2) Auerbachs Keller** (p284), where sections of Goethe's *Faust* took place. The following day, explore the **(3) Thomaskirche** (p283) – where Johann Sebastian Bach worked as a cantor – and be sure to visit the **(4) Bach-Museum** (p283). Stop off for coffee at **(5) Zum Arabischen Coffe Baum** (p285), where composer Robert Schumann used to hang his hat. Spend the next few days doing day trips, all reachable by train. Head out to **(6) Lutherstadt Wittenberg** (p291), where – during the Reformation – Martin Luther wrote his 95 theses, priests were married and educators argued for schools to accept female pupils. Continue with the Luther theme with a day in **(7) Erfurt** (p285), where the reformer studied philosophy between 1501 and 1505. On your final excursion from Leipzig, head to **(8) Weimar** (p287), where scores of intellectual heavyweights lived and worked. The most notable sights are the former homes of Goethe and his pal Schiller, where they penned, respectively, *Faust* and *William Tell.*

CASTLES & CHURCHES One Week

This tour takes in some of the region's most impressive castles and churches, in the region's most famous towns; this entire itinerary

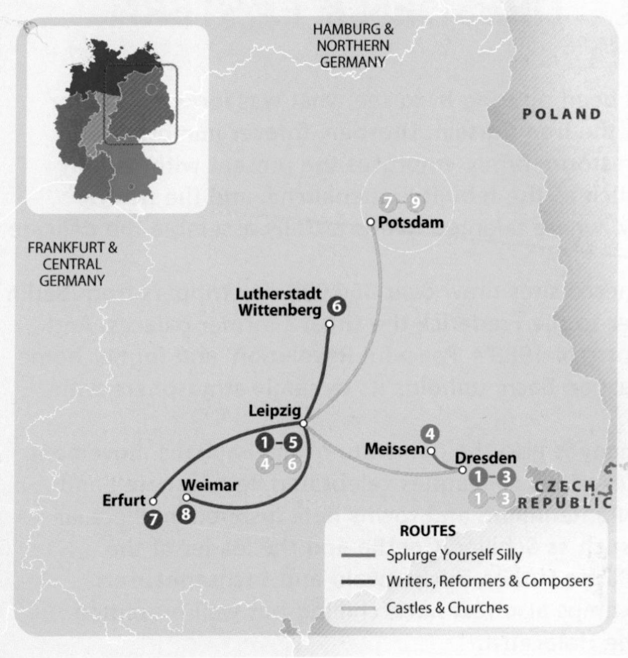

can be done by train. Start in (1) Dresden (p277) at the restored (2) Frauenkirche (p277), the salt-and-pepper facade of which is on account of the old (dark) and new (light) materials they used to rebuild the church after the Wall came down. Down the street is the new Renaissance (3) Residenzschloss (p279), home to 3000 precious treasures across two wings. Next head to (4) Leipzig (p282) to visit the (5) Nikolaikirche (p283), the Romanesque and Gothic beauty that played a key role in the fall of the Wall, and the (6) Thomaskirche (p283), where Bach worked as a cantor. Last, visit the mother lode of castles in (7) Potsdam (p272); its most famous (and popular) is (8) Schloss Sanssouci (p274). Be sure to include a stop at Potsdam's (9) Nikolaikirche (p275) and snap a photo of its magnificent neoclassical dome.

DISCOVER DRESDEN & EASTERN GERMANY

Travellers have been pouring in to see what was locked away for so long behind the Iron Curtain. Dresden, forever immortalised by the WWII firestorm, firmly embraces the present with its fully restored sites such as the rebuilt Frauenkirche, and the nearby Meissen factory, where talented hands artfully assemble the delicate porcelain.

Potsdam's Unesco sites draw over 350,000 day trippers from Berlin each year, eager to see Frederick the Great's former palaces. And Leipzig, the centre of 1989's 'Peaceful Revolution' and former home to Johann Sebastian Bach, upholds its dynamic atmosphere with vigour and fun.

Eastern Germany is also the epicentre of the Bauhaus movement (where Gropius and his colleagues celebrated 'less is more') and the German Enlightenment, and towns here inspired intellectual heavyweights such as Schiller, Goethe and the leader of the Reformation, Martin Luther. Buchenwald and Sachsenhausen concentration camps also rest here, chilling but well-presented reminders of the Holocaust.

BRANDENBURG

POTSDAM

Potsdam is the capital and crown jewel of the state of Brandenburg. Scores of visitors arrive every year to admire the stunning architecture of this former Prussian royal seat and to soak up the elegant air of history that hangs over its parks and gardens. A visit here is essential if you're spending any time in the region at all. All this splendour didn't go unnoticed by Unesco, which gave World Heritage status to large parts of the city in 1990.

No single individual shaped Potsdam more than King Friedrich II (Frederick the Great), the visionary behind many of Sanssouci's fabulous palaces and parks. In April 1945, Royal Air Force bombers devastated the historic centre, including the City Palace on Am Alten Markt, but fortunately most other palaces escaped with nary a shrapnel wound. When the shooting stopped, the Allies chose Schloss Cecilienhof for the Potsdam Conference of August 1945, which set the stage for the division of Berlin and Germany into occupation zones.

TOURIST INFORMATION

For pretrip planning, visit www.potsdam tourismus.de.

Sanssouci Besucherzentrum (☎ 969 4200; www.spsg.de; An der Orangerie 1; 🕑 8.30am-5pm Mar-Oct, 9am-4pm Nov-Feb)

Tourist office Brandenburger Tor (☎ 275 580; Brandenburger Strasse 3; 🕑 9.30am-6pm Mon-Fri, to 4pm Sat & Sun Apr-Oct, 10am-6pm Mon-Fri, 9.30am-2pm Sat & Sun Nov-Mar)

Tourist office Potsdam Hauptbahnhof (☎ 275 580; Bahnhofspassagen, Babelsberger Strasse 16; 🕑 9.30am-8pm Mon-Fri, 9am-8pm Sat)

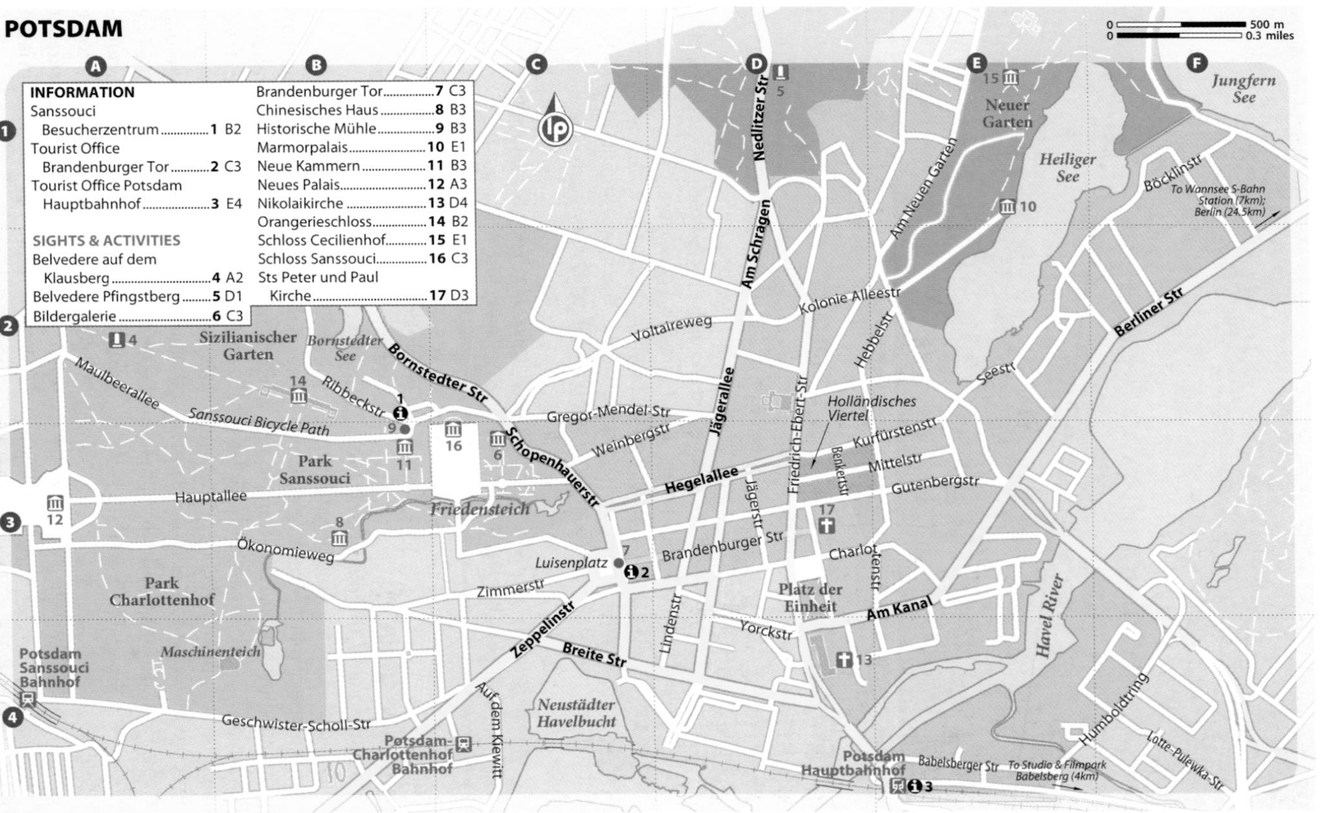
POTSDAM
0 500 m
0 0.3 miles
A
B
C
D
E
F
1
2
3
4
INFORMATION
Sanssouci Besucherzentrum 1 B2
Tourist Office Brandenburger Tor 2 C3
Tourist Office Potsdam Hauptbahnhof 3 E4
SIGHTS & ACTIVITIES
Belvedere auf dem Klausberg 4 A2
Belvedere Pfingstberg 5 D1
Bildergalerie 6 C3
Brandenburger Tor 7 C3
Chinesisches Haus 8 B3
Historische Mühle 9 B3
Marmorpalais 10 E1
Neue Kammern 11 B3
Neues Palais 12 A3
Nikolaikirche 13 D4
Orangerieschloss 14 B2
Schloss Cecilienhof 15 E1
Schloss Sanssouci 16 C3
Sts Peter und Paul Kirche 17 D3
Jungfern See
Neuer Garten
Heiliger See
Böcklinstr
To Wannsee S-Bahn Station (7km); Berlin (24.5km)
Nedlitzer Str
Am Schragen
Am Neuen Garten
Kolonie Alleestr
Berliner Str
Voltaireweg
Hebbelstr
Seestr
Sizilianischer Garten
Bornstedter See
Bornstedter Str
Maulbeerallee
Ribbeckstr
Gregor-Mendel-Str
Jägerallee
Friedrich-Ebert-Str
Holländisches Viertel
Kurfürstenstr
Sanssouci Bicycle Path
Weinbergstr
Benkertstr
Mittelstr
Park Sanssouci
Schopenhauerstr
Hegelallee
Jägerstr
Gutenbergstr
Hauptallee
Friedensteich
Ökonomieweg
Brandenburger Str
Charlottenstr
Luisenplatz
Park Charlottenhof
Zimmerstr
Platz der Einheit
Am Kanal
Havel River
Zeppelinstr
Lindenstr
Yorckstr
Maschinenteich
Breite Str
Potsdam Sanssouci Bahnhof
Auf dem Kiewitt
Neustädter Havelbucht
Humboldtring
Geschwister-Scholl-Str
Potsdam-Charlottenhof Bahnhof
Potsdam Hauptbahnhof
Babelsberger Str
To Studio & Filmpark Babelsberg (4km)
Lotte-Pulewka-Str

EWR/IMAGEBROKER

Schloss Sanssouci, Potsdam

SCHLOSS SANSSOUCI & AROUND

The biggest stunner, and what everyone comes to see, is **Schloss Sanssouci**, the celebrated rococo palace designed by Georg Wenzeslaus von Knobelsdorff in 1747.

Among the rooms you'll see on your self-guided audio tour, the exquisite circular **Bibliothek** (Library), with its cedar panelling and gilded sunburst ceiling, is undoubtedly a highlight, even if you can only see it through a glass door. Other favourites include the **Konzertsaal** (Concert Room), playfully decorated with vines, grapes, seashells and even a cobweb where spiders frolic. The most elegant room is the domed **Marmorhalle** (Marble Hall), a symphony in white Carrara marble.

Things you need to know: (☎ 969 4190; adult/concession incl audioguide Apr-Oct €12/8, incl tour or audioguide Nov-Mar €8/5; ⌚ 10am-6pm Tue-Sun Apr-Oct, to 5pm Nov-Mar)

SIGHTS

PARK SANSSOUCI

Park Sanssouci is the oldest and most splendid of Potsdam's many gardens, a vast expanse of mature trees, rare plants and magnificent palaces. Its trump card is Schloss Sanssouci, Frederick the Great's favourite summer retreat, a place where he could be *'sans souci'* (without cares). In the 19th century, Friedrich Wilhelm IV also left his mark by adding a few buildings

The park is open from dawn till dusk. Admission is free, but there are machines by the entrance where you can make a voluntary donation of €2. The buildings have different hours and admission prices.

ORANGERIESCHLOSS & AROUND

The dominant building in this corner of the park is the elegantly ageing **Orangerieschloss** (Orangery Palace; ☎ 969 4280; mandatory tour adult/concession €4/3; ⌚ 10am-6pm Tue-Sun May-Oct), a 300m-long Renaissance-style palace built in 1864 by Italophile Friedrich Wilhelm IV as a guesthouse for visiting royalty. There are some nice views from the **tower** (admission €2) but otherwise the most interesting room is the

Raphaelsaal, featuring 19th-century copies of the painter's masterpieces.

NEUES PALAIS

At the far western end of the park, the **Neues Palais** (New Palace; ☎ 969 4361; adult/concession with tour or audioguide €6/5; ⏱ 10am-6pm Wed-Mon Apr-Oct, to 5pm Nov-Mar) has made-to-impress dimensions, a central dome and a lavish exterior. It was the last palace built by Frederick the Great, but he never really camped out here, preferring the intimacy of Schloss Sanssouci.

Inside await about a dozen splendid rooms, the most memorable of which are the **Grottensaal** (Grotto Hall), a rococo delight with shells, fossils and baubles set into the walls and ceilings; the **Marmorsaal**, a large banquet hall of Carrara marble with a wonderful ceiling fresco; and the **Jagdkammer** (Hunting Chamber), with lots of dead furry things and fine gold tracery on the walls.

PFINGSTBERG

For the best view over Potsdam and surrounds, head uphill to the beautifully restored **Belvedere Pfingstberg** (☎ 2005 7930; adult/concession €3.50/2.50; ⏱ 10am-8pm Jun-Aug, 10am-6pm Apr, May, Sep & Oct, 10am-4pm Sat & Sun Mar & Nov). Built in Italian Renaissance style, this massive twin-towered palace was commissioned by Friedrich Wilhelm IV but not completed until 1863, two years after his death.

Northeast of the Roman Baths, the adorable **Chinesisches Haus** (Chinese House; ☎ 969 4225; admission €2; ⏱ 10am-6pm Tue-Sun May-Oct) reflects the 18th-century fascination with the Far East. It is one of the prettiest and most photographed buildings in the park, largely because of the gilded sandstone figures, with oriental dress, shown sipping tea, dancing and playing musical instruments.

ALTSTADT

Moving into old town Potsdam, the baroque **Brandenburger Tor** (Brandenburg Gate) on Luisenplatz is actually older than its more famous cousin in Berlin. From this square, the pedestrianised Brandenburger Strasse runs east to the **Sts Peter und Paul Kirche** (Church of Sts Peter & Paul; ☎ 230 7990; admission free; ⏱ 10am-5pm Mon-Sat, 11.30am-3.30pm Sun), dating from 1868.

Northwest of the church, bounded by Friedrich-Ebert-Strasse, Hebbelstrasse, Kurfürstenstrasse and Gutenbergstrasse, is the picturesque **Holländisches Viertel** (Dutch Quarter). It consists of 134 gabled red-brick houses built for Dutch workers who came to Potsdam in the 1730s at the invitation of Friedrich Wilhelm I.

Southeast of the GDR-era Platz der Einheit looms the great neoclassical dome of Schinkel's **Nikolaikirche** (☎ 270 8602; Am Alten Markt; ⏱ 9am-7pm Mon-Sat, 11.30am-7pm Sun), built in 1850, complemented by an obelisk and a small pavilion on the old market square.

NEUER GARTEN

The winding lakeside Neuer Garten (New Garden), laid out in natural English style on the western shore of the Heiliger See, is another fine park in which to relax. Right on the lake, the neoclassical **Marmorpalais** (Marble Palace; ☎ 969 4246; tour adult/concession €5/4; ⏱ 10am-6pm Tue-Sun May-Oct, 10am-4pm Sat & Sun Nov-Apr) was built in 1792 for Friedrich Wilhelm II by Carl Gotthard Langhans (he of Berlin's Brandenburger Tor fame).

Further north, **Schloss Cecilienhof** (☎ 969 4200; adult/concession with tour or audioguide €6/5; ⏱ 10am-6pm Tue-Sun Apr-Oct, to 5pm Nov-Mar) is a rustic English-style country manor completed in 1917 for crown prince Wilhelm and his wife Cecilie.

HBA/IMAGEBROKER

Neue Kammern (New Chambers), Park Sanssouci, Potsdam

IF YOU LIKE...

If you're enchanted by **Potsdam's extravagant palaces**, you might be suitably impressed by what else is on offer in this historic town. It's no wonder it's the most popular day trip from Berlin:

- **Bildergalerie** (Picture Gallery; ☎ 969 4181) Just east of the Schloss (Sanssouci), this stunning 1763 structure houses a feast of 17th-century paintings by Rubens, Caravaggio, van Dyck and others.
- **Neue Kammern** (New Chambers; ☎ 969 4206) To the west is a former orangery and guesthouse, the fancy interior of which includes the festive Ovidsaal, a grand ballroom with a patterned marble floor surrounded by gilded reliefs.
- **Historische Mühle** (☎ 550 6581) Maulbeerallee is the only road cutting straight through Park Sanssouci. On the northeast corner is a functioning replica of an 18th-century windmill. Parents enjoy the historic exhibits and kids love watching the enormous grinding mechanism.
- **Belvedere auf dem Klausberg** (☎ 969 4206) From the Orangerieschloss, a tree-lined path forms a visual axis to the rococo templelike pavilion whose sumptuous interior was beautifully restored following war damage.

BABELSBERG

Babelsberg is synonymous with film-making. The mighty UFA began shooting flicks here in 1912, and by the 1920s was producing such blockbusters as Fritz Lang's *Metropolis* and *The Blue Angel* with Marlene Dietrich. After WWII it became the base of the East German production company DEFA, and today cameras are rolling in what is called **Studio Babelsberg**.

For visitors, the main reason to come here is the attached **Filmpark Babelsberg** (☎ 721 2750; www.filmpark.de; enter on Grossbeerenstrasse; adult/4-14yr/concession €19/13/16; 🕑 10am-6pm Apr-Oct), a movie-themed amusement park with live shows (great stunt show!), a 4-D cinema and a few poky rides. A highlight is the guided tram ride where you'll be whisked past working sound stages to the studio backlot and such outdoor sets as 'Berlin Wall' and 'Berlin Street'.

GETTING THERE & AWAY

Regional trains leaving from Berlin-Hauptbahnhof and Zoologischer Garten take only 25 minutes to reach Potsdam Hauptbahnhof; some continue on to Potsdam-Charlottenhof and Potsdam-Sanssouci, which are closer to Park Sanssouci than Hauptbahnhof. The S-Bahn line S7 from central Berlin makes the trip in about 40 minutes. Berlin transit tickets must cover zones A, B and C (€2.80) to be valid for the trip to Potsdam.

SACHSENHAUSEN CONCENTRATION CAMP

The **Gedenkstätte und Museum Sachsenhausen** (**☎ 03301-2000; www.stiftung-bg.de; Strasse der Nationen 22; admission free; 8.30am-6pm mid-Mar–mid-Oct, to 4.30pm mid-Oct–mid-Mar, most exhibits closed Mon**) consists of several parts. Even before you enter you'll see a **memorial** to the 6000 prisoners who died on the *Todesmarsch* (Death March) of April 1945, when the Nazis tried to drive the camp's 33,000 inmates to the Baltic in advance of the Red Army.

About 100m inside the camp is a mass grave of 300 prisoners who died in the infirmary after liberation in April 1945. Further on, in the camp commander's house and the so-called 'Green Monster' building, SS troops were trained in camp maintenance and other, more brutal, activities. At the end of the road, the **Neues Museum** (New Museum) has a permanent exhibit about the camp's precursor, the KZ Oranienburg, which was set up in a disused brewery shortly after Hitler's rise to power in 1933.

GETTING THERE & AWAY

Oranienburg is served every 20 minutes by the S1 from Berlin-Friedrichstrasse (€2.80, 45 minutes) and by hourly regional trains from Berlin-Hauptbahnhof (€2.80, 25 minutes). From Oranienburg station it's a signposted 20-minute walk to the camp; bus 804 comes by hourly.

SAXONY

DRESDEN

There are few city silhouettes more striking than Dresden's. The classic view from the Elbe's northern bank takes in a playful phalanx of delicate spires, soaring towers and dominant domes belonging to palaces, churches and stately buildings.

'Florence of the north', the Saxon capital was called in the 18th century, when it was a centre of artistic activity presided over by the cosmopolitan Augustus the Strong (August der Starke) and his son Augustus III. Their vision produced many of Dresden's iconic buildings, including the Zwinger, the Frauenkirche and the Hofkirche. But following the seemingly indiscriminate destruction of the city by Allied bombers in 1945 during which most of the city centre was turned into landfill, it's a miracle some of these monumental edifices are here today.

INFORMATION

Tourist office (**☎ 5016 0160; www.dresden-tourist.de; Kulturpalast, Schlossstrasse; 10am-7pm Mon-Fri, to 6pm Sat, to 3pm Sun**)

SIGHTS

FRAUENKIRCHE

The domed **Frauenkirche** (**☎ visitor centre 6560 6100, tickets 6560 6701; www.frauenkirche-dresden.de; admission free; 10am-noon & 1-6pm Mon-Fri, limited hours on weekends**), which is one of Dresden's most beloved symbols, has literally risen from the ashes of the city. The original, designed by Georg

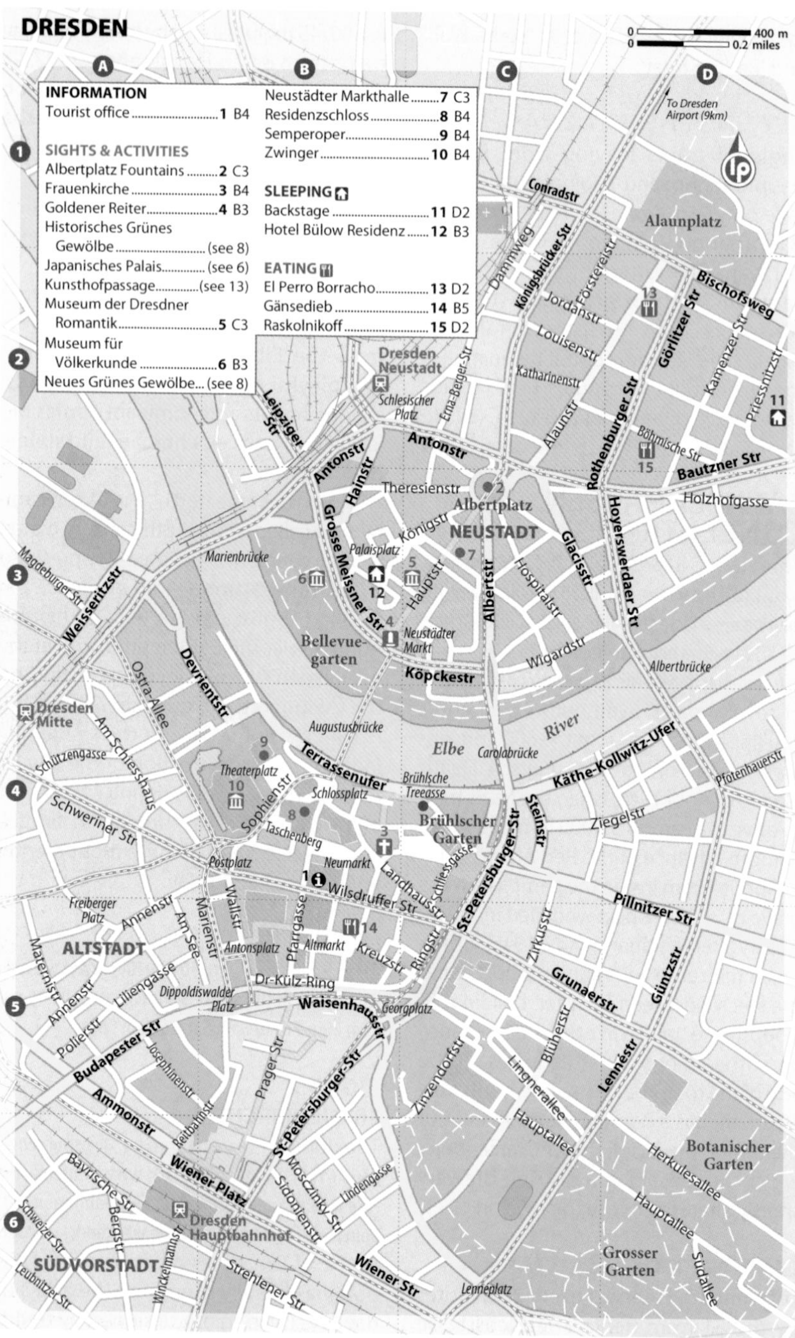
DRESDEN
0 400 m
0 0.2 miles
A
B
C
D
1
2
3
4
5
6
INFORMATION
Tourist office 1 B4
SIGHTS & ACTIVITIES
Albertplatz Fountains 2 C3
Frauenkirche 3 B4
Goldener Reiter 4 B3
Historisches Grünes Gewölbe ..... (see 8)
Japanisches Palais ..... (see 6)
Kunsthofpassage ..... (see 13)
Museum der Dresdner Romantik 5 C3
Museum für Völkerkunde 6 B3
Neues Grünes Gewölbe ..... (see 8)
Neustädter Markthalle 7 C3
Residenzschloss 8 B4
Semperoper 9 B4
Zwinger 10 B4
SLEEPING
Backstage 11 D2
Hotel Bülow Residenz 12 B3
EATING
El Perro Borracho 13 D2
Gänsedieb 14 B5
Raskolnikoff 15 D2
To Dresden Airport (9km)
Conradstr
Alaunplatz
Bischofsweg
Dammweg
Königsbrücker Str
Förstereistr
Jordanstr
Louisenstr
Görlitzer Str
Kamenzer Str
Priessnitzstr
Katharinenstr
Dresden Neustadt
Schlesischer Platz
Erna-Berger-Str
Leipziger Str
Alaunstr
Rothenburger Str
Böhmische Str
Antonstr
Bautzner Str
Holzhofgasse
Hainstr
Theresienstr
Albertplatz
NEUSTADT
Königstr
Glacisstr
Hoyerswerdaer Str
Marienbrücke
Grosse Meissner Str
Palaisplatz
Hauptstr
Albertstr
Hospitalstr
Magdeburger Str
Weisseritzstr
Neustädter Markt
Bellevue-garten
Wigardstr
Albertbrücke
Köpckestr
Devrientstr
Ostra-Allee
Dresden Mitte
Am Schiesshaus
Augustusbrücke
River
Elbe
Carolabrücke
Schützengasse
Theaterplatz
Terrassenufer
Brühlsche Treeasse
Käthe-Kollwitz-Ufer
Pfotenhauerstr
Schlossplatz
Sophienstr
Schweriner Str
Taschenberg
Brühlscher Garten
Steinstr
Ziegelstr
Postplatz
Neumarkt
Landhausstr
Schliessgasse
St-Petersburger-Str
Wilsdruffer Str
Pillnitzer Str
Freiberger Platz
Annenstr
Am See
Marienstr
Wallstr
Pfarrgasse
ALTSTADT
Antonsplatz
Altmarkt
Kreuzstr
Ringstr
Zirkusstr
Grunaerstr
Güntzstr
Maternistr
Liliengasse
Dippoldiswalder Platz
Dr-Külz-Ring
Waisenhausstr
Georgplatz
Annenstr
Poliersr
Budapester Str
Josephinenstr
Prager Str
Zinzendorfstr
Blüherstr
Lennéstr
Lingnerallee
Ammonstr
Reitbahnstr
Hauptallee
Botanischer Garten
Herkulesallee
Bayrische Str
Wiener Platz
Mosczinky Str
Lindengasse
Sidonienstr
Hauptallee
Bergstr
Dresden Hauptbahnhof
Schweizer Str
Winckelmannstr
Grosser Garten
Südallee
SÜDVORSTADT
Strehlener Str
Wiener Str
Lenneplatz
Leubnitzer Str

Bähr, graced Dresden's skyline for two centuries before collapsing two days after the February 1945 bombing. The GDR left the rubble there as a war memorial, but after reunification a grass-roots movement to rebuild the landmark gained momentum. It was consecrated in November 2005, a year ahead of schedule.

A spitting image of the original, it may not bear the gravitas of age but that only slightly detracts from its festive beauty inside and out. The altar, reassembled from nearly 2000 fragments, is especially striking.

RESIDENZSCHLOSS

Home of Saxon kings until 1918, the highlight of the neo-Renaissance Residenzschloss is the must-see **Grünes Gewölbe** (Green Vault), returned to the palace after postwar reconstruction had been completed.

The **Neues Grünes Gewölbe** (New Green Vault; ☎ 4914 2000; adult/concession incl audioguide €6/3.50; 10am-6pm Wed-Mon) presents some 1000 objects in 10 modern rooms on the upper floor. Among the most prized items are a frigate fashioned from ivory with wafer-thin sails, a cherry pit with 185 faces carved into it, and an exotic ensemble of 132 gem-studded figurines representing a royal court in India.

A further 3000 items are exhibited below in the show-stopping **Historisches Grünes Gewölbe** (Historical Green Vault; ☎ tickets & information 4914 2000; www.skd-dresden.de; admission incl audioguide €10; 10am-7pm Wed-Mon), displayed on shelves and tables in a series of increasingly lavish rooms, just as they were during the time of August der Starke.

SEMPEROPER

The original **Semperoper** (Opera House; ☎ 491 1496; www.semperoper.de; tours adult/concession €7/3.50) burned down a mere three decades after its 1841 inauguration. When it reopened in 1878, the neo-Renaissance jewel entered its most dazzling period, which saw the premieres of works by Richard Strauss, Carl Maria von Weber and Richard Wagner. Alas, WWII put an end to the fun, and it wasn't until 1985 that music again filled the grand hall.

ZWINGER

Next to the opera house, the sprawling **Zwinger** (☎ 4914 2000; 10am-6pm Tue-Sun) is among the most ravishing baroque buildings in all of Germany. A collaboration between the architect Matthäus Pöppelmann and the sculptor Balthasar Permoser, it was primarily a party palace for royals, despite the odd name (which means dungeon). Atlas with the world on his shoulders; opposite him is a cutesy carillon of 40 Meissen porcelain bells, which emit a tinkle every 15 minutes.

NEUSTADT

Despite its name, Neustadt is actually an older part of Dresden that was considerably less smashed up in WWII than the Altstadt. The first thing that catches the eye when crossing Augustusbrücke is the gleaming **Goldener Reiter** (1736) statue of Augustus the Strong. North of the statue, Hauptstrasse is a tree-lined pedestrian shopping street where the **Museum der Dresdner Romantik** (Museum of Dresden Romanticism; ☎ 804 4760; Hauptstrasse 13; adult/concession €3/2; 10am-6pm Wed-Sun) documents the city's artistic and intellectual movements during the early 19th century.

Across Hauptstrasse, the **Neustädter Markthalle**, a gorgeously restored old market hall (enter on Metzer Strasse), provides a laid-back retail experience with stalls selling everything from Russian groceries to kid's wooden toys. There's also a supermarket.

Hauptstrasse culminates at **Albertplatz** with its two striking **fountains** representing turbulent and still waters. Königstrasse runs southwest of Albertplatz, all the way to the not-very-Japanese **Japanisches Palais** (1737). Inside is Dresden's **Museum für Völkerkunde** (**Museum of Ethnology; ☎ 814 4814; Palaisplatz 11; adult/concession €4/2; 10am-6pm Tue-Sun**), which boasts well over 70,000 anthropological items from far-flung corners of the world.

North of Albertplatz, the Äussere Neustadt is a spidery web of narrow streets, late-19th-century patrician houses and hidden courtyards, all chock-full of pubs, clubs, galleries and one-of-a-kind shops. A highlight here is the **Kunsthofpassage** (enter from Alaunstrasse 70 or Görlitzer Strasse 21), a series of five whimsically designed courtyards each reflecting the vision of a different Dresden artist.

SLEEPING & EATING

our pick **Backstage** (**☎ 8887 777; www.backstage-dresden.de; Priessnitzstrasse 12; r from €74;**) A cool converted factory where rooms, each designed by a local artist, will blow your mind but not your budget. One has a four-poster made entirely of bamboo; others have swirling Gaudi-esque bathrooms.

Hotel Bülow Residenz (**☎ 800 30; www.buelow-residenz.de; Rähnitzstrasse 19; s/d €195/250, breakfast €19;**) This place is a class act all round, from the welcome drink to the cute bears delivered at turndown, the free minibar to free wi-fi. Even the standard rooms are spacious, and the restaurant has a fine reputation as well.

El Perro Borracho (**☎ 803 6723; Alaunstrasse 70, Kunsthof; tapas €3.30**) Almost blocking an entrance to the Kunsthofpassage, this buzzy eatery is a great place to enjoy a glass of Rioja and a platter of tapas on the cobblestone courtyard when the mercury heads north.

our pick **Raskolnikoff** (**☎ 804 5706; Böhmische Strasse 34; mains €5-14**) This bohemian cafe behind an extremely tatty facade was one of the Neustadt's first post-*Wende* (postcommunist) pubs. The menu is sorted by compass direction (from borscht to quiche Lorraine to smoked fish), there's a sweet little beer garden out the back, and a gallery and basic guest rooms can be found upstairs (singles and doubles €40 to €55).

Gänsedieb (**☎ 485 0905; Weisse Gasse 1; mains €8-17**) Worth a gander in the Weisse Gasse, the 'Goose Thief' serves hearty schnitzels, goulash and steaks alongside a full range of Bavarian Paulaner beers. The name was inspired by the fountain outside.

GETTING THERE & AWAY

Dresden airport (**☎ 881 3360; www.dresden-airport.de**) deals mainly in domestic and charter flights.

Dresden is 2¼ hours south of Berlin-Hauptbahnhof (€36). For Leipzig choose from hourly ICE trains (€29, 1½ hours) or RE trains (€20.80, 1½ hours). The S-Bahn runs half-hourly to Meissen (€5.30, 40 minutes) and Bad Schandau (€5.30, 50 minutes). There are connections to Frankfurt (€85, five hours) and Prague (€30.70, two hours).

MEISSEN

Straddling the Elbe around 25km upstream from Dresden, Meissen is a compact, perfectly preserved Saxon town, popular with day trippers. Crowning a rocky ridge above it is the Albrechtsburg palace, which in 1710 became the cradle

WER/IMAGEBROKER

Porcelain-painting demonstration, Meissen

of European porcelain manufacture. The world-famous Meissen china, easily recognised by its trademark insignia of blue crossed swords, is still the main draw for coach parties. Fortunately, the Altstadt's cobbled lanes, dreamy nooks and idyllic courtyards make escaping from the shuffling crowds a snap.

INFORMATION

Tourist office (☎ 419 40; www.touristinfo-meissen.de; Markt 3; 10am-6pm Mon-Fri, 10am-4pm Sat & Sun Apr-Oct, 10am-5pm Mon-Fri, 10am-3pm Sat Nov, Dec, Feb & Mar)

SIGHTS

The Markt is framed by the **Rathaus** (town hall;1472) and the Gothic **Frauenkirche** (☎ 453 832; tower adult/concession €2/1; 10am-noon & 2-4pm Apr-Oct) whose carillon is the world's oldest made from porcelain; it chimes a different ditty six times daily. Climb the tower for fine red-roof views of the Altstadt.

Next to the palace is Meissen's modest and rather soot-blackened **Dom** (cathedral; ☎ 452 490; Domplatz 7; adult/concession/family €2.50/1.50/6; 10am-6pm Mar-Oct, to 4pm Nov-Feb), a Gothic masterpiece with medieval stained-glass windows and delicately carved statues in the choir. Combination tickets for both buildings are €6/3/15.

There's no 'quiet time' to arrive at the understandably popular and utterly unmissable **Porzellan-Museum** (☎ 468 208; Talstrasse 9; adult/concession/family €8.50/4.50/18; 9am-6pm May-Oct, to 5pm Nov-Apr), but it's worth braving the crush (and the waiting) to witness the astonishing artistry and craftsmanship that makes Meissen porcelain truly unique.

GETTING THERE & AROUND

From Dresden, take the half-hourly S1 (€5.30, 37 minutes) to Meissen. For the porcelain factory, get off at Meissen-Triebischtal.

A slower but more fun way to get there is by steam boat operated by **Sächsische Dampfschiffahrt** (☎ 866 090; www.saechsische-dampfschiffahrt.de). These leave the Terrassenufer in Dresden. Boats return upstream to Dresden at 2.45pm but take three hours to make the trip. Many people opt to go up by boat and back by train.

LEIPZIG

In Goethe's *Faust,* a character named Frosch calls Leipzig 'a little Paris'. He was wrong – Leipzig is more fun and infinitely less self-important than the Gallic capital. It's an important business and transport centre, a trade-fair mecca, and arguably the most dynamic city in eastern Germany.

Leipzig became known as the *Stadt der Helden* (City of Heroes) for its leading role in the 1989 'Peaceful Revolution'. Its residents organised protests against the communist regime in May of that year; by October, hundreds of thousands were taking to the streets, placing candles on the steps of Stasi headquarters and attending peace services at the Nikolaikirche.

INFORMATION

Leipzig Tourist Service (☎ 710 4260; www.leipzig.de; Richard-Wagner-Strasse 1;

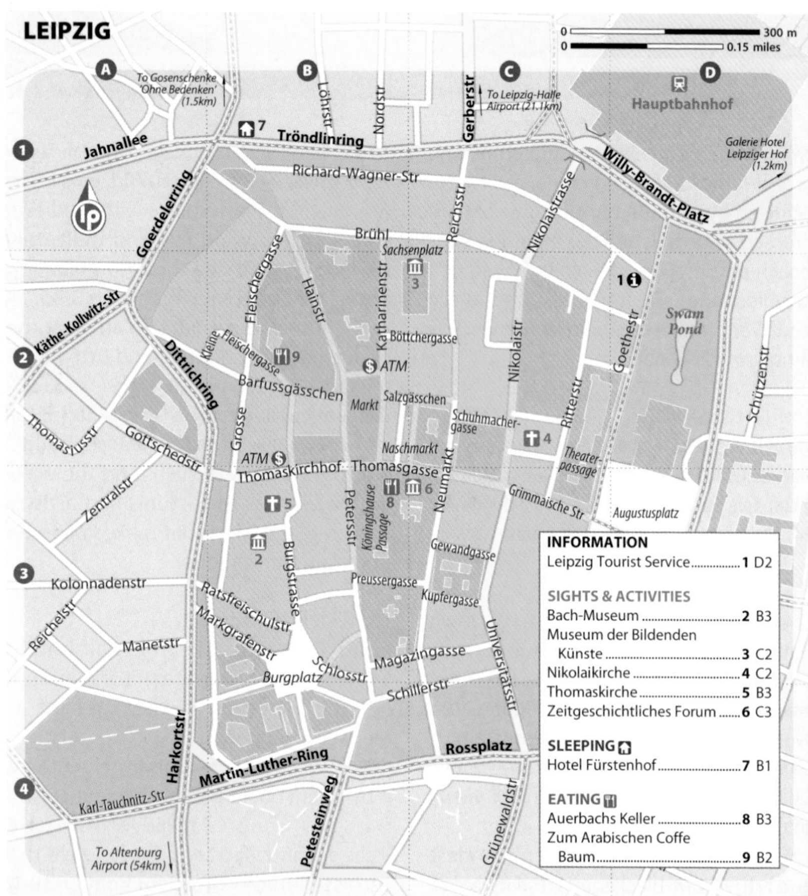

9.30am-6pm Mon-Fri, to 4pm Sat, to 3pm Sun)

SIGHTS

Opened in 1999, the excellent **Zeitgeschichtliches Forum** (**Forum of Contemporary History; ☎ 222 00; Grimmaische Strasse 6; admission free; 9am-6pm Tue-Fri, 10am-6pm Sat & Sun**) depicts the history of the GDR from division and dictatorship to fall-of-the-Wall ecstasy and post-*Wende* blues. Highlights include the actual sign from Checkpoint Charlie, film clips showing Berliners looking on in stunned dis- belief as the Wall goes up and a mock-up of a GDR-era living room.

In the GDR the walls had ears, as is vividly documented in this **museum** (**☎ 961 2443; www.runde-ecke-leipzig.de; Dittrichring 24; admission free; 10am-6pm**) on the all-pervasive power of the Ministry for State Security (Stasi for short), the country's secret police. It's housed in the former Leipzig Stasi headquarters, in a building known as the Runde Ecke (Round Corner). The all-German displays on propaganda, preposterous disguises, cunning surveillance devices, Stasi recruitment among children, scent storage and other chilling machinations reveal the GDR's all-out zeal when it came to controlling, manipulating and repressing its own people.

Leipzig's largest church, the **Nikolaikirche** (**St Nicholas Church; ☎ 960 5270; 10am-6pm**), has Romanesque and Gothic roots, but now sports an amazing classical-style interior with palmlike pillars and cream-coloured pews. More recently the church played a key role in the nonviolent movement that eventually brought down the GDR regime. In 1982 it began hosting 'peace prayers' every Monday at 5pm (still held today) and in 1989 it became the chief meeting point for peaceful demonstrators.

The composer Johann Sebastian Bach worked in the **Thomaskirche** (**St Thomas Church; ☎ 2222 4200; www.thomaskirche.org; Thomaskirchhof 18; 9am-6pm**) as a cantor from 1723 until his death in 1750, and his remains lie buried beneath a bronze epitaph near the altar. The Thomanerchor, once led by Bach, is still going strong and now includes 100 boys aged eight to 18. Opposite the Thomaskirche, the **Bach-Museum** (**☎ 964 110; www.bach-leipzig.de; Thomaskirchhof 16; adult/concession €6/4; 10am-6pm Tue-Sat**) presents the life and work of Bach with sound experiments and interactive multimedia stations as well as the console of an organ examined by Bach in 1743.

SBE/IMAGEBROKER

Nikolaikirche (St Nicholas Church) interior, Leipzig

An edgy glass cube is the home of the **Museum der Bildenden Künste** (**Museum of Fine Arts; ☎ 216 990; Katharinenstrasse 10; adult/concession permanent exhibit €5/3.50, temporary exhibit from €6/4, combination ticket from €8/5.50; 10am-6pm Tue & Thu-Sun, noon-8pm Wed**), which has a well-respected collection of paintings from the 15th century to today, including works by Caspar David Friedrich, Lucas Cranach the Younger and Claude Monet.

SLEEPING & EATING

our pick **Galerie Hotel Leipziger Hof** (**☎ 697 40; www.leipziger-hof.de; Hedwigstrasse 1-3; s €69-150, d €89-180;**) Leipzig's most unique place to unpack your bags is this 'gallery with rooms', which brims with originals created by local artists since 1989. It's a first-rate stay, yet relatively affordable, as is the restaurant.

Hotel Fürstenhof (**☎ 1400; www.luxurycollection.com/fuerstenhof; Tröndlinring 8; r from €200, breakfast €25;**) The *dame vieille* of the Leipzig hotel scene, with a 200-year pedigree, finds umpteen ways to spoil its guests. It has updated old-world flair, impeccable service, a gourmet restaurant and an oh-so-soothing grotto-style pool and spa.

Gosenschenke 'Ohne Bedenken' (**☎ 566 2360; Menckestrasse 5; mains €6-16; noon-1am**) This historic Leipzig institution, backed by the city's prettiest beer garden, is *the* place to sample *Gose,* a local top-fermented beer often served with a shot of liqueur. The menu has a distinctly carnivorous bent.

Zum Arabischen Coffe Baum (**☎ 961 0061; Kleine Fleischergasse 4; mains €7.50-17; 11am-midnight**) Hosting six different eateries, Leipzig's oldest inn is as stuffy as your grandma's attic, but the cakes and meals are excellent and there's a free coffee museum to boot. Composer Robert Schumann used to come here for his daily caffeine fix.

Auerbachs Keller (**☎ 216 100; Grimmaische Strasse 2-4, Mädlerpassage; mains €8-25**) Founded in 1525, Auerbachs Keller is one of Germany's best-known restaurants. It's cosy and touristy, but the food's actually

JMW/IMAGEBROKER

Domplatz, Erfurt

quite good and the setting memorable. In Goethe's *Faust – Part I*, Mephistopheles and Faust carouse here with some students before they ride off on a barrel. The scene is depicted on a carved tree trunk in what is now the Goethe Room (where the great writer allegedly came for 'inspiration').

GETTING THERE & AWAY

AIR

Leipzig-Halle airport (☎ 224 1155; www.leipzig-halle-airport.de) is served by domestic and international flights from two dozen airlines, including Lufthansa, Germanwings, Air Berlin, Condor and Austrian Airlines. Ryanair flies into **Altenburg airport** (www.flughafen-altenburg.de) from London-Stansted and Edinburgh.

TRAIN

Leipzig is an important link between eastern and western Germany, with connections to all major cities. There are frequent services to Frankfurt (€70, 3½ hours), Munich (€87, five hours), Dresden (€20.80, 1½ hours) and Berlin (€42, 1¼ hours).

THURINGIA

ERFURT

Thuringia's capital is a scene-stealing combination of sweeping squares, time-worn alleyways, perky church towers, idyllic river scenery and vintage inns and taverns. On the little Gera River, Erfurt was founded by the indefatigable missionary St Boniface as a bishopric in 742 and was catapulted to prominence and prosperity in the Middle Ages when it began producing a precious blue pigment from the woad plant. In 1392 rich merchants founded the university, allowing students to study common law, rather than religious law. Its most famous graduate was Martin Luther, who studied philosophy here before becoming a monk at the local Augustinian monastery in 1505.

INFORMATION

Erfurt Tourist Office (www.erfurt-tourismus.de) Benediktsplatz (☎ 664 00; Benediktsplatz 1; ⌚ 10am-7pm Mon-Fri, 10am-6pm Sat, 10am-4pm Sun Apr-Dec, 10am-6pm Mon-Sat, 10am-4pm Sun Jan-Mar); Petersberg (☎ 6015 384; ⌚ 11am-6.30pm Apr-Oct, 11am-4pm Nov & Dec) Sells the ErfurtCard (€12.90 per 48 hours), which includes a city tour, public transport and free or discounted admissions.

SIGHTS

The **Mariendom** (St Mary's Cathedral; ☎ 646 1265; Domplatz; ⌚ 9am-6pm Mon-Sat, 1-6pm Sun May-Oct, 10-11.30am & 12.30pm-4pm Mon-Sat, 2-4pm Sun Nov-Apr) has origins as a simple chapel founded in 742 by St Boniface, but the Gothic pile you see today has the hallmarks of the 14th century.

The **Severikirche** (☎ 576 960; Domplatz; ⌚ 9am-6pm Mon-Sat, 1-6pm Sun May-Oct, 10-11.30am & 12.30-4pm Mon-Sat, 2-4pm Sun Nov-Apr) is a five-aisled hall church (1280) that counts a stone **Madonna** (1345), a 15m-high baptismal **font** (1467), and the sarcophagus of **St Severus** among its most prized treasures.

On the Petersberg hill northwest of Domplatz, the **Zitadelle Petersberg** ranks among Europe's largest and best-preserved baroque fortresses. It sits above a honeycomb of tunnels, which can be explored on **guided tours** (adult/concession €8/4; ⌚ tours 7pm Fri & Sat May-Oct) run by the tourist office.

It's Luther lore galore at the **Augustinerkloster** (Augustinian monastery; ☎ 576 600; Augustinerstrasse 10, enter on Comthurgasse; tours adult/concession €5/3; ⌚ tours

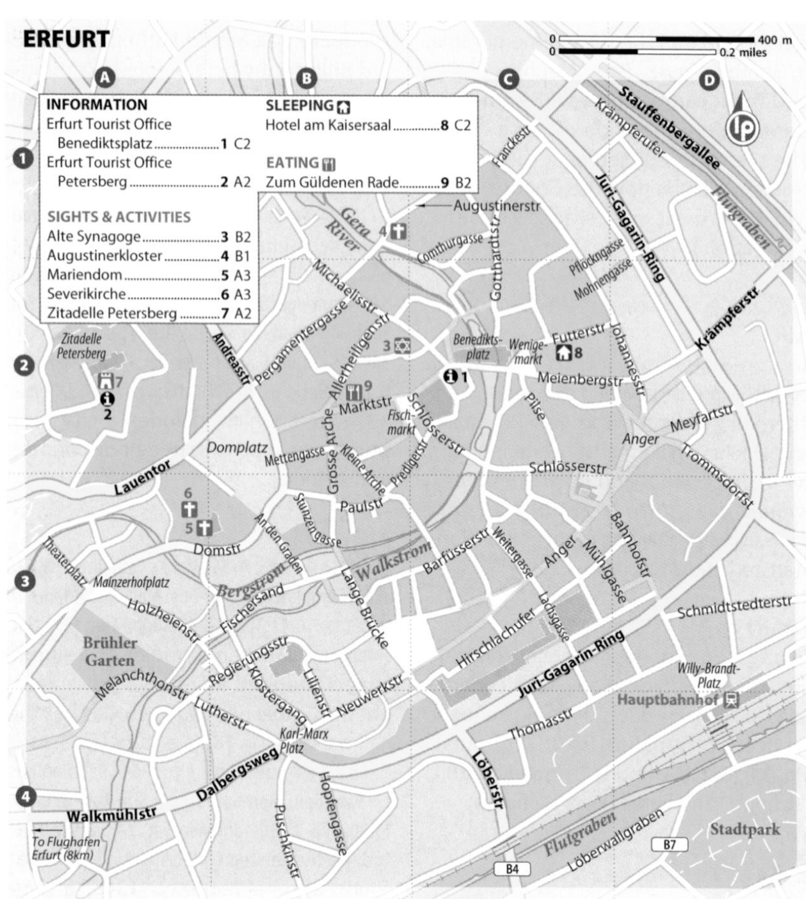

hourly 10am-noon & 2-5pm Mon-Sat, 11am, 2pm & 3pm Sun Apr-Oct, to 4pm Mon-Sat Nov-Mar). This is where the reformer lived from 1505 to 1511, and where he was ordained as a monk and read his first mass.

The **Alte Synagoge** (**Old Synagogue; ☎ 655 1608; http://alte-synagoge.erfurt.de; Waagegasse 8; admission adult/student under 27/child €5/1.50/1.50; 10am-6pm Tue-Sun**) in Erfurt is one of the oldest Jewish houses of worship in Europe, with roots in the 12th century. After the pogrom of 1349, it was converted into a storehouse and, after later standing empty for decades, has now been restored as an exhibit space and museum.

SLEEPING & EATING

Hotel am Kaisersaal (**☎ 658 560; www.hotel-am-kaisersaal.de, in German; Futterstrasse 8; s €84-94, d €100-110; P**) Rooms are tip-top and appointed with all expected mod cons in this highly rated hotel. Request a room facing the yard, though, if street noise disturbs.

Zum Güldenen Rade (**☎ 561 3506; Marktstrasse 50; mains €8.50-15; 11am-midnight**) For the best potato dumplings in town, report to this gorgeous patrician town house that, centuries ago, housed a tobacco factory. Aside from the classic version with gravy, you can also order them with stuffings, such as spinach and salmon, or with black pudding and liver pâté.

GETTING THERE & AWAY

The tiny **Flughafen Erfurt** (☎ **656 2200; www.flughafen-erfurt.de; Binderlebener Landstrasse 100**) is about 6km west of the city centre and is served by Air Berlin and a few charter airlines.

Erfurt has direct IC train links to Berlin-Hauptbahnhof (€54, 2½ hours) and ICE connections with Dresden (€48, 2½ hours) and Frankfurt am Main (€51, 2¼ hours). Regional trains to Weimar (€4.40, 15 minutes) and Eisenach (€10.30, 50 minutes) run at least once hourly.

WEIMAR

Neither a monumental town nor a medieval one, Weimar appeals to those whose tastes run to cultural and intellectual pleasures. After all, this is the epicentre of the German Enlightenment, a symbol for all that is good and great in German culture. An entire pantheon of intellectual and creative giants lived and worked here: Goethe, Schiller, Bach, Cranach, Liszt, Nietzsche, Gropius, Herder, Feininger, Kandinsky, Klee...the list goes on (and on, and on).

The ghostly ruins of the Buchenwald concentration camp, on the other hand, provide haunting evidence of the terrors of the Nazi regime. The Bauhaus and classical Weimar locations are protected as Unesco World Heritage Sites.

INFORMATION

Tourist office (☎ **7450; www.weimar.de; Markt 10; 9.30am-6pm Mon-Fri, to 3pm Sat & Sun Apr-Oct, 9.30am-6pm Mon-Fri, to 2pm Sat & Sun Nov-Mar**) Sells the WeimarCard (€10 for 72 hours) for free or discounted museum admissions and travel on city buses and other benefits.

SIGHTS

No other individual is as closely associated with Weimar as Johann Wolfgang von Goethe, who lived in this town from 1775 until his death in 1832, the last 50 years in what is now the **Goethe Haus** (☎ **545 401; Frauenplan 1; adult/under 16yrs/concession €8.50/free/7; 9am-6pm Tue-Fri & Sun, to 7pm Sat Apr-Sep, to 6pm Tue-Sun Oct, to 4pm Tue-Sun Nov-Mar**). This is where he worked, studied, researched and penned *Faust* and other immortal works.

Dramatist and Goethe buddy Friedrich von Schiller lived in Weimar from 1799 until his early death in 1805. Unlike Goethe, however, he had to buy his own house, now the **Schiller Haus** (☎ **545 401; Schillerstrasse 12; adult/concession/under 16 €5/4/free; 9am-6pm Tue-Fri & Sun, 9am-7pm Sat Apr-Sep, 9am-6pm Tue-Sun Oct, 9am-4pm Tue-Sun Nov-Mar**). Study up on the man, his family and life in Thuringia in a new permanent exhibit before plunging on to the private quarters, including the study with his deathbed and the desk where he wrote *Wilhelm Tell* and other famous works.

The sprawling Park an der Ilm (Ilm Park), just east of the Altstadt, is as inspiring and romantic now as it was when Goethe lived here from 1776 until 1782 in what is now **Goethes Gartenhaus** (☎ **545 401; adult/under 16yrs/concession €4.50/free/3.50; 10am-6pm Apr-Oct, to 4pm Nov-Mar**). By giving him this simple cottage, Carl August successfully induced Goethe to stay in Weimar.

On the western edge of the park, the **Liszt-Museum** (☎ **545 401; Marienstrasse 17; adult/under 16yrs/concession €4/free/3; 10am-6pm Wed-Mon Apr-Oct**) is where the composer and pianist resided in Weimar in 1848 and

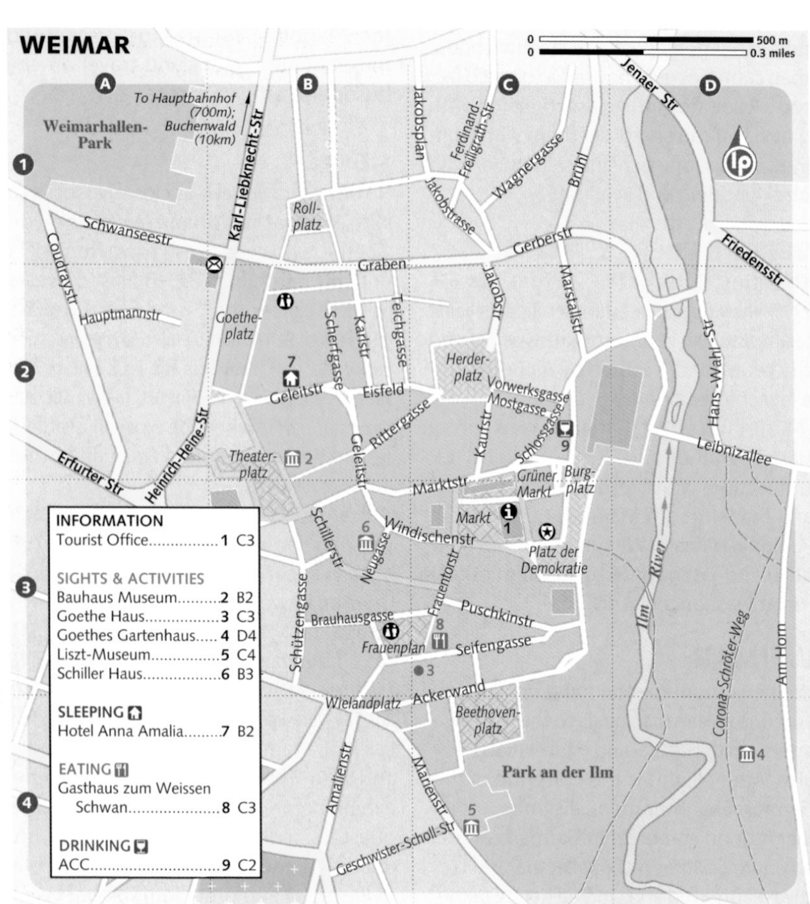

again from 1869 to 1886, writing such key works as the *Hungarian Rhapsodies* and the *Faust Symphony*.

Considering that Weimar is the birthplace of the influential Bauhaus school, the **Bauhaus Museum** (☎ **545 401; Theaterplatz; adult/concession €4.50/3.50; 10am-6pm**) is a rather modest affair. But if all goes according to plan, that'll change when it moves into splashy new digs in 2013. Meanwhile, the old building will present temporary exhibits on the group's profound impact on modern design and construction.

SLEEPING & EATING

Hotel Anna Amalia (☎ **495 60; www.hotel-anna-amalia.de; Geleitstrasse 8-12; s €60-75, d €85-120, apt €120-180;**) The Mediterranean look, with its nice, fresh colour scheme, exudes feel-good cheer in this family-run hotel near Goetheplatz. For more panache and elbow room, book one of the apartments, which sleep up to four.

ACC (☎ **851 161; www.acc-cafe.de; Burgplatz 1; dishes €5-10; 11am-midnight Mon-Fri, 10am-midnight Sat & Sun;**) Goethe had his first pad after arriving in Weimar in this building, now home to an alt-vibe, artsy hang-out, where the food and wine are organic whenever possible and the upstairs gallery delivers a primer on the local art scene. The owners also rent out a room and a holiday flat (www.goethezimmer.de), both handsomely furnished.

Gasthaus zum Weissen Schwan (☎ 908 751; Frauentorstrasse 23; mains €11-20; noon-midnight Wed-Sun; ☒) Fill your tummy with Goethe's favourite dish, which actually hails from his home town of Frankfurt (boiled beef with herb sauce, red beet salad and potatoes); or, the rest of the menu is upmarket Thuringian.

GETTING THERE & AWAY

Regular ICE services go to Frankfurt (€55, 2½ hours), Leipzig (€25, 50 minutes) and Dresden (€44, 2¼ hours); the IC train serves Berlin-Hauptbahnhof (€51, 2¼ hours). Erfurt (€5, 15 minutes) and Eisenach (€13.30, 1¼ hours) are served several times hourly, plus there's frequent service to Jena-West (€5, 15 minutes).

BUCHENWALD CONCENTRATION CAMP

The Buchenwald concentration camp **museum and memorial** (☎ 03643-4300; www.buchenwald.de; Ettersberg; admission free; buildings & exhibits 10am-6pm Tue-Sun Apr-Oct, 10am-4pm Tue-Sun Nov-Mar, grounds open until sunset) are 10km northwest of Weimar. You first pass the memorial erected above the mass graves of some of the 56,500 victims from 18 nations that died here – including Jews, German antifascists and Soviet and Polish prisoners of war. The concentration camp and museum are 1km beyond the memorial. Many prominent German communists and social democrats, Ernst Thälmann and Rudolf Breitscheid among them, were murdered here. Between 1937 and 1945, more than one-fifth of the 250,000 people incarcerated here died.

To get here, take bus 6 (direction Buchenwald) from Goetheplatz in Weimar. By car, head north on Ettersburger Strasse from Weimar train station and turn left onto Blutstrasse.

SAXONY-ANHALT

DESSAU-ROSSLAU

For Bauhaus junkies, Dessau represents the mother lode. Nowhere else in the world will you find a greater concentration of original 1920s Bauhaus structures than in this city on the Elbe River. Considered the 'built manifesto of Bauhaus ideas', Dessau was the home of the most influential design school of the 20th century during its most creative period from 1925 to 1932.

DAVID PEEVERS

Fence at Buchenwald concentration camp

INFORMATION

Tourist office (☎ 204 1442, accommodation 220 3003; www.dessau-rosslau-tourismus.de; Zerbster Strasse 2c; ⌚ 9am-6pm Mon-Fri, 9am-1pm Sat Apr-Oct, 9am-5pm Mon-Fri, 10am-1pm Sat Nov-Mar).

SIGHTS

BAUHAUSGEBÄUDE

Across the world, many modernist masterpieces have fallen into ruin and, for a while, it looked as though a similar fate might befall the seminal **Bauhausgebäude**

KAS/IMAGEBROKER

Lutherhaus interior, Einsach

↘ IF YOU LIKE...

If you are diehard **Bach** fan and can't get enough of **Luther**'s old stomping grounds, head to **Eisenach** (www.eisenach.info), just west of Erfurt, whose modest appearance belies its association with these two German heavyweights:

- **Wartburg** (☎ 2500; www.wartburg-eisenach.de; tour adult/concession €8/5, museum & Luther study only €4/2.50; ⌚ tours 8.30am-5pm Mar-Oct, 9am-3.30pm Nov-Feb) This medieval castle is where Martin Luther went into hiding in 1521 under the assumed name of Junker Jörg after being excommunicated and placed under papal ban. During his 10-month stay, he translated the New Testament from Greek into German, contributing enormously to the development of the written German language.
- **Lutherhaus** (☎ 298 30; www.lutherhaus-eisenach.de; Lutherplatz 8; adult/concession €3.50/2; ⌚ 10am-5pm) As a school boy, Luther lived in this half-timbered house; a partly interactive exhibit reveals how the eager pupil became one of the world's most influential religious reformers.
- **Bachhaus** (☎ 793 40; www.bachhaus.de; Frauenplan 21; adult/concession/family €6.50/3.50/12; ⌚ 10am-6pm) Johann Sebastian Bach, who was born in Eisenach in 1685, takes the spotlight in one of the best biographical museums we've ever seen. Exhibits are set up in the type of wattle-and-daub town house where Bach lived (the original was destroyed) and trace both his professional and private life through concise, intelligent and engaging bilingual panelling.

(**Bauhaus Bldg; ☎ 650 8251; www.bauhaus-dessau.de; Gropiusallee 38; admission free, exhibition adult/concession €5/4; ⏰ 10am-6pm**). Fortunately, major restoration, completed in 2006, successfully staved off the wrecking ball.

If you consider the history of this school building, it's almost impossible to overstate its significance. Two key pioneers of modern architecture, Walter Gropius and Ludwig Mies van der Rohe, served as its directors. Gropius claimed that the ultimate of all artistic endeavours was architecture, and this building was the first real-life example of his vision. It was revolutionary, bringing industrial construction techniques, such as curtain walling and wide spans, into the public domain and presaging untold buildings worldwide. The tubular steel-frame chair and other enduring industrial designs were born here.

MEISTERHÄUSER

On leafy Ebertallee, a 15-minute walk west of the Hauptbahnhof, the three remaining **Meisterhäuser** (**Masters' Houses; www.meisterhaeuser.de; admission to all 3 houses adult/concession €5/4, combination ticket with Bauhausgebäude €9/6; ⏰ 10am-6pm Tue-Sun mid-Feb–Oct, 10am-5pm Nov–mid-Feb**) line up for inspection. The leading lights of the Bauhaus movement lived together as neighbours in these white cubist structures that exemplify the Bauhaus aim of 'design for living' in a modern industrial world.

Haus Feininger, former home of Lyonel Feininger, now pays homage to another German icon with the **Kurt-Weill-Zentrum** (**☎ 619 595; Ebertallee 63**). There's a room devoted to Dessau-born Weill, who later became playwright Bertolt Brecht's musical collaborator in Berlin, and composed *The Threepenny Opera*.

Next up is the **Haus Muche/Schlemmer** (**☎ 882 2138; Ebertallee 65/67**), which makes it apparent that the room proportions and some of the experiments, such as low balcony rails, don't really cut it in the modern world.

The **Haus Kandinsky/Klee** (**☎ 661 0934; Ebertallee 69/71**) is most notable for the varying pastel shades in which Wassily Kandinsky and Paul Klee painted their walls (re-created today).

GETTING THERE & AWAY

Regional trains serve Dessau from Berlin-Hauptbahnhof (€21, 1¾ hours), Lutherstadt Wittenberg (€6.90, 40 minutes) as well as Leipzig, Halle and Magdeburg (all €10.30, one hour). The Berlin–Munich autobahn (A9) runs east of town.

LUTHERSTADT WITTENBERG

As its full name suggests, Wittenberg is first and foremost associated with Martin Luther (1483–1546), the monk who triggered the German Reformation by publishing his 95 theses against church corruption in 1517. Sometimes called the 'Rome of the Protestants', its many Reformation-related sites garnered it the World Heritage Site nod from Unesco in 1996.

INFORMATION

Tourist office (**☎ 498 610; www.wittenberg.de; Schlossplatz 2; ⏰ 9am-6.30pm Mon-Fri, 10am-4pm Sat & Sun Apr-Oct, 10am-4pm Mon-Fri, 10am-2pm Sat, 11am-3pm Sun Nov-Mar, closed Sat & Sun Jan & Feb**)

SIGHTS

Even those with no previous interest in the Reformation will likely be fascinated by the state-of-the-art exhibits in the **Lutherhaus** (**☎ 420 30; www.martinluther.de; Collegienstrasse 54; adult/concession €5/3; ⏰ 9am-6pm daily Apr-Oct, 10am-5pm Tue-Sun Nov-Mar**), the former monastery turned Luther family home. Through an engaging mix

SOM/IMAGEBROKER

Bauhausgebäude (Bauhaus Building; p290), Dessau-Rosslau

of accessible narrative (in German and English), spotlit artefacts (eg his lectern from the Stadtkirche, indulgences chests, Bibles, cloaks), famous oil paintings and interactive multimedia stations, you'll learn about the man, his times and his impact on world history.

Did or didn't he nail those 95 theses to the door of the **Schlosskirche** (**Castle Church; ☎ 402 585; Schlossplatz; admission free; 🕑 10am-6pm Mon-Sat, 11.30am-6pm Sun, to 4pm Nov-Easter**)? We'll never know for sure, for the original portal was destroyed by fire in 1760 and replaced in 1858 with a massive bronze version inscribed with the theses in Latin.

If the Schlosskirche was the billboard used to advertise the forthcoming Reformation, the twin-towered **Stadtkirche St Marien** (**Town Church of St Mary; ☎ 403 201; Jüdenstrasse 35; admission free; 🕑 10am-6pm Mon-Sat, 11.30am-6pm Sun, to 4pm Nov-Easter**) was where the ecumenical revolution began, with the world's first Protestant worship services in 1521. It was also here that Luther preached his famous Lectern sermons in 1522, and where he married ex-nun Katharina von Bora three years later.

GETTING THERE & AWAY

Wittenberg is on the main train line to Halle and Leipzig (both €11.30, one hour). ICE (€29, one hour) and RE trains (€20, 1¼ hours) travel to Berlin. Coming from Berlin, be sure to board for 'Lutherstadt-Wittenberg', as there's also a Wittenberge west of the capital.

HAMBURG & NORTHERN GERMANY

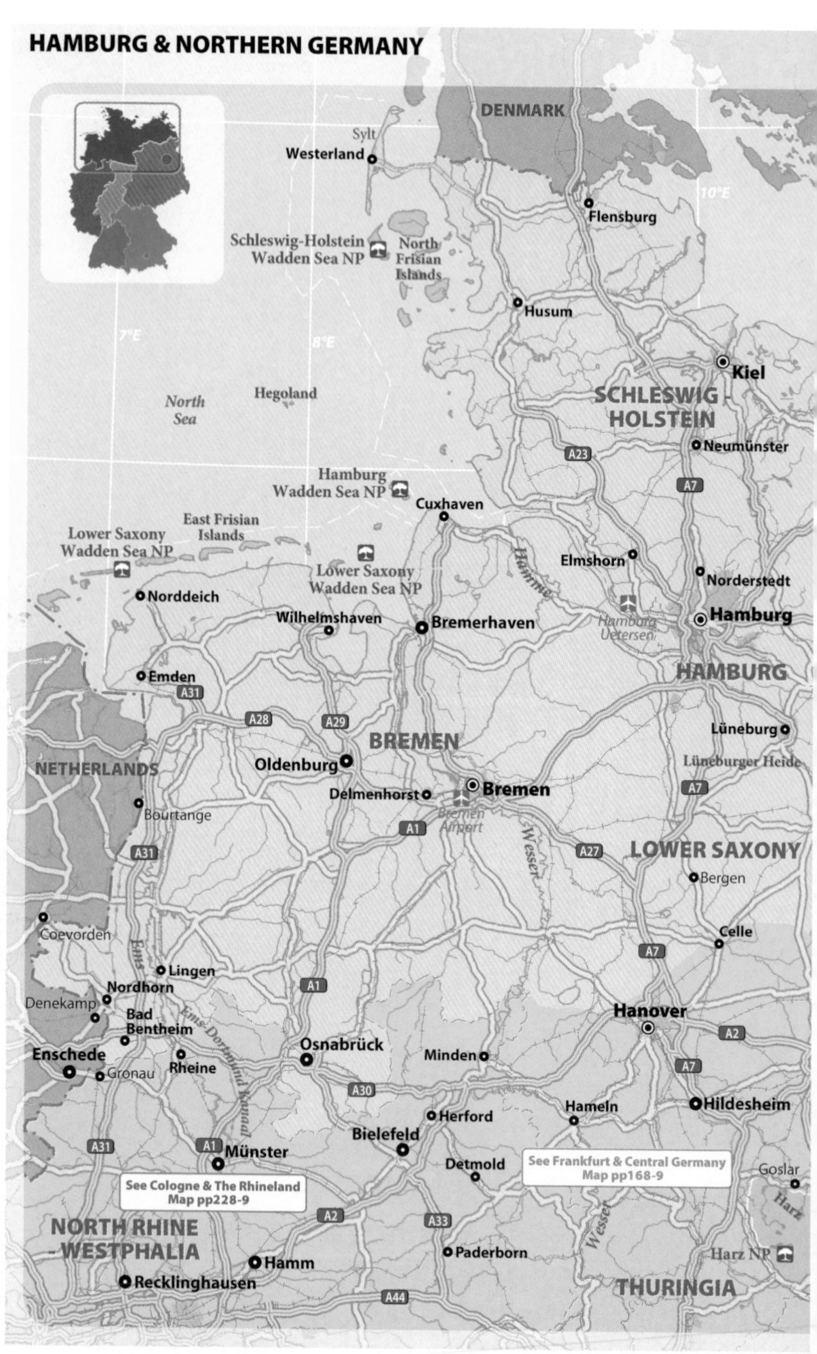
HAMBURG & NORTHERN GERMANY
DENMARK
Sylt
Westerland
Flensburg
10°E
Schleswig-Holstein
Wadden Sea NP
North
Frisian
Islands
Husum
7°E
8°E
Kiel
North
Sea
Hegoland
SCHLESWIG-
HOLSTEIN
Neumünster
A23
A7
Hamburg
Wadden Sea NP
Cuxhaven
East Frisian
Islands
Lower Saxony
Wadden Sea NP
Elmshorn
Lower Saxony
Wadden Sea NP
Norderstedt
Norddeich
Hamme
Wilhelmshaven
Bremerhaven
Hamburg
Uetersen
Hamburg
Emden
A31
HAMBURG
A28
A29
Lüneburg
BREMEN
Oldenburg
Lüneburger Heide
NETHERLANDS
Delmenhorst
Bremen
A7
Bourtange
Bremen
Airport
A1
Weser
A31
A27
LOWER SAXONY
Bergen
Celle
Coevorden
Ems
A7
Lingen
A1
Nordhorn
Denekamp
Bad
Bentheim
Ems-Dortmund Kanaal
Hanover
A2
Enschede
Gronau
Rheine
Osnabrück
Minden
A7
A30
Hameln
Hildesheim
Herford
Bielefeld
A31
A1
Münster
Detmold
See Frankfurt & Central Germany
Map pp168-9
Goslar
See Cologne & The Rhineland
Map pp228-9
Harz
A2
A33
Weser
NORTH RHINE
-WESTPHALIA
Paderborn
Harz NP
Hamm
Recklinghausen
THURINGIA
A44

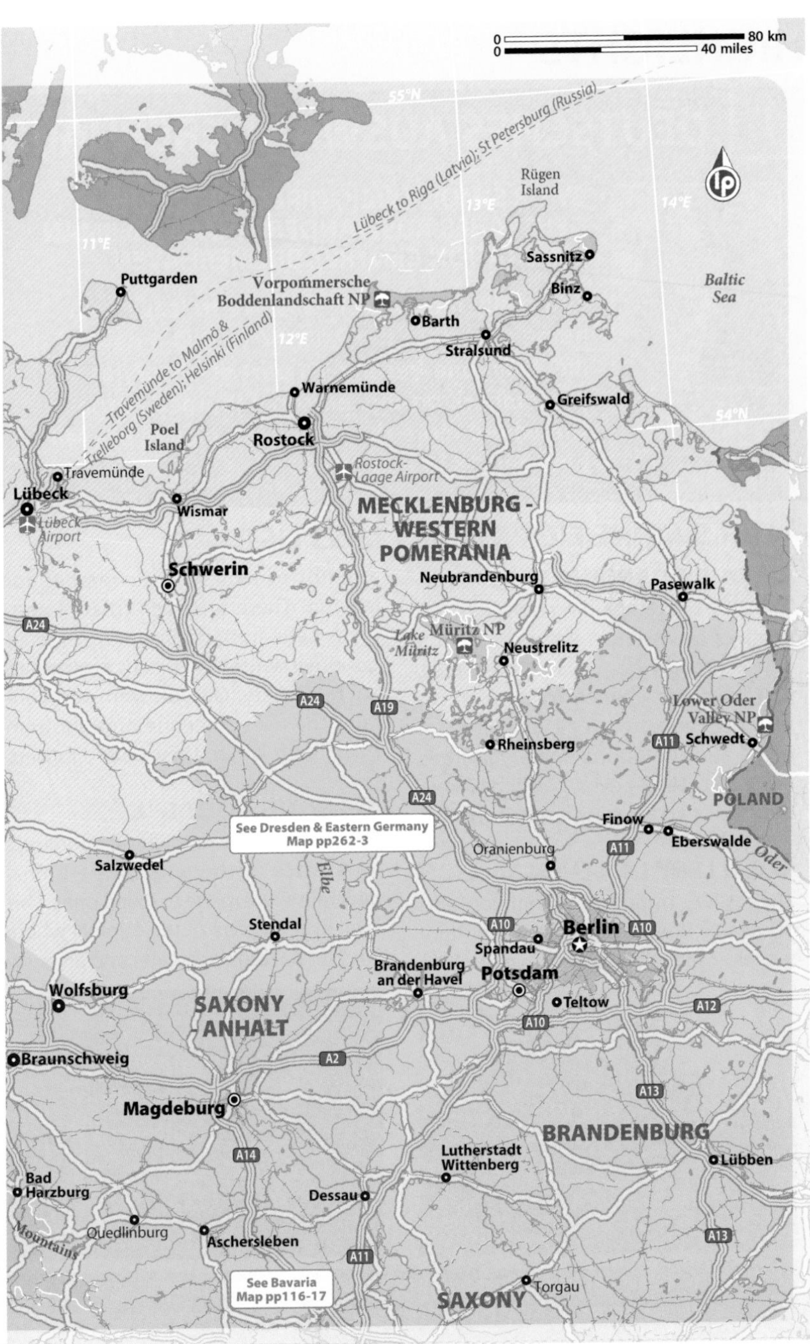

0 80 km
0 40 miles
Lübeck to Riga (Latvia); St Petersburg (Russia)
Rügen Island
Baltic Sea
Puttgarden
Vorpommersche Boddenlandschaft NP
Sassnitz
Binz
Barth
Stralsund
Travemünde to Malmö & Trelleborg (Sweden); Helsinki (Finland)
Warnemünde
Greifswald
Poel Island
Rostock
Rostock-Laage Airport
Travemünde
Lübeck
Lübeck Airport
Wismar
MECKLENBURG - WESTERN POMERANIA
Schwerin
Neubrandenburg
Pasewalk
Lake Müritz
Müritz NP
Neustrelitz
Lower Oder Valley NP
Schwedt
Rheinsberg
POLAND
See Dresden & Eastern Germany Map pp262-3
Finow
Eberswalde
Oder
Oranienburg
Salzwedel
Elbe
Stendal
Berlin
Spandau
Brandenburg an der Havel
Potsdam
Teltow
Wolfsburg
SAXONY - ANHALT
Braunschweig
Magdeburg
BRANDENBURG
Lutherstadt Wittenberg
Lübben
Bad Harzburg
Dessau
Quedlinburg
Aschersleben
See Bavaria Map pp116-17
Torgau
SAXONY

HIGHLIGHTS

1 DEUTSCHES AUSWANDERERHAUS

BY DR SIMONE EICK, DIRECTOR OF THE DEUTSCHES AUSWANDERERHAUS (GERMAN EMIGRATION CENTRE), BREMERHAVEN

You really feel what it was like to leave your home and cross the Atlantic to find a new life. Everyone becomes a part of history as you embark on this personal journey at the site where more than 7 million people set sail between 1830 and 1974.

DR SIMONE EICK'S DON'T MISS LIST

❶ YOUR BOARDING PASS

Everyone gets a boarding card, with the name of a passenger whose story you follow through their voyage. Afterwards, you have the chance to track down your own ancestors – all you need is a name and the approximate year they emigrated. Nearly everyone finds something – it's an amazing experience.

❷ GALLERY OF SEVEN MILLION

The Gallery of Seven Million contains oodles of tiny drawers, each containing emigrants' personal items, which attempt to explain their reasons for leaving. There are over 2000 biographies here, from photos and words of goodbye written on pieces of paper to an 1850 diary. One drawer even contains the nails someone brought from the church where they were baptised.

❸ SAYING GOODBYE

The most heart-wrenching moments took place at the wharf, where final farewells were made to loved ones. This is an exact replica of the original wharf, with menacing dark water and an enor-

Clockwise from top: Deutsches Auswandererhaus; Try the questions required for emigration approval; Re-creation of 3rd-class living quarters on board a ship; Replica of the original wharf; Boats in Bremerhaven's harbour

GERMAN EMIGRATION CENTRE

mous ship towering over passengers waiting to board. As you stand among the people leaving, it's extraordinary – the tears, hope and fear are immediately palpable in this emotional place.

❹ SLEEPING QUARTERS

This seems so real, it makes some people feel a little ill. Every detail of the cramped, overcrowded environment of an 1890 steamship sleeping quarters has been re-created – from the feel of the boat rocking to the dour smell. Passengers spent months sleeping in these dismal conditions.

❺ ELLIS ISLAND RECEPTION HALL

Upon arrival you sit on long wooden benches and await the immigration inspector, who asks questions and examines you. It's easy to imagine how nervous the immigrants were – if they answered wrongly or were disabled, they were denied entry to the land of their hopes and dreams and promptly shipped back to Europe.

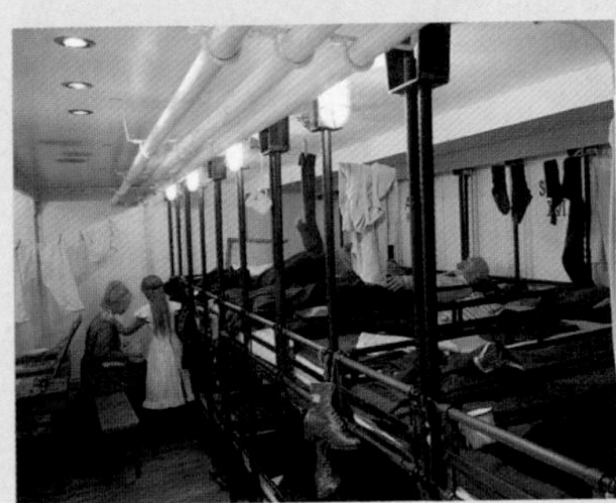

➘ THINGS YOU NEED TO KNOW

Top tip Avoid weekday mornings – the centre is often crowded with school groups **Eating on location** The outdoor restaurant has a deck where you can eat and take in a view of the port immigrants departed from. **See our author's review on p320**

HIGHLIGHTS

2

➘ SEX & THE BEATLES

It's tamer than Amsterdam's, but Europe's largest red light district, the **Reeperbahn** (p309), is a huge draw. Coming to life around 4pm, within a few hours thousands stream in to check out its dim bars, peep shows and sex shops. Not your cup of tea? Then just come to visit **Beatles-platz** (p309) at the corner of Reeperbahn and Grosse Freiheit – the Beatles' first taste of fame took place in this neighbourhood.

3

➘ MARZIPAN'S MULTIPLE PERSONALITIES

Sometimes it's a log, happy to be naked (how very German, see p337); sometimes it wears a thin chocolate coat. It's often a piece of fruit, an endearing pig or that old staple, the potato. When it's feeling fancy, it likes to drape itself across cakes and sweets, like a luxurious silk blanket. But one thing never changes – it's always an almond and sugar concoction, and **Lübeck** (p311) produces the world's best.

4

WISMAR

Wismar's (p316) enticing scenery is no secret, and countless film-makers have deemed it cinema-worthy – if its *Alter Hafen* (old harbour) looks familiar, it might be because you saw it in the 1922 Dracula movie *Nosferatu*. Don't be surprised if you stumble across a film crew on your way to its Unesco-listed Altstadt (old town).

5

SCHWERIN'S SCHLOSS

With six facades, combining styles from mainly the 16th and 17th centuries, you'll find Gothic and Renaissance turrets, a golden dome and vaguely Ottoman features (among others) at Schwerin's magnificent **castle** (p315). And it's not just a pretty attraction – it's the official seat of Mecklenburg–Western Pomerania's parliament.

6

THE FANTASTIC FOUR

In the Brothers Grimm fairy tale, the *Bremer Stadtmusikanten* (Town Musicians of Bremen) never actually make it to **Bremen** (p318). But when you arrive you'll find the donkey, dog, cat and rooster who ran away from their owners (intending to make their fortune as musicians) standing on each other's backs.

2 WAYNE WALTON; 3 DAVID PEEVERS; 4 NMI/IMAGEBROKER; 5 WITOLD SKRYPCZAK; 6 PSF/IMAGEBROKER

2 Advertising for a show in the Reeperbahn (p309), Hamburg; 3 Marzipan in Lübeck (p311); 4 View down to Wismar's St-Nikolai-Kirche (p317); 5 Schwerin's Schloss (p315); 6 Gerhard Marcks' *Bremer Stadtmusikanten* statue (p319)

THE BEST...

↘ THINGS FOR FREE

- **HafenCity InfoCenter** (p308) Check out Hamburg's ambitious plans to extend the city limits by 40%.
- **Marzipan Salon** (p312) Learn what marzipan was previously used for (sweet treat is not the correct answer).
- **Dom St Petri** (p318) Bremen's 1200-year-old cathedral.

↘ GRIN-INDUCING MONUMENTS

- **Beatles-Platz** (p309) All you need is love, and a city square shaped like a vinyl record.
- **Town Musicians of Bremen** statue (p319) Why is the rooster standing on a cat, perched on a dog that is sitting on a donkey?
- **Pig statuettes** (p318) A metal *oink oink* parade graces Wismar's *Schweinsbrücke* (pig bridge).

↘ HARBOURSIDE HIGHLIGHTS

- **International Maritime Museum** (p305) Perched at the edge of the gargantuan HafenCity.
- **Ozeanum** (p317) Located in Stralsund, this aquarium, housed in an architecturally stunning swirl of white, takes you on a journey through northern seas and oceans.
- **Deutsches Auswandererhaus** (German Emigration Centre; p320) Set on the very harbour emigrants departed from.

↘ BOAT TOURS

- **Trave River** (p314) Glide around Lübeck.
- **Wismar's Harbour** (p318) Cruise around this Hanseatic town, or catch a boat to nearby Poel Island, a traditional fishing community.
- **Port and Elbe River cruises** (p309) You haven't experienced Hamburg until you've seen it from the water.

HafenCity (p308), Hamburg

THINGS YOU NEED TO KNOW

VITAL STATISTICS

- **Population** Hamburg 1.77 million; Schleswig-Holstein 2.37 million; Mecklenburg–Western Pomerania 1.68 million; Bremen 663,082
- **Points of entry** Hamburg, Lübeck and Bremen airports
- **Best time to visit** May to September

ADVANCE PLANNING

- **One month before** Reserve a table at one of Hamburg's Elbmeile (p308) hotspots.
- **One day before** Make sure you've packed an umbrella, a raincoat and a sweater, even if the weather forecast is sunny and warm: the weather here is notoriously fickle.

RESOURCES

- **www.thehamburgexpress.com** General Hamburg news and services in English.
- **www.szene-hamburg-online.de** Hamburg's *Szene* magazine is chock-full of local listings and events. German only, but highlights and headlines are intuitive enough for you to be able to figure out what's going on in town while you visit.

GETTING AROUND

- **Train** The trains in this region are comfortable, efficient and relaxing – there's absolutely no reason to hire a car, and parking in cities like Hamburg gets expensive. Plan your journey and book tickets in advance on www.bahn.de.
- **Bicycle** Hamburg is relatively flat and filled with oodles of well-designated bike paths, many along the city's waterways. Rent a bike at Fahrradladen St Georg (p311).

BE FOREWARNED

- **Reeperbahn** (p309) This area is not for the faint of heart: you will pass strip clubs, peep shows, and insalubrious characters mingling among the throngs of normal folk and tourists.
- **Women travellers** Don't even consider trying to walk down Herbertstrasse (p309).
- **Food** Northern Germany's local specialities look to the sea for inspiration – if you're seeking the epicentre of bratwurst, you're better off sticking to more southern regions.

HAMBURG & NORTHERN GERMANY ITINERARIES

UNESCO WORLD HERITAGE SITES Three Days

Northern Germany is a cornucopia of Unesco Heritage Sites. Start in **(1) Bremen City** (p318), whose **(2) Roland Statue** (p318) and **(3) Rathaus** (town hall; p318) have both been recognised. Next hop on a train and base yourself in **(4) Lübeck** (p311) for a couple of nights to explore the buzzing Hanseatic city. Cross through the impressive red-brick **(5) Holstentor** (p313) city gate to get to the protected Altstadt, where you can sample the world's best marzipan at **(6) Café Niederegger** (p312) after gaping at the architecture. From here it's an easy day trip by train (the surrounding countryside en route is beautiful) to medieval **(7) Wismar** (p316), the entire historic centre of which is a Unesco Site, including the **(8) Alter Schwede** (p316), a striking example of the red brick that graces many structures in this region.

WATER, WATER EVERYWHERE Five Days

From the Baltic Sea to endless lakes to canals that rival Venice and Amsterdam's, Northern Germany is all about embracing the water. Base yourself in **(1) Lübeck** (p311), which is surrounded by the **(2) Trave River** (p314) and never forgets its role as a Hanseatic city. When you want more action (and more water), head into **(3) Hamburg** (p304) where you can choose to float your way around several bodies of water: cruise the **(4) Alster Lakes** (p309) or the **(5) port and Elbe River** (p309), or take a small barge trip up the **(6) Speicherstadt** (p305) canals. More lakes await you in **(7) Schwerin** (an easy train journey from Hamburg; p315), which boasts a whopping 12 lakes within its city limits. Between late April and mid-October, hop on the toylike passenger ferry that crosses the **(8) Pfaffenteich** (p316), a tiny lake in the middle of town. If you're up for some exercise or you visit outside of those months, take a pleasant 40-minute stroll around the lake.

FROM SEA TO SEA One Week

Germany's coastline extends from the North Sea (due west) to the Baltic Sea (due east), with a gamut of extraordinary sites in between. Set yourself up in a **(1) Hamburg** hotel close to the main train hub, like literary-fave **(2) Hotel Wedina** (p310), a pleasant 15-minute walk from the station. Spend a few days strolling around Hamburg's **(3) Alsterarkaden** (p304), a canal-hugging arcade of shops and restaurants; hit the **(4) Reeperbahn** (p309), Europe's largest red-light district; and stop off at the **(5) Beatlemania Museum** (p309) to learn how Paul and his buddies got their first shot of fame in the port city. After you've explored Hamburg, rent a car for the next few days; spend

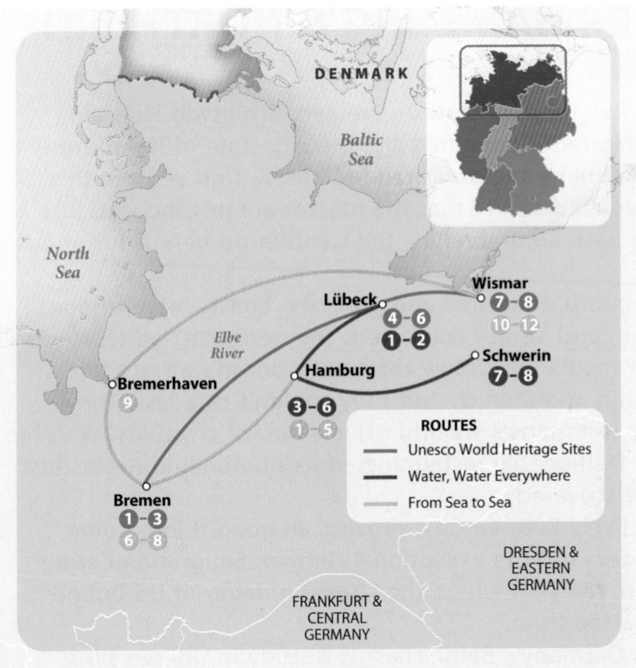

a morning in (6) Bremen City (p318). Check out the pretty town and its two famous statues: (7) Knight Roland (p318) and (8) The Town Musicians of Bremen (p319) before popping up to Bremerhaven's (9) Deutsches Auswandererhaus (p320) – situated on the North Sea harbour, millions of New World-bound emigrants departed from here. Spend the next day in (10) Wismar (p316); be sure to get a picture of its famous (11) Swedish Heads (p318) and take a (12) harbour cruise (p318) for a first-hand view of Baltic port life. Before or after your cruise, grab a bite from the harbourside boats selling smoked-fish sandwiches – it doesn't get much fresher than this.

DISCOVER HAMBURG & NORTHERN GERMANY

Encompassing five German states – Bremen, Schleswig-Holstein, Mecklenburg–Western Pomerania and the city-state of Hamburg – this is one of Germany's least-visited regions. But do venture this far north and you'll discover that the masses are missing out; just make sure you pack an umbrella – the weather up here is notoriously fickle.

Dynamic Hamburg, the canal and port city, boasts more bridges than Amsterdam and Venice combined. The designer-clad residents cycling to their media jobs know their town doesn't attract foreign visitors like Berlin and Munich, but they couldn't care less. They know their city (Germany's wealthiest) is a hub of creativity, with hip boutiques and fashionable restaurants in its photogenic streets just waiting to be discovered.

Then there's lively Bremen City, proving all good things come in small packages; and the exceptional German Emigration Centre in Bremerhaven, the port where the largest number of US-bound emigrants departed from.

Moving east, Germany's Baltic coast is a study in Unesco sites, notably Lübeck, which is also known as the home of marzipan; and the former Hanseatic town of Wismar, with its magnificent medieval centre.

HAMBURG

'Gateway to the world' may be a bold claim, but Germany's second-largest city and biggest port has never been shy. Hamburg's maritime spirit infuses the entire city – from its architecture (such as red-brick, copper-roofed neo-Gothic warehouses rising above the canal-woven Speicherstadt, and buildings shaped like cruise liners and stacked shipping crates) to its rowdy fish market, along with the sailboats gracing the Alster Lakes, and ships the size of city blocks sounding their horns as they navigate the mighty Elbe River.

INFORMATION

Hamburg Tourismus (☎ 3005 1300; www.hamburg-tourismus.de) Airport (arrivals hall; 🕑 6am-11pm); Hauptbahnhof (Kirchenallee exit; 🕑 8am-9pm Mon-Sat, 10am-6pm Sun); Landungsbrücken (btwn Brücke 4 & Brücke 5; 🕑 8am-6pm Apr-Oct, 10am-6pm Nov-Mar)

SIGHTS

ALTSTADT, MERCHANT'S DISTRICT & AROUND

Hamburg's baroque **Rathaus** (town hall; ☎ 428 312 010; Rathausmarkt; tour adult/child €3/0.50; 🕑 English-language tours hourly 10.15am-3.15pm Mon-Thu, to 1.15pm Fri, to 5.15pm Sat, to 4.15pm Sun) is one of Europe's most opulent, renowned for the Emperor's Hall and the Great Hall, with its spectacular coffered ceiling. To the northwest, the elegant Renaissance-style arcades of the **Alsterarkaden** shelter shops and cafes alongside a canal.

The brown-brick **Chilehaus** (**www.chilehaus-hamburg.de, in German; Burchardstrasse**) is shaped like an ocean liner, with remarkable curved walls meeting in the shape of a ship's bow and staggered balconies that look like decks. Designed by architect Fritz Höger for a merchant who derived his wealth from trading with Chile, the 1924 building is a leading example of German expressionist architecture. Nearby **St Nikolai** (**☎ 371 125; Ost-West-Strasse; adult/child €3.70/2; ⏰ 10am-8pm May-Sep, to 6pm Oct-Apr**), not to be confused with the new Hauptkirche St Nikolai in Harvestehude, was the world's tallest building from 1874 to 1876, and remains Hamburg's second-tallest structure (after the TV tower).

A treasure trove of art from the Renaissance to the present day, Hamburg's **Kunsthalle** (**☎ 428 131 200; www.hamburger-kunsthalle.de; Glockengiesserwall; adult/under 18yr/concession €8.50/free/5; ⏰ 10am-6pm Tue, Wed & Fri-Sun, to 9pm Thu**) spans two buildings – one old, one new – linked by an underground passage. The main building houses works ranging from medieval portraiture to 20th-century classics, such as Klee and Kokoschka. Its stark white new building, the **Galerie der Gegenwart**, showcases contemporary German artists, including Rebecca Horn, Georg Baselitz and Gerhard Richter, alongside international stars, including David Hockney, Jeff Koons and Barbara Kruger.

SPEICHERSTADT

The seven-storey red-brick warehouses lining the Speicherstadt archipelago are a well-recognised Hamburg symbol, stretching to Baumwall in the world's largest continuous warehouse complex.

Kapitän Prüsse (**☎ 313 130; www.kapitaen-pruesse.de, in German; Landungsbrücken 3; tours from €12.50**) offers regular Speicherstadt tours, leaving from the port.

In the postindustrial age, many of the warehouses have been put to new use as museums. The centrepiece is the new **International Maritime Museum** (**☎ 3009 2300; www.internationales-maritimes-museum.de; Koreastrasse 1; adult/child €10/7; ⏰ 10am-6pm Tue-Wed & Fri-Sun, to 8pm Thu**) It takes 10 floors

CLX/IMAGEBROKER

Hamburg's Speicherstadt

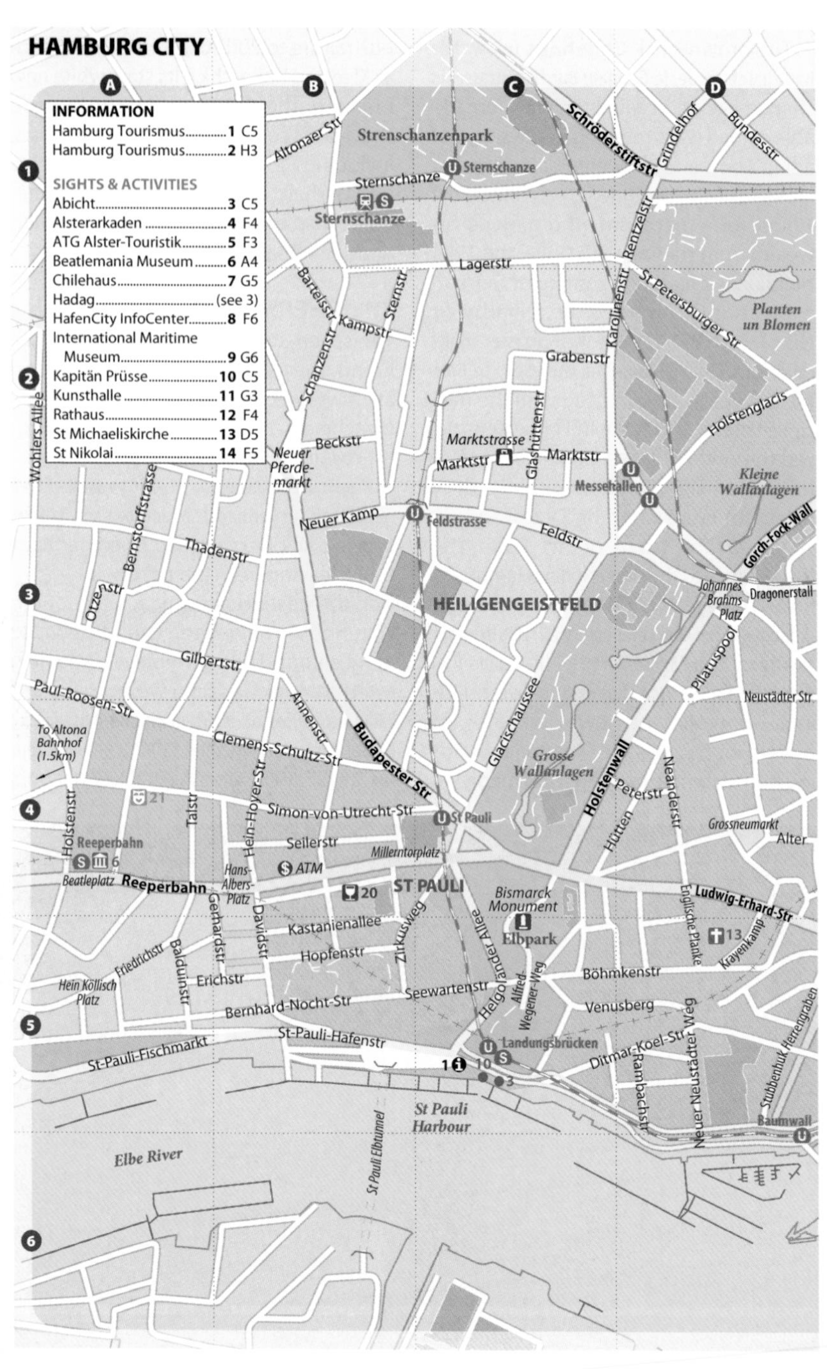
HAMBURG CITY
INFORMATION
Hamburg Tourismus 1 C5
Hamburg Tourismus 2 H3
SIGHTS & ACTIVITIES
Abicht 3 C5
Alsterarkaden 4 F4
ATG Alster-Touristik 5 F3
Beatlemania Museum 6 A4
Chilehaus 7 G5
Hadag (see 3)
HafenCity InfoCenter 8 F6
International Maritime Museum 9 G6
Kapitän Prüsse 10 C5
Kunsthalle 11 G3
Rathaus 12 F4
St Michaeliskirche 13 D5
St Nikolai 14 F5
Strenschanzenpark
Sternschanze
Schröderstiftstr
Grindelhof
Bundesstr
Altonaer Str
Lagerstr
Rentzelstr
St Petersburger Str
Planten un Blomen
Bartelsstr
Kampstr
Sternstr
Schanzenstr
Karolinenstr
Grabenstr
Holstenglacis
Glashüttenstr
Marktstrasse
Marktstr
Beckstr
Neuer Pferdemarkt
Messehallen
Kleine Wallanlagen
Neuer Kamp
Feldstrasse
Feldstr
Gorch-Fock-Wall
Wohlers Allee
Bernstorffstrasse
Thadenstr
Otzenstr
HEILIGENGEISTFELD
Johannes Brahms Platz
Dragonerstall
Gilbertstr
Pilatuspool
Neustädter Str
Paul-Roosen-Str
To Altona Bahnhof (1.5km)
Annenstr
Budapester Str
Clemens-Schultz-Str
Glacischaussee
Grosse Wallanlagen
Holstenwall
Peterstr
Neanderstr
Hein-Hoyer-Str
Simon-von-Utrecht-Str
St Pauli
Hütten
Grossneumarkt
Alter
Holstenstr
Talstr
Reeperbahn
Seilerstr
Millerntorplatz
ATM
Beatleplatz
Hans-Albers-Platz
ST PAULI
Bismarck Monument
Ludwig-Erhard-Str
Gerhardstr
Davidstr
Kastanienallee
Zirkusweg
Helgoländer Allee
Elbpark
Englische Planke
Krayenkamp
Friedrichstr
Balduinstr
Hopfenstr
Alfred-Wegener-Weg
Böhmkenstr
Hein Köllisch Platz
Erichstr
Seewartenstr
Venusberg
Bernhard-Nocht-Str
St-Pauli-Hafenstr
Landungsbrücken
Ditmar-Koel-Str
Herrengraben
St-Pauli-Fischmarkt
Rambachstr
Neuer Neustädter Weg
Stubbenhuk
St Pauli Harbour
St Pauli Elbtunnel
Baumwall
Elbe River

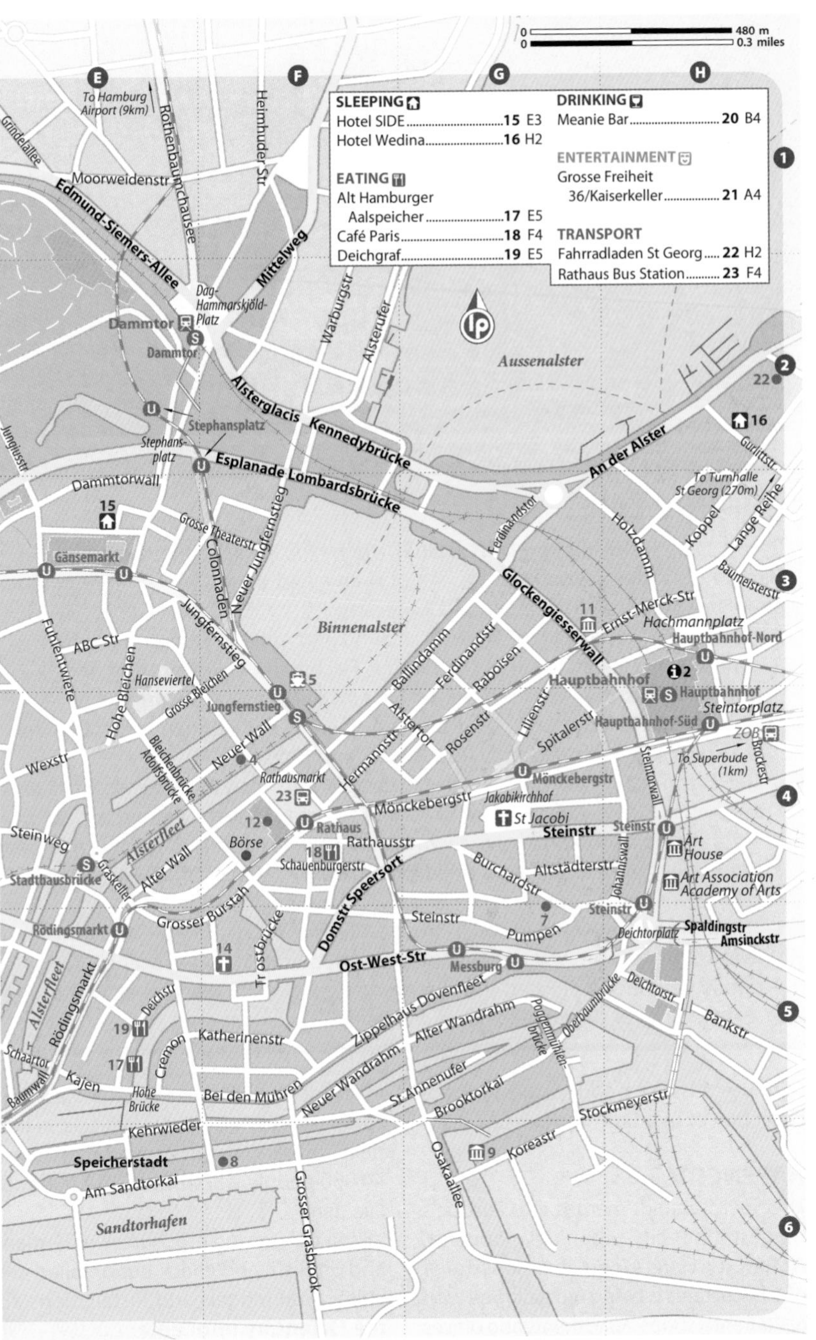
0 480 m
0 0.3 miles
E
F
G
H
1
2
3
4
5
6
SLEEPING
Hotel SIDE 15 E3
Hotel Wedina 16 H2
EATING
Alt Hamburger Aalspeicher 17 E5
Café Paris 18 F4
Deichgraf 19 E5
DRINKING
Meanie Bar 20 B4
ENTERTAINMENT
Grosse Freiheit 36/Kaiserkeller 21 A4
TRANSPORT
Fahrradladen St Georg 22 H2
Rathaus Bus Station 23 F4
To Hamburg Airport (9km)
Grindelallee
Rothenbaumchaussee
Heimhuder Str
Moorweidenstr
Edmund-Siemers-Allee
Mittelweg
Dag-Hammarskjöld-Platz
Dammtor
Warburgstr
Alsterufer
Aussenalster
Alsterglacis
Kennedybrücke
Stephansplatz
Esplanade
Lombardsbrücke
An der Alster
Gurlittstr
To Turnhalle St Georg (270m)
Jungiusstr
Dammtorwall
Grosse Theaterstr
Colonnaden
Neuer Jungfernstieg
Ferdinandstor
Holzdamm
Koppel
Lange Reihe
Baumeisterstr
Gänsemarkt
Glockengiesserwall
Ernst-Merck-Str
Hachmannplatz
Hauptbahnhof-Nord
Jungfernstieg
Binnenalster
Fuhlentwiete
ABC Str
Hohe Bleichen
Hanseviertel
Grosse Bleichen
Ballindamm
Ferdinandstr
Raboisen
Hauptbahnhof
Hauptbahnhof-Süd
Steintorplatz
ZOB
Brockestr
To Superbude (1km)
Wexstr
Neuer Wall
Bleichenbrücke
Adolfsbrücke
Rathausmarkt
Hermannstr
Alstertor
Rosenstr
Lilienstr
Spitalerstr
Steintorwall
Mönckebergstr
Jakobikirchhof
St Jacobi
Steinstr
Steinweg
Alsterfleet
Börse
Rathaus
Rathausstr
Schauenburgerstr
Art House
Art Association Academy of Arts
Stadthausbrücke
Graskeller
Alter Wall
Domstr
Speersort
Burchardstr
Altstädterstr
Johanniswall
Grosser Burstah
Rödingsmarkt
Trostbrücke
Pumpen
Deichtorplatz
Spaldingstr
Amsinckstr
Ost-West-Str
Messberg
Oberbaumbrücke
Deichtorstr
Bankstr
Deichstr
Zippelhaus
Dovenfleet
Alter Wandrahm
Poggenmühlenbrücke
Katherinenstr
Cremon
Schaartor
Baumwall
Kajen
Hohe Brücke
Bei den Mühren
Neuer Wandrahm
St Annenufer
Brooktorkai
Stockmeyerstr
Kehrwieder
Osakaallee
Koreastr
Speicherstadt
Am Sandtorkai
Sandtorhafen
Grosser Grasbrook

WST/IMAGEBROKER

A steamer cruising in front of the Fischmarkt, Hamburg

IF YOU LIKE...

If you like the **Speicherstadt** (p305), then you clearly like experiencing Hamburg's water action. But this is a port city, and there's much more going on in and around those canals and waterways:

- **Fischmarkt** (www.fischmarkt-hamburg.de) Sundays between 5am and 10am, curious tourists join locals at the famous Fischmarkt in St Pauli. Running since 1703, its stars are the *Marktschreier* (market criers) hawking their wares at full volume. Live cover bands also crank out German pop songs in the adjoining *Fischauktionshalle* (Fish Auction Hall).
- **Deichgraf** (☎ 364 208; www.deichgraf-hamburg.de; Deichstrasse 23; lunch mains €7-14.50, dinner mains €14.50-24.50; lunch & dinner Mon-Fri, noon-10pm Sat) Seafood is king here, and you shouldn't leave town before trying Hamburg's famous *Aalsuppe* (eel soup), spiced with dried fruit, ham, vegetables and herbs, at this leading local restaurant.
- **The Elbmeile** (www.elbmeile.de) In the past few years, Hamburg's western riverfront has morphed into one of Germany's hottest dining scenes. The trendy eateries are housed in contemporary, industrial spaces – all with serene views of the wide expanse of water.

to house this, the world's largest private collection of maritime treasures.

HAFENCITY

The Speicherstadt merges into Europe's biggest inner-city urban development, **HafenCity**. Here, a long-abandoned area of 155 hectares is being redeveloped with restaurants, shops, apartments and offices in an enormous regeneration project encompassing 12 distinctive quarters. In the next 20 years, it's anticipated that some 40,000 people will work and 12,000 will live here.

You can pick up brochures (in German and English) and check out detailed architectural models and installations at the **HafenCity InfoCenter** (☎ 3690 1799;

www.hafencity.com; Am Sandtorkai 30; admission free; 10am-6pm Tue, Wed & Fri-Sun, to 8pm Thu May-Sep), which also has a cafe.

PORT OF HAMBURG

Each year some 12,000 ships deliver and take on some 70 million tonnes of goods at Hamburg's huge port, which sprawls over 75 sq km (12% of Hamburg's entire surface area).

Climbing the steps above the Landungsbrücken U-/S-Bahn station to the Stintfang stone balcony offers an interesting snapshot, while dozens of **port and Elbe River cruises**, starting at the St Pauli Harbour Landungsbrücken, put you right in the middle of the action.

Operators at the Landungsbrücken include the following:

Abicht (**☎ 317 8220; www.abicht.de; Brücke 1; 1hr tour adult/child €12/6; English-language tours noon Apr-Oct**) Also offers Saturday evening tours taking you past the illuminated warehouses (departure times vary according to tides).

Hadag (**☎ 311 7070; www.hadag.de; Brücke 2; adult/under 16yr 1hr tour incl audioguide €11/5; tours up to 4 times daily year-round) Has a Lower Elbe service, too.**

Northeast of the landing piers, the **St Michaeliskirche** (**☎ 3767 8100; www.st-michaelis.de, in German; Englische Planke 1a; adult/under 16yr tower €3/2, tower & crypt €5/3; 9am-7.30pm May-Oct, 10am-5.30pm Nov-Apr**), or 'Der Michel' as it's commonly called, is one of Hamburg's most recognisable landmarks and northern Germany's largest Protestant baroque church.

REEPERBAHN

Even those who are not interested in strip shows usually pay a quick visit to the red-light **Reeperbahn** to see what all the fuss is about. Long established as a party place for incoming sailors, crowds of thousands start to stream in from around 4pm, cruising the rip-roaring collection of bars, sex clubs, variety acts, pubs and cafes collectively known as the 'Kiez'.

Just north of the S-Bahn station is the **Grosse Freiheit** (literally 'great freedom') street, with its bright lights, dark doorways and live sex shows. Along Davidstrasse, a painted tin wall bars views into **Herbertstrasse**, a block-long bordello that's off limits to men under 18 and to women of all ages (this is no joke: women have been met not only with verbal abuse but buckets of urine).

In the swinging '60s, the Beatles cut their musical teeth at the area's now-defunct Star-Club. At the intersection of the Reeperbahn and Grosse Freiheit, the new **Beatles-Platz** is designed like a vinyl record. Standing on this circular, 29m-diameter black-paved plaza are abstract steel sculptures resembling cookie cutters of the fab four (including a hybrid of Ringo Starr and Pete Best) plus Stuart Sutcliffe.

You can take a slightly surreal journey through the Beatles' career at the **Beatlemania Museum** (**☎ 8538 8888; www.beatlemania-hamburg.de, in German; Nobistor 10; adult/child €10/6; 10am-10pm**).

TOURS

In addition to the boat tours in the Speicherstadt (p305) and Port of Hamburg (p309), you can also float past elegant buildings aboard an Alster Lakes cruise.

ATG Alster-Touristik (**☎ 3574 2419; www.alstertouristik.de; adult/under 16yr single stage €1.50/0.75, 2hr round trip €9.50/4.25; Apr-Sep**) runs a hop-on, hop-off service between nine landing stages around the lakes, as well as various canal and waterway tours.

SLEEPING

our pick Superbude (☎ 380 8780; www.superbude.de; dm €16-22, d €59-89, breakfast €7; P ⊠ 💻 wifi; 🅖 Berliner Tor) A games room (with Wii, table football and punching bags), large-screen cinema (and seat covers stitched from old jeans) and an open-plan kitchen and dining area (with bar stools made from recycled beer crates) are among the innovations at Hamburg's hippest hostel-budget hotel.

Hotel Wedina (☎ 280 8900; www.wedina.de; Gurlittstrasse 23; s/d main bldg incl breakfast from €98/118, other bldg incl breakfast from €108/138; P wifi) You might find a novel instead of a chocolate on your pillow at this literary hotel. Margaret Atwood, Jonathan Safran Foer, Jonathan Franzen, Michel Houellebecq, Vladimir Nabokov and JK Rowling are just some of the authors who've stayed and left behind signed books.

Hotel SIDE (☎ 309 990; www.side-hamburg.de; Drehbahn 49; r incl breakfast €170-300; P ⊠ ❄ 💻 wifi) A stylish alternative to the city centre's chain hotels, this Matteo Thun–designed stunner is built around a soaring prism-shaped central atrium. The 8th-floor chill-out lounge, strewn with 1950s-style saucers-from-outer-space sofas, opens to a panoramic sun deck.

EATING

Café Paris (☎ 3252 7777; Rathausstrasse 4; mains €5.50-26; 🕑 from 9am Mon-Fri, from 10am Sat, closing times vary) Within a spectacularly tiled 1882 butchers' hall and adjoining art-deco salon, this elegant yet relaxed brasserie serves classical French fare like *croque-monsieur* (toasted ham-and-cheese sandwich), *croque-madame* (the same, but with a fried egg), and *steak tartare* (minced meat, but pan-fried, not raw).

Turnhalle St Georg (☎ 2800 8480; Lange Reihe 107; mains €9.50-25.50, brunch Sat/Sun €11.90/17.90; 🕑 9.30am-midnight Mon-Sat, 11am-midnight Sun) Intimate is not a word you could use for this converted gymnasium, inside an elegant 1882 red-brick building, serving modern international cuisine – but you still sometimes have trouble getting a seat.

Alt Hamburger Aalspeicher (☎ 362 990; Deichstrasse 43; mains €12-26.50, set menus €29.50-47.50; 🕑 lunch & dinner) Despite its tourist-friendly canalside location, the knick-knack-filled dining room and warm service at this avocado-coloured restaurant make you feel like you're dining in your *Oma's* (grandma's) house.

DRINKING & ENTERTAINMENT

Meanie Bar (☎ 310 845; www.molotowclub.com, in German; Spielbudenplatz 5; 🕑 from 6pm) One of the few venues along the Reeperbahn with local cred, the retro Meanie Bar is a hang-out for musos and artists.

Grosse Freiheit 36/Kaiserkeller (☎ 3177 7811; www.grossefreiheit36.de, in German; Grosse Freiheit 36; 🕑 from 10pm Tue-Sat) The Beatles once played in the basement Kaiserkeller at this now-mainstream venue mounting pop and rock concerts.

GETTING THERE & AWAY

AIR

Hamburg Airport (HAM; ☎ 507 50; www.flughafen-hamburg.de) has frequent flights to domestic and European cities, including on Lufthansa, British Airways and Air France, and low-cost carriers Air Berlin and Germanwings.

TRAIN

Hamburg has four mainline train stations: the Hauptbahnhof, Dammtor, Altona and Harburg.

Frequent trains serve Lübeck (€18.50, 40 minutes), Kiel (€27, 1¼ hours), Hanover (€40, 1¼ hours) and Bremen (€20.80 to €28, 55 minutes).

There are direct ICE services to Berlin-Hauptbahnhof (€68, 2¼ hours), Cologne (€79, four hours), Munich (€127, six hours) and Frankfurt (€106, three hours).

GETTING AROUND

TO/FROM THE AIRPORT

The S1 S-Bahn connects the airport directly with the city centre, including the Hauptbahnhof. The journey takes 24 minutes and costs €2.70.

BICYCLE

Many hostels and some hotels arrange bike rental for guests, or try **Fahrradladen St Georg** (☎ 243 908; Schmilinskystrasse 6; per 24hr €10-12, refundable cash deposit €50; 🕑 10am-7pm Mon-Fri, to 1pm Sat).

PUBLIC TRANSPORT

The **HVV** (☎ 194 49; www.hvv.de) operates buses, ferries, U-Bahn and S-Bahn (plus A-Bahn commuter services), and has several offices, including at the Jungfernstieg S-/U-Bahn station, and the Hauptbahnhof.

SCHLESWIG-HOLSTEIN

LÜBECK

A 12th-century gem boasting more than 1000 historical buildings, Lübeck's picture-book appearance is an enduring reminder of its role as one of the founding cities of the mighty Hanseatic League and its moniker of the 'Queen of the Hanse'. Behind its landmark Holstentor (gate), you'll find streets lined with medieval merchants' homes and spired churches forming Lübeck's 'crown'.

COF/IMAGEBROKER

Alster Lakes landing stage, Hamburg

Recognised by Unesco as a World Heritage Site in 1987, today this thriving provincial city retains many enchanting corners to explore.

INFORMATION

Lübeck & Travemünde tourist office (☎ 01805-882 233; www.lubeck-tourism.de; Holstentorplatz 1; 🕑 9.30am-7pm Mon-Fri, 10am-3pm Sat, 10am-2pm Sun Jun-Sep, 9.30am-6pm Mon-Fri, 10am-3pm Sat Oct-May) Sells the Happy Day Card (per 1/3 days €7/14) offering free public transport and museum discounts. Also has a cafe and internet terminals.

SIGHTS & ACTIVITIES

Just behind the Holstentor (to the east) stand the **Salzspeicher**: six gabled brick buildings once used to store salt transported from Lüneburg. It was then bartered for furs from Scandinavia and used to preserve the herrings that formed a substantial chunk of Lübeck's Hanseatic trade.

Sometimes described as a 'fairy tale in stone', Lübeck's 13th- to 15th-century **Rathaus** (**town hall; ☎ 122 1005; Breite Strasse; guided tours in German adult/concession €3/1.50; tours 11am, noon & 3pm Mon-Fri**) is widely regarded as one of the most beautiful in Germany.

Across the street from the Markt, **Café Niederegger** (**☎ 530 1126; www.niederegger.de; Breite Strasse 89; 9am-7pm Mon-Fri, 9am-6pm Sat, 10am-6pm Sun**) is Lübeck's mecca for marzipan, the almond confectionery from Arabia that has been made in Lübeck for centuries. In its **Marzipan-Salon** (**admission free**) you'll learn that in medieval Europe marzipan was considered medicine, not a treat.

Near the Markt rise the 125m twin spires of Germany's third-largest church, the **Marienkirche** (**Schüsselbuden 13; admission €1; 10am-6pm Apr-Sep, to 5pm Oct, 10am-4pm Tue-Sun Nov-Mar**). It's most famous for its shattered bells, which have been left

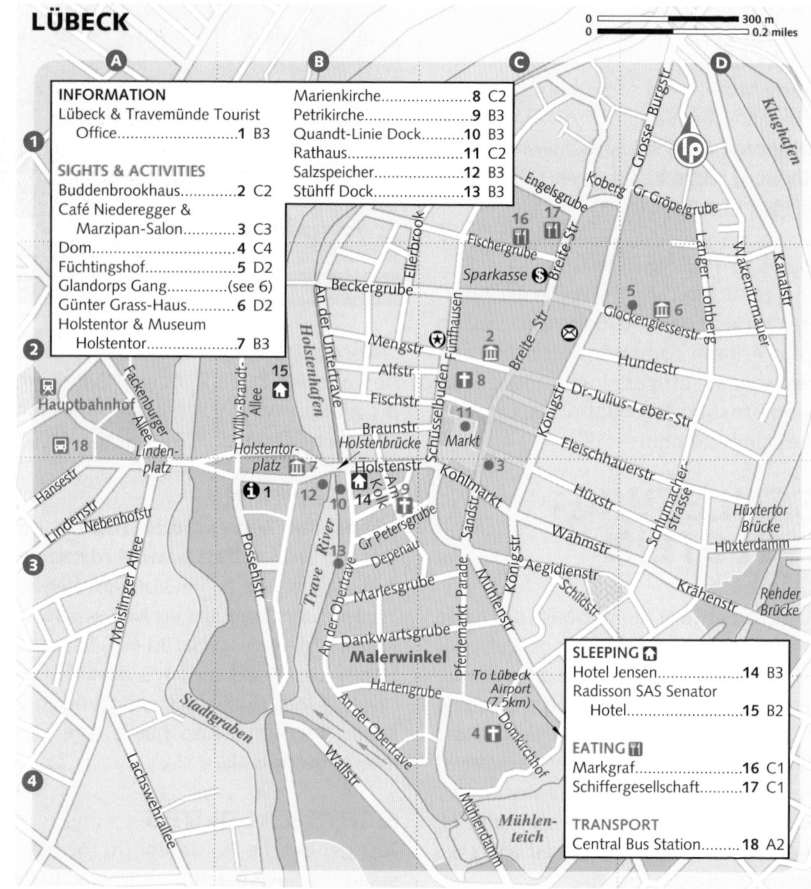

where they fell after a WWII bombing raid, as a peace memorial. Turn left upon entering the church and go to the end of the aisle. Outside there's a little devil sculpture with an amusing folk tale (in German and English).

Panoramic views over the city unfold from the **Petrikirche** (**Schmiedstrasse; lift adult/concession €2.50/1.50; 9am-9pm Apr-Sep, 10am-7pm Oct-Mar**), which has a tower lift to the 7th floor.

The **Dom** (**cathedral; 10am-6pm Apr-Oct, to 4pm Nov-Mar**) was founded in 1173 by Heinrich der Löwe when he took over Lübeck. Locals like to joke that if you approach the Dom from the northeast, you have to go through *Hölle* (hell) and *Fegefeuer* (purgatory) – the actual names of streets – to see **Paradies**, the lavish vestibule to the Dom.

In the Middle Ages, Lübeck was home to numerous craftspeople and artisans. Their presence caused demand for housing to outgrow the available space, so tiny single-storey homes were built in courtyards behind existing rows of houses. These were then made accessible via little walkways from the street. Almost 90 such *Gänge* (walkways) and *Höfe* (courtyards) still exist, among them charitable housing estates built for the poor, the *Stiftsgänge* and *Stiftshöfe*. The most famous of the latter are the beautiful **Füchtingshof** (**Glockengiesserstrasse 25; 9am-noon & 3-6pm**) and the **Glandorps Gang** (**Glockengiesserstrasse 41-51**), which you can peer into.

The winner of the 1929 Nobel Prize for Literature, Thomas Mann, was born in Lübeck in 1875 and his family's former home is now the **Buddenbrookhaus** (**122 4190; www.buddenbrookhaus.de; Mengstrasse 4; adult/child under 18yr/concession €5/2/2.50; 11am-6pm Apr-Dec, to 5pm Jan-Mar**).

WITOLD SKRYPCZAK

Holstentor, Lübeck

HOLSTENTOR

Built in 1464 and looking so settled-in that it appears to sag, Lübeck's charming red-brick Holstentor **city gate** is a national icon. Its twin pointed cylindrical towers, leaning together across the stepped gable that joins them, captivated Andy Warhol, and have graced postcards, paintings, posters, marzipan souvenirs and even the old DM50 note, as you'll discover inside its **Museum Holstentor**.

Things you need to know: **Museum Holstentor (122 4129; adult/child under 18yr/concession €5/2/2.50; 10am-6pm Apr-Dec, 11am-5pm Tue-Sun Jan-Mar)**

Born in Danzig (now Gdansk), Poland, Günter Grass had been living just outside Lübeck for 13 years when he collected his Nobel Prize in 1999. But this postwar literary colossus initially trained as an artist, and has always continued to draw and sculpt. The **Günter Grass-Haus** (**Günter Grass House; 122 4192; www.guenter-grass-haus.de; Glockengiesserstrasse 21; adult/child under 18yr/concession €5/2/2.50; 10am-5pm Apr-Dec, 11am-5pm Jan-Mar**) is filled with the author's leitmotifs – flounders, rats, snails and eels – brought to life in bronze and charcoal, as well as in prose.

TOURS

The **Trave River** forms a moat around the Altstadt, and cruising it aboard a boat is the best way to get a feel for the city. You start off viewing an industrial harbour, but soon float past beautiful leafy surrounds.

Quandt-Linie (☎ 777 99; www.quandt-linie.de; adult/child under 15yr €10/6) Leaves from just south of the Holstenbrücke bridge. One-hour city tours leave every half-hour between 10am and 6pm from May to October (plus limited services November to April).

Stühff (☎ 707 8222; www.luebecker-barkassenfahrt.de, in German; adult/child under 12yr/concession €7.50/3.50/6.50) Runs boat tours up to six times daily (call ahead outside the summer months).

SLEEPING & EATING

Hotel Jensen (☎ 702 490; www.hotel-jensen.de; An der Obertrave 4-5; s €75-85, d €93-115) This old *Patrizierhaus* (mansion house) dating from the early 14th century overlooks the Salzspeicher across the Trave River. Alas, rooms aren't as characterful as the gabled exterior suggests, with modern and comfortable if somewhat pedestrian furnishings. Beautiful stained glass and tiling, however, adorn its excellent regional restaurant. Rates include breakfast.

Radisson SAS Senator Hotel (☎ 1420; www.senatorhotel.de; Willy-Brandt-Allee 6; s €131-179, d €142-198; P ⊠ ✲ 🖳 ᯤ ♿) The Lübeck option that really wows, the Senator resembles something from *War of the Worlds* with its three parallel rectangular wings cantilevered out into the Trave River.

our pick **Schiffergesellschaft** (☎ 767 76; Breite Strasse 2; mains €11.50-24.50; ⏰ 10am-11pm) Opened in 1535 as the dining room for the Blue Water Captains' Guild, Lübeck's best restaurant is a veritable museum. Ships' lanterns, original model ships dating from 1607 and orange Chinese-style lamps with revolving maritime silhouettes adorn the wood-lined rooms, which include an elevated banquet room up the back.

RBB/IMAGEBROKER

Schloss, Schwerin

Markgraf (☎ 706 0343; Fischergrube 18; mains €14.50-23.50, 3-/4-/5-course menu €33/41/48; ⌚ dinner Tue-Sun) White tablecloths and silverware are laid out under the chandeliers and black ceiling beams of this historic, ochre-coloured 14th-century house.

GETTING THERE & AWAY

AIR

Low-cost carriers **Ryanair** (www.ryanair.com) and **Wizzair** (www.wizzair.com) serve **Lübeck airport** (www.luebeckairport.com), which they euphemistically call Hamburg-Lübeck.

TRAIN

Lübeck has connections every hour to Hamburg (€18.50, 40 minutes), Kiel (€15.20, 1¼ hours) and Rostock (€22.90, two hours 20 minutes) with a change in Bad Kleinen.

MECKLENBURG–WESTERN POMERANIA

SCHWERIN

Picturesquely sited around seven lakes (or possibly more depending on how you tally them), the centrepiece of this engaging city is its Schloss (castle), built in the 14th century during the city's time as the former seat of the Grand Duchy of Mecklenburg.

Schwerin has shrugged off the 45 years of communist rule that followed WWII. Today there's an upbeat, vibrant energy on its streets that befits its role as the reinstated capital of Mecklenburg–Western Pomerania (beating Rostock for the mantle), and creative new shops and restaurants occupy its preserved 16th- to 19th-century buildings.

INFORMATION

Tourist-Information Schwerin (☎ 592 5212; www.schwerin.com; Rathaus, Am Markt 14; ⌚ 9am-7pm Mon-Fri, 10am-6pm Sat & Sun Apr-Oct, 9am-6pm Mon-Fri, 10am-4pm Sat & Sun Nov-Mar)

SIGHTS

Gothic and Renaissance turrets, Slavic onion domes, Ottoman features and terracotta Hanseatic step gables are among the mishmash of architectural styles that make up Schwerin's inimitable **Schloss** (☎ 525 2920; www.schloss-schwerin.de; adult/concession €4/2.50, audioguide €2; ⌚ 10am-6pm mid-Apr–mid-Oct, 10am-5pm Tue-Sun mid-Oct–mid-Apr), which is crowned by a main golden dome. Nowadays the Schloss earns its keep as the state's parliament building.

Schwerin derives its name from a Slavic castle known as Zuarin (Animal Pasture) that was formerly on the site, and which was first mentioned in 973 AD. In a niche over the main gate, the **statue of Niklot** depicts a Slavic prince, who was defeated by Heinrich der Löwe in 1160.

Inside the castle's opulently furnished rooms, highlights include a huge collection of Meissen porcelain.

Crossing the causeway south from the Burggarten brings you to the baroque **Schlossgarten** (Palace Garden), intersected by several canals.

In the Alter Garten, opposite the Schloss, the **Staatliches Museum** (State Museum Schwerin; ☎ 595 80; www.museum-schwerin.de; Alter Garten 3; adult/concession €6/4; ⌚ 10am-6pm Tue-Sun Apr-Oct, to 5pm Tue-Sun Nov-Mar) has a substantial collection spanning the ages. The 15 statues in the Ernst Barlach room provide a small taste of the sculptor's work. There's also a typically amusing and irreverent Marcel Duchamp collection. Those with more traditional tastes will prefer the oils by Lucas Cranach the

Elder, as well as works by Rembrandt and Rubens.

Above the Markt, the tall 14th-century Gothic **Dom** (cathedral; Am Dom 4; 11am-2pm Mon-Fri, 11am-4pm Sat, noon-3pm Sun) is a superb example of north German red-brick architecture.

The bustling Markt is home to the **Rathaus** (town hall) and the colonnaded neoclassical **Neues Gebäude** (1780–83), which houses a classy cafe. The latter is fronted by a lion monument honouring the town's founder, Heinrich der Löwe.

GETTING THERE & AWAY

Trains arrive regularly from Hamburg (from €21.50, one hour), Rostock (from €15.20, one hour), Stralsund (from €26.30, two hours) and Wismar (€6.90, 30 minutes), with less frequent direct connections to/from Berlin (€32.30, 2¾ hours). A ferry crosses the Pfaffenteich (€1) from late April to mid-October.

EBO/IMAGEBROKER

Alter Schwede, Wismar

WISMAR

With its gabled facades and cobbled streets, this small, photogenic city looks essentially Hanseatic. But although it joined the Hanseatic trading league in the 13th century, it spent most of the 16th and 17th centuries as part of Sweden. There are numerous reminders of this era all over town, including some striking buildings, a clock and a tomb. The entire Altstadt was Unesco-listed in 2002.

INFORMATION

Tourist-Information (☎ 251 3025; www.wismar.de, with English sections; Am Markt 11; 9am-6pm Mar-Dec, 9am-6pm Mon-Sat, 10am-4pm Sun Jan & Feb)

SIGHTS

Dominating the middle of the Markt is the 1602-built **Wasserkunst** (waterworks), an ornate, 12-sided well that supplied Wismar's drinking water until 1897. Today it remains the town's landmark.

Behind it, the red-brick **Alter Schwede** dates from 1380 and features a striking step buttress gable facade. Today it houses a restaurant and guesthouse, as well as a copy of one of the so-called 'Swedish Heads' (see p318).

The large **Rathaus** at the square's northern end was built between 1817 and 1819 and today houses the excellent **Rathaus Historical Exhibition** (adult/concession €1/0.50; 10am-6pm) in its basement. Displays include an original 15th-century *Wandmalerei* (mural) uncovered by archaeologists in 1985, a glass-covered medieval well, and the Wrangel tomb – the coffin of influential Swedish General

View over Straslund from Marienkirche

IF YOU LIKE...

If you like the Baltic atmosphere of **Wismar** (opposite), head to these seaside spots dotted along Mecklenburg–Western Pomerania's magnificent coastline:

- **Stralsund** (www.strasundtourismus.de) For an immense dose of Baltic culture, explore Stralsund's Unesco historic centre and learn about the Baltic, the North Sea and North Atlantic ecosystems at the Ozeanum, the snazzy harbourside aquarium. Like Wismar, this town was a Hanseatic League trading centre in the 14th and 15th centuries. It's also the gateway to Rügen (below).
- **Rügen Island** (www.ruegen.de or www.binz.de) Formerly the holiday choice for dedicated Nazis and later, GDR comrades, Germany's largest island is a mix of towering chalk cliffs, national parkland and a bird refuge. Prora, the former 2km-long workers' retreat built by Hitler, houses a fascinating documentation centre; and the island's main base, Binz, is a quintessential Baltic resort town.

Helmut V Wrangel and his wife, with outsized wooden figures carved on top.

Of the three great red-brick churches that once rose above the rooftops before WWII, only the enormous red-brick **St-Nikolai-Kirche** (admission by donation; 8am-8pm May-Sep, 10am-6pm Apr & Oct, 11am-4pm Nov-Mar), the largest of its kind in Europe, was left intact.

All that remains of the 13th-century **St-Marien-Kirche** (admission by donation; 10am-8pm Jul & Aug, 10am-6pm Mar-Jun & Sep-Dec, 10am-6pm Mon-Sat, 10am-4pm Sun Jan & Feb) is its great brick steeple (1339), which rises above the city.

The town's historical museum is in the Renaissance **Schabbellhaus** (☎ 282 350; www.schabbellhaus.de; Schweinsbrücke 8; adult/child under 18yr/concession €2/free/1; 10am-8pm Tue-Sun May-Oct, to 5pm Nov-Apr) in a former brewery (1571), just south of St-Nikolai-Kirche across the canal. Pride of place goes to one of the original **Swedish Heads** (the originals were two baroque busts of Hercules, once mounted on mooring posts at the harbour entrance).

Regional artist Christian Wetzel's four charming metal **pig statuettes** grace the **Schweinsbrücke** between the church and the museum.

TOURS

Clermont Reederei (☎ 224 646; www.reederei-clermont.de, in German) runs hour-long harbour cruises five times daily, May to September, leaving from the *Alter Hafen* (old harbour; adult/child €8/4); and boats, up to four times daily, to Poel Island (adult one way/return €8/14, bicycle €2/3), which despite its close proximity to Wismar has the atmosphere of a remote fishing community.

PSF/IMAGEBROKER

Bremen's Rathaus

GETTING THERE & AWAY

Trains travel every hour to/from Rostock (€10.30, 70 minutes) and Schwerin (€6.90, 40 minutes). The fastest connection to Hamburg (€26.30, 1¾ hours) requires a change in Bad Kleinen.

BREMEN

BREMEN CITY

Bremen has a highly justified reputation for being one of Germany's most outward-looking and hospitable places, and the people of Bremen seem to strike a very good balance between style, earthiness and good living.

INFORMATION

Tourist-Info Bremen (☎ 01805-101 030; www.bremen-tourism.de) City (Obernstrasse/Liebfrauenkirchhof; 🕑 10am-6.30pm Mon-Fri, to 4pm Sat & Sun) Hauptbahnhof (Hauptbahnhof; 🕑 9am-7pm Mon-Fri, 9.30am-6pm Sat & Sun)

SIGHTS & ACTIVITIES

With high, historic buildings looming over a relatively small space, Bremen's Markt is one of the most remarkable in northern Germany. The two towers of the 1200-year-old **Dom St Petri** (St Petri Cathedral; 🕑 10am-5pm Mon-Fri, 10am-2pm Sat, 2-5pm Sun) dominate the northeastern edge, beside the ornate and imposing **Rathaus**. Although the Rathaus was first erected in 1410, the Weser Renaissance balcony in the middle, crowned by three gables, was added between 1595 and 1618.

Bremers boast that the 13m-high **Knight Roland statue** (1404) situated in front of the Rathaus is Germany's tallest representation of this just, freedom-loving knight, and his belt buckle is certainly in an interesting position. However, it's the statue tucked away

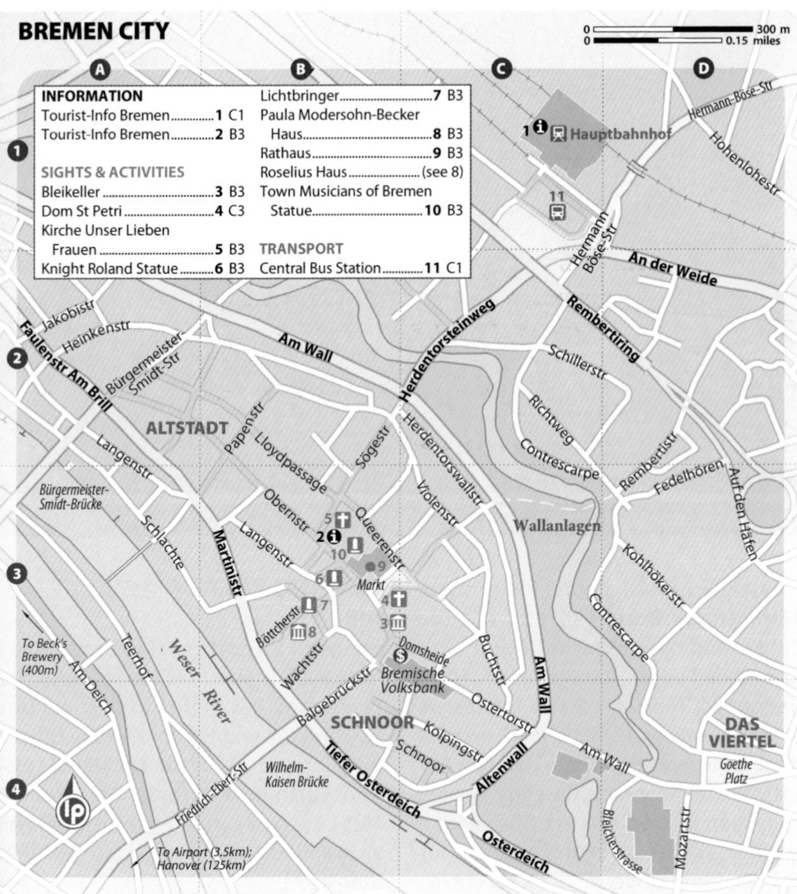

on the Rathaus' western side, in front of the **Kirche Unser Lieben Frauen** (Church of our Beloved Lady) that people more readily identify with this city. Sculptor Gerhard Marcks has cast the *Bremer Stadtmusikanten* in their famous pose – one on top of the other, on the shoulders of the donkey – in the **Town Musicians of Bremen statue** (1951).

What's most unusual about Dom St Petri is what lies beneath. In the incredibly dry air of its **Bleikeller** (**Lead Cellar; ☎ 365 0441; adult/concession €1.40/1; ⏰ 10am-5pm Mon-Fri, 10am-2pm Sat, noon-5pm Sun Easter-Oct**) corpses mummify, and you can still spy eight preserved bodies in open coffins here.

If Bremen's Markt is striking, the nearby Böttcherstrasse (1931) is unique. A charming lane with a golden entrance and staggered red-brick walls as you approach from the Markt, it's a superb example of expressionism.

Most of the street's design was by Bernhard Hoetger (1874–1959), including the **Lichtbringer** (Bringer of Light), the golden relief at the northern entrance, showing a scene from the Apocalypse with the Archangel Michael fighting a dragon.

PSF/IMAGEBROKER

Knight Roland statue (p318), Bremen

Hoetger worked around the existing, 16th-century **Roselius Haus**, but the **Paula Modersohn-Becker Haus**, with its rounded edges and wall reliefs, is his design too. Today these two houses are adjoining **museums** (☎ 336 5077; combined ticket adult/concession €5/3; 11am-6pm Tue-Sun). The first contains Roselius' private collection of medieval art. The second showcases the art of the eponymous painter, Paula Modersohn-Becker (1876–1907), an early expressionist and member of the Worpswede colony.

Germany has well over 1200 breweries, and about half of these are found in Bavaria, not the north. The beer of one brewery in particular, though, has long washed beyond the shores of Germany to establish itself as an international brand. You can see where the wares come from during a two-hour tour of the **Beck's brewery** (☎ 5094 5555; Am Deich; tours €9; tours 2pm & 3.30pm Thu & Fri, 12.30pm, 2pm, 3.30pm & 5pm Sat Jan-Apr, additionally 11am & 12.30pm Thu & Fri, 9.30am & 11am Sat May-Dec).

GETTING THERE & AWAY

AIR

Bremen's **airport** (☎ 559 50; www.airport-bremen.de) is about 3.5km south of the centre and has flights to destinations in Germany and Europe. Airline offices here include **Air Berlin** (☎ 0421-552 035) and **Lufthansa Airlines** (☎ 01803-803 803). Low-cost carrier **RyanAir** (www.ryanair.com) flies to Edinburgh and London Stansted.

TRAIN

Frequent trains go to Hamburg (€20.80 to €28, one hour to 1¼ hours), Hanover (€21 to €30, one hour to 80 minutes) and Cologne (€60, three hours).

BREMERHAVEN

'Give me your tired, your poor, your huddled masses,' invites the Statue of Liberty in New York harbour. Well, Bremerhaven is one place that most certainly did. Millions of those landing at Ellis Island departed from here, and the **Deutsches Auswandererhaus** (German Emigration

Centre; ☎ 902 200; www.dah-bremerhaven.de; Columbusstrasse 65; adult/child/concession/family €10.50/6/8.50/26; ⌚ 10am-6pm Mar-Oct, to 5pm Nov-Feb) now chronicles and commemorates some of their stories.

This is Europe's largest exhibition on emigration, and it does a superb job of conjuring up the experience. For added piquancy, it's located on the very spot where more than seven million people set sail, for the USA and other parts of the world, between 1830 and 1974.

The exhibition re-creates their travelling conditions, as you move from a 3rd-class passengers' waiting room, to dockside, to the gangway, into the bowels of a ship. You also stop in the huge 'Gallery of Seven Million', which contains emigrants' personal details (a few thousand of them) in pull-out drawers and tries to explain why people left home. Your electronic entry card contains the biographical details of one particular traveller, whom you can follow throughout the exhibition.

GETTING THERE & AWAY

Frequent trains connect Bremen and Bremerhaven (€10.60, 52 minutes), but consider buying a €20 return Niedersachsen Single ticket.

↘ GERMANY IN FOCUS

ARTS & ARCHITECTURE

REK/IMAGEBROKER

Sculpture by Henry Moore in front of the Alte Pinakothek (p103), Munich

Germany's meticulously creative population has made major contributions to international culture, particularly during the 18th century when the Saxon courts at Weimar and Dresden attracted some of the greatest minds of Europe. With such rich traditions to fall back on, inspiration has seldom been in short supply for the new generations of German artists, despite the upheavals of the country's recent history.

LITERARY GIANTS

The undisputed colossus of the German arts was Johann Wolfgang von Goethe: poet, dramatist, painter, politician, scientist, philosopher, landscape gardener and perhaps the last European to achieve the Renaissance ideal of excellence in many fields. His greatest work, the drama *Faust,* is the definitive version of the legend showing the archetypal human search for meaning and knowledge. Goethe's buddy Friedrich Schiller was a poet, dramatist and novelist known best for his dramatic cycle *Wallenstein,* based on the life of a treacherous general of the Thirty Years War who plotted to make himself arbiter of the empire. Schiller's other great play, *Wilhelm Tell,* dealt with the right of the oppressed to rise against tyranny.

Postwar literature was influenced by the politically focused Gruppe 47. This group included writers such as Günter Grass, winner of the 1999 Nobel Prize for Literature, whose modern classic, *Die Blechtrommel* (The Tin Drum), humorously follows German history through the eyes of a young boy who refuses to grow up; and Christa Wolf, an East German novelist who won high esteem throughout Germany. Wolf's 1963 story

Der geteilte Himmel (Divided Heaven) tells of a young woman whose fiancé abandons her for life in the west.

A wave of recent novelists has addressed modern history in a lighter fashion. *Helden Wie Wir* (Heroes Like Us) by Thomas Brussig, an eastern German, tells the story of a man whose penis brings about the collapse of the Berlin Wall; while Russian-born Wladimir Kaminer's books document stranger-than-fiction lives in the capital. Kaminer's *Russian Disco* has been translated into English.

Bitterness in the east over the reunification is given a full airing in the darkly satirical *New Lives*, by Ingo Schulze. The same subject matter is given a more entertaining take in *Settlement*, by Christoph Hein, which follows the rise of Germany's richest man.

CAUGHT ON FILM

Since the foundation of the UFA studios in Potsdam in 1917, Germany has had an active and successful film industry. Marlene Dietrich (1901–92) became the country's first international superstar and sex symbol, starting out in silent films and later moving to Hollywood. Director Fritz Lang also made a name for himself, with complex films such as *Metropolis* (1926) and *M* (1931).

During the Third Reich the arts were devoted mainly to propaganda, with grandiose projects and realist art extolling the virtues of German nationhood. The best-known Nazi-era director was Leni Riefenstahl (1902–2003), whose *Triumph of the Will* (1934), depicting the Nuremberg rallies, won great acclaim but later rendered her unemployable. The controversy surrounding her personal politics dogged her for much of her life.

The 1960s and 1970s saw a great revival of German cinema, spearheaded by energetic, politically aware young directors such as Rainer Werner Fassbinder, Wim Wenders, Volker Schlöndorff and Margarethe von Trotta. Most recently, Wolfgang Becker's GDR comedy *Good Bye Lenin!* (2003) was a surprise smash hit worldwide; and, not to be missed, Florian Henckel von Donnersmarck's *The Lives of Others* (2006) is a brilliant film about mistrust and betrayal in the old GDR. It won the Oscar for Best Foreign Film.

BEST GDR RETRO FILMS

Sonnenallee (Sun Alley; 1999) Set in a fantastical Wall-clad East Berlin in the 1970s.

Helden Wie Wir (Heroes Like Us; 1999) The protagonist recounts the story of his life, including how his penis allegedly led to the collapse of the Wall.

Halbe Treppe (Grill Point; 2001) Ellen and Chris in Frankfurt an der Oder are caught doing it.

Herr Lehmann (Berlin Blues; 2003) The Wall falls the day a bartender hits 30 in West Berlin's bohemian Kreuzberg district.

Good Bye, Lenin! (2003) A son tries to re-create the GDR for a bedridden mother whose health couldn't stand the shock of a fallen Wall.

CLASSICAL TO CLUB MUSIC

Forget brass bands and oompah music – few countries can claim the impressive musical heritage of Germany. Even a partial list of household names would have to include Johann Sebastian Bach, Georg Friedrich Händel, Ludwig van Beethoven,

Richard Strauss, Robert Schumann, Johannes Brahms, Felix Mendelssohn-Bartholdy and Richard Wagner, all of whom are celebrated in museums around the country.

Germany has also made significant contributions to the contemporary-music scene. Internationally renowned artists include punk icon Nina Hagen, '80s balloon girl Nena, and rock bands from the Scorpions to Die Toten Hosen and current darlings Wir sind Helden. Gothic and hard rock have a disproportionately large following in Germany, largely thanks to the success of death-obsessed growlers Rammstein.

For real innovation, though, German dance music is second to none, particularly in Frankfurt am Main and Berlin. Kraftwerk pioneered the original electronic sounds, which were then popularised in raves and clubs such as Berlin's Tresor in the early '90s. Paul van Dyk was among the first proponents of euphoric trance, which pushed club music firmly into the commercial mainstream. Germany has the largest electronic-music scene in the world, and DJs such as Ian Pooley, Westbam and Ellen Allien play all around the globe.

ROMANESQUE TO BAUHAUS

The scope of German architecture is so extraordinary you could make an entire trip based solely on the subject.

The first great wave of buildings came with the Romanesque period (800–1200), examples of which include Trier Cathedral, the churches of Cologne and the chapel of Charlemagne's palace in Aachen.

The Gothic style (1200–1500) is best viewed at Freiburg's Münster cathedral, Cologne's Dom (cathedral) and the Marienkirche in Lübeck. Red-brick Gothic structures are common in the north of Germany, with buildings such as Schwerin's Dom and Stralsund's Nikolaikirche.

ALFREDO MAIQUEZ

Kölner Dom (p230) and Hohenzollernbrücke, Cologne

For classic baroque, Balthasar Neumann's superb Residenz in Würzburg, the magnificent cathedral in Passau and the many classics of Dresden's old centre are must-sees. The neoclassical period of the 19th century was led by Karl Friedrich Schinkel, whose name crops up all over Germany.

In 1919 Walter Gropius founded the Bauhaus movement in an attempt to meld theoretical concerns of architecture with the practical problems faced by artists and craftspeople. The Bauhaus flourished in Dessau-Rosslau, but with the arrival of the Nazis, Gropius left for Harvard University.

Albert Speer was Hitler's favourite architect, known for his pompous neoclassical buildings and grand plans to change the face of Berlin. Most of his epic works ended up unbuilt or flattened by WWII.

Frankfurt shows Germany's take on the modern high-rise. For a glimpse of the future of German architecture, head to Potsdamer Platz, Leipziger Platz and the government area north of the Reichstag in Berlin, which are glitzy swaths of glass, concrete and chrome.

THE BEST

SZM/IMAGEBROKER

Kaiserthermen (p258), Trier

UNESCO WORLD HERITAGE SITES

- **Aachen Dom** (Cathedral; p249)
- **Berlin's Museumsinsel** (Museum Island; p66)
- **Cologne's Dom** (p230)
- **Lübeck** (p311)
- **Potsdam's parks and palaces** (p274)
- **Trier's Roman monuments, Dom and Liebfrauenkirche** (p257)

KANDINSKY & BEYOND

The Renaissance came late to Germany, but flourished once it took hold, replacing the predominant Gothic style. The draughtsman Albrecht Dürer of Nuremberg was one of the world's finest portraitists, as was the prolific Lucas Cranach the Elder, who worked in Wittenberg for more than 45 years. The baroque period brought great sculpture, including works by Andreas Schlüter in Berlin; while romanticism produced some of Germany's most famous paintings, best exemplified by Caspar David Friedrich and Otto Runge.

At the turn of the 20th century, expressionism established itself with great names such as Swiss-born Paul Klee and the Russian-born painter Wassily Kandinsky, who were also associated with the Bauhaus design school. By the 1920s art had become more radical and political, with artists such as George Grosz, Otto Dix and Max Ernst exploring the new concepts of Dada and surrealism. Käthe Kollwitz is one of the era's few major female artists, known for her social-realist drawings.

The only works encouraged by the Nazis were of the epic style of propaganda artists such as Mjölnir; nonconforming artists such as sculptor Ernst Barlach and painter Emil Nolde were declared 'degenerate' and their pieces destroyed or appropriated for secret private collections.

Since 1945 abstract art has been a mainstay of the German scene, with key figures such as Joseph Beuys, Monica Bonvicini and Anselm Kiefer achieving worldwide reputations. In Leipzig, a Neue Leipziger Schule (New Leipzig School) of artists has emerged recently and achieved success at home and abroad – figurative painters such as Neo Rauch are generating much acclaim.

BRECHT TO FORSYTHE

In the 1920s Berlin was the theatrical capital of Germany; its most famous practitioner was the poet and playwright Bertolt Brecht (1898–1956). Brecht introduced Marxist concepts into his plays, aiming to encourage moral debate by detaching the audience from what was happening on stage.

During the Nazi occupation of Germany, the arts were repressed – they were strictly monitored and by and large focused on exemplifying nationalism, racial purity, militarism, power and obedience. In the 1950s Heiner Müller (1929–95) – a Marxist who was critical of the reality of the GDR – became unpalatable in both Germanys, but he still earned an avant-garde label in the 1980s.

Today Berlin once again has the most dynamic theatre scene in the country, as Volksbühne director Frank Castorf vies with Schaubühne head Thomas Ostermeier to capture the attention of young audiences neglected by the major stages, choosing mainly modern, provocative works. Dance, too, is undergoing something of a renaissance – although this is primarily in Frankfurt. American William Forsythe has put together what is possibly the world's most innovative dance troupe, the Forsythe Company (www.theforsythecompany.de), which tours almost constantly – they peform often in Dresden.

LEFT: CHR/IMAGEBROKER; RIGHT: BAI/IMAGEBROKER

Left: Installation on Bebelplatz (p66), Berlin; Right: Joseph Beuys piece at the Pinakothek der Moderne (p104), Munich

CHRISTMAS MARKETS

MSZ/IMAGEBROKER

Christmas market at Konstanz (p223)

In late November clusters of miniature chalets erupt in cities and towns across Germany. These temporary villages lay claim to town squares, stand in the shadow of Unesco-designated cathedrals, squeeze into busy shopping areas or erect swanky tents. It all means one thing: the *Christkindlmarkt* (Christmas market) is in town.

Take *Glühwein* (mulled wine); add *Lebkuchen* (gingerbread), classic nutcrackers and shimmering ornaments; place them in a fairy-tale village of wooden stalls and *ta da!*, it's obvious why Germany's Christmas markets are such popular social affairs and tourist magnets. Nearly every sizeable town across the country has its own market, and larger cities often have a dozen or so, each with their own unique personality. Berlin's Schloss Charlottenburg is backdrop to a sprawling collection of goodies, while the Gendarmenmarkt hosts a more swanky affair (some of the best restaurants in town set up mini-restaurants, with heating) and charges admission (usually a euro or two). Cologne holds several markets in town; its best sits adjacent to the gleaming Dom (cathedral).

But two markets draw the most attention (and crowds): Nuremberg's highlight is its opening event when the Christmas Angel, played by a local girl, reads a prologue from the balcony of the Nuremberg Cathedral; while Dresden's *Striezelmarkt* is Germany's oldest Christmas market (1434). *Striezelmarkt* also marks a festival on the second Saturday of advent, when a 3000kg *Striezel* (Dresden's name for *Stollen*, a moist fruit cake served around the holidays) is paraded through the old city until a baker cuts it with a ceremonial 1.6m knife.

FAMILY TRAVEL

THOMAS STANKIEWICZ/PHOTOLIBRARY

Hiking in Bavaria

(Tiny) hands down, travelling to Germany with tots can be child's play, especially if you keep a light schedule and involve the little ones in the day-to-day trip planning. Plus they're a great excuse if you secretly yearn to ride roller coasters or go ape in a zoo.

THE LOW-DOWN

Germany is a very family-friendly destination and most places are happy to cater to kids, whether with smaller dinner portions, a high chair or special attention on a tour, or by making up a special bed or giving them a little extra attention.

Practically every accommodation option can provide cots (cribs), though sometimes for a small charge. Some properties, especially those in the countryside, don't charge any extra for small children staying in their parents' room without requiring extra bedding. In vehicles, children's safety seats are compulsory and available through car-hire companies (make sure to book them in advance). Taxis are not equipped with car seats.

Baby food, infant formulas, soy and cow's milk and disposable nappies (diapers) are widely available in supermarkets and pharmacies (drugstores). Breast feeding in public is commonly practised, especially in the cities, but most women are discreet about it. Most tourist offices can direct you to local resources for children's facilities and babysitters. Agentur Mary Poppins (www.agenturmarypoppins.de, in German) offers babysitting across nine cities; in Berlin, try Babysitter Express (www.babysitter-express.de).

KIDDING AROUND

It's easy to keep the kids entertained no matter where you travel in Germany. The great outdoors, of course, yields endless possibilities. Germany's legend-shrouded castles, including the stately Wartburg in Thuringia or dreamy Schloss Neuschwanstein in Bavaria, are sure to fuel the imagination of many a Harry Potter fan. Older kids might get a kick out of Hollywood magic at Filmpark Babelsberg in Potsdam near Berlin.

Parks and playgrounds are ubiquitous, or try such kid-friendly museums as the Schokoladen Museum (Chocolate Museum) in Cologne; the Deutsches Technikmuseum (Technology museum) in Berlin; and Wolfsburg's Autostadt, home to the Volkswagen Beetle. Even the world's largest beer festival is kid-friendly: those jolly beer tents at Munich's Oktoberfest are surrounded by over-the-top amusement rides, including the famous Olympialooping, which loops around five dizzying times.

THE BEST

ARCO IMAGES/ALAMY

Pied Piper of Hamelin parade, Hamelin (p188)

CHILDRENS ACTIVITIES

- **Scooting down the Schauinsland** (p221)
- **Canoeing in Altmühltal Nature Park** (p159)
- **Puppet shows at the Augsburger Puppenkiste** (p139)
- **The Pied Piper Trail, Hamelin** (p188)

ROOSTERS WOKE ME UP

A holiday on a working farm *(Urlaub auf dem Bauernhof)* is inexpensive and a great opportunity for the family to get close to nature in relative comfort. Accommodation ranges from bare-bones rooms with shared facilities to fully-furnished holiday flats. A variety of farm types are on offer, including organic, dairy and equestrian farms, as well as wine estates.

In summer you can also kip on clean, sweet hay at about a dozen *Heuhotels* (www.strohtour.de, in German); bring your own sleeping bag. Surrounded by glorious countryside, these family-friendly barns offer an authentic farm experience, often with animals that kids can pet and home-grown goodies such as fresh eggs and apple juice at breakfast.

To learn more about farm holidays, check www.landtourismus.de, www.bauernhofurlaub-deutschland.de or www.bauernhofurlaub.com (in German).

THE NITTY GRITTY

- **Cots/Cribs** Available upon request in midrange and top-end hotels; best to reserve in advance
- **Highchairs & Kids' menu** (*Kindermenü*) Standard in most restaurants
- **Nappies/diapers** Easy to buy in supermarkets and pharmacies
- **Changing facilities** Rare; best bring a towel to be safe
- **Strollers** Bring your own

GERMAN CUISINE

RUSSELL MOUNTFORD

Various wursts on display in Frankfurt

In the international imagination, German cuisine is often just something – usually a wurst (sausage) – to accompany its superlative beer. Relying heavily on meat, cabbage and potato, the country's traditional cuisine has a not entirely undeserved reputation as gut clinging and banal.

But, as in Britain, Germany has redeemed itself gastronomically in the past decade. Top chefs have been experimenting with time-honoured dishes in a wave that's referred to as the Neue Deutsche Küche (New German Cuisine), and *multi-kulti* (multicultural) influences – ranging from Turkish to Mediterranean to Asian – have put baba ganoush, burritos and curries on menus.

As a rule, you still won't find the exuberant love of excellent food – and the ability to produce it – permeating every neighbourhood haunt as you will in some other European locales, such as, say, Italy. But exceptions do abound in urban centres like Berlin and Hamburg, and the global trend to source local, seasonal ingredients is gaining strength here, too. The *Imbiss* fast-food stall, however, is a ubiquitous phenomenon, and eating a wurst or kebab (while standing) is a simple, quintessential German experience.

When ordering food in some parts of the country, sometimes confidence in your little knowledge of German can be a dangerous thing: don't expect to be given half a chicken when you order a *Halve Hahn* in Cologne – it's actually a rye-bread roll with gouda cheese, gherkin and mustard. *Kölscher Kaviar* is similarly confusing – it's not caviar, but black pudding. And *Nordseekrabben* in Hamburg? They're small prawns…of course.

SPARGELZEIT

Asparagus season kicks off with the harvesting of the first crop in mid-April and lasts until 24 June – the feast day of St John the Baptist – which is fitting, given the almost religious intensity with which this 'king of vegetables' is celebrated. Germans spend the season devouring great quantities (mostly white) of the long stalks and many restaurants feature special asparagus menus.

SAUSAGE COUNTRY

In the Middle Ages German peasants found a way to package and disguise animals' less appetising bits – the birth of the wurst. Today it's a noble and highly respected element of German cuisine, with strict rules determining the authenticity of wurst varieties. In some cases, as with the finger-sized Nuremberg sausage, regulations even ensure offal no longer enters the equation.

While there are more than 1500 sausage species, all are commonly served with bread and a sweet *(süss)* or spicy *(scharf)* mustard *(Senf)*. Bratwurst, served countrywide, is made from minced pork, veal and spices, and is cooked in different ways (boiled in beer, baked with apples and cabbage, stewed in a casserole or simply grilled or barbecued).

The availability of other sausages differs regionally. A *Thüringer* is long, thin and spiced, while a *Wiener* is what hot-dog fiends call a frankfurter. *Blutwurst* is blood sausage (not to be confused with black pudding, which is *Rotwurst*), *Leberwurst* is liver sausage, and *Knackwurst* is lightly tickled with garlic.

Saxony is all about the brain sausage *(Bregenwurst)*, Bavaria sells white rubbery *Weisswurst*, made from veal, and Berliners are addicted to the *Currywurst* (slices of sausage topped with curry powder and ketchup).

A CRUSTY ROLL

In exile in California in 1941, German playwright Bertolt Brecht confessed that what he missed most about his homeland was the bread. German bread is a world-beater, in a league of its own. Its 300 varieties are tasty and textured, often mixing wheat and rye flour.

FOODFOLIO/IMAGELIBRARY

Crusty bread

'Black' rye bread *(Schwarzbrot)* is actually brown, but a much darker shade than the slightly sour *Bauernbrot* – divine with a slab of butter. Pumpernickel bread is steam-cooked instead of baked, making it extra moist, and actually is black. *Vollkorn* means wholemeal, while bread coated in sunflower seeds is *Sonnenblumenbrot*. If you insist on white bread *(Weissbrot)*, the Germans have that, too.

Fresh bread rolls (*Brötchen* in the north, *Semmel* in Bavaria, *Wecken* in the rest of southern Germany) can be covered in poppy seeds *(Mohnbrötchen)*, cooked with sweet raisins *(Rosinenbrötchen)*, sprinkled with salt *(Salzstangel)* or treated in dozens of other, different ways.

Brezeln are traditional pretzels covered in rock salt.

MOVING ON TO POTATOES

Germans are almost as keen as Russians on the potato. The *Kartoffel* is not only Vegetable Nummer Eins in any meat-and-three-veg dish, it can also be incorporated into any course of a meal, from potato soup *(Kartoffelsuppe)* as a starter, to potato waffles *(Kartoffelwaffeln)* or potato pancakes *(Reibekuchen)* as a sweet treat.

In between, you can try *Himmel und Erde* (Heaven and Earth), a dish of mashed potatoes and stewed apples served with black pudding; or potato-based *Klösse* dumplings.

THE BEST

KOCH, KARSTEN/ALAMY

Pier 51 (p187), Hanover

EATS

- **Brauerei im Füchschen** (p245) Earthy Rhenish hospitality
- **Cookies Cream** (p79) Meat-free gourmet fare
- **Eisgrubbräu** (p210) Hearty German classics
- **Délice** (p210) Stuttgart's Michelin-starred restaurant.
- **Pier 51** (p187) Culinary fireworks with a view.
- **Villa Mittermeier** (p132) Top-end dining astride the Romantic Road.

IT'S PICKLED CABBAGE

Finally comes a quintessential German side dish that many outside the country find impossible to fathom: sauerkraut. Before the 2006 FIFA World Cup one football magazine suggested, with typical abrasiveness: 'It's pickled cabbage; don't try to make it sound interesting.' Okay, we won't. It's shredded cabbage, doused in white-wine vinegar and slowly simmered. But if you haven't at least tried *Rotkohl* (the red-cabbage version), you don't know what you're missing. Braising the cabbage with sliced apples and wine turns it into *Bayrischkraut* or *Weinkraut*.

WHEN IN THE NORTH

Regional variations in German cuisine are significant, particularly if you compare the north, where root vegetables such as potatoes predominate and there's a much greater focus on fish, to the southern states, which feature many pork and veal dishes, accompanied by noodles or dumplings. Towards the country's borders, French, Scandinavian and even Slavic flavours sneak into dishes – but it's a subtle difference and the taste usually remains recognisably German.

KAFFEE UND KUCHEN

Germans *love* sweets, but they tend to exercise their sweet tooth over *Kaffee und Kuchen* (coffee and cakes) more than they do after a meal. After all, this is the country that brought the world the sugary, creamy, calorie-laden, over-the-top *Schwarzwälder Kirschtorte* (Black Forest gateau), which is a perfectly acceptable indulgence on your afternoon coffee break. When Germans do eat desserts (*Nachspeisen* or *Nachtische*) after a savoury plate, they are usually light affairs, such as custard and fruit, *Rote Grütze* (a tart fruit compote topped with vanilla sauce), ice cream or fruit salad.

Christmas brings its own specialities. *Stollen* is a spiced cake loaded with sultanas, raisins and candied peel, sprinkled with icing sugar and occasionally spruced up inside with a ball of marzipan. It's rarely baked in German homes today (although when it is, it's exquisite), but you'll find it in abundance in Christmas markets – *Stollen* from Dresden is reputedly the best.

THE BEST

ABR/IMAGEBROKER

Lebkuchen (gingerbread) at a Christmas market

MOREISH CONFECTIONS

- **Lebkuchen** (gingerbread) Available in spades at Christmas markets, year-round at many bakeries
- **Nürnberger Lebkuchen** Nuremberg's soft cookies with nuts, fruit peel, honey and spices
- **Aachener Printen** Aachen's crunchy spiced cookie, similar to gingerbread
- **Lübecker Marzipan** A blend of almonds and sugar – from Lübeck

GERMANS

OLF/IMAGEBROKER

A bathing ship on the Spree River, Berlin (p62)

The German state of mind is always a favourite for speculation – two 20th-century wars and the memory of the Jewish Holocaust are reasons. Throw in the chilling razor's edge of Cold War division, a modern juggernaut economy that draws half of Europe in its wake and pumps more goods into the world economy than any other, and a crucial geographical location at the crossroads of Europe – and continued fascination becomes understandable.

CULTURE

It pays to ignore the stereotypes, jingoism and those occasional headlines at home describing Germany in military terms – and maybe even forgive Germans for the way they go about life in such an orderly, systematic fashion, or conduct conversations in such a serious manner even in social settings (German's don't tend to engage in small talk). Sometimes it helps to see the country through its regional nuances. Germany was very slow to become a nation, so, if you look closely, you will begin to notice many different local cultures within the one set of borders. You will also find that it's one of Europe's most multicultural countries, with Turkish, Greek, Italian, Russian and Balkan influences.

THE FORMER EAST

Around 15 million people today live in the former GDR, a part of Germany where until 1989 travel was restricted, the state was almighty, and life was secure – but also strongly regulated – from the cradle to the grave. Not surprisingly, many former East Germans are still coming to terms with a more competitive, unified Germany. According to one poll conducted by the Emnid research group, 49% of eastern Germans say the GDR had more good sides than bad, and 8% say they were happier or lived better at that time.

The former East Germany continues to lose people hand over fist. In the past badly affected regions have tried to lure their youngest and brightest back from cities such as Munich and Stuttgart with novel ideas such as a 'returnees package' – containing things like mouse pads, internet links and local newspaper subscriptions – but the trend is irreversible. According to some estimates, Saxony-Anhalt and the Chemnitz region can expect to lose a quarter of their population by 2030, and Thuringia will shrink by about 20%.

CANDID

Germans generally fall within the mental topography of northern Europe and are sometimes described as culturally 'low context'. That means Germans like to pack what they mean right into the words they use rather than hint or suggest. Facing each other squarely in conversation, firm handshakes, and a hug or a kiss on the cheek among friends are par for the course.

DIRNDLS TO STILETTOS

Most Germans look fondly upon the flourishing practice of chimney sweeps (some of them women these days) donning traditional attire – pitch-black suits and top hats – in towns and villages. And a young Bavarian from, say, a financial firm, might don the dirndl (traditional Bavarian skirt and blouse ensemble) around Oktoberfest time and swill like a rollicking peasant. Monday they'll be soberly back at the desk, in their stylish stilettos, crunching the numbers like it was all just good fun – which it was, of course.

NEX/IMAGEBROKER

Women dressed in dirndls

NAKED

For all this popular tradition, Germans are not prudish. Nude bathing on beaches and naked mixed saunas are both commonplace, although many women prefer single-sex saunas. Wearing your swimming suit or covering yourself with a towel in the sauna is definitely *not* the done thing.

GET OUTSIDE

CHT/IMAGEBROKER

Berchtesgaden National Park (p146), Bavaria

No matter what kind of outdoor activity gets you off that couch, you'll be able to pursue it in this land of lakes, rivers, mountains and forests. There's plenty to do year-round, with each season offering its own special delights, be it hiking among spring wildflowers, swimming in a lake warmed by the summer sun, biking among a kaleidoscope of autumn foliage or celebrating winter by schussing through deep powder. Wherever you go, you'll find outfitters and local operators eager to gear you up.

STRAP ON YOUR HELMET

Germany is superb cycling territory, whether you're after a leisurely spin along the beach, an adrenalin-fuelled mountain exploration or a multiday bike-touring adventure. Practically every town and region has a network of signposted bike routes; most towns have at least one bike-hire station (often at or near the train station).

Germany is also criss-crossed by more than 200 long-distance trails covering 70,000km, making it ideal for *Radwandern* (bike touring). Routes are well signposted and are typically a combination of lightly travelled back roads, forestry tracks and paved highways with dedicated bike lanes. Many traverse nature reserves, meander along rivers or venture into steep mountain terrain.

For inspiration and route planning, check out www.germany-tourism.de/cycling, which provides (in English) an overview of routes and free downloads of route maps and descriptions.

For on-the-road navigating, the best maps are those published by the national cycling organization Allgemeiner Deutscher Fahrrad Club (ADFC). Its regional maps for day and weekend tours, and cycle tour maps for longer excursions, are available in book stores, at tourist offices and online (www.adfc.de, in German). ADFC also publishes a useful online directory called Bett & Bike (www.bettundbike.de, in German), which lists thousands of bicycle-friendly hotels, inns and hostels.

HIKING & NORDIC WALKING

Got wanderlust? Germany is perfect for exploring on foot. Ramble through romantic river valleys, hike among fragrant pines, bag Alpine peaks or simply go for a walk by the lake or through the dunes. Many of the nicest trails traverse national and nature parks or biosphere reserves. Nordic walking – where you strut with poles just like a cross-country skier – has taken Germany by storm in recent years.

Trails are usually well signposted, sometimes with symbols quaintly painted on tree trunks. To find a route matching your fitness level and time frame, pick the brains of local tourist-office staff, who can also supply you with maps and tips.

The www.wanderbares-deutschland.de is an excellent resource – it features comprehensive information on dozens of walking trails throughout Germany. It's mostly in German, but some routes are also detailed in English.

THE BEST

ANDREW BAIN

Cycling the Bodensee-Königssee Radweg

LONG-DISTANCE CYCLING ROUTES

- **Altmühltal Radweg** (190km) Easy to moderate; Rothenburg ob der Tauber to Beilngries, following the Altmühl River through the Altmühltal Nature Park.
- **Bodensee-Königssee Radweg** (414km) Moderate; Lindau to Berchtesgaden along the foot of the Alps with magnificent views of the mountains, lakes and forests.
- **Donauradweg** (434km) Easy to moderate; Neu-Ulm to Passau – a delightful riverside trip along one of Europe's great streams.
- **Romantische Strasse** (359km) Easy to moderate; Würzburg to Füssen – one of the nicest ways to explore Germany's most famous holiday route; can get busy during the summer peak season.

MOUNTAINEERING

'Climb every mountain…' the Mother Superior belts out in the *Sound of Music*, and the Bavarian Alps – the centre of mountaineering in Germany – will give you plenty of opportunity to do just that. You can venture out on day treks or plan multiday clambers from hut to hut – as long as you keep in mind that hiking in the Alps is no walk in the park. You need to be in reasonable condition and come equipped with the right shoes,

KPW/IMAGEBROKER

Cross-country skiing

gear and topographic maps or GPS. Trails can be narrow, steep and have icy patches, even in summer.

The **Deutscher Alpenverein** (**DAV; German Alpine Club; ☎ 089-140 030; www.alpenverein.de, in German**) is a goldmine of information on hiking and mountaineering and has local chapters in practically every German town. It also maintains hundreds of Alpine mountain huts, many of them open to the public, where you can spend the night and get a meal. Local DAV chapters also organise various courses (climbing, mountaineering etc), as well as guided treks, with which you can link up.

HITTING THE SLOPES

Modern lifts, primed ski slopes from 'Sesame Street' to 'Death Wish', solitary cross-country trails through untouched nature, cosy mountain huts, steaming mulled wine, hearty dinners by a crackling fire – all are hallmarks of a German skiing holiday.

The Bavarian Alps, only an hour's drive south of Munich, offer the best downhill slopes and most reliable snow conditions. The most famous resort town here is, of course, Garmisch-Partenkirchen (p146), which hosted the 1936 Olympic Games and is popular with the international set.

There's also plenty of skiing, snowboarding and cross-country skiing to be done elsewhere in the country, where the mountains may not soar as high as the Alps, but assets include cheaper prices, smaller crowds and a less frenetic atmosphere. Among Germany's lower mountain ranges, the Bavarian Forest (p165) has the most reliable snow levels, with plenty of good downhill action on the Grosser Arber mountain. Cross-country skiing is especially wonderful in the Bavarian Forest National Park.

HISTORY

SZM/IMAGEBROKER

Port Nigra (p257), Trier

Events in Germany have often dominated the European stage, but the country itself is a relatively recent invention: for most of its history Germany has been a patchwork of semi-independent principalities and city-states, occupied first by the Roman Empire, then the Holy Roman Empire and finally the Austrian Habsburgs. Perhaps because of this, many Germans retain a strong regional identity despite the momentous national events that have occurred since.

TRIBES & THE ROMANS

The early inhabitants of Germany were Celts and, later, the Germanic tribes. In the Iron Age (from around 800 BC), Germanic tribes on the North German Plain and in the Central Uplands lived on the fringes of Celtic regions and were influenced by that culture, but without ever melting into it.

The Romans fought pitched battles with the Germanic tribes from about 100 BC. The Germanic tribes east of the Rhine and the Romans fought for control of territory across

800–300 BC

Germanic tribes and Celts inhabit large parts of northern and central Germany.

AD 9

The Battle of the Teutoburg Forest halts Roman expansion eastwards.

482

Clovis becomes king of the Franks and lays the foundations for a Frankish Reich.

STEVE RAYMER/CORBIS

Wax seals on a German trade document, as used by the Hanseatic League

the river until AD 9, when the Roman general Varus lost three legions – about 20,000 men – in the bloody Battle of the Teutoburg Forest, and the Romans abandoned their plans to extend eastwards. By AD 300, four main groups of tribes had formed along the Rhine and the Danube: Alemans, Franks, Saxons and Goths.

THE FRANKISH REICH

The Frankish Reich became Europe's most important political power in medieval times. This was due, in part, to the Merovingian king Clovis (r 482–511), who united diverse populations.

When fighting broke out among aristocratic clans in the 7th century, the Merovingians were replaced by the Carolingians, who introduced hierarchical Church structures. From his grandiose residence in Aachen, Charlemagne (r 768–814) conquered Lombardy, won territory in Bavaria, waged a 30-year war against the Saxons in the north and was crowned Kaiser (emperor) by the pope in 800. The cards were reshuffled in the 9th century, when attacks by Danes, Saracens and Magyars threw the eastern portion of Charlemagne's empire into turmoil; four dominant duchies emerged – Bavaria, Franconia, Swabia and Saxony.

Charlemagne's burial in Aachen Dom turned a court chapel into a major pilgrimage site. The Treaty of Verdun (843) saw a gradual carve-up of the Reich and, when Louis

486

Clovis defeats the Romans in the Battle of Soissons in France.

732

Frankish king Charles Martel wins the Battle of Tours (in France) and stops the progress of Muslims into Western Europe.

768–814

The Carolingian Charlemagne is crowned Kaiser and under him the Frankish Reich grows in power and extent.

the Child (r 900–11) – a grandson of Charlemagne's brother – died heirless, the East Frankish (ie German) dukes elected a king from their own ranks. The first German monarchy was created.

EARLY MIDDLE AGES

In the early Middle Ages dynasties squabbled and intrigued over territorial spoils, while a toothless, Roman-inspired central state watched on helplessly. The symbolic heart of power was Aachen Dom, which hosted the coronation and burial of dozens of German kings from 936. In 962 Otto I renewed Charlemagne's pledge to protect the papacy and the pope reciprocated with a pledge of loyalty to the Kaiser. This made the Kaiser and pope acrimonious bedfellows for the next 800 years and created the Holy Roman Empire, a nebulous state that survived until 1806.

Under Friedrich I Barbarossa (r 1152–90), Aachen assumed the role of Reich capital and was granted liberty in 1165, the year Charlemagne was canonised. Meanwhile, Heinrich der Löwe (Henry the Lion) extended influence eastwards in campaigns to Germanise and convert the Slavs who populated much of today's eastern Germany. Heinrich was very well connected, and founded not only Braunschweig but Munich and Lübeck, too.

The Reich gained territory to the east and in Italy, but soon fell apart. At this time kings were being elected by *Kurfürsten* (prince-electors) but crowned kaiser by the pope – a system that made an unwilling lackey out of a kaiser. In 1245 the Reich plunged into an era called the Great Interregnum, or the Terrible Time, when central authority collapsed in a political heap.

Although the central Reich was only a shadow of its former self, expansion eastwards continued unabated.

THE HOUSE OF HABSBURG

In 1273 a Habsburg dynasty emerged from the royal heap, mastered the knack of the politically expedient arranged marriage, and dominated European affairs until the 20th century. The Declaration of Rhense (1338) dispensed with the pope's role in crowning a Kaiser. Now the king, elected by the *Kurfürsten*, was automatically Kaiser. In 1356 the Golden Bull set out precise rules for elections and defined the relationship between the Kaiser and the princes. It was an improvement, but the Kaiser was still dancing to the tune of the princes.

Dancing, however, was the last thing on the minds of ordinary Germans. They battled with panic lynching, pogroms against Jews and labour shortages – all sparked off by the plague (1348–50) that wiped out 25% of Europe's population. While death gripped the (Ger)man on the street, universities were being established all over the country around this time.

911

Louis the Child dies and Frankish dukes bypass Charles the Simple in favour of their own monarch.

962

Otto I is crowned Holy Roman Emperor by the pope, reaffirming the precedent established by Charlemagne.

1152

Friedrich I Barbarossa is crowned in Aachen.

A QUESTION OF FAITH

The religious fabric of Germany was cut from a pattern created in the 16th-century Reformation. In 1517 Martin Luther (1483–1546) made public his *Ninety-Five Theses,* which questioned the papal practice of selling indulgences to exonerate sins. Threatened with excommunication, Luther refused to recant, broke from the Catholic Church and was banned by the Reich.

It was not until 1555 that the Catholic and Lutheran churches were ranked as equals, thanks to Karl V (r 1520–58), who signed the Peace of Augsburg (1555), allowing princes to decide the religion of their principality. The more secular northern principalities adopted Lutheran teachings, while the clerical lords in the south, southwest and Austria stuck with Catholicism.

But the religious issue degenerated into the bloody Thirty Years War, which Sweden and France had joined by 1635. Calm was restored with the Peace of Westphalia (1648), but it left the Reich a nominal, impotent state. Switzerland and the Netherlands gained formal independence, France won chunks of Alsace and Lorraine, and Sweden helped itself to the mouths of the Elbe, Oder and Weser Rivers.

THE ENLIGHTENMENT & THE INDUSTRIAL AGE

In the 18th century the Enlightenment breathed new life into Germany, inspiring a rabble of autocratic princes to build stunning grand palaces and gardens across the German lands. Meanwhile, Johann Sebastian Bach and Georg Friedrich Händel were ushered on stage and a wave of *Hochkultur* (high culture) swept through society's top sliver.

Brandenburg-Prussia became an entity to be reckoned with, kick-started by the acquisition of former Teutonic Knights' territories and assisted by Hohenzollern king Friedrich Wilhelm I (the Soldier King) and his son, Friedrich II (r 1740–86). After the Seven Years' War (1756–63) with Austria, Brandenburg-Prussia annexed Silesia and sliced up Poland.

At the behest of French emperor Napoleon Bonaparte, an imperial deputation secularised and reconstituted German territory between 1801 and 1803. In 1806 the Confederation of the Rhine eradicated about 100 principalities. Sniffing the end of the Holy Roman Empire, Kaiser Franz II (r 1792–1806) packed his bags and abdicated the throne. That same year Brandenburg-Prussia fell to the French, but humiliating defeat prompted reforms that brought it closer to civil statehood: Jews were granted equality and bonded labour was abolished.

In 1815 at the Congress of Vienna Germany was reorganised into a confederation of 35 states and a Reichstag (legislative assembly) was established in Frankfurt. The ineffective Reichstag poorly represented the most populous states and failed to rein in Austro-Prussian rivalry.

1241	1273	1356
Hamburg and Lübeck create the basis for the powerful Hanseatic League.	The House of Habsburg begins its rise to become Europe's most powerful dynasty.	The Golden Bull formalises the election of the Kaiser.

By the mid-19th century the engines of the industrial age were purring across the country. A newly created urban proletarian movement fuelled calls for central government, while the Young Germany movement of satirists lampooned the powerful of the day and called for a central state.

Berlin, along with much of the southwest, erupted in riots in 1848, prompting German leaders to bring together Germany's first ever freely elected parliamentary delegation in Frankfurt's Paulskirche. Austria, meanwhile, broke away from Germany, came up with its own constitution and promptly relapsed into monarchism. As revolution fizzled in 1850, Prussian king Friedrich Wilhelm IV drafted his own constitution, which would remain in force until 1918.

THE BEST

AKG-IMAGES/ALAMY

Germany declares war on Russia, 1914

BEST HISTORIC READS

- **Heinrich the Fowler: Father of the Ottoman Empire** (Mirella Patzer) Brings 10th - century Germany to life in a blend of history and fiction
- **The Great War 1914–18** (Marc Ferro) A compelling account of WWI
- **This Way for the Gas, Ladies and Gentlemen** (Tadeusz Borowski) A set of short stories, by an author who spent time in concentration camps
- **Stasiland** (Anna Funder) An Australian journalist's account of interviewing former Stasi men in the 1990s

'HONEST OTTO' VON BISMARCK

The creation of a unified Germany with Prussia at the helm was the glorious ambition of Otto von Bismarck (1815–98), a former member of the Reichstag and Prussian prime minister. An old-guard militarist, he used intricate diplomacy and a series of wars with neighbours Denmark and France to achieve his aims. Germany was unified in 1871, with Berlin the proud capital of Western Europe's largest state. The Prussian king was crowned Kaiser of the Reich – a bicameral, constitutional monarchy – at Versailles on 18 January 1871 and Bismarck became its 'Iron Chancellor'.

Bismarck's power was based on the support of merchants and *Junker,* a noble class of nonknighted landowners. An ever-skilful diplomat and power broker, Bismarck achieved much through a dubious 'honest Otto' policy, whereby he brokered deals

1455

Johannes Gutenberg of Mainz prints the Gutenberg Bible using a moveable type system, revolutionising book printing.

1517

Martin Luther makes public his *Ninety-Five Theses* in the town of Wittenburg.

1555

The Peace of Augsburg allows princes to decide their principality's religion.

THE BEST

NIT/IMAGEBROKER

Dresden's Zwinger (p279)

EXAMPLES OF THE ENLIGHTENMENT SPIRIT

- Berlin's **Schloss Charlottenburg** (p77)
- Potsdam's **Park Sanssouci** (p274)
- Dresden's **Zwinger** (p279)

between European powers and encouraged colonial vanities to distract others from his own deeds.

When pressed, Bismarck made concessions to the growing and increasingly antagonistic socialist movement, enacting Germany's first modern social reforms. By 1888 Germany found itself burdened with a new Kaiser, Wilhelm II, who wanted to extend social reform, and an Iron Chancellor who wanted stricter antisocialist laws. Finally, in 1890, the Kaiser's scalpel excised Bismarck from the political scene. After that the legacy of Bismarck's brilliant diplomacy unravelled and a wealthy, unified and industrially powerful Germany paddled into the new century with incompetent leaders at the helm.

WWI

Technological advances and the toughening of Europe into colonial power blocs made WWI far from 'great'. The conflict began with the assassination of the heir to the Austro-Hungarian throne, Archduke Franz-Ferdinand, in Sarajevo in 1914 and quickly escalated into a European and Middle Eastern affair: Germany, Austria-Hungary and Turkey against Britain, France, Italy and Russia. In 1915 a German submarine attack on a British passenger liner killed 120 US citizens. By 1917 the USA had also entered the war.

Russia, in the grip of revolution, accepted humiliating peace terms from Germany. Germany, militarily broken, itself teetering on the verge of revolution and caught in a no man's land between monarchy and modern democracy, signed the Treaty of Versailles (1919), which made it responsible for all losses incurred by its enemies. Its borders were trimmed back and it was forced to pay high reparations.

THE RISE OF HITLER

The reparations from the Treaty of Versailles were impossible to meet and the subsequent hyperinflation and miserable economic conditions in Germany provided fertile ground for political extremists. One of these was Adolf Hitler, an Austrian drifter, would-be artist and German army veteran. Led by Hitler, the National Socialist German Workers'

1618–48

The Thirty Years War sweeps through Germany and leaves it with a depleted population.

1806

Napoleon Bonaparte takes Berlin and pays homage at the grave of Friedrich the Great.

1815

The Congress of Vienna redraws the map of Europe, creating the German Alliance with 35 states.

HULTON ARCHIVE/GETTY
German Junkers Ju 87 dive bombers flying in formation during WWII

Party (or Nazi Party) staged an abortive coup in Munich in 1923. This landed Hitler in prison for nine months, during which time he wrote *Mein Kampf*.

From 1929 the Depression hit Germany hard, leading to unemployment, strikes and demonstrations. Wealthy industrialists began to support the Nazis and police turned a blind eye to the Nazis' stance against Jews, intellectuals and non-Aryans. They increased their strength in general elections and in 1933 replaced the Social Democrats as the largest party in the Reichstag (parliament), with about one-third of the seats. Hitler was appointed chancellor and one year later assumed absolute control as Führer (leader).

WWII

From 1935 Germany began to re-arm and build its way out of the depression with strategic public works such as the autobahns (freeways). Hitler reoccupied the Rhineland in 1936, and in 1938 annexed Austria.

All of this took place against a backdrop of growing racism at home. The Nuremberg Laws of 1935 deprived non-Aryans – mostly Jews and Roma (sometimes called Gypsies) – of their German citizenship and many other rights. On 9 November 1938 the horror escalated into *Kristallnacht* (see the boxed text, p348).

1834
The German Customs Union reinforces the idea of a Germany without Austria.

1848
The Communist Manifesto, by Karl Marx and Friedrich Engels, is published by a group of Germans living in exile in Britain.

1871
Chancellor Otto von Bismarck creates a North German Confederation that excludes Austria.

THE NIGHT OF BROKEN GLASS

Nazi horror escalated on 9 November 1938 with the *Reichspogromnacht* (often called *Kristallnacht* or the 'Night of Broken Glass'). In retaliation for the assassination of a German consular official by a Polish Jew in Paris, synagogues and Jewish cemeteries, property and businesses across Germany were desecrated, burnt or demolished. About 90 Jews died that night. The next day another 30,000 were incarcerated, and Jewish businesses were transferred to non-Jews through forced sale at below-market prices.

In September 1939, after signing a pact that allowed both Stalin and himself a free hand in the east of Europe, Hitler attacked Poland, which led to war with Britain and France. Germany quickly occupied large parts of Europe, but after 1942 began to suffer increasingly heavy losses. Massive bombing reduced Germany's cities to rubble, and the country lost 10% of its population. Germany surrendered unconditionally in May 1945, soon after Hitler's suicide.

THE DIVISION OF GERMANY

After the war, the full scale of Nazi racism was exposed. 'Concentration camps', intended to rid Europe of people considered undesirable according to Nazi doctrine, had exterminated some six million Jews and one million more Roma, communists, homosexuals and others in what has come to be known as the Holocaust, history's first 'assembly line' genocide.

At conferences in Yalta and Potsdam, the Allies (the Soviet Union, the USA, the UK and France) redrew the borders of Germany, making it around 25% smaller than it had become after the Treaty of Versailles 26 years earlier. Germany was divided into four occupation zones.

In the Soviet zone of the country, the communist Socialist Unity Party (SED) won the 1946 elections and began a rapid nationalisation of industry. In September 1949 the Federal Republic of Germany (FRG) was created out of the three western zones; in response the German Democratic Republic (GDR) was founded in the Soviet zone the following month, with (East) Berlin as its capital.

A WALL

As the West's bulwark against communism, the FRG received massive injections of US capital, and experienced rapid economic development (the *Wirtschaftswunder* or 'economic miracle') under the leadership of Konrad Adenauer. The GDR, on the other hand, had to pay US$10 billion in war reparations to the Soviet Union and rebuild itself from scratch.

1914–18

WWI: Germany, Austria-Hungary and Turkey go to war against Britain, France, Italy and Russia.

1919

The Treaty of Versailles' 'war guilt' makes Germany and its allies financially responsible for all loss suffered by its enemies.

1933

Hitler becomes chancellor of Germany and creates a dictatorship through the Enabling Law.

A better life in the west increasingly attracted skilled workers away from the miserable economic conditions in the east. As these were people the GDR could ill afford to lose, it built a wall around West Berlin in 1961 and sealed its border with the FRG.

In 1971 a change to the more flexible leadership of Erich Honecker in the east, combined with the *Ostpolitik* (East Politics) of FRG chancellor Willy Brandt, allowed an easier political relationship between the two Germanys. In the same year the four occupying powers formally accepted the division of Berlin.

GALERIE BILDERWELT/GETTY

Concentration camp in German-occupied Poland, WWII

DPA/CORBIS

John F Kennedy visits Berlin, 1963

STASI SECRETS

The Ministry of State Security, commonly called the Stasi, was based on the Soviet KGB and served as the 'shield and sword' of the SED. Almost a state within the state, it boasted a spy network of about 90,000 full-time employees and 180,000 *inoffizielle Mitarbeiter* (unofficial coworkers) by 1989. Since 1990 only 250 Stasi agents have been prosecuted and since the 10-year limit ended in 2000, future trials are unlikely.

The Stasi utilised unusual methods to track down dissidents. One collection of files found in its Berlin archive kept a record of dissidents' body odour. Some dissidents brought in for interrogation unknowingly delivered an odour sample, usually taken with a cotton-wool pad hidden under the chair the victim sat upon. The sample was then stored in a hermetic glass jar for later use if a dissident suddenly disappeared. To track down a missing dissident by odour, Stasi sniffer dogs were employed. These specially trained groin-sniffing curs were euphemistically known as 'smell differentiation dogs'.

The Stasi allegedly accumulated around six million files on suspected dissidents in its lifetime. In January 1990, protestors stormed the Stasi headquarters in Berlin (today a museum, memorial and research centre – see p70 for details), demanding to see the

1935

The Nuremberg Laws are enacted forbidding marriage between 'Aryans' and 'non-Aryans'.

1939–45

WWII: Hitler invades Poland; France and Britain declare war on Germany.

1949

Allied-occupied West Germany becomes the FRG; a separate East Germany is founded in the Soviet-occupied zone.

ROBERT WALLIS/CORBIS

People climbing on the Berlin Wall, 10 November 1989

files. Since then, the controversial records have been assessed and safeguarded by a Berlin-based public body. In mid-2000, 1000-odd information-packed CDs, removed by the US Central Intelligence Agency's (CIA's) Operation Rosewood immediately after the fall of the Wall in 1989, were returned to Germany. A second batch of CIA files (apparently acquired by the CIA from a Russian KGB officer in 1992) were handed over in 2003. The files, for the first time, matched code names with real names. Some of those with an *inoffizieller Mitarbeiter* file are fully fledged informants; others are 'contact' people who either knew they were giving information to someone from the Stasi or were unfortunate enough to be pumped for information without knowing it. While there is no way for certain to know precisely how many people were spies, it is estimated that when official spies, fully fledged informants and unofficial informants are included, the Stasi had approximately one spy per 6.5 citizens.

REUNIFIED

Honecker's policies produced higher living standards in the GDR, yet East Germany barely managed to achieve a level of prosperity half that of the FRG's. After Mikhail Gorbachev came to power in the Soviet Union in March 1985, the East German communists gradually lost Soviet backing. Events in 1989 rapidly overtook the GDR government, which resisted pressure to introduce reforms. When Hungary relaxed its border controls

1951–61
The economic vision of Ludwig Erhard unleashes West Germany's *Wirtschaftswunder.*

1961
The GDR government begins building the Berlin Wall between East and West Germany.

1971
Social Democrat chancellor Willy Brandt's *Ostpolitik* thaws relations between the two Germanys.

in May 1989, East Germans began crossing to the west. Tighter travel controls resulted in would-be defectors taking refuge in the FRG's embassy in Prague.

Meanwhile, mass demonstrations in Leipzig spread to other cities and Honecker was replaced by his security chief, Egon Krenz, who introduced cosmetic reforms. Then, suddenly, on 9 November 1989 a decision to allow direct travel to the west was mistakenly interpreted as the immediate opening of all GDR borders with West Germany. That same night thousands of people streamed into the west past stunned border guards. Millions more followed in the next few days, and the dismantling of the Berlin Wall began soon thereafter.

The trend at first was to reform the GDR but, in East German elections held in early 1990, citizens voted clearly in favour of the pro-reunification Christian Democratic Union (CDU). A Unification Treaty was drawn up to integrate East Germany into the Federal Republic of Germany, and was enacted on 3 October 1990. All-German elections were held on 2 December that year and, in the midst of national euphoria, the CDU-led coalition, which strongly favoured reunification, soundly defeated the Social Democrat opposition. CDU-leader Helmut Kohl earned the enviable position of 'unification chancellor'.

THE ENIGMATIC MERKEL

Some say that she's enigmatic; others say she likes to keep a low profile when political dissonance breaks out, especially within her own party. But indisputably Angela Merkel's rise to German chancellor in 2005 brought a number of firsts. She was Germany's first woman and the first former East German in the job.

Political commentators often compare her to the former UK prime minister Margaret Thatcher – Merkel's leadership style rarely has the bite of Britain's 'Iron Lady,' but both have been ranked among the *Forbes* 100 most powerful women in the world – Merkel has topped the list three times.

TWO DECADES OF UNITY

In 1998 a coalition of Social Democrats, led by Gerhard Schröder, and Bündnis 90/die Grünen (the Greens party) took political office from Kohl and the CDU amid allegations of widespread financial corruption in the unification-era government.

Schröder and the SDP-Greens only narrowly managed to retain office in the 2002 general election. In 2004 things looked even worse. The slashing of university funding brought students out in protest for several weeks, and an unpopular reform of the public health-insurance system resulted in massive gains for the supposedly discredited CDU at subsequent local elections.

1989
Hungary opens its border with Austria, and East Germans are allowed to travel to the West; the Wall falls.

1990
Berlin becomes the capital of reunified Germany. Helmut Kohl's conservative coalition promises East-West economic integration.

1998
Helmut Kohl's CDU/CSU–FDP coalition is replaced by an SPD–Bündnis 90/Die Grünen government.

SJF/IMAGEBROKER

Holocaust Memorial (p65), Berlin

These advances paid off in September 2005 as Schröder lost the national elections. The winner by a very narrow margin was Angela Merkel (see the boxed text, p351) and the CDU.

During her first term in office, Merkel proved to be a cautious leader, forming a coalition with the SPD. Her calm-and-collected style struck a chord with many Germans and her popularity remained at over 50% even as the CDU's fell somewhat in increasingly harsh economic times.

Meanwhile Germany's export-based economy has been battered by global recession and the mood is glum. And two decades after reunification, overall stereotypes of the west and the old east – that the *Wessis* are arrogant while the *Ossis* simply complain – still exist to varying degrees in German society.

2005

Angela Merkel becomes Germany's first woman chancellor.

2008

German banks are propped up by state funds as unemployment and state debt begin to rise.

2009

The CDU/CSU and FDP form a new coalition government; Angela Merkel is re-elected as chancellor.

PILSNERS TO RIESLINGS

MSI/IMAGEBROKER

Oktoberfest (p92), Munich

BEER

It's not as cheap as the Czech Republic's world-famous lagers, but German beer is patently up there with the best and is well worth the premium. Brewing here goes back to Germanic tribes, and later monks, so it follows in hallowed tradition. Unsurprisingly, a trip to an atmospheric Bavarian beer garden or a Cologne beer hall is one of the first things on many foreign visitors' to-do lists.

The 'secret' of the country's golden nectar dates back to the *Reinheitsgebot* (purity law), demanding breweries use just four ingredients – malt, yeast, hops and water. Passed in Bavaria in 1516, the *Reinheitsgebot* stopped being a legal requirement in 1987, when the EU struck it down as uncompetitive. However, many German brewers still conform to it anyway, seeing it as a good marketing tool against mass-market, chemical-happy competitors.

Thanks to the tradition of the *Reinheitsgebot,* German beer is supposed to be unique in not giving you a *Katzenjammer* or *Kater* (hangover). However, party-goers downing 5 million litres of the stuff at Munich's Oktoberfest (see the boxed text, p108) must surely disagree!

SO MANY VARIETIES

Despite frequently tying their own hands and giving themselves just four ingredients to play with, German brewers turn out 5000 distinctively different beers.

They achieve this via subtle variations in the basic production process. At the simplest level, a brewer can choose a particular yeast for top or bottom fermenting (the terms indicating where the yeast lives while working – at the top or bottom of the brewing vessel).

THE BEST

CHRISTIAN REISTER/ALAMY

Berlin's Prater beer garden (p81)

BEER GARDENS

- **Biergarten im Schlossgarten** (p210), Stuttgart
- **Braunauer Hof** (p109), Munich
- **Spitalgarten** (p162), Regensburg
- **Prater** (p81), Berlin
- **Klosterschenke Weltenburg** (p183), near Regensburg

The most popular form of brewing is bottom fermentation, which accounts for about 85% of German beers, notably the *Pils* (pilsner), most *Bock* beers and the *Helles* (pale lager) type found in Bavaria. Top fermentation is used for the *Weizenbier/Weissbier* (wheat/white beer) popular in Berlin and Bavaria, Cologne's *Kölsch* and the very few stouts brewed in the country.

One of the most ubiquitous and popular beers is the golden *Pils,* a bottom-fermented full beer with a pronounced hop flavour and a creamy head. It has an alcohol content of around 4.8% and is served throughout Germany. But many other beers are regional, meaning that, for example, a Saxon Rechenberger cannot be found in Düsseldorf, where the locally brewed *Altbier* is the taste of choice.

OVER 1200 BREWERIES

German beer is brewed by more than 1200 breweries, although many traditionally family-run concerns have been swallowed up by the big-boy brewers. Bremen-based Beck's, producer of one of Germany's best-known beers since 1873, was bought out by Belgian beer-giant Interbrew in 2002, while Hamburg's Holsten (founded 1879) now has its roots firmly embedded in the USA.

Still, 11 German monasteries continue to produce beer. Kloster Weltenburg, near Kelheim on the Danube north of Munich, is the world's oldest monastery brewery; its Weltenburg Barock Dunckel won a medal at the 2006 World Beer Cup in Seattle. This light, smooth beer has a malty, toasty finish.

Other connoisseurs believe the earthy Andechs Doppelbock Dunkel – produced by the Benedictines in Andechs, near Munich – to be among the world's best.

WINE

Its name sullied for decades by the cloyingly sugary taste of *Liebfraumilch* white wine, German wine has been making a comeback in the 21st century. Following the 2002 marketing campaign – 'If you think you know German wine, drink again' – in the industry's biggest export market, the UK, sellers have been talking of a renaissance. Even discerning critics have been pouring praise on German winemakers, with *Decanter* magazine awarding *Weingut* Meyer-Näkel's Dernauer Pfarrwingert Spätburgunder Grosses Gewächs 2005 the top international trophy for Pinot noir in 2008, much to the astonishment of wine experts globally. It's been reported that a symphony of gasps filled the room when the winner was announced at the prestigious awards ceremony.

RIESLING, *BITTE*

Germany is most commonly associated with white wines made from riesling grapes. According to Tim Atkin, wine correspondent for the UK's *Observer,* 'Germany makes the best rieslings of all'. At the same time, the country itself has had 'a tremendous run of vintages since 2000', and its midrange wines have markedly improved, with brands like Devil's Rock (www.devils-rock.com), Dr Loosen (www.drloosen.com) and the Vineyard Creatures series (www.lingen-felder.com).

Having produced wines since Roman times, Germany now has more than 100,000 hectares of vineyards, mostly on the Rhine and Moselle riverbanks. Despite the common association with riesling grapes (particularly in its best wine regions), the less acidic Müller-Thurgau *(Rivaner)* grape is more wide-spread. Meanwhile, the *Gewürztraminer* grape produces spicy wines with an intense bouquet. What Germans call *Grauburgunder* is known to the rest of the world as Pinot gris.

German reds are light and lesser known. *Spätburgunder* (Pinot noir) is the best of the bunch and goes into some velvety, full-bodied reds with an occasional almond taste.

THE BEST

NIGEL BLYTHE/ALAMY

Egon Müller Scharzhof

GERMAN WINE PRODUCERS

- **Dönnhoff** (☎ 06755-263; www.doennhoff.com; Oberhausen, Nahe region)
- **Egon Müller Scharzhof** (www.scharzhof.de; Saar region)
- **JJ Prüm** (www.jjpruem.de; Bernkastel-Wehlen, Mosel region)
- **Weingut Meyer-Näkel** (☎ 02643-1628; www.meyer-naekel.de; Dernau, Ahr region)
- **Wittmann** (☎ 06244-905036; www.weingutwittman.com; Westhofen bei Worms, Rheinhessen region)

VINES ON THE HILL

There are 13 official grape-growing areas, the best being the Mosel-Saar-Ruwer region. It boasts some of the world's steepest vineyards, where the predominantly riesling grapes are still hand-picked. Slate soil on the hillsides gives the wines a flinty taste. Chalkier riverside soils are planted with the Elbling grape, an ancient Roman variety.

East of the Moselle, the Nahe region produces fragrant, fruity and full-bodied wines using Müller-Thurgau and Silvaner grapes, as well as riesling.

Riesling grapes are also the mainstay in Rheingau and Mittelrhein (Middle Rhine), two other highly respected wine-growing pockets. Rheinhessen, south of Rheingau, is responsible for *Liebfraumilch,* but also some top rieslings.

The region around Stuttgart produces some of the country's best reds, while Saxony-Anhalt is home to Rotkäppchen (Little Red Riding Hood) sparkling wine, a former GDR brand that's been a big hit in the new Germany.

THE BEST

BLU/IMAGEBROKER

Road through vineyards in Baden-Württemberg

SWEET & SPARKLY WINES

- **Auslese** A 'selected harvest'; usually intense and sweet
- **Beerenauslese (BA)** Grapes are picked overripe; usually a dessert wine
- **Eiswein** Grapes are picked and pressed while frozen; a dessert wine
- **Sekt** Sparkling wine

BETTER THAN GLÜHWEIN

Served in winter and designed to inure you to the sudden drop in temperatures, hot spiced *Glühwein* is a common commodity at Germany's popular Christmas markets. However, a far more spectacular and intoxicating mulled wine is *Feuerzangenbowle* (literally 'fire-tongs-punch'), where a flaming rum-soaked sugar cube falls into the spiced red wine, producing a delicious and heady drink. It's become a cult tipple, thanks to a movie of the same name.

WHERE TO DRINK

Weinkeller or *Bierkeller* (cellars serving wine or beer) are your best bets for sampling the local tipple. In summer hit the closest *Biergarten* (beer garden), a relaxing, alfresco spot – often covered by trees, surrounded by a wall and filled with long wooden tables – to while away a lazy sunny day. Both cook up light meals as well.

↘ DIRECTORY & TRANSPORT

DIRECTORY

ACCOMMODATION

Germany has all types of places to unpack your suitcase, from hostels, camping grounds and family hotels to chains, business hotels and luxury resorts. Reservations are a good idea between June and September, around major holidays (p265), festivals and cultural events (mentioned throughout this book and also on p46) and trade shows.

PRACTICALITIES

- **Electrical supply** is 220V AC, 50 Hz.
- Widely read **daily newspapers** include the *Süddeutsche Zeitung, Die Welt* and *Der Tagesspiegel* (all quite centrist), as well as the more conservative *Frankfurter Allgemeine Zeitung*. *Die Zeit* is a high-brow weekly with in-depth reporting.
- *Der Spiegel* and *Focus* **magazines** are popular German news weeklies, and the *Economist, Time* and *Newsweek* are sold in train stations and major news-stands.
- **Radio stations** are regional with most featuring a mixed format of news, talk and music.
- Germany uses the **metric system** (see conversion chart on inside front cover).
- GSM 900/1800 is used for mobile (cell) phones.
- For women's **clothing sizes**, a German size 36 equals size 6 in the US and size 10 in the UK, then increases in increments of two, making size 38 a US 8 and UK 12.

This book lists accommodation in ascending order of price. Unless noted, rates include VAT and breakfast, which is usually a generous all-you-can-eat buffet. Places we consider extra special have been identified as **our pick**.

Some regional variation notwithstanding, budget stays will have you checking in at hostels, country inns, *Pensionen* (B&Bs or small hotels) or simple family hotels charging €80 or less (per double, less in rural areas).

Midrange properties (between €80 and €150) generally offer the best value for money. For that price you can expect a clean, comfortable, decent-sized double with at least a modicum of style, a private bathroom, cable TV and direct-dial telephone. Communal saunas and basic fitness facilities are quite common as well.

Top-end places (starting at €150) offer luxurious amenities, perhaps a scenic location, special decor or historical ambience. Many also have pools, saunas, business centres or other upmarket facilities.

To help you determine whether a property listed in this book is right for you, we've devised a handful of icons. Hotels with on-site parking, for instance, sport the parking icon, P. Properties with designated nonsmoking rooms or floors are identified with ☒. These are very common now and the number of properties that are completely nonsmoking is on the rise. By contrast, rooms with air-con are exceedingly rare, except in upmarket chain hotels; properties that do have at least some rooms with air-con are denoted with ❄. Hostels and hotels offering guest PCs with internet access are identified with an internet icon 💻, while 📶 indicates the availability of wi-fi. Places with their own swimming pool are denoted by 🏊.

BOOK YOUR STAY ONLINE

For more accommodation reviews and recommendations by Lonely Planet authors, check out the online booking service at www.lonelyplanet.com. You'll find the true, insider low-down on the best places to stay. Reviews are thorough and independent. Best of all, you can book online.

Prices listed in this book do not take into account promotional discounts. City hotels geared to the suit brigade often try to lure leisure travellers with lower weekend rates. Also check hotel websites (listed throughout this book) for discount rates or packages.

RESERVATIONS

Many tourist-office and hotel websites let you check for room availability and make advance reservations. Quite a few of those reviewed in this book can also be booked via Lonely Planet's own website (see the boxed text, above). Other online booking services include www.venere.com and www.hotel.de. Last-minute bargains can often be found at www.hrs.de (in German). For independent hostels, try www.hostelworld.com, www.gomio.com and www.hostels.com.

If you're already in town, swing by the tourist office, where staff can assist you in finding last-minute lodging. After hours, vacancies may be posted in the window or in a display case.

When making a room reservation directly with a property, tell your host what time they can expect you and stick to your plan or ring again. Many well-meaning visitors have lost rooms by showing up late.

FARM STAYS

A holiday on a working farm *(Urlaub auf dem Bauernhof)* is inexpensive and a great opportunity to get close to nature in relative comfort. This type of vacation is especially popular with families. Kids get to interact with their favourite barnyard animals and maybe help with everyday chores. Accommodation ranges from bare-bones rooms with shared facilities to fully-furnished holiday flats. Minimum stays are common. A variety of farm types are on offer, including organic, dairy and equestrian farms as well as wine estates. Places advertising *Landurlaub* (country holiday) no longer actively work their farms. The best establishments are quality controlled by the Deutsche Landwirtschafts-Gesellschaft (DLG; German Agricultural Association). To learn more about farm holidays, check www.landtourismus.de, www.bauernhofurlaub-deutschland.de or www.bauernhofurlaub.com (in German).

HOLIDAY FLATS & HOMES

If you want to get to know a place better, renting for a week or two can be ideal, especially for budget-minded travellers, self-caterers, families and small groups. Tourist offices have lists of holiday flats *(Ferienwohnungen* or *Ferien-Appartements)*. Some *Pensionen,* inns, hotels and even farmhouses also rent out apartments. Stays under a week usually incur a surcharge, and there's almost always a 'cleaning fee' payable at the end. A central online booking service is www.atraveo.de.

HOSTELS

DJH HOSTELS

Germany's 600 Hostelling International-affiliated hostels are run by the **Deutsches Jugendherbergswerk** (DJH; www.jugendherberge.de) and are open to people of all ages, although they're especially popular with school and youth groups, families and sports clubs. Most have recently been modernised but often can't quite shake that institutional feel. Still, smaller dorms and private rooms for families and couples, often with private bathroom, are increasingly common. Almost all hostels can accommodate mobility-impaired travellers.

Rates in gender-segregated dorms or in family rooms range from €13 to €29 per person, including linen and breakfast; optional lunch and dinner cost around €5 extra each. People over 27 are charged an extra €3 or €4. If space is tight, hostels may give priority to people under 27, except for those travelling as a family.

Unless you're a member of your home country's HI association, you need to buy either a Hostelling International Card for €15.50 (valid for one year) or six individual stamps costing €3.10 per night. Both are available at any DJH hostel. Around half of German DJH hostels can now be booked online at www.jugendherberge.de and about 60 can also be booked on the HI website (www.hihostels.com). Alternatively, just contact the hostel directly by phone, fax or email.

INDEPENDENT HOSTELS

Germany was slow to embrace the backpacker hostel concept, but in recent years indies have been popping up all over the country. Although they sometimes accept school groups, they generally cater for individual travellers, welcome people of all ages and attract a more convivial, international crowd than DJH hostels. Most now offer private quarters with bathrooms, and even apartments with kitchens, alongside multibed dorms, making them an excellent budget choice even if you've traded your backpack for a rolling suitcase.

No two hostels are alike, but typical facilities include communal kitchens, bars, cafes, TV lounges, lockers, internet terminals and laundry facilities. There are no curfews, and staff tend to be savvy, energetic, eager to help and multilingual. Dorms are mixed, although women-only dorms can usually be set up on request. Most hostels charge an extra fee (around €3) for linen; some also serve optional breakfast but no other meals.

Several dozen indies have joined together in an alliance known as the **Backpacker Network** (**www.backpackernetwork.de, partly in English**). Some hostels can also be booked via this site. Other recommended online booking systems are www.gomio.com, www.hostelworld.com, www.hostels.com and www.hostels.net.

HOTELS

Hotels range from small family-run properties to cookie-cutter international chains to luxurious designer abodes. Those serving only breakfast are called *Hotel garni.* An official classification system exists, based on a scale of one to five stars, but it's voluntary and few hotels participate. Even so, this being Germany, you can generally expect even budget abodes to be spotlessly clean, comfortable and well run.

In older, family-run hotels, individual rooms often vary dramatically in terms of size, decor and amenities. The cheapest might have shared facilities, while others come with a shower cubicle installed but no private toilet; only the pricier ones will have their own bathrooms. If possible, ask to see several rooms before committing to one.

If you're the romantic type, consider staying in a *Schlosshotel,* a modernised castle, palace or country manor that drips with character and history. Some belong to an association called Romantik Hotels (www.romantikhotels.com). Also try www.castles.de.

PENSIONEN, INNS & PRIVATE ROOMS

Pensionen and *Gasthöfe/Gasthäuser* (inns) are smaller and less formal, and are an excellent low-cost alternative to hotels; the latter usually have restaurants serving regional and German food to a local clientele. Expect clean rooms but minimal amenities – maybe a radio, sometimes a small TV, almost never a phone. Facilities may be shared. What rooms lack in amenities, though, they often make up for in charm and authenticity, often augmented by friendly hosts who take a personal interest in ensuring that you enjoy your stay. Rates always include breakfast.

Privatzimmer – essentially guest rooms in private homes – are ubiquitous and great for catching a glimpse into how locals live, although privacy seekers may find these places a bit too intimate. Tourist offices keep lists of available rooms; you can also look around for *'Zimmer Frei'* (rooms available) signs in house or shop windows. They're usually quite cheap, with per-person rates starting at €13 and usually topping out at €25, including breakfast. If a landlord is reluctant to rent for a single night, offer to pay a little extra. For advance reservations, try www.bed-and-breakfast.de or www.bedandbreakfast.de.

BUSINESS HOURS

Most shops open between 9am and 10am, except for bakeries and kiosks that may open as early as 6am and some supermarkets which open at 7am or 8am. Closing times vary from 6pm or 6.30pm (1pm or 2pm on Saturday) for shops in rural areas and suburbs to 8pm or 9pm for malls, department stores and stores in the bigger city centres. There is no Sunday shopping except in December and a few times throughout the year. After hours and on Sundays you can get basic (and overpriced) supplies at petrol stations and larger train stations. Bakeries open for a few hours on Sunday mornings.

Banks do business from 8.30am to 4pm Monday to Friday (sometimes 6pm on Thursday), while core hours at post offices are 9am to 6pm Monday to Friday and to noon or 1pm on Saturday.

Museums usually take Monday off but stay open late one evening a week.

In villages and suburbs, shops and businesses often observe a two- to three-hour lunch break. And speaking of lunch, it's generally served between 11.30am and 2pm, while dinner feedings are from 5.30pm to 9.30pm, although many restaurants continue to dish up throughout the afternoon. Some also observe a *Ruhetag* (day of rest), usually Monday or Tuesday.

Pubs and bars pour libations from around 6pm, unless they serve food, in which case they're also open during the day. In cities without closing hours, such as Hamburg and Berlin, bars stay open until the last tippler leaves; otherwise, 1am or 2am are typical closing times. Big-city clubs open around 11pm but don't kick into high gear until 1am or 2am and keep buzzing until sunrise or later. Cities like Berlin have a growing number of day-time clubs, so it's quite possible not to go home at all at weekends!

Variations on the above are noted in individual reviews.

CLIMATE CHARTS

The German weather is highly capricious: on any given day it can be cold or warm, sunny or rainy, windy or calm – or any combination thereof. Meteorologists blame this lack of stability on colliding

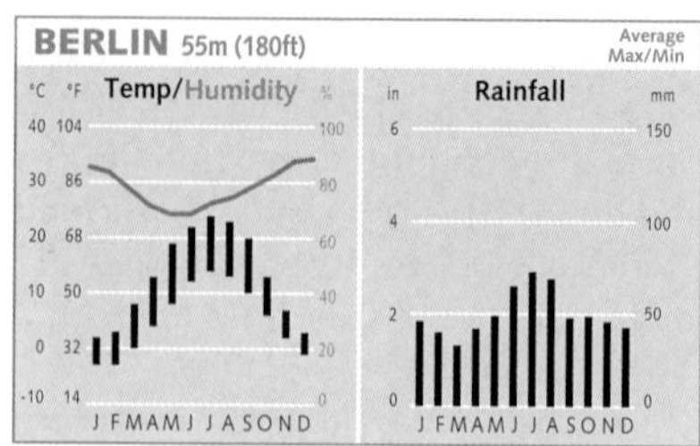

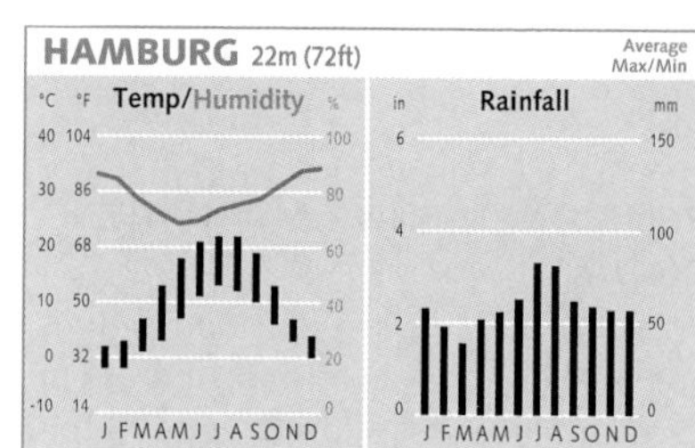

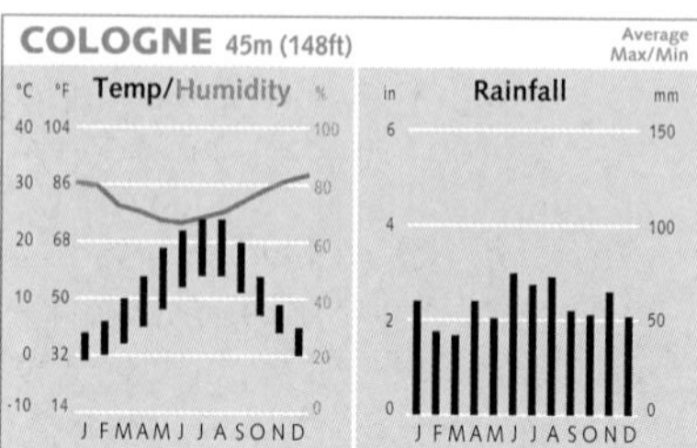

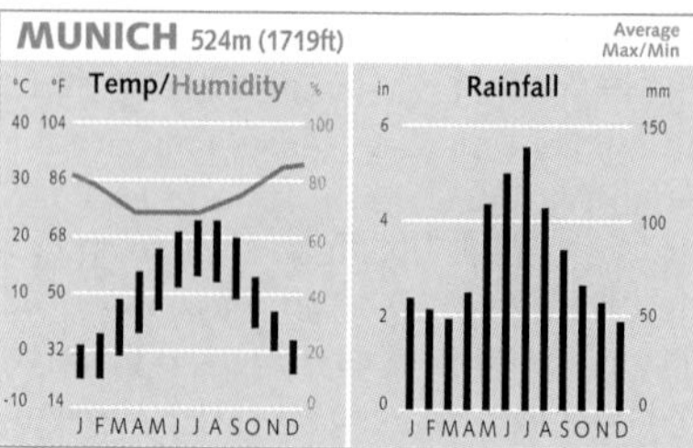

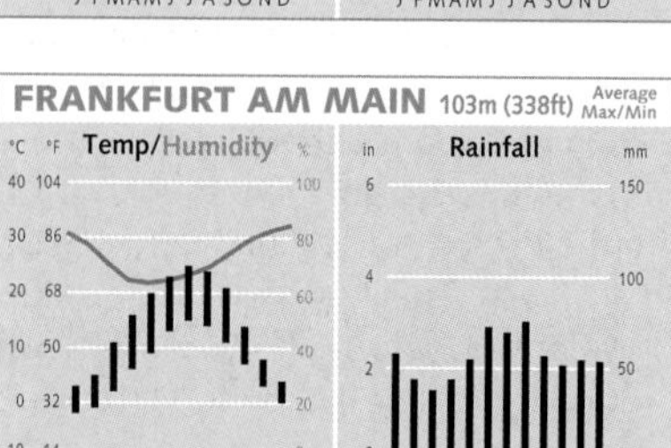
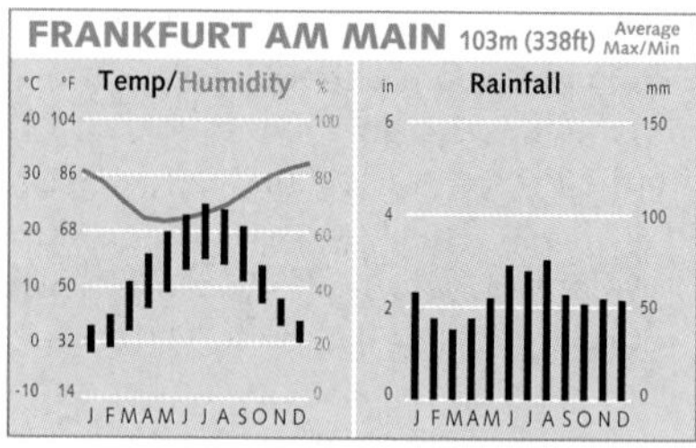

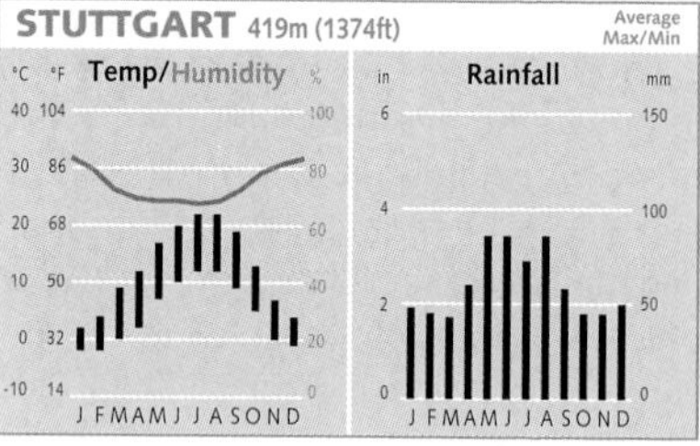

maritime and continental air masses, but for you this simply means packing a wardrobe that's as flexible as possible.

The weather tends to be most pleasant in summer, which is rarely suffocatingly hot (usually around 28°C/82°F), the occasional heat wave notwithstanding. Humidity levels tend to be quite high, making afternoon thunderstorms fairly common. Spring is beautiful but it can be slow to arrive, even if jackets are sometimes stripped off as early as April. Autumn arrives in September and brings the added bonus of bright foliage. Temperatures can still be quite pleasant, which may keep beer gardens and outdoor cafes open until October. Predictably, December to February is the coldest period, when the mercury can plunge well below 0°C/32°F. At the higher elevations, snowfall is possible from November.

For general advice on the best times to travel around the country, see p44. The climate charts (above) provide a snapshot of local weather patterns.

CUSTOMS & REGULATIONS

Most articles that you take to Germany for your personal use may be imported free of duty and tax. Duty-free allowances for goods purchased in a non-EU country were recently changed. Anyone over 17 may now bring in 1L of strong liquor *or* 2L of less than 22% alcohol by volume *plus* 4L of wine *plus* 16L of beer. Duty-free tobacco imports are capped at 200 cigarettes *or* 100 cigarillos *or* 50 cigars *or* 250g of loose tobacco. If you're over 15, you may also bring in other products up to the value of €300 if arriving by land or €430 if arriving by sea or air. The limit for those under 15 is €175.

DANGERS & ANNOYANCES

Germany is a very safe country in which to live and travel, with crime rates that are quite low by international standards. Theft and other crimes against travellers occur rarely. Of course, you should still take all the usual sensible precautions, such as locking hotel rooms and cars, not leaving valuables unattended, keeping an eye out for pickpockets in crowded places and not taking midnight strolls in city parks. Many hostels provide lockers, but you need your own padlock. Train stations tend to be magnets for the destitute and drug dependent who might harass you or make you feel otherwise uncomfortable, especially if you are in the area at night.

In big cities, especially Berlin, large-scale political protests and demonstrations are quite common. Despite a high police presence, these can turn rowdy or violent on rare occasions, so it's best to stay away from them altogether. Police are also very visible on game days of soccer matches to prevent clashes between fans of rival teams. Always avoid groups of intoxicated hooligans, as many belong to neo-Nazi and skinhead organisations and are erratic, unpredictable and often violent. Although they do not target tourists, innocent bystanders they perceive as 'foreign looking' or as members of rival left-wing groups could potentially be harassed. If you do find yourself in a threatening situation, try not to provoke these aggressors, get away from the scene as fast as possible and notify the police.

DISCOUNT CARDS

If you're a full-time student, the **International Student Identity Card** (ISIC; www.isic.org) is your ticket to savings on airfares, travel insurance and many local attractions. The **International Youth Travel Card** (IYTC; www.istc.org) grants similar savings and benefits for nonstudents under 26, while the **Euro<26 Youth Card** (www.euro26.org) is available to anyone under 30, despite the name. All cards are issued online, by student unions, hostelling organisations and youth-oriented travel agencies such as STA Travel.

Discounts are also available for seniors, children, families and the disabled. Although no special cards are needed, you may be asked to show ID to prove your age.

In cities, many tourist offices sell **Welcome Cards** entitling visitors to discounts on museums, sights and tours, plus unlimited trips on local public transportation. They can be good value if you plan on taking advantage of most of the benefits and don't qualify for any of the standard discounts.

EMBASSIES & CONSULATES

All foreign embassies are in Berlin, but many countries have consular offices in such cities as Frankfurt, Munich, Hamburg and Düsseldorf. Call the embassy number listed here to find out which consulate is closest to your location. For German missions around the world, as well as foreign missions in Germany not listed here, go to www.auswaertiges-amt.de (click on 'English', then 'Addresses').

Australia (Map p64; ☎ 030-880 0880; www.germany.embassy.gov.au; Wallstrasse 76-79)

Canada (Map pp72-3; ☎ 030-203 120; www.kanada-info.de; Leipziger Platz 17)

France (Map p64; ☎ 030-590 039 000; www.botschaft-frankreich.de; Pariser Platz 5)

Ireland (Map p64; ☎ 030-220 720; www.embassyofireland.de; Friedrichstrasse 200)

Italy (Map pp52-3; ☎ 030-254400; www.ambberlino.esteri.it; Hiroshimastrasse 1)

Japan (Map pp52-3; ☎ 030-210 940; www.de.emb-japan.go.jp; Hiroshimastrasse 6)

New Zealand (Map p64; ☎ 030-206 210; www.nzembassy.com/germany; Friedrichstrasse 60)

Russia (Map p64; ☎ 030-229 111 029; www.russische-botschaft.de; Unter den Linden 63-65)

South Africa (Map pp52-3; ☎ 030-220 730; www.suedafrika.org; Tiergartenstrasse 18)

Spain (Map pp52-3; ☎ 030-254 0070; www.spanischebotschaft.de; Lichtensteinallee 1)

Switzerland (Map p64; ☎ 030-390 4000; www.eda.admin.ch; Otto-von-Bismarck-Allee 4a)

UK (Map p64; ☎ 030-204 570; www.britischebotschaft.de; Wilhelmstrasse 70)

USA (Map p64; ☎ 030-830 50; www.usembassy.de; Pariser Platz 2)

FOOD

Eating recommendations in this guide match all tastes and travel budgets. Budget eateries include takeaways, delis, cafes, *Imbisse* (snack bars), markets and basic restaurants where you can get a meal (defined as a main course and one drink) for less than €10. At midrange establishments expect tablecloths, full menus, beer and wine lists and a bill that shouldn't exceed €20 per person. Top-end places tend to be full gourmet affairs with expert service, creative and freshly prepared food and matching wine lists. Main courses alone here will cost €20 or more; set three- or four-course menus are usually a better deal. Places with a good selection for vegetarians are denoted with Ⓥ.

If our reviews do not mention opening hours, standard hours (11am to 11pm) apply. Note that food service may stop earlier, depending on how busy the place is that night.

For more on cuisine and eating customs, see p332.

GAY & LESBIAN TRAVELLERS

Germany is a magnet for gay travellers with the rainbow flag flying especially proudly in Berlin, which is helmed by Germany's first openly gay mayor, Klaus Wowereit. For an overview of the Berlin scene, see the boxed text on p86. Berlin, Cologne and Hamburg have humming nightlife scenes, magazines, associations and support groups, and major Gay Pride celebrations. Frankfurt, Munich and Bremen have smaller but still vibrant scenes.

Overall, Germans are tolerant of gays *(Schwule)* and lesbians *(Lesben)* although, as elsewhere in the world, cities are more liberal than rural areas, and younger people tend to be more open-minded than older generations. Homophobic hostility is more likely in eastern Germany and in the conservative south where gays and lesbians tend to keep a lower profile.

For online info, listings and contacts, see www.gayscape.com, a search tool with hundreds of links, www.gay-web.de or www.blu.fm, the online version of the magazine. Lesbians should check out www.lesarion.de and the online version of *L-Mag* (www.l-mag.de), a bimonthly magazine. An LGBT travel specialist is www.damronvacations.com. Another good general source is www.outtraveler.com.

HEALTH

While Germany does have excellent health care, prevention is always the key to staying healthy while abroad. A little planning before departure, particularly for pre-existing illnesses, will save trouble later. Bring medications in their original, clearly labelled containers. A signed and dated letter from your physician describing your medical conditions and medications, including generic names, is also a good idea. If carrying syringes or needles, be sure to have a physician's letter documenting their medical necessity. Carry a spare pair of contact lenses and glasses, and take your optical prescription with you.

INSURANCE

If you're an EU citizen, an E111 form, available from health centres or, in the UK, post offices, covers you for most medical care. E111 will not cover you for non-emergencies, or emergency repatriation home. Citizens from other countries should find out if there is a reciprocal arrangement for free medical care between their country and Germany. If you do need health insurance, make sure you get a policy that covers you for the worst possible case, such as an accident requiring an emergency flight home. Find out in advance if your insurance plan will make payments directly to providers or reimburse you later for overseas health expenditures.

RECOMMENDED VACCINATIONS

No jabs are required to travel to Germany. The World Health Organization (WHO), however, recommends that all travellers should be covered for diphtheria, tetanus, measles, mumps, rubella and polio, regardless of their destination.

AVAILABILITY & COST OF HEALTH CARE

Excellent health care is readily available but rather expensive. For minor illnesses, pharmacists are able to dispense valuable advice and over-the-counter medication. They can also advise when more specialised help is required and point you in the right direction.

TRAVELLING WITH CHILDREN

Make sure the children are up to date with routine vaccinations, and discuss possible travel vaccines well before departure as some vaccines are not suitable for children aged under one year.

If your child has vomiting or diarrhoea, lost fluid and salts must be replaced. It may be helpful to take rehydration powders with boiled water.

HOLIDAYS

PUBLIC HOLIDAYS

Germany observes eight religious and three secular holidays nationwide. Shops, banks, government offices and post offices are closed on these days. States with predominantly Catholic populations, such as Bavaria and Baden-Württemberg, also celebrate Epiphany (6 January), Corpus Christi (10 days after Pentecost), Assumption Day (15 August) and All Saints' Day (1 November). Reformation Day (31 October) is only observed in eastern Germany (but not in Berlin).

The following are *gesetzliche Feiertage* (public holidays):

Neujahrstag (New Year's Day) 1 January

Ostern (Easter) March/April; Good Friday, Easter Sunday and Easter Monday

Christi Himmelfahrt (Ascension Day) 40 days after Easter

Maifeiertag/Tag der Arbeit (Labour Day) 1 May

Pfingsten (Whit/Pentecost Sunday & Monday) 50 days after Easter
Tag der Deutschen Einheit (Day of German Unity) 3 October
Weihnachtstag (Christmas Day) 25 December
Zweiter Weihnachtstag (Boxing Day) 26 December

SCHOOL HOLIDAYS

Each state sets its own school holidays but, in general, kids get six weeks off in summer and two weeks each around Christmas, Easter and October. In some states, schools are also closed for a few days in February and around Whitsun/Pentecost.

Traffic is worst at the beginning of school holidays in population-rich states like North Rhine–Westphalia and can become a nightmare if several states let out their schools at the same time.

Germans are big fans of miniholidays built around public holidays, when you can expect heavy crowds on the roads, in the towns, on boats, in beer gardens and everywhere else. Lodging is at a premium at these times as well.

INSURANCE

No matter how long or short your trip, make sure you have adequate travel insurance. EU citizens should obtain the European Health Insurance Card (EHIC), which entitles you to reduced-cost or free medical treatment due to illness or accident, although not for emergency repatriation home. Non-EU citizens should check if a similar reciprocal agreement exists between their country and Germany, or if their policy at home provides worldwide health-care coverage.

If you do need to buy travel health insurance, be sure to get a policy that also covers emergency flights back home. While some plans pay doctors or hospitals directly, some health-care providers may still require immediate payment from non-locals. Most do not accept credit cards. Except in emergencies, call around for a doctor willing to accept your insurance. Check your policy for what supporting documentation you need to file a claim and be sure to keep all receipts.

Also consider coverage for luggage theft or loss. If you already have a home-owners or renters policy, check what it will cover and only get supplemental insurance to protect against the rest. If you have prepaid a large portion of your vacation, trip-cancellation insurance is a worthwhile expense.

Worldwide travel insurance is available at www.lonelyplanet.com/travel_services. You can buy, extend and claim online anytime – even if you're already on the road.

For information about what kind of insurance coverage you need while driving in Germany, see p378.

INTERNET ACCESS

Internet cafes are listed throughout the destination chapters, but most have about the lifespan of a fruit fly, so please forgive us if our listings are outdated and ask staff at your hotel for a recommendation. Public libraries offer free terminals and sometimes wi-fi access, but downsides may include time limits, reservation requirements and queues. Internet access is also available at slightly seedy 'telephone call shops', which cluster near train stations.

In hotels and hostels, broadband and wi-fi (*W-LAN* in German) have become quite commonplace. Some hotels, especially in eastern Germany, have ISDN data service which was state-of-the-art in the '90s but has since been supplanted by DSL. Unless you have an ISDN-compatible modem, access may be difficult, if not impossible. Laptop users may also need adapters for German electrical outlets and telephone sockets, which are widely available in such electronics stores as Saturn and Media Markt.

Wi-fi is available on select ICE train routes, including Frankfurt to Hamburg and Frankfurt to Munich. More than 20 stations, including those in Berlin, Munich, Hamburg and Frankfurt, also offer wi-fi in their DB Lounges.

Throughout this book, we use 💻 to indicate that a place has PCs with internet access for public use and 📶 for places with wi-fi. Access fees range from free to exorbitant, with some top-end business chain hotels charging as much as €25 per day.

To locate wi-fi hot spots, check the directories at www.jiwire.com or www.hotspot-locations.com. For a full rundown on connectivity issues, see www.kropla.com or www.teleadapt.com.

LEGAL MATTERS

By law you must carry some form of photographic identification, such as your passport, national identity card or driving licence. Reporting theft to the police is usually a simple, if occasionally time-consuming, matter. Remember that the first thing to do is show some form of identification.

If driving in Germany, you should carry your driving licence and obey road rules carefully (see p379). The permissible blood-alcohol limit is 0.05%; drivers caught exceeding this amount are subject to stiff fines, a confiscated licence and even jail time. Drinking in public is not illegal, but please be discreet about it.

Illegal drugs are widely available, especially in clubs. Cannabis possession is a criminal offence and punishment may range from a warning to a court appearance. Dealers face far stiffer penalties, as do people caught with any other 'recreational' drugs.

If you are arrested, you have the right to make a phone call and are presumed innocent until proven guilty. If you don't know a lawyer, contact your embassy (p363).

THE LEGAL AGE FOR...

- **Drinking beer or wine**: 14
- **Being served beer or wine in a pub**: 16
- **Buying cigarettes**: 18
- **Driving a car**: 18
- **Military service**: 17
- **Sexual consent**: 14 (with restrictions)
- **Voting in an election**: 18

MONEY

Euros come in seven notes (€5, €10, €20, €50, €100, €200 and €500) and eight coins (€0.01, €0.02, €0.05, €0.10, €0.20, €0.50, €1 and €2). At press time, the euro was a strong and stable currency, although some minor fluctuations are common. A guide to exchange rates is given on the inside front cover of this book; for pointers on costs, see p43.

Cash is still king in Germany, so you can't really avoid having at least some notes and coins, say €100 or so, on you at all times. Plan to pay in cash almost everywhere.

You can exchange money at airports, some banks and currency exchange offices, such as ReiseBank. In rural areas such facilities are rare, so make sure you have plenty of cash.

ATMS

The easiest and quickest way to obtain cash is by using your debit (bank) card at

SMOKE & MIRRORS

Germany was one of the last countries in Europe to legislate smoking, which it did in 2007–08, and, by all accounts, it hasn't done a very effective job. Each of the 16 states was allowed to introduce its own antismoking laws, creating a rather confusing patchwork. In most states, smoking is a no-no in schools, hospitals, airports, train stations and other public facilities. But when it comes to bars, pubs, cafes and restaurants, every state does it just a little differently. Bavaria has the toughest laws, which ban smoking practically everywhere, although an exception was made for Oktoberfest tents; so-called 'smoking clubs' are also permitted. In most states, lighting up is allowed in designated smoking rooms. However, in July 2008 Germany's highest court ruled this scheme unconstitutional because it discriminates against one-room establishments. These may now allow smoking provided they serve no food and only admit patrons over 18. So far only Berlin has introduced this compromise, but other states are likely to follow suit. In any case, enforcement has been sporadic, to say the least, despite the threat of fines. The situation is fluid.

an ATM *(Geldautomat)* linked to international networks such as Cirrus, Plus, Star and Maestro. ATMs are ubiquitous and accessible 24/7. Make sure you know your PIN and check with your bank for fees, daily withdrawal limits and contact information for reporting lost or stolen cards. Some shops, hotels, restaurants and other businesses also accept payment by debit card. Since 2006 nearly all cards use the 'chip and pin' system: instead of signing, you enter your PIN. If you're from overseas and your card isn't chip-and-pin enabled, you may be able to sign it in the usual way, although not all places will accept your card, so enquire first.

CREDIT CARDS

Credit cards are becoming more widely accepted, but it's best not to assume that you'll be able to use one – enquire first. Even so, a piece of plastic is vital in emergencies and also useful for phone or internet bookings. Visa and MasterCard are more commonly accepted than American Express. Avoid getting cash advances on your credit card via ATMs since fees are steep and you'll be charged interest immediately (in other words, there's no grace period as with purchases). Report lost or stolen cards to the following:

American Express (☎ 01805-840 840)
MasterCard (☎ 0800-819 1040)
Visa (☎ 0800-811 8440)

TIPPING

Restaurant bills always include a *Bedienung* (service charge) but most people add 5% or 10% unless the service was truly abhorrent. At hotels, bellboys get about €1 per bag and it's also nice to leave some cash for the room cleaners. Tip bartenders about 5% and taxi drivers around 10%.

TRAVELLERS CHEQUES

Travellers cheques are becoming increasingly obsolete in the age of network-linked ATMs. It doesn't help that German businesses generally don't accept them, even if denominated in euros, and banks charge exorbitant fees for cashing them (currency exchange offices are usually better). American Express offices cash Amex cheques free of charge.

PHOTOGRAPHY

Germany is a photographer's dream, with its gorgeous countryside, fabulous architecture, quaint villages, exciting cities, lordly cathedrals, lively cafes and picture-perfect castles, palaces and old towns. A good general reference guide is Lonely Planet's *Travel Photography* by Richard I'Anson.

Germans tend to be deferential around photographers and will make a point of not walking in front of your camera, even if you want them to. No one seems to mind being photographed in the context of an overall scene, but if you want a close-up shot, you should ask first.

SHOPPING

Germany is a fun place to shop, with a big selection of everyday and unique items. Much of the shopping is done in pedestrianised shopping areas in the city centres rather than in big shopping malls, which are often relegated to the suburbs. Famous shopping strips include the Kurfürstendamm in Berlin; the Königsallee in Düsseldorf; the Hohe Strasse in Cologne; Kaufingerstrasse, Neuhauser Strasse and Maximilianstrasse in Munich; and the Zeil in Frankfurt.

There's really nothing you can't buy in Germany, but even in the age of globalisation, there are still some treasures you'll unearth here better than anywhere else.

Regional products include traditional Bavarian outfits, including dirndl dresses, lederhosen and loden jackets. Beer mugs are the classic souvenir, no matter whether made of glass or stoneware, plain or decorated, with or without pewter lids – the choice is endless. Famous food products include marzipan from Lübeck, *Lebkuchen* (gingerbread) from Nuremberg and *Printen* (spicy cookies) from Aachen.

The Black Forest is the birthplace of German clockmaking, and not only of the cuckoo variety. Precision instruments, such as microscopes and binoculars, are also a speciality. Cutlery is first-rate, with Wüsthof and JA Henckels being leading brands.

Good-quality woodcarvings are widely available in the Alpine regions (Oberammergau's are especially famous, see p145). Fans of the fragile can pick up exquisite china made by Meissen, Villeroy & Boch, Rosenthal, KPM or Porzellanmanufaktur Nymphenburg. The glass artisans in the Bavarian Forest make beautiful vases, bowls and ornaments.

Famous toy brands include stuffed animals by Steiff (the inventor of the teddy bear) and collectible Käthe Kruse dolls. At

TAXES & REFUNDS

Prices for goods and services include a value-added tax (VAT), called *Mehrwertsteuer,* which is 19% for regular goods and 7% for food and books. If your permanent residence is outside the EU, you can have a large portion of the VAT refunded, provided you shop at a store displaying the 'Tax-Free for Tourists' sign and obtain a tax-free form for your purchase from the sales clerk. At the airport, show this form, your unused goods and your receipt to a custom official before checking your luggage. The customs official will stamp the form, which you can then take straight to the cash refund office at the airport.

Christmas markets you'll discover wonderful ornaments, classic nutcrackers and other decorations.

German wine is another excellent purchase, especially since some of the best bottles are not available outside the country. If you're into street fashion, head to Berlin, which makes the most Zeitgeist-capturing outfits.

Bargaining almost never occurs, except at flea markets.

TELEPHONE & FAX

FAX

Faxes can be sent from and received at most hotels, photocopy shops, internet cafes and telephone call shops.

MOBILE PHONES

Mobile (cell) phones are called *'Handys'* and work on GSM 900/1800. If your home country uses a different standard, you'll need a multiband GSM phone in Germany. If you're staying for a while and have an unlocked multiband phone, buying a prepaid, rechargeable SIM card with a local number might work out cheaper than using your own network. Cards are available at any telecommunications store (eg T-Online, Vodafone, E-Plus or O_2). These places also sell prepaid GSM900/1800 phones, including some credit, starting at €30. Recharge credit by buying scratch-off cards sold at newsagents, supermarkets, petrol stations and general stores.

Calls made to a mobile phone are more expensive than those to a landline, but incoming calls are free.

PHONE CODES

German phone numbers consist of an area code, which starts with ☎ 0, and the local number. Area codes can be up to six digits long; local numbers, up to nine digits. If dialling from a landline within the same city, you don't need to dial the area code. If using a mobile, you must dial it.

If calling Germany from abroad, first dial your country's international access code, then ☎ 49 (Germany's country code), then the area code (dropping the initial ☎ 0) and the local number. Germany's international access code is ☎ 00.

Deutsche Telekom directory assistance charges a ridiculous €1.39 per minute for numbers within Germany (☎ 118 37 for an English-speaking operator; ☎ 118 33 for German-speaking) and €1.99 for numbers outside Germany (☎ 118 34). Get the same information for free at www.telefonbuch.de. A much cheaper provider is the fully automated Telix (☎ 118 10), which charges €0.39 per minute.

Numbers starting with ☎ 0800 are toll free, ☎ 01801 numbers are charged at €0.046 per minute, ☎ 01803 at €0.09 and ☎ 01805 at €0.14. Calls to numbers starting with ☎ 01802 cost a flat €0.06, while those to ☎ 01804 numbers cost a flat €0.20. Avoid numbers starting with ☎ 0190 or ☎ 900, which are charged at exorbitant rates. Direct-dialled calls made from hotel rooms are also usually charged at a premium.

If you have access to a private phone, you can benefit from cheaper rates by using a *'Call-by-Call'* access code (eg ☎ 01016 or ☎ 010090). Rates change daily and are published in the newspapers or online at www.billigertelefonieren.de (in German).

Telephone call shops, which tend to cluster around train stations, may also offer competitive calling rates but often charge steep connection fees. Always make sure you understand the charges involved.

With a high-speed internet connection, you can talk for free via **Skype** (**www.skype.**

com), or use its SkypeOut service, which allows you to call landlines from your computer.

PHONECARDS

Most public pay phones only work with Deutsche Telekom (DT) phonecards, available in denominations of €5, €10 and €20 from DT stores, as well as post offices, newsagents and tourist offices. Occasionally you'll see non-DT pay phones, but these may not necessarily offer better rates.

For long-distance or international calls, prepaid calling cards issued by other companies tend to offer better rates than DT's phonecards. Look for them at newsagents and telephone call shops. Most of these cards also work with payphones but usually at a surcharge – read the fine print on the card itself. Those sold at ReiseBank outlets have some of the most competitive rates.

TIME

Clocks in Germany are set to central European time (GMT/UTC plus one hour). Daylight-saving time kicks in at 2am on the last Sunday in March and ends on the last Sunday in October. Without taking daylight-saving times into account, when it's noon in Berlin, it's 11am in London, 6am in New York, 3am in San Francisco, 8pm in Tokyo, 9pm in Sydney and 11pm in Auckland. The use of the 24-hour clock (eg 6.30pm is 18.30) is the norm.

TOURIST INFORMATION

The best pretrip planning source is the **German National Tourist Office** (GNTO; www.deutschland-tourismus.de); its website is available in almost 30 languages and has links to subsites catering specifically for visitors from various countries. Regional websites and tourist organisations are listed at the start of each destination chapter throughout this book.

LOCAL TOURIST OFFICES

Just about every community in Germany has a walk-in tourist office where you can get advice and pick up maps and pamphlets, sometimes in English. Many also offer a room and ticket-reservation service, usually free but sometime for a small fee. With few exceptions, there's at least one staff member more or less fluent in English and willing to make the effort to help you. Contact details are listed throughout this book in the Information section of each town.

TRAVELLERS WITH DISABILITIES

If you happen to be in a wheelchair, use crutches or can't see or hear so well, Germany is a mixed bag. The mobility impaired will find access ramps and/or lifts in many public buildings, including train stations, museums, theatres and cinemas, especially in the cities. In historic towns, though, cobblestone streets make getting around quite cumbersome.

Newer hotels have lifts and rooms with extra-wide doors and spacious bathrooms. Trains, trams, underground trains and buses are becoming increasingly accessible. Some stations also have grooved platform borders to assist blind passengers. Seeing-eye dogs are allowed on all forms of public transport. For the hearing impaired, upcoming station names are often displayed electronically on all forms of public transport.

Some car-hire agencies offer hand-controlled vehicles and vans with wheelchair lifts at no charge; you must reserve them well in advance. In parking lots and garages, look for designated disabled spots marked with a wheelchair symbol.

Many local and regional tourist offices have special brochures for people with disabilities, although usually in German. Good general resources include:

Deutsche Bahn Mobility Service Centre (☎ 01805-512 512, 01805-996 633, ext 9 for English operator; www.bahn.de; 🕑 8am-8pm Mon-Fri, to 4pm Sat) Train access information and help with route planning. The website has useful information in English.

German National Tourism Office (www.deutschland-tourismus.de) Has an entire section (under Travel Tips) about barrier-free travel in Germany.

Natko (☎ 0211-336 8001; www.natko.de, in German) Central clearing house for inquiries about 'tourism without barriers' in Germany.

VISAS

Most EU nationals only need their national identity card or passport to enter, stay and work in Germany. Citizens of Australia, Canada, Israel, Japan, New Zealand, Poland, Switzerland and the US are among those countries that need only a valid passport but no visa if entering Germany as tourists for up to three months within a six-month period. Passports should be valid for at least another four months from the planned date of departure from Germany.

Nationals from most other countries need a so-called Schengen Visa, named for the 1995 Schengen Agreement that abolished passport controls between Austria, Belgium, Denmark, Finland, France, Germany, Iceland, Italy, Greece, Luxembourg, Netherlands, Norway, Portugal, Spain and Sweden. In late 2007 the following nine countries joined the agreement: Czech Republic, Estonia, Hungary, Latvia, Lithuania, Malta, Poland, Slovakia and Slovenia. Switzerland joined in 2008.

Applications for a Schengen Visa must be filed with the embassy or consulate of the country that is your primary destination. It is valid for stays up to 90 days. Legal residency in any Schengen country makes a visa unnecessary, regardless of your nationality.

Visa applications are usually processed within two to 10 days, but it's always best to start the process as early as possible. For details, see www.auswaertiges-amt.de and check with a German consulate in your country.

WOMEN TRAVELLERS

Germany is a safe place for women to explore, even solo. Of course, this doesn't mean you can let your guard down and trust your life to every stranger. Simply use the same common sense you would at home. Getting hassled in the streets happens infrequently and is usually limited to wolf whistles and unwanted stares. In crowded situations, like public transport and events, groping is possible but rare.

If assaulted, call the police (☎ 110) or contact a women's crisis hotline (selected numbers follow). They can help you deal with the emotional trauma and make referrals to medical, legal and social-service providers. For a complete list, see www.frauennotrufe.de (click to '*Hilfsangebote*') or call ☎ 030-3229 9500. They're not staffed around the clock, but don't get discouraged - try again later or leave a message and someone will call you back.

TRANSPORT

GETTING THERE & AWAY

ENTERING THE COUNTRY

Entering Germany is usually a very straightforward procedure. If you're arriving in Germany from any of the 25 Schengen countries, such as the

CLIMATE CHANGE & TRAVEL

Travel – especially air travel – is a significant contributor to global climate change. At Lonely Planet, we believe that all who travel have a responsibility to limit their personal impact. As a result, we have teamed with Rough Guides and other concerned industry partners to support Climate Care, which allows people to offset the greenhouse gases they are responsible for with contributions to energy-saving projects and other climate-friendly initiatives in the developing world. Lonely Planet offsets all staff and author travel.

For more information, turn to the responsible travel pages on www.lonelyplanet.com. For details on offsetting your carbon emissions and a carbon calculator, go to www.climatecare.org.

Netherlands or Austria, you no longer have to show your passport or go through customs in Germany, no matter which nationality you are.

PASSPORT

Passports must be valid for at least six months after the end of your trip. Citizens of most Western countries can enter Germany without a visa; other nationals may need a Schengen Visa; see opposite for details.

AIR

AIRPORTS

Frankfurt International Airport (FRA; ☎ 01805-372 4636; www.frankfurt-airport.de) is the main gateway for transcontinental flights, although **Düsseldorf** (DUS; ☎ 0211-4210; www.duesseldorf-international.de) and **Munich** (MUC; ☎ 089-975 00; www.munich-airport.de) also receive their share of overseas air traffic. Berlin has two international airports, **Tegel** (TXL; ☎ 0180-500 0186; www.berlin-airport.de) and **Schönefeld** (SXF; ☎ 0180-500 0186; www.berlin-airport.de). There are also sizeable airports in **Hamburg** (HAM; ☎ 040-507 50; www.flughafen-hamburg.de), **Cologne/Bonn** (CGN; ☎ 02203-404 001; www.airport-cgn.de) and **Stuttgart** (STR; ☎ 01805-948 444; www.stuttgart-airport.com), and smaller ones in such cities as Bremen, Dresden, Erfurt, Hanover, Leipzig, Münster-Osnabrück and Nuremberg.

Some of the budget airlines – Ryanair in particular – keep their fares low by flying to remote airports, which are often recycled military airstrips. The biggest of these is **Frankfurt-Hahn** (HHN; ☎ 06543-509 200; www.hahn-airport.de), which is actually near the Moselle River, about 110km northwest of Frankfurt proper.

TICKETS

AUSTRALIA & NEW ZEALAND

The dominant carriers to central Europe are Qantas, British Airways and Singapore Airlines. Flights go either via Asia or the Middle East (with possible stopovers in such cities as Singapore or Dubai), or across Canada or the US (with possible stopovers in Honolulu, Los Angeles or San Francisco).

CANADA

Lufthansa and Air Canada fly to Frankfurt and Munich from all major Canadian airports.

CONTINENTAL EUROPE

Lufthansa and other national carriers connect all major European cities with destinations in Germany. The dominant discount carriers – Air Berlin, easyJet, Germanwings and Ryanair – have flights to all major and minor German airports from throughout Europe.

UK & IRELAND

Numerous airlines fly to destinations throughout Germany from practically every airport in the UK and Ireland. Lufthansa and British Airways are the main national carriers, but prices are usually lower on Ryanair, easyJet, TUIfly, Air Berlin and Germanwings. Their extensive route networks have made travelling even to smaller, regional destinations, such as Dortmund, Nuremberg and Münster, very inexpensive.

USA

Lufthansa and all major US carriers operate flights from nearly every big US city to Germany. In addition, German carriers Air Berlin and Condor operate seasonal (ie summer) services from selected US cities. (Condor flies from Anchorage and Fairbanks, for instance.) Good fares are often available from Asia-based airlines, such as Air India and Singapore Airlines, which stop in the US en route to their final destination.

Most flights land in Frankfurt, but Düsseldorf and Munich are also seeing more incoming traffic. But even if you land in Frankfurt – and it's not your final destination – it's a snap to catch a connecting domestic flight or continue your travels on Germany's ever-efficient train system.

STA Travel (☎ 800-781-4040; www.statravel.com) and **Flight Centre** (☎ 877-233-9999; www.flightcentre.us) are both reliable budget travel agencies offering online bookings and brick-and-mortar branches throughout the country.

LAND

BUS

Eurolines (www.eurolines.com) is the umbrella organisation of 32 European coach operators connecting 500 destinations across Europe. Children between the ages of four and 12 pay half price, while teens, students and seniors get 10% off regular fares. In Germany Eurolines is represented by **Deutsche Touring** (☎ 069-790 3501; www.touring.de).

Backpacker-geared **Busabout** (☎ in the UK 08450 267 514; www.busabout.com) is a hop-on, hop-off service that runs coaches along three interlocking European loops between May and October. Germany is part of the northern loop, which includes stops in Berlin, Dresden, Munich and Stuttgart.

CAR & MOTORCYCLE

When bringing your own vehicle to Germany, you need a valid driving licence, your car registration certificate and proof of insurance. Foreign cars must display a nationality sticker unless they have official European plates. You also need to carry a warning (hazard) triangle and a first-aid kit. For road rules and other driving-related information, see p377.

Coming from the UK, the fastest way to the continent is via the **Eurotunnel** (☎ in the UK 08705-353 535, in Germany 01805-000 248; www.eurotunnel.com). These shuttle trains whisk cars, motorbikes, bicycles and coaches from Folkestone in England through the Channel Tunnel to Coquelles (near Calais, in France) in about 35 minutes. From there, you can be in Germany in about three hours.

TRAIN

Long-distance trains connecting major German cities with those in other countries are called EuroCity (EC) trains. Seat reservations are highly recommended, especially during the peak summer season and around major holidays (p365).

There are direct overnight trains (City Night Line, CNL) to Germany from such cities as Amsterdam, Copenhagen, Belgrade, Budapest, Bucharest, Florence, Milan, Prague, Rome, Venice and Vienna. For full details, contact Deutsche Bahn's **night train specialists** (☎ in Germany 01805-141 514; www.nachtzugreise.de, in German).

EUROSTAR

The Channel Tunnel makes train travel between the UK and Germany a fast and enjoyable option. High-speed **Eurostar** (☎ in the UK 08705-186 186; www.eurostar.com) passenger trains hurtle at least 10 times daily between London and Paris (the journey takes 2½ hours) or Brussels (two hours). At either city you can change to regular or other high-speed trains to destinations in Germany.

LAKE

The Romanshorn–Friedrichshafen car ferry provides the quickest way across Lake Constance between Switzerland and Germany. It's operated year-round by **Schweizerische Bodensee Schifffahrt** (☎ in Switzerland 071-466 7888; www.bodenseeschiffe.ch), takes 40 minutes and costs €7.50 per person (children €3.50). Bicycles are €5, cars start at €28.50.

SEA

Germany's main ferry ports are Kiel and Travemünde (near Lübeck) in Schleswig-Holstein, and Rostock and Sassnitz (on Rügen Island) in Mecklenburg–Western Pomerania. All have services to Scandinavia and the Baltic states. Return tickets are often cheaper than two one-way tickets. All prices quoted are for one-way fares. Car prices are for a standard passenger vehicle up to 6m in length and include all passengers.

DENMARK

GEDSER–ROSTOCK

Scandlines (☎ 01805-116 688; www.scandlines.de) runs year-round ferries every two hours to/from Gedser, about 100km south of Copenhagen. The 1¾-hour trip costs €87 per car in high season. Walk-on passengers pay €7/5 per adult/child. It's €16 for a bike and you.

RØDBY–PUTTGARDEN

Scandlines (☎ 01805-116 688; www.scandlines.de) operates a 45-minute ferry every half-hour for €64 for a regular car. Foot passengers pay €6/4 per adult/child in peak season one way or same-day return. It's €13 if you bring a bicycle.

FINLAND

HELSINKI–TRAVEMÜNDE

Finnlines (☎ 04502-805 43; www.finnlines.de) goes to Travemünde (near Lübeck) daily, year-round in 27 to 36 hours. Berths start at €196; food is another €60. Bikes are €20, cars start at €100.

NORWAY

OSLO–KIEL

Color Line (☎ 0431-730 0300; www.colorline.de) makes this 20-hour journey almost daily. The fare, including a berth in the most basic two-bed cabin, is around €225. Children, seniors and students pay half-price on selected departures. Cars start at €84.

SWEDEN

GOTHENBURG–KIEL

The daily overnight ferry run by **Stena Line** (☎ 0431-9099, 01895-916 666; www.stenaline.de) takes 14 hours and costs €71 for foot passengers (€46 for children, students and seniors). Taking your car will cost €171 in peak season, including all passengers. Berths are compulsory and start at €78.

MALMÖ–TRAVEMÜNDE

Finnlines (☎ 04502-805 43; www.finnlines.de) makes the trip in nine hours. It's primarily geared to passengers travelling with their own car. Tickets start at €60 for daytime sailings and €120 for overnight departures, including car and one person.

UK

There are no longer any direct ferry services between Germany and the UK, but you can just as easily go via the Netherlands, Belgium or France and drive or train it from there. Competition from Eurotunnel and budget airlines has forced ferry operators to significantly lower their fares, meaning great bargains may be available at quiet times of the day or year. Check the ferries' websites for fare details or check www.ferrybooker.com, a single site covering all sea-ferry routes and operators, plus Eurotunnel.

TO BELGIUM

P&O Ferries (☎ in the UK 08716-645 645, in Germany 01805-500 9437; www.poferries.com) Hull–Zeebrugge; 13½ hours.

TO FRANCE

Norfolkline (☎ in the UK 0844-499 007, in Germany 01801-600 31; www.norfolkline.com) Dover–Dunkirk; two hours.

P&O Ferries (☎ in the UK 08716-645 645, in Germany 01805-500 9437; www.poferries.com) Dover–Calais; 75 minutes.

TO THE NETHERLANDS

DFDS Seaways (☎ 0871-522 9955; www.dfds.co.uk) Newcastle–Amsterdam; 15 hours.

P&O Ferries (☎ in the UK 08716-645 645, in Germany 01805-500 9437; www.poferries.com) Hull–Rotterdam; 14 hours.

Stena Line (☎ 0431-9099, 01895-916 666; www.stenaline.co.uk) Harwich–Hoek van Holland; 3¾ hours.

GETTING AROUND

AIR

Most large and many smaller German cities have their own airports (see also p373) and numerous carriers operate domestic flights within Germany. Lufthansa, of course, has the most dense route network. Other airlines offering domestic flights include Air Berlin, Cirrus Air and Germanwings.

Unless you're flying from one end of the country to the other, say Berlin to Munich or Hamburg to Munich, planes are only marginally quicker than trains if you factor in the time it takes to get to and from the airports.

BICYCLE

Cycling is allowed on all roads and highways but not on the autobahns (motorways). Cyclists must follow the same rules of the road as cars and motorcycles. Helmets are not compulsory, not even for children, but wearing one is simply common sense.

HIRE & PURCHASE

Most towns and cities have some sort of bicycle-hire station, which is often at or near the train station. Hire costs range from €9 to €25 per day and €35 to €85 per week, depending on the model of bicycle you hire. A minimum deposit of €30 (more for fancier bikes) and/or ID are required. Many agencies are listed in the Getting Around sections of the destination chapters in this book. Some outfits also offer repair service or bicycle storage facilities.

TRANSPORT

Bicycles may be taken on most trains but require purchasing a separate ticket *(Fahrrad-karte)*. These cost €9 per trip on long-distance trains (IC and EC; reservations required) and €4.50 per day on local and regional trains (IRE, RB, RE and S-Bahn). Bicycles are not allowed on high-speed ICE trains. There is no charge at all on some trains. For full details, enquire at a local station or call ☎01805-151 415. Free lines are also listed in Deutsche Bahn's complimentary *Bahn & Bike* brochure (in German), as are the almost 250 stations where you can rent bikes. Both are available for downloading from www.bahn.de/bahnundbike.

Many regional companies use buses with special bike racks. Bicycles are also allowed on practically all boat and ferry services on Germany's lakes and rivers.

BOAT

With two seas and a lake- and river-filled interior, don't be surprised to find yourself in a boat at some point. Scheduled boat services operate along sections of the Rhine, the Elbe and the Danube. There are also ferry services in areas with no or only a few bridges as well as on major lakes such as the Chiemsee and Lake Starnberg in Bavaria and Lake Constance in Baden-Württemberg. For details, see the individual entries in the destination chapters.

BUS

LOCAL & REGIONAL

Basically, wherever there is a train, take it. Buses are generally slower, less dependable and more polluting than trains, but in some rural areas they may be your only option for getting around without your own vehicle. This is especially true of the Harz Mountains, sections of the Bavarian Forest and the Alpine foothills. Separate bus companies, each with its own tariffs and schedules, operate in the different regions.

In cities, buses generally converge at the *Busbahnhof* or *Zentraler Omnibus Bahnhof* (ZOB; central bus station), which is often near the Hauptbahnhof (central train station).

LONG DISTANCE

Deutsche Touring (☎**069-790 3501; www.touring.de**) runs daily overnight services between Hamburg and Mannheim via Hannover, Frankfurt, Göttingen, Kassel and Heidelberg. If you book early, trips between any two cities cost just €9. Fares top out at €49 for the full Hannover–Mannheim route for tickets bought on the bus. Children under 12 pay half-price.

Berlin Linien Bus (☎**030-861 9331; www.berlinlinien bus.de**) connects major cities (primarily Berlin, but also Munich, Düsseldorf and Frankfurt) with each other as well as holiday regions such as the Harz, the islands of Rügen and Usedom and the Bavarian Alps. One of the most popular routes is the express bus to Hamburg, which makes the journey from Berlin in 3¼ hours 12 times daily with one-way fares ranging from €9 to €21.50.

For details on the Europabus service along the Romantic Road, see p126.

CAR & MOTORCYCLE

German roads are excellent and motoring around the country can be a lot of fun. The country's pride and joy is its 11,000km network of autobahns. Every 40km to 60km, you'll find service areas with fuel, toilets and restaurants; many open 24 hours. In between are rest stops *(Rastplatz)*, which usually have picnic tables and toilets. Orange emergency call boxes are spaced about 2km apart.

Autobahns are supplemented by an extensive network of *Bundesstrassen* (secondary 'B' roads, highways) and smaller *Landstrassen* (country roads). These are generally more scenic and fun as you wind through the countryside from village to village – ideal for car or motorcycle touring. You can't travel fast, but you won't care. No tolls are charged on any public roads.

Seat belts are mandatory for all passengers and there's a €30 fine if you get caught not wearing one. If you're in an accident, not wearing a seatbelt may invalidate your insurance. Children need a child seat if under four years and a seat cushion if under 12; they may not ride in the front until age 13. Motorcyclists must wear a helmet. The use of hand-held mobile phones while driving is very much *verboten* (forbidden).

Many cities have electronic parking guidance systems directing you to the nearest garage and indicating the number of available spaces. Street parking usually works on the pay-and-display system and tends to be short-term (one or two hours) only.

AUTOMOBILE ASSOCIATIONS

Germany's main motoring organisation, the **Allgemeiner Deutscher Automobil-Club** (ADAC; ☎ for roadside assistance 0180-222 2222, from a mobile phone 222 222; www.adac.de) has offices in all major cities and many smaller ones. Its roadside assistance program is also available to members of its affiliates, including the British (AA), American (AAA) and Canadian (CAA) ones.

DRIVING LICENCE

Drivers need a valid driving licence. International Driving Permits (IDP) are not compulsory, but having one may help Germans make sense of your home licence (always carry that one, too) and may simplify the car or motorcycle hire process.

HIRE

In order to hire your own wheels, you'll need to be at least 25 years old, and possess a valid driving licence and a major credit card. Some companies hire out to drivers between the ages of 21 and 24 for an additional charge (about €12 to €20 per day). Younger people or those without a credit card are often out of luck, although some local car-hire outfits may accept cash or travellers-cheque deposits. Taking your hire car into an Eastern European country, such as the Czech Republic or Poland, is often a no-no, so check in advance if that's where you're planning to head.

All the main international companies, including **Avis** (☎ 01805-217 702; www.avis.com), **Europcar** (☎ 01805-8000; www.europcar.com), **Hertz** (☎ 01805-333 535; www.hertz.com) and **Budget** (☎ 01805-244 388; www.budget.com), maintain branches at airports, major train stations and towns.

Prebooked and prepaid packages arranged in your home country usually work out much cheaper than on-the-spot rentals. The same is true of fly/drive packages. Check for deals with the online travel agencies, travel agents or car-hire brokers, such as the US-based company **Auto Europe** (☎ in the US 888-223-5555; www.autoeurope.com) or the UK-based **Holiday Autos** (☎ in the UK 0871-472 5229; www.holidayautos.co.uk).

INSURANCE

German law requires that all registered vehicles carry third-party liability insurance. You could get seriously screwed by driving uninsured or underinsured.

Germans are very fussy about their cars, and even nudging someone's bumper when jostling out of a tight parking space may well result in you having to pay for an entirely new one.

When hiring a vehicle, make sure your contract includes adequate liability insurance at the very minimum. Rental agencies almost never include insurance that covers damage to the vehicle itself, called Collision Damage Waiver (CDW) or Loss Damage Waiver (LDW). It's optional but driving without it is not recommended. Some credit-card companies cover CDW/LDW for a certain period if you charge the entire rental to your card.

ROAD RULES

Driving is on the right-hand side of the road and standard international signs are in use. Speed and red-light cameras are common and notices are sent to the car's registration address wherever that may be. If you're renting a car, the police will obtain your home address from the rental agency.

The usual speed limits for German roads are 50km/h on city streets and 100km/h on highways, unless they are otherwise marked. And yes, it's true, there really are no speed limits on autobahns. However, there are many stretches where slower speeds must be observed (eg near towns, road construction), so be sure to keep an eye out for those signs or risk getting ticketed.

Drivers unaccustomed to the high speeds on autobahns should be extra careful when passing another vehicle. It takes only seconds for a car in the rear-view mirror to close in at 200km/h. Pass as quickly as possible, then quickly return to the right lane. Try to ignore those annoying drivers who will flash their headlights or tailgate you to make you drive faster and get out of the way. It's an illegal practice anyway, as is passing on the right.

The highest permissible blood-alcohol level for drivers is 0.05%, which for most people equates to one glass of wine or two small beers.

Pedestrians at crossings have absolute right of way over all motor vehicles. Always watch out for bicyclists when turning right; they have the right of way. Right turns at a red light are only legal if there's a green arrow pointing to the right.

HITCHING & RIDE-SHARES

Hitching *(trampen)* is never entirely safe in any country and we don't recommend it. A safer, inexpensive and eco-conscious form of travelling is ride-shares, where you travel as a passenger in a private car in exchange for some petrol money. Most arrangements are now set up via free online ride boards, such as www.mitfahrzentrale.de, www.mitfahrgelegenheit.de (in German) and www.drive2day.de. You can advertise a ride yourself or link up with a driver going to your destination. **Citynetz** (**☎ 01805-194 444; www.citynetz-mitfahrzentrale.de, in German**) still maintains a few staffed offies in major cities, but they do charge a small commission for linking you up with a driver.

LOCAL TRANSPORT

Most towns have efficient public transport systems. Bigger cities, such as Berlin and Munich, integrate buses, trams, U-Bahn (underground, subway) trains and S-Bahn (suburban) trains into a single network.

Fares are either determined by zones or time travelled, or sometimes by both. A multiticket strip *(Streifenkarte)* or a day pass *(Tageskarte)* generally offers better value than a single-ride ticket. Normally, tickets must be stamped upon boarding in order to be valid.

BUS & TRAM

Buses are the most ubiquitous form of public transport and practically all towns have their own comprehensive network. Buses run at regular intervals, with restricted services in the evenings and at weekends. Some cities operate night buses along the most popular routes to get night owls safely back home.

Occasionally, buses are supplemented by trams, which are usually faster because they travel on their own tracks, largely independent of other traffic. In city centres, they sometimes go underground. Bus and tram drivers normally sell single tickets and day passes only.

S-BAHN

Metropolitan areas, such as Berlin and Munich, have a system of suburban trains called the S-Bahn. They are faster and cover a wider area than buses or trams but tend to be less frequent. S-Bahn lines are often linked to the national rail network and sometimes connect urban centres. Rail passes are generally valid on these services. Specific S-Bahn lines are abbreviated with 'S' followed by the number (eg S1, S7) in the destination chapters.

TAXI

Taxis are expensive and, given the excellent public transport systems, not recommended unless you're in a real hurry. (They can actually be slower than trains or trams if you're stuck in rush-hour traffic.) Cabs are metered and charged at a base rate (flag fall) plus a per-kilometre fee. It's rarely possible to flag down a taxi. Rather, order one by phone (look up *Taxiruf* in the phone book) or board at a taxi rank.

U-BAHN

Underground (subway) trains are known as U-Bahn and are generally the fastest form of travel in big cities. Route maps are posted in all stations, and a printed copy is often available from the stationmaster or ticket office. Specific U-Bahn lines are abbreviated with 'U' followed by the number (eg U7) in the destination chapters.

TRAIN

Germany's rail system is operated almost entirely by **Deutsche Bahn** (**DB; ☎ 01805-996 633, free automated timetable information 0800-150 7090; www.bahn.de**), with a variety of train types serving just about every corner in the country.

Most stations have coin-operated lockers ranging in cost from €1 to €4 per 24-hour period. Larger stations have staffed left-luggage offices *(Gepäckaufbewahrung)*, but these are more expensive than lockers.

See p377 for details on taking your bicycle on the train.

CLASSES

German trains have 1st- and 2nd-class cars, both of them modern and comfortable. Paying extra for 1st class is usually not worth it, except perhaps on busy travel days (eg Friday, Sunday afternoon and holidays) when 2nd-class cars can get very crowded. On ICE trains you'll enjoy such extras as reclining seats, tables, free newspapers and audio systems in your armrest. Newer generation ICE trains also have individual laptop outlets, unimpeded cell-phone reception in 1st class and, on some routes, wi-fi access.

Trains and stations are completely non-smoking. ICE, IC and EC trains are fully air-conditioned and have a restaurant or self-service bistro.

COSTS

Standard, nondiscounted train tickets tend to be quite expensive, but promotions, discounted tickets and special offers become available all the time. Always check www.bahn.de for the latest rail promotions. Permanent rail deals include the Schönes-Wochenende-Ticket and Ländertickets.

SCHÖNES-WOCHENENDE-TICKET

The 'Nice-Weekend-Ticket' is Europe's finest rail deal. It allows you and up to four accompanying passengers (or one or both parents or grandparents plus all their children or grandchildren up to 14 years) to travel anywhere in Germany on *one day* from midnight Saturday or Sunday until 3am the next day for just €37. The catch is that you can only use IRE, RE, RB and S-Bahn trains in 2nd class, plus local buses and other forms of public transport.

LÄNDERTICKETS

These are essentially a variation of the Schönes-Wochenende-Ticket, except that they are valid any day of the week and are limited to travel within one of the German states (or, in some cases, also in bordering states). Prices vary slightly from state to state but are in the €26 to €34 range. Some states also offer cheaper tickets for solo travellers costing between €18 and €25.

RESERVATIONS

Seat reservation for long-distance travel is highly recommended, especially if you're travelling on a Friday or Sunday afternoon, during holiday periods or in summer. Reservations cost €4 in 2nd class if bought from an agent and €2 if bought online or from a vending machine (€5/3 in 1st class). They can be made online and at ticket counters as late as 10 minutes before departure.

TRAIN PASSES

If your permanent residence is outside Europe, you qualify for the **German Rail Pass**. It entitles you to unlimited 1st- or 2nd-class travel for four to 10 days within a one-month period. The pass is valid on all trains within Germany and some Köln-Düsseldorfer river services on the Rhine and Moselle Rivers. The four-day pass costs €236 in 1st and €180 in 2nd class, with extra days being charged at €32/22. Children between six and 11 pay half-fare. Children under six travel free.

If you are between the ages of 12 and 25, you qualify for the **German Rail Youth Pass**, which costs €150 for four days and is only good for 2nd-class travel. Additional days are €10. Two adults travelling together should check out the four-day **German Rail Twin Pass** for €270 in 2nd class and €370 in 1st class. More days cost €30/42.

Tickets are sold online (www.bahn.de), at some ticket counters in Germany and through agents in your home country. In the US, try www.raileurope.com; in the UK, www.raileurope.co.uk.

GLOSSARY

ADAC – Allgemeiner Deutscher Automobil-Club (automobile association)
Altstadt – old town
Apotheke – pharmacy
Autobahn – motorway, freeway

Bahnhof – train station
Bedienung – service; service charge
Berg – mountain
Bibliothek – library
Bierkeller – cellar pub
BRD – Bundesrepublik Deutschland (FRG; Federal Republic of Germany); the name for Germany today; before reunification it applied to West Germany
Brücke – bridge
Brunnen – fountain, well
Burg – castle
Busbahnhof – bus station

Christkindlmarkt – Christmas market; also called *Weihnachtsmarkt*
City Night Line (CNL) – night trains with sleeper cars and couchettes

DB – Deutsche Bahn; German national railway
DDR – Deutsche Demokratische Republik (GDR; German Democratic Republic); the name for former East Germany
Dirndl – traditional women's dress (Bavaria only)
DJH – Deutsches Jugendherbergswerk; German youth hostels association
Dom – cathedral

Ebbelwei – apple wine

Fahrrad – bicycle
Ferienwohnung – holiday flat or apartment
Flohmarkt – flea market
Flughafen – airport
FRG – see *BRD*

Garten – garden
Gästehaus – guesthouse
Gaststätte, Gasthaus – informal restaurant, inn
GDR – see *DDR*
Gedenkstätte – memorial site
Gepäckaufbewahrung – left-luggage office

Hafen – harbour, port
Hauptbahnhof – central train station
Hof – courtyard
Hotel garni – hotel without a restaurant where you are only served breakfast

Imbiss – stand-up food stall; also called *Schnellimbiss*
Insel – island
InterCity (IC), EuroCity (EC) – long-distance trains; slower than the ICE and stop in major cities; EC trains go to major cities in neighbouring countries
InterCity Express (ICE) – long-distance, bullet trains; stop at major cities only
InterRegio-Express (IRE) – slower medium-distance trains connecting cities

Jugendherberge – youth hostel

Kapelle – chapel
Karte – ticket
Kirche – church
Kloster – monastery, convent
Kreuzgang – cloister
Kunst – art

Kurhaus – literally 'cure house', usually a spa town's central building, used for social gatherings and events
Kurtaxe – resort tax

Land – state
Lebkuchen – gingerbread
Lederhosen – traditional leather trousers with attached braces (Bavaria only)
Lesbe – lesbian (n)

Markt – market; often used instead of *Marktplatz*
Marktplatz – marketplace or square; often abbreviated to *Markt*
Mass – 1L tankard or stein of beer
Mehrwertsteuer (MwST) – value-added tax
Mitfahrzentrale – ride-sharing agency
multi-kulti – multicultural
Münster – large church/cathedral

Neustadt – new town

Palais, Palast – palace, residential quarters of a castle
Pension – cheap boarding house
Pfarrkirche – parish church
Platz – square

Radwandern – bicycle touring
Radweg – bicycle path
Rathaus – town hall
Regional Express (RE) – local trains with limited stops that link rural areas with metropolitan centres and the S-Bahn
RegionalBahn (RB) – local trains, mostly in rural areas, with frequent stops
Reich – empire
Reisezentrum – travel centre in train or bus stations
Ruhetag – literally 'rest day'; closing day at a shop or restaurant

Saal – hall, room
Sammlung – collection
Säule – column, pillar
S-Bahn – suburban-metropolitan trains; short for 'Schnellbahn'
Schatzkammer – treasury room
Schiffahrt – shipping, navigation
Schloss – palace, castle
Schwuler – gay (n)
See – lake
Sesselbahn – chairlift
Stadt – city, town
StadtExpress (SE) – local trains primarily connecting cities and geared towards commuters
Stollen – a moist fruitcake served around the holidays
Striezel – Dresden's word for *Stollen*

Tageskarte – daily menu; day ticket on public transport
Tor – gate
trampen – hitchhike
Turm – tower

U-Bahn – underground train system
Ufer – bank (of river etc)

verboten – forbidden
Verkehrsamt, Verkehrsverein – tourist office
Viertel – quarter, district

Wald – forest
Weihnachtsmarkt – Christmas market; also called *Christkindlmarkt*
Weingut – wine-growing estate
Weinkeller – wine cellar
Weinstube – traditional wine bar/tavern
Wende – 'change' of 1989, ie the fall of communism that led to the collapse of the GDR and German reunification
Wurst – sausage

Zimmer frei – rooms available

↘ BEHIND THE SCENES

THE AUTHORS

ANDREA SCHULTE-PEEVERS

Coordinating Author, This is Germany, Germany's Top 25 Experiences, Germany's Top Itineraries, Planning Your Trip, Berlin, Brandenburg, Saxony-Anhalt, Thuringia, North Rhine–Westphalia, Directory & Transport

Andrea has logged countless miles travelling in nearly 60 countries on five continents and carries her dog-eared passport like a badge of honour. Born and raised in Germany and educated in London and at UCLA, she's built a career on writing about her native country for almost two decades. She's authored or contributed to more than 40 Lonely Planet titles, including all six editions of the Germany country guide as well as the city guide to Berlin, the *Berlin Encounter* guide and the guide to Munich, Bavaria & the Black Forest.

Author thanks Big thanks to all the wonderful experts who've made themselves available for interviews at short notice: Dr Elisabeth Südkamp, Miriam Bers, Martin Wollenberg, Matthias Deml and Cornelia Ziegler. Thanks to my coauthor Caroline Sieg for being such fun to work with and to all the production folks at LP for answering our many questions. Last but not least, thanks to David, simply for being there.

CAROLINE SIEG

Contributing Author, Munich, Hamburg & Northern Germany, Dresden & Eastern Germany, Stuttgart & the Black Forest, Frankfurt & Central Germany, Germany In Focus

Half-American and half-Swiss, Caroline has spent most of her life moving back and forth across the Atlantic Ocean, with lengthy stops in Zurich, Miami and New York City. When not cycling around Berlin's Tiergarten or beside Hamburg's waterways in an effort to work off a daily dose of *Kaffee und Kuchen*, Caroline spends her days writing and editing, with a focus on anything involving travel and food.

Author thanks Thank you to Cliff for the assignment. Thanks to Andrea Schulte-Peevers for all the tips and ideas when word-count limits seemed impossible, and for always maintaining a sense of humour. Special thanks to Regina Ebert, Dr Simone Eick, Óscar Hernández, Hans Spindler and Angela Cullen for so graciously granting me interviews and taking the time to email me photos; to the tourism offices in Munich and Potsdam for putting me in touch with local experts; and to Anthony Haywood and Ryan ver Berkmoes for passing along the names of their contacts.

KERRY CHRISTIANI — Baden-Württemberg

Big wilderness, the promise of snow in winter and a husband born in Villingen lured Kerry from London to the Black Forest four years ago. When not on the road, Kerry can be found hiking, cycling or cross-country skiing in the woods and hills close to her home. On recent research she was delighted to rediscover Baden-Württemberg, from canoeing on Lake Constance to testing – well it would be rude not to! – Black Forest cake in Triberg. Kerry's incurably itchy feet have taken her to some 40 countries, inspiring numerous travel articles, online features and around 15 guidebooks, including Lonely Planet's guides to Austria, Switzerland, Munich, Bavaria & the Black Forest and Portugal.

MARC DI DUCA — Saxony, Bavaria

From a library job in the Ruhrgebiet during that balmy and barmy summer of '89 to scrambling up the Alps more recently, Germany and German have been with Marc throughout his adult life. Instilled with a love of irregular verbs, Brecht and bratwurst, Marc has explored many corners of Germany over the last 20 years, but it's to the variety and friendliness of Bavaria that he returns most willingly. Marc has also enjoyed the opportunity to explore Saxony where he became smitten with the Trabant. If anyone has one to sell, he's buying. When not Trabi hugging in Zwickau or leaving beer rings in Munich, Marc can usually be found in Sandwich, Kent, where he lives with his Kievite wife, Tanya, and son Taras. Marc has also written for Lonely Planet's *Russia*, *Trans-Siberian Railway* and *Cycling Britain*.

ANTHONY HAYWOOD — Harz Mountains, Lower Saxony, Bremen

Anthony was born in the port city of Fremantle, Western Australia, and pulled anchor early on to hitchhike through Europe and the USA. Aberystwyth in Wales and Ealing in London were his wintering grounds at the time. He later studied comparative literature in Perth and Russian language in Melbourne. In the 1990s, fresh from a spell in post-Soviet, pre-anything Moscow, he moved to Germany. Today he works as a German-based freelance writer and journalist and divides his time between Göttingen (Lower Saxony) and Berlin. Anthony worked on the first and most subsequent editions of *Germany*.

CATHERINE LE NEVEZ — Hamburg, Schleswig-Holstein, Mecklenburg–Western Pomerania

Catherine's wanderlust kicked in when she road-tripped across Europe, including Germany, aged four, and she's been hitting the road at every opportunity since, completing her Doctorate of Creative Arts in Writing, Masters in Professional Writing, and postgrad qualifications in editing and publishing along the way. Catherine has authored or coauthored well over a dozen Lonely Planet guidebooks, mostly for Europe, including two editions of *Munich, Bavaria & the Black Forest*. On a recent trip she jumped at the chance to celebrate Hamburg's Hafengeburtstag (harbour birthday), head into northern Germany's national parks, and soak up the sun, sea air and scenery (and, yes, the beer) on the country's spectacular Baltic and North Sea coastline and islands.

DANIEL ROBINSON **Hesse, Rhineland-Palatinate & Saarland**

Brought up in Northern California, Illinois and Israel, Daniel holds degrees from Princeton and Tel Aviv University and now lives with his wife Rachel in Los Angeles and Tel Aviv. In his two decades with Lonely Planet, he has covered both sides of the Franco-German border and has had his work translated into 10 languages. The Moselle's medieval wine villages and the area's many *Radwege* (cycling paths) keep bringing Daniel back to Rhineland-Palatinate, but he's equally enchanted by the trains that slither along both banks of the Romantic Rhine, past cargo barges and car ferries. In the Saarland he's as captivated by the hulking Völklinger Hütte ironworks as he is at peace on the leafy Saar River.

THIS BOOK

This 1st edition of *Discover Germany* was coordinated by Andrea Schulte-Peevers, and researched and written by Caroline Sieg, Kerry Christiani, Marc Di Duca, Anthony Haywood, Catherine Le Nevez and Daniel Robinson. This guidebook was commissioned in Lonely Planet's London office, and produced by the following:
Commissioning Editor Clifton Wilkinson
Coordinating Editor Angela Tinson
Coordinating Cartographer Valentina Kremenchutskaya
Coordinating Layout Designer Kerrianne Southway
Managing Editor Brigitte Ellemor
Managing Cartographer Herman So
Managing Layout Designers Sally Darmody, Celia Wood
Assisting Editor Charlotte Orr
Assisting Cartographer Birgit Jordan
Cover Research Naomi Parker, lonelyplanetimages.com
Internal Image Research Jane Hart, lonelyplanetimages.com
Project Manager Craig Kilburn
Language Content Branislava Vladisavljevic

Thanks to Glenn Beanland, Trent Paton, Juan Winata

Internal photographs
p4 Hackescher Hof, Berlin, JHX/imagebroker; pp10-11 Schloss Neuschwanstein, FBE/imagebroker; pp12-13 Heidelberg, Richard l'Anson; p31 Marienplatz, Munich, STF/imagebroker; p39 Schwerin's Schloss, Witold Skrypczak; p3, pp50-1 Brandenburger Tor,

Berlin, David Peevers; p3, p89 Antiquarium, Residenz, Munich, BAI/imagebroker; p3, p115 Schloss Linderhof, JBE/imagebroker; p3, p167 Bank of the River Main, Frankfurt, MOX/imagebroker; p3, p195 Gertelbach brook, Gertelbachschlucht, the Black Forest, JKI/imagebroker; p3, p227 Vineyard near Bacharach, KIM/imagebroker; p3, p261 Zwinger, Dresden, EWR/imagebroker; p3, p293 Speicherstadt, Hamburg, JOT/imagebroker; pp322-3 Alsterakaden, Hamburg, SHU/imagebroker; p357 Beach bar on the Spree River, Berlin, STN/imagebroker.

ACKNOWLEDGMENTS

Many thanks to the following for the use of their content:

Berlin S+U-Bahn Map © 2010 Berliner Verkehrsbetriebe (BVG)

Munich S+U-Bahn Map © 2010 Münchner Verkehrs- und Tarifverbund GmbH (MVV)

SEND US YOUR FEEDBACK

We love to hear from travellers – your comments keep us on our toes and help make our books better. Our well-travelled team reads every word on what you loved or loathed about this book. Although we cannot reply individually to postal submissions, we always guarantee that your feedback goes straight to the appropriate authors, in time for the next edition. Each person who sends us information is thanked in the next edition and the most useful submissions are rewarded with a free book.

To send us your updates – and find out about Lonely Planet events, newsletters and travel news – visit our award-winning website: **lonelyplanet.com/contact**.

Note: we may edit, reproduce and incorporate your comments in Lonely Planet products such as guidebooks, websites and digital products, so let us know if you don't want your comments reproduced or your name acknowledged. For a copy of our privacy policy visit **lonelyplanet.com/privacy**.

INDEX

C

000 Map pages
000 Photograph pages

000 Map pages
000 Photograph pages

000 Map pages
000 Photograph pages

Y

Z

MAP LEGEND

ROUTES

Tollway
Freeway
Primary
Secondary
Tertiary
Lane
Under Construction
Unsealed Road
One-Way Street
Mall/Steps
Tunnel
Pedestrian Overpass
Walking Tour
Walking Tour Detour
Walking Path
Track

TRANSPORT

Ferry
Metro
Monorail
Rail/Underground
Tram
Cable Car, Funicular

HYDROGRAPHY

River, Creek
Intermittent River
Swamp/Mangrove
Reef
Canal
Water
Dry Lake/Salt Lake
Glacier

BOUNDARIES

International
State, Provincial
Disputed
Regional, Suburb
Marine Park
Cliff/Ancient Wall

AREA FEATURES

Area of Interest
Beach, Desert
Building/Urban Area
Cemetery, Christian
Cemetery, Other
Forest
Mall/Market
Park
Restricted Area
Sports

POPULATION

CAPITAL (NATIONAL)
LARGE CITY
Small City
CAPITAL (STATE)
Medium City
Town, Village

SYMBOLS

Sights/Activities

Buddhist
Canoeing, Kayaking
Castle, Fortress
Christian
Confucian
Diving
Hindu
Islamic
Jain
Jewish
Monument
Museum, Gallery
Point of Interest
Pool
Ruin
Sento (Public Hot Baths)
Shinto
Sikh
Skiing
Surfing, Surf Beach
Taoist
Trail Head
Winery, Vineyard
Zoo, Bird Sanctuary

Information

Bank, ATM
Embassy/Consulate
Hospital, Medical
Information
Internet Facilities
Police Station
Post Office, GPO
Telephone
Toilets
Wheelchair Access

Eating

Eating

Drinking

Cafe
Drinking

Entertainment

Entertainment

Shopping

Shopping

Sleeping

Camping
Sleeping

Transport

Airport, Airfield
Border Crossing
Bus Station
Bicycle Path/Cycling
FFCC (Barcelona)
Metro (Barcelona)
Parking Area
Petrol Station
S-Bahn
Taxi Rank
Tube Station
U-Bahn

Geographic

Beach
Lighthouse
Lookout
Mountain, Volcano
National Park
Pass, Canyon
Picnic Area
River Flow
Shelter, Hut
Waterfall

LONELY PLANET OFFICES

Australia
Head Office
Locked Bag 1, Footscray, Victoria 3011
☎ 03 8379 8000, fax 03 8379 8111
talk2us@lonelyplanet.com.au

USA
150 Linden St, Oakland, CA 94607
☎ 510 250 6400, toll free 800 275 8555,
fax 510 893 8572
info@lonelyplanet.com

UK
2nd fl, 186 City Rd,
London EC1V 2NT
☎ 020 7106 2100, fax 020 7106 2101
go@lonelyplanet.co.uk

Published by Lonely Planet
ABN 36 005 607 983

Printed through Colorcraft Ltd, Hong Kong.
Printed in China.